POEMS OF

Robert Browning

SELECTED WITH AN
INTRODUCTION AND NOTES BY
DONALD SMALLEY
UNIVERSITY OF ILLINOIS

HOUGHTON MIFFLIN COMPANY
Boston

POEMS OF

ROBERT BROWNING

RIVERSIDE EDITIONS

RIVERSIDE EDITIONS

UNDER THE GENERAL EDITORSHIP OF

Gordon N. Ray

CONTENTS

INTRODUCTION   ix

    Browning's Life: A Chronological Outline   xxvii
    Selected Bibliography   xxxi

PIPPA PASSES: A Drama (1841)   3

FROM *Dramatic Lyrics* (1842)
    Cavalier Tunes   47
        1. Marching Along   47
        2. Give a Rouse   48
        3. Boot and Saddle   49
    My Last Duchess ✓   49
    Count Gismond   51
    Incident of the French Camp   55
    Soliloquy of the Spanish Cloister   56
    In a Gondola   59
    Artemis Prologizes   66
    Rudel to the Lady of Tripoli   69
    Cristina   70
    Johannes Agricola in Meditation   72
    Porphyria's Lover   73
    The Pied Piper of Hamelin   75

FROM *Dramatic Romances and Lyrics* (1845)
    "How They Brought the Good News from Ghent to Aix"   83
    Pictor Ignotus   85
    The Italian in England   87

The Englishman in Italy   91

The Lost Leader   98

Home-Thoughts, from Abroad   99

Home-Thoughts, from the Sea   99

The Bishop Orders His Tomb at Saint Praxed's Church   100

Garden Fancies   103

    1. The Flower's Name   103

    2. Sibrandus Schafnaburgensis   104

The Laboratory   107

The Boy and the Angel   109

Meeting at Night   111

Parting at Morning   112

Time's Revenges   112

The Glove   114

FROM *Men and Women* (1855)

Love Among the Ruins   119

Evelyn Hope   121

Up at a Villa — Down in the City   123

A Woman's Last Word   126

Fra Lippo Lippi   127

A Toccata of Galuppi's   136

By the Fire-side   138

Any Wife to Any Husband   147

An Epistle Containing the Strange Medical Experience of

    Karshish, the Arab Physician   152

A Serenade at the Villa   159

My Star   161

"Childe Roland to the Dark Tower Came"   162

Respectability   169

A Light Woman   170

The Statue and the Bust   172

Love in a Life   180

Life in a Love   180
✳ How It Strikes a Contemporary   181
The Last Ride Together   184
The Patriot   187
Bishop Blougram's Apology   188
Memorabilia   213
✓ Andrea del Sarto   213
In Three Days   220
Old Pictures in Florence   221
Saul   230
"De Gustibus —"   240
Cleon   241
Popularity   249
Two in the Campagna   252
A Grammarian's Funeral   254
"Transcendentalism: A Poem in Twelve Books"   257
One Word More   259

FROM *Dramatis Personae* (1864)
James Lee's Wife   265
Abt Vogler   278
Rabbi Ben Ezra   281
Caliban Upon Setebos; or, Natural Theology in the Island   288
Confessions   295
Prospice   296
✳ Youth and Art   297
Apparent Failure   300
Epilogue: "On the first of the Feast of Feasts"   302

FROM *The Ring and the Book* (1868-1869)
Book VI.   Giuseppe Caponsacchi   306
Book VII. Pompilia   356
Book X.   The Pope   400

FROM *Pacchiarotto* (1876)
House   450
Shop   451
Hervé Riel   455

FROM *Dramatic Idylls* [First Series] (1879)
I vàn Ivànovitch   460

FROM *Jocoseria* (1883)
Never the Time and the Place   472

Why I Am a Liberal (1885)   473

FROM *Asolando* (1889)
Summum Bonum   474
Epilogue: "At the midnight in the silence"   475

NOTES   477

INDEX OF TITLES   542

INTRODUCTION

by Donald Smalley

[This introduction attempts to trace for the reader Browning's gradual working out of his special theory and practice. Emphasis is given to a few aspects of Browning's life and habits of thought which go far in themselves to make clear the distinctive characteristics of his poetry. A chronological outline of Browning's life is provided at the end of the introduction, and a number of Browning's ideas that are sometimes given much space in introducing his poems are discussed and cross-referenced from poem to poem in the notes at the back of this edition.]

I. BROWNING'S EARLY LIFE (1812-33)

The headlong energy and the zest for experience that are manifest in much of Browning's poetry can probably be linked with his unusually happy childhood. Robert Browning was born on May 7, 1812, in Camberwell, then a leafy suburb on the far shore of the Thames from the busy center of London. Browning's father was a clerk at a modest salary in the Bank of England; but he was also a man of culture with a love for painting and a passion for rare books, both for collecting them and reading them. Browning's mother, a gentle, quietly religious woman, taught her son a love of plants and animals and shared with him her delight in music.

Browning's parents gave their son every encouragement to develop his talents. At two years and three months, employing lead pencil and currant juice ("paint being rank poison, as they said when I sucked my brushes"), he produced a sketch of a cottage and rocks that his proud father thought worth dating and preserving. As for poetry: "I never can recollect *not* writing rhymes," Browning wrote later; but he remembered composing, at about the age of five, an imitation of Ossian and thinking so well of the piece that he deposited it for the benefit of posterity "under the cushion of a great armchair." Sent to a private elementary school at about this same time, he proved to be so far advanced in his knowledge, even beyond the older boys, that he had to be withdrawn for fear of arousing jealousy among the pupils and their parents. When, some four years later, he was again entered in a school, he found his lessons absurdly easy and became a great pet of the master's. He kept his own pace in his omnivorous reading and in his exploration of the arts. By his twelfth year, Browning had discovered Byron. Writing in the flush of his enthusiasm for Byron, he produced a whole volume of poems. These seemed so good to his father and mother that they seriously, though in vain, attempted to interest a publisher in the manuscript. Browning twenty years later was to confess to Elizabeth Barrett that he had been "spoiled" by his parents. "Since I was a child," he added, "I never looked for the least or greatest thing within the compass of their means to give, but given it was . . . ." The pets which the parents permitted their son to maintain as part of the household included spiders, frogs, owls, monkeys, ladybirds, magpies, an eagle, hedgehogs, and two large snakes. Browning's sister Sarianna, two years his junior, seems to have fitted willingly into the role of admirer and subordinate to her brilliant brother. When he chose to play, as a child, at being preacher, she was his congregation; later, when he wished to have fair copies made of his manuscripts, she was his amanuensis.

At sixteen Browning was enrolled at the recently founded University of London; but he missed his pleasant days at home and attended only for a few months. His education, both before and after his brief university training, came primarily from hours of voracious but relatively undisciplined reading in his father's library of six thousand volumes and from private instruction. Greek and Latin he learned probably with his father's assistance; and his parents provided him with lessons from excellent tutors in French, Italian, and music. For art, he was free to visit the fine collections at the Dulwich Gallery across green meadows from his home in Camberwell. For exercise, he rode, boxed, and fenced.

II. *Pauline* (1833) AND BROWNING'S ZEST FOR EXPERIENCE

Browning's discovery of Shelley's poetry when he was fourteen had been a momentous event in the history of his development. Under the influence of Shelley, the young disciple had declared himself an atheist; and Shelley's long note on vegetarianism in *Queen Mab* had so impressed him, it is said, that he lived for some time on a diet of **bread and** potatoes.

By the time of his first published work, Browning had abandoned his atheism and his vegetarianism; but the influence of Shelley was still strong upon him. *Pauline: a Fragment of a Confession* appeared anonymously early in 1833, the thirty pounds required for publication being paid by an admiring aunt. The poem avows its indebtedness to Shelley in idolatrous lines addressed to him as "Sun-treader." There are echoes of Shelley's poetry, and especially of *Alastor,* throughout the work. But there is also much that is original. Many descriptive passages show a jewel-like clarity and a concreteness of detail that are distinctly new and fresh. Moreover, Browning at twenty shows an independent bent for intensive analysis of character. In spite of the poem's fictional framework, the character of the hero of *Pauline* is patently based upon that of the author himself; the young Browning has anticipated his future studies of men and women by elaborately analyzing his own nature. One passage of analysis is especially suggestive:

> I am made up of an intensest life,
> Of a most clear idea of consciousness
> Of self, distinct from all its qualities,
> From all affections, passions, feelings, powers;
> And thus far it exists, if tracked, in all:
> But linked, in me, to self-supremacy, . . .
> And to a principle of restlessness
> Which would be all, have, see, know, taste, feel, all —
> This is myself; . . .

The possession of "intensest life"; the belief in a central selfhood or central core of consciousness in human character distinct from incidental moods or concerns of the moment; the restless desire to experience life as intensely as possible in its concrete detail — these were to remain essential characteristics of Robert Browning. Five years after the publication of *Pauline,* Browning wrote his friend Fanny Haworth that he would sometimes bite flowers and leaves — "some leaves" — to bits "in an impatience at being unable to possess myself of them thoroughly, to see them quite, [to] satiate myself with their scent. . . ."

Browning's urge to experience the essential nature of flowers or of leaves or of any aspect of experience is as characteristic of him in his mature works as it is of the speaker of *Pauline.* In his famous dramatic monologue of 1855, Browning gives the Renaissance painter Fra Lippo Lippi lines that could with few changes be used to describe his own artistic creed in his poetry:

> This world's no blot for us,
> Nor blank; it means intensely, and means good:
> To find its meaning is my meat and drink.
>
> ... you've seen the world
> — The Beauty and the wonder and the power,
> The shapes of things, their colors, lights and shades,
> Changes, surprises, — ...
>   What's it all about?
> To be passed over, despised? or dwelt upon,
> Wondered at? oh, this last of course! — you say.
> But why not do as well as say, — paint these
> Just as they are, careless what comes of it?
> God's works — paint any one, and count it crime
> To let a truth slip.

In *How It Strikes a Contemporary*, another poem of Browning's collection *Men and Women* (1855), Browning does indeed present a poet working in much the same spirit as Fra Lippo Lippi, "Scenting the world, looking it full in face." This poet was fascinated by the detail of the life that surrounded him. He could be found poking the ferrel of his cane into the mortar of a new shop in process of being built, or peering close to learn the peculiarities in the construction of an ancient window. He studied people with the same intense interest:

> He stood and watched the cobbler at his trade,
> The man who slices lemons into drink,
> The coffee-roaster's brazier, and the boys
> That volunteer to help him turn its winch.
> He glanced o'er books on stalls with half an eye,
> And fly-leaf ballads on the vendor's string, ...
>
> He took such cognizance of men and things,
> If any beat a horse, you felt he saw;
> If any cursed a woman, he took note; ...

In "*Transcendentalism*," still another poem of 1855, Browning returns to the idea that good art entails perceiving and filling one's work with the immediate and intensely realized sights and sounds of the world. Two poets are contrasted. The one is preoccupied with conveying "stark naked thought" in his poetry, devoting his verses to abstractions and generalizations "Instead of draping them in sights and sounds"; but the true poet, Browning makes clear, is the one who causes the vividness of life itself to surround us as we read his work. Such a poet is like a magician who does not stop at merely generalizing about roses but, through the exercise of his craft, suddenly causes the room to be filled with the very roses themselves:

> He with a "look you!" vents a brace of rhymes,
> And in there breaks the sudden rose herself,
> Over us, under, round us every side,
> Nay, in and out the tables and the chairs,
> And musty volumes, . . .
> Buries us with a glory, young once more,
> Pouring heaven into this shut house of life.

Certainly the vivid effect of immediacy that characterizes Browning's poetry even in passages of *Pauline* and *Paracelsus* comes in good part from the profusion of intensely realized sights and sounds with which he manages to freight his lines.

Some readers may feel that the magician's roses of "*Transcendentalism*" inadequately represent the types of sights and sounds that often find their way into Browning's verse; but Browning, with his zest for life in its concrete detail, can write as enthusiastically of what is conventionally considered ugly as he can of roses. One can cite, for example, the gusto with which he describes the depredations of the rats among the burghers in *The Pied Piper of Hamelin;* or that revel in the raw color and steaming fertility of the Neapolitan countryside that makes up *The Englishman in Italy;* or the evocation of romping insect life among wet moss and toadstools in *Sibrandus Schafnaburgensis;* or the absurdly graphic mosaic of busyness in the square of a provincial Italian city in *Up at a Villa;* or the celebration of fire-tongs, prints, dresser knobs, wrecked tapestry, and other multitudinous "odds and ends of ravage" in the market at Florence which adds lustre to the first book of *The Ring and the Book.* Browning's mastery of the grotesque* in such passages as these is a notable aspect of his art. For another note, there are the powerfully repellent images of "*Childe Roland to the Dark Tower Came.*" And finally, for still another note that is nearly as far removed from conventional prettiness as the images of "*Childe Roland,*" there are the lines that conjure up the intensity of Tyrian blue in *Popularity.* The range is enormous: Brown-

---

*J. Cotter Morrison's description of grotesque art in a paper on Browning's *Caliban Upon Setebos* is suggestive:

"Its proper province would seem to be the exhibition of fanciful power by the artist; not beauty or truth in the literal sense at all, but inventive affluence of unreal yet absurdly comic forms, with just a flavour of the terrible added, to give a grim dignity, and save from the triviality of caricature." — Quoted in Arthur Symons, p. 125.

ing leaves the reader of his poetry convinced of the truth with which he wrote in *Pauline* of possessing "an intensest life," a restless vitality that "would be all, have, see, know, taste, feel, all —. . ." A few critics, including George Santayana (*The Poetry of Barbarism*) have considered Browning's absorption with the vivid detail of life a major vice rather than one of the prime virtues of his poetry. They object that in his zest for the immediate he loses restraint and simplicity. Fortunately, there is room for a variety of tastes. Restraint and simplicity are seldom marked qualities in Browning's poetry, but a great many critics and readers feel that there are compensating virtues of the sort Walter Savage Landor singled out for praise early in Browning's career:

> Since Chaucer was alive and hale
> No man has walked along our road with step
> So active, so enquiring eye, and tongue
> So varied in discourse.

III. *Paracelsus* (1835)

Though *Pauline* was enthusiastically praised by two notable critics — William J. Fox and Allan Cunningham — not a copy of the poem was sold. How amazingly confident of his own capabilities Browning had been at twenty when he produced *Pauline*, and how little he had been chastened by contact with the world outside his sheltered Camberwell environment, can be gathered from the note he inscribed some years later inside the cover of a copy of the poem. He had written *Pauline*, he said, "in pursuance of a foolish plan" which had occupied him "mightily for a time." He had dreamed of creating whole operas, novels, speeches, which the world would never guess had been produced by one and the same author. (Perhaps he meant to astound the world eventually by revealing the secret.) "Only this crab," Browning ended ruefully, "remains of the shapely Tree of Life in this Fool's paradise of mine." At another point in the same copy he added: "I don't know whether I had not made up my mind to *act* as well as make verses, music, and God knows what, — *que de châteaux en Espagne* [what castles in Spain]!"

The absolute failure of *Pauline* to gain a reading public must have given a severe check to Browning's soaring egoism; but he was soon active in other projects. In March and April of 1834, he made his first trip outside England, traveling as a companion to the Chevalier George de Benkhausen, the Russian consul general, through the Low Countries and across the plains of western Russia to St. Petersburg. By fall of the same year, he was hard at work on *Paracelsus*, his second piece to reach print and the first to bear his name on the title-page. It was published the following spring.

Paracelsus, written in the form of a drama but not designed for stage presentation, is supposed to present the experiences of the famous Renaissance scientist and physician. The history of the learned sixteenth-century Paracelsus does not actually go far, however, to determine the character of the hero or the true subject matter of the poem. In the extended speeches which take up a large part of the work, it is really the young poet who speaks, and his subject is the proper relation of love and knowledge in human life. Though Browning's lines still have Shelleyan echoes in them, *Paracelsus* is an authentic and highly original poem. More than one critic of the nineteenth century and the early twentieth judged that though Browning went on to write in a much different vein, he never surpassed his achievement in this work written in his twenty-second year.

In *Paracelsus* as in *Pauline* Browning has concentrated upon the internal experiences of his hero rather than upon incidents that could be acted out on the stage. Browning states in the preface to the first edition that he has dispensed with "an external machinery of incident," such as ordinarily characterizes drama, in order "to display somewhat minutely the mood itself in its rise and progress." In the preface to his next drama, *Strafford* (1837), he was to present the idea somewhat more succinctly by stating that his play dealt primarily with "Action in Character, rather than Character in Action."

There are relatively few passages in *Paracelsus* that rival the fresh, detailed vividness that Browning had given to many passages in *Pauline;* but *Paracelsus* is a coherent poem, as *Pauline* is not. Though *Paracelsus* failed to attract a large audience, important critics, writers, and other men of influence, including the actor William Charles Macready, recognized the poem as the work of an authentic poet of great promise. Browning seemed well launched upon his career.

IV. Browning and the Drama (1836-46)

The next years did not bring the recognition that *Paracelsus* seemed to promise. With the encouragement of Macready, Browning set out to write a successful play for the Victorian stage. His first attempt, *Strafford* (1837), closed after five performances. Browning next made a series of attempts at actable drama that failed to reach production. Then *A Blot in the 'Scutcheon* (1843), put upon the boards by Macready under adverse circumstances, played to thinning audiences for three performances. Browning failed as a writer for the Victorian stage; in retrospect it is not hard to see why he should do so. Victorian audiences favored plays that offered them not merely a lively machinery of external incident. but even lavish spectacle. In contrast, Browning's driving interest throughout his dramas was upon "Action in Character, rather than Character in Action." He could not create upon the stage the illusion of a world in action. Browning's heroes are prone to reveal their hidden purposes and to justify their decisions in lengthy speeches. There are few clashes of will externalized in fierce dialogue; there is seldom a sense of decisions brought about upon the stage itself. Browning's characters convey the impression that their actions on the stage are merely outward and visible signs of special traits, special points of view, that had taken shape in their natures long ago. Upon the printed page, many of the intricate speeches Browning wrote for his actors challenge the reader by their subtle revelation of character; but they are probably better on the page. *Pippa Passes* (1841), which Browning did not design for stage presentation, is probably for the majority of readers his most compelling play — the most "dramatic" so far as creating an illusion of a world in motion is concerned.

V. *Sordello* (1840) AND BROWNING'S THEORY AND PRACTICE

a. The Two Soliloquies of *Madhouse Cells*

In the same years, Browning was writing poems not designed for the stage. Both in these and in his dramas he was gradually feeling his way toward the form and subject matter best suited to his special abilities and interests. Two poems published only five months after *Paracelsus*, and possibly written before it, show Browning already attempting something different from what he had done in either that poem or earlier in *Pauline*. The two pieces were published in the *Monthly Repository* for January, 1836, under their separate titles. Later, in 1842, Browning published them jointly under the caption *Madhouse Cells*. They represent Browning's first known studies in portraying in brief monologues points of view widely differing from his own.

In *Porphyria's Lover*, Browning attempts to give the reader a glimpse into the point of view of a crazed speaker who explains what has led him to do away with the woman he loved. The speaker's reason is a very special one — nothing that the world would be likely to hit upon by viewing his case from the outside: He was sure he could crystallize and hold to a single good moment in time:

> That moment she was mine, mine, fair,
> Perfectly pure and good . . . .

And so he strangled Porphyria to isolate and preserve the moment. It is apparently next morning when he speaks; but he is sure there has been no change:

> And thus we sit together now,
> And all night long we have not stirred,
> And yet God has not said a word!

Johannes Agricola in Meditation, the other poem of *Madhouse Cells*, is a vivid soliloquy in which Browning attempts to portray the intimate point of view of a type of religious fanatic. Browning manages to convey more than a little of the magnificence that envelops Johannes' private vision. To the external view, he is a pitiable figure huddled on the straw of a madhouse cell; but within himself he is leading a life of glory:

> There's heaven above, and night by night
> I look right through its gorgeous roof;
> No suns and moons though e'er so bright
> Avail to stop me; splendor-proof
> I keep the broods of stars aloof: . . .

Like the speaker of *Porphyria's Lover*, Johannes Agricola is obsessed by a very special attitude toward time — and the world has ceased to have any normal meaning for him because of this special point of view:

> I lie where I have always lain,
> God smiles as he has always smiled;
> Ere suns and moons could wax and wane,
> Ere stars were thundergirt and piled
> The heavens, God thought on me his child; . . .

In their concentration upon the speaker's special point of view, his special way of perceiving the world, the two soliloquies of *Madhouse Cells* foreshadow the manner of the great dramatic monologues which were to constitute Browning's most distinctive contribution to literature.

b. *Sordello* (1840)

In 1840 Browning published *Sordello*, a poem of nearly six thousand lines in rhymed couplets, which he had begun even before writing *Paracelsus*. This work presents the story of a thirteenth-century troubadour and involves a good deal of very complicated Italian history. As Dean W. C. DeVane has shown,* Browning had revised the poem to an extent that amounted to rewriting it at least four separate times, though in each revision remnants of the earlier tellings remained. The final poem as a result suffers from a lack of any real unity. Moreover, Browning attempted here as a bold experiment an extremely elliptical style. Victorian readers of the work were badly confused. Later critics tend to regret the poem's lack of coherence and many opaquenesses but incline to admire its frequent passages of intense beauty and its wealth in original ideas.

Sordello severely damaged Browning's standing with the Victorian reading public for well over two decades. It was unfortunate for his reputation that Browning published the poem; but it was probably necessary for him to write it. Part of the obscurity of *Sordello* comes from the fact that into the final version of his poem about a thirteenth-century troubadour Browning crammed much of what he had been thinking and feeling about his own poetry and his future. In writing his ideas out in the tangled verses of *Sordello*, Browning managed to clarify for himself many of his own ideas regarding his proper function as a poet.

Browning's conclusions in *Sordello* are approximately those he was to hold to throughout the best part of his career. They can be briefly summarized thus:

1. Each human being, in the way he copes with the world, represents a special point of view, an individual reading of life, a separate spiritual drama. Even those we speak of as "losels" — worthless fellows — or "evil men past hope," have their inner struggles and try to hold to some conception of virtue, however twisted and unapparent in what the world sees of them:

> . . . ask moreover, when they prate
> Of evil men past hope, "Don't each contrive,
> Despite the evil you abuse, to live? —
> Keeping, each losel, through a maze of lies,
> His own conceit of truth? to which he hies
> By obscure windings, tortuous, if you will,
> But to himself not inaccessible;

---

*A *Browning Handbook,* p. 72.

> He sees truth, and his lies are for the crowd
> Who cannot see; some fancied right allowed
> His vilest wrong. . . . (III. 787-95)

2. The "best" type of poet is able to "read profound Disclosures" in the faces of the men and women about him — to penetrate far more deeply into what goes on inside them than other men are able to do. (III, 869-72)

3. The "best" type of poet possesses as his chief power the ability to "impart the gift of seeing" to his audience, making the scene and the character come alive before them. Browning calls this poet the "Maker-see." (III. 928 ff.) Inferior poets lack this power:

> The office of ourselves [the poets] . . .
> has been,
> For the worst of us, to say they so have seen;
> For the better, what it was they saw; the best
> Impart the gift of seeing to the rest: . . . (III. 864-68)

The threefold classification is very like that of T. S. Eliot in his lecture *The Three Voices of Poetry*. It is also somewhat similar to Leon Edel's clever method of describing types of novelists* which can perhaps be adapted to Browning's lines with profit: The "worst" poet looks out a window and tells his readers, who are seated in a room, that he sees something outside. The "better" poet gives his readers a detailed running account of what he is seeing out the window. The "Maker-see" in effect puts his readers at the window and affords them the opportunity of viewing for themselves what is going on.

c. Browning's Vision of Humanity

Browning was to restate or imply these ideas from time to time in his later verse. The poet of *How It Strikes a Contemporary* (1855), for example, "took such cognizance of men and things" that the citizens felt he saw into the intimate secrets of everyone about him and was to all intents "a recording chief-inquisitor." In the *Epilogue* to *Dramatis Personae* (1864), Browning speaks frankly in his own person as a poet whose business it is to penetrate the minds of the men and women about him and witness in each of them, even the worst, a private struggle for self-respect, a unique outlook on the world:

> Take the least man of all mankind, as I;
> Look at his head and heart, find how and why
> He differs from his fellows utterly:

The Psychological Novel, 1900-1950 (New York, 1955), pp. 208-209.

> Then, like me, watch when nature by degrees
> Grows alive round him, . . .

The miracle of individual personality, the sight of each man's life as a separate spiritual drama, is for Browning his sufficient proof that Spirit is at work in the world:

> When you acknowledge that one world could do
> All the diverse work, old yet ever new,
> Divide us, each from other, me from you,—. . .
>
> That one Face, far from vanish, rather grows,
> Or decomposes but to recompose,
> Become my universe that feels and knows.

But it was seldom in his best years (before the eighteen-seventies) that Browning spoke so directly of the meaning that might be derived from his work. It was ineffective, Browning held, for the poet to fill his verse with moral maxims or to attempt direct teaching of any sort. The poet's function was to give his reader portrayals of life and to fill them with such vitality that the reader would be stimulated by them to work out conclusions regarding their meaning for himself. Browning, if he read it, must have highly approved Thomas DeQuincey's observation on the futility of attempting to convey important truths wholesale by direct statement:

> No complex or very important truth was ever yet transferred in full development from one mind to another: truth of that character is not a piece of furniture to be shifted; it is a seed which must be sown, and pass through the several stages of growth. No doctrine of importance can be transferred in a matured shape into any man's understanding from without: it must arise by an act of genesis within the understanding itself. — *Letters to a Young Man,* Letter V.

Browning's conviction that the poet must hold by his art and merely plant the seed of truth in his reader's mind, rather than attempt teaching whole truths directly,* is conveyed at length in *Sordello* (III. 803-61, 924-37); but it is more clearly and succinctly stated at the end of *The Ring and the Book:*

---

*Browning in his later years came to indulge more and more in direct teaching. Even by 1864, as in *Rabbi Ben Ezra* and the *Epilogue* to *Dramatis Personae,* he often seems more concerned with teaching and less with portraying life as it is than his theory would allow for. Throughout his works, of course, Browning assumes that there is an ultimate truth that the reader will be inevitably drawn toward if he is stimulated to give much thought to the subject.

> . . . it is the glory and good of Art,
> That Art remains the one way possible
> Of speaking truth, to mouths like mine at least.
>
> . . . Art may tell a truth
> Obliquely, do the thing shall breed the thought,
> Nor wrong the thought, missing the mediate word.
> So may you paint your picture, twice show truth,
> Beyond mere imagery on the wall, —. . .
> So write a book shall mean beyond the facts . . . .

Earlier, in *Fra Lippo Lippi* (1855), Browning had suggested the way works of art might "do the thing shall breed the thought." Fra Lippo had completed at Prato a painting that showed Saint Laurence being tortured over a gridiron by three slaves. Lippo's painting created such a lively sense of reality in the natives of Prato as they viewed the picture that in the excitement and religious zeal it stirred in them they attacked the slaves with sticks and stones. The monks were greatly pleased and informed Fra Lippo that his work was a huge success:

> "Already not one phiz of your three slaves
> Who turn the Deacon off his toasted side,
> But's scratched and prodded to our heart's content,
> The pious people have so eased their own
> With coming to say prayers there in a rage:
> We get on fast to see the bricks beneath.
> Expect another job this time next year,
> For pity and religion grow i' the crowd —
> Your painting serves its purpose!"

It is seldom that the artist can produce so immediate an effect upon the people; but the artist's (or poet's) function, Browning believed, is to work as Fra Lippo had worked — to isolate a meaningful scene or character and to attempt through the aliveness of his piece to quicken in the beholder a fresh view of life, a new awareness of significance in the world about him:

> For, don't you mark? we're made so that we love
> First when we see them painted, things we have passed
> Perhaps a hundred times nor cared to see;
> And so they are better, painted — better to us,
> Which is the same thing. Art was given for that;
> God uses us to help each other so,
> Lending our minds out.

Browning believed that his own special work as a poet was to portray men and women, revealing their intimate points of view with such aliveness that his reader became aware of profounder meanings in the human scene he had passed day after day "a hundred times nor cared to see." "Can't you imagine a clever sort of angel who plots and plans and tries to build up something," Browning wrote a correspondent (Madame du Quaire) in the late eighteen-fifties, "— he wants to make you see it as he sees it — shows you one point of view, carries you off to another, hammering into your head the thing he wants you to understand." And in a letter of 1863 to Isabella Blagden, Browning agreed that his poetry was "meant to have 'one central meaning, seen only by reflexion in details.'"

Browning's "central meaning," it seems clear, was his vision of humanity (which is at the same time a vision of Spirit at work in the world) as he presents it most directly in Book III of *Sordello* and in the *Epilogue* to *Dramatis Personae*.* He restates the idea, though in less direct terms, in introducing his masterpiece, *The Ring and the Book* (1868-69). Here again he is speaking in his own person. He might have chosen to tell the story simply and from his own point of view, he says, "Landscaping what I saved, not what I saw."** (To do so, however, would be to work in the manner of the inferior poets as described in *Sordello*, who merely tell us what they have seen.) Instead, he prefers to work as a "Maker-see," causing us to witness the events and draw our own conclusions:

> See it for yourselves,
> This man's act, changeable because alive!

Man is like a glass ball with a point of light placed above it, and sends out mingled bright and dark gleams from his troubled inner life. People are prone to judge men superficially as either good or bad:

> Action now shrouds, nor shows the informing thought;
> Man, like a glass ball with a spark a-top,
> Out of the magic fire that lurks inside,
> Shows one tint at a time to take the eye:
> Which, let a finger touch the silent sleep,
> Shifted a hair's-breadth shoots you dark for bright,
> Suffuses bright with dark, and baffles so
> Your sentence absolute for shine or shade.

---

*Browning's most elaborate (though most intricate and indirect) statement occurs in *Fifine at the Fair* (1872).

**The passages quoted from *The Ring and the Book* in this paragraph and the next occur in Book I, lines 1340-70, and Book XII, lines 829-36.

See such men intimately, catching glimpses of the "other side" they normally hide from the world, and simple judgments are impossible. There are mixed qualities in each man, whether judged simply good or bad by the world as it sees him; and even famous villains like Guy Faux, or Browning's own villain Guido Franceschini of *The Ring and the Book*, reveal that a unique spiritual drama is going on inside each of them:

> Once set such orbs, — white styled, black stigmatized, —
> A-rolling, see them once on the other side
> Your good men and your bad men every one
> From Guido Franceschini to Guy Faux,
> Oft would you rub your eyes and change your names.

Browning returns to the idea at the end of the last book of his poem, again speaking in his own person. His work is valuable, he says, if it affords insight into the hearts (or souls) of his characters:

> It lives,
> If precious be the soul of man to man.

Its chief lesson is that appearances in the world are not to be trusted, that one must learn to question the easy judgments of the casual beholder and to probe beneath the surface of life for profounder meanings:

> . . . learn one lesson hence
> Of many which whatever lives should teach:
> This lesson, that our human speech is naught,
> Our human testimony false, our fame
> And human estimation words and wind.

VI. THE DRAMATIC MONOLOGUE

So much for Browning's theories concerning his function as a poet. They color, and help to explain, a great deal of his best work; but fortunately even in theory Browning held that his business was not so much to preach a doctrine as it was to work like his Fra Lippo Lippi, portraying things "Just as they are," counting it "crime to let a truth slip," and stimulating his audience to work out conclusions for themselves. Browning's characteristic vehicle for enabling his men and women to express their special points of view — the literary form that he came to make peculiarly his own — was the dramatic monologue.

The dramatic monologue differs from the simple monologue or soliloquy in that while there is only one speaker, his words make us aware of both a setting and an auditor. Thus while in *Andrea del Sarto,* for example, only Andrea speaks, we are given through his words a vivid awareness of the presence of his wife Lucrezia and a sense of the scene or setting. We are made to visualize the painter and his wife sitting at the window of a room of their house filled with Andrea's canvases, looking out into an autumn twilight, with the hill town of Fiesole in the distance and a length of convent wall and garden in the foreground. But it is our awareness of Andrea's auditor, his wife Lucrezia, that figures more significantly in the total effect of the piece. Browning could conceivably have written a soliloquy, allowing Andrea to present substantially the same subject matter but without Lucrezia sitting beside him bored, half-listening, interrupting — we are made aware — at one place to ask what Andrea is talking about, while she waits for "the Cousin's whistle." If Browning had written the poem as a soliloquy, however, much of the special interest of the work as it stands, its psychological complexity, its irony, its effect of immediacy, would have been lost. In the dramatic monologue as Browning employs it at his best, the fact that an auditor figures in the poem constitutes much more than a technical difference from the soliloquy; it represents a potent element in the effect of the work. This can be true even when, as in *An Epistle,* the person addressed does not actually hear the speaker's words. What the Arabian Karshish of *An Epistle* writes about Lazarus, the strange man with a disturbing tale of being raised from the dead, is powerfully modified by the fact that in his letter Karshish is addressing a fellow scientist and man of medicine. It should be added that Browning on occasion, as in *Pictor Ignotus* or *The Last Ride Together,* can portray a speaker and his point of view quite effectively without laying much stress upon either auditor or setting. In the great majority of his most notable poems aside from his brief lyrics, however, Browning makes highly profitable use of both.

Two of Browning's most brilliant dramatic monologues — *My Last Duchess* and *The Bishop Orders His Tomb at Saint Praxed's Church* — appeared in 1842 and 1845, respectively; but it was in *Men and Women,* the famous collection of 1855, that Browning showed his full power and scope in handling the form, with such poems as *Fra Lippo Lippi, An Epistle, Cleon, Andrea del Sarto,* and *Bishop Blougram's Apology.* The poems named in this paragraph and the great monologues of *The Ring and the Book* (1868-69) would be enough in

themselves to establish him as the master of the dramatic monologue
— a title he is likely to hold without serious challenge for a good
while to come.

ACKNOWLEDGMENTS

The text of this edition follows that of *The Complete Works of
Robert Browning* (*Florentine Edition*), prepared with care and discernment by Charlotte Porter and Helen A. Clarke (New York,
1898). For helpful criticism of the Introduction, the editor is grateful
to Professor Merritt E. Lawlis of Indiana University, and, for her
assistance with proof and her good advice at all stages of the project,
to Barbara Jane Smalley. Any one who writes anything about the
life and poetry of Robert Browning owes a very considerable debt
to Dean W. C. DeVane of Yale College.

BROWNING'S LIFE

A Chronological Outline

[Dates given for Browning's works are those of publication unless there is a statement to the contrary.]

1812   May 7. Born at Camberwell, a pleasant suburb of London. (For details of Browning's early life, see Section I of the Introduction.)

1833   *Pauline: A Fragment of a Confession* (Discussed at some length in Section II of the Introduction.)

1834   March and April. Browning's trip to St. Petersburg, Russia.

1835   *Paracelsus* (Discussed at some length in Section III of the Introduction.)

1837   *Strafford* performed and published. (See Section IV of the Introduction, "Browning and the Drama.")

1838   Browning's first visit to Italy, including Venice and Asolo, setting of *Pippa Passes.*

1840   *Sordello* (Discussed at length in Section V of the Introduction.)

1841   *Pippa Passes,* published as Number 1 of *Bells and Pomegranates,* a series of eight pamphlets which appeared 1841-46 containing Browning's plays and poems.

1842   *Dramatic Lyrics,* containing, among other poems, *My Last Duchess* and *The Pied Piper of Hamelin.*

1843   *A Blot in the 'Scutcheon* performed and published. (See Section IV of the Introduction.)

1844   Browning's second visit to Italy, including Naples and Rome.

1845   *Dramatic Romances and Lyrics,* containing, among other poems, *The Bishop Orders His Tomb at Saint Praxed's Church, Saul* (the first nine sections — see the notes), and *The Glove.*

1845-46. Courtship and marriage. Browning wrote Elizabeth Barrett, praising her poetry (she was already recognized as a writer of importance), on January 10, 1845. Six years older than Browning, and resigned, at thirty-nine, to what seemed hopeless invalidism, she was under the dominance of her father, who ruled his large family with the high-handedness of an Old Testament patriarch and forbade any of his offspring to think of marriage. The correspondence carried on between Browning and Miss Barrett runs to two thick (and very interesting) printed volumes. In May, 1845, Elizabeth at last allowed Browning to call on her. Shortly thereafter, Browning wrote her passionately declaring his love. The spiritual history of the courtship from this point is recorded in Elizabeth's famous *Sonnets from the Portuguese*. After at first rejecting his suit because of her age and her invalidism, Elizabeth was gradually won by Browning's letters and his visits into accepting him as her lover.

1846 September 12. Knowing the father was adamant against his daughter's marrying, Robert Browning and Elizabeth Barrett were secretly wedded, and a week later Elizabeth fled with Browning to the continent. Her father never forgave her.

1847-61 The Brownings made their home in Italy, at Florence. Though her health was always frail, Mrs. Browning improved sufficiently to lead a varied and eventful life, seeing much of the colorful society that visited Florence or made part of the brilliant English and American colony of the city. In 1849 she gave birth to a son, Robert Wiedemann Barrett Browning. The Brownings spent brief periods in Rome and Paris and made occasional visits to London and to other cities and places of interest. Browning painted and worked in clay (under the tutelage of his good friend, the American sculptor William W. Story), read much, studied deeply in Italian art of the Renaissance, and wrote less poetry, possibly, than he would have written if he had not been so pleasantly occupied in the present.

1850 *Christmas-Eve and Easter-Day,* Browning's "dramatic" and indirect but ambitious exposition of his religious views, revealing his awareness of Strauss, Comte, and the rationalistic tendencies in mid-Victorian thought.

1855   *Men and Women,* the two-volume collection of Browning's poetry containing much of his best work, including *Fra Lippo Lippi, Andrea del Sarto, An Epistle, Cleon,* and *Bishop Blougram's Apology.*

1856   Death of John Kenyon, kinsman of Elizabeth and friend of both the Brownings, who left them a bequest of £11,000.

1860   In June, Browning discovered the "Old Yellow Book," source of *The Ring and the Book,* in a second-hand stall in the market at Florence.

1861   Death of Mrs. Browning on June 29. Browning left Florence forever. He returned to England to watch over the education of his son, now twelve.

1862   Browning, after his first grief at the death of Elizabeth, began to see much of London social life.

1864   *Dramatis Personae.* Many poems of this collection reflect Browning's return to English life and his consequent interest in the political, scientific, and religious issues of the day, especially Evolution (as in *Caliban Upon Setebos*) and Higher Criticism of the Bible (as in *A Death in the Desert* and the *Epilogue* to the collection). A second edition was soon called for. Browning's works began to be widely read among the students of Cambridge and Oxford.

1868-69   *The Ring and the Book,* Browning's great work, the writing of which had been his major occupation since 1864. The volumes appeared at intervals of a month, beginning on November 21, 1868. The poem established Browning with the public as second in honor only to Tennyson among the living poets of England.

1871-89   Browning became a social lion in the eighteen-seventies and after. He wrote voluminously, producing occasional fine lyrics and vivid narrative poems. Often even in his longer works he managed splendid passages of poetry, or brilliant flashes of ingenuity where the poetry is less than splendid. The general quality of his output, however, was decidedly inferior to that of his best years, and he was all too frequently guilty of garrulity.

1871* *Balaustion's Adventure*, on August 8, a pleasant if overlong tribute to Browning's favorite Greek dramatist, Euripides, including a translation of his *Alcestis*.

1871 *Prince Hohenstiel-Schwangau, Saviour of Society*, on December 16, a lengthy and intricate dramatic monologue, probably begun as early as 1860. The speaker is patently Napoleon III, the exiled former Emperor of France, who reviews his career and attempts to defend his devious courses as a ruler.

1872 *Fifine at the Fair*, an extremely casuistical but highly interesting poem in which a modern Don Juan is made to present some of Browning's most ingenious ideas.

1873 *Red Cotton Night-Cap Country*, a long psychological narrative that presents Browning's curious version of a notorious contemporary French scandal and suicide.

1875 *Aristophanes' Apology*, in April — another, and more garrulous, defense of Euripides and, at the same time, a defense of Browning's own practice as a poet.

1875 *The Inn Album*, in November — a narrative involving much dialogue, its story based primarily upon a criminal incident that had occurred four decades earlier. Swinburne, who liked it, called it Browning's "new sensation novel."

1878 Browning traveled to Italy for the first time since the death of his wife. Thereafter he made frequent sojourns at Venice or Asolo, though he never revisited Florence.

1881 Founding of the Browning Society. Browning was both pleased and embarrassed by the attentions of the Society to his work and to himself.

1887 *Parleyings with Certain People of Importance in Their Day*. This book, divided into seven "parleyings" with men whose works had influenced Browning's thinking, is essentially "notes for Browning's mental autobiography." See DeVane, *Browning's Parleyings*, in the bibliography below.

1889 December 12. Browning died at the Palazzo Rezzonico, the home of his son in Venice. He was buried on December 31 in Westminster Abbey.

---

*Only longer works of special interest are mentioned from this point on.

SELECTED BIBLIOGRAPHY

[Only works of special interest for the undergraduate student of Browning are included. A splendid selection along more ambitious lines appears at the end of Dean DeVane's *Handbook,* and a discerning review of Browning scholarship 1910-1949 makes up chapter 11 of W. O. Raymond's *The Infinite Moment.* The standard (and excellent) Browning bibliography that aims at completeness is listed with works of reference below.]

1. EDITIONS OF BROWNING'S WORKS

The Complete Works of Robert Browning (Florentine Edition), 12 vols., edited with Introductions and Notes by Charlotte Porter and Helen A. Clarke, New York, 1898, 1926.

The Works of Robert Browning (Centenary Edition), 10 vols., edited with Introductions by F. G. Kenyon, London, 1912.

2. LETTERS

The Letters of Elizabeth Barrett Browning, ed. F. G. Kenyon, 2 vols., New York, 1897.

The Letters of Robert Browning and Elizabeth Barrett Barrett, 1845-1846, 2 vols., New York and London, 1899.

Letters of Robert Browning, Collected by T. J. Wise, ed. with introduction, notes, and appendix by T. L. Hood, New Haven, 1933.

New Letters of Robert Browning, ed. with introduction, notes, and appendices by William C. De Vane and K. L. Knickerbocker, New Haven, 1950.

3. BIOGRAPHIES*

Burdett, O., *The Brownings,* London, 1929.

Chesterton, G. K., *Robert Browning* (English Men of Letters Series), London, 1903.

---

*The student will find highly interesting two creative works based upon Browning biography: Rudolf Besier's play, *The Barretts of Wimpole Street,* New York, 1931; and Virginia Woolf's *Flush,* New York, 1933, the narrative of Browning's courtship told from the point of view of Elizabeth Barrett's dog, Flush.

Dowden, E., *The Life of Robert Browning* (Everyman's Library), London, 1904.

Griffin, W. H., and Minchin, H. C., *The Life of Robert Browning,* London, 1910 (new edition, 1938).

Miller, Betty, *Robert Browning: A Portrait,* New York, 1953.

Orr, Mrs. Sutherland, *Life and Letters of Robert Browning,* revised by F. G. Kenyon, New York, 1908.

4. WORKS OF REFERENCE

Berdoe, Edward, *The Browning Cyclopaedia,* London, 1891.

Broughton, L. N., Northrup, C. S., and Pearsall, R., *Robert Browning: A Bibliography,* Ithaca, 1953.

Broughton, L. N., and Stelter, B. F., *A Concordance to the Poems of Robert Browning,* 2 vols., New York, 1924-25.

Cooke, G. W., *A Guide-Book to the Poetic and Dramatic Works of Robert Browning,* Boston, 1891.

De Vane, William C., *A Browning Handbook,* (Second — Revised — Edition), New York, 1955.

Orr, Mrs. Sutherland, *A Handbook to the Works of Robert Browning,* London, 1886, and successive editions with revisions.

5. STUDIES

Cook, A. K., *A Commentary Upon Browning's "The Ring and the Book,"* London, 1920.

De Vane, William C., *Browning's Parleyings: The Autobiography of a Mind,* New Haven, 1927.

Duckworth, F. G. R., *Browning: Background and Conflict,* London, 1931.

Jones, Henry, *Browning as a Philosophical and Religious Teacher,* London, 1891.

Phelps, William Lyon, *Robert Browning,* Indianapolis, 1931.

Raymond, William O., *The Infinite Moment and Other Essays in Robert Browning,* Toronto, 1950.

Santayana, George, "The Poetry of Barbarism," in *Interpretations of Poetry and Religion,* New York, 1900.

Symons, Arthur, *An Introduction to the Study of Browning,* London, 1906.

POEMS OF

ROBERT BROWNING

Pippa Passes: A Drama

(1841)

⊓⊔⊓⊔⊓⊔⊓⊔⊓⊔⊓⊔⊓⊔⊓⊔⊓⊔⊓⊔⊓⊔⊓⊔⊓⊔⊓⊔⊓⊔⊓⊔⊓⊔

I dedicate my best intentions, in this poem, admiringly to the author of "Ion," affectionately to Mr. Sergeant Talfourd.

R. B.

LONDON: 1841

PERSONS

Pippa

Ottima

Sebald

Foreign Students

Gottlieb

Schramm

Jules

Phene

Austrian Police

Bluphocks

Luigi *and his mother*

Poor Girls

Monsignor *and his attendants*

INTRODUCTION

New Year's Day at Asolo in the Trevisan

SCENE — *A large mean airy chamber. A girl,* PIPPA, *from the silk-mills, springing out of bed.*

DAY!
Faster and more fast,
O'er night's brim, day boils at last:
Boils, pure gold, o'er the cloud-cup's brim
Where spurting and suppressed it lay,
For not a froth-flake touched the rim
Of yonder gap in the solid gray

3

Of the eastern cloud, an hour away;
But forth one wavelet, then another, curled,
Till the whole sunrise, not to be suppressed,   10
Rose, reddened, and its seething breast
Flickered in bounds, grew gold, then overflowed the world.

Oh, Day, if I squander a wavelet of thee,
A mite of my twelve hours' treasure,
The least of thy gazes or glances,
(Be they grants thou art bound to or gifts above measure)
One of thy choices or one of thy chances,
(Be they tasks God imposed thee or freaks at thy pleasure)
— My Day, if I squander such labor or leisure,
Then shame fall on Asolo, mischief on me!   20

Thy long blue solemn hours serenely flowing,
Whence earth, we feel, gets steady help and good —
Thy fitful sunshine-minutes, coming, going,
As if earth turned from work in gamesome mood —
All shall be mine! But thou must treat me not
As prosperous ones are treated, those who live
At hand here, and enjoy the higher lot,
In readiness to take what thou wilt give,
And free to let alone what thou refusest;
For, Day, my holiday, if thou ill-usest   30
Me, who am only Pippa, — old-year's sorrow,
Cast off last night, will come again to-morrow:
Whereas, if thou prove gentle, I shall borrow
Sufficient strength of thee for new-year's sorrow.
All other men and women that this earth
Belongs to, who all days alike possess,
Make general plenty cure particular dearth,
Get more joy one way, if another, less:
Thou art my single day, God lends to leaven
What were all earth else, with a feel of heaven, —   40
Sole light that helps me through the year, thy sun's!
Try now! Take Asolo's Four Happiest Ones —
And let thy morning rain on that superb
Great haughty Ottima; can rain disturb
Her Sebald's homage? All the while thy rain
Beats fiercest on her shrub-house window-pane,
He will but press the closer, breathe more warm
Against her cheek; how should she mind the storm?
And, morning past, if mid-day shed a gloom

O'er Jules and Phene, — what care bride and groom   50
Save for their dear selves? 'Tis their marriage-day;
And while they leave church and go home their way,
Hand clasping hand, within each breast would be
Sunbeams and pleasant weather spite of thee.
Then, for another trial, obscure thy eve
With mist, — will Luigi and his mother grieve —
The lady and her child, unmatched, forsooth,
She in her age, as Luigi in his youth,
For true content? The cheerful town, warm, close
And safe, the sooner that thou art morose,   60
Receives them. And yet once again, outbreak
In storm at night on Monsignor, they make
Such stir about, — whom they expect from Rome
To visit Asolo, his brothers' home,
And say here masses proper to release
A soul from pain, — what storm dares hurt his peace?
Calm would he pray, with his own thoughts to ward
Thy thunder off, nor want the angels' guard.
But Pippa — just one such mischance would spoil
Her day that lightens the next twelvemonth's toil   70
At wearisome silk-winding, coil on coil!
          And here I let time slip for naught!
Aha, you foolhardy sunbeam, caught
With a single splash from my ewer!
You that would mock the best pursuer,
Was my basin over-deep?
One splash of water ruins you asleep,
And up, up, fleet your brilliant bits
Wheeling and counterwheeling,
Reeling, broken beyond healing: 80
Now grow together on the ceiling!
That will task your wits.
Whoever it was quenched fire first, hoped to see
Morsel after morsel flee
As merrily, as giddily . . .
Meantime, what lights my sunbeam on,
Where settles by degrees the radiant cripple?
Oh, is it surely blown, my martagon?
New-blown and ruddy as St. Agnes' nipple,
Plump as the flesh-bunch on some Turk bird's poll!   90
Be sure if corals, branching 'neath the ripple
Of ocean, bud there, — fairies watch unroll
Such turban-flowers; I say, such lamps disperse

Thick red flame through that dusk green universe!
I am queen of thee, floweret!
And each fleshy blossom
Preserve I not — (safer
Than leaves that embower it,
Or shells that embosom)
— From weevil and chafer?   100
Laugh through my pane then; solicit the bee;
Gibe him, be sure; and, in midst of thy glee,
Love thy queen, worship me!

— Worship whom else? For am I not, this day,
Whate'er I please? What shall I please to-day?
My morn, noon, eve and night—how spend my day?
To-morrow I must be Pippa who winds silk,
The whole year round, to earn just bread and milk:
But, this one day, I have leave to go,
And play out my fancy's fullest games;   110
I may fancy all day — and it shall be so —
That I taste of the pleasures, am called by the names
Of the Happiest Four in our Asolo!

See! Up the hill-side yonder, through the morning,
Some one shall love me, as the world calls love:
I am no less than Ottima, take warning!
The gardens, and the great stone house above,
And other house for shrubs, all glass in front,
Are mine; where Sebald steals, as he is wont,
To court me, while old Luca yet reposes: 120
And therefore, till the shrub-house door uncloses,
I . . . what now? — give abundant cause for prate
About me — Ottima, I mean — of late,
Too bold, too confident she'll still face down
The spitefullest of talkers in our town.
How we talk in the little town below!
        But love, love, love—there's better love, I know!
This foolish love was only day's first offer;
I choose my next love to defy the scoffer:
For do not our Bride and Bridegroom sally   130
Out of Possagno church at noon?
Their house looks over Orcana valley:
Why should not I be the bride as soon
As Ottima? For I saw, beside,
Arrive last night that little bride —

Saw, if you call it seeing her, one flash
Of the pale snow-pure cheek and black bright tresses,
Blacker than all except the black eyelash;
I wonder she contrives those lids no dresses!
— So strict was she, the veil 140
Should cover close her pale
Pure cheeks — a bride to look at and scarce touch,
Scarce touch, remember, Jules! For are not such
Used to be tended, flower-like, every feature,
As if one's breath would fray the lily of a creature?
A soft and easy life these ladies lead:
Whiteness in us were wonderful indeed.
Oh, save that brow its virgin dimness,
Keep that foot its lady primness,
Let those ankles never swerve 150
From their exquisite reserve,
Yet have to trip along the streets like me,
All but naked to the knee!
How will she ever grant her Jules a bliss
So startling as her real first infant kiss?
Oh, no — not envy, this!

— Not envy, sure! — for if you gave me
Leave to take or to refuse,
In earnest, do you think I'd choose
That sort of new love to enslave me? 160
Mine should have lapped me round from the beginning;
As little fear of losing it as winning:
Lovers grow cold, men learn to hate their wives,
And only parents' love can last our lives.
At eve the Son and Mother, gentle pair,
Commune inside our turret: what prevents
My being Luigi? While that mossy lair
Of lizards through the winter-time is stirred
With each to each imparting sweet intents
For this new-year, as brooding bird to bird — 170
(For I observe of late, the evening walk
Of Luigi and his mother, always ends
Inside our ruined turret, where they talk,
Calmer than lovers, yet more kind than friends)
— Let me be cared about, kept out of harm,
And schemed for, safe in love as with a charm;
Let me be Luigi! If I only knew
What was my mother's face — my father, too!

Nay, if you come to that, best love of all
Is God's; then why not have God's love befall   180
Myself as, in the palace by the Dome,
Monsignor? — who to-night will bless the home
Of his dead brother; and God bless in turn
That heart which beats, those eyes which mildly burn
With love for all men! I, to-night at least,
Would be that holy and beloved priest.

Now wait! — even I already seem to share
In God's love: what does New-year's hymn declare?
What other meaning do these verses bear?

> *All service ranks the same with God:*   190
> *If now, as formerly he trod*
> *Paradise, his presence fills*
> *Our earth, each only as God wills*
> *Can work —God's puppets, best and worst,*
> *Are we; there is no last nor first.*
> *Say not "a small event!" Why "small"?*
> *Costs it more pain that this, ye call*
> *A "great event," should come to pass,*
> * Than that? Untwine me from the mass*
> *Of deeds which make up life, one deed*   200
> *Power shall fall short in or exceed!*

And more of it, and more of it! — oh yes —
I will pass each, and see their happiness,
And envy none — being just as great, no doubt,
Useful to men, and dear to God, as they!
A pretty thing to care about
So mightily, this single holiday!
But let the sun shine! Wherefore repine?
— With thee to lead me, O Day of mine,
Down the grass path gray with dew,   210
Under the pine-wood, blind with boughs
Where the swallow never flew
Nor yet cicala dared carouse —
No, dared carouse!   [*She enters the street.*

1. MORNING

SCENE — *Up the Hill-side, inside the Shrub-house.* LUCA'S *wife,* OTTIMA, *and her paramour, the German* SEBALD.

Sebald [*sings*].

> Let the watching lids wink!
> Day's a-blaze with eyes, think!
> Deep into the night, drink!

Ottima. Night? Such may be your Rhineland nights perhaps;
But this blood-red beam through the shutter's chink
— We call such light, the morning: let us see!
Mind how you grope your way, though! How these tall
Naked geraniums straggle! Push the lattice
Behind that frame! — Nay, do I bid you? — Sebald,
It shakes the dust down on me! Why, of course   10
The slide-bolt catches. Well, are you content,
Or must I find you something else to spoil?
Kiss and be friends, my Sebald! Is't full morning?
Oh, don't speak then!
　　　Sebald. 　　　　　Ay, thus it used to be.
Ever your house was, I remember, shut
Till mid-day; I observed that, as I strolled
On mornings through the vale here; country girls
Were noisy, washing-garments in the brook,
Hinds drove the slow white oxen up the hills:
But no, your house was mute, would ope no eye.   20
And wisely: you were plotting one thing there,
Nature, another outside. I looked up —
Rough white wood shutters, rusty iron bars,
Silent as death, blind in a flood of light.
Oh, I remember! — and the peasants laughed
And said, "The old man sleeps with the young wife."
This house was his, this chair, this window — his.
　　　Ottima. Ah, the clear morning! I can see St. Mark's;
That black streak is the belfry. Stop: Vicenza
Should lie . . . there's Padua, plain enough, that blue!   30
Look o'er my shoulder, follow my finger!

Sebald.   Morning?
It seems to me a night with a sun added.
Where's dew, where's freshness? That bruised plant, I bruised
In getting through the lattice yestereve,
Droops as it did. See, here's my elbow's mark
I' the dust o' the sill.
          Ottima.   Oh, shut the lattice, pray!
          Sebald. Let me lean out. I cannot scent blood here,
Foul as the morn may be.
                         There, shut the world out!
How do you feel now, Ottima? There, curse
The world and all outside! Let us throw off   40
This mask: how do you bear yourself? Let's out
With all of it.
          Ottima. Best never speak of it.
          Sebald. Best speak again and yet again of it,
Till words cease to be more than words. "His blood,"
For instance — let those two words mean "His blood"
And nothing more. Notice, I'll say them now,
"His blood."
          Ottima. Assuredly if I repented
The deed —
          Sebald. Repent? Who should repent, or why?
What puts that in your head? Did I once say
That I repented?
          Ottima.   No, I said the deed.   50
          Sebald. "The deed" and "the event" — just now it was
"Our passion's fruit" — the devil take such cant!
Say, once and always, Luca was a wittol,
I am his cut-throat, you are . . .
          Ottima.   Here's the wine;
I brought it when we left the house above,
And glasses too — wine of both sorts. Black? White then?
          Sebald. But am not I his cut-throat? What are you?
          Ottima. There trudges on his business from the Duomo
Benet the Capuchin, with his brown hood
And bare feet; always in one place at church,   60
Close under the stone wall by the south entry.
I used to take him for a brown cold piece
Of the wall's self, as out of it he rose
To let me pass — at first, I say, I used:
Now, so has that dumb figure fastened on me,
I rather should account the plastered wall

A piece of him, so chilly does it strike.
This, Sebald?
    Sebald. No, the white wine — the white wine!
Well, Ottima, I promised no new year
Should rise on us the ancient shameful way;   70
Nor does it rise. Pour on! To your black eyes!
Do you remember last damned New Year's day?
    Ottima. You brought those foreign prints. We looked at them
Over the wine and fruit. I had to scheme
To get him from the fire. Nothing but saying
His own set wants the proof-mark, roused him up
To hunt them out.
    Sebald.   'Faith, he is not alive
To fondle you before my face.
    Ottima.   Do you
Fondle me then! Who means to take your life
For that, my Sebald?
    Sebald.   Hark you, Ottima!   80
One thing to guard against. We'll not make much
One of the other — that is, not make more
Parade of warmth, childish officious coil,
Than yesterday: as if, sweet, I supposed
Proof upon proof were needed now, now first,
To show I love you — yes, still love you — love you
In spite of Luca and what's come to him
— Sure sign we had him ever in our thoughts,
White sneering old reproachful face and all!
We'll even quarrel, love, at times, as if   90
We still could lose each other, were not tied
By this: conceive you?
    Ottima.   Love!
    Sebald.   Not tied so sure.
Because though I was wrought upon, have struck
His insolence back into him — am I
So surely yours? — therefore forever yours?
    Ottima. Love, to be wise, (one counsel pays another)
Should we have — months ago, when first we loved,
For instance that May morning we two stole
Under the green ascent of sycamores —
If we had come upon a thing like that   100
Suddenly . . .
    Sebald. "A thing" — there again — "a thing!"
    Ottima. Then, Venus' body, had we come upon
My husband Luca Gaddi's murdered corpse

Within there, at his couch-foot, covered close —
Would you have pored upon it? Why persist
In poring now upon it? For 'tis here
As much as there in the deserted house:
You cannot rid your eyes of it. For me,
Now he is dead I hate him worse: I hate . . .
Dare you stay here? I would go back and hold   110
His two dead hands, and say, "I hate you worse,
Luca, than . . ."
    Sebald.   Off, off — take your hands off mine,
'Tis the hot evening — off! oh, morning is it?
    Ottima. There's one thing must be done; you know what thing.
Come in and help to carry. We may sleep
Anywhere in the whole wide house to-night.
    Sebald. What would come, think you, if we let him lie
Just as he is? Let him lie there until
The angels take him! He is turned by this
Off from his face beside, as you will see.   120
    Ottima. This dusty pane might serve for looking-glass.
Three, four — four gray hairs! Is it so you said
A plait of hair should wave across my neck?
No — this way.
    Sebald.   Ottima, I would give your neck,
Each splendid shoulder, both those breasts of yours,
That this were undone! Killing! Kill the world
So Luca lives again! — ay, lives to sputter
His fulsome dotage on you — yes, and feign
Surprise that I return at eve to sup,
When all the morning I was loitering here —   130
Bid me despatch my business and begone.
I would . . .
    Ottima. See!
    Sebald.   No, I'll finish. Do you think
I fear to speak the bare truth once for all?
All we have talked of, is, at bottom, fine
To suffer; there's a recompense in guilt;
One must be venturous and fortunate:
What is one young for, else? In age we'll sigh
O'er the wild reckless wicked days flown over;
Still, we have lived: the vice was in its place.
But to have eaten Luca's bread, have worn   140
His clothes, have felt his money swell my purse —
Do lovers in romances sin that way?
Why, I was starving when I used to call

And teach you music, starving while you plucked me
These flowers to smell!
    Ottima.   My poor lost friend!
    Sebald.   He gave me
Life, nothing less: what if he did reproach
My perfidy, and threaten, and do more —
Had he no right? What was to wonder at?
He sat by us at table quietly:
Why must you lean across till our cheeks touched?   150
Could he do less than make pretence to strike?
'Tis not the crime's sake — I'd commit ten crimes
Greater, to have this crime wiped out, undone!
And you — O how feel you? Feel you for me?
    Ottima. Well then, I love you better now than ever,
And best (look at me while I speak to you) —
Best for the crime; nor do I grieve, in truth,
This mask, this simulated ignorance,
This affectation of simplicity,
Falls off our crime; this naked crime of ours   160
May not now be looked over: look it down!
Great? let it be great; but the joys it brought,
Pay they or no its price? Come: they or it!
Speak not! The past, would you give up the past
Such as it is, pleasure and crime together?
Give up that noon I owned my love for you?
The garden's silence: even the single bee
Persisting in his toil, suddenly stopped,
And where he hid you only could surmise
By some campanula chalice set a-swing.   170
Who stammered — "Yes, I love you"?
    Sebald.   And I drew
Back; put far back your face with both my hands
Lest you should grow too full of me — your face
So seemed athirst for my whole soul and body!
    Ottima. And when I ventured to receive you here,
Made you steal hither in the mornings —
    Sebald.   When
I used to look up 'neath the shrub-house here,
Till the red fire on its glazed windows spread
To a yellow haze?
    Ottima.   Ah — my sign was, the sun
Inflamed the sere side of yon chestnut-tree   180
Nipped by the first frost.

  Sebald.   You would always laugh
At my wet boots. I had to stride thro' grass
Over my ankles.
  Ottima. Then our crowning night!
  Sebald. The July night?
  Ottima.   The day of it too, Sebald!
When heaven's pillars seemed o'erbowed with heat,
Its black-blue canopy suffered descend
Close on us both, to weigh down each to each,
And smother up all life except our life.
So lay we till the storm came.
  Sebald.   How it came!
  Ottima. Buried in woods we lay, you recollect;   190
Swift ran the searching tempest overhead;
And ever and anon some bright white shaft
Burned thro' the pine-tree roof, here burned and there,
As if God's messenger thro' the close wood screen
Plunged and replunged his weapon at a venture,
Feeling for guilty thee and me: then broke
The thunder like a whole sea overhead —
  Sebald. Yes!
  Ottima. — While I stretched myself upon you, hands
To hands, my mouth to your hot mouth, and shook
All my locks loose, and covered you with them —   200
You, Sebald, the same you!
  Sebald.   Slower, Ottima!
  Ottima. And as we lay —
  Sebald.   Less vehemently! Love me!
Forgive me! Take not words, mere words, to heart!
Your breath is worse than wine! Breathe slow, speak slow!
Do not lean on me!
  Ottima. Sebald, as we lay,
Rising and falling only with our pants,
Who said, "Let death come now! 'Tis right to die!
Right to be punished! Naught completes such bliss
But woe!" Who said that? Who said that?
  Sebald.   How did we ever rise?
Was't that we slept? Why did it end?
  Ottima.   I felt you   210
Taper into a point the ruffled ends
Of my loose locks 'twixt both your humid lips.
My hair is fallen now: knot it again!
  Sebald. I kiss you now, dear Ottima, now and now!

This way? Will you forgive me — be once more
My great queen?
     Ottima.   Bind it thrice about my brow;
Crown me your queen, your spirit's arbitress,
Magnificent in sin. Say that!
     Sebald.   I crown you
My great white queen, my spirit's arbitress,
Magnificent . . .   220

        [*From without is heard the voice of* PIPPA, *singing* —

          The year's at the spring
          And day's at the morn;
          Morning's at seven;
          The hill-side's dew-pearled;
          The lark's on the wing;
          The snail's on the thorn:
          God's in his heaven —
          All's right with the world!   [PIPPA *passes.*

     Sebald. God's in his heaven! Do you hear that? Who spoke?
You, you spoke!
     Ottima.   Oh — that little ragged girl!   230
She must have rested on the step: we give them
But this one holiday the whole year round.
Did you ever see our silk-mills — their inside?
There are ten silk-mills now belong to you.
She stoops to pick my double heartsease . . . Sh!
She does not hear: call you out louder!
     Sebald.   Leave me!
Go, get your clothes on — dress those shoulders!
     Ottima.   Sebald?
     Sebald. Wipe off that paint! I hate you.
     Ottima.   Miserable!
     Sebald. My God, and she is emptied of it now!
Outright now! — how miraculously gone   240
All of the grace — had she not strange grace once?
Why, the blank cheek hangs listless as it likes,
No purpose holds the features up together,
Only the cloven brow and puckered chin
Stay in their places: and the very hair,
That seemed to have a sort of life in it,
Drops, a dead web!
     Ottima.   Speak to me — not of me!

Sebald. — That round great full-orbed face, where not an angle
Broke the delicious indolence — all broken!

    Ottima. To me — not of me! Ungrateful, perjured cheat!   250
A coward too: but ingrate's worse than all.
Beggar — my slave — a fawning, cringing lie!
Leave me! Betray me! I can see your drift!
A lie that walks and eats and drinks!

    Sebald.   My God!
Those morbid olive faultless shoulder-blades —
I should have known there was no blood beneath!

    Ottima. You hate me then? You hate me then?

    Sebald.   To think
She would succeed in her absurd attempt,
And fascinate by sinning, show herself
Superior — guilt from its excess superior   260
To innocence! That little peasant's voice
Has righted all again. Though I be lost,
I know which is the better, never fear,
Of vice or virtue, purity or lust,
Nature or trick! I see what I have done,
Entirely now! Oh I am proud to feel
Such torments — let the world take credit thence —
I, having done my deed, pay too its price!
I hate, hate — curse you! God's in his heaven!

    Ottima.   — Me!
Me! no, no, Sebald, not yourself — kill me!   270
Mine is the whole crime. Do but kill me — then
Yourself — then — presently — first hear me speak!
I always meant to kill myself — wait, you!
Lean on my breast — not as a breast; don't love me
The more because you lean on me, my own
Heart's Sebald! There, there, both deaths presently!

    Sebald. My brain is drowned now — quite drowned: all I feel
Is . . . is, at swift-recurring intervals,
A hurry-down within me, as of waters
Loosened to smother up some ghastly pit: 280
There they go — whirls from a black fiery sea!

    Ottima. Not me — to him, O God, be merciful!

Talk by the way, while PIPPA *is passing from the hill-side to Orcana.
Foreign* Students *of painting and sculpture, from Venice, assembled opposite the house of* JULES, *a young French statuary,
at Possagno.*

1st Student. Attention! My own post is beneath this window, but the pomegranate clump yonder will hide three or four of you with a little squeezing, and Schramm and his pipe must lie flat in the balcony. Four, five — who's a defaulter? We want everybody, for Jules must not be suffered to hurt his bride when the jest's found out.

2nd Student. All here! Only our poet's away — never having much meant to be present, moonstrike him! The airs of that fellow, that Giovacchino! He was in violent love with himself, and 290 had a fair prospect of thriving in his suit, so unmolested was it, — when suddenly a woman falls in love with him, too; and out of pure jealousy he takes himself off to Trieste, immortal poem and all: whereto is this prophetical epitaph appended already, as Bluphocks assures me, — *"Here a mammoth-poem lies, Fouled to death by butter-flies."* His own fault, the simpleton! Instead of cramp couplets, each like a knife in your entrails, he should write, says Bluphocks, both classically and intelligibly. — *Æsculapius, an Epic. Catalogue of the drugs: Hebe's plaister — One strip Cools your lip. Phœbus' emulsion — One bottle Clears your throttle. Mercury's bolus — One 300 box Cures . . .*

3rd Student. Subside, my fine fellow! If the marriage was over by ten o'clock, Jules will certainly be here in a minute with his bride.

2nd Student. Good! — only, so should the poet's muse have been universally acceptable, says Bluphocks, *et canibus nostris . . .* and Delia not better known to our literary dogs than the boy Giovacchino!

1st Student. To the point, now. Where's Gottlieb, the new-comer? Oh, — listen, Gottlieb, to what has called down this piece of friendly vengeance on Jules, of which we now assemble to witness the winding-up. We are all agreed, all in a tale, observe, when Jules shall 310 burst out on us in a fury by and by: I am spokesman — the verses that are to undeceive Jules bear my name of Lutwyche — but each professes himself alike insulted by this strutting stone-squarer, who came alone from Paris to Munich, and thence with a crowd of us to Venice and Possagno here, but proceeds in a day or two alone again — oh, alone indubitably! — to Rome and Florence. He, forsooth, take up his portion with these dissolute, brutalized, heartless bunglers! — so he was heard to call us all: now, is Schramm brutalized, I should like to know? Am I heartless?

Gottlieb. Why, somewhat heartless; for, suppose Jules a 320 coxcomb as much as you choose, still, for this mere coxcombry, you will have brushed off — what do folks style it? — the bloom of his life. Is it too late to alter? These love-letters now, you call his — I can't laugh at them.

4th Student. Because you never read the sham letters of our inditing which drew forth these.

Gottlieb. His discovery of the truth will be frightful.

4th Student. That's the joke. But you should have joined us at the beginning: there's no doubt he loves the girl — loves a model he might hire by the hour!   330

Gottlieb. See here! "He has been accustomed," he writes, "to have Canova's women about him, in stone, and the world's women beside him, in flesh; these being as much below, as those above, his soul's aspiration: but now he is to have the reality." There you laugh again! I say, you wipe off the very dew of his youth.

1st Student. Schramm! (Take the pipe out of his mouth, somebody!) Will Jules lose the bloom of his youth?

Schramm. Nothing worth keeping is ever lost in this world: look at a blossom — it drops presently, having done its service and lasted its time; but fruits succeed, and where would be the blossom's   340 place could it continue? As well affirm that your eye is no longer in your body, because its earliest favorite, whatever it may have first loved to look on, is dead and done with — as that any affection is lost to the soul when its first object, whatever happened first to satisfy it, is superseded in due course. Keep but ever looking, whether with the body's eye or the mind's, and you will soon find something to look on! Has a man done wondering at women? — there follow men, dead and alive, to wonder at. Has he done wondering at men? — there's God to wonder at: and the faculty of wonder may be, at the same time, old and tired enough with respect to its first object, and   350 yet young and fresh sufficiently, so far as concerns its novel one. Thus . . .

1st Student. Put Schramm's pipe into his mouth again! There, you see! Well, this Jules . . . a wretched fribble — oh, I watched his disportings at Possagno, the other day! Canova's gallery — you know: there he marches first resolvedly past great works by the dozen without vouchsafing an eye: all at once he stops full at the *Psiche-fanciulla* — cannot pass that old acquaintance without a nod of encouragement — "In your new place, beauty? Then behave yourself as well here as at Munich — I see you!" Next he posts himself deliberately   360 before the unfinished *Pietà* for half an hour without moving, till up he starts of a sudden, and thrusts his very nose into — I say, into — the group; by which gesture you are informed that precisely the sole point he had not fully mastered in Canova's practice was a certain method of using the drill in the articulation of the knee-joint — and that, likewise, has he mastered at length! Good-bye, therefore, to poor Canova — whose gallery no longer needs detain his successor Jules, the predestinated novel thinker in marble!

5th Student. Tell him about the women: go on to the women!

1st Student. Why, on that matter he could never be super-   370 cilious enough. How should we be other (he said) than the poor devils you see, with those debasing habits we cherish? He was not to wallow in that mire, at least: he would wait, and love only at the proper time, and meanwhile put up with the *Psiche-fanciulla*. Now, I happened to hear of a young Greek — real Greek girl at Malamocco; a true Islander, do you see, with Alciphron's "hair like sea-moss" — Schramm knows! — white and quiet as an apparition, and fourteen years old at farthest, — a daughter of Natalia, so she swears — that hag Natalia, who helps us to models at three *lire* an hour. We selected this girl for the heroine of our jest. So first, Jules received a   380 scented letter — somebody had seen his Tydeus at the Academy, and my picture was nothing to it: a profound admirer bade him persevere — would make herself known to him ere long. (Paolina, my little friend of the *Fenice*, transcribes divinely.) And in due time, the mysterious correspondent gave certain hints of her peculiar charms — the pale cheeks, the black hair — whatever, in short, had struck us in our Malamocco model: we retained her name, too — Phene, which is, by interpretation, sea-eagle. Now, think of Jules finding himself distinguished from the herd of us by such a creature! In his very first answer he proposed marrying his monitress: and fancy us over   390 these letters, two, three times a day, to receive and despatch! I concocted the main of it: relations were in the way — secrecy must be observed — in fine, would he wed her on trust, and only speak to her when they were indissolubly united? St — st — Here they come!

6th Student. Both of them! Heaven's love, speak softly, speak within yourselves!

5th Student. Look at the bridegroom! Half his hair in storm and half in calm, — patted down over the left temple, — like a frothy cup one blows on to cool it: and the same old blouse that he murders the marble in.   400

2nd Student. Not a rich vest like yours, Hannibal Scratchy! — rich, that your face may the better set it off.

6th Student. And the bride! Yes, sure enough, our Phene! Should you have known her in her clothes? How magnificently pale!

Gottlieb. She does not also take it for earnest, I hope?

1st Student. Oh, Natalia's concern, that is! We settle with Natalia.

6th Student. She does not speak — has evidently let out no word. The only thing is, will she equally remember the rest of her lesson, and repeat correctly all those verses which are to break the secret to Jules?   410

Gottlieb. How he gazes on her! Pity — pity!

1st Student. They go in: now, silence! You three, — not nearer the window, mind, than that pomegranate: just where the little girl, who a few minutes ago passed us singing, is seated!

2. NOON

SCENE — *Over Orcana. The house of* JULES, *who crosses its threshold with* PHENE: *she is silent, on which* JULES *begins* —

Do not die, Phene! I am yours now, you
Are mine now; let fate reach me how she likes,
If you'll not die: so, never die! Sit here —
My work-room's single seat. I over-lean
This length of hair and lustrous front; they turn
Like an entire flower upward: eyes, lips, last
Your chin — no, last your throat turns: 'tis their scent
Pulls down my face upon you. Nay, look ever
This one way till I change, grow you — I could
Change into you, beloved!
                                    You by me,   10
And I by you; this is your hand in mine,
And side by side we sit: all's true. Thank God!
I have spoken: speak you!
                                    O my life to come!
My Tydeus must be carved that's there in clay;
Yet how be carved, with you about the room?
Where must I place you? When I think that once
This room-full of rough block-work seemed my heaven
Without you! Shall I ever work again,
Get fairly into my old ways again,
Bid each conception stand while, trait by trait,   20
My hand transfers its lineaments to stone?
Will my mere fancies live near you, their truth —
The live truth, passing and repassing me,
Sitting beside me?
                        Now speak!
                              Only first,
See, all your letters! Was't not well contrived?
Their hiding-place is Psyche's robe; she keeps
Your letters next her skin: which drops out foremost?
Ah, — this that swam down like a first moonbeam
Into my world!
                  Again those eyes complete
Their melancholy survey, sweet and slow,   30

Of all my room holds; to return and rest
On me, with pity, yet some wonder too:
As if God bade some spirit plague a world,
And this were the one moment of surprise
And sorrow while she took her station, pausing
O'er what she sees, finds good, and must destroy!
What gaze you at? Those? Books, I told you of;
Let your first word to me rejoice them, too:
This minion, a Coluthus, writ in red
Bistre and azure by Bessarion's scribe —   40
Read this line . . . no, shame — Homer's be the Greek
First breathed me from the lips of my Greek girl!
This Odyssey in coarse black vivid type
With faded yellow blossoms 'twixt page and page,
To mark great places with due gratitude;
*"He said, and on Antinous directed
A bitter shaft"* . . . a flower blots out the rest!
Again upon your search? My statues, then!
— Ah, do not mind that — better that will look
When cast in bronze — an Almaign Kaiser, that,   50
Swart-green and gold, with truncheon based on hip.
This, rather, turn to! What, unrecognized?
I thought you would have seen that here you sit
As I imagined you, — Hippolyta,
Naked upon her bright Numidian horse.
Recall you this then? "Carve in bold relief" —
So you commanded — "carve, against I come,
A Greek, in Athens, as our fashion was,
Feasting, bay-filleted and thunder-free,
Who rises 'neath the lifted myrtle-branch.   60
'Praise those who slew Hipparchus! cry the guests,
'While o'er thy head the singer's myrtle waves
As erst above our champion: stand up, all!' "
See, I have labored to express your thought.
Quite round, a cluster of mere hands and arms,
(Thrust in all senses, all ways, from all sides,
Only consenting at the branch's end
They strain toward) serves for frame to a sole face,
The Praiser's, in the centre: who with eyes
Sightless, so bend they back to light inside   70
His brain where visionary forms throng up,
Sings, minding not that palpitating arch
Of hands and arms, nor the quick drip of wine
From the drenched leaves o'erhead, nor crowns cast off,

Violet and parsley crowns to trample on —
Sings, pausing as the patron-ghosts approve,
Devoutly their unconquerable hymn.
But you must say a "well" to that — say "well!"
Because you gaze — am I fantastic, sweet?
Gaze like my very life's-stuff, marble — marbly   80
Even to the silence! Why, before I found
The real flesh Phene, I inured myself
To see, throughout all nature, varied stuff
For better nature's birth by means of art:
With me, each substance tended to one form
Of beauty — to the human archetype.
On every side occurred suggestive germs
Of that — the tree, the flower — or take the fruit, —
Some rosy shape, continuing the peach,
Curved beewise o'er its bough; as rosy limbs,   90
Depending, nestled in the leaves; and just
From a cleft rose-peach the whole Dryad sprang.
But of the stuffs one can be master of,
How I divined their capabilities!
From the soft-rinded smoothening facile chalk
That yields your outline to the air's embrace,
Half-softened by a halo's pearly gloom;
Down to the crisp imperious steel, so sure
To cut its one confided thought clean out
Of all the world. But marble! — 'neath my tools   100
More pliable than jelly — as it were
Some clear primordial creature dug from depths
In the earth's heart, where itself breeds itself,
And whence all baser substance may be worked;
Refine it off to air, you may, — condense it
Down to the diamond; — is not metal there,
When o'er the sudden speck my chisel trips?
— Not flesh, as flake off flake I scale, approach,
Lay bare those bluish veins of blood asleep?
Lurks flame in no strange windings where, surprised   110
By the swift implement sent home at once,
Flushes and glowings radiate and hover
About its track?
                    Phene? what — why is this?
That whitening cheek, those still dilating eyes!
Ah, you will die — I knew that you would die!

PHENE *begins, on his having long remained silent.*

Now the end's coming; to be sure, it must
Have ended sometime! Tush, why need I speak
Their foolish speech? I cannot bring to mind
One half of it, beside; and do not care
For old Natalia now, nor any of them.   120
Oh, you — what are you? — if I do not try
To say the words Natalia made me learn,
To please your friends, — it is to keep myself
Where your voice lifted me, by letting that
Proceed: but can it? Even you, perhaps,
Cannot take up, now you have once let fall,
The music's life, and me along with that —
No, or you would! We'll stay, then, as we are:
Above the world.
          You creature with the eyes!
If I could look forever up to them,   130
As now you let me, — I believe, all sin,
All memory of wrong done, suffering borne,
Would drop down, low and lower, to the earth
Whence all that's low comes, and there touch and stay
— Never to overtake the rest of me,
All that, unspotted, reaches up to you,
Drawn by those eyes! What rises is myself,
Not me the shame and suffering; but they sink,
Are left, I rise above them. Keep me so,
Above the world!
          But you sink, for your eyes   140
Are altering — altered! Stay — "I love you, love" . . .
I could prevent it if I understood:
More of your words to me: was't in the tone
Or the words, your power?
          Or stay — I will repeat
Their speech, if that contents you! Only change
No more, and I shall find it presently
Far back here, in the brain yourself filled up.
Natalia threatened me that harm should follow
Unless I spoke their lesson to the end,
But harm to me, I thought she meant, not you.   150
Your friends, — Natalia said they were your friends
And meant you well, — because, I doubted it,
Observing (what was very strange to see)
On every face, so different in all else,
The same smile girls like me are used to bear,
But never men, men cannot stoop so low;

Yet your friends, speaking of you, used that smile,
That hateful smirk of boundless self-conceit
Which seems to take possession of the world
And make of God a tame confederate,   160
Purveyor to their appetites . . . you know!
But still Natalia said they were your friends,
And they assented though they smiled the more.
And all came round me, — that thin Englishman
With light lank hair seemed leader of the rest;
He held a paper — "What we want," said he,
Ending some explanation to his friends —
"Is something slow, involved and mystical,
To hold Jules long in doubt, yet take his taste
And lure him on until, at innermost   170
Where he seeks sweetness' soul, he may find — this!
— As in the apple's core, the noisome fly:
For insects on the rind are seen at once,
And brushed aside as soon, but this is found
Only when on the lips or loathing tongue."
And so he read what I have got by heart:
I'll speak it, — "Do not die, love! I am yours."
No — is not that, or like that, part of words
Yourself began by speaking? Strange to lose
What cost such pains to learn! Is this more right?   180

> I am a painter who cannot paint;
> In my life, a devil rather than saint;
> In my brain, as poor a creature too:
> No end to all I cannot do!
> Yet do one thing at least I can —
> Love a man or hate a man
> Supremely: thus my lore began.
> Through the Valley of Love I went,
> In the lovingest spot to abide,
> And just on the verge where I pitched my tent,   190
> I found Hate dwelling beside.
> (Let the Bridegroom ask what the painter meant,
> Of his Bride, of the peerless Bride!)
> And further, I traversed Hate's grove,
> In the hatefullest nook to dwell;
> But lo, where I flung myself prone, couched Love
> Where the shadow threefold fell.
> (The meaning — those black bride's-eyes above,
> Not a painter's lip should tell!)

"And here," said he, "Jules probably will ask,   200
'You have black eyes, Love, — you are, sure enough,
My peerless bride, — then do you tell indeed
What needs some explanation! What means this?' "
— And I am to go on, without a word —

    So, I grew wise in Love and Hate,
    From simple that I was of late.
    Once, when I loved, I would enlace
    Breast, eyelids, hands, feet, form and face
    Of her I loved, in one embrace —
    As if by mere love I could love immensely!   210
    Once, when I hated, I would plunge
    My sword, and wipe with the first lunge
    My foe's whole life out like a sponge —
    As if by mere hate I could hate intensely!
    But now I am wiser, know better the fashion
    How passion seeks aid from its opposite passion:
    And if I see cause to love more, hate more
    Than ever man loved, ever hated before —
    And seek in the Valley of Love,
    The nest, or the nook in Hate's Grove,   220
    Where my soul may surely reach
    The essence, naught less, of each,
    The Hate of all Hates, the Love
    Of all Loves, in the Valley or Grove, —
    I find them the very warders
    Each of the other's borders.
    When I love most, Love is disguised
    In Hate; and when Hate is surprised
    In Love, then I hate most: ask
    How Love smiles through Hate's iron casque,   230
    Hate grins through Love's rose-braided mask, —
    And how, having hated thee,
    I sought long and painfully
    To reach thy heart, nor prick
    The skin but pierce to the quick —
    Ask this, my Jules, and be answered straight
    By thy bride — how the painter Lutwyche can hate!

        Jules *interposes.*

Lutwyche! Who else? But all of them, no doubt,
Hated me: they at Venice — presently

Their turn, however! You I shall not meet: 240
If I dreamed, saying this would wake me.
                                          Keep
What's here, the gold — we cannot meet again,
Consider! and the money was but meant
For two years' travel, which is over now,
All chance or hope or care or need of it.
This — and what comes from selling these, my casts
And books and medals, except . . . let them go
Together, so the produce keeps you safe
Out of Natalia's clutches! If by chance
(For all's chance here) I should survive the gang   250
At Venice, root out all fifteen of them,
We might meet somewhere, since the world is wide.
        [*From without is heard the voice of* PIPPA, *singing —*

        Give her but a least excuse to love me!
        When — where —
        How — can this arm establish her above me,
        If fortune fixed her as my lady there,
        There already, to eternally reprove me?
                ("Hist!" — said Kate the Queen;
                But "Oh!" — cried the maiden, binding her tresses,
                " 'Tis only a page that carols unseen,   260
                Crumbling your hounds their messes!")

        Is she wronged? — To the rescue of her honor,
        My heart!
        Is she poor? — What costs it to be styled a donor?
        Merely an earth to cleave, a sea to part.
        But that fortune should have thrust all this upon her!
                ("Nay, list!" — bade Kate the Queen;
                And still cried the maiden, binding her tresses,
                " 'Tis only a page that carols unseen,
                Fitting your hawks their jesses!")   270
                                        [PIPPA *passes*

                JULES *resumes.*

What name was that the little girl sang forth?
Kate? The Cornaro, doubtless, who renounced
The crown of Cyprus to be lady here
At Asolo, where still her memory stays,
And peasants sing how once a certain page

Pined for the grace of her so far above
His power of doing good to, "Kate the Queen —
She never could be wronged, be poor," he sighed,
"Need him to help her!"
                Yes, a bitter thing
To see our lady above all need of us;   280
Yet so we look ere we will love; not I,
But the world looks so. If whoever loves
Must be, in some sort, god or worshipper,
The blessing or the blest one, queen or page,
Why should we always choose the page's part?
Here is a woman with utter need of me, —
I find myself queen here, it seems!
                    How strange!
Look at the woman here with the new soul,
Like my own Psyche, — fresh upon her lips
Alit, the visionary butterfly,   290
Waiting my word to enter and make bright,
Or flutter off and leave all blank as first.
This body had no soul before, but slept
Or stirred, was beauteous or ungainly, free
From taint or foul with stain, as outward things
Fastened their image on its passiveness:
Now, it will wake, feel, live — or die again!
Shall to produce form out of unshaped stuff
Be Art — and further, to evoke a soul
From form be nothing? This new soul is mine!   300

Now, to kill Lutwyche, what would that do? — save
A wretched dauber, men will hoot to death
Without me, from their hooting. Oh, to hear
God's voice plain as I heard it first, before
They broke in with their laughter! I heard them
Henceforth, not God.
             To Ancona — Greece — some isle!
I wanted silence only; there is clay
Everywhere. One may do whate'er one likes
In Art: the only thing is, to make sure
That one does like it — which takes pains to know.   310
    Scatter all this, my Phene — this mad dream!
Who, what is Lutwyche, what Natalia's friends,
What the whole world except our love — my own,
Own Phene? But I told you, did I not,
Ere night we travel for your land — some isle

With the sea's silence on it? Stand aside —
I do but break these paltry models up
To begin Art afresh. Meet Lutwyche, I —
And save him from my statue meeting him?
Some unsuspected isle in the far seas!   320
Like a god going through his world, there stands
One mountain for a moment in the dusk,
Whole brotherhoods of cedars on its brow:
And you are ever by me while I gaze
— Are in my arms as now — as now — as now!
Some unsuspected isle in the far seas!
Some unsuspected isle in far-off seas!

Talk by the way, while PIPPA *is passing from Orcana to the Turret.
Two or three of the Austrian Police loitering with* BLUPHOCKS,
an English vagabond, just in view of the Turret.

Bluphocks. So, that is your Pippa, the little girl who passed us singing? Well, your Bishop's Intendant's money shall be honestly earned:
— now, don't make me that sour face because I bring the   330
Bishop's name into the business; we know he can have nothing to do
with such horrors: we know that he is a saint and all that a bishop
should be, who is a great man beside. *Oh were but every worm a
maggot, Every fly a grig, Every bough a Christmas faggot, Every tune
a jig!* In fact, I have abjured all religions; but the last I inclined to,
was the Armenian: for I have travelled, do you see, and at Koenigs-
berg, Prussia Improper (so styled because there's a sort of bleak
hungry sun there), you might remark over a venerable house-porch,
a certain Chaldee inscription; and brief as it is, a mere glance at it
used absolutely to change the mood of every bearded pas-   340
senger. In they turned, one and all; the young and lightsome, with no
irreverent pause, the aged and decrepit, with a sensible alacrity: 'twas
the Grand Rabbi's abode, in short. Struck with curiosity, I lost no time
in learning Syriac — (these are vowels, you dogs, — follow my stick's
end in the mud — *Celarent, Darii, Ferio!*), and one morning presented
myself, spelling-book in hand, a, b, c, — I picked it out letter by
letter, and what was the purport of this miraculous posy? Some cher-
ished legend of the past, you'll say — *"How Moses hocuspocussed
Egypt's land with fly and locust,"* — or, *"How to Jonah sounded
harshish, Get thee up and go to Tarshish,"* — or, *"How the   350
angel meeting Balaam, Straight his ass returned a salaam."* In no
wise! *"Shackabrack — Boach — somebody or other — Isaach, Re-cei-
ver, Pur-cha-ser and Ex-chan-ger of — Stolen Goods!"* So, talk to me
of the religion of a bishop! I have renounced all bishops save Bishop

Beveridge — mean to live so — and die — *As some Greek dog-sage, dead and merry, Hellward bound in Charon's wherry, With food for both worlds, under and upper, Lupine-seed and Hecate's supper, And never an obolus* . . . (Though thanks to you, or this Intendant through you, or this Bishop through his Intendant — I possess a burning pocketful of *zwanzigers*) . . . *To pay the Stygian Ferry!*   360

1st Policeman. There is the girl, then; go and deserve them the moment you have pointed out to us Signor Luigi and his mother. [*To the rest.*] I have been noticing a house yonder, this long while: not a shutter unclosed since morning!

2nd Policeman. Old Luca Gaddi's, that owns the silk-mills here: he dozes by the hour, wakes up, sighs deeply, says he should like to be Prince Metternich, and then dozes again, after having bidden young Sebald, the foreigner, set his wife to playing draughts. Never molest such a household, they mean well.

Bluphocks. Only, cannot you tell me something of this little   370 Pippa, I must have to do with? One could make something of that name. Pippa — that is, short for Felippa — rhyming to *Panurge consults Hertrippa — Believest thou, King Agrippa?* Something might be done with that name.

2nd Policeman. Put into rhyme that your head and a ripe musk-melon would not be dear at half a *zwanziger!* Leave this fooling, and look out; the afternoon's over or nearly so.

3rd Policeman. Where in this passport of Signor Luigi does our Principal instruct you to watch him so narrowly? There? What's there beside a simple signature? (That English fool's busy watching.)   380

2nd Policeman. Flourish all round — "Put all possible obstacles in his way;" oblong dot at the end — "Detain him till further advices reach you;" scratch at bottom — "Send him back on pretence of some informality in the above;" ink-spirt on right-hand side (which is the case here) — "Arrest him at once." Why and wherefore, I don't concern myself, but my instructions amount to this: if Signor Luigi leaves home to-night for Vienna — well and good, the passport deposed with us for our *visa* is really for his own use, they have misinformed the Office, and he means well; but let him stay over to-night — there has been the pretence we suspect, the accounts of his corre-   390 sponding and holding intelligence with the Carbonari are correct, we arrest him at once, to-morrow comes Venice, and presently Spielberg. Bluphocks makes the signal, sure enough! That is he, entering the turret with his mother, no doubt.

3. EVENING

SCENE — *Inside the Turret on the Hill above Asolo.* LUIGI *and his*
Mother *entering.*

Mother. If there blew wind, you'd hear a long sigh, easing
The utmost heaviness of music's heart.
    Luigi. Here in the archway?
    Mother.   Oh no, no — in farther,
Where the echo is made, on the ridge.
    Luigi.   Here surely, then.
How plain the tap of my heel as I leaped up!
Hark — "Lucius Junius!" The very ghost of a voice
Whose body is caught and kept by . . . what are those?
Mere withered wallflowers, waving overhead?
They seem an elvish group with thin bleached hair
That lean out of their topmost fortress — look   **10**
And listen, mountain men, to what we say,
Hand under chin of each grave earthy face.
Up and show faces all of you! — "All of you!"
That's the king dwarf with the scarlet comb; old Franz,
Come down and meet your fate? Hark — "Meet your fate!"
    Mother. Let him not meet it, my Luigi — do not
Go to his City! Putting crime aside,
Half of these ills of Italy are feigned:
Your Pellicos and writers for effect,
Write for effect.
    Luigi.   Hush! Say A. writes, and B.   **20**
    Mother. These A.s and B.s write for effect, I say.
Then, evil is in its nature loud, while good
Is silent; you hear each petty injury.
None of his virtues; he is old beside,
Quiet and kind, and densely stupid. Why
Do A. and B. not kill him themselves?
    Luigi.   They teach
Others to kill him — me — and, if I fail,
Others to succeed; now, if A. tried and failed,
I could not teach that: mine's the lesser task.
Mother, they visit night by night . . .

Mother.   — You, Luigi?   30
Ah, will you let me tell you what you are?
   Luigi. Why not? Oh, the one thing you fear to hint,
You may assure yourself I say and say
Ever to myself! At times — nay, even as now
We sit — I think my mind is touched, suspect
All is not sound: but is not knowing that,
What constitutes one sane or otherwise?
I know I am thus — so, all is right again.
I laugh at myself as through the town I walk,
And see men merry as if no Italy   40
Were suffering; then I ponder — "I am rich,
Young, healthy; why should this fact trouble me,
More than it troubles these?" But it does trouble.
No, trouble's a bad word; for as I walk
There's springing and melody and giddiness,
And old quaint turns and passages of my youth,
Dreams long forgotten, little in themselves,
Return to me — whatever may amuse me:
And earth seems in a truce with me, and heaven
Accords with me, all things suspend their strife,   50
The very cicala laughs "There goes he, and there!
Feast him, the time is short; he is on his way
For the world's sake: feast him this once, our friend!"
And in return for all this, I can trip
Cheerfully up the scaffold-steps. I go
This evening, mother!
   Mother.   But mistrust yourself —
Mistrust the judgment you pronounce on him!
   Luigi. Oh, there I feel — am sure that I am right!
   Mother. Mistrust your judgment then, of the mere means
To this wild enterprise. Say, you are right, —   60
How should one in your state e'er bring to pass
What would require a cool head, a cold heart,
And a calm hand? You never will escape.
   Luigi. Escape? To even wish that, would spoil all.
The dying is best part of it. Too much
Have I enjoyed these fifteen years of mine,
To leave myself excuse for longer life:
Was not life pressed down, running o'er with joy,
That I might finish with it ere my fellows
Who, sparelier feasted, make a longer stay?   70
I was put at the board-head, helped to all
At first; I rise up happy and content.

God must be glad one loves his world so much.
I can give news of earth to all the dead
Who ask me: — last year's sunsets, and great stars
Which had a right to come first and see ebb
The crimson wave that drifts the sun away —
Those crescent moons with notched and burning rims
That strengthened into sharp fire, and there stood,
Impatient of the azure — and that day   80
In March, a double rainbow stopped the storm —
May's warm slow yellow moonlit summer nights —
Gone are they, but I have them in my soul!
   Mother. (He will not go!)
   Luigi.   You smile at me? 'Tis true, —
Voluptuousness, grotesqueness, ghastliness,
Environ my devotedness as quaintly
As round about some antique altar wreathe
The rose festoons, goats' horns, and oxen's skulls.
   Mother. See now: you reach the city, you must cross
His threshold — how?
   Luigi.   Oh, that's if we conspired!   90
Then would come pains in plenty, as you guess —
But guess not how the qualities most fit
For such an office, qualities I have,
Would little stead me, otherwise employed,
Yet prove of rarest merit only here.
Every one knows for what his excellence
Will serve, but no one ever will consider
For what his worst defect might serve: and yet
Have you not seen me range our coppice yonder
In search of a distorted ash? — I find   100
The wry spoilt branch a natural perfect bow.
Fancy the thrice-sage, thrice-precautioned man
Arriving at the palace on my errand!
No, no! I have a handsome dress packed up —
White satin here, to set off my black hair;
In I shall march — for you may watch your life out
Behind thick walls, make friends there to betray you;
More than one man spoils everything. March straight —
Only, no clumsy knife to fumble for.
Take the great gate, and walk (not saunter) on   110
Thro' guards and guards — I have rehearsed it all
Inside the turret here a hundred times.
Don't ask the way of whom you meet, observe!
But where they cluster thickliest is the door

Of doors; they'll let you pass — they'll never blab
Each to the other, he knows not the favorite,
Whence he is bound and what's his business now.
Walk in — straight up to him; you have no knife:
Be prompt, how should he scream? Then, out with you!
Italy, Italy, my Italy!   120
You're free, you're free! Oh mother, I could dream
They got about me — Andrea from his exile,
Pier from his dungeon, Gualtier from his grave!
    Mother. Well, you shall go. Yet seems this patriotism
The easiest virtue for a selfish man
To acquire: he loves himself — and next, the world —
If he must love beyond, — but naught between:
As a short-sighted man sees naught midway
His body and the sun above. But you
Are my adored Luigi, ever obedient   130
To my least wish, and running o'er with love:
I could not call you cruel or unkind.
Once more, your ground for killing him! — then go!
    Luigi. Now do you try me, or make sport of me?
How first the Austrians got these provinces . . .
(If that is all, I'll satisfy you soon)
— Never by conquest but by cunning, for
That treaty whereby . . .
    Mother.   Well?
    Luigi   (Sure, he's arrived,
The tell-tale cuckoo: spring's his confidant,
And he lets out her April purposes!)   140
Or . . . better go at once to modern time,
He has . . . they have . . . in fact, I understand
But can't restate the matter; that's my boast:
Others could reason it out to you, and prove
Things they have made me feel.
    Mother.   Why go to-night?
Morn's for adventure. Jupiter is now
A morning-star. I cannot hear you, Luigi!
    Luigi. "I am the bright and morning-star," saith God —
And, "to such an one I give the morning-star,"
The gift of the morning-star! Have I God's gift   150
Of the morning-star?
    Mother.   Chiara will love to see
That Jupiter an evening-star next June.
    Luigi. True, mother. Well for those who live through June!
Great noontides, thunder-storms, all glaring pomps

That triumph at the heels of June the god
Leading his revel through our leafy world.
Yes, Chiara will be here.
    Mother.   In June: remember,
Yourself appointed that month for her coming.
    Luigi. Was that low noise the echo?
    Mother.   The night-wind.
She must be grown — with her blue eyes upturned   160
As if life were one long and sweet surprise:
In June she comes.
    Luigi.   We were to see together
The Titian at Treviso. There, again!

              [*From without is heard the voice of* PIPPA, *singing —*

       A king lived long ago,
       In the morning of the world,
       When earth was nigher heaven than now:
       And the king's locks curled,
       Disparting o'er a forehead full
       As the milk-white space 'twixt horn and horn
       Of some sacrificial bull —   170
       Only calm as a babe new-born:
       For he was got to a sleepy mood,
       So safe from all decrepitude,
       Age with its bane, so sure gone by,
       (The gods so loved him while he dreamed)
       That, having lived thus long, there seemed
       No need the king should ever die.

   Luigi. No need that sort of king should ever die!

       Among the rocks his city was:
       Before his palace, in the sun,   180
       He sat to see his people pass,
       And judge them every one
       From its threshold of smooth stone.
       They haled him many a valley-thief
       Caught in the sheep-pens, robber-chief
       Swarthy and shameless, beggar-cheat,
       Spy-prowler, or rough pirate found ·
       On the sea-sand left aground;
       And sometimes clung about his feet.
       With bleeding lip and burning cheek.   190

A woman, bitterest wrong to speak
Of one with sullen thickset brows:
And sometimes from the prison-house
The angry priests a pale wretch brought,
Who through some chink had pushed and pressed
On knees and elbows, belly and breast,
Worm-like into the temple, — caught
He was by the very god,
Who ever in the darkness strode
Backward and forward, keeping watch 200
O'er his brazen bowls, such rogues to catch!
These, all and every one,
The king judged, sitting in the sun.

Luigi. That king should still judge sitting in the sun!

His councillors, on left and right,
Looked anxious up, — but no surprise
Disturbed the king's old smiling eyes
Where the very blue had turned to white.
'Tis said, a Python scared one day
The breathless city, till he came, 210
With forky tongue and eyes on flame,
Where the old king sat to judge alway;
But when he saw the sweepy hair
Girt with a crown of berries rare
Which the god will hardly give to wear
To the maiden who singeth, dancing bare
In the altar-smoke by the pine-torch lights,
At his wondrous forest rites, —
Seeing this, he did not dare
Approach that threshold in the sun, 220
Assault the old king smiling there.
Such grace had kings when the world begun!

[PIPPA *passes.*

Luigi. And such grace have they, now that the world ends!
The Python at the city, on the throne,
And brave men, God would crown for slaying him,
Lurk in bye-corners lest they fall his prey.
Are crowns yet to be won in this late time,
Which weakness makes me hesitate to reach?
'Tis God's voice calls: how could I stay? Farewell!

Talk by the way, while PIPPA *is passing from the Turret to the
Bishop's Brother's House, close to the Duomo S. Maria. Poor
Girls sitting on the steps.*

   1st Girl. There goes a swallow to Venice — the stout seafarer!   230
Seeing those birds fly, makes one wish for wings.
Let us all wish; you wish first!
   2nd Girl.   I? This sunset
To finish.
   3rd Girl. That old — somebody I know,
Grayer and older than my grandfather,
To give me the same treat he gave last week —
Feeding me on his knee with fig-peckers,
Lampreys and red Breganze-wine, and mumbling
The while some folly about how well I fare,
Let sit and eat my supper quietly:
Since had he not himself been late this morning   240
Detained at — never mind where, — had he not . . .
"Eh, baggage, had I not!" —
   2nd Girl.   How she can lie!
   3rd Girl. Look there — by the nails!
   2nd Girl.   What makes your fingers red!
   3rd Girl. Dipping them into wine to write bad words with
On the bright table: how he laughed!
   1st Girl.   My turn.
Spring's come and summer's coming. I would wear
A long loose gown, down to the feet and hands,
With plaits here, close about the throat, all day;
And all night lie, the cool long nights, in bed;
And have new milk to drink, apples to eat,   250
Deuzans and junetings, leather-coats . . . ah, I should say,
This is away in the fields — miles!
   3rd Girl.   Say at once
You'd be at home: she'd always be at home!
Now comes the story of the farm among
The cherry orchards, and how April snowed
White blossoms on her as she ran. Why, fool,
They've rubbed the chalk-mark out, how tall you were,
Twisted your starling's neck, broken his cage,
Made a dung-hill of your garden!
   1st Girl.   They, destroy
My garden since I left them? well — perhaps!   260
I would have done so: so I hope they have!

A fig-tree curled out of our cottage wall;
They called it mine, I have forgotten why,
It must have been there long ere I was born:
Cric — cric — I think I hear the wasps o'erhead
Pricking the papers strung to flutter there
And keep off birds in fruit-time — coarse long papers,
And the wasps eat them, prick them through and through.

 3rd Girl. How her mouth twitches! Where was I? — before
She broke in with her wishes and long gowns   270
And wasps — would I be such a fool! — oh, here!
This is my way: I answer every one
Who asks me why I make so much of him —
(If you say, "you love him" — straight "he'll not be gulled!")
"He that seduced me when I was a girl
Thus high — had eyes like yours, or hair like yours,
Brown, red, white," — as the case may be: that pleases!
See how that beetle burnishes in the path!
There sparkles he along the dust: and, there —
Your journey to that maize-tuft spoiled at least!   280

 1st Girl. When I was young, they said if you killed one
Of those sunshiny beetles, that his friend
Up there, would shine no more that day nor next.

 2nd Girl. When you were young? Nor are you young, that's true.
How your plump arms, that were, have dropped away!
Why, I can span them. Cecco beats you still?
No matter, so you keep your curious hair.
I wish they'd find a way to dye our hair
Your color — any lighter tint, indeed,
Than black: the men say they are sick of black,   290
Black eyes, black hair!

 4th Girl.   Sick of yours, like enough.
Do you pretend you ever tasted lampreys
And ortolans? Giovita, of the palace,
Engaged (but there's no trusting him) to slice me
Polenta with a knife that had cut up
An ortolan.

 2nd Girl. Why, there! Is not that Pippa
We are to talk to, under the window, — quick, —
Where the lights are?

 1st Girl.   That she? No, or she would sing,
For the Intendant said . . .

 3rd Girl.   Oh, you sing first!
Then, if she listens and comes close . . . I'll tell you, —   300
Sing that song the young English noble made,

Who took you for the purest of the pure,
And meant to leave the world for you — what fun!

    2nd Girl [*sings*].

> *You'll love me yet! — and I can tarry*
> > *Your love's protracted growing:*
> *June reared that bunch of flowers you carry,*
> > *From seeds of April's sowing.*
>
> *I plant a heartful now: some seed*
> > *At least is sure to strike,*
> *And yield — what you'll not pluck indeed,*   310
> > *Not love, but, may be, like.*
>
> *You'll look at least on love's remains,*
> > *A grave's one violet:*
> *Your look? — that pays a thousand pains.*
> > *What's death? You'll love me yet!*

    3rd Girl [*to* Pippa, *who approaches*]. Oh, you may come closer —
we shall not eat you! Why, you seem the very person that the great
rich handsome Englishman has fallen so violently in love with. I'll
tell you all about it.

4. NIGHT

Scene — *Inside the Palace by the Duomo.* Monsignor, *dismissing his*
Attendants.

Monsignor. Thanks, friends, many thanks! I chiefly desire life now,
that I may recompense every one of you. Most I know something of
already. What, a repast prepared? *Benedicto benedicatur* . . . ugh, ugh!
Where was I? Oh, as you were remarking, Ugo, the weather is mild,
very unlike winter-weather: but I am a Sicilian, you know, and shiver
in your Julys here. To be sure, when 'twas full summer at Messina, as
we priests used to cross in procession the great square on Assumption
Day, you might see our thickest yellow tapers twist suddenly in two,
each like a falling star, or sink down on themselves in a gore of wax.
But go, my friends, but go! [*To the* Intendant.] Not you, Ugo!   10
[*The others leave the apartment.*] I have long wanted to converse
with you, Ugo.

Intendant. Uguccio —

Monsignor. . . . 'guccio Stefani, man! of Ascoli, Fermo and Fossom-
bruno; — what I do need instructing about, are these accounts of
your administration of my poor brother's affairs. Ugh! I shall never get
through a third part of your accounts: take some of these dainties
before we attempt it, however. Are you bashful to that degree? For
me, a crust and water suffice.

Intendant. Do you choose this especial night to question me?   20

Monsignor. This night, Ugo. You have managed my late brother's
affairs since the death of our elder brother: fourteen years and a
month, all but three days. On the Third of December, I find him . . .

Intendant. If you have so intimate an acquaintance with your
brother's affairs, you will be tender of turning so far back: they will
hardly bear looking into, so far back.

Monsignor. Ay, ay, ugh, ugh, — nothing but disappointments here
below! I remark a considerable payment made to yourself on this
Third of December. Talk of disappointments! There was a young
fellow here, Jules, a foreign sculptor I did my utmost to ad-   30
vance, that the Church might be a gainer by us both: he was going
on hopefully enough, and of a sudden he notifies to me some marvellous change that has happened in his notions of Art. Here's his letter,
— "He never had a clearly conceived Ideal within his brain till to-day.
Yet since his hand could manage a chisel, he has practised expressing

other men's Ideals; and, in the very perfection he has attained to, he foresees an ultimate failure: his unconscious hand will pursue its prescribed course of old years, and will reproduce with a fatal expertness the ancient types, let the novel one appear never so palpably to his spirit. There is but one method of escape: confiding the   40 virgin type to as chaste a hand, he will turn painter instead of sculptor, and paint, not carve, its characteristics," — strike out, I dare say, a school like Correggio: how think you, Ugo?

Intendant. Is Correggio a painter?

Monsignor. Foolish Jules! and yet, after all, why foolish? He may — probably will — fail egregiously; but if there should arise a new painter, will it not be in some such way, by a poet now, or a musician (spirits who have conceived and perfected an Ideal through some other channel), transferring it to this, and escaping our conventional roads by pure ignorance of them; eh, Ugo? If you have no appetite,   50 talk at least, Ugo!

Intendant. Sir, I can submit no longer to this course of yours. First, you select the group of which I formed one, — next you thin it gradually, — always retaining me with your smile, — and so do you proceed till you have fairly got me alone with you between four stone walls. And now then? Let this farce, this chatter end now: what is it you want with me?

Monsignor. Ugo!

Intendant. From the instant you arrived, I felt your smile on me as you questioned me about this and the other article in those   60 papers — why your brother should have given me this villa, that *podere,* — and your nod at the end meant, — what?

Monsignor. Possibly that I wished for no loud talk here. If once you set me coughing, Ugo! —

Intendant. I have your brother's hand and seal to all I possess: now ask me what for! what service I did him — ask me!

Monsignor. I would better not: I should rip up old disgraces, let out my poor brother's weaknesses. By the way, Maffeo of Forli (which, I forgot to observe, is your true name), was the interdict ever taken off you, for robbing that church at Casena?   70

Intendant. No, nor needs be: for when I murdered your brother's friend, Pasquale, for him . . .

Monsignor. Ah, he employed you in that business, did he? Well, I must let you keep, as you say, this villa and that *podere,* for fear the world should find out my relations were of so indifferent a stamp? Maffeo, my family is the oldest in Messina, and century after century have my progenitors gone on polluting themselves with every wickedness under heaven: my own father . . . rest his soul! — I have, I know, a chapel to support that it may rest: my dear two dead brothers were,

— what you know tolerably well; I, the youngest, might have 80
rivalled them in vice, if not in wealth: but from my boyhood I came
out from among them, and so am not partaker of their plagues. My
glory springs from another source; or if from this, by contrast only, —
for I, the bishop, am the brother of your employers, Ugo. I hope to
repair some of their wrong, however; so far as my brother's ill-gotten
treasure reverts to me, I can stop the consequences of his crime: and
not one *soldo* shall escape me. Maffeo, the sword we quiet men spurn
away, you shrewd knaves pick up and commit murders with; what
opportunities the virtuous forego, the villainous seize. Because, to
pleasure myself apart from other considerations, my food 90
would be millet-cake, my dress sackcloth, and my couch straw, —
am I therefore to let you, the offscouring of the earth, seduce the
poor and ignorant by appropriating a pomp these will be sure to think
lessens the abominations so unaccountably and exclusively associated
with it? Must I let villas and *poderi* go to you, a murderer and thief,
that you may beget by means of them other murderers and thieves?
No — if my cough would but allow me to speak!

Intendant. What am I to expect? You are going to punish me?

Monsignor. — Must punish you, Maffeo. I cannot afford to cast
away a chance. I have whole centuries of sin to redeem, and 100
only a month or two of life to do it in. How should I dare to say . . .

Intendant. "Forgive us our trespasses"?

Monsignor. My friend, it is because I avow myself a very worm,
sinful beyond measure, that I reject a line of conduct you would applaud perhaps. Shall I proceed, as it were, a pardoning? — I? — who
have no symptom of reason to assume that aught less than my strenu-
ousest efforts will keep myself out of mortal sin, much less keep others
out. No: I do trespass, but will not double that by allowing you to
trespass.

Intendant. And suppose the villas are not your brother's to 110
give, nor yours to take? Oh, you are hasty enough just now!

Monsignor. 1, 2 — N° 3! — ay, can you read the substance of a
letter, N° 3, I have received from Rome? It is precisely on the ground
there mentioned, of the suspicion I have that a certain child of my
late elder brother, who would have succeeded to his estates, was murdered in infancy by you, Maffeo, at the instigation of my late younger
brother — that the Pontiff enjoins on me not merely the bringing that
Maffeo to condign punishment, but the taking all pains, as guardian of
the infant's heritage for the Church, to recover it parcel by parcel,
howsoever, whensoever, and wheresoever. While you are now 120
gnawing those fingers, the police are engaged in sealing up your
papers, Maffeo, and the mere raising my voice brings my people from
the next room to dispose of yourself. But I want you to confess quietly,

and save me raising my voice. Why, man, do I not know the old story?
The heir between the succeeding heir, and this heir's ruffianly instrument, and their complot's effect, and the life of fear and bribes and
ominous smiling silence? Did you throttle or stab my brother's infant?
Come now!

Intendant. So old a story, and tell it no better? When did such an
instrument ever produce such an effect? Either the child   130
smiles in his face; or, most likely, he is not fool enough to put himself
in the employer's power so thoroughly: the child is always ready to
produce — as you say — howsoever, wheresoever, and whensoever.

Monsignor. Liar!

Intendant. Strike me? Ah, so might a father chastise! I shall sleep
soundly to-night at least, though the gallows await me to-morrow; for
what a life did I lead! Carlo of Cesena reminds me of his connivance,
every time I pay his annuity; which happens commonly thrice a year.
If I remonstrate, he will confess all to the good bishop — you!

Monsignor. I see through the trick, caitiff! I would you spoke   140
truth for once. All shall be sifted, however — seven times sifted.

Intendant. And how my absurd riches encumbered me! I dared
not lay claim to above half my possessions. Let me but once unbosom
myself, glorify Heaven, and die!

Sir, you are no brutal dastardly idiot like your brother I frightened
to death: let us understand one another. Sir, I will make away with her
for you — the girl — here close at hand; not the stupid obvious kind of
killing; do not speak — know nothing of her nor of me! I see her every
day — saw her this morning: of course there is to be no killing; but
at Rome the courtesans perish off every three years, and I can   150
entice her thither — have indeed begun operations already. There's a
certain lusty blue-eyed florid-complexioned English knave, I and the
Police employ occasionally. You assent, I perceive — no, that's not it —
assent I do not say — but you will let me convert my present havings
and holdings into cash, and give me time to cross the Alps? 'Tis but
a little black-eyed pretty singing Felippa, gay silk-winding girl. I have
kept her out of harm's way up to this present; for I always intended
to make your life a plague to you with her. 'Tis as well settled once
and forever. Some women I have procured will pass Bluphocks, my
handsome scoundrel, off for somebody; and once Pippa en-   160
tangled! — you conceive? Through her singing? Is it a bargain?

[*From without is heard the voice of* PIPPA, *singing* —

> *Overhead the tree-tops meet,*
> *Flowers and grass spring 'neath one's feet;*
> *There was naught above me, naught below,*

My childhood had not learned to know:
For, what are the voices of birds
— Ay, and of beasts, — but words, our words,
Only so much more sweet?
The knowledge of that with my life begun.
But I had so near made out the sun, 170
And counted your stars, the seven and one,
Like the fingers of my hand:
Nay, I could all but understand
Wherefore through heaven the white moon ranges;
And just when out of her soft fifty changes
No unfamiliar face might overlook me —
Suddenly God took me.

[PIPPA *passes.*

    Monsignor [*springing up*]. My people — one and all — all — all
within there! Gag this villain — tie him hand and foot! He dares . . . I
know not half he dares — but remove him — quick! *Miserere* 180
mei, Domine! Quick, I say!

SCENE — PIPPA's *chamber again. She enters it.*

The bee with his comb,
The mouse at her dray,
The grub in his tomb,
Wile winter away;
But the fire-fly and hedge-shrew and lob-worm, I pray,
How fare they?
Ha, ha, thanks for your counsel, my Zanze!
"Feast upon lampreys, quaff Breganze" —
The summer of life so easy to spend, 190
And care for to-morrow so soon put away!
But winter hastens at summer's end,
And fire-fly, hedge-shrew, lob-worm, pray,
How fare they?
No bidding me then to . . . what did Zanze say?
"Pare your nails pearlwise, get your small feet shoes
More like" . . . (what said she?) — "and less like canoes!"
How pert that girl was! — would I be those pert
Impudent staring women! It had done me,
However, surely no such mighty hurt 200
To learn his name who passed that jest upon me:
No foreigner, that I can recollect,

Came, as she says, a month since, to inspect
Our silk-mills — none with blue eyes and thick rings
Of raw-silk-colored hair, at all events.
Well, if old Luca keep his good intents,
We shall do better, see what next year brings.
I may buy shoes, my Zanze, not appear
More destitute than you perhaps next year!
Bluph . . . something! I had caught the uncouth name   210
But for Monsignor's people's sudden clatter
Above us — bound to spoil such idle chatter
As ours: it were indeed a serious matter
If silly talk like ours should put to shame
The pious man, the man devoid of blame,
The . . . ah but — ah but, all the same,
No mere mortal has a right
To carry that exalted air;
Best people are not angels quite:
While — not the worst of people's doings scare   220
The devil; so there's that proud look to spare!
    Which is mere counsel to myself, mind! for
I have just been the holy Monsignor:
And I was you too, Luigi's gentle mother,
And you too, Luigi! — how that Luigi started
Out of the turret — doubtlessly departed
On some good errand or another,
For he passed just now in a traveller's trim,
And the sullen company that prowled
About his path, I noticed, scowled   230
As if they had lost a prey in him.
And I was Jules the sculptor's bride,
And I was Ottima beside,
And now what am I? — tired of fooling.
Day for folly, night for schooling!
New Year's day is over and spent,
Ill or well, I must be content.
    Even my lily's asleep, I vow:
Wake up — here's a friend I've plucked you:
Call this flower a heart's-ease now!   240
Something rare, let me instruct you,
Is this, with petals triply swollen,
Three times spotted, thrice the pollen;
While the leaves and parts that witness
Old proportions and their fitness,
Here remain unchanged, unmoved now;

Call this pampered thing improved now!
Suppose there's a king of the flowers
And a girl-show held in his bowers —
"Look ye, buds, this growth of ours,"   250
Says he, "Zanze from the Brenta,
I have made her gorge polenta
Till both cheeks are near as bouncing
As her . . . name there's no pronouncing!
See this heightened color too,
For she swilled Breganze wine
Till her nose turned deep carmine;
'Twas but white when wild she grew.
And only by this Zanze's eyes
Of which we could not change the size,   260
The magnitude of all achieved
Otherwise, may be perceived."

Oh what a drear dark close to my poor day!
How could that red sun drop in that black cloud?
Ah Pippa, morning's rule is moved away,
Dispensed with, never more to be allowed!
Day's turn is over, now arrives the night's.
Oh lark, be day's apostle
To mavis, merle and throstle,
Bid them their betters jostle   270
From day and its delights!
But at night, brother howlet, over the woods,
Toll the world to thy chantry;
Sing to the bat's sleek sisterhoods
Full complines with gallantry:
Then, owls and bats,
Cowls and twats,
Monks and nuns, in a cloister's moods,
Adjourn to the oak-stumped pantry!
                       [*After she has begun to undress herself.*
Now, one thing I should like to really know: 280
How near I ever might approach all these
I only fancied being, this long day:
— Approach, I mean, so as to touch them, so
As to . . . in some way . . . move them — if you please,
Do good or evil to them some slight way.
For instance, if I wind
Silk to-morrow, my silk may bind
                         [*Sitting on the bedside.*

And border Ottima's cloak's hem.
Ah me, and my important part with them,
This morning's hymn half promised when I rose!   290
True in some sense or other, I suppose.

> [*As she lies down.*

God bless me! I can pray no more to-night.
No doubt, some way or other, hymns say right.

> *All service ranks the same with God —*
> *With God, whose puppets, best and worst,*
> *Are we: there is no last nor first.*

> [*She sleeps.*

FROM *Dramatic Lyrics*

(1842)

CAVALIER TUNES

1. MARCHING ALONG

I

KENTISH Sir Byng stood for his King,
Bidding the crop-headed Parliament swing:
And, pressing a troop unable to stoop
And see the rogues flourish and honest folk droop,
Marched them along, fifty-score strong,
Great-hearted gentlemen, singing this song.

II

God for King Charles! Pym and such carles
To the Devil that prompts 'em their treasonous parles!
Cavaliers, up! Lips from the cup,
Hands from the pasty, nor bite take nor sup   10
Till you're —
  CHORUS. *Marching along, fifty-score strong,*
     Great-hearted gentlemen, singing this song.

III

Hampden to hell, and his obsequies' knell
Serve Hazelrig, Fiennes, and young Harry as well!
England, good cheer! Rupert is near!
Kentish and loyalists, keep we not here
  CHORUS. *Marching along, fifty-score strong,*
     Great-hearted gentlemen, singing this song?

47

IV

Then, God for King Charles! Pym and his snarls
To the Devil that pricks on such pestilent carles!   20
Hold by the right, you double your might;
So, onward to Nottingham, fresh for the fight,
    CHORUS. *March we along, fifty-score strong,*
            Great-hearted gentlemen, singing this song!

2. GIVE A ROUSE

I

King Charles, and who'll do him right now?
King Charles, and who's ripe for fight now?
Give a rouse: here's, in hell's despite now,
King Charles!

II

Who gave me the goods that went since?
Who raised me the house that sank once?
Who helped me to gold I spent since?
Who found me in wine you drank once?
    CHORUS. *King Charles, and who'll do him right now?*
            King Charles, and who's ripe for fight now?   10
            Give a rouse: here's, in hell's despite now,
            King Charles!

III

To whom used my boy George quaff else,
By the old fool's side that begot him?
For whom did he cheer and laugh else,
While Noll's damned troopers shot him?
    CHORUS. *King Charles, and who'll do him right now?*
            King Charles, and who's ripe for fight now?
            Give a rouse: here's, in hell's despite now,
            King Charles!   20

3. Boot and Saddle

I

Boot, saddle, to horse, and away!
Rescue my castle before the hot day
Brightens to blue from its silvery gray,
    Chorus. *Boot, saddle, to horse, and away!*

II

Ride past the suburbs, asleep as you'd say;
Many's the friend there, will listen and pray
"God's luck to gallants that strike up the lay —
    Chorus. *"Boot, saddle, to horse, and away!"*

III

Forty miles off, like a roebuck at bay,
Flouts Castle Brancepeth the Roundheads' array:
Who laughs, "Good fellows ere this, by my fay,
    Chorus. *"Boot, saddle, to horse, and away!"*

10

IV

Who? My wife Gertrude; that, honest and gay,
Laughs when you talk of surrendering, "Nay!
I've better counsellors; what counsel they?
    Chorus. *"Boot, saddle, to horse, and away!"*

MY LAST DUCHESS

Ferrara

That's my last Duchess painted on the wall,
Looking as if she were alive. I call
That piece a wonder, now: Frà Pandolf's hands
Worked busily a day, and there she stands.
Will't please you sit and look at her? I said

"Frà Pandolf" by design, for never read
Strangers like you that pictured countenance,
The depth and passion of its earnest glance,
But to myself they turned (since none puts by
The curtain I have drawn for you, but I)   10
And seemed as they would ask me, if they durst,
How such a glance came there; so, not the first
Are you to turn and ask thus. Sir, 'twas not
Her husband's presence only, called that spot
Of joy into the Duchess' cheek: perhaps
Frà Pandolf chanced to say "Her mantle laps
Over my lady's wrist too much," or "Paint
Must never hope to reproduce the faint
Half-flush that dies along her throat:" such stuff
Was courtesy, she thought, and cause enough   20
For calling up that spot of joy. She had
A heart — how shall I say? — too soon made glad,
Too easily impressed; she liked whate'er
She looked on, and her looks went everywhere.
Sir, 'twas all one! My favor at her breast,
The dropping of the daylight in the West,
The bough of cherries some officious fool
Broke in the orchard for her, the white mule
She rode with round the terrace — all and each
Would draw from her alike the approving speech,   30
Or blush, at least. She thanked men, — good! but thanked
Somehow — I know not how — as if she ranked
My gift of a nine-hundred-years-old name
With anybody's gift. Who'd stoop to blame
This sort of trifling? Even had you skill
In speech — (which I have not) — to make your will
Quite clear to such an one, and say, "Just this
Or that in you disgusts me; here you miss,
Or there exceed the mark" — and if she let
Herself be lessoned so, nor plainly set   40
Her wits to yours, forsooth, and made excuse,
— E'en then would be some stooping; and I choose
Never to stoop. Oh sir, she smiled, no doubt,
Whene'er I passed her; but who passed without
Much the same smile? This grew; I gave commands;
Then all smiles stopped together. There she stands
As if alive. Will't please you rise? We'll meet
The company below, then. I repeat,
The Count your master's known munificence

Is ample warrant that no just pretence   50
Of mine for dowry will be disallowed;
Though his fair daughter's self, as I avowed
At starting, is my object. Nay, we'll go
Together down, sir. Notice Neptune, though,
Taming a sea-horse, thought a rarity,   *Osmond*
Which Claus of Innsbruck cast in bronze for me!

COUNT GISMOND

AIX IN PROVENCE

I

CHRIST God who savest man, save most
    Of men Count Gismond who saved me!
Count Gauthier, when he chose his post,
    Chose time and place and company
To suit it; when he struck at length
My honor, 'twas with all his strength.

II

And doubtlessly ere he could draw
    All points to one, he must have schemed!
That miserable morning saw
    Few half so happy as I seemed,   10
While being dressed in queen's array
To give our tourney prize away.

III

I thought they loved me, did me grace
    To please themselves; 'twas all their deed;
God makes, or fair or foul, our face;
    If showing mine so caused to bleed
My cousins' hearts, they should have dropped
A word, and straight the play had stopped.

IV

They, too, so beauteous! Each a queen
    By virtue of her brow and breast;   20
Not needing to be crowned, I mean,
    As I do. E'en when I was dressed,

Had either of them spoke, instead
Of glancing sideways with still head!

V

But no: they let me laugh, and sing
 My birthday song quite through, adjust
The last rose in my garland, fling
 A last look on the mirror, trust
My arms to each an arm of theirs,
And so descend the castle-stairs —   30

VI

And come out on the morning-troop
 Of merry friends who kissed my cheek,
And called me queen, and made me stoop
 Under the canopy — (a streak
That pierced it, of the outside sun,
Powdered with gold its gloom's soft dun) —

VII

And they could let me take my state
 And foolish throne amid applause
Of all come there to celebrate
 My queen's-day — Oh I think the cause   40
Of much was, they forgot no crowd
Makes up for parents in their shroud!

VIII

However that be, all eyes were bent
 Upon me, when my cousins cast
Theirs down; 'twas time I should present
 The victor's crown, but . . . there, 'twill last
No long time . . . the old mist again
Blinds me as then it did. How vain!

IX

See! Gismond's at the gate, in talk
 With his two boys: I can proceed.   50
Well, at that moment, who should stalk
 Forth boldly — to my face, indeed —
But Gauthier, and he thundered "Stay!"
And all stayed. "Bring no crowns, I say!

X

"Bring torches! Wind the penance-sheet
 About her! Let her shun the chaste,
Or lay herself before their feet!
 Shall she whose body I embraced
A night long, queen it in the day?
For honor's sake no crowns, I say!"   60

XI

I? What I answered? As I live,
 I never fancied such a thing
As answer possible to give.
 What says the body when they spring
Some monstrous torture-engine's whole
 Strength on it? No more says the soul.

XII

Till out strode Gismond; then I knew
 That I was saved. I never met
His face before, but, at first view,
 I felt quite sure that God had set   70
Himself to Satan; who would spend
A minute's mistrust on the end?

XIII

He strode to Gauthier, in his throat
 Gave him the lie, then struck his mouth
With one back-handed blow that wrote
 In blood men's verdict there. North, South,
East, West, I looked. The lie was dead,
And damned, and truth stood up instead.

XIV

This glads me most, that I enjoyed
 The heart of the joy, with my content   80
In watching Gismond unalloyed
 By any doubt of the event:
God took that on him — I was bid
Watch Gismond for my part: I did.

xv

Did I not watch him while he let
> His armorer just brace his greaves,
Rivet his hauberk, on the fret
> The while! His foot . . . my memory leaves
No least stamp out, nor how anon
He pulled his ringing gauntlets on.   90

xvi

And e'en before the trumpet's sound
> Was finished, prone lay the false knight,
Prone as his lie, upon the ground:
> Gismond flew at him, used no sleight
O' the sword, but open-breasted drove,
Cleaving till out the truth he clove.

xvii

Which done, he dragged him to my feet
> And said "Here die, but end thy breath
In full confession, lest thou fleet
> From my first, to God's second death!   100
Say, hast thou lied?" And, "I have lied
To God and her," he said, and died.

xviii

Then Gismond, kneeling to me, asked
> — What safe my heart holds, though no word
Could I repeat now, if I tasked
> My powers forever, to a third
Dear even as you are. Pass the rest
Until I sank upon his breast.

xix

Over my head his arm he flung
> Against the world; and scarce I felt   110
His sword (that dripped by me and swung)
> A little shifted in its belt:
For he began to say the while
How South our home lay many a mile.

XX

So 'mid the shouting multitude
    We two walked forth to never more
Return. My cousins have pursued
    Their life, untroubled as before
I vexed them. Gauthier's dwelling-place
God lighten! May his soul find grace!   120

XXI

Our elder boy has got the clear
    Great brow; tho' when his brother's black
Full eye shows scorn, it . . . Gismond here?
    And have you brought my tercel back?
I just was telling Adela
How many birds it struck since May.

INCIDENT OF THE FRENCH CAMP

I

You know, we French stormed Ratisbon:
    A mile or so away,
On a little mound, Napoleon
    Stood on our storming-day;
With neck out-thrust, you fancy how,
    Legs wide, arms locked behind,
As if to balance the prone brow
    Oppressive with its mind.

II

Just as perhaps he mused "My plans
    That soar, to earth may fall,
Let once my army-leader Lannes   10
    Waver at yonder wall," —
Out 'twixt the battery-smokes there flew
    A rider, bound on bound
Full-galloping; nor bridle drew
    Until he reached the mound.

III

Then off there flung in smiling joy,
    And held himself erect
By just his horse's mane, a boy:
    You hardly could suspect —   20
(So tight he kept his lips compressed,
    Scarce any blood came through)
You looked twice ere you saw his breast
    Was all but shot in two.

IV

"Well," cried he, "Emperor, by God's grace
    We've got you Ratisbon!
The Marshal's in the market-place,
    And you'll be there anon
To see your flag-bird flap his vans
    Where I, to heart's desire,   30
Perched him!" The chief's eye flashed; his plans
    Soared up again like fire.

V

The chief's eye flashed; but presently
    Softened itself, as sheathes
A film the mother-eagle's eye
    When her bruised eaglet breathes;
"You're wounded!" "Nay," the soldier's pride
    Touched to the quick, he said:
"I'm killed, sire!" And his chief beside
    Smiling the boy fell dead.   40

SOLILOQUY OF THE SPANISH CLOISTER

I

Gr-r-r — there go, my heart's abhorrence!
    Water your damned flower-pots, do!
If hate killed men, Brother Lawrence,
    God's blood, would not mine kill you!

What? your myrtle-bush wants trimming?
    Oh, that rose has prior claims —
Needs its leaden vase filled brimming?
    Hell dry you up with its flames!

II

At the meal we sit together:
    Salve tibi! I must hear   10
Wise talk of the kind of weather,
    Sort of season, time of year:
Not a plenteous cork-crop: scarcely
    Dare we hope oak-galls, I doubt:
What's the Latin name for "parsley"?
    What's the Greek name for Swine's Snout?

III

Whew! We'll have our platter burnished,
    Laid with care on our own shelf!
With a fire-new spoon we're furnished,
    And a goblet for ourself,   20
Rinsed like something sacrificial
    Ere 'tis fit to touch our chaps —
Marked with L. for our initial!
    (He-he! There his lily snaps!)

IV

Saint, forsooth! While brown Dolores
    Squats outside the Convent bank
With Sanchicha, telling stories,
    Steeping tresses in the tank,
Blue-black, lustrous, thick like horsehairs,
    — Can't I see his dead eye glow,   30
Bright as 'twere a Barbary corsair's?
    (That is, if he'd let it show!)

V

When he finishes refection,
    Knife and fork he never lays
Cross-wise, to my recollection,
    As do I, in Jesu's praise.
I the Trinity illustrate,
    Drinking watered orange-pulp —

In three sips the Arian frustrate;
    While he drains his at one gulp.   40

VI

Oh, those melons? If he's able
    We're to have a feast! so nice!
One goes to the Abbot's table,
    All of us get each a slice.
How go on your flowers? None double?
    Not one fruit-sort can you spy?
Strange! — And I, too, at such trouble,
    Keep them close-nipped on the sly!

VII

There's a great text in Galatians,
    Once you trip on it, entails   50
Twenty-nine distinct damnations,
    One sure, if another fails:
If I trip him just a-dying,
    Sure of heaven as sure can be,
Spin him round and send him flying
    Off to hell, a Manichee?

VIII

Or, my scrofulous French novel
    On gray paper with blunt type!
Simply glance at it, you grovel
    Hand and foot in Belial's gripe: 60
If I double down its pages
    At the woeful sixteenth print,
When he gathers his greengages,
    Ope a sieve and slip it in't?

IX

Or, there's Satan! — one might venture
    Pledge one's soul to him, yet leave
Such a flaw in the indenture
    As he'd miss till, past retrieve,
Blasted lay that rose-acacia
    We're so proud of! *Hy, Zy, Hine.*   70
'St, there's Vespers! *Plena gratiâ*
    Ave, Virgo! Gr-r-r — you swine!

IN A GONDOLA

He sings.

I SEND my heart up to thee, all my heart
    In this my singing.
For the stars help me, and the sea bears part;
    The very night is clinging
Closer to Venice' streets to leave one space
    Above me, whence thy face
May light my joyous heart to thee its dwelling-place.

She speaks.

Say after me, and try to say
My very words, as if each word
Came from you of your own accord,
In your own voice, in your own way: 10
"This woman's heart and soul and brain
Are mine as much as this gold chain
She bids me wear; which" (say again)
"I choose to make by cherishing
A precious thing, or choose to fling
Over the boat-side, ring by ring."
And yet once more say . . . no word more!
Since words are only words. Give o'er!

Unless you call me, all the same,   20
Familiarly by my pet name,
Which if the Three should hear you call,
And me reply to, would proclaim
At once our secret to them all.
Ask of me, too, command me, blame —
Do, break down the partition-wall
'Twixt us, the daylight world beholds
Curtained in dusk and splendid folds!
What's left but — all of me to take?
I am the Three's: prevent them, slake   30
Your thirst! 'Tis said, the Arab sage,
In practising with gems, can loose

Their subtle spirit in his cruce
And leave but ashes: so, sweet mage,
Leave them my ashes when thy use
Sucks out my soul, thy heritage!

He sings.

I

Past we glide, and past, and past!
    What's that poor Agnese doing
Where they make the shutters fast?
    Gray Zanobi's just a-wooing   40
To his couch the purchased bride:
    Past we glide!

II

Past we glide, and past, and past!
    Why's the Pucci Palace flaring
Like a beacon to the blast?
    Guests by hundreds, not one caring
If the dear host's neck were wried:
    Past we glide!

She sings.

I

The moth's kiss, first!
Kiss me as if you made believe   50
You were not sure, this eve,
How my face, your flower, had pursed
Its petals up; so, here and there
You brush it, till I grow aware
Who wants me, and wide ope I burst.

II

The bee's kiss, now!
Kiss me as if you entered gay
My heart at some noonday,
A bud that dares not disallow
The claim, so all is rendered up,   60
And passively its shattered cup
Over your head to sleep I bow.

He sings.

I

What are we two?
I am a Jew,
And carry thee, farther than friends can pursue,
To a feast of our tribe;
Where they need thee to bribe
The devil that blasts them unless he imbibe
Thy . . . Scatter the vision forever! And now,
As of old, I am I, thou art thou!   **70**

II

Say again, what we are?
The sprite of a star,
I lure thee above where the destinies bar
My plumes their full play
Till a ruddier ray
Than my pale one announce there is withering away
Some . . . Scatter the vision forever! And now,
As of old, I am I, thou art thou!

He muses.

Oh, which were best, to roam or rest?
The land's lap or the water's breast?   **80**
To sleep on yellow millet-sheaves,
Or swim in lucid shallows just
Eluding water-lily leaves,
An inch from Death's black fingers, thrust
To lock you, whom release he must;
Which life were best on Summer eves?

He speaks, musing.

Lie back; could thought of mine improve you?
From this shoulder let there spring
A wing; from this, another wing;
Wings, not legs and feet, shall move you!   **90**
Snow-white must they spring, to blend
With your flesh, but I intend
They shall deepen to the end,
Broader, into burning gold,

Till both wings crescent-wise enfold
Your perfect self, from 'neath your feet
To o'er your head, where, lo, they meet
As if a million sword-blades hurled
Defiance from you to the world!

Rescue me thou, the only real!   100
And scare away this mad ideal
That came, nor motions to depart!
Thanks! Now, stay ever as thou art!

Still he muses.

I

What if the Three should catch at last
Thy serenader? While there's cast
Paul's cloak about my head, and fast
Gian pinions me, Himself has past
His stylet thro' my back; I reel;
And . . . is it thou I feel?

II

They trail me, these three godless knaves,   110
Past every church that saints and saves,
Nor stop till, where the cold sea raves
By Lido's wet accursed graves,
They scoop mine, roll me to its brink,
And . . . on thy breast I sink!

She replies, musing.

Dip your arm o'er the boat-side, elbow-deep,
As I do: thus: were death so unlike sleep,
Caught this way? Death's to fear from flame or steel,
Or poison doubtless; but from water — feel!
Go find the bottom! Would you stay me? There!   120
Now pluck a great blade of that ribbon-grass
To plait in where the foolish jewel was,
I flung away: since you have praised my hair,
'Tis proper to be choice in what I wear.

He speaks.

Row home? must we row home? Too surely
Know I where its front's demurely
Over the Giudecca piled;
Window just with window mating,
Door on door exactly waiting,
All's the set face of a child: 130
But behind it, where's a trace
Of the staidness and reserve,
And formal lines without a curve,
In the same child's playing-face?
No two windows look one way
O'er the small sea-water thread
Below them. Ah, the autumn day
I, passing, saw you overhead!
First, out a cloud of curtain blew,
Then a sweet cry, and last came you —   140
To catch your lory that must needs
Escape just then, of all times then,
To peck a tall plant's fleecy seeds,
And make me happiest of men.
I scarce could breathe to see you reach
So far back o'er the balcony
To catch him ere he climbed too high
Above you in the Smyrna peach
That quick the round smooth cord of gold,
This coiled hair on your head, unrolled,   150
Fell down you like a gorgeous snake
The Roman girls were wont, of old,
When Rome there was, for coolness' sake
To let lie curling o'er their bosoms.
Dear lory, may his beak retain
Ever its delicate rose stain
As if the wounded lotus-blossoms
Had marked their thief to know again!

Stay longer yet, for others' sake
Than mine! What should your chamber do?   160
— With all its rarities that ache
In silence while day lasts, but wake
At night-time and their life renew,
Suspended just to pleasure you

Who brought against their will together
These objects, and, while day lasts, weave
Around them such a magic tether
That dumb they look: your harp, believe,
With all the sensitive tight strings
Which dare not speak, now to itself   170
Breathes slumberously, as if some elf
Went in and out the chords, his wings
Make murmur wheresoe'er they graze,
As an angel may, between the maze
Of midnight palace-pillars, on
And on, to sow God's plagues, have gone
Through guilty glorious Babylon.
And while such murmurs flow, the nymph
Bends o'er the harp-top from her shell
As the dry limpet for the lymph   180
Come with a tune he knows so well.
And how your statues' hearts must swell!
And how your pictures must descend
To see each other, friend with friend!
Oh, could you take them by surprise,
You'd find Schidone's eager Duke
Doing the quaintest courtesies
To that prim saint by Haste-thee-Luke!
And, deeper into her rock den,
Bold Castelfranco's Magdalen   190
You'd find retreated from the ken
Of that robed counsel-keeping Ser —
As if the Tizian thinks of her,
And is not, rather, gravely bent
On seeing for himself what toys
Are these, his progeny invent,
What litter now the board employs
Whereon he signed a document
That got him murdered! Each enjoys
Its night so well, you cannot break   200
The sport up, so, indeed must make
More stay with me, for others' sake.

She speaks.

I

To-morrow, if a harp-string, say,
Is used to tie the jasmine back
That overfloods my room with sweets,
Contrive your Zorzi somehow meets
My Zanze! If the ribbon's black,
The Three are watching: keep away!

II

Your gondola — let Zorzi wreathe
A mesh of water-weeds about   210
Its prow, as if he unaware
Had struck some quay or bridge-foot stair!
That I may throw a paper out
As you and he go underneath.

There's Zanze's vigilant taper; safe are we.
Only one minute more to-night with me?
Resume your past self of a month ago!
Be you the bashful gallant, I will be
The lady with the colder breast than snow.
Now bow you, as becomes, nor touch my hand   220
More than I touch yours when I step to land,
And say, "All thanks, Siora!" —
                              Heart to heart
And lips to lips! Yet once more, ere we part,
Clasp me and make me thine, as mine thou art!
                        [*He is surprised, and stabbed.*
It was ordained to be so, sweet! — and best
Comes now, beneath thine eyes, upon thy breast.
Still kiss me! Care not for the cowards! Care
Only to put aside thy beauteous hair
My blood will hurt! The Three, I do not scorn
To death, because they never lived: but I   230
Have lived indeed, and so — (yet one more kiss) — can die!

ARTEMIS PROLOGIZES

I AM a Goddess of the ambrosial courts,
And save by Here, Queen of Pride, surpassed
By none whose temples whiten this the world.
Through heaven I roll my lucid moon along;
I shed in hell o'er my pale people peace;
On earth I, caring for the creatures, guard
Each pregnant yellow wolf and fox-bitch sleek,
And every feathered mother's callow brood,
And all that love green haunts and loneliness.
Of men, the chaste adore me, hanging crowns   10
Of poppies red to blackness, bell and stem,
Upon my image at Athenai here;
And this dead Youth, Asclepios bends above,
Was dearest to me. He, my buskined step
To follow through the wild-wood leafy ways,
And chase the panting stag, or swift with darts
Stop the swift ounce, or lay the leopard low,
Neglected homage to another god:
Whence Aphrodite, by no midnight smoke
Of tapers lulled, in jealousy despatched   20
A noisome lust that, as the gadbee stings,
Possessed his stepdame Phaidra for himself
The son of Theseus her great absent spouse.
Hippolutos exclaiming in his rage
Against the fury of the Queen, she judged
Life insupportable; and, pricked at heart
An Amazonian stranger's race should dare
To scorn her, perished by the murderous cord:
Yet, ere she perished, blasted in a scroll
The fame of him her swerving made not swerve.   30
And Theseus, read, returning, and believed,
And exiled, in the blindness of his wrath,
The man without a crime who, last as first,
Loyal, divulged not to his sire the truth.
Now Theseus from Poseidon had obtained
That of his wishes should be granted three,
And one he imprecated straight — "Alive
May ne'er Hippolutos reach other lands!"

Poseidon heard, ai ai! And scarce the prince
Had stepped into the fixed boots of the car   40
That give the feet a stay against the strength
Of the Henetian horses, and around
His body flung the rein, and urged their speed
Along the rocks and shingles of the shore,
When from the gaping wave a monster flung
His obscene body in the coursers' path.
These, mad with terror, as the sea-bull sprawled
Wallowing about their feet, lost care of him
That reared them; and the master-chariot-pole
Snapping beneath their plunges like a reed,   50
Hippolutos, whose feet were trammelled fast,
Was yet dragged forward by the circling rein
Which either hand directed; nor they quenched
The frenzy of their flight before each trace,
Wheel-spoke and splinter of the woful car,
Each boulder-stone, sharp stub and spiny shell,
Huge fish-bone wrecked and wreathed amid the sands
On that detested beach, was bright with blood
And morsels of his flesh: then fell the steeds
Head foremost, crashing in their mooned fronts,   60
Shivering with sweat, each white eye horror-fixed.
His people, who had witnessed all afar,
Bore back the ruins of Hippolutos.
But when his sire, too swoln with pride, rejoiced
(Indomitable as a man foredoomed)
That vast Poseidon had fulfilled his prayer,
I, in a flood of glory visible,
Stood o'er my dying votary and, deed
By deed, revealed, as all took place, the truth.
Then Theseus lay the wofullest of men,   70
And worthily; but ere the death-veils hid
His face, the murdered prince full pardon breathed
To his rash sire. Whereat Athenai wails.
   So I, who ne'er forsake my votaries,
Lest in the cross-way none the honey-cake
Should tender, nor pour out the dog's hot life;
Lest at my fane the priests disconsolate
Should dress my image with some faded poor
Few crowns, made favors of, nor dare object
Such slackness to my worshippers who turn   80
Elsewhere the trusting heart and loaded hand,
As they had climbed Olumpos to report

Of Artemis and nowhere found her throne —
I interposed: and, this eventful night, —
(While round the funeral pyre the populace
Stood with fierce light on their black robes which bound
Each sobbing head, while yet their hair they clipped
O'er the dead body of their withered prince,
And, in his palace, Theseus prostrated
On the cold hearth, his brow cold as the slab   90
'Twas bruised on, groaned away the heavy grief —
As the pyre fell, and down the cross logs crashed
Sending a crowd of sparkles through the night,
And the gay fire, elate with mastery,
Towered like a serpent o'er the clotted jars
Of wine, dissolving oils and frankincense,
And splendid gums like gold), — my potency
Conveyed the perished man to my retreat
In the thrice-venerable forest here.
And this white-bearded sage who squeezes now   100
The berried plant, is Phoibos' son of fame,
Asclepios, whom my radiant brother taught
The doctrine of each herb and flower and root,
To know their secret'st virtue and express
The saving soul of all: who so has soothed
With lavers the torn brow and murdered cheeks,
Composed the hair and brought its gloss again,
And called the red bloom to the pale skin back,
And laid the strips and jagged ends of flesh
Even once more, and slacked the sinew's knot   110
Of every tortured limb — that now he lies
As if mere sleep possessed him underneath
These interwoven oaks and pines. Oh cheer,
Divine presenter of the healing rod,
Thy snake, with ardent throat and lulling eye,
Twines his lithe spires around! I say, much cheer!
Proceed thou with thy wisest pharmacies!
And ye, white crowd of woodland sister-nymphs,
Ply, as the sage directs, these buds and leaves
That strew the turf around the twain! While I   120
Await, in fitting silence, the event.

RUDEL TO THE LADY OF TRIPOLI

I

I KNOW a Mount, the gracious Sun perceives
First, when he visits, last, too, when he leaves
The world; and, vainly favored, it repays
The day-long glory of his steadfast gaze
By no change of its large calm front of snow.
And underneath the Mount, a Flower I know,
He cannot have perceived, that changes ever
At his approach; and, in the lost endeavor
To live his life, has parted, one by one,
With all a flower's true graces, for the grace   10
Of being but a foolish mimic sun,
With ray-like florets round a disk-like face.
Men nobly call by many a name the Mount
As over many a land of theirs its large
Calm front of snow like a triumphal targe
Is reared, and still with old names, fresh names vie,
Each to its proper praise and own account:
Men call the Flower, the Sunflower, sportively.

II

Oh, Angel of the East, one, one gold look
Across the waters to this twilight nook,   20
— The far sad waters, Angel, to this nook!

III

Dear Pilgrim, art thou for the East indeed?
Go! — saying ever as thou dost proceed,
That I, French Rudel, choose for my device
A sunflower outspread like a sacrifice
Before its idol. See! These inexpert
And hurried fingers could not fail to hurt
The woven picture; 'tis a woman's skill
Indeed; but nothing baffled me, so, ill
Or well, the work is finished. Say, men feed   30
On songs I sing, and therefore bask the bees
On my flower's breast as on a platform broad:
But, as the flower's concern is not for these
But solely for the sun, so men applaud
In vain this Rudel, he not looking here
But to the East — the East! Go, say this, Pilgrim dear!

CRISTINA

I

SHE should never have looked at me
  If she meant I should not love her!
There are plenty . . . men, you call such,
  I suppose . . . she may discover
All her soul to, if she pleases,
  And yet leave much as she found them:
But I'm not so, and she knew it
  When she fixed me, glancing round them.

II

What? To fix me thus meant nothing?
  But I can't tell (there's my weakness)   10
What her look said! — no vile cant, sure,
  About "need to strew the bleakness
Of some lone shore with its pearl-seed
  That the sea feels" — no "strange yearning
That such souls have, most to lavish
  Where there's chance of least returning."

III

Oh, we're sunk enough here, God knows!
  But not quite so sunk that moments,
Sure tho' seldom, are denied us,
  When the spirit's true endowments   20
Stand out plainly from its false ones,
  And apprise it if pursuing
Or the right way or the wrong way,
  To its triumph or undoing.

IV

There are flashes struck from midnights,
  There are fire-flames noondays kindle,
Whereby piled-up honors perish,
  Whereby swollen ambitions dwindle,
While just this or that poor impulse,
  Which for once had played unstifled,   30
Seems the sole work of a life-time
  That away the rest have trifled.

V

Doubt you if, in some such moment,
    As she fixed me, she felt clearly,
Ages past the soul existed,
    Here an age 'tis resting merely,
And hence fleets again for ages,
    While the true end, sole and single,
It stops here for is, this love-way,
    With some other soul to mingle?   40

VI

Else it loses what it lived for,
    And eternally must lose it;
Better ends may be in prospect,
    Deeper blisses (if you choose it),
But this life's end and this love-bliss
    Have been lost here. Doubt you whether
This she felt as, looking at me,
    Mine and her souls rushed together?

VII

Oh, observe! Of course, next moment,
    The world's honors, in derision,   50
Trampled out the light forever:
    Never fear but there's provision
Of the devil's to quench knowledge
    Lest we walk the earth in rapture!
— Making those who catch God's secret
    Just so much more prize their capture!

VIII

Such am I: the secret's mine now!
    She has lost me, I have gained her;
Her soul's mine: and thus, grown perfect,
    I shall pass my life's remainder.   60
Life will just hold out the proving
    Both our powers, alone and blended:
And then, come next life quickly!
    This world's use will have been ended.

JOHANNES AGRICOLA IN MEDITATION

THERE's heaven above, and night by night
    I look right through its gorgeous roof;
No suns and moons though e'er so bright
    Avail to stop me; splendor-proof
    I keep the broods of stars aloof:
For I intend to get to God,
    For 'tis to God I speed so fast,
For in God's breast, my own abode,
    Those shoals of dazzling glory, past,
    I lay my spirit down at last.   10
I lie where I have always lain,
    God smiles as he has always smiled;
Ere suns and moons could wax and wane,
    Ere stars were thundergirt, or piled
    The heavens, God thought on me his child;
Ordained a life for me, arrayed
    Its circumstances, every one
To the minutest; ay, God said
    This head this hand should rest upon
    Thus, ere he fashioned star or sun.   20
And having thus created me,
    Thus rooted me, he bade me grow,
Guiltless forever, like a tree
    That buds and blooms, nor seeks to know
    The law by which it prospers so:
But sure that thought and word and deed
    All go to swell his love for me,
Me, made because that love had need
    Of something irreversibly
    Pledged solely its content to be.   30
Yes, yes, a tree which must ascend,
    No poison-gourd foredoomed to stoop!
I have God's warrant, could I blend
    All hideous sins, as in a cup,
    To drink the mingled venoms up;
Secure my nature will convert
    The draught to blossoming gladness fast:
While sweet dews turn to the gourd's hurt,

And bloat, and while they bloat it, blast,
  As from the first its lot was cast.   40
For as I lie, smiled on, full-fed
  By unexhausted power to bless,
I gaze below on hell's fierce bed,
  And those its waves of flame oppress,
  Swarming in ghastly wretchedness;
Whose life on earth aspired to be
  One altar-smoke, so pure! — to win
If not love like God's love for me,
  At least to keep his anger in;
  And all their striving turned to sin.   50
Priest, doctor, hermit, monk grown white
  With prayer, the broken-hearted nun,
The martyr, the wan acolyte,
  The incense-swinging child, — undone
  Before God fashioned star or sun!
God, whom I praise; how could I praise,
  If such as I might understand,
Make out and reckon on his ways,
  And bargain for his love, and stand,
Paying a price, at his right hand?   60

PORPHYRIA'S LOVER

The rain set early in to-night,
  The sullen wind was soon awake,
It tore the elm-tops down for spite,
  And did its worst to vex the lake:
  I listened with heart fit to break.
When glided in Porphyria; straight
  She shut the cold out and the storm,
And kneeled and made the cheerless grate
  Blaze up, and all the cottage warm;
  Which done, she rose, and from her form   10
Withdrew the dripping cloak and shawl,
  And laid her soiled gloves by, untied
Her hat and let the damp hair fall,
  And, last, she sat down by my side
  And called me. When no voice replied,
She put my arm about her waist,

And made her smooth white shoulder bare,
And all her yellow hair displaced,
    And, stooping, made my cheek lie there,
    And spread, o'er all, her yellow hair,   20
Murmuring how she loved me — she
    Too weak, for all her heart's endeavor,
To set its struggling passion free
    From pride, and vainer ties dissever,
    And give herself to me forever.
But passion sometimes would prevail,
    Nor could to-night's gay feast restrain
A sudden thought of one so pale
    For love of her, and all in vain:
    So, she was come through wind and rain.   30
Be sure I looked up at her eyes
    Happy and proud; at last I knew
Porphyria worshipped me: surprise
    Made my heart swell, and still it grew
    While I debated what to do.
That moment she was mine, mine, fair,
    Perfectly pure and good: I found
A thing to do, and all her hair
    In one long yellow string I wound
    Three times her little throat around,   40
And strangled her. No pain felt she;
    I am quite sure she felt no pain.
As a shut bud that holds a bee,
    I warily oped her lids: again
    Laughed the blue eyes without a stain.
And I untightened next the tress
    About her neck; her cheek once more
Blushed bright beneath my burning kiss:
    I propped her head up as before,
    Only, this time my shoulder bore   50
Her head, which droops upon it still:
    The smiling rosy little head,
So glad it has its utmost will,
    That all it scorned at once is fled,
    And I, its love, am gained instead!
Porphyria's love: she guessed not how
    Her darling one wish would be heard.
And thus we sit together now,
    And all night long we have not stirred,
    And yet God has not said a word!   60

THE PIED PIPER OF HAMELIN

A CHILD'S STORY

(Written for, and inscribed to, W. M. the Younger.)

I

HAMELIN TOWN's in Brunswick,
       By famous Hanover city;
The river Weser, deep and wide,
Washes its wall on the southern side;
A pleasanter spot you never spied;
       But, when begins my ditty,
Almost five hundred years ago,
To see the townsfolk suffer so
       From vermin, was a pity.

II

Rats!   10
They fought the dogs and killed the cats,
       And bit the babies in the cradles,
And ate the cheeses out of the vats,
       And licked the soup from the cooks' own ladles,
Split open the kegs of salted sprats,
Made nests inside men's Sunday hats,
And even spoiled the women's chats
              By drowning their speaking
              With shrieking and squeaking
In fifty different sharps and flats.   20

III

At last the people in a body
       To the Town Hall came flocking:
" 'Tis clear," cried they, "our Mayor's a noddy;
       And as for our Corporation — shocking
To think we buy gowns lined with ermine
For dolts that can't or won't determine
What's best to rid us of our vermin!
You hope, because you're old and obese,

To find in the furry civic robe ease?
Rouse up, sirs! Give your brains a racking   00
To find the remedy we're lacking,
Or, sure as fate, we'll send you packing!"
At this the Mayor and Corporation
Quaked with a mighty consternation.

IV

An hour they sat in council,
      At length the Mayor broke silence:
"For a guilder I'd my ermine gown sell,
      I wish I were a mile hence!
It's easy to bid one rack one's brain —
I'm sure my poor head aches again,   40
I've scratched it so, and all in vain.
Oh for a trap, a trap, a trap!"
Just as he said this, what should hap
At the chamber door but a gentle tap?
"Bless us," cried the Mayor, "what's that?"
(With the Corporation as he sat,
Looking little though wondrous fat;
Nor brighter was his eye, nor moister
Than a too-long-opened oyster,
Save when at noon his paunch grew mutinous   50
For a plate of turtle green and glutinous)
"Only a scraping of shoes on the mat?
Anything like the sound of a rat
Makes my heart go pit-a-pat!"

V

"Come in!" — the Mayor cried, looking bigger:
And in did come the strangest figure
His queer long coat from heel to head
Was half of yellow and half of red,
And he himself was tall and thin,
With sharp blue eyes, each like a pin,   60
And light loose hair, yet swarthy skin,
No tuft on cheek nor beard on chin,
But lips where smiles went out and in;
There was no guessing his kith and kin:
And nobody could enough admire
The tall man and his quaint attire.
Quoth one: "It's as my great-grandsire,

Starting up at the Trump of Doom's tone,
Had walked this way from his painted tombstone!"

VI

He advanced to the council-table: 70
And, "Please your honors," said he, "I'm able,
By means of a secret charm, to draw
    All creatures living beneath the sun,
     That creep or swim or fly or run,
After me so as you never saw!
And I chiefly use my charm
On creatures that do people harm,
The mole and toad and newt and viper;
And people call me the Pied Piper."
(And here they noticed round his neck   80
    A scarf of red and yellow stripe,
To match with his coat of the self-same cheque;
    And at the scarf's end hung a pipe;
And his fingers, they noticed, were ever straying
As if impatient to be playing
Upon this pipe, as low it dangled
Over his vesture so old-fangled.)
"Yet," said he, "poor piper as I am,
In Tartary I freed the Cham,
    Last June, from his huge swarms of gnats;   90
I eased in Asia the Nizam
    Of a monstrous brood of vampyre-bats:
And as for what your brain bewilders,
    If I can rid your town of rats
Will you give me a thousand guilders?"
"One? fifty thousand!" — was the exclamation
Of the astonished Mayor and Corporation.

VII

Into the street the Piper stept,
    Smiling first a little smile,
As if he knew what magic slept   100
    In his quiet pipe the while;
Then, like a musical adept,
To blow the pipe his lips he wrinkled,
And green and blue his sharp eyes twinkled,
Like a candle-flame where salt is sprinkled;
And ere three shrill notes the pipe uttered,

You heard as if an army muttered;
And the muttering grew to a grumbling;
And the grumbling grew to a mighty rumbling;
And out of the houses the rats came tumbling.   110
Great rats, small rats, lean rats, brawny rats,
Brown rats, black rats, gray rats, tawny rats,
Grave old plodders, gay young friskers,
        Fathers, mothers, uncles, cousins,
Cocking tails and pricking whiskers,
        Families by tens and dozens,
Brothers, sisters, husbands, wives —
Followed the Piper for their lives.
From street to street he piped advancing,
And step for step they followed dancing,   120
Until they came to the river Weser,
        Wherein all plunged and perished!
— Save one who, stout as Julius Cæsar,
Swam across and lived to carry
        (As he, the manuscript he cherished)
To Rat-land home his commentary:
Which was, "At the first shrill notes of the pipe,
I heard a sound as of scraping tripe,
And putting apples, wondrous ripe,
Into a cider-press's gripe: 130
And a moving away of pickle-tub-boards,
And a leaving ajar of conserve-cupboards,
And a drawing the corks of train-oil-flasks,
And a breaking the hoops of butter-casks:
And it seemed as if a voice
        (Sweeter far than by harp or by psaltery
Is breathed) called out, 'Oh rats, rejoice!
        The world is grown to one vast drysaltery!
So munch on, crunch on, take your nuncheon,
Breakfast, supper, dinner, luncheon!'   140
And just as a bulky sugar-puncheon,
All ready staved, like a great sun shone
Glorious scarce an inch before me,
Just as methought it said, 'Come, bore me!'
— I found the Weser rolling o'er me."

VIII

You should have heard the Hamelin people
Ringing the bells till they rocked the steeple.

"Go," cried the Mayor, "and get long poles,
Poke out the nests and block up the holes!
Consult with carpenters and builders,   150
And leave in our town not even a trace
Of the rats!" — when suddenly, up the face
Of the Piper perked in the market-place,
With a, "First, if you please, my thousand guilders!"

IX

A thousand guilders! The Mayor looked blue;
So did the Corporation too.
For council dinners made rare havoc
With Claret, Moselle, Vin-de-Grave, Hock;
And half the money would replenish
Their cellar's biggest butt with Rhenish.   160
To pay this sum to a wandering fellow
With a gipsy coat of red and yellow!
"Beside," quoth the Mayor with a knowing wink,
"Our business was done at the river's brink;
We saw with our eyes the vermin sink,
And what's dead can't come to life, I think.
So, friend, we're not the folks to shrink
From the duty of giving you something for drink,
And a matter of money to put in your poke;
But as for the guilders, what we spoke   170
Of them, as you very well know, was in joke.
Beside, our losses have made us thrifty.
A thousand guilders! Come, take fifty!"

X

The Piper's face fell, and he cried
"No trifling! I can't wait, beside!
I've promised to visit by dinnertime
Bagdat, and accept the prime
Of the Head-Cook's pottage, all he's rich in,
For having left, in the Caliph's kitchen,
Of a nest of scorpions no survivor: 180
With him I proved no bargain-driver,
With you, don't think I'll bate a stiver!
And folks who put me in a passion
May find me pipe after another fashion."

XI

"How?" cried the Mayor, "d'ye think I brook
Being worse treated than a Cook?
Insulted by a lazy ribald
With idle pipe and vesture piebald?
You threaten us, fellow? Do your worst,
Blow your pipe there till you burst!"   190

XII

Once more he stept into the street
     And to his lips again
     Laid his long pipe of smooth straight cane;
And ere he blew three notes (such sweet
Soft notes as yet musician's cunning
     Never gave the enraptured air)
There was a rustling that seemed like a bustling
Of merry crowds justling at pitching and hustling,
Small feet were pattering, wooden shoes clattering,
Little hands clapping and little tongues chattering.   200
And, like fowls in a farm-yard when barley is scattering,
Out came the children running.
All the little boys and girls,
With rosy cheeks and flaxen curls,
And sparkling eyes and teeth like pearls,
Tripping and skipping, ran merrily after
The wonderful music with shouting and laughter.

XIII

The Mayor was dumb, and the Council stood
As if they were changed into blocks of wood,
Unable to move a step, or cry   210
To the children merrily skipping by,
— Could only follow with the eye
That joyous crowd at the Piper's back.
But how the Mayor was on the rack,
And the wretched Council's bosoms beat,
As the Piper turned from the High Street
To where the Weser rolled its waters
Right in the way of their sons and daughters!
However he turned from South to West,
And to Koppelberg Hill his steps addressed,   220

And after him the children pressed;
Great was the joy in every breast.
"He never can cross that mighty top!
He's forced to let the piping drop,
And we shall see our children stop!"
When, lo, as they reached the mountain-side,
A wondrous portal opened wide,
As if a cavern was suddenly hollowed;
And the Piper advanced and the children followed,
And when all were in to the very last,   230
The door in the mountain-side shut fast.
Did I say, all? No! One was lame,
  And could not dance the whole of the way;
And in after years, if you would blame
  His sadness, he was used to say, —
"It's dull in our town since my playmates left!
I can't forget that I'm bereft
Of all the pleasant sights they see,
Which the Piper also promised me.
For he led us, he said, to a joyous land,   240
Joining the town and just at hand,
Where waters gushed and fruit-trees grew
And flowers put forth a fairer hue,
And everything was strange and new;
The sparrows were brighter than peacocks here,
And their dogs outran our fallow deer,
And honey-bees had lost their stings,
And horses were born with eagles' wings:
And just as I became assured
My lame foot would be speedily cured,   250
The music stopped and I stood still,
And found myself outside the hill,
Left alone against my will,
To go now limping as before,
And never hear of that country more!"

XIV

Alas, alas for Hamelin!
  There came into many a burgher's pate
  A text which says that heaven's gate
  Opes to the rich at as easy rate
As the needle's eye takes a camel in!   260
The mayor sent East, West, North and South,
To offer the Piper, by word of mouth,

Wherever it was men's lot to find him,
Silver and gold to his heart's content,
If he'd only return the way he went.
    And bring the children behind him.
But when they saw 'twas a lost endeavor,
And Piper and dancers were gone forever,
They made a decree that lawyers never
    Should think their records dated duly   270
If, after the day of the month and year,
These words did not as well appear,
"And so long after what happened here
    On the Twenty-second of July,
Thirteen hundred and seventy-six:"
And the better in memory to fix
The place of the children's last retreat,
They called it, the Pied Piper's Street —
Where any one playing on pipe or tabor
Was sure for the future to lose his labor.   280
Nor suffered they hostelry or tavern
    To shock with mirth a street so solemn;
But opposite the place of the cavern
    They wrote the story on a column,
And on the great church-window painted
The same, to make the world acquainted
How their children were stolen away,
And there it stands to this very day.
And I must not omit to say
That in Transylvania there's a tribe   290
Of alien people who ascribe
The outlandish ways and dress
On which their neighbors lay such stress,
To their fathers and mothers having risen
Out of some subterraneous prison
Into which they were trepanned
Long time ago in a mighty band
Out of Hamelin town in Brunswick land,
But how or why, they don't understand.

xv

So, Willy, let me and you be wipers   300
Of scores out with all men — especially pipers!
And, whether they pipe us free from rats or from mice,
If we've promised them aught, let us keep our promise!

FROM *Dramatic Romances and Lyrics*
(1845)

"HOW THEY BROUGHT THE GOOD NEWS FROM GHENT TO AIX"

[16 —]

I

I SPRANG to the stirrup, and Joris, and he;
I galloped, Dirck galloped, we galloped all three;
"Good speed!" cried the watch, as the gate-bolts undrew;
"Speed!" echoed the wall to us galloping through;
Behind shut the postern, the lights sank to rest,
And into the midnight we galloped abreast.

II

Not a word to each other; we kept the great pace
Neck by neck, stride by stride, never changing our place;
I turned in my saddle and made its girths tight,
Then shortened each stirrup, and set the pique right,   10
Rebuckled the cheek-strap, chained slacker the bit,
Nor galloped less steadily Roland a whit.

III

'Twas moonset at starting; but while we drew near
Lokeren, the cocks crew and twilight dawned clear;
At Boom, a great yellow star came out to see;
At Düffeld, 'twas morning as plain as could be;
And from Mecheln church-steeple we heard the half-chime,
So, Joris broke silence with, "Yet there is time!"

IV

At Aershot, up leaped of a sudden the sun,
And against him the cattle stood black every one,   20
To stare thro' the mist at us galloping past,
And I saw my stout galloper Roland at last,
With resolute shoulders, each butting away
The haze, as some bluff river headland its spray:

V

And his low head and crest, just one sharp ear bent back
For my voice, and the other pricked out on his track;
And one eye's black intelligence, — ever that glance
O'er its white edge at me, his own master, askance!
And the thick heavy spume-flakes which aye and anon
His fierce lips shook upwards in galloping on.   30

VI

By Hasselt, Dirck groaned; and cried Joris, "Stay spur!
Your Roos galloped bravely, the fault's not in her,
We'll remember at Aix" — for one heard the quick wheeze
Of her chest, saw the stretched neck and staggering knees,
And sunk tail, and horrible heave of the flank,
As down on her haunches she shuddered and sank.

VII

So, we were left galloping, Joris and I,
Past Looz and past Tongres, no cloud in the sky;
The broad sun above laughed a pitiless laugh,
'Neath our feet broke the brittle bright stubble like chaff;   40
Till over by Dalhem a dome-spire sprang white,
And "Gallop," gasped Joris, "for Aix is in sight!"

VIII

"How they'll greet us!" — and all in a moment his roan
Rolled neck and croup over, lay dead as a stone;
And there was my Roland to bear the whole weight
Of the news which alone could save Aix from her fate,
With his nostrils like pits full of blood to the brim,
And with circles of red for his eye-sockets' rim.

IX

Then I cast loose my buffcoat, each holster let fall,
Shook off both my jack-boots, let go belt and all,   50
Stood up in the stirrup, leaned, patted his ear,
Called my Roland his pet-name, my horse without peer;
Clapped my hands, laughed and sang, any noise, bad or good,
Till at length into Aix Roland galloped and stood.

X

And all I remember is — friends flocking round
As I sat with his head 'twixt my knees on the ground;
And no voice but was praising this Roland of mine,
As I poured down his throat our last measure of wine,
Which (the burgesses voted by common consent)
Was no more than his due who brought good news from Ghent.   60

PICTOR IGNOTUS

FLORENCE, 15 —

I COULD have painted pictures like that youth's
       Ye praise so. How my soul springs up! No bar
Stayed me — ah, thought which saddens while it soothes!
       — Never did fate forbid me, star by star,
To outburst on your night with all my gift
       Of fires from God: nor would my flesh have shrunk
From seconding my soul, with eyes uplift
       And wide to heaven, or, straight like thunder, sunk
To the centre, of an instant; or around
       Turned calmly and inquisitive, to scan   10
The license and the limit, space and bound,
       Allowed to truth made visible in man.
And, like that youth ye praise so, all I saw,
       Over the canvas could my hand have flung,
Each face obedient to its passion's law,
       Each passion clear proclaimed without a tongue;
Whether Hope rose at once in all the blood,
       A-tiptoe for the blessing of embrace,
Or Rapture drooped the eyes, as when her brood
       Pull down the nesting dove's heart to its place;   20

Or Confidence lit swift the forehead up,
    And locked the mouth fast, like a castle braved, —
O human faces, hath it spilt, my cup?
    What did ye give me that I have not saved?
Nor will I say I have not dreamed (how well!)
    Of going — I, in each new picture, — forth,
As, making new hearts beat and bosoms swell,
    To Pope or Kaiser, East, West, South, or North,
Bound for the calmly-satisfied great State,
    Or glad aspiring little burgh, it went,   30
Flowers cast upon the car which bore the freight,
    Through old streets named afresh from the event,
Till it reached home, where learned age should greet
    My face, and youth, the star not yet distinct
Above his hair, lie learning at my feet! —
    Oh, thus to live, I and my picture, linked
With love about, and praise, till life should end,
    And then not go to heaven, but linger here,
Here on my earth, earth's every man my friend, —
    The thought grew frightful, 'twas so wildly dear!   40
But a voice changed it. Glimpses of such sights
    Have scared me, like the revels through a door
Of some strange house of idols at its rites!
    This world seemed not the world it was before:
Mixed with my loving trusting ones, there trooped
    ... Who summoned those cold faces that begun
To press on me and judge me? Though I stooped
    Shrinking, as from the soldiery a nun,
They drew me forth, and spite of me ... enough!
    These buy and sell our pictures, take and give,   50
Count them for garniture and household-stuff,
    And where they live needs must our pictures live
And see their faces, listen to their prate,
    Partakers of their daily pettiness,
Discussed of, — "This I love, or this I hate,
    This likes me more, and this affects me less!"
Wherefore I chose my portion. If at whiles
    My heart sinks, as monotonous I paint
These endless cloisters and eternal aisles
    With the same series, Virgin, Babe and Saint,   60
With the same cold calm beautiful regard, —
    At least no merchant traffics in my heart;
The sanctuary's gloom at least shall ward
    Vain tongues from where my pictures stand apart:

Only prayer breaks the silence of the shrine
    While, blackening in the daily candle-smoke,
They moulder on the damp wall's travertine,
    'Mid echoes the light footstep never woke.
So, die my pictures! surely, gently die!
    O youth, men praise so — holds their praise its worth?   70
Blown harshly, keeps the trump its golden cry?
    Tastes sweet the water with such specks of earth?

THE ITALIAN IN ENGLAND

THAT second time they hunted me
From hill to plain, from shore to sea,
And Austria, hounding far and wide
Her blood-hounds thro' the country-side,
Breathed hot and instant on my trace, —
I made six days a hiding-place
Of that dry green old aqueduct
Where I and Charles, when boys, have plucked
The fire-flies from the roof above,
Bright creeping thro' the moss they love: 10
— How long it seems since Charles was lost!
Six days the soldiers crossed and crossed
The country in my very sight;
And when that peril ceased at night,
The sky broke out in red dismay
With signal fires; well, there I lay
Close covered o'er in my recess,
Up to the neck in ferns and cress,
Thinking on Metternich our friend,
And Charles's miserable end,   20
And much beside, two days; the third,
Hunger o'ercame me when I heard
The peasants from the village go
To work among the maize; you know,
With us in Lombardy, they bring
Provisions packed on mules, a string
With little bells that cheer their task,
And casks, and boughs on every cask
To keep the sun's heat from the wine;
These I let pass in jingling line,   30

And, close on them, dear noisy crew,
The peasants from the village, too;
For at the very rear would troop
Their wives and sisters in a group
To help, I knew. When these had passed,
I threw my glove to strike the last,
Taking the chance: she did not start,
Much less cry out, but stooped apart,
One instant rapidly glanced round,
And saw me beckon from the ground.   40
A wild bush grows and hides my crypt;
She picked my glove up while she stripped
A branch off, then rejoined the rest
With that; my glove lay in her breast.
Then I drew breath; they disappeared:
It was for Italy I feared.

An hour, and she returned alone
Exactly where my glove was thrown.
Meanwhile came many thoughts: on me
Rested the hopes of Italy.   50
I had devised a certain tale
Which, when 'twas told her, could not fail
Persuade a peasant of its truth;
I meant to call a freak of youth
This hiding, and give hopes of pay,
And no temptation to betray.
But when I saw that woman's face,
Its calm simplicity of grace,
Our Italy's own attitude
In which she walked thus far, and stood,   60
Planting each naked foot so firm,
To crush the snake and spare the worm —
At first sight of her eyes, I said,
"I am that man upon whose head
They fix the price, because I hate
The Austrians over us: the State
Will give you gold — oh, gold so much! —
If you betray me to their clutch,
And be your death, for aught I know,
If once they find you saved their foe.   70
Now, you must bring me food and drink,
And also paper, pen and ink,

And carry safe what I shall write
To Padua, which you'll reach at night
Before the duomo shuts; go in,
And wait till Tenebræ begin;
Walk to the third confessional,
Between the pillar and the wall,
And kneeling whisper, *Whence comes peace?*
Say it a second time, then cease;   80
And if the voice inside returns,
From Christ and Freedom; what concerns
The cause of Peace? — for answer, slip
My letter where you placed your lip;
Then come back happy we have done
Our mother service — I, the son,
As you the daughter of our land!"

    Three mornings more, she took her stand
In the same place, with the same eyes:
I was no surer of sun-rise   90
Than of her coming. We conferred
Of her own prospects, and I heard
She had a lover — stout and tall,
She said — then let her eyelids fall,
"He could do much" — as if some doubt
Entered her heart, — then, passing out,
"She could not speak for others, who
Had other thoughts; herself she knew."
And so she brought me drink and food.
After four days, the scouts pursued   100
Another path; at last arrived
The help my Paduan friends contrived
To furnish me: she brought the news.
For the first time I could not choose
But kiss her hand, and lay my own
Upon her head — "This faith was shown
To Italy, our mother; she
Uses my hand and blesses thee."
She followed down to the sea-shore;
I left and never saw her more.   110

    How very long since I have thought
Concerning — much less wished for — aught
Beside the good of Italy,

For which I live and mean to die!
I never was in love; and since
Charles proved false, what shall now convince
My inmost heart I have a friend?
However, if I pleased to spend
Real wishes on myself — say, three —
I know at least what one should be.   120
I would grasp Metternich until
I felt his red wet throat distil
In blood thro' these two hands. And next,
— Nor much for that am I perplexed —
Charles, perjured traitor, for his part,
Should die slow of a broken heart
Under his new employers. Last
— Ah, there, what should I wish? For fast
Do I grow old and out of strength.
If I resolved to seek at length   130
My father's house again, how scared
They all would look, and unprepared!
My brothers live in Austria's pay
— Disowned me long ago, men say;
And all my early mates who used
To praise me so — perhaps induced
More than one early step of mine —
Are turning wise: while some opine
"Freedom grows license," some suspect
"Haste breeds delay," and recollect   140
They always said, such premature
Beginnings never could endure!
So, with a sullen "All's for best,"
The land seems settling to its rest.
I think, then, I should wish to stand
This evening in that dear, lost land,
Over the sea the thousand miles,
And know if yet that woman smiles
With the calm smile; some little farm
She lives in there, no doubt: what harm   150
If I sat on the door-side bench,
And, while her spindle made a trench
Fantastically in the dust,
Inquired of all her fortunes — just
Her children's ages and their names,
And what may be the husband's aims
For each of them. I'd talk this out,

And sit there, for an hour about,
Then kiss her hand once more, and lay
Mine on her head, and go my way.   160

So much for idle wishing — how
It steals the time! To business now!

THE ENGLISHMAN IN ITALY

PIANO DI SORRENTO

FORTÙ, FORTÙ, my beloved one,
    Sit here by my side,
On my knees put up both little feet!
    I was sure, if I tried,
I could make you laugh spite of Scirocco.
    Now, open your eyes,
Let me keep you amused till he vanish
    In black from the skies,
With telling my memories over
    As you tell your beads;   10
All the Plain saw me gather, I garland
    — The flowers or the weeds.

Time for rain! for your long hot dry Autumn
    Had net-worked with brown
The white skin of each grape on the bunches,
    Marked like a quail's crown,
Those creatures you make such account of,
    Whose heads, — speckled white
Over brown like a great spider's back,
    As I told you last night, —   20
Your mother bites off for her supper.
    Red-ripe as could be,
Pomegranates were chapping and splitting
    In halves on the tree:
And betwixt the loose walls of great flint-stone,
    Or in the thick dust
On the path, or straight out of the rock-side,
    Wherever could thrust

Some burnt sprig of bold hardy rock-flower
    Its yellow face up,   30
For the prize were great butterflies fighting,
    Some five for one cup.
So, I guessed, ere I got up this morning,
    What change was in store,
By the quick rustle-down of the quail-nets
    Which woke me before
I could open my shutter, made fast
    With a bough and a stone,
And looked thro' the twisted dead vine-twigs,
    Sole lattice that's known.   40
Quick and sharp rang the rings down the net-poles,
    While, busy beneath,
Your priest and his brother tugged at them,
    The rain in their teeth.
And out upon all the flat house-roofs
    Where split figs lay drying,
The girls took the frails under cover:
    Nor use seemed in trying
To get out the boats and go fishing,
    For, under the cliff,   50
Fierce the black water frothed o'er the blind-rock.
    No seeing our skiff
Arrive about noon from Amalfi,
    — Our fisher arrive,
And pitch down his basket before us,
    All trembling alive
With pink and gray jellies, your sea-fruit;
    You touch the strange lumps,
And mouths gape there, eyes open, all manner
    Of horns and of humps,   60
Which only the fisher looks grave at,
    While round him like imps
Cling screaming the children as naked
    And brown as his shrimps;
Himself too as bare to the middle
    — You see round his neck
The string and its brass coin suspended,
    That saves him from wreck.
But to-day not a boat reached Salerno,
    So back, to a man,   70
Came our friends, with whose help in the vineyards
    Grape-harvest began.

In the vat, halfway up in our house-side,
  Like blood the juice spins,
While your brother all bare-legged is dancing
  Till breathless he grins
Dead-beaten in effort on effort
  To keep the grapes under,
Since still when he seems all but master,
  In pours the fresh plunder   80
From girls who keep coming and going
  With basket on shoulder,
And eyes shut against the rain's driving;
  Your girls that are older, —
For under the hedges of aloe,
  And where, on its bed
Of the orchard's black mould, the love-apple
  Lies pulpy and red,
All the young ones are kneeling and filling
  Their laps with the snails   90
Tempted out by this first rainy weather, —
  Your best of regales,
As to-night will be proved to my sorrow,
  When, supping in state,
We shall feast our grape-gleaners (two dozen,
  Three over one plate)
With lasagne so tempting to swallow
  In slippery ropes,
And gourds fried in great purple slices,
  That color of popes.   100
Meantime, see the grape bunch they've brought you:
  The rain-water slips
O'er the heavy blue bloom on each globe
  Which the wasp to your lips
Still follows with fretful persistence:
  Nay, taste, while awake,
This half of a curd-white smooth cheese-ball
  That peels, flake by flake,
Like an onion, each smoother and whiter;
  Next, sip this weak wine   110
From the thin green glass flask, with its stopper,
  A leaf of the vine;
And end with the prickly-pear's red flesh
  That leaves thro' its juice
The stony black seeds on your pearl-teeth.
  Scirocco is loose!

Hark, the quick, whistling pelt of the olives
    Which, thick in one's track,
Tempt the stranger to pick up and bite them,
    Tho' not yet half black! 120
How the old twisted olive trunks shudder,
    The medlars let fall
Their hard fruit, and the brittle great fig-trees
    Snap off, figs and all,
For here comes the whole of the tempest!
    No refuge, but creep
Back again to my side and my shoulder,
    And listen or sleep.
O how will your country show next week,
    When all the vine-boughs 130
Have been stripped of their foliage to pasture
    The mules and the cows?
Last eve, I rode over the mountains:
    Your brother, my guide,
Soon left me, to feast on the myrtles
    That offered, each side,
Their fruit-balls, black, glossy and luscious, —
    Or strip from the sorbs
A treasure, or, rosy and wondrous,
    Those hairy gold orbs! 140
But my mule picked his sure sober path out,
    Just stopping to neigh
When he recognizd down in the valley
    His mates on their way
With the faggots and barrels of water;
    And soon we emerged
From the plain, where the woods could scarce follow;
    And still as we urged
Our way, the woods wondered, and left us,
    As up still we trudged 150
Though the wild path grew wilder each instant,
    And place was e'en grudged
'Mid the rock-chasms and piles of loose stones
    Like the loose broken teeth
Of some monster which climbed there to die
    From the ocean beneath —
Place was grudged to the silver-gray fume-weed
    That clung to the path,
And dark rosemary ever a-dying
    That, 'spite the wind's wrath, 160

So loves the salt rock's face to seaward,
 And lentisks as staunch
To the stone where they root and bear berries,
 And . . . what shows a branch
Coral-colored, transparent, with circlets
 Of pale seagreen leaves;
Over all trod my mule with the caution
 Of gleaners o'er sheaves,
Still, foot after foot like a lady,
 Till, round after round,   170
He climbed to the top of Calvano,
 And God's own profound
Was above me, and round me the mountains,
 And under, the sea,
And within me my heart to bear witness
 What was and shall be.
Oh, heaven and the terrible crystal!
 No rampart excludes
Your eye from the life to be lived
 In the blue solitudes.   180
Oh, those mountains, their infinite movement!
 Still moving with you;
For, ever some new head and breast of them
 Thrusts into view
To observe the intruder; you see it
 If quickly you turn
And, before they escape you surprise them.
 They grudge you should learn
How the soft plains they look on, lean over
 And love (they pretend)   190
— Cower beneath them, the flat sea-pine crouches,
 The wild fruit-trees bend,
E'en the myrtle-leaves curl, shrink and shut:
 All is silent and grave:
'Tis a sensual and timorous beauty,
 How fair! but a slave.
So, I turned to the sea; and there slumbered
 As greenly as ever
Those isles of the siren, your Galli;
 No ages can sever   200
The Three, nor enable their sister
 To join them, — halfway
On the voyage, she looked at Ulysses —
 No farther to-day,

Tho' the small one, just launched in the wave,
    Watches breast-high and steady
From under the rock, her bold sister
    Swum halfway already.
Fortù, shall we sail there together
    And see from the sides   210
Quite new rocks show their faces, new haunts
    Where the siren abides?
Shall we sail round and round them, close over
    The rocks, tho' unseen,
That ruffle the gray glassy water
    To glorious green?
Then scramble from splinter to splinter,
    Reach land and explore,
On the largest, the strange square black turret
    With never a door,   220
Just a loop to admit the quick lizards;
    Then, stand there and hear
The birds' quiet singing, that tells us
    What life is, so clear?
— The secret they sang to Ulysses
    When, ages ago,
He heard and he knew this life's secret
    I hear and I know.

Ah, see! The sun breaks o'er Calvano;
    He strikes the great gloom   230
And flutters it o'er the mount's summit
    In airy gold fume.
All is over. Look out, see the gipsy,
    Our tinker and smith,
Has arrived, set up bellows and forge,
    And down-squatted forthwith
To his hammering, under the wall there;
    One eye keeps aloof
The urchins that itch to be putting
    His jews'-harps to proof,   240
While the other, thro' locks of curled wire,
    Is watching how sleek
Shines the hog, come to share in the windfall
    — Chew, abbot's own cheek!
All is over. Wake up and come out now,
    And down let us go,

And see the fine things got in order
    At church for the show
Of the Sacrament, set forth this evening.
    To-morrow's the Feast   250
Of the Rosary's Virgin, by no means
    Of Virgins the least,
As you'll hear in the off-hand discourse
    Which (all nature, no art)
The Dominican brother, these three weeks,
    Was getting by heart.
Not a pillar nor post but is dizened
    With red and blue papers;
All the roof waves with ribbons, each altar
    A-blaze with long tapers;   260
But the great masterpiece is the scaffold
    Rigged glorious to hold
All the fiddlers and fifers and drummers
    And trumpeters bold,
Not afraid of Bellini nor Auber,
    Who, when the priest's hoarse,
Will strike us up something that's brisk
    For the feast's second course.
And then will the flaxen-wigged Image
    Be carried in pomp   270
Thro' the plain, while in gallant procession
    The priests mean to stomp.
All round the glad church lie old bottles
    With gunpowder stopped,
Which will be, when the Image re-enters,
    Religiously popped;
And at night from the crest of Calvano
    Great bonfires will hang,
On the plain will the trumpets join chorus,
    And more poppers bang.   280
At all events, come — to the garden
    As far as the wall;
See me tap with a hoe on the plaster
    Till out there shall fall
A scorpion with wide angry nippers!

    — "Such trifles!" you say?
Fortù, in my England at home,
    Men meet gravely to-day

And debate, if abolishing Corn-laws
        De righteous and wise   290
    — If't were proper, Scirocco should vanish
        In black from the skies!

THE LOST LEADER

I

Just for a handful of silver he left us,
    Just for a riband to stick in his coat —
Found the one gift of which fortune bereft us,
    Lost all the others she lets us devote;
They, with the gold to give, doled him out silver,
    So much was theirs who so little allowed:
How all our copper had gone for his service!
    Rags — were they purple, his heart had been proud!
We that had loved him so, followed him, honored him,
    Lived in his mild and magnificent eye,   10
Learned his great language, caught his clear accents,
    Made him our pattern to live and to die!
Shakespeare was of us, Milton was for us,
    Burns, Shelley, were with us, — they watch from their graves!
He alone breaks from the van and the freemen,
    — He alone sinks to the rear and the slaves!

II

We shall march prospering, — not thro' his presence;
    Songs may inspirit us, — not from his lyre;
Deeds will be done, — while he boasts his quiescence,
    Still bidding crouch whom the rest bade aspire: 20
Blot out his name, then, record one lost soul more,
    One task more declined, one more footpath untrod,
One more devils'-triumph and sorrow for angels,
    One wrong more to man, one more insult to God!
Life's night begins: let him never come back to us!
    There would be doubt, hesitation and pain,
Forced praise on our part — the glimmer of twilight,
    Never glad confident morning again!
Best fight on well, for we taught him — strike gallantly,
    Menace our heart ere we master his own;   30
Then let him receive the new knowledge and wait us,
    Pardoned in heaven, the first by the throne!

HOME-THOUGHTS, FROM ABROAD

I

Oh, to be in England
Now that April's there,
And whoever wakes in England
Sees, some morning, unaware,
That the lowest boughs and the brushwood sheaf
Round the elm-tree bole are in tiny leaf,
While the chaffinch sings on the orchard bough
In England — now!

II

And after April, when May follows,
And the whitethroat builds, and all the swallows!   10
Hark, where my blossomed pear-tree in the hedge
Leans to the field and scatters on the clover
Blossoms and dewdrops — at the bent spray's edge —
That's the wise thrush; he sings each song twice over,
Lest you should think he never could recapture
The first fine careless rapture!
And though the fields look rough with hoary dew,
All will be gay when noontide wakes anew
The buttercups, the little children's dower
— Far brighter than this gaudy melon-flower!   20

HOME-THOUGHTS, FROM THE SEA

Nobly, nobly Cape Saint Vincent to the North-west died away;
Sunset ran, one glorious blood-red, reeking into Cadiz Bay;
Bluish 'mid the burning water, full in face Trafalgar lay;
In the dimmest North-east distance dawned Gibraltar grand and gray;
"Here and here did England help me: how can I help England?" —
    say,
Whoso turns as I, this evening, turn to God to praise and pray,
While Jove's planet rises yonder, silent over Africa.

[handwritten: worldly]
[handwritten: leverage petty revenge envy]

THE BISHOP ORDERS HIS TOMB
AT SAINT PRAXED'S CHURCH

ROME, 15 —

VANITY, saith the preacher, vanity! *[handwritten: ecc. 1:2]*
Draw round my bed: is Anselm keeping back?
Nephews — sons mine . . . ah God, I know not! Well —
She, men would have to be your mother once,
Old Gandolf envied me, so fair she was!
What's done is done, and she is dead beside,
Dead long ago, and I am Bishop since,
And as she died so must we die ourselves,
And thence ye may perceive the world's a dream.
Life, how and what is it? As here I lie   10
In this state-chamber, dying by degrees,
Hours and long hours in the dead night, I ask
"Do I live, am I dead?" Peace, peace seems all.
Saint Praxed's ever was the church for peace;
And so, about this tomb of mine. I fought
With tooth and nail to save my niche, ye know:
— Old Gandolf cozened me, despite my care;
Shrewd was that snatch from out the corner South
He graced his carrion with, God curse the same!
Yet still my niche is not so cramped but thence   20
One sees the pulpit o' the epistle-side,
And somewhat of the choir, those silent seats,
And up into the aery dome where live
The angels, and a sunbeam's sure to lurk:
And I shall fill my slab of basalt there,
And 'neath my tabernacle take my rest,
With those nine columns round me, two and two,
The odd one at my feet where Anselm stands:
Peach-blossom marble all, the rare, the ripe
As fresh-poured red wine of a mighty pulse.   30
— Old Gandolf with his paltry onion-stone,
Put me where I may look at him! True peach,
Rosy and flawless: how I earned the prize!
Draw close: that conflagration of my church
— What then? So much was saved if aught were missed!
My sons, ye would not be my death? Go dig
The white-grape vineyard where the oil-press stood,

Drop water gently till the surface sink,
And if ye find . . . Ah God, I know not, I! . . .
Bedded in store of rotten fig-leaves soft,   40
And corded up in a tight olive-frail,
Some lump, ah God, of *lapis lazuli*,
Big as a Jew's head cut off at the nape,
Blue as a vein o'er the Madonna's breast . . .
Sons, all have I bequeathed you, villas, all,
That brave Frascati villa with its bath,
So, let the blue lump poise between my knees,
Like God the Father's globe on both his hands
Ye worship in the Jesu Church so gay,
For Gandolf shall not choose but see and burst!   50
Swift as a weaver's shuttle fleet our years:
Man goeth to the grave, and where is he?
Did I say basalt for my slab, sons? Black —
'Twas ever antique-black I meant! How else
Shall ye contrast my frieze to come beneath?
The bas-relief in bronze ye promised me,
Those Pans and Nymphs ye wot of, and perchance   *order*
Some tripod, thyrsus, with a vase or so,
The Saviour at his sermon on the mount,
Saint Praxed in a glory, and one Pan   60
Ready to twitch the Nymph's last garment off,   *order*
And Moses with the tables . . . but I know
Ye mark me not! What do they whisper thee,
Child of my bowels, Anselm? Ah, ye hope
To revel down my villas while I gasp
Bricked o'er with beggar's mouldy travertine
Which Gandolf from his tomb-top chuckles at!
Nay, boys, ye love me — all of jasper, then!
'Tis jasper ye stand pledged to, lest I grieve
My bath must needs be left behind, alas!   70
One block, pure green as a pistachio-nut,
There's plenty jasper somewhere in the world —
And have I not Saint Praxed's ear to pray
Horses for ye, and brown Greek manuscripts,
And mistresses with great smooth marbly limbs?
— That's if ye carve my epitaph aright,
Choice Latin, picked phrase, Tully's every word,
No gaudy ware like Gandolf's second line —
Tully, my masters? Ulpian serves his need!
And then how I shall lie through centuries,   80
And hear the blessed mutter of the mass,

And see God made and eaten all day long,
And feel the steady candle-flame, and taste
Good strong thick stupefying incense-smoke!
For as I lie here, hours of the dead night,
Dying in state and by such slow degrees,
I fold my arms as if they clasped a crook,
And stretch my feet forth straight as stone can point,
And let the bedclothes, for a mortcloth, drop
Into great laps and folds of sculptor's-work: 90
And as yon tapers dwindle, and strange thoughts
Grow, with a certain humming in my ears,
About the life before I lived this life,
And this life too, popes, cardinals and priests,
Saint Praxed at his sermon on the mount,
Your tall pale mother with her talking eyes,
And new-found agate urns as fresh as day,
And marble's language, Latin pure, discreet,
— Aha, ELUCESCEBAT quoth our friend?
No Tully, said I, Ulpian at the best!   100
Evil and brief hath been my pilgrimage.
All *lapis,* all, sons! Else I give the Pope
My villas! Will ye ever eat my heart?
Ever your eyes were as a lizard's quick,
They glitter like your mother's for my soul,   stomach? (Carlyle)
Or ye would heighten my impoverished frieze,
Piece out its starved design, and fill my vase
With grapes, and add a vizor and a Term,
And to the tripod ye would tie a lynx
That in his struggle throws the thyrsus down,   110
To comfort me on my entablature
Whereon I am to lie till I must ask
"Do I live, am I dead?" There, leave me, there!
For ye have stabbed me with ingratitude
To death — ye wish it — God, ye wish it! Stone —
Gritstone, a-crumble! Clammy squares which sweat   horror
As if the corpse they keep were oozing through —
And no more *lapis* to delight the world!
Well go! I bless ye. Fewer tapers there,
But in a row: and, going, turn your backs   120
— Ay, like departing altar-ministrants,
And leave me in my church, the church for peace,
That I may watch at leisure if he leers —
Old Gandolf, at me, from his onion-stone,
As still he envied me, so fair she was!

GARDEN FANCIES

1. THE FLOWER'S NAME

I

HERE's the garden she walked across,
  Arm in my arm, such a short while since:
Hark, now I push its wicket, the moss
  Hinders the hinges and makes them wince!
She must have reached this shrub ere she turned,
  As back with that murmur the wicket swung;
For she laid the poor snail, my chance foot spurned,
  To feed and forget it the leaves among.

II

Down this side of the gravel-walk
  She went while her robe's edge brushed the box: 10
And here she paused in her gracious talk
  To point me a moth on the milk-white phlox.
Roses, ranged in valiant row,
  I will never think that she passed you by!
She loves you noble roses, I know;
  But yonder, see, where the rock-plants lie!

III

This flower she stopped at, finger on lip,
  Stooped over, in doubt, as settling its claim;
Till she gave me, with pride to make no slip,
  Its soft meandering Spanish name: 20
What a name! Was it love, or praise?
  Speech half-asleep or song half-awake?
I must learn Spanish, one of these days,
  Only for that slow sweet name's sake.

IV

Roses, if I live and do well,
  I may bring her, one of these days,
To fix you fast with as fine a spell,
  Fit you each with his Spanish phrase

But do not detain me now; for she lingers
    There, like sunshine over the ground,   30
And ever I see her soft white fingers
    Searching after the bud she found.

V

Flower, you Spaniard, look that you grow not,
    Stay as you are and be loved for ever!
Bud, if I kiss you 'tis that you blow not:
    Mind, the shut pink mouth opens never!
For while it pouts, her fingers wrestle,
    Twinkling the audacious leaves between,
Till round they turn and down they nestle —
    Is not the dear mark still to be seen?   40

VI

Where I find her not, beauties vanish;
    Whither I follow her, beauties flee;
Is there no method to tell her in Spanish
    June's twice June since she breathed it with me?
Come, bud, show me the least of her traces,
    Treasure my lady's lightest footfall!
— Ah, you may flout and turn up your faces —
    Roses, you are not so fair after all!

2. SIBRANDUS SCHAFNABURGENSIS

I

Plague take all your pedants, say I!
    He who wrote what I hold in my hand,
Centuries back was so good as to die,
    Leaving this rubbish to cumber the land;
This, that was a book in its time,
    Printed on paper and bound in leather,
Last month in the white of a matin-prime
    Just when the birds sang all together.

II

Into the garden I brought it to read,
    And under the arbute and laurustine   10

Read it, so help me grace in my need,
    From title-page to closing line.
Chapter on chapter did I count,
    As a curious traveller counts Stonehenge;
Added up the mortal amount;
    And then proceeded to my revenge.

III

Yonder's a plum-tree with a crevice
    An owl would build in, were he but sage;
For a lap of moss, like a fine pont-levis
    In a castle of the Middle Age,   20
Joins to a lip of gum, pure amber;
    When he'd be private, there might he spend
Hours alone in his lady's chamber:
    Into this crevice I dropped our friend.

IV

Splash, went he, as under he ducked,
    — At the bottom, I knew, rain-drippings stagnate:
Next, a handful of blossoms I plucked
    To bury him with, my bookshelf's magnate;
Then I went in-doors, brought out a loaf,
    Half a cheese, and a bottle of Chablis;   30
Lay on the grass and forgot the oaf
    Over a jolly chapter of Rabelais.

V

Now, this morning, betwixt the moss
    And gum that locked our friend in limbo,
A spider had spun his web across,
    And sat in the midst with arms akimbo:
So, I took pity, for learning's sake,
    And, *de profundis, accentibus lætis,*
Cantate! quoth I, as I got a rake;
    And up I fished his delectable treatise.   40

VI

Here you have it, dry in the sun,
    With all the binding all of a blister,
And great blue spots where the ink has run,
    And reddish streaks that wink and glister

O'er the page so beautifully yellow:
    Oh, well have the droppings played their tricks!
Did he guess how toadstools grow, this fellow?
    Here's one stuck in his chapter six!

VII

How did he like it when the live creatures
    Tickled and toused and browsed him all over,   50
And worm, slug, eft, with serious features,
    Came in, each one, for his right of trover?
— When the water-beetle with great blind deaf face
    Made of her eggs the stately deposit
And the newt borrowed just so much of the preface
    As tiled in the top of his black wife's closet?

VIII

All that life and fun and romping,
    All that frisking and twisting and coupling,
While slowly our poor friend's leaves were swamping
    And clasps were cracking and covers suppling!   60
As if you had carried sour John Knox
    To the play-house at Paris, Vienna or Munich,
Fastened him into a front-row box,
    And danced off the ballet with trousers and tunic.

IX

Come, old martyr! What, torment enough is it?
    Back to my room shall you take your sweet self.
Good-bye, mother-beetle; husband-eft, *sufficit!*
    See the snug niche I have made on my shelf!
A.'s book shall prop you up, B.'s shall cover you,
    Here's C. to be grave with, or D. to be gay,   70
And with E. on each side, and F. right over you,
    Dry-rot at ease till the Judgment-day!

THE LABORATORY

ANCIEN RÉGIME

I

Now that I, tying thy glass mask tightly,
May gaze thro' these faint smokes curling whitely,
As thou pliest thy trade in this devil's-smithy —
Which is the poison to poison her, prithee?

II

He is with her, and they know that I know
Where they are, what they do: they believe my tears flow
While they laugh, laugh at me, at me fled to the drear
Empty church, to pray God in, for them! — I am here.

III

Grind away, moisten and mash up thy paste,
Pound at thy powder, — I am not in haste!
Better sit thus, and observe thy strange things,
Than go where men wait me and dance at the King's.

10

IV

That in the mortar — you call it a gum?
Ah, the brave tree whence such gold oozings come!
And yonder soft phial, the exquisite blue,
Sure to taste sweetly, — is that poison too?

V

Had I but all of them, thee and thy treasures,
What a wild crowd of invisible pleasures!
To carry pure death in an earring, a casket,
A signet, a fan-mount, a filigree basket!

20

VI

Soon, at the King's, a mere lozenge to give,
And Pauline should have just thirty minutes to live!
But to light a pastile, and Elise, with her head
And her breast and her arms and her hands, should drop dead!

VII

Quick — is it finished? The color's too grim!
Why not soft like the phial's, enticing and dim?
Let it brighten her drink, let her turn it and stir,
And try it and taste, ere she fix and prefer!

VIII

What a drop! She's not little, no minion like me!
That's why she ensnared him: this never will free   30
The soul from those masculine eyes, — say, "no!"
To that pulse's magnificent come-and-go.

IX

For only last night, as they whispered, I brought
My own eyes to bear on her so, that I thought
Could I keep them one half minute fixed, she would fall
Shrivelled; she fell not; yet this does it all!

X

Not that I bid you spare her the pain;
Let death be felt and the proof remain:
Brand, burn up, bite into its grace —
He is sure to remember her dying face!   40

XI

Is it done? Take my mask off! Nay, be not morose;
It kills her, and this prevents seeing it close:
The delicate droplet, my whole fortune's fee!
If it hurts her, beside, can it ever hurt me?

XII

Now, take all my jewels, gorge gold to your fill,
You may kiss me, old man, on my mouth if you will!
But brush this dust off me, lest horror it brings
Ere I know it — next moment I dance at the King's!

THE BOY AND THE ANGEL

MORNING, evening, noon and night,
"Praise God!" sang Theocrite.

Then to his poor trade he turned,
Whereby the daily meal was earned.

Hard he labored, long and well;
O'er his work the boy's curls fell.

But ever, at each period,
He stopped and sang, "Praise God!"

Then back again his curls he threw,
And cheerful turned to work anew.			10

Said Blaise, the listening monk, "Well done;
I doubt not thou art heard, my son:

"As well as if thy voice to-day
Were praising God, the Pope's great way.

"This Easter Day, the Pope at Rome
Praises God from Peter's dome."

Said Theocrite, "Would God that I
Might praise him, that great way, and die!"

Night passed, day shone,
And Theocrite was gone.			20

With God a day endures alway,
A thousand years are but a day.

God said in heaven, "Nor day nor night
Now brings the voice of my delight."

Then Gabriel, like a rainbow's birth,
Spread his wings and sank to earth;

Entered, in flesh, the empty cell,
Lived there, and played the craftsman well;

And morning, evening, noon and night,
Praised God in place of Theocrite.   30

And from a boy, to youth he grew:
The man put off the stripling's hue:

The man matured and fell away
Into the season of decay:

And ever o'er the trade he bent,
And ever lived on earth content.

(He did God's will; to him, all one
If on the earth or in the sun.)

God said, "A praise is in mine ear;
There is no doubt in it, no fear: 40

"So sing old worlds, and so
New worlds that from my footstool go.

"Clearer loves sound other ways:
I miss my little human praise."

Then forth sprang Gabriel's wings, off fel:
The flesh disguise, remained the cell.

'Twas Easter Day: he flew to Rome,
And paused above Saint Peter's dome.

In the tiring-room close by
The great outer gallery,   50

With his holy vestments dight,
Stood the new Pope, Theocrite:

And all his past career
Came back upon him clear,

Since when, a boy, he plied his trade,
Till on his life the sickness weighed;

And in his cell, when death drew near,
An angel in a dream brought cheer:

And rising from the sickness drear
He grew a priest, and now stood here.   60

To the East with praise he turned,
And on his sight the angel burned.

"I bore thee from thy craftsman's cell
And set thee here; I did not well.

"Vainly I left my angel-sphere,
Vain was thy dream of many a year.

"Thy voice's praise seemed weak; it dropped—
Creation's chorus stopped!

"Go back and praise again
The early way, while I remain.   70

"With that weak voice of our disdain,
Take up creation's pausing strain.

"Back to the cell and poor employ:
Resume the craftsman and the boy!"

Theocrite grew old at home;
A new Pope dwelt in Peter's dome.

One vanished as the other died:
They sought God side by side.

MEETING AT NIGHT

I
THE gray sea and the long black land;
And the yellow half-moon large and low;
And the startled little waves that leap
In fiery ringlets from their sleep,
As I gain the cove with pushing prow,
And quench its speed i' the slushy sand.

II

Then a mile of warm sea-scented beach;
Three fields to cross till a farm appears;
A tap at the pane, the quick sharp scratch
And blue spurt of a lighted match,
And a voice less loud, thro' its joys and fears,
Than the two hearts beating each to each!

10

PARTING AT MORNING

ROUND the cape of a sudden came the sea,
And the sun looked over the mountain's rim:
And straight was a path of gold for him,
And the need of a world of men for me.

TIME'S REVENGES

I'VE a Friend, over the sea;
I like him, but he loves me.
It all grew out of the books I write;
They find such favor in his sight
That he slaughters you with savage looks
Because you don't admire my books.
He does himself though, — and if some vein
Were to snap to-night in this heavy brain,
To-morrow month, if I lived to try,
Round should I just turn quietly,
Or out of the bedclothes stretch my hand
Till I found him, come from his foreign land,
To be my nurse in this poor place,
And make my broth and wash my face
And light my fire and, all the while,
Bear with his old good-humored smile
That I told him "Better have kept away
Than come and kill me, night and day,
With, worse than fever throbs and shoots,
The creaking of his clumsy boots."
I am as sure that this he would do,
As that Saint Paul's is striking two.
And I think I rather . . . woe is me!
— Yes, rather would see him than not see,

10

20

If lifting a hand could seat him there
Before me in the empty chair
To-night, when my head aches indeed,
And I can neither think nor read
Nor make these purple fingers hold
The pen; this garret's freezing cold!   30

And I've a Lady — there he wakes,
The laughing fiend and prince of snakes
Within me, at her name, to pray
Fate send some creature in the way
Of my love for her, to be down-torn,
Upthrust and outward-borne,
So I might prove myself that sea
Of passion which I needs must be!
Call my thoughts false and my fancies quaint
And my style infirm and its figures faint,   40
All the critics say, and more blame yet,
And not one angry word you get.
But, please you, wonder I would put
My cheek beneath that lady's foot
Rather than trample under mine
The laurels of the Florentine,
And you shall see how the devil spends
A fire God gave for other ends!
I tell you, I stride up and down
This garret, crowned with love's best crown,   50
And feasted with love's perfect feast,
To think I kill for her, at least,
Body and soul and peace and fame,
Alike youth's end and manhood's aim,
— So is my spirit, as flesh with sin,
Filled full, eaten out and in
With the face of her, the eyes of her,
The lips, the little chin, the stir
Of shadow round her mouth; and she
— I'll tell you, — calmly would decree   60
That I should roast at a slow fire,
If that would compass her desire
And make her one whom they invite
To the famous ball to-morrow night.

There may be heaven; there must be hell;
Meantime, there is our earth here — well!

THE GLOVE

(PETER RONSARD *loquitur*)

"HEIGHO!" yawned one day King Francis,
"Distance all value enhances!
When a man's busy, why, leisure
Strikes him as wonderful pleasure:
'Faith, and at leisure once is he?
Straightway he wants to be busy.
Here we've got peace; and aghast I'm
Caught thinking war the true pastime.
Is there a reason in metre?
Give us your speech, master Peter!"   10
I who, if mortal dare say so,
Ne'er am at loss with my Naso,
"Sire," I replied, "joys prove cloudlets:
Men are the merest Ixions" —
Here the King whistled aloud, "Let's
— Heigho — go look at our lions!"
Such are the sorrowful chances
If you talk fine to King Francis.

And so, to the courtyard proceeding,
Our company, Francis was leading,   20
Increased by new followers tenfold
Before he arrived at the penfold;
Lords, ladies, like clouds which bedizen
At sunset the western horizon.
And Sir De Lorge pressed 'mid the foremost
With the dame he professed to adore most.
Oh, what a face! One by fits eyed
Her, and the horrible pitside;
For the penfold surrounded a hollow
Which led where the eye scarce dared follow,   30
And shelved to the chamber secluded
Where Bluebeard, the great lion, brooded.
The King hailed his keeper, an Arab
As glossy and black as a scarab,
And bade him make sport and at once stir

Up and out of his den the old monster.
They opened a hole in the wire-work
Across it, and dropped there a firework,
And fled: one's heart's beating redoubled;
A pause, while the pit's mouth was troubled,   40
The blackness and silence so utter,
By the firework's slow sparkling and sputter;
Then earth in a sudden contortion
Gave out to our gaze her abortion.
Such a brute! Were I friend Clement Marot
(Whose experience of nature's but narrow,
And whose faculties move in no small mist
When he versifies David the Psalmist)
I should study that brute to describe you
Illum Juda Leonem de Tribu.   50
One's whole blood grew curdling and creepy
To see the black mane, vast and heapy,
The tail in the air stiff and straining,
The wide eyes, nor waxing nor waning,
As over the barrier which bounded
His platform, and us who surrounded
The barrier, they reached and they rested
On space that might stand him in best stead:
For who knew, he thought, what the amazement,
The eruption of clatter and blaze meant,   60
And if, in this minute of wonder,
No outlet, 'mid lightning and thunder,
Lay broad, and, his shackles all shivered,
The lion at last was delivered?
Ay, that was the open sky o'erhead!
And you saw by the flash on his forehead,
By the hope in those eyes wide and steady,
He was leagues in the desert already,
Driving the flocks up the mountain,
Or catlike couched hard by the fountain   70
To waylay the date-gathering negress:
So guarded he entrance or egress.
"How he stands!" quoth the King: "we may well swear,
(No novice, we'ye won our spurs elsewhere
And so can afford the confession,)
We exercise wholesome discretion
In keeping aloof from his threshold;
Once hold you, those jaws want no fresh hold,
Their first would too pleasantly purloin

The visitor's brisket or surloin: 80
But who's he would prove so fool-hardy?
Not the best man of Marignan, pardie!"

The sentence no sooner was uttered,
Than over the rails a glove fluttered,
Fell close to the lion, and rested:
The dame 'twas, who flung it and jested
With life so, De Lorge had been wooing
For months past; he sat there pursuing
His suit, weighing out with nonchalance
Fine speeches like gold from a balance.   90

Sound the trumpet, no true knight's a tarrier!
De Lorge made one leap at the barrier,
Walked straight to the glove, — while the lion
Ne'er moved, kept his far-reaching eye on
The palm-tree-edged desert-spring's sapphire,
And the musky oiled skin of the Kaffir, —
Picked it up, and as calmly retreated,
Leaped back where the lady was seated,
And full in the face of its owner
Flung the glove.

        "Your heart's queen, you dethrone her?   100
So should I!" — cried the King — " 'twas mere vanity,
Not love, set that task to humanity!"
Lords and ladies alike turned with loathing
From such a proved wolf in sheep's clothing.

Not so, I; for I caught an expression
In her brow's undisturbed self-possession
Amid the Court's scoffing and merriment, —
As if from no pleasing experiment
She rose, yet of pain not much heedful
So long as the process was needful, —   110
As if she had tried in a crucible,
To what "speeches like gold" were reducible,
And, finding the finest prove copper,
Felt the smoke in her face was but proper;
To know what she had *not* to trust to,
Was worth all the ashes and dust too.
She went out 'mid hooting and laughter;
Clement Marot stayed; I followed after.

And asked, as a grace, what it all meant?
If she wished not the rash deed's recallment?   120
"For I" — so I spoke — "am a poet:
Human nature, — behoves that I know it!"

She told me, "Too long had I heard
Of the deed proved alone by the word:
For my love — what De Lorge would not dare!
With my scorn — what De Lorge could compare!
And the endless descriptions of death
He would brave when my lip formed a breath,
I must reckon as braved, or, of course,
Doubt his word — and moreover, perforce,   130
For such gifts as no lady could spurn,
Must offer my love in return.
When I looked on your lion, it brought
All the dangers at once to my thought,
Encountered by all sorts of men,
Before he was lodged in his den,—
From the poor slave whose club or bare hands
Dug the trap, set the snare on the sands,
With no King and no Court to applaud,
By no shame, should he shrink, overawed,   140
Yet to capture the creature made shift,
That his rude boys might laugh at the gift,
— To the page who last leaped o'er the fence
Of the pit, on no greater pretence
Than to get back the bonnet he dropped,
Lest his pay for a week should be stopped.
So, wiser I judged it to make
One trial what 'death for my sake'
Really meant, while the power was yet mine,
Than to wait until time should define   150
Such a phrase not so simply as I,
Who took it to mean just 'to die.'
The blow a glove gives is but weak:
Does the mark yet discolor my cheek?
But when the heart suffers a blow,
Will the pain pass so soon, do you know?"

I looked, as away she was sweeping,
And saw a youth eagerly keeping
As close as he dared to the doorway.
No doubt that a noble should more weigh   160

His life than befits a plebeian;
And yet, had our brute been Nemean —
(I judge by a certain calm fervor
The youth stepped with, forward to serve her)
— He'd have scarce thought you did him the worst turn
If you whispered "Friend, what you'd get, first earn!"
And when, shortly after, she carried
Her shame from the Court, and they married,
To that marriage some happiness, maugre
The voice of the Court, I dared augur.   170

For De Lorge, he made women with men vie,
Those in wonder and praise, these in envy;
And in short stood so plain a head taller
That he wooed and won . . . How do you call her?
The beauty, that rose in the sequel
To the King's love, who loved her a week well.
And 'twas noticed he never would honor
De Lorge (who looked daggers upon her)
With the easy commission of stretching
His legs in the service, and fetching   180
His wife, from her chamber, those straying
Sad gloves she was always mislaying,
While the King took the closet to chat in, —
But of course this adventure came pat in.
And never the King told the story,
How bringing a glove brought such glory,
But the wife smiled — "His nerves are grown firmer:
Mine he brings now and utters no murmur."

Venienti occurrite morbo!
With which moral I drop my theorbo.   190

FROM *Men and Women*

(1855)

LOVE AMONG THE RUINS

I

WHERE the quiet-colored end of evening smiles,
    Miles and miles
On the solitary pastures where our sheep
    Half-asleep
Tinkle homeward thro' the twilight, stray or stop
    As they crop —
Was the site once of a city great and gay,
    (So they say)
Of our country's very capital, its prince
    Ages since   10
Held his court in, gathered councils, wielding far
    Peace or war.

II

Now, — the country does not even boast a tree,
    As you see,
To distinguish slopes of verdure, certain rills
    From the hills
Intersect and give a name to, (else they run
    Into one)
Where the domed and daring palace shot its spires
    Up like fires   20
O'er the hundred-gated circuit of a wall
    Bounding all,
Made of marble, men might march on nor be pressed,
    Twelve abreast.

III

And such plenty and perfection, see, of grass
    Never was!
Such a carpet as, this summer-time, o'erspreads
    And embeds
Every vestige of the city, guessed alone,
    Stock or stone —   30
Where a multitude of men breathed joy and woe
    Long ago;
Lust of glory pricked their hearts up, dread of shame
    Struck them tame;
And that glory and that shame alike, the gold
    Bought and sold.

IV

Now, — the single little turret that remains
    On the plains,
By the caper overrooted, by the gourd
    Overscored,   40
While the patching houseleek's head of blossom winks
    Through the chinks —
Marks the basement whence a tower in ancient time
    Sprang sublime,
And a burning ring, all round, the chariots traced
    As they raced,
And the monarch and his minions and his dames
    Viewed the games.

V

And I know, while thus the quiet-colored eve
    Smiles to leave   50
To their folding, all our many-tinkling fleece
    In such peace,
And the slopes and rills in undistinguished gray
    Melt away —
That a girl with eager eyes and yellow hair
    waits me there
In the turret whence the charioteers caught soul
    For the goal,
When the king looked, where she looks now, breathless, dumb
    Till I come.   60

VI

But he looked upon the city, every side,
    Far and wide,
All the mountains topped with temples, all the glades'
    Colonnades,
All the causeys, bridges, aqueducts, — and then,
    All the men!
When I do come, she will speak not, she will stand,
    Either hand
On my shoulder, give her eyes the first embrace
    Of my face,   70
Ere we rush, ere we extinguish sight and speech
    Each on each.

VII

In one year they sent a million fighters forth
    South and North,
And they built their gods a brazen pillar high
    As the sky,
Yet reserved a thousand chariots in full force —
    Gold, of course.
Oh heart! oh blood that freezes, blood that burns!
    Earth's returns   80
For whole centuries of folly, noise and sin!
    Shut them in,
With their triumphs and their glories and the rest!
    Love is best.

EVELYN HOPE

I

BEAUTIFUL Evelyn Hope is dead!
    Sit and watch by her side an hour.
That is her book-shelf, this her bed;
    She plucked that piece of geranium-flower,
Beginning to die too, in the glass;
    Little has yet been changed, I think:
The shutters are shut, no light may pass
    Save two long rays thro' the hinge's chink.

II

Sixteen years old when she died!
 Perhaps she had scarcely heard my name;   **10**
It was not her time to love; beside,
 Her life had many a hope and aim,
Duties enough and little cares,
 And now was quiet, now astir, —
Till God's hand beckoned unawares, —
 And the sweet white brow is all of her.

III

Is it too late then, Evelyn Hope?
 What, your soul was pure and true,
The good stars met in your horoscope,
 Made you of spirit, fire and dew —   **20**
And, just because I was thrice as old
 And our paths in the world diverged so wide,
Each was naught to each, must I be told?
 We were fellow mortals, naught beside?

IV

No, indeed! for God above
 Is great to grant, as mighty to make,
And creates the love to reward the love:
 I claim you still, for my own love's sake!
Delayed it may be for more lives yet,
 Through worlds I shall traverse, not a few: **30**
Much is to learn, much to forget
 Ere the time be come for taking you.

V

But the time will come, — at last it will,
 When, Evelyn Hope, what meant (I shall say)
In the lower earth, in the years long still,
 That body and soul so pure and gay?
Why your hair was amber, I shall divine,
 And your mouth of your own geranium's red —
And what you would do with me, in fine,
 In the new life come in the old one's stead.   **40**

VI

I have lived (I shall say) so much since°then,
    Given up myself so many times,
Gained me the gains of various men,
    Ransacked the ages, spoiled the climes;
Yet one thing, one, in my soul's full scope,
    Either I missed or itself missed me:
And I want and find you, Evelyn Hope!
    What is the issue? let us see!

VII

I loved you, Evelyn, all the while.
    My heart seemed full as it could hold?   **50**
There was place and to spare for the frank young smile,
    And the red young mouth, and the hair's young gold.
So, hush, — I will give you this leaf to keep:
    See, I shut it inside the sweet cold hand!
There, that is our secret: go to sleep!
    You will wake, and remember, and understand.

UP AT A VILLA — DOWN IN THE CITY

(As Distinguished by an Italian Person of Quality)

I

Had I but plenty of money, money enough and to spare,
The house for me, no doubt, were a house in the city-square;
Ah, such a life, such a life, as one leads at the window there!

II

Something to see, by Bacchus, something to hear, at least!
There, the whole day long, one's life is a perfect feast;
While up at a villa one lives, I maintain it, no more than a beast.

III

Well now, look at our villa! stuck like the horn of a bull
Just on a mountain-edge as bare as the creature's skull,
Save a mere shag of a bush with hardly a leaf to pull!
— I scratch my own, sometimes, to see if the hair's turned wool.   **10**

IV

But the city, oh the city — the square with the houses! Why?
They are stone-faced, white as a curd, there's something to take the
    eye!
Houses in four straight lines, not a single front awry;
You watch who crosses and gossips, who saunters, who hurries by;
Green blinds, as a matter of course, to draw when the sun gets high;
And the shops with fanciful signs which are painted properly.

V

What of a villa? Though winter be over in March by rights,
'Tis May perhaps ere the snow shall have withered well off the heights:
You've the brown ploughed land before, where the oxen steam and
    wheeze,
And the hills over-smoked behind by the faint gray olive-trees.   20

VI

Is it better in May, I ask you? You've summer all at once;
In a day he leaps complete with a few strong April suns.
'Mid the sharp short emerald wheat, scarce risen three fingers well,
The wild tulip, at end of its tube, blows out its great red bell
Like a thin clear bubble of blood, for the children to pick and sell.

VII

Is it ever hot in the square? There's a fountain to spout and splash!
In the shade it sings and springs; in the shine such foam-bows flash
On the horses with curling fish-tails, that prance and paddle and pash
Round the lady atop in her conch — fifty gazers do not abash,
Though all that she wears is some weeds round her waist in a sort of
    sash.   30

VIII

All the year long at the villa, nothing to see though you linger,
Except yon cypress that points like death's lean lifted forefinger.
Some think fireflies pretty, when they mix i' the corn and mingle,
Or thrid the stinking hemp till the stalks of it seem a-tingle.
Late August or early September, the stunning cicala is shrill,
And the bees keep their tiresome whine round the resinous firs on the
    hill.
Enough of the seasons, — I spare you the months of the fever and
    chill.

IX

Ere you open your eyes in the city, the blessed church-bells begin:
No sooner the bells leave off than the diligence rattles in:
You get the pick of the news, and it costs you never a pin.   40
By-and-by there's the travelling doctor gives pills, lets blood, draws
    teeth;
Or the Pulcinello-trumpet breaks up the market beneath.
At the post-office such a scene-picture — the new play, piping hot!
And a notice how, only this morning, three liberal thieves were shot.
Above it, behold the Archbishop's most fatherly of rebukes,
And beneath, with his crown and his lion, some little new law of the
    Duke's!
Or a sonnet with flowery marge, to the Reverend Don So-and-so
Who is Dante, Boccaccio, Petrarca, Saint Jerome and Cicero,
"And moreover," (the sonnet goes rhyming,) "the skirts of Saint Paul
    has reached,
Having preached us those six Lent-lectures more unctuous than ever
    he preached."   50
Noon strikes, — here sweeps the procession! our Lady borne smiling
    and smart
With a pink gauze gown all spangles, and seven swords stuck in her
    heart!
Bang-whang-whang goes the drum, *tootle-te-tootle* the fife;
No keeping one's haunches still: it's the greatest pleasure in life.

X

But bless you, it's dear — it's dear! fowls, wine, at double the rate.
They have clapped a new tax upon salt, and what oil pays passing the
    gate
It's a horror to think of. And so, the villa for me, not the city!
Beggars can scarcely be choosers: but still — ah, the pity, the pity!
Look, two and two go the priests, then the monks with cowls and
    sandals,
And the penitents dressed in white shirts, a-holding the yellow candles;
One, he carries a flag up straight, and another a cross with handles, 61
And the Duke's guard brings up the rear, for the better prevention of
    scandals:
Bang-whang-whang goes the drum, *tootle-te-tootle* the fife.
Oh, a day in the city-square, there is no such pleasure in life!

A WOMAN'S LAST WORD

I

Let's contend no more, Love,
    Strive nor weep:
All be as before, Love,
    — Only sleep!

II

What so wild as words are?
    I and thou
In debate, as birds are,
    Hawk on bough!

III

See the creature stalking
    While we speak!   10
Hush and hide the talking,
    Cheek on cheek!

IV

What so false as truth is,
    False to thee?
Where the serpent's tooth is
    Shun the tree —

V

Where the apple reddens
    Never pry —
Lest we lose our Edens,
    Eve and I.   20

VI

Be a god and hold me
    With a charm!
Be a man and fold me
    With thine arm!

VII

Teach me, only teach, Love!
   As I ought
I will speak thy speech, Love,
   Think thy thought —

VIII

Meet, if thou require it,
   Both demands,
Laying flesh and spirit
   In thy hands.

30

IX

That shall be to-morrow
   Not to-night:
I must bury sorrow
   Out of sight:

X

— Must a little weep, Love,
   (Foolish me!)
And so fall asleep, Love,
   Loved by thee.

40

FRA LIPPO LIPPI

I AM poor brother Lippo, by your leave!
You need not clap your torches to my face.
Zooks, what's to blame? you think you see a monk!
What, 'tis past midnight, and you go the rounds,
And here you catch me at an alley's end
Where sportive ladies leave their doors ajar?
The Carmine's my cloister: hunt it up,
Do, — harry out, if you must show your zeal,
Whatever rat, there, haps on his wrong hole,
And nip each softling of a wee white mouse,
Weke, weke, that's crept to keep him company!
Aha, you know your betters! Then, you'll take

10

Your hand away that's fiddling on my throat,
And please to know me likewise. Who am I?
Why, one, sir, who is lodging with a friend
Three streets off — he's a certain . . . how d'ye call?
Master — a . . . Cosimo of the Medici,
I' the house that caps the corner. Boh! you were best!
Remember and tell me, the day you're hanged,
How you affected such a gullet's-gripe!   20
But you, sir, it concerns you that your knaves
Pick up a manner nor discredit you:
Zooks, are we pilchards, that they sweep the streets
And count fair prize what comes into their net?
He's Judas to a tittle, that man is!
Just such a face! Why, sir, you make amends.
Lord, I'm not angry! Bid your hangdogs go
Drink out this quarter-florin to the health
Of the munificent House that harbors me
(And many more beside, lads! more beside!)   30
And all's come square again. I'd like his face —
His, elbowing on his comrade in the door
With the pike and lantern, — for the slave that holds
John Baptist's head a-dangle by the hair
With one hand ("Look you, now," as who should say)
And his weapon in the other, yet unwiped!
It's not your chance to have a bit of chalk,
A wood-coal or the like? or you should see!
Yes, I'm the painter, since you style me so.
What, brother Lippo's doings, up and down,   40
You know them and they take you? like enough!
I saw the proper twinkle in your eye —
'Tell you, I liked your looks at very first.
Let's sit and set things straight now, hip to haunch.
Here's spring come, and the nights one makes up bands
To roam the town and sing out carnival,
And I've been three weeks shut within my mew,
A-painting for the great man, saints and saints
And saints again. I could not paint all night —
Ouf! I leaned out of window for fresh air.   50
There came a hurry of feet and little feet,
A sweep of lute-strings, laughs, and whiffs of song, —
Flower o' the broom,
Take away love, and our earth is a tomb!
Flower o' the quince,
I let Lisa go, and what good in life since?

Flower o' the thyme — and so on. Round they went.
Scarce had they turned the corner when a titter
Like the skipping of rabbits by moonlight, — three slim shapes,
And a face that looked up . . . zooks, sir, flesh and blood,   60
That's all I'm made of! Into shreds it went,
Curtain and counterpane and coverlet,
All the bed-furniture — a dozen knots,
There was a ladder! Down I let myself,
Hands and feet, scrambling somehow, and so dropped,
And after them. I came up with the fun
Hard by Saint Laurence, hail fellow, well met, —
Flower o' the rose,
If I've been merry, what matter who knows?
And so as I was stealing back again   70
To get to bed and have a bit of sleep
Ere I rise up to-morrow and go work
On Jerome knocking at his poor old breast
With his great round stone to subdue the flesh,
You snap me of the sudden. Ah, I see!
Though your eye twinkles still, you shake your head —
Mine's shaved — a monk, you say — the sting's in that!
If Master Cosimo announced himself,
Mum's the word naturally; but a monk!
Come, what am I a beast for? tell us, now!   80
I was a baby when my mother died
And father died and left me in the street.
I starved there, God knows how, a year or two
On fig-skins, melon-parings, rinds and shucks,
Refuse and rubbish. One fine frosty day,
My stomach being empty as your hat,
The wind doubled me up and down I went.
Old Aunt Lapaccia trussed me with one hand,
(Its fellow was a stinger as I knew)
And so along the wall, over the bridge,   90
By the straight cut to the convent. Six words there,
While I stood munching my first bread that month:
"So, boy, you're minded," quoth the good fat father
Wiping his own mouth, 'twas refection-time, —
"To quit this very miserable world?
Will you renounce" . . . "the mouthful of bread?" thought I;
By no means! Brief, they made a monk of me;
I did renounce the world, its pride and greed,
Palace, farm, villa, shop and banking-house,
Trash, such as these poor devils of Medici   100

Have given their hearts to — all at eight years old.
Well, sir, I found in time, you may be sure,
'Twas not for nothing — the good bellyful,
The warm serge and the rope that goes all round,
And day-long blessed idleness beside!
"Let's see what the urchin's fit for" — that came next.
Not overmuch their way, I must confess.
Such a to-do! They tried me with their books:
Lord, they'd have taught me Latin in pure waste!
  Flower o' the clove,   110
  All the Latin I construe is, "amo" I love!
But, mind you, when a boy starves in the streets
Eight years together, as my fortune was,
Watching folk's faces to know who will fling
The bit of half-stripped grape-bunch he desires,
And who will curse or kick him for his pains, —
Which gentleman processional and fine,
Holding a candle to the Sacrament,
Will wink and let him lift a plate and catch
The droppings of the wax to sell again,   120
Or holla for the Eight and have him whipped, —
How say I? — nay, which dog bites, which lets drop
His bone from the heap of offal in the street, —
Why, soul and sense of him grow sharp alike,
He learns the look of things, and none the less
For admonition from the hunger-pinch.
I had a store of such remarks, be sure,
Which, after I found leisure, turned to use.
I drew men's faces on my copy-books,
Scrawled them within the antiphonary's marge,   130
Joined legs and arms to the long music-notes,
Found eyes and nose and chin for A's and B's,
And made a string of pictures of the world
Betwixt the ins and outs of verb and noun,
On the wall, the bench, the door. The monks looked black.
"Nay," quoth the Prior, "turn him out, d' ye say?
In no wise. Lose a crow and catch a lark.
What if at last we get our man of parts,
We Carmelites, like those Camaldolese
And Preaching Friars, to do our church up fine   140
And put the front on it that ought to be!"
And hereupon he bade me daub away.
Thank you! my head being crammed, the walls a blank,
Never was such prompt disemburdening.

First, every sort of monk, the black and white,
I drew them, fat and lean: then, folk at church,
From good old gossips waiting to confess
Their cribs of barrel-droppings, candle-ends, —
To the breathless fellow at the altar-foot,
Fresh from his murder, safe and sitting there   150
With the little children round him in a row
Of admiration, half for his beard and half
For that white anger of his victim's son
Shaking a fist at him with one fierce arm,
Signing himself with the other because of Christ
(Whose sad face on the cross sees only this
After the passion of a thousand years)
Till some poor girl, her apron o'er her head,
(Which the intense eyes looked through) came at eve
On tiptoe, said a word, dropped in a loaf,   160
Her pair of earrings and a bunch of flowers
(The brute took growling), prayed, and so was gone.
I painted all, then cried " 'Tis ask and have;
Choose, for more's ready!" — laid the ladder flat,
And showed my covered bit of cloister-wall.
The monks closed in a circle and praised loud
Till checked, taught what to see and not to see,
Being simple bodies, — "That's the very man!
Look at the boy who stoops to pat the dog!
That woman's like the Prior's niece who comes   170
To care about his asthma: it's the life!"
But there my triumph's straw-fire flared and funked;
Their betters took their turn to see and say:
The Prior and the learned pulled a face
And stopped all that in no time. "How? what's here?
Quite from the mark of painting, bless us all!
Faces, arms, legs and bodies like the true
As much as pea and pea! it's devil's-game!
Your business is not to catch men with show,
With homage to the perishable clay,   180
But lift them over it, ignore it all,
Make them forget there's such a thing as flesh.
Your business is to paint the souls of men —
Man's soul, and it's a fire, smoke . . . no, it's not . . .
It's vapor done up like a new-born babe —
(In that shape when you die it leaves your mouth)
It's . . . well, what matters talking, it's the soul!
Give us no more of body than shows soul!

Here's Giotto, with his Saint a-praising God,
That sets us praising, — why not stop with him? 190
Why put all thoughts of praise out of our head
With wonder at lines, colors, and what not?
Paint the soul, never mind the legs and arms!
Rub all out, try at it a second time.
Oh, that white smallish female with the breasts,
She's just my niece . . . Herodias, I would say, —
Who went and danced and got men's heads cut off!
Have it all out!" Now, is this sense, I ask?
A fine way to paint soul, by painting body
So ill, the eye can't stop there, must go further 200
And can't fare worse! Thus, yellow does for white
When what you put for yellow's simply black,
And any sort of meaning looks intense
When all beside itself means and looks naught.
Why can't a painter lift each foot in turn,
Left foot and right foot, go a double step,
Make his flesh liker and his soul more like,
Both in their order? Take the prettiest face,
The Prior's niece . . . patron-saint — is it so pretty
You can't discover if it means hope, fear, 210
Sorrow or joy? won't beauty go with these?
Suppose I've made her eyes all right and blue,
Can't I take breath and try to add life's flash,
And then add soul and heighten them three-fold?
Or say there's beauty with no soul at all —
(I never saw it — put the case the same —)
If you get simple beauty and naught else,
You get about the best thing God invents:
That's somewhat: and you'll find the soul you have missed,
Within yourself, when you return him thanks. 220
"Rub all out!" Well, well, there's my life, in short,
And so the thing has gone on ever since.
I'm grown a man no doubt, I've broken bounds:
You should not take a fellow eight years old
And make him swear to never kiss the girls.
I'm my own master, paint now as I please —
Having a friend, you see, in the Corner-house!
Lord, it's fast holding by the rings in front —
Those great rings serve more purposes than just
To plant a flag in, or tie up a horse! 230
And yet the old schooling sticks, the old grave eyes
Are peeping o'er my shoulder as I work,

The heads shake still — "It's art's decline, my son!
You're not of the true painters, great and old;
Brother Angelico's the man, you'll find;
Brother Lorenzo stands his single peer:
Fag on at flesh, you'll never make the third!"
Flower o' the pine,
You keep your mistr . . . manners, and I'll stick to mine!
I'm not the third, then: bless us, they must know!   240
Don't you think they're the likeliest to know,
They with their Latin? So, I swallow my rage,
Clench my teeth, suck my lips in tight, and paint
To please them — sometimes do and sometimes don't;
For, doing most, there's pretty sure to come
A turn, some warm eve finds me at my saints —
A laugh, a cry, the business of the world —
(*Flower o' the peach,*
Death for us all, and his own life for each!)
And my whole soul revolves, the cup runs over,   250
The world and life's too big to pass for a dream,
And I do these wild things in sheer despite,
And play the fooleries you catch me at,
In pure rage! The old mill-horse, out at grass
After hard years, throws up his stiff heels so,
Although the miller does not preach to him
The only good of grass is to make chaff.
What would men have? Do they like grass or no —
May they or mayn't they? all I want's the thing
Settled forever one way. As it is,   260
You tell too many lies and hurt yourself:
You don't like what you only like too much,
You do like what, if given you at your word,
You find abundantly detestable.
For me, I think I speak as I was taught;
I always see the garden and God there
A-making man's wife: and, my lesson learned,
The value and significance of flesh,
I can't unlearn ten minutes afterwards.

    You understand me: I'm a beast, I know.   270
But see, now — why, I see as certainly
As that the morning-star's about to shine,
What will hap some day. We've a youngster here
Comes to our convent, studies what I do,
Slouches and stares and lets no atom drop:

His name is Guidi — he'll not mind the monks —
They call him Hulking Tom, he lets them talk —
He picks my practice up — he'll paint apace,
I hope so — though I never live so long,
I know what's sure to follow. You be judge!   280
You speak no Latin more than I, belike;
However, you're my man, you've seen the world
— The beauty and the wonder and the power,
The shapes of things, their colors, lights and shades,
Changes, surprises, — and God made it all!
— For what? Do you feel thankful, ay or no,
For this fair town's face, yonder river's line,
The mountain round it and the sky above,
Much more the figures of man, woman, child,
These are the frame to? What's it all about?   290
To be passed over, despised? or dwelt upon,
Wondered at? oh, this last of course! — you say.
But why not do as well as say, — paint these
Just as they are, careless what comes of it?
God's works — paint any one, and count it crime
To let a truth slip. Don't object, "His works
Are here already; nature is complete:
Suppose you reproduce her — (which you can't)
There's no advantage! You must beat her, then."
For, don't you mark? we're made so that we love   300
First when we see them painted, things we have passed
Perhaps a hundred times nor cared to see;
And so they are better, painted — better to us,
Which is the same thing. Art was given for that;   *Art < Truth*
God uses us to help each other so,
Lending our minds out. Have you noticed, now,
Your cullion's hanging face? A bit of chalk,
And trust me but you should, though! How much more,
If I drew higher things with the same truth!
That were to take the Prior's pulpit-place,   310
Interpret God to all of you! Oh, oh,
It makes me mad to see what men. shall do
And we in our graves! This world's no blot for us,
Nor blank; it means intensely, and means good:
To find its meaning is my meat and drink.
"Ay, but you don't so instigate to prayer!"
Strikes in the Prior: "when your meaning's plain
It does not say to folk — remember matins,
Or, mind you fast next Friday!" Why, for this

What need of art at all? A skull and bones,   320
Two bits of stick nailed crosswise, or, what's best,
A bell to chime the hour with, does as well.
I painted a Saint Laurence six months since
At Prato, splashed the fresco in fine style:
"How looks my painting, now the scaffold's down?"
I ask a brother: "Hugely," he returns —
"Already not one phiz of your three slaves
Who turn the Deacon off his toasted side,
But's scratched and prodded to our heart's content,
The pious people have so eased their own   330
With coming to say prayers there in a rage:
We get on fast to see the bricks beneath.
Expect another job this time next year,
For pity and religion grow i' the crowd —
Your painting serves its purpose!" Hang the fools!

     — That is — you'll not mistake an idle word
Spoke in a huff by a poor monk, God wot,
Tasting the air this spicy night which turns
The unaccustomed head like Chianti wine!
Oh, the church knows! don't misreport me, now!   340
It's natural a poor monk out of bounds
Should have his apt word to excuse himself:
And hearken how I plot to make amends.
I have bethought me: I shall paint a piece
. . . There's for you! Give me six months, then go, see
Something in Sant' Ambrogio's! Bless the nuns!
They want a cast o' my office. I shall paint
God in the midst, Madonna and her babe,
Ringed by a bowery flowery angel-brood,
Lilies and vestments and white faces, sweet   350
As puff on puff of grated orris-root
When ladies crowd to Church at midsummer.
And then i' the front, of course a saint or two —
Saint John, because he saves the Florentines,
Saint Ambrose, who puts down in black and white
The convent's friends and gives them a long day,
And Job, I must have him there past mistake,
The man of Uz (and Us without the z,
Painters who need his patience). Well, all these
Secured at their devotion, up shall come   360
Out of a corner when you least expect,
As one by a dark stair into a great light,

Music and talking, who but Lippo! I! —
Mazed, motionless and moonstruck — I'm the man!
Back I shrink — what is this I see and hear?
I, caught up with my monk's-things by mistake,
My old serge gown and rope that goes all round,
I, in this presence, this pure company!
Where's a hole, where's a corner for escape?
Then steps a sweet angelic slip of a thing   370
Forward, puts out a soft palm — "Not so fast!"
— Addresses the celestial presence, "nay —
He made you and devised you, after all,
Though he's none of you! Could Saint John there draw —
His camel-hair make up a painting-brush?
We come to brother Lippo for all that,
Iste perfecit opus!" So, all smile —
I shuffle sideways with my blushing face
Under the cover of a hundred wings
Thrown like a spread of kirtles when you're gay   380
And play hot cockles, all the doors being shut,
Till, wholly unexpected, in there pops
The hothead husband! Thus I scuttle off
To some safe bench behind, not letting go
The palm of her, the little lily thing
That spoke the good word for me in the nick,
Like the Prior's niece . . . Saint Lucy, I would say.
And so all's saved for me, and for the church
A pretty picture gained. Go, six months hence!
Your hand, sir, and good-bye: no lights, no lights!   390
The street's hushed, and I know my own way back,
Don't fear me! There's the gray beginning. Zooks!

A TOCCATA OF GALUPPI'S

I

Oh, Galuppi, Baldassaro, this is very sad to find!
I can hardly misconceive you; it would prove me deaf and blind;
But although I take your meaning, 'tis with such a heavy mind!

II

Here you come with your old music, and here's all the good it brings.
What, they lived once thus at Venice where the merchants were the
    kings,

Where Saint Mark's is, where the Doges used to wed the sea with
    rings?

III

Ay, because the sea's the street there; and 'tis arched by . . . what you
    call
. . . Shylock's bridge with houses on it, where they kept the carnival:
I was never out of England — it's as if I saw it all.

IV

Did young people take their pleasure when the sea was warm in May?
Balls and masks begun at midnight, burning ever to mid-day,   11
When they made up fresh adventures for the morrow, do you say?

V

Was a lady such a lady, cheeks so round and lips so red, —
On her neck the small face buoyant, like a bell-flower on its bed,
O'er the breast's superb abundance where a man might base his head?

VI

Well, and it was graceful of them — they'd break talk off and afford
— She, to bite her mask's black velvet — he, to finger on his sword,
While you sat and played Toccatas, stately at the clavichord?

VII

What? Those lesser thirds so plaintive, sixths diminished, sigh on sigh,
Told them something? Those suspensions, those solutions — "Must we
    die?"   20
Those commiserating sevenths — "Life might last! we can but try!"

VIII

"Were you happy?" — "Yes." — "And are you still as happy?" —
    "Yes. And you?"
— "Then, more kisses!" — "Did *I* stop them, when a million seemed so
    few?"
Hark, the dominant's persistence till it must be answered to!

IX

So, an octave struck the answer. Oh, they praised you, I dare say!
"Brave Galuppi! that was music; good alike at grave and gay!
I can always leave off talking when I hear a master play!"

x

Then they left you for their pleasure: till in due time, one by one,
Some with lives that came to nothing, some with deeds as well undone,
Death stepped tacitly and took them where they never see the sun. 30

XI

But when I sit down to reason, think to take my stand nor swerve,
While I triumph o'er a secret wrung from nature's close reserve,
In you come with your cold music till I creep thro' every nerve.

XII

Yes, you, like a ghostly cricket, creaking where a house was burned:
"Dust and ashes, dead and done with, Venice spent what Venice
    earned.
The soul, doubtless, is immortal — where a soul can be discerned.

XIII

"Yours for instance: you know physics, something of geology,
Mathematics are your pastime; souls shall rise in their degree;
Butterflies may dread extinction, — you'll not die, it cannot be!

XIV

"As for Venice and her people, merely born to bloom and drop,   40
Here on earth they bore their fruitage, mirth and folly were the crop:
What of soul was left, I wonder, when the kissing had to stop?

XV

"Dust and ashes!" So you creak it, and I want the heart to scold.
Dear dead women, with such hair, too — what's become of all the gold
Used to hang and brush their bosoms? I feel chilly and grown old.

BY THE FIRE-SIDE

I

How well I know what I mean to do
    When the long dark autumn-evenings come:
And where, my soul, is thy pleasant hue?
    With the music of all thy voices, dumb
In life's November too!

II

I shall be found by the fire, suppose,
　　O'er a great wise book as beseemeth age,
While the shutters flap as the cross-wind blows
　　And I turn the page, and I turn the page,
Not verse now, only prose!　　　　　　　　　　10

III

Till the young ones whisper, finger on lip,
　　"There he is at it, deep in Greek:
Now then, or never, out we slip
　　To cut from the hazels by the creek
A mainmast for our ship!"

IV

I shall be at it indeed, my friends:
　　Greek puts already on either side
Such a branch-work forth as soon extends
　　To a vista opening far and wide,
And I pass out where it ends.　　　　　　　　　20

V

The outside-frame, like your hazel-trees:
　　But the inside-archway widens fast,
And a rarer sort succeeds to these,
　　And we slope to Italy at last
And youth, by green degrees.

VI

I follow wherever I am led,
　　Knowing so well the leader's hand:
Oh woman-country, wooed not wed,
　　Loved all the more by earth's male-lands,
Laid to their hearts instead!　　　　　　　　　30

VII

Look at the ruined chapel again
　　Half-way up in the Alpine gorge!
Is that a tower, I point you plain,
　　Or is it a mill, or an iron-forge
Breaks solitude in vain?

VIII

A turn, and we stand in the heart of things;
    The woods are round us, heaped and dim;
From slab to slab how it slips and springs,
    The thread of water single and slim,
Through the ravage some torrent brings!   40

IX

Does it feed the little lake below?
    That speck of white just on its marge
Is Pella; see, in the evening-glow,
    How sharp the silver spear-heads charge
When Alp meets heaven in snow!

X

On our other side is the straight-up rock;
    And a path is kept 'twixt the gorge and it
By boulder-stones where lichens mock
    The marks on a moth, and small ferns fit
Their teeth to the polished block.   50

XI

Oh the sense of the yellow mountain-flowers,
    And thorny balls, each three in one,
The chestnuts throw on our path in showers!
    For the drop of the woodland fruit's begun,
These early November hours,

XII

That crimson the creeper's leaf across
    Like a splash of blood, intense, abrupt,
O'er a shield else gold from rim to boss,
    And lay it for show on the fairy-cupped
Elf-needled mat of moss,   60

XIII

By the rose-flesh mushrooms, undivulged
    Last evening — nay, in to-day's first dew
Yon sudden coral nipple bulged,
    Where a freaked fawn-colored flaky crew
Of toadstools peep indulged.

XIV

And yonder, at foot of the fronting ridge
    That takes the turn to a range beyond,
Is the chapel reached by the one-arched bridge
    Where the water is stopped in a stagnant pond
Danced over by the midge.   **70**

XV

The chapel and bridge are of stone alike,
    Blackish-gray and mostly wet;
Cut hemp-stalks steep in the narrow dyke.
    See here again, how the lichens fret
And the roots of the ivy strike!

XVI

Poor little place, where its one priest comes
    On a festa-day, if he comes at all,
To the dozen folk from their scattered homes,
    Gathered within that precinct small
By the dozen ways one roams —   **80**

XVII

To drop from the charcoal-burners' huts,
    Or climb from the hemp-dressers' low shed,
Leave the grange where the woodman stores his nuts,
    Or the wattled cote where the fowlers spread
Their gear on the rock's bare juts.

XVIII

It has some pretension too, this front,
    With its bit of fresco half-moon-wise
Set over the porch, Art's early wont:
    'Tis John in the Desert, I surmise,
But has borne the weather's brunt —   **90**

XIX

Not from the fault of the builder, though,
    For a pent-house properly projects
Where three carved beams make a certain show,
    Dating — good thought of our architect's —
'Five, six, nine, he lets you know.

XX

And all day long a bird sings there,
    And a stray sheep drinks at the pond at times;
The place is silent and aware;
    It has had its scenes, its joys and crimes,
But that is its own affair.   100

XXI

My perfect wife, my Leonor,
    Oh heart, my own, oh eyes, mine too,
Whom else could I dare look backward for,
    With whom beside should I dare pursue
The path gray heads abhor?

XXII

For it leads to a crag's sheer edge with them;
    Youth, flowery all the way, there stops —
Not they; age threatens and they contemn,
    Till they reach the gulf wherein youth drops,
One inch from life's safe hem!   110

XXIII

With me, youth led . . . I will speak now,
    No longer watch you as you sit
Reading by fire-light, that great brow
    And the spirit-small hand propping it,
Mutely, my heart knows how —

XXIV

When, if I think but deep enough,
    You are wont to answer, prompt as rhyme;
And you, too, find without rebuff
    Response your soul seeks many a time
Piercing its fine flesh-stuff.   120

XXV

My own, confirm me! If I tread
    This path back, is it not in pride
To think how little I dreamed it led
    To an age so blest that, by its side,
Youth seems the waste instead?

XXVI

My own, see where the years conduct!
    At first, 'twas something our two souls
Should mix as mists do; each is sucked
    In each now: on, the new stream rolls,
Whatever rocks obstruct.   130

XXVII

Think, when our one soul understands
    The great Word which makes all things new,
When earth breaks up and heaven expands,
    How will the change strike me and you
In the house not made with hands?

XXVIII

Oh I must feel your brain prompt mine,
    Your heart anticipate my heart,
You must be just before, in fine,
    See and make me see, for your part,
New depths of the divine!   140

XXIX

But who could have expected this
    When we two drew together first
Just for the obvious human bliss,
    To satisfy life's daily thirst
With a thing men seldom miss?

XXX

Come back with me to the first of all,
    Let us lean and love it over again,
Let us now forget and now recall,
    Break the rosary in a pearly rain,
And gather what we let fall!   150

XXXI

What did I say? — that a small bird sings
    All day long, save when a brown pair
Of hawks from the wood float with wide wings
    Strained to a bell: 'gainst noon-day glare
You count the streaks and rings.

XXXII

But at afternoon or almost eve
    'Tis better; then the silence grows
To that degree, you half believe
    It must get rid of what it knows,
Its bosom does so heave.   160

XXXIII

Hither we walked then, side by side,
    Arm in arm and cheek to cheek,
And still I questioned or replied,
    While my heart, convulsed to really speak,
Lay choking in its pride.

XXXIV

Silent the crumbling bridge we cross,
    And pity and praise the chapel sweet,
And care about the fresco's loss,
    And wish for our souls a like retreat,
And wonder at the moss.

XXXV

Stoop and kneel on the settle under,
    Look through the window's grated square:
Nothing to see! For fear of plunder,
    The cross is down and the altar bare,
As if thieves don't fear thunder.

XXXVI

We stoop and look in through the grate,
    See the little porch and rustic door,
Read duly the dead builder's date;
    Then cross the bridge that we crossed before,
Take the path again — but wait!   180

XXXVII

Oh moment, one and infinite!
    The water slips o'er stock and stone;
The West is tender, hardly bright:
    How gray at once is the evening grown —
One star, its chrysolite!

XXXVIII

We two stood there with never a third,
    But each by each, as each knew well:
The sights we saw and the sounds we heard,
    The lights and the shades made up a spell
Till the trouble grew and stirred.   190

XXXIX

Oh, the little more, and how much it is!
    And the little less, and what worlds away!
How a sound shall quicken content to bliss,
    Or a breath suspend the blood's best play,
And life be a proof of this!

XL

Had she willed it, still had stood the screen
    So slight, so sure, 'twixt my love and her:
I could fix her face with a guard between,
    And find her soul as when friends confer,
Friends — lovers that might have been.   200

XLI

For my heart had a touch of the woodland-time,
    Wanting to sleep now over its best.
Shake the whole tree in the summer-prime,
    But bring to the last leaf no such test!
"Hold the last fast!" runs the rhyme.

XLII

For a chance to make your little much,
    To gain a lover and lose a friend,
Venture the tree and a myriad such,
    When nothing you mar but the year can mend:
But a last leaf — fear to touch!   210

XLIII

Yet should it unfasten itself and fall
    Eddying down till it find your face
At some slight wind — best chance of all!
    Be your heart henceforth its dwelling-place
You trembled to forestall!

XLIV

Worth how well, those dark gray eyes,
    That hair so dark and dear, how worth
That a man should strive and agonize,
    And taste a veriest hell on earth
For the hope of such a prize!   220

XLV

You might have turned and tried a man,
    Set him a space to weary and wear,
And prove which suited more your plan,
    His best of hope or his worst despair,
Yet end as he began.

XLVI

But you spared me this, like the heart you are,
    And filled my empty heart at a word.
If two lives join, there is oft a scar,
    They are one and one, with a shadowy third;
One near one is too far.   230

XLVII

A moment after, and hands unseen
    Were hanging the night around us fast;
But we knew that a bar was broken between
    Life and life: we were mixed at last
In spite of the mortal screen.

XLVIII

The forests had done it; there they stood;
    We caught for a moment the powers at play:
They had mingled us so, for once and good,
    Their work was done — we might go or stay,
They relapsed to their ancient mood.   240

XLIX

How the world is made for each of us!
    How all we perceive and know in it
Tends to some moment's product thus,
    When a soul declares itself — to wit,
By its fruit, the thing it does!

L

Be hate that fruit or love that fruit,
    It forwards the general deed of man,
And each of the Many helps to recruit
    The life of the race by a general plan;
Each living his own, to boot.   250

LI

I am named and known by that moment's feat;
    There took my station and degree;
So grew my own small life complete,
    As nature obtained her best of me —
One born to love you, sweet!

LII

And to watch you sink by the fire-side now
    Back again, as you mutely sit
Musing by fire-light, that great brow
    And the spirit-small hand propping it,
Yonder, my heart knows how!   260

LIII

So, earth has gained by one man the more,
    And the gain of earth must be heaven's gain too;
And the whole is well worth thinking o'er
    When autumn comes: which I mean to do
One day, as I said before.

ANY WIFE TO ANY HUSBAND

I

MY LOVE, this is the bitterest, that thou —
Who art all truth, and who dost love me now
    As thine eyes say, as thy voice breaks to say —
Shouldst love so truly, and couldst love me still
A whole long life through, had but love its will,
    Would death that leads me from thee brook delay.

II

I have but to be by thee, and thy hand
Will never let mine go, nor heart withstand
    The beating of my heart to reach its place.
When shall I look for thee and feel thee gone?   10
When cry for the old comfort and find none?
    Never, I know! Thy soul is in thy face.

III

Oh, I should fade — 'tis willed so! Might I save,
Gladly I would, whatever beauty gave
    Joy to thy sense, for that was precious too.
It is not to be granted. But the soul
Whence the love comes, all ravage leaves that whole;
    Vainly the flesh fades; soul makes all things new.

IV

It would not be because my eye grew dim
Thou couldst not find the love there, thanks to Him   20
    Who never is dishonored in the spark
He gave us from his fire of fires, and bade
Remember whence it sprang, nor be afraid
    While that burns on, though all the rest grow dark.

V

So, how thou wouldst be perfect, white and clean
Outside as inside, soul and soul's demesne
    Alike, this body given to show it by!
Oh, three-parts through the worst of life's abyss,
What plaudits from the next world after this,
    Couldst thou repeat a stroke and gain the sky!   30

VI

And is it not the bitterer to think
That, disengage our hands and thou wilt sink
    Although thy love was love in very deed?
I know that nature! Pass a festive day,
Thou dost not throw its relic-flower away
    Nor bid its music's loitering echo speed.

VII

Thou let'st the stranger's glove lie where it fell;
If old things remain old things all is well,
    For thou art grateful as becomes man best:
And hadst thou only heard me play one tune,   40
Or viewed me from a window, not so soon
    With thee would such things fade as with the rest.

VIII

I seem to see! We meet and part; 'tis brief;
The book I opened keeps a folded leaf,
    The very chair I sat on, breaks the rank;
That is a portrait of me on the wall —
Three lines, my face comes at so slight a call:
    And for all this, one little hour to thank!

IX

But now, because the hour through years was fixed,
Because our inmost beings met and mixed,   50
    Because thou once hast loved me — wilt thou dare
Say to thy soul and Who may list beside,
"Therefore she is immortally my bride;
    Chance cannot change my love, nor time impair.

X

"So, what if in the dusk of life that's left,
I, a tired traveller of my sun bereft,
    Look from my path when, mimicking the same,
The fire-fly glimpses past me, come and gone?
— Where was it till the sunset? where anon
    It will be at the sunrise! What's to blame?"   60

XI

Is it so helpful to thee? Canst thou take
The mimic up, nor, for the true thing's sake,
    Put gently by such efforts at a beam?
Is the remainder of the way so long,
Thou need'st the little solace, thou the strong?
    Watch out thy watch, let weak ones doze and dream!

XII

— Ah, but the fresher faces! "Is it true,"
Thou'lt ask, "some eyes are beautiful and new?
    Some hair, — how can one choose but grasp such wealth?
And if a man would press his lips to lips   70
Fresh as the wilding hedge-rose-cup there slips
    The dew-drop out of, must it be by stealth?

XIII

"It cannot change the love still kept for Her,
More than if such a picture I prefer
    Passing a day with, to a room's bare side:
The painted form takes nothing she possessed,
Yet, while the Titian's Venus lies at rest,
    A man looks. Once more, what is there to chide?"

XIV

So must I see, from where I sit and watch,
My own self sell myself, my hand attach   80
    Its warrant to the very thefts from me —
Thy singleness of soul that made me proud,
Thy purity of heart I loved aloud,
    Thy man's-truth I was bold to bid God see!

XV

Love so, then, if thou wilt! Give all thou canst
Away to the new faces — disentranced,
    (Say it and think it) obdurate no more:
Re-issue looks and words from the old mint,
Pass them afresh, no matter whose the print
    Image and superscription once they bore!   90

XVI

Re-coin thyself and give it them to spend, —
It all comes to the same thing at the end,
    Since mine thou wast, mine art and mine shalt be,
Faithful or faithless, sealing up the sum
Or lavish of my treasure, thou must come
    Back to the heart's place here I keep for thee!

XVII

Only, why should it be with stain at all?
Why must I, 'twixt the leaves of coronal,
    Put any kiss of pardon on thy brow?
Why need the other women know so much,   100
And talk together, "Such the look and such
    The smile he used to love with, then as now!"

XVIII

Might I die last and show thee! Should I find
Such hardship in the few years left behind,
    If free to take and light my lamp, and go
Into thy tomb, and shut the door and sit,
Seeing thy face on those four sides of it
    The better that they are so blank, I know!

XIX

Why, time was what I wanted, to turn o'er
Within my mind each look, get more and more   110
    By heart each word, too much to learn at first;
And join thee all the fitter for the pause
'Neath the low doorway's lintel. That were cause
    For lingering, though thou calledst, if I durst!

XX

And yet thou art the nobler of us two:
What dare I dream of, that thou canst not do,
    Outstripping my ten small steps with one stride?
I'll say then, here's a trial and a task —
Is it to bear? — if easy, I'll not ask:
    Though love fail, I can trust on in thy pride.   120

XXI

Pride? — when those eyes forestall the life behind
The death I have to go through! — when I find,
    Now that I want thy help most, all of thee!
What did I fear? Thy love shall hold me fast
Until the little minute's sleep is past
    And I wake saved. — And yet it will not be!

AN EPISTLE

*Containing the Strange Medical Experience of Karshish,
The Arab Physician*

KARSHISH, the picker-up of learning's crumbs,
The not-incurious in God's handiwork
(This man's-flesh he hath admirably made,
Blown like a bubble, kneaded like a paste,
To coop up and keep down on earth a space
That puff of vapor from his mouth, man's soul)
— To Abib, all-sagacious in our art,
Breeder in me of what poor skill I boast,
Like me inquisitive how pricks and cracks
Befall the flesh through too much stress and strain,   10
Whereby the wily vapor fain would slip
Back and rejoin its source before the term, —
And aptest in contrivance (under God)
To baffle it by deftly stopping such: —
The vagrant Scholar to his Sage at home
Sends greeting (health and knowledge, fame with peace)
Three samples of true snakestone — rarer still,
One of the other sort, the melon-shaped,
(But fitter, pounded fine, for charms than drugs)
And writeth now the twenty-second time.   20

    My journeyings were brought to Jericho:
Thus I resume. Who studious in our art
Shall count a little labor unrepaid?
I have shed sweat enough, left flesh and bone
On many a flinty furlong of this land.
Also, the country-side is all on fire
With rumors of a marching hitherward:
Some say Vespasian cometh, some, his son.
A black lynx snarled and pricked a tufted ear:
Lust of my blood inflamed his yellow balls: 30
I cried and threw my staff and he was gone.
Twice have the robbers stripped and beaten me,
And once a town declared me for a spy;
But at the end, I reach Jerusalem,
Since this poor covert where I pass the night,

This Bethany, lies scarce the distance thence
A man with plague-sores at the third degree
Runs till he drops down dead. Thou laughest here!
'Sooth, it elates me, thus reposed and safe,
To void the stuffing of my travel-scrip   40
And share with thee whatever Jewry yields.
A viscid choler is observable
In tertians, I was nearly bold to say;
And falling-sickness hath a happier cure
Than our school wots of: there's a spider here
Weaves no web, watches on the ledge of tombs,
Sprinkled with mottles on an ash-gray back;
Take five and drop them . . . but who knows his mind,
The Syrian runagate I trust this to?
His service payeth me a sublimate   50
Blown up his nose to help the ailing eye.
Best wait: I reach Jerusalem at morn,
There set in order my experiences,
Gather what most deserves, and give thee all —
Or I might add, Judæa's gum-tragacanth
Scales off in purer flakes, shines clearer-grained,
Cracks 'twixt the pestle and the porphyry,
In fine exceeds our produce. Scalp-disease
Confounds me, crossing so with leprosy —
Thou hadst admired one sort I gained at Zoar —   60
But zeal outruns discretion. Here I end.

Yet stay: my Syrian blinketh gratefully,
Protesteth his devotion is my price —
Suppose I write what harms not, though he steal?
I half resolve to tell thee, yet I blush,
What set me off a-writing first of all.
An itch I had, a sting to write, a tang!
For, be it this town's barrenness — or else
The Man had something in the look of him —
His case has struck me far more than 'tis worth.   70
So, pardon if — (lest presently I lose
In the great press of novelty at hand
The care and pains this somehow stole from me)
I bid thee take the thing while fresh in mind,
Almost in sight — for, wilt thou have the truth?
The very man is gone from me but now,
Whose ailment is the subject of discourse.
Thus then, and let thy better wit help all!

'Tis but a case of mania — subinduced
By epilepsy, at the turning-point   80
Of trance prolonged unduly some three days:
When, by the exhibition of some drug
Or spell, exorcisation, stroke of art
Unknown to me and which 'twere well to know,
The evil thing out-breaking all at once
Left the man whole and sound of body indeed, —
But, flinging (so to speak) life's gates too wide,
Making a clear house of it too suddenly,
The first conceit that entered might inscribe
Whatever it was minded on the wall   90
So plainly at that vantage, as it were,
(First come, first served) that nothing subsequent
Attaineth to erase those fancy-scrawls
The just-returned and new-established soul
Hath gotten now so thoroughly by heart
That henceforth she will read or these or none.
And first — the man's own firm conviction rests
That he was dead (in fact they buried him)
— That he was dead and then restored to life
By a Nazarene physician of his tribe: 100
— 'Sayeth, the same bade "Rise," and he did rise.
"Such cases are diurnal," thou wilt cry.
Not so this figment! — not, that such a fume,
Instead of giving way to time and health,
Should eat itself into the life of life,
As saffron tingeth flesh, blood, bones and all!
For see, how he takes up the after-life.
The man — it is one Lazarus a Jew,
Sanguine, proportioned, fifty years of age,
The body's habit wholly laudable,   110
As much, indeed, beyond the common health
As he were made and put aside to show.
Think, could we penetrate by any drug
And bathe the wearied soul and worried flesh,
And bring it clear and fair, by three days' sleep!
Whence has the man the balm that brightens all?
This grown man eyes the world now like a child.
Some elders of his tribe, I should premise,
Led in their friend, obedient as a sheep,
To bear my inquisition. While they spoke,   120
Now sharply, now with sorrow, — told the case, —
He listened not except I spoke to him,

But folded his two hands and let them talk,
Watching the flies that buzzed: and yet no fool.
And that's a sample how his years must go.
Look, if a beggar, in fixed middle-life,
Should find a treasure, — can he use the same
With straitened habits and with tastes starved small,
And take at once to his impoverished brain
The sudden element that changes things,   130
That sets the undreamed-of rapture at his hand
And puts the cheap old joy in the scorned dust?
Is he not such an one as moves to mirth —
Warily parsimonious, when no need,
Wasteful as drunkenness at undue times?
All prudent counsel as to what befits
The golden mean, is lost on such an one:
The man's fantastic will is the man's law.
So here — we call the treasure knowledge, say,
Increased beyond the fleshly faculty —   140
Heaven opened to a soul while yet on earth,
Earth forced on a soul's use while seeing heaven:
The man is witless of the size, the sum,
The value in proportion of all things,
Or whether it be little or be much.
Discourse to him of prodigious armaments
Assembled to besiege his city now,
And of the passing of a mule with gourds —
'Tis one! Then take it on the other side,
Speak of some trifling fact, — he will gaze rapt   150
With stupor at its very littleness,
(Far as I see) as if in that indeed
He caught prodigious import, whole results;
And so will turn to us the bystanders
In ever the same stupor (note this point)
That we too see not with his opened eyes.
Wonder and doubt come wrongly into play,
Preposterously, at cross purposes.
Should his child sicken unto death, — why, look
For scarce abatement of his cheerfulness,   160
Or pretermission of the daily craft!
While a word, gesture, glance from that same child
At play or in the school or laid asleep,
Will startle him to an agony of fear,
Exasperation, just as like. Demand
The reason why — " 'tis but a word," object —

"A gesture" — he regards thee as our lord
Who lived there in the pyramid alone,
Looked at us (dost thou mind?) when, being young,
We both would unadvisedly recite   170
Some charm's beginning, from that book of his,
Able to bid the sun throb wide and burst
All into stars, as suns grown old are wont.
Thou and the child have each a veil alike
Thrown o'er your heads, from under which ye both
Stretch your blind hands and trifle with a match
Over a mine of Greek fire, did ye know!
He holds on firmly to some thread of life —
(It is the life to lead perforcedly)
Which runs across some vast distracting orb   180
Of glory on either side that meagre thread,
Which, conscious of, he must not enter yet —
The spiritual life around the earthly life:
The law of that is known to him as this,
His heart and brain move there, his feet stay here.
So is the man perplext with impulses
Sudden to start off crosswise, not straight on,
Proclaiming what is right and wrong across,
And not along, this black thread through the blaze —
"It should be" balked by "here it cannot be."   190
And oft the man's soul springs into his face
As if he saw again and heard again
His sage that bade him "Rise" and he did rise.
Something, a word, a tick o' the blood within
Admonishes: then back he sinks at once
To ashes, who was very fire before,
In sedulous recurrence to his trade
Whereby he earneth him the daily bread;
And studiously the humbler for that pride,
Professedly the faultier that he knows   200
God's secret, while he holds the thread of life.
Indeed the especial marking of the man
Is prone submission to the heavenly will —
Seeing it, what it is, and why it is.
'Sayeth, he will wait patient to the last
For that same death which must restore his being
To equilibrium, body loosening soul
Divorced even now by premature full growth:
He will live, nay, it pleaseth him to live
So long as God please, and just how God please.   210

He even seeketh not to please God more
(Which meaneth, otherwise) than as God please.
Hence, I perceive not he affects to preach
The doctrine of his sect whate'er it be,
Make proselytes as madmen thirst to do:
How can he give his neighbor the real ground,
His own conviction? Ardent as he is —
Call his great truth a lie, why, still the old
"Be it as God please" reassureth him.
I probed the sore as thy disciple should: 220
"How, beast," said I, "this stolid carelessness
Sufficeth thee, when Rome is on her march
To stamp out like a little spark thy town,
Thy tribe, thy crazy tale and thee at once?"
He merely looked with his large eyes on me.
The man is apathetic, you deduce?
Contrariwise, he loves both old and young,
Able and weak, affects the very brutes
And birds — how say I? flowers of the field —
As a wise workman recognizes tools   230
In a master's workshop, loving what they make.
Thus is the man as harmless as a lamb:
Only impatient, let him do his best,
At ignorance and carelessness and sin —
An indignation which is promptly curbed:
As when in certain travel I have feigned
To be an ignoramus in our art
According to some preconceived design,
And happed to hear the land's practitioners
Steeped in conceit sublimed by ignorance,   240
Prattle fantastically on disease,
Its cause and cure — and I must hold my peace!

      Thou wilt object — why have I not ere this
Sought out the sage himself, the Nazarene
Who wrought this cure, inquiring at the source,
Conferring with the frankness that befits?
Alas! it grieveth me, the learned leech
Perished in a tumult many years ago,
Accused, — our learning's fate, — of wizardry,
Rebellion, to the setting up a rule   250
And creed prodigious as described to me.
His death, which happened when the earthquake fell
(Prefiguring, as soon appeared, the loss

To occult learning in our lord the sage
Who lived there in the pyramid alone)
Was wrought by the mad people — that's their wont!
On vain recourse, as I conjecture it,
To his tried virtue, for miraculous help —
How could he stop the earthquake? That's their way!
The other imputations must be lies;   260
But take one, though I loathe to give it thee,
In mere respect for any good man's fame.
(And after all, our patient Lazarus
Is stark mad; should we count on what he says?
Perhaps not: though in writing to a leech
'Tis well to keep back nothing of a case.)
This man so cured regards the curer, then,
As — God forgive me! who but God himself,
Creator and sustainer of the world,
That came and dwelt in flesh on it awhile!   270
— 'Sayeth that such an one was born and lived,
Taught, healed the sick, broke bread at his own house,
Then died, with Lazarus by, for aught I know,
And yet was . . . what I said nor choose repeat,
And must have so avouched himself, in fact,
In hearing of this very Lazarus
Who saith — but why all this of what he saith?
Why write of trivial matters, things of price
Calling at every moment for remark?
I noticed on the margin of a pool   280
Blue-flowering borage, the Aleppo sort,
Aboundeth, very nitrous. It is strange!

        Thy pardon for this long and tedious case,
Which, now that I review it, needs must seem
Unduly dwelt on, prolixly set forth!
Nor I myself discern in what is writ
Good cause for the peculiar interest
And awe indeed this man has touched me with.
Perhaps the journey's end, the weariness
Had wrought upon me first. I met him thus: 290
I crossed a ridge of short sharp broken hills
Like an old lion's cheek teeth. Out there came
A moon made like a face with certain spots
Multiform, manifold and menacing:
Then a wind rose behind me. So we met
In this old sleepy town at unaware,

The man and I. I send thee what is writ.
Regard it as a chance, a matter risked
To this ambiguous Syrian — he may lose,
Or steal, or give it thee with equal good.   300
Jerusalem's repose shall make amends
For time this letter wastes, thy time and mine;
Till when, once more thy pardon and farewell!

    The very God! think, Abib; dost thou think?
So, the All-Great, were the All-Loving too —
So, through the thunder comes a human voice
Saying, "O heart I made, a heart beats here!
Face, my hands fashioned, see it in myself!
Thou hast no power nor mayst conceive of mine,
But love I gave thee, with myself to love,   310
And thou must love me who have died for thee!"
The madman saith He said so: it is strange.

A SERENADE AT THE VILLA

I

THAT was I, you heard last night,
    When there rose no moon at all,
Nor, to pierce the strained and tight
    Tent of heaven, a planet small:
Life was dead and so was light.

II

Not a twinkle from the fly,
    Not a glimmer from the worm;
When the crickets stopped their cry,
    When the owls forebore a term,
You heard music; that was I.   10

III

Earth turned in her sleep with pain,
    Sultrily suspired for proof:
In at heaven and out again,
    Lightning! — where it broke the roof.
Bloodlike, some few drops of rain.

IV

What they could my words expressed,
    O my love, my all, my one!
Singing helped the verses best,
    And when singing's best was done,
To my lute I left the rest.   20

V

So wore night; the East was gray,
    White the broad-faced hemlock-flowers:
There would be another day;
    Ere its first of heavy hours
Found me, I had passed away.

VI

What became of all the hopes,
    Words and song and lute as well?
Say, this struck you — "When life gropes
    Feebly for the path where fell
Light last on the evening slopes,   30

VII

"One friend in that path shall be,
    To secure my step from wrong;
One to count night day for me,
    Patient through the watches long,
Serving most with none to see."

VIII

Never say — as something bodes —
    "So, the worst has yet a worse!
When life halts 'neath double loads,
    Better the taskmaster's curse
Than such music on the roads!   40

IX

"When no moon succeeds the sun,
    Nor can pierce the midnight's tent
Any star, the smallest one,
    While some drops, where lightning rent,
Show the final storm begun —

x

"When the fire-fly hides its spot,
    When the garden-voices fail
In the darkness thick and hot, —
    Shall another voice avail,
That shape be where these are not?   50

xi

"Has some plague a longer lease,
    Proffering its help uncouth?
Can't one even die in peace?
    As one shuts one's eyes on youth,
Is that face the last one sees?"

xii

Oh how dark your villa was,
    Windows fast and obdurate!
How the garden grudged me grass
    Where I stood — the iron gate
Ground its teeth to let me pass!   60

MY STAR

All that I know
    Of a certain star
Is, it can throw
    (Like the angled spar)
Now a dart of red,
    Now a dart of blue;
Till my friends have said
    They would fain see, too,
My star that dartles the red and the blue!
Then it stops like a bird; like a flower, hangs furled: 10
    They must solace themselves with the Saturn above it.
What matter to me if their star is a world?
    Mine has opened its soul to me; therefore I love it.

"CHILDE ROLAND TO THE DARK TOWER CAME"

(*See Edgar's song in* "LEAR")

I

My FIRST thought was, he lied in every word,
 That hoary cripple, with malicious eye
 Askance to watch the working of his lie
On mine, and mouth scarce able to afford
Suppression of the glee, that pursed and scored
 Its edge, at one more victim gained thereby.

II

What else should he be set for, with his staff?
 What, save to waylay with his lies, ensnare
 All travellers who might find him posted there,
And ask the road? I guessed what skull-like laugh   10
Would break, what crutch 'gin write my epitaph
 For pastime in the dusty thoroughfare,

III

If at his counsel I should turn aside
 Into that ominous tract which, all agree,
 Hides the Dark Tower. Yet acquiescingly
I did turn as he pointed: neither pride
Nor hope rekindling at the end descried,
 So much as gladness that some end might be.

IV

For, what with my whole world-wide wandering,
 What with my search drawn out thro' years, my hope 20
 Dwindled into a ghost not fit to cope
With that obstreperous joy success would bring,
I hardly tried now to rebuke the spring
 My heart made, finding failure in its scope.

V

As when a sick man very near to death
Seems dead indeed, and feels begin and end
The tears and takes the farewell of each friend,
And hears one bid the other go, draw breath
Freelier outside, ("since all is o'er," he saith,
"And the blow fallen no grieving can amend;")   30

Death

VI

While some discuss if near the other graves
Be room enough for this, and when a day
Suits best for carrying the corpse away,
With care about the banners, scarves and staves:
And still the man hears all, and only craves
He may not shame such tender love and stay.

VII

Thus, I had so long suffered in this quest,
Heard failure prophesied so oft, been writ
So many times among "The Band" — to wit,
The knights who to the Dark Tower's search addressed   40
Their steps — that just to fail as they, seemed best,
And all the doubt was now — should I be fit?

Quest

gray

VIII

So, quiet as despair, I turned from him,
That hateful cripple, out of his highway
Into the path he pointed. All the day
Had been a dreary one at best, and dim
Was settling to its close, yet shot one grim
Red leer to see the plain catch its estray.

sun

IX

For mark! no sooner was I fairly found
Pledged to the plain, after a pace or two,   50
Than, pausing to throw backward a last view
O'er the safe road, 'twas gone; gray plain all round:
Nothing but plain to the horizon's bound.
I might go on; naught else remained to do.

resignation

waste land

X

So, on I went. I think I never saw
    Such starved ignoble nature; nothing throve:
    For flowers — as well expect a cedar grove!
But cockle, spurge, according to their law
Might propagate their kind, with none to awe,
    You'd think; a burr had been a treasure-trove.   60

X nature

XI

No! penury, inertness and grimace,
    In some strange sort, were the land's portion. "See
    Or shut your eyes," said Nature peevishly,
"It nothing skills: I cannot help my case:
'Tis the Last Judgment's fire must cure this place,
    Calcine its clods and set my prisoners free."

predictive

X N FIRE

XII

If there pushed any ragged thistle-stalk
    Above its mates, the head was chopped; the bents
    Were jealous else. What made those holes and rents
In the dock's harsh swarth leaves, bruised as to balk   70
All hope of greenness? 'tis a brute must walk
    Pashing their life out, with a brute's intents.

parallel to Quester

HORSE XIII

As for the grass, it grew as scant as hair
    In leprosy; thin dry blades pricked the mud
    Which underneath looked kneaded up with blood.
One stiff blind horse, his every bone a-stare,
Stood stupefied, however he came there:
    Thrust out past service from the devil's stud!

HORSE

XIV

Alive? he might be dead for aught I know,
    With that red gaunt and colloped neck a-strain,   80
    And shut eyes underneath the rusty mane;
Seldom went such grotesqueness with such woe;
I never saw a brute I hated so;
    He must be wicked to deserve such pain.

moral

Job

XV

I shut my eyes and turned them on my heart.
    As a man calls for wine before he fights,
    I asked one draught of earlier, happier sights,
Ere fitly I could hope to play my part.
Think first, fight afterwards — the soldier's art:
    One taste of the old time sets all to rights.   90

[margin, handwritten: R 11 to horse]

XVI

[margin, handwritten: Post]

Not it! I fancied Cuthbert's reddening face
    Beneath its garniture of curly gold,
    Dear fellow, till I almost felt him fold
An arm in mine to fix me to the place,
That way he used. Alas, one night's disgrace!
    Out went my heart's new fire and left it cold.

[margin, handwritten: adultery? Fires]

XVII

Giles then, the soul of honour — there he stands
    Frank as ten years ago when knighted first.
    What honest man should dare (he said) he durst.
Good — but the scene shifts — faugh! what hangman hands 100
Pin to his breast a parchment? His own bands
    Read it. Poor traitor, spit upon and curst!

[margin, handwritten: traitor]

XVIII

Better this present than a past like that;
    Back therefore to my darkening path again!
    No sound, no sight as far as eye could strain.
Will the night send a howlet or a bat?
I asked: when something on the dismal flat
    Came to arrest my thoughts and change their train.

XIX

A sudden little river crossed my path
    As unexpected as a serpent comes.
    No sluggish tide congenial to the glooms;
This, as it frothed by, might have been a bath
For the fiend's glowing hoof — to see the wrath
    Of its black eddy bespate with flakes and spumes.

[margin, handwritten: demonic rill]   110

XX

So petty yet so spiteful! All along,
        Low scrubby alders kneeled down over it;
        Drenched willows flung them headlong in a fit
Of mute despair, a suicidal throng:
The river which had done them all the wrong,
        Whate'er that was, rolled by, deterred no whit.   120

XXI

Which, while I forded, — good saints, how I feared
        To set my foot upon a dead man's cheek,
        Each step, or feel the spear I thrust to seek
For hollows, tangled in his hair or beard!
— It may have been a water-rat I speared,
        But, ugh! it sounded like a baby's shriek.

XXII

Glad was I when I reached the other bank.
        Now for a better country. Vain presage!
        Who were the strugglers, what war did they wage,
Whose savage trample thus could pad the dank   130
Soil to a plash? Toads in a poisoned tank,
        Or wild cats in a red-hot iron cage —

XXIII

The fight must so have seemed in that fell cirque.
        What penned them there, with all the plain to choose?
        No foot-print leading to that horrid mews,
None out of it. Mad brewage set to work
Their brains, no doubt, like galley-slaves the Turk
        Pits for his pastime, Christians against Jews.

XXIV

And more than that — a furlong on — why, there!
        What bad use was that engine for, that wheel,   140
        Or brake, not wheel — that harrow fit to reel
Men's bodies out like silk? with all the air
Of Tophet's tool, on earth left unaware,
        Or brought to sharpen its rusty teeth of steel.

XXV

Then came a bit of stubbed ground, once a wood,
    Next a marsh, it would seem, and now mere earth
    Desperate and done with; (so a fool finds mirth,
Makes a thing and then mars it, till his mood
Changes and off he goes!) within a rood —
    Bog, clay and rubble, sand and stark black dearth.   150

XXVI

Now blotches rankling, colored gay and grim,
    Now patches where some leanness of the soil's
    Broke into moss or substances like boils;
Then came some palsied oak, a cleft in him
Like a distorted mouth that splits its rim
    Gaping at death, and dies while it recoils.

XXVII

And just as far as ever from the end!
    Naught in the distance but the evening, naught
    To point my footstep further! At the thought,
A great black bird, Apollyon's bosom-friend,   160
Sailed past, nor beat his wide wing dragon-penned
    That brushed my cap — perchance the guide I sought.

XXVIII

For, looking up, aware I somehow grew,
    'Spite of the dusk, the plain had given place
    All round to mountains — with such name to grace
Mere ugly heights and heaps now stolen in view.
How thus they had surprised me, — solve it, you!
    How to get from them was no clearer case.

XXIX

Yet half I seemed to recognize some trick
    Of mischief happened to me, God knows when —   170
    In a bad dream perhaps. Here ended, then,
Progress this way. When, in the very nick
Of giving up, one time more, came a click
    As when a trap shuts — you're inside the den!

XXX

Burningly it came on me all at once,
    This was the place! those two hills on the right,
    Crouched like two bulls locked horn in horn in fight;
While to the left, a tall scalped mountain . . . Dunce,
Dotard, a-dozing at the very nonce,
    After a life spent training for the sight!   **180**

XXXI

What in the midst lay but the Tower itself?
    The round squat turret, blind as the fool's heart,
    Built of brown stone, without a counterpart
In the whole world. The tempest's mocking elf
Points to the shipman thus the unseen shelf
    He strikes on, only when the timbers start.

XXXII

Not see? because of night perhaps? — why, day
    Came back again for that! before it left,
    The dying sunset kindled through a cleft:
The hills, like giants at a hunting, lay,   **190**
Chin upon hand, to see the game at bay, —
    "Now stab and end the creature — to the heft!"

XXXIII

Not hear? when noise was everywhere! it tolled
    Increasing like a bell. Names in my ears
    Of all the lost adventurers my peers, —
How such a one was strong, and such was bold,
And such was fortunate, yet each of old
    Lost, lost! one moment knelled the woe of years.

XXXIV

There they stood, ranged along the hill-sides, met
    To view the last of me, a living frame   **200**
    For one more picture! in a sheet of flame
I saw them and I knew them all. And yet
Dauntless the slug-horn to my lips I set,
    And blew. "*Childe Roland to the Dark Tower came.*"

RESPECTABILITY

I

DEAR, had the world in its caprice
    Deigned to proclaim "I know you both,
    Have recognized your plighted troth,
Am sponsor for you: live in peace!" —
How many precious months and years
    Of youth had passed, that speed so fast,
    Before we found it out at last,
The world, and what it fears?

II

How much of priceless life were spent
    With men that every virtue decks,   10
    And women models of their sex,
Society's true ornament, —
Ere we dared wander, nights like this,
    Thro' wind and rain, and watch the Seine,
    And feel the Boulevard break again
To warmth and light and bliss?

III

I know! the world proscribes not love;
    Allows my fingers to caress
    Your lips' contour and downiness,
Provided it supply a glove.   20
The world's good word! — the Institute!
    Guizot receives Montalembert!
    Eh? Down the court three lampions flare:
Put forward your best foot!

A LIGHT WOMAN

I

So FAR as our story approaches the end,
  Which do you pity the most of us three? —
My friend, or the mistress of my friend
  With her wanton eyes, or me?

II

My friend was already too good to lose,
  And seemed in the way of improvement yet,
When she crossed his path with her hunting-noose
  And over him drew her net.

III

When I saw him tangled in her toils,
  A shame, said I, if she adds just him   10
To her nine-and-ninety other spoils,
  The hundredth for a whim!

IV

And before my friend be wholly hers,
  How easy to prove to him, I said,
An eagle's the game her pride prefers,
  Though she snaps at a wren instead!

V

So, I gave her eyes my own eyes to take,
  My hand sought hers as in earnest need,
And round she turned for my noble sake,
  And gave me herself indeed.   20

VI

The eagle am I, with my fame in the world,
  The wren is he, with his maiden face.
— You look away and your lip is curled?
  Patience, a moment's space!

VII

For see, my friend goes shaking and white;
 He eyes me as the basilisk:
I have turned, it appears, his day to night,
  Eclipsing his sun's disk.

VIII

And I did it, he thinks, as a very thief:
 "Though I love her — that, he comprehends —   30
One should master one's passions, (love, in chief)
  And be loyal to one's friends!"

IX

And she, — she lies in my hand as tame
 As a pear late basking over a wall;
Just a touch to try and off it came;
  'Tis mine, — can I let it fall?

X

With no mind to eat it, that's the worst!
 Were it thrown in the road, would the case assist?
'Twas quenching a dozen blue-flies' thirst
  When I gave its stalk a twist.   40

XI

And I, — what I seem to my friend, you see:
 What I soon shall seem to his love, you guess:
What I seem to myself, do you ask of me?
  No hero, I confess.

XII

'Tis an awkward thing to play with souls,
 And matter enough to save one's own:
Yet think of my friend, and the burning coals
  He played with for bits of stone!

XIII

One likes to show the truth for the truth;
 That the woman was light is very true: 50
But suppose she says, — Never mind that youth!
  What wrong have I done to you?

XIV

Well, anyhow, here the story stays,
    So far at least as I understand;
And, Robert Browning, you writer of plays,
    Here's a subject made to your hand!

THE STATUE AND THE BUST

THERE'S a palace in Florence, the world knows well,
And a statue watches it from the square,
And this story of both do our townsmen tell.

Ages ago, a lady there,
At the farthest window facing the East
Asked, "Who rides by with the royal air?"

The bridesmaids' prattle around her ceased;
She leaned forth, one on either hand;
They saw how the blush of the bride increased —

They felt by its beats her heart expand —
As one at each ear and both in a breath
Whispered, "The Great-Duke Ferdinand."

That selfsame instant, underneath,
The Duke rode past in his idle way,
Empty and fine like a swordless sheath.

Gay he rode, with a friend as gay,
Till he threw his head back — "Who is she?"
— "A bride the Riccardi brings home to-day."

Hair in heaps lay heavily
Over a pale brow spirit-pure —
Carved like the heart of a coal-black tree,

Crisped like a war-steed's encolure —
And vainly sought to dissemble her eyes
Of the blackest black our eyes endure.

      10

      20

And lo, a blade for a knight's emprise
Filled the fine empty sheath of a man, —
The Duke grew straightway brave and wise.

He looked at her, as a lover can;
She looked at him, as one who awakes:
The past was a sleep, and her life began.   30

Now, love so ordered for both their sakes,
A feast was held that selfsame night
In the pile which the mighty shadow makes.

(For Via Larga is three-parts light,
But the palace overshadows one,
Because of a crime which may God requite!

To Florence and God the wrong was done,
Through the first republic's murder there
By Cosimo and his cursed son.)

The Duke (with the statue's face in the square)
Turned in the midst of his multitude
At the bright approach of the bridal pair.

Face to face the lovers stood
A single minute and no more,
While the bridegroom bent as a man subdued —

Bowed till his bonnet brushed the floor —
For the Duke on the lady a kiss conferred,
As the courtly custom was of yore.

In a minute can lovers exchange a word?
If a word did pass, which I do not think,
Only one out of the thousand heard.

That was the bridegroom. At day's brink
He and his bride were alone at last
In a bedchamber by a taper's blink.

Calmly he said that her lot was cast,
That the door she had passed was shut on her
Till the final catafalk repassed.

The world meanwhile, its noise and stir,
Through a certain window facing the East,
She could watch like a convent's chronicler. 60

Since passing the door might lead to a feast,
And a feast might lead to so much beside,
He, of many evils, chose the least.

"Freely I choose too," said the bride —
"Your window and its world suffice,"
Replied the tongue, while the heart replied —

"If I spend the night with that devil twice,
May his window serve as my loop of hell
Whence a damned soul looks on paradise!

"I fly to the Duke who loves me well, 70
Sit by his side and laugh at sorrow
Ere I count another ave-bell.

" 'Tis only the coat of a page to borrow,
And tie my hair in a horse-boy's trim,
And I save my soul — but not to-morrow" —

(She checked herself and her eye grew dim)
"My father tarries to bless my state:
I must keep it one day more for him.

"Is one day more so long to wait?
Moreover the Duke rides past, I know; 80
We shall see each other, sure as fate."

She turned on her side and slept. Just so!
So we resolve on a thing and sleep:
So did the lady, ages ago.

That night the Duke said, "Dear or cheap
As the cost of this cup of bliss may prove
To body or soul, I will drain it deep."

And on the morrow, bold with love,
He beckoned the bridegroom (close on call,
As his duty bade, by the Duke's alcove) 90

And smiled " 'Twas a very funeral,
Your lady will think, this feast of ours, —
A shame to efface, whate'er befall!

"What if we break from the Arno bowers,
And try if Petraja, cool and green,
Cure last night's fault with this morning's flowers?"

The bridegroom, not a thought to be seen
On his steady brow and quiet mouth,
Said, "Too much favor for me so mean!

"But, alas! my lady leaves the South;   100
Each wind that comes from the Apennine
Is a menace to her tender youth:

"Nor a way exists, the wise opine,
If she quits her palace twice this year,
To avert the flower of life's decline."

Quoth the Duke, "A sage and a kindly fear.
Moreover Petraja is cold this spring:
Be our feast to-night as usual here!"

And then to himself — "Which night shall bring
Thy bride to her lover's embraces, fool —   110
Or I am the fool, and thou art the king!

"Yet my passion must wait a night, nor cool —
For to-night the Envoy arrives from France
Whose heart I unlock with thyself, my tool.

"I need thee still and might miss perchance.
To-day is not wholly lost, beside,
With its hope of my lady's countenance:

"For I ride — what should I do but ride?
And passing her palace, if I list,
May glance at its window — well betide!"   120

So said, so done; nor the lady missed
One ray that broke from the ardent brow,
Nor a curl of the lips where the spirit kissed.

Be sure that each renewed the vow,
No morrow's sun should arise and set
And leave them then as it left them now.

But next day passed, and next day yet,
With still fresh cause to wait one day more
Ere each leaped over the parapet.

And still, as love's brief morning wore,   130
With a gentle start, half smile, half sigh,
They found love not as it seemed before.

They thought it would work infallibly,
But not in despite of heaven and earth:
The rose would blow when the storm passed by

Meantime they could profit in winter's dearth
By store of fruits that supplant the rose:
The world and its ways have a certain worth·

And to press a point while these oppose
Were simple policy; better wait: 140
We lose no friends and we gain no foes.

Meantime, worse fates than a lover's fate,
Who daily may ride and pass and look
Where his lady watches behind the grate!

And she — she watched the square like a book
Holding one picture and only one,
Which daily to find she undertook:

When the picture was reached the book was done,
And she turned from the picture at night to scheme
Of tearing it out for herself next sun.   150

So weeks grew months, years; gleam by gleam
The glory dropped from their youth and love,
And both perceived they had dreamed a dream;

Which hovered as dreams do, still above:
But who can take a dream for a truth?
Oh, hide our eyes from the next remove!

One day as the lady saw her youth
Depart, and the silver thread that streaked
Her hair, and, worn by the serpent's tooth,

The brow so puckered, the chin so peaked, —   160
And wondered who the woman was,
Hollow-eyed and haggard-cheeked,

Fronting her silent in the glass —
"Summon here," she suddenly said,
"Before the rest of my old self pass,

"Him, the Carver, a hand to aid,
Who fashions the clay no love will change,
And fixes a beauty never to fade.

"Let Robbia's craft so apt and strange
Arrest the remains of young and fair,   170
And rivet them while the seasons range.

"Make me a face on the window there,
Waiting as ever, mute the while,
My love to pass below in the square!

"And let me think that it may beguile
Dreary days which the dead must spend
Down in their darkness under the aisle,

"To say, 'What matters it at the end?
I did no more while my heart was warm
Than does that image, my pale-faced friend.'   180

"Where is the use of the lip's red charm,
The heaven of hair, the pride of the brow,
And the blood that blues the inside arm —

"Unless we turn, as the soul knows how,
The earthly gift to an end divine?
A lady of clay is as good, I trow."

But long ere Robbia's cornice, fine,
With flowers and fruits which leaves enlace,
Was set where now is the empty shrine —

(And, leaning out of a bright blue space,   190
As a ghost might lean from a chink of sky,
The passionate pale lady's face —

Eyeing ever, with earnest eye
And quick-turned neck at its breathless stretch,
Some one who ever is passing by —)

The Duke had sighed like the simplest wretch
In Florence, "Youth — my dream escapes!
Will its record stay?" And he bade them fetch

Some subtle moulder of brazen shapes —
"Can the soul, the will, die out of a man   200
Ere his body find the grave that gapes?

"John of Douay shall effect my plan,
Set me on horseback here aloft,
Alive, as the crafty sculptor can,

"In the very square I have crossed so oft:
That men may admire, when future suns
Shall touch the eyes to a purpose soft,

"While the mouth and the brow stay brave in bronze —
Admire and say, 'When he was alive
How he would take his pleasure once!'   210

"And it shall go hard but I contrive
To listen the while, and laugh in my tomb
At idleness which aspires to strive."

———

So! While these wait the trump of doom,
How do their spirits pass, I wonder,
Nights and days in the narrow room?

Still, I suppose, they sit and ponder
What a gift life was, ages ago,
Six steps out of the chapel yonder.

Only they see not God, I know,   220
Nor all that chivalry of his,
The soldier-saints who, row on row,

Burn upward each to his point of bliss —
Since, the end of life being manifest,
He had burned his way thro' the world to this.

I hear you reproach, "But delay was best,
For their end was a crime." — Oh, a crime will do
As well, I reply, to serve for a test,

As a virtue golden through and through,
Sufficient to vindicate itself   230
And prove its worth at a moment's view!

Must a game be played for the sake of pelf?
Where a button goes, 'twere an epigram
To offer the stamp of the very Guelph.

The true has no value beyond the sham:
As well the counter as coin, I submit,
When your table's a hat, and your prize a dram.

Stake your counter as boldly every whit,
Venture as warily, use the same skill,
Do your best, whether winning or losing it,   240

If you choose to play! — is my principle.
Let a man contend to the uttermost
For his life's set prize, be it what it will!

The counter our lovers staked was lost
As surely as if it were lawful coin:
And the sin I impute to each frustrate ghost

Is — the unlit lamp and the ungirt loin,
Though the end in sight was a vice, I say.
You of the virtue (we issue join)
How strive you? *De te, fabula!*   250

LOVE IN A LIFE

I

Room after room,
I hunt the house through
We inhabit together.
Heart, fear nothing, for, heart, thou shalt find her —
Next time, herself! — not the trouble behind her
Left in the curtain, the couch's perfume!
As she brushed it, the cornice-wreath blossomed anew:
Yon looking-glass gleamed at the wave of her feather.

II

Yet the day wears,
And door succeeds door;   10
I try the fresh fortune —
Range the wide house from the wing to the centre.
Still the same chance! she goes out as I enter.
Spend my whole day in the quest, — who cares?
But 'tis twilight, you see, — with such suites to explore,
Such closets to search, such alcoves to importune!

LIFE IN A LOVE

Escape me?
Never —
Beloved!
While I am I, and you are you,
    So long as the world contains us both,
    Me the loving and you the loth,
While the one eludes, must the other pursue.
My life is a fault at last, I fear:
    It seems too much like a fate, indeed!
    Though I do my best I shall scarce succeed.   10

But what if I fail of my purpose here?
It is but to keep the nerves at strain,
    To dry one's eyes and laugh at a fall,
And baffled, get up and begin again, —
    So the chace takes up one's life, that's all.
While, look but once from your farthest bound
    At me so deep in the dust and dark,
No sooner the old hope goes to ground
    Than a new one, straight to the self-same mark,
I shape me —   20
Ever
Removed!

HOW IT STRIKES A CONTEMPORARY

I ONLY knew one poet in my life:
And this, or something like it, was his way.

    You saw go up and down Valladolid,
A man of mark, to know next time you saw.
His very serviceable suit of black
Was courtly once and conscientious still,
And many might have worn it, though none did:
The cloak, that somewhat shone and showed the threads,
Had purpose, and the ruff, significance.
He walked and tapped the pavement with his cane,   10
Scenting the world, looking it full in face,
An old dog, bald and blindish, at his heels.
They turned up, now, the alley by the church,
That leads nowhither; now, they breathed themselves
On the main promenade just at the wrong time:
You'd come upon his scrutinizing hat,
Making a peaked shade blacker than itself
Against the single window spared some house
Intact yet with its mouldered Moorish work, —
Or else surprise the ferrel of his stick   20
Trying the mortar's temper 'tween the chinks
Of some new shop a-building, French and fine.
He stood and watched the cobbler at his trade,
The man who slices lemons into drink,
The coffee-roaster's brazier, and the boys

That volunteer to help him turn its winch.
He glanced o'er books on stalls with half an eye,
And fly-leaf ballads on the vendor's string,
And broad-edge bold-print posters by the wall.
He took such cognizance of men and things,   30
If any beat a horse, you felt he saw;
If any cursed a woman, he took note;
Yet stared at nobody, — you stared at him,
And found, less to your pleasure than surprise,
He seemed to know you and expect as much.
So, next time that a neighbor's tongue was loosed,
It marked the shameful and notorious fact,
We had among us, not so much a spy,
As a recording chief-inquisitor,
The town's true master if the town but knew!   40
We merely kept a governor for form,
While this man walked about and took account
Of all thought, said and acted, then went home,
And wrote it fully to our Lord the King
Who has an itch to know things, he knows why,
And reads them in his bedroom of a night.
Oh, you might smile! there wanted not a touch,
A tang of . . . well, it was not wholly ease
As back into your mind the man's look came.
Stricken in years a little, — such a brow   50
His eyes had to live under! — clear as flint
On either side the formidable nose
Curved, cut and colored like an eagle's claw.
Had he to do with A.'s surprising fate?
When altogether old B. disappeared
And young C. got his mistress, — was't our friend,
His letter to the King, that did it all?
What paid the bloodless man for so much pains?
Our Lord the King has favorites manifold,
And shifts his ministry some once a month;   60
Our city gets new governors at whiles, —
But never word or sign, that I could hear,
Notified to this man about the streets
The King's approval of those letters conned
The last thing duly at the dead of night.
Did the man love his office? Frowned our Lord,
Exhorting when none heard — "Beseech me not!
Too far above my people, — beneath me!
I set the watch, — how should the people know?

Forget them, keep me all the more in mind!" 70
Was some such understanding 'twixt the two?

I found no truth in one report at least —
That if you tracked him to his home, down lanes
Beyond the Jewry, and as clean to pace,
You found he ate his supper in a room
Blazing with lights, four Titians on the wall,
And twenty naked girls to change his plate!
Poor man, he lived another kind of life
In that new stuccoed third house by the bridge,
Fresh-painted, rather smart than otherwise! 80
The whole street might o'erlook him as he sat,
Leg crossing leg, one foot on the dog's back,
Playing a decent cribbage with his maid
(Jacynth, you're sure her name was) o'er the cheese
And fruit, three red halves of starved winter-pears,
Or treat of radishes in April. Nine,
Ten, struck the church clock, straight to bed went he.

My father, like the man of sense he was,
Would point him out to me a dozen times;
" 'St — 'St," he'd whisper, "the Corregidor!" 90
I had been used to think that personage
Was one with lacquered breeches, lustrous belt,
And feathers like a forest in his hat,
Who blew a trumpet and proclaimed the news,
Announced the bull-fights, gave each church its turn,
And memorized the miracle in vogue!
He had a great observance from us boys;
We were in error; that was not the man.

I'd like now, yet had haply been afraid,
To have just looked, when this man came to die, 100
And seen who lined the clean gay garret-sides
And stood about the neat low truckle-bed,
With the heavenly manner of relieving guard.
Here had been, mark, the general-in-chief,
Thro' a whole campaign of the world's life and death,
Doing the King's work all the dim day long,
In his old coat and up to knees in mud,
Smoked like a herring, dining on a crust, —
And, now the day was won, relieved at once!
No further show or need for that old coat. 110

You are sure, for one thing! Bless us, all the while
How sprucely we are dressed out, you and I!
A second, and the angels alter that.
Well, I could never write a verse, — could you?
Let's to the Prado and make the most of time.

THE LAST RIDE TOGETHER

I

I SAID — Then, dearest, since 'tis so,
Since now at length my fate I know,
Since nothing all my love avails,
Since all, my life seemed meant for, fails,
  Since this was written and needs must be —
My whole heart rises up to bless
Your name in pride and thankfulness!
Take back the hope you gave, — I claim
Only a memory of the same,
 — And this beside, if you will not blame,   10
  Your leave for one more last ride with me.

II

My mistress bent that brow of hers;
Those deep dark eyes where pride demurs
When pity would be softening through,
Fixed me a breathing-while or two
  With life or death in the balance: right!
The blood replenished me again;
My last thought was at least not vain:
I and my mistress, side by side
Shall be together, breathe and ride,   20
So, one day more am I deified.
  Who knows but the world may end to-night?

III

Hush! if you saw some western cloud
All billowy-bosomed, over-bowed
By many benedictions — sun's
And moon's and evening-star's at once —
  And so, you, looking and loving best,

Conscious grew, your passion drew
Cloud, sunset, moonrise, star-shine too,
Down on you, near and yet more near,   30
Till flesh must fade for heaven was here! —
Thus leant she and lingered — joy and fear!
    Thus lay she a moment on my breast.

IV

Then we began to ride. My soul
Smoothed itself out, a long-cramped scroll
Freshening and fluttering in the wind.
Past hopes already lay behind.
    What need to strive with a life awry?
Had I said that, had I done this,
So might I gain, so might I miss.   40
Might she have loved me? just as well
She might have hated, who can tell!
Where had I been now if the worst befell?
    And here we are riding, she and I.

V

Fail I alone, in words and deeds?
Why, all men strive and who succeeds?
We rode; it seemed my spirit flew,
Saw other regions, cities new,
    As the world rushed by on either side.
I thought, — All labor, yet no less   50
Bear up beneath their unsuccess.
Look at the end of work, contrast
The petty done, the undone vast,
This present of theirs with the hopeful past!
    I hoped she would love me; here we ride.

VI

What hand and brain went ever paired?
What heart alike conceived and dared?
What act proved all its thought had been?
What will but felt the fleshly screen?
    We ride and I see her bosom heave.   60
There's many a crown for who can reach.
Ten lines, a statesman's life in each!

The flag stuck on a heap of bones,
A soldier's doing! what atones?
They scratch his name on the Abbey-stones.
 My riding is better, by their leave.

VII

What does it all mean, poet? Well,
Your brains beat into rhythm, you tell
What we felt only; you expressed
You hold things beautiful the best,   **70**
 And pace them in rhyme so, side by side.
'Tis something, nay 'tis much: but then,
Have you yourself what's best for men?
Are you — poor, sick, old ere your time —
Nearer one whit your own sublime
Than we who never have turned a rhyme?
 Sing, riding's a joy! For me, I ride.

VIII

And you, great sculptor — so, you gave
A score of years to Art, her slave,
And that's your Venus, whence we turn   **80**
To yonder girl that fords the burn!
 You acquiesce, and shall I repine?
What, man of music, you grown gray
With notes and nothing else to say,
Is this your sole praise from a friend,
"Greatly his opera's strains intend,
But in music we know how fashions end!"
 I gave my youth; but we ride, in fine.

IX

Who knows what's fit for us? Had fate
Proposed bliss here should sublimate   90
My being — had I signed the bond —
Still one must lead some life beyond,
 Have a bliss to die with, dim-descried.
This foot once planted on the goal,
This glory-garland round my soul,
Could I descry such? Try and test!
I sink back shuddering from the quest.
Earth being so good, would Heaven seem best?
 Now, Heaven and she are beyond this ride.

x

And yet — she has not spoke so long!   100
What if heaven be that, fair and strong
At life's best, with our eyes upturned
Whither life's flower is first discerned,
    We, fixed so, ever should so abide?
What if we still ride on, we two
With life for ever old yet new,
Changed not in kind but in degree,
The instant made eternity, —
And heaven just prove that I and she
    Ride, ride together, forever ride?   110

THE PATRIOT

An Old Story

I

It was roses, roses, all the way,
    With myrtle mixed in my path like mad:
The house-roofs seemed to heave and sway,
    The church-spires flamed, such flags they had,
A year ago on this very day.

II

The air broke into a mist with bells,
    The old walls rocked with the crowd and cries.
Had I said, "Good folk, mere noise repels —
    But give me your sun from yonder skies!"
They had answered, "And afterward, what else?"   10

III

Alack, it was I who leaped at the sun
    To give it my loving friends to keep!
Naught man could do, have I left undone:
    And you see my harvest, what I reap
This very day, now a year is run.

IV

There's nobody on the house-tops now —
  Just a palsied few at the windows set;
For the best of the sight is, all allow,
  At the Shambles' Gate — or, better yet,
By the very scaffold's foot, I trow.   20

V

I go in the rain, and, more than needs,
  A rope cuts both my wrists behind;
And I think, by the feel, my forehead bleeds,
  For they fling, whoever has a mind,
Stones at me for my year's misdeeds.

VI

Thus I entered, and thus I go!
  In triumphs, people have dropped down dead.
"Paid by the world, what dost thou owe
  Me?" — God might question; now instead,
'Tis God shall repay: I am safer so.   30

BISHOP BLOUGRAM'S APOLOGY

No more wine? then we'll push back chairs and talk.
A final glass for me, though: cool i' faith!
We ought to have our Abbey back, you see.
It's different, preaching in basilicas,
And doing duty in some masterpiece
Like this of brother Pugin's, bless his heart!
I doubt if they're half baked, those chalk rosettes,
Ciphers and stucco-twiddlings everywhere;
It's just like breathing in a lime-kiln: eh?
These hot long ceremonies of our church   10
Cost us a little — oh, they pay the price,
You take me — amply pay it! Now, we'll talk.

So, you despise me, Mr. Gigadibs.
No deprecation, — nay, I beg you, sir!
Beside 'tis our engagement: don't you know,
I promised, if you'd watch a dinner out,

We'd see truth dawn together? — truth that peeps
Over the glasses' edge when dinner's done,
And body gets its sop and holds its noise
And leaves soul free a little. Now's the time: 20
Truth's break of day! You do despise me then.
And if I say, "despise me," — never fear!
I know you do not in a certain sense —
Not in my arm-chair, for example: here,
I well imagine you respect my place
(*Status, entourage,* worldly circumstance)
Quite to its value — very much indeed:
— Are up to the protesting eyes of you
In pride at being seated here for once —
You'll turn it to such capital account!   30
When somebody, through years and years to come,
Hints of the bishop, — names me — that's enough:
"Blougram? I knew him" — (into it you slide)
"Dined with him once, a Corpus Christi Day,
All alone, we two; he's a clever man:
And after dinner, — why, the wine you know, —
Oh, there was wine, and good! — what with the wine . . .
'Faith, we began upon all sorts of talk!
He's no bad fellow, Blougram; he had seen
Something of mine he relished, some review: 40
He's quite above their humbug in his heart,
Half said as much, indeed — the thing's his trade.
I warrant, Blougram's sceptical at times:
How otherwise? I liked him, I confess!"
Che che, my dear sir, as we say at Rome,
Don't you protest now! It's fair give and take;
You have had your turn and spoken your home-truths:
The hand's mine now, and here you follow suit.

        Thus much conceded, still the first fact stays —
You do despise me; your ideal of life   50
Is not the bishop's: you would not be I.
You would like better to be Goethe, now,
Or Buonaparte, or, bless me, lower still,
Count D'Orsay, — so you did what you preferred,
Spoke as you thought, and, as you cannot help,
Believed or disbelieved, no matter what,
So long as on that point, whate'er it was,
You loosed your mind, were whole and sole yourself.
— That, my ideal never can include,

Upon that element of truth and worth   60
Never be based! for say they make me Pope —
(They can't — suppose it for our argument!)
Why, there I'm at my tether's end, I've reached
My height, and not a height which pleases you:
An unbelieving Pope won't do, you say.
It's like those eerie stories nurses tell,
Of how some actor on a stage played Death,
With pasteboard crown, sham orb and tinselled dart,
And called himself the monarch of the world;
Then, going in the tire-room afterward,   70
Because the play was done, to shift himself,
Got touched upon the sleeve familiarly,
The moment he had shut the closet door,
By Death himself. Thus God might touch a Pope
At unawares, ask what his baubles mean,
And whose part he presumed to play just now.
Best be yourself, imperial, plain and true!

So, drawing comfortable breath again,
You weigh and find, whatever more or less
I boast of my ideal realized   80
Is nothing in the balance when opposed
To your ideal, your grand simple life,
Of which you will not realize one jot.
I am much, you are nothing; you would be all,
I would be merely much: you beat me there.

No, friend you do not beat me: hearken why!
The common problem, yours, mine, every one's,
Is — not to fancy what were fair in life
Provided it could be, — but, finding first
What may be, then find how to make it fair   90
Up to our means: a very different thing!
No abstract intellectual plan of life
Quite irrespective of life's plainest laws,
But one, a man, who is man and nothing more,
May lead within a world which (by your leave)
Is Rome or London, not Fool's-paradise.
Embellish Rome, idealize away,
Make paradise of London if you can,
You're welcome, nay, you're wise.

A simile!
We mortals cross the ocean of this world   100
Each in his average cabin of a life;
The best's not big, the worst yields elbow-room.
Now for our six months' voyage — how prepare?
You come on shipboard with a landsman's list
Of things he calls convenient: so they are!
An India screen is pretty furniture,
A piano-forte is a fine resource,
All Balzac's novels occupy one shelf,
The new edition fifty volumes long;
And little Greek books, with the funny type   110
They get up well at Leipsic, fill the next:
Go on! slabbed marble, what a bath it makes!
And Parma's pride, the Jerome, let us add!
'Twere pleasant could Correggio's fleeting glow
Hang full in face of one where'er one roams,
Since he more than the others brings with him
Italy's self, — the marvellous Modenese! —
Yet was not on your list before, perhaps.
— Alas, friend, here's the agent . . . is't the name?
The captain, or whoever's master here —   120
You see him screw his face up; what's his cry
Ere you set foot on shipboard? "Six feet square!"
If you won't understand what six feet mean,
Compute and purchase stores accordingly —
And if, in pique because he overhauls
Your Jerome, piano, bath, you come on board
Bare — why, you cut a figure at the first
While sympathetic landsmen see you off;
Not afterward, when long ere half seas over,
You peep up from your utterly naked boards   130
Into some snug and well-appointed berth,
Like mine for instance (try the cooler jug —
Put back the other, but don't jog the ice!)
And mortified you mutter "Well and good;
He sits enjoying his sea-furniture;
'Tis stout and proper, and there's store of it:
Though I've the better notion, all agree,
Of fitting rooms up. Hang the carpenter,
Neat ship-shape fixings and contrivances —
I would have brought my Jerome, frame and all!"   140
And meantime you bring nothing: never mind —

You've proved your artist-nature: what you don't
You might bring, so despise me, as I say.

    Now come, let's backward to the starting-place.
See my way: we're two college friends, suppose.
Prepare together for our voyage, then;
Each note and check the other in his work, —
Here's mine, a bishop's outfit; criticise!
What's wrong? why won't you be a bishop too?

    Why first, you don't believe, you don't and can't,   **150**
(Not statedly, that is, and fixedly
And absolutely and exclusively)
In any revelation called divine.
No dogmas nail your faith; and what remains
But say so, like the honest man you are?
First, therefore, overhaul theology!
Nay, I too, not a fool, you please to think,
Must find believing every whit as hard:
And if I do not frankly say as much,
The ugly consequence is clear enough.   **160**

    Now wait, my friend: well, I do not believe —
If you'll accept no faith that is not fixed,
Absolute and exclusive, as you say.
You're wrong — I mean to prove it in due time.
Meanwhile, I know where difficulties lie
I could not, cannot solve, nor ever shall,
So give up hope accordingly to solve —
(To you, and over the wine). Our dogmas then
With both of us, though in unlike degree,
Missing full credence — overboard with them!   **170**
I mean to meet you on your own premise:
Good, there go mine in company with yours!

    And now what are we? unbelievers both,
Calm and complete, determinately fixed
To-day, to-morrow and forever, pray?
You'll guarantee me that? Not so, I think!
In no wise! all we've gained is, that belief,
As unbelief before, shakes us by fits,
Confounds us like its predecessor. Where's
The gain? how can we guard our unbelief,   **180**

Make it bear fruit to us? — the problem here.
Just when we are safest, there's a sunset-touch,
A fancy from a flower-bell, some one's death,
A chorus-ending from Euripides, —
And that's enough for fifty hopes and fears
As old and new at once as nature's self,
To rap and knock and enter in our soul,
Take hands and dance there, a fantastic ring,
Round the ancient idol, on his base again, —
The grand Perhaps! We look on helplessly.   190
There the old misgivings, crooked questions are —
This good God, — what he could do, if he would,
Would, if he could — then must have done long since:
If so, when, where and how? some way must be, —
Once feel about, and soon or late you hit
Some sense, in which it might be, after all.
Why not, "The Way, the Truth, the Life?"

                              — That way
Over the mountain, which who stands upon
Is apt to doubt if it be meant for a road;
While, if he views it from the waste itself,   200
Up goes the line there, plain from base to brow,
Not vague, mistakable! what's a break or two
Seen from the unbroken desert either side?
And then (to bring in fresh philosophy)
What if the breaks themselves should prove at last
The most consummate of contrivances
To train a man's eye, teach him what is faith?
And so we stumble at truth's very test!
All we have gained then by our unbelief
Is a life of doubt diversified by faith,   210
For one of faith diversified by doubt:
We called the chess-board white, — we call it black.

     "Well," you rejoin, "the end's no worse, at least;
We've reason for both colors on the board:
Why not confess then, where I drop the faith
And you the doubt, that I'm as right as you?"

     Because, friend, in the next place, this being so,
And both things even, — faith and unbelief
Left to a man's choice, — we'll proceed a step,
Returning to our image, which I like.   220

A man's choice, yes — but a cabin-passenger's —
The man made for the special life o' the world —
Do you forget him? I remember though!
Consult our ship's conditions and you find
One and but one choice suitable to all;
The choice, that you unluckily prefer,
Turning things topsy-turvy — they or it
Going to the ground. Belief or unbelief
Bears upon life, determines its whole course,
Begins at its beginning. See the world   230
Such as it is, — you made it not, nor I;
I mean to take it as it is, — and you,
Not so you'll take it, — though you get naught else.
I know the special kind of life I like,
What suits the most my idiosyncrasy,
Brings out the best of me and bears me fruit
In power, peace, pleasantness and length of days.
I find that positive belief does this
For me, and unbelief, no whit of this.
— For you, it does, however? — that, we'll try!   240
'Tis clear, I cannot lead my life, at least,
Induce the world to let me peaceably,
Without declaring at the outset, "Friends,
I absolutely and peremptorily
Believe!" — I say, faith is my waking life:
One sleeps, indeed, and dreams at intervals,
We know, but waking's the main point with us,
And my provision's for life's waking part.
Accordingly, I use heart, head and hand
All day, I build, scheme, study, and make friends;   250
And when night overtakes me, down I lie,
Sleep, dream a little, and get done with it,
The sooner the better, to begin afresh.
What's midnight doubt before the dayspring's faith?
You, the philosopher, that disbelieve,
That recognize the night, give dreams their weight —
To be consistent you should keep your bed,
Abstain from healthy acts that prove you man,
For fear you drowse perhaps at unawares!
And certainly at night you'll sleep and dream,   260
Live through the day and bustle as you please.
And so you live to sleep as I to wake,
To unbelieve as I to still believe?

Well, and the common sense o' the world calls you
Bed-ridden, — and its good things come to me.
Its estimation, which is half the fight,
That's the first-cabin comfort I secure:
The next . . . but you perceive with half an eye!
Come, come, it's best believing, if we may;
You can't but own that!

                       Next, concede again,   270
If once we choose belief, on all accounts
We can't be too decisive in our faith,
Conclusive and exclusive in its terms,
To suit the world which gives us the good things.
In every man's career are certain points
Whereon he dares not be indifferent;
The world detects him clearly, if he dare,
As baffled at the game, and losing life.
He may care little or he may care much
For riches, honor, pleasure, work, repose,   280
Since various theories of life and life's
Success are extant which might easily
Comport with either estimate of these;
And whoso chooses wealth or poverty,
Labor or quiet, is not judged a fool
Because his fellow would choose otherwise:
We let him choose upon his own account
So long as he's consistent with his choice.
But certain points, left wholly to himself,
When once a man has arbitrated on,   290
We say he must succeed there or go hang.
Thus, he should wed the woman he loves most
Or needs most, whatsoe'er the love or need —
For he can't wed twice. Then, he must avouch,
Or follow, at the least, sufficiently,
The form of faith his conscience holds the best,
Whate'er the process of conviction was:
For nothing can compensate his mistake
On such a point, the man himself being judge:
He cannot wed twice, nor twice lose his soul.   300

   Well now, there's one great form of Christian faith
I happened to be born in — which to teach
Was given me as I grew up, on all hands,
As best and readiest means of living by;

The same on examination being proved
The most pronounced moreover, fixed, precise
And absolute form of faith in the whole world —
Accordingly, most potent of all forms
For working on the world. Observe, my friend!
Such as you know me, I am free to say,   310
In these hard latter days which hamper one,
Myself — by no immoderate exercise
Of intellect and learning, but the tact
To let external forces work for me,
— Bid the street's stones be bread and they are bread:
Bid Peter's creed, or rather, Hildebrand's,
Exalt me o'er my fellows in the world
And make my life an ease and joy and pride;
It does so, — which for me's a great point gained,
Who have a soul and body that exact   320
A comfortable care in many ways.
There's power in me and will to dominate
Which I must exercise, they hurt me else:
In many ways I need mankind's respect,
Obedience, and the love that's born of fear:
While at the same time, there's a taste I have,
A toy of soul, a titillating thing,
Refuses to digest these dainties crude.
The naked life is gross till clothed upon:
I must take what men offer, with a grace   330
As though I would not, could I help it, take!
An uniform I wear though over-rich —
Something imposed o   no choice of mine;
No fancy-dress worn f   re fancy's sake
And despicable therefore! now folk kneel
And kiss my hand — of course the Church's hand.
Thus I am made, thus life is best for me,
And thus that it should be I have procured;
And thus it could not be another way,
I venture to imagine.

                    You'll reply,   340
So far my choice, no doubt, is a success;
But were I made of better elements,
With nobler instinct   'astes, like ,
I hardly would accou   hing success
Though it did all for me I say.

But, friend,
We speak of what is; not of what might be,
And how 'twere better if 'twere otherwise.
I am the man you see here plain enough:
Grant I'm a beast, why, beasts must lead beasts' lives!
Suppose I own at once to tail and claws;   350
The tailless man exceeds me: but being tailed
I'll lash out lion fashion, and leave apes
To dock their stump and dress their haunches up.
My business is not to remake myself,
But make the absolute best of what God made.
Or — our first simile — though you prove me doomed
To a viler berth still, to the steerage-hole,
The sheep-pen or the pig-stye, I should strive
To make what use of each were possible;
And as this cabin gets upholstery,   360
That hutch should rustle with sufficient straw.

But, friend, I don't acknowledge quite so fast
I fail of all your manhood's lofty tastes
Enumerated so complacently,
On the mere ground that you forsooth can find
In this particular life I choose to lead
No fit provision for them. Can you not?
Say you, my fault is I address myself
To grosser estimators than should judge?
And that's no way of holding up the soul,   370
Which, nobler, needs men's praise perhaps, yet knows
One wise man's verdict outweighs all the fools' —
Would like the two, but, forced to choose, takes that.
I pine among my million imbeciles
(You think) aware some dozen men of sense
Eye me and know me, whether I believe
In the last winking Virgin, as I vow,
And am a fool, or disbelieve in her
And am a knave, — approve in neither case,
Withhold their voices though I look their way: 380
Like Verdi when, at his worst opera's end
(The thing they gave at Florence, — what's its name?)
While the mad houseful's plaudits near outbang
His orchestra of salt-box, tongs and bones,
He looks through all the roaring and the wreaths
Where sits Rossini patient in his stall.

        Nay, friend, I meet you with an answer here —
That even your prime men who appraise their kind
Are men still, catch a wheel within a wheel,
See more in a truth than the truth's simple self,   390
Confuse themselves. You see lads walk the street
Sixty the minute; what's to note in that?
You see one lad o'erstride a chimney-stack;
Him you must watch — he's sure to fall, yet stands!
Our interest's on the dangerous edge of things.
The honest thief, the tender murderer,
The superstitious atheist, demirep
That loves and saves her soul in new French books —
We watch while these in equilibrium keep
The giddy line midway: one step aside,   400
They're classed and done with. I, then, keep the line
Before your sages, — just the men to shrink
From the gross weights, coarse scales and labels broad
You offer their refinement. Fool or knave?
Why needs a bishop be a fool or knave
When there's a thousand diamond weights between?
So, I enlist them. Your picked twelve, you'll find,
Profess themselves indignant, scandalized
At thus being held unable to explain
How a superior man who disbelieves   410
May not believe as well: that's Schelling's way!
It's through my coming in the tail of time,
Nicking the minute with a happy tact.
Had I been born three hundred years ago
They'd say, "What's strange? Blougram of course believes;"
And, seventy years since, "disbelieves of course."
But now, "He may believe; and yet, and yet
How can he?" All eyes turn with interest.
Whereas, step off the line on either side —
You, for example, clever to a fault,   420
The rough and ready man who write apace,
Read somewhat seldomer, think perhaps even less —
You disbelieve! Who wonders and who cares?
Lord So-and-so — his coat bedropped with wax,
All Peter's chains about his waist, his back
Brave with the needlework of Noodledom —
Believes! Again, who wonders and who cares?
But I, the man of sense and learning too,
The able to think yet act, the this, the that,

I, to believe at this late time of day!   430
Enough; you see, I need not fear contempt.

      — Except it's yours! Admire me as these may,
You don't. But whom at least do you admire?
Present your own perfection, your ideal,
Your pattern man for a minute — oh, make haste,
Is it Napoleon you would have us grow?
Concede the means; allow his head and hand,
(A large concession, clever as you are)
Good! In our common primal element
Of unbelief (we can't believe, you know —   440
We're still at that admission, recollect!)
Where do you find — apart from, towering o'er
The secondary temporary aims
Which satisfy the gross taste you despise —
Where do you find his star? — his crazy trust
God knows through what or in what? it's alive
And shines and leads him, and that's all we want.
Have we aught in our sober night shall point
Such ends as his were, and direct the means
Of working out our purpose straight as his,   450
Nor bring a moment's trouble on success
With after-care to justify the same?
— Be a Napoleon, and yet disbelieve —
Why, the man's mad, friend, take his light away!
What's the vague good o' the world, for which you dare
With comfort to yourself blow millions up?
We neither of us see it! we do see
The blown-up millions — spatter of their brains
And writhing of their bowels and so forth,
In that bewildering entanglement   460
Of horrible eventualities
Past calculation to the end of time!
Can I mistake for some clear word of God
(Which were my ample warrant for it all)
His puff of hazy instinct, idle talk,
"The State, that's I," quack-nonsense about crowns,
And (when one beats the man to his last hold)
A vague idea of setting things to rights,
Policing people efficaciously,
More to their profit, most of all to his own;   470
The whole to end that dismallest of ends
By an Austrian marriage, cant to us the Church,

And resurrection of the old *régime?*
Would I, who hope to live a dozen years,
Fight Austerlitz for reasons such and such?
No: for, concede me but the merest chance
Doubt may be wrong — there's judgment, life to come!
With just that chance, I dare not. Doubt proves right?
This present life is all? — you offer me
Its dozen noisy years, without a chance   480
That wedding an archduchess, wearing lace,
And getting called by divers new-coined names,
Will drive off ugly thoughts and let me dine,
Sleep, read and chat in quiet as I like!
Therefore I will not.

            Take another case;
Fit up the cabin yet another way.
What say you to the poets? shall we write
Hamlet, Othello — make the world our own,
Without a risk to run of either sort?
I can't! — to put the strongest reason first.   490
"But try," you urge, "the trying shall suffice;
The aim, if reached or not, makes great the life:
Try to be Shakespeare, leave the rest to fate!"
Spare my self-knowledge — there's no fooling me!
If I prefer remaining my poor self,
I say so not in self-dispraise but praise.
If I'm a Shakespeare, let the well alone;
Why should I try to be what now I am?
If I'm no Shakespeare, as too probable, —
His power and consciousness and self-delight   500
And all we want in common, shall I find —
Trying forever? while on points of taste
Wherewith, to speak it humbly, he and I
Are dowered alike — I'll ask you, I or he,
Which in our two lives realizes most?
Much, he imagined — somewhat, I possess.
He had the imagination; stick to that!
Let him say, "In the face of my soul's works
Your world is worthless and I touch it not
Lest I should wrong them" — I'll withdraw my plea.   510
But does he say so? look upon his life!
Himself, who only can, gives judgment there.
He leaves his towers and gorgeous palaces
To build the trimmest house in Stratford town;

Saves money, spends it, owns the worth of things,
Giulio Romano's pictures, Dowland's lute;
Enjoys a show, respects the puppets, too,
And none more, had he seen its entry once,
Than "Pandulph, of fair Milan cardinal."
Why then should I who play that personage,   520
The very Pandulph Shakespeare's fancy made,
Be told that had the poet chanced to start
From where I stand now (some degree like mine
Being just the goal he ran his race to reach)
He would have run the whole race back, forsooth,
And left being Pandulph, to begin write plays?
Ah, the earth's best can be but the earth's best!
Did Shakespeare live, he could but sit at home
And get himself in dreams the Vatican,
Greek busts, Venetian paintings, Roman walls,   530
And English books, none equal to his own,
Which I read, bound in gold (he never did).
— Terni's fall, Naples' bay and Gothard's top —
Eh, friend? I could not fancy one of these;
But, as I pour this claret, there they are:
I've gained them — crossed St. Gothard last July
With ten mules to the carriage and a bed
Slung inside; is my hap the worse for that?
We want the same things, Shakespeare and myself,
And what I want, I have: he, gifted more,   540
Could fancy he too had them when he liked,
But not so thoroughly that, if fate allowed,
He would not have them also in my sense.
We play one game; I send the ball aloft
No less adroitly that of fifty strokes
Scarce five go o'er the wall so wide and high
Which sends them back to me: I wish and get.
He struck balls higher and with better skill,
But at a poor fence level with his head,
And hit — his Stratford house, a coat of arms,   550
Successful dealings in his grain and wool, —
While I receive heaven's incense in my nose
And style myself the cousin of Queen Bess.
Ask him, if this life's all, who wins the game?

　　Believe — and our whole argument breaks up.
Enthusiasm's the best thing, I repeat;

Only, we can't command it; fire and life
Are all, dead matter's nothing, we agree:
And be it a mad dream or God's very breath,
The fact's the same, — belief's fire, once in us,   560
Makes of all else mere stuff to show itself:
We penetrate our life with such a glow
As fire lends wood and iron — this turns steel,
That burns to ash — all's one, fire proves its power
For good or ill, since men call flare success.
But paint a fire, it will not therefore burn.
Light one in me, I'll find it food enough!
Why, to be Luther — that's a life to lead,
Incomparably better than my own.
He comes, reclaims God's earth for God, he says,   570
Sets up God's rule again by simple means,
Re-opens a shut book, and all is done.
He flared out in the flaring of mankind;
Such Luther's luck was: how shall such be mine?
If he succeeded, nothing's left to do:
And if he did not altogether — well,
Strauss is the next advance. All Strauss should be
I might be also. But to what result?
He looks upon no future: Luther did.
What can I gain on the denying side?   580
Ice makes no conflagration. State the facts,
Read the text right, emancipate the world —
The emancipated world enjoys itself
With scarce a thank-you: Blougram told it first
It could not owe a farthing, — not to him
More than Saint Paul! 'twould press its pay, you think?
Then add there's still that plaguy hundredth chance
Strauss may be wrong. And so a risk is run —
For what gain? not for Luther's, who secured
A real heaven in his heart throughout his life,   590
Supposing death a little altered things.

   "Ay, but since really you lack faith," you cry,
"You run the same risk really on all sides,
In cool indifference as bold unbelief.
As well be Strauss as swing 'twixt Paul and him.
It's not worth having, such imperfect faith,
No more available to do faith's work
Than unbelief like mine. Whole faith, or none!"

Softly, my friend! I must dispute that point.
Once own the use of faith, I'll find you faith.   600
We're back on Christian ground. You call for faith:
I show you doubt, to prove that faith exists.
The more of doubt, the stronger faith, I say,
If faith o'ercomes doubt. How I know it does?
By life and man's free will, God gave for that!
To mould life as we choose it, shows our choice:
That's our one act, the previous work's his own.
You criticize the soul? it reared this tree —
This broad life and whatever fruit it bears!
What matter though I doubt at every pore,   610
Head-doubts, heart-doubts, doubts at my fingers' ends,
Doubts in the trivial work of every day,
Doubts at the very bases of my soul
In the grand moments when she probes herself —
If finally I have a life to show,
The thing I did, brought out in evidence
Against the thing done to me underground
By hell and all its brood, for aught I know?
I say, whence sprang this? shows it faith or doubt?
All's doubt in me; where's break of faith in this?   620
It is the idea, the feeling and the love,
God means mankind should strive for and show forth
Whatever be the process to that end, —
And not historic knowledge, logic sound,
And metaphysical acumen, sure!
"What think ye of Christ," friend? when all's done and said,
Like you this Christianity or not?
It may be false, but will you wish it true?
Has it your vote to be so if it can?
Trust you an instinct silenced long ago   630
That will break silence and enjoin you love
What mortified philosophy is hoarse,
And all in vain, with bidding you despise?
If you desire faith — then you've faith enough:
What else seeks God — nay, what else seek ourselves?
You form a notion of me, we'll suppose,
On hearsay; it's a favorable one:
"But still" (you add), "there was no such good man,
Because of contradiction in the facts.
One proves, for instance, he was born in Rome,   640
This Blougram; yet throughout the tales of him
I see he figures as an Englishman."

Well, the two things are reconcilable,
But would I rather you discovered that,
Subjoining — "Still, what matter though they be?
Blougram concerns me naught, born here or there."

    Pure faith indeed — you know not what you ask!
Naked belief in God the Omnipotent,
Omniscient, Omnipresent, sears too much
The sense of conscious creatures to be borne.   650
It were the seeing him, no flesh shall dare.
Some think, Creation's meant to show him forth:
I say it's meant to hide him all it can,
And that's what all the blessed evil's for.
Its use in Time is to environ us,
Our breath, our drop of dew, with shield enough
Against that sight till we can bear its stress.
Under a vertical sun, the exposed brain
And lidless eye and disemprisoned heart
Less certainly would wither up at once   660
Than mind, confronted with the truth of him.
But time and earth case-harden us to live;
The feeblest sense is trusted most; the child
Feels God a moment, ichors o'er the place,
Plays on and grows to be a man like us.
With me, faith means perpetual unbelief
Kept quiet like the snake 'neath Michael's foot
Who stands calm just because he feels it writhe.
Or, if that's too ambitious, — here's my box —
I need the excitation of a pinch   670
Threatening the torpor of the inside-nose
Nigh on the imminent sneeze that never comes.
"Leave it in peace" advise the simple folk:
Make it aware of peace by itching-fits,
Say I — let doubt occasion still more faith!

    You'll say, once all believed, man, woman, child,
In that dear middle-age these noodles praise.
How you'd exult if I could put you back
Six hundred years, blot out cosmogony,
Geology, ethnology, what not,   680
(Greek endings, each the little passing-bell
That signifies some faith's about to die),
And set you square with Genesis again, —
When such a traveller told you his last news,

He saw the ark a-top of Ararat
But did not climb there since 'twas getting dusk
And robber-bands infest the mountain's foot!
How should you feel, I ask, in such an age,
How act? As other people felt and did;
With soul more blank than this decanter's knob,   690
Believe — and yet lie, kill, rob, fornicate
Full in belief's face, like the beast you'd be!

    No, when the fight begins within himself,
A man's worth something. God stoops o'er his head,
Satan looks up between his feet — both tug —
He's left, himself, i' the middle: the soul wakes
And grows. Prolong that battle through his life!
Never leave growing till the life to come!
Here, we've got callous to the Virgin's winks
That used to puzzle people wholesomely: 700
Men have outgrown the shame of being fools.
What are the laws of nature, not to bend
If the Church bid them? — brother Newman asks.
Up with the Immaculate Conception, then —
On to the rack with faith! — is my advice.
Will not that hurry us upon our knees,
Knocking our breasts, "It can't be — yet it shall!
Who am I, the worm, to argue with my Pope?
Low things confound the high things!" and so forth.
That's better than acquitting God with grace   710
As some folk do. He's tried — no case is proved,
Philosophy is lenient — he may go!

    You'll say, the old system's not so obsolete
But men believe still: ay, but who and where?
King Bomba's lazzaroni foster yet
The sacred flame, so Antonelli writes;
But even of these, what ragamuffin-saint
Believes God watches him continually,
As he believes in fire that it will burn,
Or rain that it will drench him? Break fire's law,   720
Sin against rain, although the penalty
Be just a singe or soaking? "No," he smiles;
"Those laws are laws that can enforce themselves."

    The sum of all is — yes, my doubt is great,
My faith's still greater, then my faith's enough.

I have read much, thought much, experienced much,
Yet would die rather than avow my fear
The Naples' liquefaction may be false,
When set to happen by the palace-clock
According to the clouds or dinner-time.   **730**
I hear you recommend, I might at least
Eliminate, decrassify my faith
Since I adopt it; keeping what I must
And leaving what I can — such points as this.
I won't — that is, I can't throw one away.
Supposing there's no truth in what I hold
About the need of trial to man's faith,
Still, when you bid me purify the same,
To such a process I discern no end.
Clearing off one excrescence to see two,   **740**
There's ever a next in size, now grown as big,
That meets the knife: I cut and cut again!
First cut the Liquefaction, what comes last
But Fichte's clever cut at God himself?
Experimentalize on sacred things!
I trust nor hand nor eye nor heart nor brain
To stop betimes: they all get drunk alike.
The first step, I am master not to take.

    You'd find the cutting-process to your taste
As much as leaving growths of lies unpruned,   **750**
Nor see more danger in it, — you retort.
Your taste's worth mine; but my taste proves more wise
When we consider that the steadfast hold
On the extreme end of the chain of faith
Gives all the advantage, makes the difference
With the rough purblind mass we seek to rule:
We are their lords, or they are free of us,
Just as we tighten or relax our hold.
So, other matters equal, we'll revert
To the first problem — which, if solved my way   **760**
And thrown into the balance, turns the scale —
How we may lead a comfortable life,
How suit our luggage to the cabin's size.

    Of course you are remarking all this time
How narrowly and grossly I view life,
Respect the creature-comforts, care to rule
The masses, and regard complacently

"The cabin," in our old phrase. Well, I do.
I act for, talk for, live for this world now,
As this world prizes action, life and talk: 770
No prejudice to what next world may prove,
Whose new laws and requirements, my best pledge
To observe then, is that I observe these now,
Shall do hereafter what I do meanwhile.
Let us concede (gratuitously though)
Next life relieves the soul of body, yields
Pure spiritual enjoyment: well, my friend,
Why lose this life i' the meantime, since its use
May be to make the next life more intense?

    Do you know, I have often had a dream   780
(Work it up in your next month's article)
Of man's poor spirit in its progress, still
Losing true life forever and a day
Through ever trying to be and ever being —
In the evolution of successive spheres —
Before its actual sphere and place of life,
Halfway into the next, which having reached,
It shoots with corresponding foolery
Halfway into the next still, on and off!
As when a traveller, bound from North to South,   790
Scouts fur in Russia: what's its use in France?
In France spurns flannel: where's its need in Spain?
In Spain drops cloth, too cumbrous for Algiers!
Linen goes next, and last the skin itself,
A superfluity at Timbuctoo.
When, through his journey, was the fool at ease?
I'm at ease now, friend; worldly in this world,
I take and like its way of life; I think
My brothers, who administer the means,
Live better for my comfort — that's good too;   800
And God, if he pronounce upon such life,
Approves my service, which is better still.
If he keep silence, — why, for you or me
Or that brute beast pulled-up in to-day's "Times,"
What odds is 't, save to ourselves, what life we lead?

    You meet me at this issue: you declare, —
All special-pleading done with — truth is truth,
And justifies itself by undreamed ways.
You don't fear but it's better, if we doubt,

To say so, act up to our truth perceived 810
However feebly. Do then, — act away!
'Tis there I'm on the watch for you. How one acts
Is, both of us agree, our chief concern:
And how you'll act is what I fain would see
If, like the candid person you appear,
You dare to make the most of your life's scheme
As I of mine, live up to its full law
Since there's no higher law that counterchecks.
Put natural religion to the test
You've just demolished the revealed with — quick 820
Down to the root of all that checks your will,
All prohibition to lie, kill and thieve,
Or even to be an atheistic priest!
Suppose a pricking to incontinence —
Philosophers deduce you chastity
Or shame, from just the fact that at the first
Whoso embraced a woman in the field,
Threw club down and forewent his brains beside,
So, stood a ready victim in the reach
Of any brother savage, club in hand; 830
Hence saw the use of going out of sight
In wood or cave to prosecute his loves:
I read this in a French book t' other day,
Does law so analyzed coerce you much?
Oh, men spin clouds of fuzz where matters end,
But you who reach where the first thread begins,
You'll soon cut that! — which means you can, but won't,
Through certain instincts, blind, unreasoned-out,
You dare not set aside, you can't tell why,
But there they are, and so you let them rule. 840
Then, friend, you seem as much a slave as I,
A liar, conscious coward and hypocrite,
Without the good the slave expects to get,
In case he has a master after all!
You own your instincts? why, what else do I,
Who want, am made for, and must have a God
Ere I can be aught, do aught? — no mere name
Want, but the true thing with what proves its truth,
To wit, a relation from that thing to me,
Touching from head to foot — which touch I feel, 850
And with it take the rest, this life of ours!
I live my life here; yours you dare not live.

    — Not as I state it, who (you please subjoin)
Disfigure such a life and call it names.
While, to your mind, remains another way
For simple men: knowledge and power have rights,
But ignorance and weakness have rights too.
There needs no crucial effort to find truth
If here or there or anywhere about:
We ought to turn each side, try hard and see,   860
And if we can't, be glad we've earned at least
The right, by one laborious proof the more,
To graze in peace earth's pleasant pasturage.
Men are not angels, neither are they brutes:
Something we may see, all we cannot see.
What need of lying? I say, I see all,
And swear to each detail the most minute
In what I think a Pan's face — you, mere cloud:
I swear I hear him speak and see him wink,
For fear, if once I drop the emphasis,   870
Mankind may doubt there's any cloud at all.
You take the simple life — ready to see,
Willing to see (for no cloud's worth a face) —
And leaving quiet what no strength can move,
And which, who bids you move? who has the right?
I bid you; but you are God's sheep, not mine:
"*Pastor est tui Dominus.*" You find
In this the pleasant pasture of our life
Much you may eat without the least offence,
Much you don't eat because your maw objects,   880
Much you would eat but that your fellow-flock
Open great eyes at you and even butt,
And thereupon you like your mates so well
You cannot please yourself, offending them;
Though when they seem exorbitantly sheep,
You weigh your pleasure with their butts and bleats
And strike the balance. Sometimes certain fears
Restrain you, real checks since you find them so;
Sometimes you please yourself and nothing checks:
And thus you graze through life with not one lie,   890
And like it best.
                But do you, in truth's name?
If so, you beat — which means you are not I —
Who needs must make earth mine and feed my fill
Not simply unbutted at, unbickered with,

But motioned to the velvet of the sward
By those obsequious wethers' very selves.
Look at me, sir; my age is double yours:
At yours, I knew beforehand, so enjoyed,
What now I should be — as, permit the word,
I pretty well imagine your whole range   900
And stretch of tether twenty years to come.
We both have minds and bodies much alike:
In truth's name, don't you want my bishopric,
My daily bread, my influence and my state?
You're young. I'm old; you must be old one day;
Will you find then, as I do hour by hour,
Women their lovers kneel to, who cut curls
From your fat lap-dog's ear to grace a brooch —
Dukes, who petition just to kiss your ring —
With much beside you know or may conceive?   910
Suppose we die to-night: well, here am I,
Such were my gains, life bore this fruit to me,
While writing all the same my articles
On music, poetry, the fictile vase
Found at Albano, chess, Anacreon's Greek.
But you — the highest honor in your life,
The thing you'll crown yourself with, all your days,
Is — dining here and drinking this last glass
I pour you out in sign of amity
Before we part forever. Of your power   920
And social influence, worldly worth in short,
Judge what's my estimation by the fact,
I do not condescend to enjoin, beseech,
Hint secrecy on one of all these words!
You're shrewd and know that should you publish one
The world would brand the lie — my enemies first,
Who'd sneer — "the bishop's an arch-hypocrite
And knave perhaps, but not so frank a fool."
Whereas I should not dare for both my ears
Breathe one such syllable, smile one such smile,   930
Before the chaplain who reflects myself —
My shade's so much more potent than your flesh.
What's your reward, self-abnegating friend?
Stood you confessed of those exceptional
And privileged great natures that dwarf mine —
A zealot with a mad ideal in reach,
A poet just about to print his ode,
A statesman with a scheme to stop this war,

An artist whose religion is his art —
I should have nothing to object: such men   940
Carry the fire, all things grow warm to them,
Their drugget's worth my purple, they beat me.
But you, — you're just as little those as I —
You, Gigadibs, who, thirty years of age,
Write stately for Blackwood's Magazine,
Believe you see two points in Hamlet's soul
Unseized by the Germans yet — which view you'll print —
Meantime the best you have to show being still
That lively lightsome article we took
Almost for the true Dickens, — what's its name?   950
"The Slum and Cellar, or Whitechapel life
Limned after dark!" it made me laugh, I know,
And pleased a month, and brought you in ten pounds.
— Success I recognize and compliment,
And therefore give you, if you choose, three words
(The card and pencil-scratch is quite enough)
Which whether here, in Dublin or New York,
Will get you, prompt as at my eyebrow's wink,
Such terms as never you aspired to get
In all our own reviews and some not ours.   960
Go write your lively sketches! be the first
"Blougram, or The Eccentric Confidence" —
Or better simply say, "The Outward-bound."
Why, men as soon would throw it in my teeth
As copy and quote the infamy chalked broad
About me on the church-door opposite.
You will not wait for that experience though,
I fancy, howsoever you decide,
To discontinue — not detesting, not
Defaming, but at least — despising me!   970

<hr />

        Over his wine so smiled and talked his hour
Sylvester Blougram, styled *in partibus*
Episcopus, nec non — (the deuce knows what
It's changed to by our novel hierarchy)
With Gigadibs the literary man,
Who played with spoons, explored his plate's design,
And ranged the olive-stones about its edge,
While the great bishop rolled him out a mind
Long crumpled, till creased consciousness lay smooth.

For Blougram, he believed, say, half he spoke.   900
The other portion, as he shaped it thus
For argumentatory purposes,
He felt his foe was foolish to dispute.
Some arbitrary accidental thoughts
That crossed his mind, amusing because new,
He chose to represent as fixtures there,
Invariable convictions (such they seemed
Beside his interlocutor's loose cards
Flung daily down, and not the same way twice)
While certain hell-deep instincts, man's weak tongue   990
Is never bold to utter in their truth
Because styled hell-deep ('tis an old mistake
To place hell at the bottom of the earth)
He ignored these, — not having in readiness
Their nomenclature and philosophy:
He said true things, but called them by wrong names.
"On the whole," he thought, "I justify myself
On every point where cavillers like this
Oppugn my life: he tries one kind of fence,
I close, he's worsted, that's enough for him.   1000
He's on the ground: if ground should break away
I take my stand on, there's a firmer yet
Beneath it, both of us may sink and reach.
His ground was over mine and broke the first:
So, let him sit with me this many a year!"

He did not sit five minutes. Just a week
Sufficed his sudden healthy vehemence.
Something had struck him in the "Outward-bound"
Another way than Blougram's purpose was:
And having bought, not cabin-furniture   1010
But settler's-implements (enough for three)
And started for Australia — there, I hope,
By this time he has tested his first plough,
And studied his last chapter of St. John.

MEMORABILIA

I

AH, DID you once see Shelley plain,
 And did he stop and speak to you
And did you speak to him again?
 How strange it seems and new!

II

But you were living before that,
 And also you are living after;
And the memory I started at —
 My starting moves your laughter.

III

I crossed a moor, with a name of its own
 And a certain use in the world no doubt,   10
Yet a hand's-breadth of it shines alone
 'Mid the blank miles round about:

IV

For there I picked up on the heather
 And there I put inside my breast
A moulted feather, an eagle-feather!
 Well, I forget the rest.

ANDREA DEL SARTO

(Called "The Faultless Painter")

BUT do not let us quarrel any more,
No, my Lucrezia; bear with me for once:
Sit down and all shall happen as you wish.
You turn your face, but does it bring your heart?
I'll work then for your friend's friend, never fear,
Treat his own subject after his own way,

Fix his own time, accept too his own price,
And shut the money into this small hand
When next it takes mine. Will it? tenderly?
Oh, I'll content him, — but to-morrow, Love!   10
I often am much wearier than you think,
This evening more than usual, and it seems
As if — forgive now — should you let me sit
Here by the window with your hand in mine
And look a half-hour forth on Fiesole,
Both of one mind, as married people use,
Quietly, quietly the evening through,
I might get up to-morrow to my work
Cheerful and fresh as ever. Let us try.
To-morrow, how you shall be glad for this!   20
Your soft hand is a woman of itself,
And mine the man's bared breast she curls inside.
Don't count the time lost, neither; you must serve
For each of the five pictures we require:
It saves a model. So! keep looking so —
My serpentining beauty, rounds on rounds!
— How could you ever prick those perfect ears,
Even to put the pearl there! oh, so sweet —
My face, my moon, my everybody's moon,
Which everybody looks on and calls his,   30
And, I suppose, is looked on by in turn,
While she looks — no one's: very dear, no less.
You smile? why, there's my picture ready made,
There's what we painters call our harmony!
A common grayness silvers everything, —
All in a twilight, you and I alike
— You, at the point of your first pride in me
(That's gone you know), — but I, at every point;
My youth, my hope, my art, being all toned down
To yonder sober pleasant Fiesole.   40
There's the bell clinking from the chapel-top;
That length of convent-wall across the way
Holds the trees safer, huddled more inside;
The last monk leaves the garden; days decrease,
And autumn grows, autumn in everything.
Eh? the whole seems to fall into a shape
As if I saw alike my work and self
And all that I was born to be and do,
A twilight-piece. Love, we are in God's hand.
How strange now, looks the life he makes us lead;   50

So free we seem, so fettered fast we are!
I feel he laid the fetter: let it lie!
This chamber for example — turn your head —
All that's behind us! You don't understand
Nor care to understand about my art,
But you can hear at least when people speak:
And that cartoon, the second from the door
— It is the thing, Love! so such things should be —
Behold Madonna! — I am bold to say.
I can do with my pencil what I know,   60
What I see, what at bottom of my heart
I wish for, if I ever wish so deep —
Do easily, too — when I say, perfectly,
I do not boast, perhaps: yourself are judge,
Who listened to the Legate's talk last week,
And just as much they used to say in France.
At any rate 'tis easy, all of it!
No sketches first, no studies, that's long past:
I do what many dream of, all their lives,
— Dream? strive to do, and agonize to do,   70
And fail in doing. I could count twenty such
On twice your fingers, and not leave this town,
Who strive — you don't know how the others strive
To paint a little thing like that you smeared
Carelessly passing with your robes afloat, —
Yet do much less, so much less, Someone says,
(I know his name, no matter) — so much less!
Well, less is more, Lucrezia: I am judged.
There burns a truer light of God in them,
In their vexed beating stuffed and stopped-up brain,   80
Heart, or whate'er else, than goes on to prompt
This low-pulsed forthright craftsman's hand of mine.
Their works drop groundward, but themselves, I know,
Reach many a time a heaven that's shut to me,
Enter and take their place there sure enough,
Though they come back and cannot tell the world.
My works are nearer heaven, but I sit here.
The sudden blood of these men! at a word —
Praise them, it boils, or blame them, it boils too.
I, painting from myself and to myself,   90
Know what I do, am unmoved by men's blame
Or their praise either. Somebody remarks
Morello's outline there is wrongly traced,
His hue mistaken; what of that? or else,

Rightly traced and well ordered; what of that?
Speak as they please, what does the mountain care?
Ah, but a man's reach should exceed his grasp,
Or what's a heaven for? All is silver-gray
Placid and perfect with my art: the worse!
I know both what I want and what might gain,   100
And yet how profitless to know, to sigh
"Had I been two, another and myself,
Our head would have o'erlooked the world!" No doubt.
Yonder's a work now, of that famous youth
The Urbinate who died five years ago.
('Tis copied, George Vasari sent it me.)
Well, I can fancy how he did it all,
Pouring his soul, with kings and popes to see,
Reaching, that heaven might so replenish him,
Above and through his art — for it gives way;   110
That arm is wrongly put — and there again —
A fault to pardon in the drawing's lines,
Its body, so to speak: its soul is right,
He means right — that, a child may understand.
Still, what an arm! and I could alter it:
But all the play, the insight and the stretch —
Out of me, out of me! And wherefore out?
Had you enjoined them on me, given me soul,
We might have risen to Rafael, I and you!
Nay, Love, you did give all I asked, I think —   120
More than I merit, yes, by many times.
But had you — oh, with the same perfect brow,
And perfect eyes, and more than perfect mouth,
And the low voice my soul hears, as a bird
The fowler's pipe, and follows to the snare —
Had you, with these the same, but brought a mind!
Some women do so. Had the mouth there urged
"God and the glory! never care for gain.
The present by the future, what is that?
Live for fame, side by side with Agnolo!   130
Rafael is waiting: up to God, all three!"
I might have done it for you. So it seems:
Perhaps not. All is as God over-rules.
Beside, incentives come from the soul's self;
The rest avail not. Why do I need you?
What wife had Rafael, or has Agnolo?
In this world, who can do a thing, will not;
And who would do it, cannot, I perceive:

Yet the will's somewhat — somewhat, too, the power —
And thus we half-men struggle. At the end,   140
God, I conclude, compensates, punishes.
'Tis safer for me, if the award be strict,
That I am something underrated here.
Poor this long while, despised, to speak the truth.
I dared not, do you know, leave home all day,
For fear of chancing on the Paris lords.
The best is when they pass and look aside;
But they speak sometimes; I must bear it all.
Well may they speak! That Francis, that first time,
And that long festal year at Fontainebleau!   150
I surely then could sometimes leave the ground,
Put on the glory, Rafael's daily wear,
In that humane great monarch's golden look, —
One finger in his beard or twisted curl
Over his mouth's good mark that made the smile,
One arm about my shoulder, round my neck,
The jingle of his gold chain in my ear,
I painting proudly with his breath on me,
All his court round him, seeing with his eyes,
Such frank French eyes, and such a fire of souls   160
Profuse, my hand kept plying by those hearts, —
And, best of all, this, this, this face beyond,
This in the background, waiting on my work,
To crown the issue with a last reward!
A good time, was it not, my kingly days?
And had you not grown restless . . . but I know —
'Tis done and past; 'twas right, my instinct said;
Too live the life grew, golden and not gray,
And I'm the weak-eyed bat no sun should tempt
Out of the grange whose four walls make his world.   170
How could it end in any other way?
You called me, and I came home to your heart.
The triumph was — to reach and stay there; since
I reached it ere the triumph, what is lost?
Let my hands frame your face in your hair's gold,
You beautiful Lucrezia that are mine!
"Rafael did this, Andrea painted that;
The Roman's is the better when you pray,
But still the other's Virgin was his wife —"
Men will excuse me. I am glad to judge   180
Both pictures in your presence; clearer grows
My better fortune, I resolve to think.

For, do you know, Lucrezia, as God lives,
Said one day Agnolo, his very self,
To Rafael . . . I have known it all these years . . .
(When the young man was flaming out his thoughts
Upon a palace-wall for Rome to see,
Too lifted up in heart because of it)
"Friend, there's a certain sorry little scrub
Goes up and down our Florence, none cares how,   190
Who, were he set to plan and execute
As you are, pricked on by your popes and kings,
Would bring the sweat into that brow of yours!"
To Rafael's! — And indeed the arm is wrong.
I hardly dare . . . yet, only you to see,
Give the chalk here — quick, thus the line should go!
Ay, but the soul! he's Rafael! rub it out!
Still, all I care for, if he spoke the truth,
(What he? why, who but Michel Agnolo?
Do you forget already words like those?)   200
If really there was such a chance, so lost, —
Is, whether you're — not grateful — but more pleased.
Well, let me think so. And you smile indeed!
This hour has been an hour! Another smile?
If you would sit thus by me every night
I should work better, do you comprehend?
I mean that I should earn more, give you more.
See, it is settled dusk now; there's a star;
Morello's gone, the watch-lights show the wall,
The cue-owls speak the name we call them by.   210
Come from the window, love, — come in, at last,
Inside the melancholy little house
We built to be so gay with. God is just.
King Francis may forgive me: oft at nights
When I look up from painting, eyes tired out,
The walls become illumined, brick from brick
Distinct, instead of mortar, fierce bright gold,
That gold of his I did cement them with!
Let us but love each other. Must you go?
That Cousin here again? he waits outside?   220
Must see you — you, and not with me? Those loans?
More gaming debts to pay? you smiled for that?
Well, let smiles buy me! have you more to spend?
While hand and eye and something of a heart
Are left me, work's my ware, and what's it worth?
I'll pay my fancy. Only let me sit

The gray remainder of the evening out,
Idle, you call it, and muse perfectly
How I could paint, were I but back in France,
One picture, just one more — the Virgin's face,   230
Not yours this time! I want you at my side
To hear them — that is, Michel Agnolo —
Judge all I do and tell you of its worth.
Will you? To-morrow, satisfy your friend.
I take the subjects for his corridor,
Finish the portrait out of hand — there, there,
And throw him in another thing or two
If he demurs; the whole should prove enough
To pay for this same Cousin's freak. Beside,
What's better and what's all I care about,   240
Get you the thirteen scudi for the ruff!
Love, does that please you? Ah, but what does he,
The Cousin! What does he to please you more?

      I am grown peaceful as old age to-night.
I regret little, I would change still less.
Since there my past life lies, why alter it?
The very wrong to Francis! — it is true
I took his coin, was tempted and complied,
And built this house and sinned, and all is said.
My father and my mother died of want.   250
Well, had I riches of my own? you see
How one gets rich! Let each one bear his lot.
They were born poor, lived poor, and poor they died:
And I have labored somewhat in my time
And not been paid profusely. Some good son
Paint my two hundred pictures — let him try!
No doubt, there's something strikes a balance. Yes,
You loved me quite enough, it seems to-night.
This must suffice me here. What would one have?
In heaven, perhaps, new chances, one more chance —   260
Four great walls in the New Jerusalem,
Meted on each side by the angel's reed,
For Leonard, Rafael, Agnolo and me
To cover — the three first without a wife,
While I have mine! So — still they overcome
Because there's still Lucrezia, — as I choose.

Again the Cousin's whistle! Go, my Love.

IN THREE DAYS

I

So, I shall see her in three days
And just one night, but nights are short,
Then two long hours, and that is morn.
See how I come, unchanged, unworn!
Feel, where my life broke off from thine,
How fresh the splinters keep and fine, —
Only a touch and we combine!

II

Too long, this time of year, the days!
But nights, at least the nights are short.
As night shows where her one moon is,   10
A hand's-breadth of pure light and bliss,
So life's night gives my lady birth
And my eyes hold her! What is worth
The rest of heaven, the rest of earth?

III

O loaded curls, release your store
Of warmth and scent, as once before
The tingling hair did, lights and darks
Outbreaking into fairy sparks,
When under curl and curl I pried
After the warmth and scent inside,   20
Thro' lights and darks how manifold —
The dark inspired, the light controlled!
As early Art embrowns the gold.

IV

What great fear, should one say, "Three days
That change the world might change as well
Your fortune; and if joy delays,
Be happy that no worse befell!"
What small fear, if another says,
"Three days and one short night beside
May throw no shadow on your ways;   30

But years must teem with change untried,
With chance not easily defied,
With an end somewhere undescried."
No fear! — or if a fear be born
This minute, it dies out in scorn.
Fear? I shall see her in three days
And one night, now the nights are short,
Then just two hours, and that is morn.

OLD PICTURES IN FLORENCE

I

THE morn when first it thunders in March,
    The eel in the pond gives a leap, they say:
As I leaned and looked over the aloed arch
    Of the villa-gate this warm March day,
No flash snapped, no dumb thunder rolled
    In the valley beneath where, white and wide
And washed by the morning water-gold,
    Florence lay out on the mountain-side.

II

River and bridge and street and square
    Lay mine, as much at my beck and call,   10
Through the live translucent bath of air,
    As the sights in a magic crystal ball.
And of all I saw and of all I praised,
    The most to praise and the best to see
Was the startling bell-tower Giotto raised:
    But why did it more than startle me?

III

Giotto, how, with that soul of yours,
    Could you play me false who loved you so?
Some slights if a certain heart endures
    Yet it feels, I would have your fellows know!   20
I' faith, I perceive not why I should care
    To break a silence that suits them best,
But the thing grows somewhat hard to bear
    When I find a Giotto join the rest.

IV

On the arch where olives overhead
    Print the blue sky with twig and leaf,
(That sharp-curled leaf which they never shed)
    'Twixt the aloes, I used to lean in chief,
And mark through the winter afternoons,
    By a gift God grants me now and then,   30
In the mild decline of those suns like moons,
    Who walked in Florence, besides her men.

V

They might chirp and chaffer, come and go
    For pleasure or profit, her men alive —
My business was hardly with them, I trow,
    But with empty cells of the human hive;
— With the chapter-room, the cloister-porch,
    The church's apsis, aisle or nave,
Its crypt, one fingers along with a torch,
    Its face set full for the sun to shave.   40

VI

Wherever a fresco peels and drops,
    Wherever an outline weakens and wanes
Till the latest life in the painting stops,
    Stands One whom each fainter pulse-tick pains:
One, wishful each scrap should clutch the brick,
    Each tinge not wholly escape the plaster,
— A lion who dies of an ass's kick,
    The wronged great soul of an ancient Master.

VII

For oh, this world and the wrong it does!
    They are safe in heaven with their backs to it,   50
The Michaels and Rafaels, you hum and buzz
    Round the works of, you of the little wit!
Do their eyes contract to the earth's old scope,
    Now that they see God face to face,
And have all attained to be poets, I hope?
    'Tis their holiday now, in any case.

VIII

Much they reck of your praise and you!
 But the wronged great souls — can they be quit
Of a world where their work is all to do,
 Where you style them, you of the little wit,   30
Old Master This and Early the Other,
 Not dreaming that Old and New are fellows:
A younger succeeds to an elder brother,
 Da Vincis derive in good time from Dellos.

IX

And here where your praise might yield returns,
 And a handsome word or two give help,
Here, after your kind, the mastiff girns
 And the puppy pack of poodles yelp.
What, not a word for Stefano there,
 Of brow once prominent and starry,   70
Called Nature's Ape and the world's despair
 For his peerless painting? (See Vasari.)

X

There stands the Master. Study, my friends,
 What a man's work comes to! So he plans it,
Performs it, perfects it, makes amends
 For the toiling and moiling, and then, *sic transit!*
Happier the thrifty blind-folk labor,
 With upturned eye while the hand is busy,
Not sidling a glance at the coin of their neighbor!
 'Tis looking downward that makes one dizzy.   80

XI

"If you knew their work you would deal your dole."
 May I take upon me to instruct you?
When Greek Art ran and reached the goal,
 Thus much had the world to boast *in fructu* —
The Truth of Man, as by God first spoken,
 Which the actual generations garble,
Was re-uttered, and Soul (which Limbs betoken)
 And Limbs (Soul informs) made new in marble.

▮▮▮▮

So, you saw yourself as you wished you were,
    As you might have been, as you cannot be;   90
Earth here, rebuked by Olympus there:
    And grew content in your poor degree
With your little power, by those statues' godhead,
    And your little scope, by their eyes' full sway,
And your little grace, by their grace embodied,
    And your little date, by their forms that stay.

XIII

You would fain be kinglier, say, than I am?
    Even so, you will not sit like Theseus.
You would prove a model? The Son of Priam
    Has yet the advantage in arms' and knees' use.   100
You're wroth — can you slay your snake like Apollo?
    You're grieved — still Niobe's the grander!
You live — there's the Racers' frieze to follow:
    You die — there's the dying Alexander.

XIV

So, testing your weakness by their strength,
    Your meagre charms by their rounded beauty,
Measured by Art in your breadth and length,
    You learned — to submit is a mortal's duty.
— When I say "you" 'tis the common soul,
    The collective, I mean: the race of Man   110
That receives life in parts to live in a whole,
    And grow here according to God's clear plan.

XV

Growth came when, looking your last on them all,
    You turned your eyes inwardly one fine day
And cried with a start — What if we so small
    Be greater and grander the while than they?
Are they perfect of lineament, perfect of stature?
    In both, of such lower types are we
Precisely because of our wider nature;
    For time, theirs — ours, for eternity.   120

XVI

To-day's brief passion limits their range;
    It seethes with the morrow for us and more.
They are perfect — how else? they shall never change:
    We are faulty — why not? we have time in store.
The Artificer's hand is not arrested
    With us; we are rough-hewn, nowise polished:
They stand for our copy, and, once invested
    With all they can teach, we shall see them abolished.

XVII

'Tis a life-long toil till our lump be leaven —
    The better! What's come to perfection perishes.   130
Things learned on earth, we shall practise in heaven:
    Works done least rapidly, Art most cherishes.
Thyself shalt afford the example, Giotto!
    Thy one work, not to decrease or diminish,
Done at a stroke, was just (was it not?) "O!"
    Thy great Campanile is still to finish.

XVIII

Is it true that we are now, and shall be hereafter,
    But what and where depend on life's minute?
Hails heavenly cheer or infernal laughter
    Our first step out of the gulf or in it?   140
Shall Man, such step within his endeavor,
    Man's face, have no more play and action
Than joy which is crystallized forever,
    Or grief, an eternal petrifaction?

XIX

On which I conclude, that the early painters,
    To cries of "Greek Art and what more wish you?" —
Replied, "To become now self-acquainters,
    And paint man man, whatever the issue!
Make new hopes shine through the flesh they fray,
    New fears aggrandize the rags and tatters: 150
To bring the invisible full into play!
    Let the visible go to the dogs — what matters?"

XX

Give these, I exhort you, their guerdon and glory
    For daring so much, before they well did it.
The first of the new, in our race's story,
    Beats the last of the old; 'tis no idle quiddit.
The worthies began a revolution,
    Which if on earth you intend to acknowledge,
Why, honor them now! (ends my allocution)
    Nor confer your degree when the folk leave college.   160

XXI

There's a fancy some lean to and others hate —
    That, when this life is ended, begins
New work for the soul in another state,
    Where it strives and gets weary, loses and wins:
Where the strong and the weak, this world's congeries,
    Repeat in large what they practised in small,
Through life after life in unlimited series;
    Only the scale's to be changed, that's all.

XXII

Yet I hardly know. When a soul has seen
    By the means of Evil that Good is best,   170
And, through earth and its noise, what is heaven's serene, —
    When our faith in the same has stood the test —
Why, the child grown man, you burn the rod,
    The uses of labor are surely done;
There remaineth a rest for the people of God:
    And I have had troubles enough, for one.

XXIII

But at any rate I have loved the season
    Of Art's spring-birth so dim and dewy;
My sculptor is Nicolo the Pisan,
    My painter — who but Cimabue?   180
Nor ever was man of them all indeed,
    From these to Ghiberti and Ghirlandajo,
Could say that he missed my critic-meed.
    So, now to my special grievance — heigh ho!

XXIV

Their ghosts still stand, as I said before,
    Watching each fresco flaked and rasped,
Blocked up, knocked out, or whitewashed o'er:
    — No getting again what the church has grasped!
The works on the wall must take their chance;
    "Works never conceded to England's thick clime!"   190
(I hope they prefer their inheritance
    Of a bucketful of Italian quick-lime.)

XXV

When they go at length, with such a shaking
    Of heads o'er the old delusion, sadly
Each master his way through the black streets taking,
    Where many a lost work breathes though badly —
Why don't they bethink them of who has merited?
    Why not reveal, while their pictures dree
Such doom, how a captive might be out-ferreted?
    Why is it they never remember me?   200

XXVI

Not that I expect the great Bigordi,
    Nor Sandro to hear me, chivalric, bellicose;
Nor the wronged Lippino; and not a word I
    Say of a scrap of Frà Angelico's:
But are you too fine, Taddeo Gaddi,
    To grant me a taste of your intonaco,
Some Jerome that seeks the heaven with a sad eye?
    Not a churlish saint, Lorenzo Monaco?

XXVII

Could not the ghost with the close red cap,
    My Pollajolo, the twice a craftsman,   210
Save me a sample, give me the hap
    Of a muscular Christ that shows the draughtsman?
No Virgin by him the somewhat petty,
    Of finical touch and tempera crumbly —
Could not Alesso Baldovinetti
    Contribute so much, I ask him humbly?

XXVIII

Margheritone of Arezzo,
    With the grave-clothes garb and swaddling barret
(Why purse up mouth and beak in a pet so,
    You bald old saturnine poll-clawed parrot?)   220
Not a poor glimmering Crucifixion,
    Where in the foreground kneels the donor?
If such remain, as is my conviction,
    The hoarding it does you but little honor.

XXIX

They pass; for them the panels may thrill,
    The tempera grow alive and tinglish;
Their pictures are left to the mercies still
    Of dealers and stealers, Jews and the English,
Who, seeing mere money's worth in their prize,
    Will sell it to somebody calm as Zeno   230
At naked High Art, and in ecstasies
    Before some clay-cold vile Carlino!

XXX

No matter for these! But Giotto, you,
    Have you allowed, as the town-tongues babble it, —
Oh, never! it shall not be counted true —
    That a certain precious little tablet
Which Buonarotti eyed like a lover, —
    Was buried so long in oblivion's womb
And, left for another than I to discover,
    Turns up at last! and to whom? — to whom?   240

XXXI

I, that have haunted the dim San Spirito,
    (Or was it rather the Ognissanti?)
Patient on altar-step planting a weary toe!
    Nay, I shall have it yet! *Detur amanti!*
My Koh-i-noor — or (if that's a platitude)
    Jewel of Giamschid, the Persian Sofi's eye;
So, in anticipative gratitude,
    What if I take up my hope and prophesy?

XXXII

When the hour grows ripe, and a certain dotard
    Is pitched, no parcel that needs invoicing,   250
To the worse side of the Mont Saint Gothard,
    We shall begin by way of rejoicing;
None of that shooting the sky (blank cartridge),
    Nor a civic guard, all plumes and lacquer,
Hunting Radetzky's soul like a partridge
    Over Morello with squib and cracker.

XXXIII

This time we'll shoot better game and bag 'em hot —
    No mere display at the stone of Dante,
But a kind of sober Witanagemot
    (Ex: "Casa Guidi," *quod videas ante*)   260
Shall ponder, once Freedom restored to Florence,
    How Art may return that departed with her.
Go, hated house, go each trace of the Loraine's,
    And bring us the days of Orgagna hither!

XXXIV

How we shall prologize, how we shall perorate,
    Utter fit things upon art and history,
Feel truth at blood-heat and falsehood at zero rate,
    Make of the want of the age no mystery;
Contrast the fructuous and sterile eras,
    Show — monarchy ever its uncouth cub licks   270
Out of the bear's shape into Chimæra's,
    While Pure Art's birth is still the republic's

XXXV

Then one shall propose in a speech (curt Tuscan,
    Expurgate and sober, with scarcely an *"issimo,"*)
To end now our half-told tale of Cambuscan,
    And turn the bell-tower's *alt* to *altissimo:*
And fine as the beak of a young beccaccia
    The Campanile, the Duomo's fit ally,
Shall soar up in gold full fifty braccia,
    Completing Florence, as Florence Italy.   280

XXXVI

Shall I be alive that morning the scaffold
    Is broken away, and the long-pent fire,
Like the golden hope of the world, unbaffled
    Springs from its sleep, and up goes the spire
While "God and the People" plain for its motto,
    Thence the new tricolor flaps at the sky?
At least to foresee that glory of Giotto
    And Florence together, the first am I!

SAUL

I

SAID Abner, "At last thou art come! Ere I tell, ere thou speak,
Kiss my cheek, wish me well!" Then I wished it, and did kiss his cheek.
And he, "Since the King, O my friend, for thy countenance sent,
Neither drunken nor eaten have we; nor until from his tent
Thou return with the joyful assurance the King liveth yet,
Shall our lip with the honey be bright, with the water be wet.
For out of the black mid-tent's silence, a space of three days,
Not a sound hath escaped to thy servants, of prayer nor of praise,
To betoken that Saul and the Spirit have ended their strife,
And that, faint in his triumph, the monarch sinks back upon life.   10

II

"Yet now my heart leaps, O beloved! God's child with his dew
On thy gracious gold hair, and those lilies still living and blue
Just broken to twine round thy harp-strings, as if no wild heat
Were now raging to torture the desert!"

III

                    Then I, as was meet,
Knelt down to the God of my fathers, and rose on my feet,
And ran o'er the sand burnt to powder. The tent was unlooped;
I pulled up the spear that obstructed, and under I stooped;
Hands and knees on the slippery grass-patch, all withered and gone,
That extends to the second enclosure, I groped my way on
Till I felt where the foldskirts fly open. Then once more I prayed,   20

And opened the foldskirts and entered, and was not afraid
But spoke, "Here is David, thy servant!" And no voice replied.
At the first I saw naught but the blackness; but soon I descried
A something more black than the blackness — the vast, the upright
Main prop which sustains the pavilion: and slow into sight
Grew a figure against it, gigantic and blackest of all.
Then a sunbeam, that burst thro' the tent-roof, showed Saul.

IV

He stood as erect as that tent-prop, both arms stretched out wide
On the great cross-support in the centre, that goes to each side;
He relaxed not a muscle, but hung there as, caught in his pangs   30
And waiting his change, the king-serpent all heavily hangs,
Far away from his kind, in the pine, till deliverance come
With the spring-time, — so agonized Saul, drear and stark, blind and
    dumb.

V

Then I tuned my harp, — took off the lilies we twine round its chords
Lest they snap 'neath the stress of the noon-tide — those sunbeams
    like swords!
And I first played the tune all our sheep know, as, one after one,
So docile they come to the pen-door till folding be done.
They are white and untorn by the bushes, for lo, they have fed
Where the long grasses stifle the water within the stream's bed;
And now one after one seeks its lodging, as star follows star   40
Into eve and the blue far above us, — so blue and so far!

VI

— Then the tune, for which quails on the cornland will each leave his
    mate
To fly after the player; then, what makes the crickets elate
Till for boldness they fight one another; and then, what has weight
To set the quick jerboa a-musing outside his sand house —
There are none such as he for a wonder, half bird and half mouse!
God made all the creatures and gave them our love and our fear,
To give sign, we and they are his children, one family here.

VII

Then I played the help-tune of our reapers, their wine-song, when
    hand
Grasps at hand, eye lights eye in good friendship, and great hearts
    expand
                                                                        50

And grow one in the sense of this world's life. — And then, the last
 song
When the dead man is praised on his journey — "Bear, bear him along
With his few faults shut up like dead flowerets! Are balm-seeds not
 here
To console us? The land has none left such as he on the bier.
Oh, would we might keep thee, my brother!" — And then, the glad
 chaunt
Of the marriage, — first go the young maidens, next, she whom we
 vaunt
As the beauty, the pride of our dwelling. — And then, the great march
Wherein man runs to man to assist him and buttress an arch
Naught can break; who shall harm them, our friends? — Then, the
 chorus intoned
As the Levites go up to the altar in glory enthroned.   60
But I stopped here: for here in the darkness Saul groaned.

VIII

And I paused, held my breath in such silence, and listened apart;
And the tent shook, for mighty Saul shuddered: and sparkles 'gan dart
From the jewels that woke in his turban, at once with a start,
All its lordly male-sapphires, and rubies courageous at heart.
So the head: but the body still moved not, still hung there erect.
And I bent once again to my playing, pursued it unchecked,
As I sang, —

IX

    "Oh, our manhood's prime vigor! No spirit feels waste,
Not a muscle is stopped in its playing nor sinew unbraced.
Oh, the wild joys of living! the leaping from rock up to rock,   70
The strong rending of boughs from the fir-tree, the cool silver shock
Of the plunge in a pool's living water, the hunt of the bear,
And the sultriness showing the lion is couched in his lair.
And the meal, the rich dates yellowed over with gold dust divine,
And the locust-flesh steeped in the pitcher, the full draught of wine,
And the sleep in the dried river-channel where bulrushes tell
That the water was wont to go warbling so softly and well.
How good is man's life, the mere living! how fit to employ
All the heart and the soul and the senses forever in joy!
Hast thou loved the white locks of thy father, whose sword thou didst
 guard   80
When he trusted thee forth with the armies, for glorious reward?
Didst thou see the thin hands of thy mother, held up as men sung

The low song of the nearly-departed, and hear her faint tongue
Joining in while it could to the witness, 'Let one more attest,
I have lived, seen God's hand thro' a lifetime, and all was for best'?
Then they sung thro' their tears in strong triumph, not much, but the
 rest.
And thy brothers, the help and the contest, the working whence grew
Such result as, from seething grape-bundles, the spirit strained true:
And the friends of thy boyhood — that boyhood of wonder and hope,
Present promise and wealth of the future beyond the eye's scope, —
Till lo, thou art grown to a monarch; a people is thine;   91
And all gifts, which the world offers singly, on one head combine!
On one head, all the beauty and strength, love and rage (like the throe
That, a-work in the rock, helps its labor and lets the gold go)
High ambition and deeds which surpass it, fame crowning them, — all
Brought to blaze on the head of one creature — King Saul!"

       x

And lo, with that leap of my spirit, — heart, hand, harp and voice,
Each lifting Saul's name out of sorrow, each bidding rejoice
Saul's fame in the light it was made for — as when, dare I say,
The Lord's army, in rapture of service, strains through its array, 100
And upsoareth the cherubim-chariot — "Saul!" cried I, and stopped,
And waited the thing that should follow. Then Saul, who hung propped
By the tent's cross-support in the centre, was struck by his name.
Have ye seen when Spring's arrowy summons goes right to the aim,
And some mountain, the last to withstand her, that held (he alone,
While the vale laughed in freedom and flowers) on a broad bust of
 stone
A year's snow bound about for a breastplate, — leaves grasp of the
 sheet?
Fold on fold all at once it crowds thunderously down to his feet,
And there fronts you, stark, black, but alive yet, your mountain of old,
With his rents, the successive bequeathings of ages untold — 110
Yea, each harm got in fighting your battles, each furrow and scar
Of his head thrust 'twixt you and the tempest — all hail, there they
 are!
— Now again to be softened with verdure, again hold the nest
Of the dove, tempt the goat and its young to the green on his crest
For their food in the ardors of summer. One long shudder thrilled
All the tent till the very air tingled, then sank and was stilled
At the King's self left standing before me, released and aware.
What was gone, what remained? All to traverse, 'twixt hope and
 despair;

Death was past, life not come: so he waited. Awhile his right hand
Held the brow, helped the eyes left too vacant forthwith to remand
To their place what new objects should enter: 'twas Saul as before.
I looked up and dared gaze at those eyes, nor was hurt any more 122
Than by slow pallid sunsets in autumn, ye watch from the shore,
At their sad level gaze o'er the ocean — a sun's slow decline
Over hills which, resolved in stern silence, o'erlap and entwine
Base with base to knit strength more intensely: so, arm folded arm
O'er the chest whose slow heavings subsided.

XI

                                   What spell or what charm,
(For, awhile there was trouble within me) what next should I urge
To sustain him where song had restored him? — Song filled to the
        verge
His cup with the wine of this life, pressing all that it yields   130
Of mere fruitage, the strength and the beauty: beyond, on what fields,
Glean a vintage more potent and perfect to brighten the eye
And bring blood to the lip, and commend them the cup they put by?
He saith, "It is good;" still he drinks not: he lets me praise life,
Gives assent, yet would die for his own part.

XII

                                   Then fancies grew rife
Which had come long ago on the pasture, when round me the sheep
Fed in silence — above, the one eagle wheeled slow as in sleep;
And I lay in my hollow and mused on the world that might lie
'Neath his ken, though I saw but the strip 'twixt the hill and the sky:
And I laughed — "Since my days are ordained to be passed with my
        flocks,   140
Let me people at least, with my fancies, the plains and the rocks,
Dream the life I am never to mix with, and image the show
Of mankind as they live in those fashions I hardly shall know!
Schemes of life, its best rules and right uses, the courage that gains,
And the prudence that keeps what men strive for." And now these old
        trains
Of vague thought came again; I grew surer; so, once more the string
Of my harp made response to my spirit, as thus —

XIII

                                   "Yea, my King,"
I began — "thou dost well in rejecting mere comforts that spring
From the mere mortal life held in common by man and by brute:
In our flesh grows the branch of this life, in our soul it bears fruit.

Thou hast marked the slow rise of the tree, — how its stem trembled
 first   151
Till it passed the kid's lip, the stag's antler; then safely outburst
The fan-branches all round; and thou mindest when these too, in turn
Broke a-bloom and the palm-tree seemed perfect: yet more was to
 learn,
E'en the good that comes in with the palm-fruit. Our dates shall we
 slight,
When their juice brings a cure for all sorrow? or care for the plight
Of the palm's self whose slow growth produced them? Not so! stem
 and branch
Shall decay, nor be known in their place, while the palm-wine shall
 staunch
Every wound of man's spirit in winter. I pour thee such wine.
Leave the flesh to the fate it was fit for! the spirit be thine!   160
By the spirit, when age shall o'ercome thee, thou still shalt enjoy
More indeed, than at first when inconscious, the life of a boy.
Crush that life, and behold its wine running! Each deed thou hast done
Dies, revives, goes to work in the world; until e'en as the sun
Looking down on the earth, though clouds spoil him, though tempests
 efface,
Can find nothing his own deed produced not, must everywhere trace
The results of his past summer-prime, — so, each ray of thy will,
Every flash of thy passion and prowess, long over, shall thrill
Thy whole people, the countless, with ardor, till they too give forth
A like cheer to their sons, who in turn, fill the South and the North
With the radiance thy deed was the germ of. Carouse in the past! 171
But the license of age has its limit; thou diest at last:
As the lion when age dims his eyeball, the rose at her height,
So with man — so his power and his beauty forever take flight.
No! Again a long draught of my soul-wine! Look forth o'er the years!
Thou hast done now with eyes for the actual; begin with the seer's!
Is Saul dead? In the depth of the vale make his tomb — bid arise
A gray mountain of marble heaped four-square, till, built to the skies,
Let it mark where the great First King slumbers: whose fame would
 ye know?
Up above see the rock's naked face, where the record shall go   180
In great characters cut by the scribe, — Such was Saul, so he did;
With the sages directing the work, by the populace chid, —
For not half, they'll affirm, is comprised there! Which fault to amend,
In the grove with his kind grows the cedar, whereon they shall spend
(See, in tablets 'tis level before them) their praise, and record
With the gold of the graver, Saul's story, — the statesman's great word
Side by side with the poet's sweet comment. The river's a-wave

With smooth paper-reeds grazing each other when prophet-winds rave;
So the pen gives unborn generations their due and their part
In thy being! Then, first of the mighty, thank God that thou art!" 190

XIV

And behold while I sang . . . but O Thou who didst grant me that day,
And before it not seldom hast granted thy help to essay,
Carry on and complete an adventure, — my shield and my sword
In that act where my soul was thy servant, thy word was my word, —
Still be with me, who then at the summit of human endeavor
And scaling the highest, man's thought could, gazed hopeless as ever
On the new stretch of heaven above me — till, mighty to save,
Just one lift of thy hand cleared that distance — God's throne from
    man's grave!
Let me tell out my tale to its ending — my voice to my heart
Which can scarce dare believe in what marvels last night I took part,
As this morning I gather the fragments, alone with my sheep,   201
And still fear lest the terrible glory evanish like sleep!
For I wake in the gray dewy covert, while Hebron upheaves
The dawn struggling with night on his shoulder, and Kidron retrieves
Slow the damage of yesterday's sunshine.

XV

                                 I say then, — my song
While I sang thus, assuring the monarch, and ever more strong
Made a proffer of good to console him — he slowly resumed
His old motions and habitudes kingly. The right-hand replumed
His black locks to their wonted composure, adjusted the swathes
Of his turban, and see — the huge sweat that his countenance bathes,
He wipes off with the robe; and he girds now his loins as of yore,   211
And feels slow for the armlets of price, with the clasp set before.
He is Saul, ye remember in glory, — ere error had bent
The broad brow from the daily communion; and still, though much
    spent
Be the life and the bearing that front you, the same, God did choose,
To receive what a man may waste, desecrate, never quite lose.
So sank he along by the tent-prop till, stayed by the pile
Of his armor and war-cloak and garments, he leaned there awhile,
And sat out my singing, — one arm round the tent-prop, to raise
His bent head, and the other hung slack — till I touched on the praise
I foresaw from all men in all time, to the man patient there;   221
And thus ended, the harp falling forward. Then first I was 'ware
That he sat, as I say, with my head just above his vast knees

Which were thrust out on each side around me, like oak-roots which
    please
To encircle a lamb when it slumbers. I looked up to know
If the best I could do had brought solace: he spoke not, but slow
Lifted up the hand slack at his side, till he laid it with care
Soft and grave, but in mild settled will, on my brow: thro' my hair
The large fingers were pushed, and he bent back my head, with kind
    power —
All my face back, intent to peruse it, as men do a flower.   230
Thus held he me there with his great eyes that scrutinized mine —
And oh, all my heart how it loved him! but where was the sign?
I yearned — "Could I help thee, my father, inventing a bliss,
I would add, to that life of the past, both the future and this;
I would give thee new life altogether, as good, ages hence,
As this moment, — had love but the warrant, love's heart to dispense!"

XVI

Then the truth came upon me. No harp more — no song more! out-
    broke —

XVII

"I have gone the whole round of creation: I saw and I spoke:
I, a work of God's hand for that purpose, received in my brain
And pronounced on the rest of his handwork — returned him again
His creation's approval or censure: I spoke as I saw: 241
I report, as a man may of God's work — all's love, yet all's law.
Now I lay down the judgeship he lent me. Each faculty tasked
To perceive him, has gained an abyss, where a dewdrop was asked.
Have I knowledge? confounded it shrivels at Wisdom laid bare.
Have I forethought? how purblind, how blank, to the Infinite Care!
Do I task any faculty highest, to image success?
I but open my eyes, — and perfection, no more and no less,
In the kind I imagined, full-fronts me, and God is seen God
In the star, in the stone, in the flesh, in the soul and the clod.   250
And thus looking within and around me, I ever renew
(With that stoop of the soul which in bending upraises it too)
The submission of man's nothing-perfect to God's all-complete,
As by each new obeisance in spirit, I climb to his feet.
Yet with all this abounding experience, this deity known,
I shall dare to discover some province, some gift of my own.
There's a faculty pleasant to exercise, hard to hoodwink,
I am fain to keep still in abeyance, (I laugh as I think)
Lest, insisting to claim and parade in it, wot ye, I worst
E'en the Giver in one gift. — Behold, I could love if I durst!   260

But I sink the pretension as fearing a man may o'ertake
God's own speed in the one way of love: I abstain for love's sake.
— What, my soul? see thus far and no farther? when doors great and
    small,
Nine-and-ninety flew ope at our touch, should the hundredth appall?
In the least things have faith, yet distrust in the greatest of all?
Do I find love so full in my nature, God's ultimate gift,
That I doubt his own love can compete with it? Here, the parts shift?
Here, the creature surpass the Creator, — the end, what Began?
Would I fain in my impotent yearning do all for this man,
And dare doubt he alone shall not help him, who yet alone can?   270
Would it ever have entered my mind, the bare will, much less power,
To bestow on this Saul what I sang of, the marvellous dower
Of the life he was gifted and filled with? to make such a soul,
Such a body, and then such an earth for insphering the whole?
And doth it not enter my mind (as my warm tears attest)
These good things being given, to go on, and give one more, the best?
Ay, to save and redeem and restore him, maintain at the height
This perfection, — succeed with life's day-spring, death's minute of
    night?
Interpose at the difficult minute, snatch Saul the mistake,
Saul the failure, the ruin he seems now, — and bid him awake   280
From the dream, the probation, the prelude, to find himself set
Clear and safe in new light and new life, — a new harmony yet
To be run, and continued, and ended — who knows? — or endure!
The man taught enough, by life's dream, of the rest to make sure;
By the pain-throb, triumphantly winning intensified bliss,
And the next world's reward and repose, by the struggles in this.

XVIII

"I believe it! 'Tis thou, God, that givest, 'tis I who receive:
In the first is the last, in thy will is my power to believe.
All's one gift: thou canst grant it moreover, as prompt to my prayer
As I breathe out this breath, as I open these arms to the air.   290
From thy will, stream the worlds, life and nature, thy dread Sabaoth:
I will? — the mere atoms despise me! Why am I not loth
To look that, even that in the face too? Why is it I dare
Think but lightly of such impuissance? What stops my despair?
This; — 'tis not what man Does which exalts him, but what man
    Would do!
See the King — I would help him but cannot, the wishes fall through.
Could I wrestle to raise him from sorrow, grow poor to enrich,
To fill up his life, starve my own out, I would — knowing which,
I know that my service is perfect. Oh, speak through me now!

Would I suffer for him that I love? So wouldst thou — so wilt thou!
So shall crown thee the topmost, ineffablest, uttermost crown —   301
And thy love fill infinitude wholly, nor leave up nor down
One spot for the creature to stand in! It is by no breath,
Turn of eye, wave of hand, that salvation joins issue with death!
As thy Love is discovered almighty, almighty be proved
Thy power, that exists with and for it, of being Beloved!
He who did most, shall bear most; the strongest shall stand the most
　　　weak.
'Tis the weakness in strength, that I cry for! my flesh, that I seek
In the Godhead! I seek and I find it. O Saul, it shall be
A Face like my face that receives thee; a Man like to me,   310
Thou shalt love and be loved by, forever: a Hand like this hand
Shall throw open the gates of new life to thee! See the Christ stand!"

XIX

I know not too well how I found my way home in the night.
There were witnesses, cohorts about me, to left and to right,
Angels, powers, the unuttered, unseen, the alive, the aware:
I repressed, I got through them as hardly, as strugglingly there,
As a runner beset by the populace famished for news —
Life or death. The whole earth was awakened, hell loosed with her
　　　crews;
And the stars of night beat with emotion, and tingled and shot
Out in fire the strong pain of pent knowledge: but I fainted not,   320
For the Hand still impelled me at once and supported, suppressed
All the tumult, and quenched it with quiet, and holy behest,
Till the rapture was shut in itself, and the earth sank to rest.
Anon at the dawn, all that trouble had withered from earth —
Not so much, but I saw it die out in the day's tender birth;
In the gathered intensity brought to the gray of the hills;
In the shuddering forests' held breath; in the sudden wind-thrills;
In the startled wild beasts that bore off, each with eye sidling still
Though averted with wonder and dread; in the birds stiff and chill
That rose heavily, as I approached them, made stupid with awe: 330
E'en the serpent that slid away silent, — he felt the new law.
The same stared in the white humid faces upturned by the flowers;
The same worked in the heart of the cedar and moved the vine-
　　　bowers:
And the little brooks witnessing murmured, persistent and low,
With their obstinate, all but hushed voices — "E'en so, it is so!"

"DE GUSTIBUS—"

I

Your ghost will walk, you lover of trees,
    (If our loves remain)
    In an English lane,
By a cornfield-side a-flutter with poppies.
Hark, those two in the hazel coppice —
A boy and a girl, if the good fates please,
    Making love, say, —
    The happier they!
Draw yourself up from the light of the moon,
And let them pass, as they will too soon,   10
    With the bean-flowers' boon,
    And the blackbird's tune,
    And May, and June!

II

What I love best in all the world
Is a castle, precipice-encurled,
In a gash of the wind-grieved Apennine
Or look for me, old fellow of mine,
(If I get my head from out the mouth
O' the grave, and loose my spirit's bands,
And come again to the land of lands) —   20
In a sea-side house to the farther South,
Where the baked cicala dies of drouth,
And one sharp tree — 'tis a cypress — stands,
By the many hundred years red-rusted,
Rough iron-spiked, ripe fruit-o'ercrusted,
My sentinel to guard the sands
To the water's edge. For, what expands
Before the house, but the great opaque
Blue breadth of sea without a break?
While, in the house, for ever crumbles   30
Some fragment of the frescoed walls,
From blisters where a scorpion sprawls.
A girl bare-footed brings, and tumbles
Down on the pavement, green-flesh melons,

And says there's news to-day — the king
Was shot at, touched in the liver-wing,
Goes with his Bourbon arm in a sling:
— She hopes they have not caught the felons.
Italy, my Italy!
Queen Mary's saying serves for me —   **40**
    (When fortune's malice
    Lost her — Calais) —
Open my heart and you will see
Graved inside of it, "Italy."
Such lovers old are I and she:
So it always was, so shall ever be!

CLEON

"As certain also of your own poets have said"—

CLEON the poet (from the sprinkled isles,
Lily on lily, that o'erlace the sea,
And laugh their pride when the light wave lisps "Greece") —
To Protus in his Tyranny: much health!

    They give thy letter to me, even now:
I read and seem as if I heard thee speak.
The master of thy galley still unlades
Gift after gift; they block my court at last
And pile themselves along its portico
Royal with sunset, like a thought of thee: **10**
And one white she-slave from the group dispersed
Of black and white slaves (like the chequer-work
Pavement, at once my nation's work and gift,
Now covered with this settle-down of doves),
One lyric woman, in her crocus vest
Woven of sea-wools, with her two white hands
Commends to me the strainer and the cup
Thy lip hath bettered ere it blesses mine.

    Well-counselled, king, in thy munificence!
For so shall men remark, in such an act   **20**
Of love for him whose song gives life its joy,
Thy recognition of the use of life;

Nor call thy spirit barely adequate
To help on life in straight ways, broad enough
For vulgar souls, by ruling and the rest.
Thou, in the daily building of thy tower, —
Whether in fierce and sudden spasms of toil,
Or through dim lulls of unapparent growth,
Or when the general work 'mid good acclaim
Climbed with the eye to cheer the architect, — 30
Didst ne'er engage in work for mere work's sake —
Hadst ever in thy heart the luring hope
Of some eventual rest a-top of it,
Whence, all the tumult of the building hushed,
Thou first of men mightst look out to the East:
The vulgar saw thy tower, thou sawest the sun.
For this, I promise on thy festival
To pour libation, looking o'er the sea,
Making this slave narrate thy fortunes, speak
Thy great words, and describe thy royal face — 40
Wishing thee wholly where Zeus lives the most,
Within the eventual element of calm.

      Thy letter's first requirement meets me here.
It is as thou hast heard: in one short life
I, Cleon, have effected all those things
Thou wonderingly dost enumerate.
That epos on thy hundred plates of gold
Is mine, — and also mine the little chant,
So sure to rise from every fishing-bark
When, lights at prow, the seamen haul their net. 50
The image of the sun-god on the phare,
Men turn from the sun's self to see, is mine;
The Pœcile, o'er-storied its whole length,
As thou didst hear, with painting, is mine too.
I know the true proportions of a man
And woman also, not observed before;
And I have written three books on the soul,
Proving absurd all written hitherto,
And putting us to ignorance again.
For music, — why, I have combined the moods, 60
Inventing one. In brief, all arts are mine;
Thus much the people know and recognize,
Throughout our seventeen islands. Marvel not
We of these latter days, with greater mind
Than our forerunners, since more composite

Look not so great, beside their simple way,
To a judge who only sees one way at once,
One mind-point and no other at a time, —
Compares the small part of a man of us
With some whole man of the heroic age,   70
Great in his way — not ours, nor meant for ours.
And ours is greater, had we skill to know:
For, what we call this life of men on earth,
This sequence of the soul's achievements here
Being, as I find much reason to conceive,
Intended to be viewed eventually
As a great whole, not analyzed to parts,
But each part having reference to all, —
How shall a certain part, pronounced complete,
Endure effacement by another part?   80
Was the thing done? — then, what's to do again?
See, in the chequered pavement opposite,
Suppose the artist made a perfect rhomb,
And next a lozenge, then a trapezoid —
He did not overlay them, superimpose
The new upon the old and blot it out,
But laid them on a level in his work,
Making at last a picture; there it lies
So, first the perfect separate forms were made,
The portions of mankind; and after, so,   90
Occurred the combination of the same.
For where had been a progress, otherwise?
Mankind, made up of all the single men, —
In such a synthesis the labor ends.
Now mark me! those divine men of old time
Have reached, thou sayest well, each at one point
The outside verge that rounds our faculty;
And where they reached, who can do more than reach?
It takes but little water just to touch
At some one point the inside of a sphere,   100
And, as we turn the sphere, touch all the rest
In due succession: but the finer air
Which not so palpably nor obviously,
Though no less universally, can touch
The whole circumference of that emptied sphere,
Fills it more fully than the water did;
Holds thrice the weight of water in itself
Resolved into a subtler element.
And yet the vulgar call the sphere first full

Up to the visible height — and after, void;   110
Not knowing air's more hidden properties.
And thus our soul, misknown, cries out to Zeus
To vindicate his purpose in our life:
Why stay we on the earth unless to grow?
Long since, I imaged, wrote the fiction out,
That he or other god descended here
And, once for all, showed simultaneously
What, in its nature, never can be shown,
Piecemeal or in succession; — showed, I say,
The worth both absolute and relative   120
Of all his children from the birth of time,
His instruments for all appointed work.
I now go on to image, — might we hear
The judgment which should give the due to each,
Show where the labor lay and where the ease,
And prove Zeus' self, the latent everywhere!
This is a dream: — but no dream, let us hope,
That years and days, the summers and the springs,
Follow each other with unwaning powers.
The grapes which dye thy wine are richer far,   130
Through culture, than the wild wealth of the rock;
The suave plum than the savage-tasted drupe;
The pastured honey-bee drops choicer sweet;
The flowers turn double, and the leaves turn flowers;
That young and tender crescent-moon, thy slave,
Sleeping above her robe as buoyed by clouds,
Refines upon the women of my youth.
What, and the soul alone deteriorates?
I have not chanted verse like Homer, no —
Nor swept string like Terpander, no — nor carved   140
And painted men like Phidias and his friend:
I am not great as they are, point by point.
But I have entered into sympathy
With these four, running these into one soul,
Who, separate, ignored each other's art.
Say, is it nothing that I know them all?
The wild flower was the larger; I have dashed
Rose-blood upon its petals, pricked its cup's
Honey with wine, and driven its seed to fruit,
And show a better flower if not so large: 150
I stand myself. Refer this to the gods
Whose gift alone it is! which, shall I dare
(All pride apart) upon the absurd pretext

That such a gift by chance lay in my hand,
Discourse of lightly or depreciate?
It might have fallen to another's hand: what then?
I pass too surely: let at least truth stay!

And next, of what thou followest on to ask.
This being with me as I declare, O king,
My works, in all these varicolored kinds,   160
So done by me, accepted so by men —
Thou askest, if (my soul thus in men's hearts)
I must not be accounted to attain
The very crown and proper end of life?
Inquiring thence how, now life closeth up,
I face death with success in my right hand:
Whether I fear death less than dost thyself
The fortunate of men? "For" (writest thou)
"Thou leavest much behind, while I leave naught.
Thy life stays in the poems men shall sing,   170
The pictures men shall study; while my life,
Complete and whole now in its power and joy,
Dies altogether with my brain and arm,
Is lost indeed; since, what survives myself?
The brazen statue to o'erlook my grave,
Set on the promontory which I named.
And that — some supple courtier of my heir
Shall use its robed and sceptred arm, perhaps,
To fix the rope to, which best drags it down.
I go then: triumph thou, who dost not go!"   180

Nay, thou art worthy of hearing my whole mind.
Is this apparent, when thou turn'st to muse
Upon the scheme of earth and man in chief,
That admiration grows as knowledge grows?
That imperfection means perfection hid,
Reserved in part, to grace the after-time?
If, in the morning of philosophy,
Ere aught had been recorded, nay perceived,
Thou, with the light now in thee, couldst have looked
On all earth's tenantry, from worm to bird,   190
Ere man, her last, appeared upon the stage —
Thou wouldst have seen them perfect, and deduced
The perfectness of others yet unseen.
Conceding which, — had Zeus then questioned thee
"Shall I go on a step, improve on this,

Do more for visible creatures than is done?"
Thou wouldst have answered, "Ay, by making each
Grow conscious in himself — by that alone.
All's perfect else: the shell sucks fast the rock,
The fish strikes through the sea, the snake both swims   200
And slides, forth range the beasts, the birds take flight,
Till life's mechanics can no further go —
And all this joy in natural life is put
Like fire from off thy finger into each,
So exquisitely perfect is the same.
But 'tis pure fire, and they mere matter are;
It has them, not they it: and so I choose
For man, thy last premeditated work
(If I might add a glory to the scheme)
That a third thing should stand apart from both,   210
A quality arise within his soul,
Which, intro-active, made to supervise
And feel the force it has, may view itself,
And so be happy." Man might live at first
The animal life: but is there nothing more?
In due time, let him critically learn
How he lives; and, the more he gets to know
Of his own life's adaptabilities,
The more joy-giving will his life become.
Thus man, who hath this quality, is best.   220

       But thou, king, hadst more reasonably said:
"Let progress end at once, — man make no step
Beyond the natural man, the better beast,
Using his senses, not the sense of sense."
In man there's failure, only since he left
The lower and inconscious forms of life.
We called it an advance, the rendering plain
Man's spirit might grow conscious of man's life,
And, by new lore so added to the old,
Take each step higher over the brute's head.   230
This grew the only life, the pleasure-house,
Watch-tower and treasure-fortress of the soul,
Which whole surrounding flats of natural life
Seemed only fit to yield subsistence to;
A tower that crowns a country. But alas,
The soul now climbs it just to perish there!
For thence we have discovered ('tis no dream —
We know this, which we had not else perceived)

That there's a world of capability
For joy, spread round about us, meant for us,   240
Inviting us; and still the soul craves all,
And still the flesh replies, "Take no jot more
Than ere thou clombst the tower to look abroad!
Nay, so much less as that fatigue has brought
Deduction to it." We struggle, fain to enlarge
Our bounded physical recipiency,
Increase our power, supply fresh oil to life,
Repair the waste of age and sickness: no,
It skills not! life's inadequate to joy,
As the soul sees joy, tempting life to take.   250
They praise a fountain in my garden here
Wherein a Naiad sends the water-bow
Thin from her tube; she smiles to see it rise.
What if I told her, it is just a thread
From that great river which the hills shut up,
And mock her with my leave to take the same?
The artificer has given her one small tube
Past power to widen or exchange — what boots
To know she might spout oceans if she could?
She cannot lift beyond her first thin thread: 260
And so a man can use but a man's joy
While he sees God's. Is it for Zeus to boast,
"See, man, how happy I live, and despair —
That I may be still happier — for thy use!"
If this were so, we could not thank our Lord,
As hearts beat on to doing; 'tis not so —
Malice it is not. Is it carelessness?
Still, no. If care — where is the sign? I ask,
And get no answer, and agree in sum,
O king, with thy profound discouragement,   270
Who seest the wider but to sigh the more.
Most progress is most failure: thou sayest well.

The last point now: — thou dost except a case —
Holding joy not impossible to one
With artist-gifts — to such a man as I
Who leave behind me living works indeed;
For, such a poem, such a painting lives.
What? dost thou verily trip upon a word,
Confound the accurate view of what joy is
(Caught somewhat clearer by my eyes than thine)   280
With feeling joy? confound the knowing how

And showing how to live (my faculty)
With actually living! — Otherwise
Where is the artist's vantage o'er the king?
Because in my great epos I display
How divers men young, strong, fair, wise, can act —
Is this as though I acted? if I paint,
Carve the young Phœbus, am I therefore young?
Methinks I'm older that I bowed myself
The many years of pain that taught me art!   290
Indeed, to know is something, and to prove
How all this beauty might be enjoyed, is more:
But, knowing naught, to enjoy is something too.   *enjoy*
Yon rower, with the moulded muscles there,
Lowering the sail, is nearer it than I.
I can write love-odes: thy fair slave's an ode.
I get to sing of love, when grown too gray
For being beloved: she turns to that young man,
The muscles all a-ripple on his back.
I know the joy of kingship: well, thou art king!   300

        "But," sayest thou — (and I marvel, I repeat,
To find thee trip on such a mere word) "what
Thou writest, paintest, stays; that does not die:
Sappho survives, because we sing her songs,
And Æschylus, because we read his plays!"
Why, if they live still, let them come and take   *poetry ≠ life*
Thy slave in my despite, drink from thy cup,
Speak in my place. Thou diest while I survive?
Say rather that my fate is deadlier still,
In this, that every day my sense of joy   310
Grows more acute, my soul (intensified
By power and insight) more enlarged, more keen;
While every day my hairs fall more and more,
My hand shakes, and the heavy years increase —
The horror quickening still from year to year,
The consummation coming past escape
When I shall know most, and yet least enjoy —
When all my works wherein I prove my worth,
Being present still to mock me in men's mouths,
Alive still, in the praise of such as thou,   320
I, I the feeling, thinking, acting man,
The man who loved his life so over-much,
Sleep in my urn. It is so horrible,
I dare at times imagine to my need

Some future state revealed to us by Zeus,
Unlimited in capability

[handwritten: Heaven?]

For joy, as this is in desire for joy,
— To seek which, the joy-hunger forces us:
That, stung by straitness of our life, made strait
On purpose to make prized the life at large —   330
Freed by the throbbing impulse we call death,
We burst there as the worm into the fly,
Who, while a worm still, wants his wings. But no!
Zeus has not yet revealed it; and alas,
He must have done so, were it possible!

[handwritten: not in Greece]

    Live long and happy, and in that thought die:
Glad for what was! Farewell. And for the rest,
I cannot tell thy messenger aright
Where to deliver what he bears of thine
To one called Paulus; we have heard his fame   340
Indeed, if Christus be not one with him —
I know not, nor am troubled much to know.

[handwritten: Answer (xty) dismissed]

Thou canst not think a mere barbarian Jew,
As Paulus proves to be, one circumcised,
Hath access to a secret shut from us?
Thou wrongest our philosophy, O king,
In stooping to inquire of such an one,
As if his answer could impose at all!
He writeth, doth he? well, and he may write.
Oh, the Jew findeth scholars! certain slaves   350
Who touched on this same isle, preached him and Christ;
And (as I gathered from a bystander)
Their doctrine could be held by no sane man.

POPULARITY

I

STAND still, true poet that you are!
    I know you; let me try and draw you.
Some night you'll fail us: when afar
    You rise, remember one man saw you,
Knew you, and named a star!

II

My star, God's glow-worm! Why extend
    That loving hand of his which leads you,
Yet locks you safe from end to end
    Of this dark world, unless he needs you,
Just saves your light to spend?   **10**

III

His clenched hand shall unclose at last,
    I know, and let out all the beauty:
My poet holds the future fast,
    Accepts the coming ages' duty,
Their present for this past.

IV

That day, the earth's feast-master's brow
    Shall clear, to God the chalice raising;
"Others give best at first, but thou
    Forever set'st our table praising,
Keep'st the good wine till now!"   **20**

V

Meantime, I'll draw you as you stand,
    With few or none to watch and wonder:
I'll say — a fisher, on the sand
    By Tyre the old, with ocean-plunder,
A netful, brought to land.

VI

Who has not heard how Tyrian shells
    Enclosed the blue, that dye of dyes
Whereof one drop worked miracles,
    And colored like Astarte's eyes
Raw silk the merchant sells?   **30**

VII

And each bystander of them all
    Could criticise, and quote tradition
How depths of blue sublimed some pall
    — To get which, pricked a king's ambition;
Worth sceptre, crown and ball.

VIII

Yet there's the dye, in that rough mesh,
    The sea has only just o'erwhispered!
Live whelks, each lip's beard dripping fresh,
    As if they still the water's lisp heard
Through foam the rock-weeds thresh.   40

IX

Enough to furnish Solomon
    Such hangings for his cedar-house,
That, when gold-robed he took the throne
    In that abyss of blue, the Spouse
Might swear his presence shone

X

Most like the centre-spike of gold
    Which burns deep in the blue-bell's womb,
What time, with ardors manifold,
    The bee goes singing to her groom,
Drunken and overbold.   50

XI

Mere conchs! not fit for warp or woof!
    Till cunning come to pound and squeeze
And clarify, — refine to proof
    The liquor filtered by degrees,
While the world stands aloof.

XII

And there's the extract, flasked and fine,
    And priced and salable at last!
And Hobbs, Nobbs, Stokes and Nokes combine
    To paint the future from the past,
Put blue into their line.   60

XIII

Hobbs hints blue, — straight he turtle eats:
    Nobbs prints blue, — claret crowns his cup:
Nokes outdares Stokes in azure feats, —
    Both gorge. Who fished the murex up?
What porridge had John Keats?

TWO IN THE CAMPAGNA

I

I WONDER do you feel to-day
    As I have felt since, hand in hand,
We sat down on the grass, to stray
    In spirit better through the land,
This morn of Rome and May?

II

For me, I touched a thought, I know,
    Has tantalized me many times,
(Like turns of thread the spiders throw
    Mocking across our path) for rhymes
To catch at and let go.   10

III

Help me to hold it! First it left
    The yellowing fennel, run to seed
There, branching from the brickwork's cleft,
    Some old tomb's ruin: yonder weed
Took up the floating weft,

IV

Where one small orange cup amassed
    Five beetles, — blind and green they grope
Among the honey-meal: and last,
    Everywhere on the grassy slope
I traced it. Hold it fast!   20

V

The champaign with its endless fleece
    Of feathery grasses everywhere!
Silence and passion, joy and peace,
    An everlasting wash of air —
Rome's ghost since her decease.

VI

Such life here, through such lengths of hours,
  Such miracles performed in play,
Such primal naked forms of flowers,
  Such letting nature have her way
While heaven looks from its towers!   30

VII

How say you? Let us, O my dove,
  Let us be unashamed of soul,
As earth lies bare to heaven above!
  How is it under our control
To love or not to love?

VIII

I would that you were all to me,
  You that are just so much, no more.
Nor yours nor mine, nor slave nor free!
  Where does the fault lie? What the core
O' the wound, since wound must be?   40

IX

I would I could adopt your will,
  See with your eyes, and set my heart
Beating by yours, and drink my fill
  At your soul's springs, — your part my part
In life, for good and ill.

X

No. I yearn upward, touch you close,
  Then stand away. I kiss your cheek,
Catch your soul's warmth, — I pluck the rose
  And love it more than tongue can speak —
Then the good minute goes.   50

XI

Already how am I so far
  Out of that minute? Must I go
Still like the thistle-ball, no bar,
  Onward, whenever light winds blow,
Fixed by no friendly star?

XII

Just when I seemed about to learn!
    Where is the thread now? Off again!
The old trick! Only I discern —
    Infinite passion, and the pain
Of finite hearts that yearn.   60

A GRAMMARIAN'S FUNERAL

Shortly after the revival of learning in Europe

LET us begin and carry up this corpse,
    Singing together.
Leave we the common crofts, the vulgar thorpes
    Each in its tether
Sleeping safe on the bosom of the plain,
    Cared-for till cock-crow:
Look out if yonder be not day again
    Rimming the rock-row!
That's the appropriate country; there, man's thought,
    Rarer, intenser,   10
Self-gathered for an outbreak, as it ought,
    Chafes in the censer.
Leave we the unlettered plain its herd and crop;
    Seek we sepulture
On a tall mountain, citied to the top,
    Crowded with culture!
All the peaks soar, but one the rest excels;
    Clouds overcome it;
No! yonder sparkle is the citadel's
    Circling its summit.   20
Thither our path lies; wind we up the heights:
    Wait ye the warning?
Our low life was the level's and the night's;
    He's for the morning.
Step to a tune, square chests, erect each head,
    'Ware the beholders!
This is our master, famous calm and dead,
    Borne on our shoulders.

Sleep, crop and herd! sleep, darkling thorpe and croft,
    Safe from the weather!   30
He, whom we convoy to his grave aloft,
    Singing together,
He was a man born with thy face and throat,
    Lyric Apollo!
Long he lived nameless: how should spring take note
    Winter would follow?
Till lo, the little touch, and youth was gone!
    Cramped and diminished,
Moaned he, "New measures, other feet anon!
    My dance is finished?"   40
No, that's the world's way: (keep the mountain-side,
    Make for the city!)
He knew the signal, and stepped on with pride
    Over men's pity;
Left play for work, and grappled with the world
    Bent on escaping:
"What's in the scroll," quoth he, "thou keepest furled?
    Show me their shaping,
Theirs who most studied man, the bard and sage, —
    Give!" — So, he gowned him,   50
Straight got by heart that book to its last page:
    Learned, we found him.
Yea, but we found him bald too, eyes like lead,
    Accents uncertain:
"Time to taste life," another would have said,
    "Up with the curtain!"
This man said rather, "Actual life comes next?
    Patience a moment!
Grant I have mastered learning's crabbed text
    Still there's the comment.   60
Let me know all! Prate not of most or least,
    Painful or easy!
Even to the crumbs I'd fain eat up the feast,
    Ay, nor feel queasy."
Oh, such a life as he resolved to live,
    When he had learned it,
When he had gathered all books had to give!
    Sooner, he spurned it.
Image the whole, then execute the parts —
    Fancy the fabric   70
Quite, ere you build, ere steel strike fire from quartz,
    Ere mortar dab brick!

(Here's the town-gate reached: there's the market-place
   Gaping before us.)
Yea, this in him was the peculiar grace
   (Hearten our chorus!)
That before living he'd learn how to live —
   No end to learning:
Earn the means first — God surely will contrive
   Use for our earning.   80
Others mistrust and say, "But time escapes:
   Live now or never!"
He said, "What's time? Leave Now for dogs and apes!
   Man has Forever."
Back to his book then: deeper drooped his head:
   Calculus racked him:
Leaden before, his eyes grew dross of lead:
   Tussis attacked him.
"Now, master, take a little rest!" — not he!
   (Caution redoubled,   90
Step two abreast, the way winds narrowly!)
   Not a whit troubled
Back to his studies, fresher than at first,
   Fierce as a dragon
He (soul-hydroptic with a sacred thirst)
   Sucked at the flagon.
Oh, if we draw a circle premature,
   Heedless of far gain,
Greedy for quick returns of profit, sure
   Bad is our bargain!   100
Was it not great? did not he throw on God,
   (He loves the burthen) —
God's task to make the heavenly period
   Perfect the earthen?
Did not he magnify the mind, show clear
   Just what it all meant?
He would not discount life, as fools do here,
   Paid by instalment.
He ventured neck or nothing — heaven's success
   Found, or earth's failure: 110
"Wilt thou trust death or not?" He answered "Yes:
   Hence with life's pale lure!"
That low man seeks a little thing to do,
   Sees it and does it:
This high man, with a great thing to pursue,
   Dies ere he knows it.

That low man goes on adding one to one,
    His hundred's soon hit:
This high man, aiming at a million,
    Misses an unit.   120
That, has the world here — should he need the next,
    Let the world mind him!
This, throws himself on God, and unperplexed
    Seeking shall find him.
So, with the throttling hands of death at strife,
    Ground he at grammar;
Still, thro' the rattle, parts of speech were rife:
    While he could stammer
He settled *Hoti's* business — let it be! —
    Properly based *Oun* —   130
Gave us the doctrine of the enclitic *De*,
    Dead from the waist down.
Well, here's the platform, here's the proper place:
    Hail to your purlieus,
All ye highfliers of the feathered race,
    Swallows and curlews!
Here's the top-peak; the multitude below
    Live, for they can, there:
This man decided not to Live but Know —
    Bury this man there?   140
Here — here's his place, where meteors shoot, clouds form,
    Lightnings are loosened,
Stars come and go! Let joy break with the storm,
    Peace let the dew send!
Lofty designs must close in like effects:
    Loftily lying,
Leave him — still loftier than the world suspects,
    Living and dying.

"TRANSCENDENTALISM: A POEM IN TWELVE BOOKS"

Stop playing, poet! May a brother speak?
'Tis you speak, that's your error. Song's our art:
Whereas you please to speak these naked thoughts
Instead of draping them in sights and sounds.

— True thoughts, good thoughts, thoughts fit to treasure up!
But why such long prolusion and display,
Such turning and adjustment of the harp,
And taking it upon your breast, at length,
Only to speak dry words across its strings?
Stark-naked thought is in request enough: 10
Speak prose and hollo it till Europe hears!
The six-foot Swiss tube, braced about with bark,
Which helps the hunter's voice from Alp to Alp —
Exchange our harp for that, — who hinders you?

But here's your fault; grown men want thought, you think;
Thought's what they mean by verse, and seek in verse.
Boys seek for images and melody,
Men must have reason — so, you aim at men.
Quite otherwise! Objects throng our youth, 'tis true;
We see and hear and do not wonder much: 20
If you could tell us what they mean, indeed!
As German Boehme never cared for plants
Until it happed, a-walking in the fields,
He noticed all at once that plants could speak,
Nay, turned with loosened tongue to talk with him.
That day the daisy had an eye indeed —
Colloquized with the cowslip on such themes!
We find them extant yet in Jacob's prose.
But by the time youth slips a stage or two
While reading prose in that tough book he wrote   30
(Collating and emendating the same
And settling on the sense most to our mind),
We shut the clasps and find life's summer past.
Then, who helps more, pray, to repair our loss —
Another Boehme with a tougher book
And subtler meanings of what roses say, —
Or some stout Mage like him of Halberstadt,
John, who made things Boehme wrote thoughts about?
He with a "look you!" vents a brace of rhymes,
And in there breaks the sudden rose herself,   40
Over us, under, round us every side,
Nay, in and out the tables and the chairs
And musty volumes, Boehme's book and all, —
Buries us with a glory, young once more,
Pouring heaven into this shut house of life.

So come, the harp back to your heart again!
You are a poem, though your poem's naught.
The best of all you showed before, believe,
Was your own boy-face o'er the finer chords
Bent, following the cherub at the top   50
That points to God with his paired half-moon wings.

ONE WORD MORE

To E. B. B.

I

THERE they are, my fifty men and women
Naming me the fifty poems finished!
Take them, Love, the book and me together:
Where the heart lies, let the brain lie also.

II

Rafael made a century of sonnets,
Made and wrote them in a certain volume
Dinted with the silver-pointed pencil
Else he only used to draw Madonnas:
These, the world might view — but one, the volume.
Who that one, you ask? Your heart instructs you.   10
Did she live and love it all her life-time?
Did she drop, his lady of the sonnets,
Die, and let it drop beside her pillow
Where it lay in place of Rafael's glory,
Rafael's cheek so duteous and so loving —
Cheek, the world was wont to hail a painter's,
Rafael's cheek, her love had turned a poet's?

III

You and I would rather read that volume,
(Taken to his beating bosom by it)
Lean and list the bosom-beats of Rafael,
Would we not? than wonder at Madonnas —
Her, San Sisto names, and Her, Foligno,
Her, that visits Florence in a vision,
Her, that's left with lilies in the Louvre —
Seen by us and all the world in circle.

IV

You and I will never read that volume.
Guido Reni, like his own eye's apple
Guarded long the treasure-book and loved it.
Guido Reni dying, all Bologna
Cried, and the world cried too, "Ours, the treasure!" 30
Suddenly, as rare things will, it vanished.

V

Dante once prepared to paint an angel:
Whom to please? You whisper "Beatrice."
While he mused and traced it and retraced it,
(Peradventure with a pen corroded
Still by drops of that hot ink he dipped for,
When, his left-hand i' the hair o' the wicked,
Back he held the brow and pricked its stigma,
Bit into the live man's flesh for parchment,
Loosed him, laughed to see the writing rankle, 40
Let the wretch go festering through Florence) —
Dante, who loved well because he hated,
Hated wickedness that hinders loving,
Dante standing, studying his angel, —
In there broke the folk of his Inferno.
Says he — "Certain people of importance"
(Such he gave his daily dreadful line to)
"Entered and would seize, forsooth, the poet."
Says the poet — "Then I stopped my painting."

VI

You and I would rather see that angel, 50
Painted by the tenderness of Dante,
Would we not? — than read a fresh Inferno.

VII

You and I will never see that picture.
While he mused on love and Beatrice,
While he softened o'er his outlined angel,
In they broke, those "people of importance."
We and Bice bear the loss forever.

VIII

What of Rafael's sonnets, Dante's picture?
This: no artist lives and loves, that longs not
Once, and only once, and for one only,   60
(Ah, the prize!) to find his love a language
Fit and fair and simple and sufficient —
Using nature that's an art to others,
Not, this one time, art that's turned his nature.
Ay, of all the artists living, loving,
None but would forego his proper dowry, —
Does he paint? he fain would write a poem, —
Does he write? he fain would paint a picture,
Put to proof art alien to the artist's,
Once, and only once, and for one only,   70
So to be the man and leave the artist,
Gain the man's joy, miss the artist's sorrow.

IX

Wherefore? Heaven's gift takes earth's abatement!
He who smites the rock and spreads the water,
Bidding drink and live a crowd beneath him,
Even he, the minute makes immortal,
Proves, perchance, but mortal in the minute,
Desecrates, belike, the deed in doing.
While he smites, how can he but remember,
So he smote before, in such a peril,   80
When they stood and mocked — "Shall smiting help us?"
When they drank and sneered — "A stroke is easy!"
When they wiped their mouths and went their journey,
Throwing him for thanks — "But drought was pleasant."
Thus old memories mar the actual triumph;
Thus the doing savors of disrelish;
Thus achievement lacks a gracious somewhat;
O'er-importuned brows becloud the mandate,
Carelessness or consciousness — the gesture.
For he bears an ancient wrong about him,   90
Sees and knows again those phalanxed faces,
Hears, yet one time more, the 'customed prelude —
"How shouldst thou, of all men, smite, and save us?"
Guesses what is like to prove the sequel —
"Egypt's flesh-pots — nay, the drought was better."

X

Oh, the crowd must have emphatic warrant!
Theirs, the Sinai-forehead's cloven brilliance,
Right-arm's rod-sweep, tongue's imperial fiat.
Never dares the man put off the prophet.

XI

Did he love one face from out the thousands, 100
(Were she Jethro's daughter, white and wifely,
Were she but the Æthiopian bondslave,)
He would envy yon dumb patient camel,
Keeping a reserve of scanty water
Meant to save his own life in the desert;
Ready in the desert to deliver
(Kneeling down to let his breast be opened)
Hoard and life together for his mistress.

XII

I shall never, in the years remaining,
Paint you pictures, no, nor carve you statues, 110
Make you music that should all-express me;
So it seems: I stand on my attainment.
This of verse alone, one life allows me;
Verse and nothing else have I to give you.
Other heights in other lives, God willing:
All the gifts from all the heights, your own, Love!

XIII

Yet a semblance of resource avails us —
Shade so finely touched, love's sense must seize it.
Take these lines, look lovingly and nearly,
Lines I write the first time and the last time. 120
He who works in fresco, steals a hair brush,
Curbs the liberal hand, subservient proudly,
Cramps his spirit, crowds its all in little,
Makes a strange art of an art familiar,
Fills his lady's missal-marge with flowerets.
He who blows thro' bronze, may breathe thro' silver,
Fitly serenade a slumbrous princess.
He who writes, may write for once as I do.

xiv

Love, you saw me gather men and women,
Live or dead or fashioned by my fancy,   130
Enter each and all, and use their service,
Speak from every mouth, — the speech, a poem.
Hardly shall I tell my joys and sorrows,
Hopes and fears, belief and disbelieving:
I am mine and yours — the rest be all men's,
Karshish, Cleon, Norbert and the fifty.
Let me speak this once in my true person,
Not as Lippo, Roland or Andrea,
Though the fruit of speech be just this sentence:
Pray you, look on these my men and women,   140
Take and keep my fifty poems finished;
Where my heart lies, let my brain lie also!
Poor the speech; be how I speak, for all things.

xv

Not but that you know me! Lo, the moon's self!
Here in London, yonder late in Florence,
Still we find her face, the thrice-transfigured.
Curving on a sky imbrued with color,
Drifted over Fiesole by twilight,
Came she, our new crescent of a hair's-breadth.
Full she flared it, lamping Samminiato,   150
Rounder 'twixt the cypresses and rounder,
Perfect till the nightingales applauded.
Now, a piece of her old self, impoverished,
Hard to greet, she traverses the houseroofs,
Hurries with unhandsome thrift of silver,
Goes dispiritedly, glad to finish.

xvi

What, there's nothing in the moon noteworthy?
Nay: for if that moon could love a mortal,
Use, to charm him (so to fit a fancy),
All her magic ('tis the old sweet mythos),   160
She would turn a new side to her mortal,
Side unseen of herdsman, huntsman, steersman —
Blank to Zoroaster on his terrace,
Blind to Galileo on his turret,
Dumb to Homer, dumb to Keats — him, even!

Think, the wonder of the moonstruck mortal —
When she turns round, comes again in heaven,
Opens out anew for worse or better!
Proves she like some portent of an iceberg
Swimming full upon the ship it founders,   170
Hungry with huge teeth of splintered crystals?
Proves she as the paved work of a sapphire
Seen by Moses when he climbed the mountain?
Moses, Aaron, Nadab and Abihu
Climbed and saw the very God, the Highest,
Stand upon the paved work of a sapphire.
Like the bodied heaven in his clearness
Shone the stone, the sapphire of that paved work,
When they ate and drank and saw God also!

XVII

What were seen? None knows, none ever shall know.   180
Only this is sure — the sight were other,
Not the moon's same side, born late in Florence,
Dying now impoverished here in London.
God be thanked, the meanest of his creatures
Boasts two soul-sides, one to face the world with,
One to show a woman when he loves her!

XVIII

This I say of me, but think of you, Love!
This to you — yourself my moon of poets!
Ah, but that's the world's side, there's the wonder,
Thus they see you, praise you, think they know you!   190
There, in turn I stand with them and praise you —
Out of my own self, I dare to phrase it.
But the best is when I glide from out them,
Cross a step or two of dubious twilight,
Come out on the other side, the novel
Silent silver lights and darks undreamed of,
Where I hush and bless myself with silence.

XIX

Oh, their Rafael of the dear Madonnas,
Oh, their Dante of the dread Inferno,
Wrote one song — and in my brain I sing it,   200
Drew one angel — borne, see, on my bosom!

R. B.

FROM *Dramatis Personae*
(1864)

⊓⊔⊓⊔⊓⊔⊓⊔⊓⊔⊓⊔⊓⊔⊓⊔⊓⊔⊓⊔⊓⊔⊓⊔⊓⊔⊓⊔

JAMES LEE'S WIFE

1 JAMES LEE'S WIFE SPEAKS AT THE WINDOW

I

Ah, Love, but a day
    And the world has changed!
The sun's away,
    And the bird estranged;
The wind has dropped,
    And the sky's deranged:
Summer has stopped.

II

Look in my eyes!
    Wilt thou change too?
Should I fear surprise?   10
    Shall I find aught new
In the old and dear,
    In the good and true,
With the changing year?

III

Thou art a man,
    But I am thy love.
For the lake, its swan;
    For the dell, its dove;
And for thee — (oh, haste!)
    Me, to bend above,
Me, to hold embraced.   20

265

2   By the Fireside

I

Is all our fire of shipwreck wood,
    Oak and pine?
Oh, for the ills half-understood,
    The dim dead woe
    Long ago
Befallen this bitter coast of France!
Well, poor sailors took their chance;
    I take mine.

II

A ruddy shaft our fire must shoot   30
    O'er the sea:
Do sailors eye the casement — mute,
    Drenched and stark,
    From their bark —
And envy, gnash their teeth for hate
O' the warm safe house and happy freight
    — Thee and me?

III

God help you, sailors, at your need!
    Spare the curse!
For some ships, safe in port indeed,   40
    Rot and rust,
    Run to dust,
All through worms i' the wood, which crept,
Gnawed our hearts out while we slept:
    That is worse.

IV

Who lived here before us two?
    Old-world pairs.
Did a woman ever — would I knew! —
    Watch the man
    With whom began   50
Love's voyage full-sail, — (now, gnash your teeth!)
When planks start, open hell beneath
    Unawares?

3 In the Doorway

I

THE swallow has set her six young on the rail,
    And looks sea-ward:
The water's in stripes like a snake, olive-pale
    To the leeward, —
On the weather-side, black, spotted white with the wind.
"Good fortune departs, and disaster's behind," —
Hark, the wind with its wants and its infinite wail!   60

II

Our fig-tree, that leaned for the saltness, has furled
    Her five fingers,
Each leaf like a hand opened wide to the world
    Where there lingers
No glint of the gold, Summer sent for her sake:
How the vines writhe in rows, each impaled on its stake!
My heart shrivels up and my spirit shrinks curled.

III

Yet here are we two; we have love, house enough,
    With the field there,
This house of four rooms, that field red and rough,   70
    Though it yield there,
For the rabbit that robs, scarce a blade or a bent;
If a magpie alight now, it seems an event;
And they both will be gone at November's rebuff.

IV

But why must cold spread? but wherefore bring change
    To the spirit,
God meant should mate his with an infinite range,
    And inherit
His power to put life in the darkness and cold?
Oh, live and love worthily, bear and be bold!   80
Whom Summer made friends of, let Winter estrange!

4 ALONG THE BEACH

I

I WILL be quiet and talk with you,
    And reason why you are wrong.
You wanted my love — is that much true?
And so I did love, so I do:
    What has come of it all along?

II

I took you — how could I otherwise?
    For a world to me, and more;
For all, love greatens and glorifies
Till God's a-glow, to the loving eyes,   90
    In what was mere earth before.

III

Yes, earth — yes, mere ignoble earth!
    Now do I mis-state, mistake?
Do I wrong your weakness and call it worth?
Expect all harvest, dread no dearth,
    Seal my sense up for your sake?

IV

Oh, Love, Love, no, Love! not so, indeed!
    You were just weak earth, I knew:
With much in you waste, with many a weed,
And plenty of passions run to seed,   100
    But a little good grain too.

V

And such as you were, I took you for mine:
    Did not you find me yours,
To watch the olive and wait the vine,
And wonder when rivers of oil and wine
    Would flow, as the Book assures?

VI

Well, and if none of these good things came,
    What did the failure prove?
The man was my whole world, all the same,
With his flowers to praise or his weeds to blame,   110
    And, either or both, to love.

VII

Yet this turns now to a fault — there! there!
    That I do love, watch too long,
And wait too well, and weary and wear;
And 'tis all an old story, and my despair
    Fit subject for some new song:

VIII

"How the light, light love, he has wings to fly
    At suspicion of a bond:
My wisdom has bidden your pleasure good-bye,
Which will turn up next in a laughing eye,   120
    And why should you look beyond?"

5   ON THE CLIFF

I

I LEANED on the turf,
I looked at a rock
Left dry by the surf;
For the turf, to call it grass were to mock:
Dead to the roots, so deep was done
The work of the summer sun.

II

And the rock lay flat
As an anvil's face:
No iron like that!   130
Baked dry; of a weed, of a shell, no trace:
Sunshine outside, but ice at the core,
Death's altar by the lone shore.

III

On the turf, sprang gay
With his films of blue,
No cricket, I'll say,
But a warhorse, barded and chanfroned too,
The gift of a quixote-mage to his knight,
Real fairy, with wings all right.

IV

On the rock, they scorch   140
Like a drop of fire
From a brandished torch,
Fall two red fans of a butterfly:
No turf, no rock: in their ugly stead,
See, wonderful blue and red!

V

Is it not so
With the minds of men?
The level and low,
The burnt and bare, in themselves; but then
With such a blue and red grace, not theirs, —   150
Love settling unawares!

6 READING A BOOK, UNDER THE CLIFF

I

"STILL ailing, Wind? Wilt be appeased or no?
    Which needs the other's office, thou or I?
Dost want to be disburthened of a woe,
    And can, in truth, my voice untie
Its links, and let it go?

II

"Art thou a dumb wronged thing that would be righted,
    Entrusting thus thy cause to me? Forbear!
No tongue can mend such pleadings; faith, requited
    With falsehood, — love, at last aware   160
Of scorn, — hopes, early blighted, —

III

"We have them; but I know not any tone
    So fit as thine to falter forth a sorrow:
Dost think men would go mad without a moan,
    If they knew any way to borrow
A pathos like thy own?

IV

"Which sigh wouldst mock, of all the sighs? The one
    So long escaping from lips starved and blue,
That lasts while on her pallet-bed the nun
    Stretches her length; her foot comes through   170
The straw she shivers on;

V

"You had not thought she was so tall: and spent,
    Her shrunk lids open, her lean fingers shut
Close, close, their sharp and livid nails indent
    The clammy palm; then all is mute:
That way, the spirit went.

VI

"Or wouldst thou rather that I understand
    Thy will to help me? — like the dog I found
Once, pacing sad this solitary strand,
    Who would not take my food, poor hound,   180
But whined and licked my hand."

VII

All this, and more, comes from some young man's pride
    Of power to see, — in failure and mistake,
Relinquishment, disgrace, on every side, —
    Merely examples for his sake,
Helps to his path untried:

VIII

Instances he must — simply recognize?
    Oh, more than so! — must, with a learner's zeal,
Make doubly prominent, twice emphasize,
    By added touches that reveal   190
The god in babe's disguise.

IX

Oh, he knows what defeat means, and the rest!
    Himself the undefeated that shall be:
Failure, disgrace, he flings them you to test, —
    His triumph, in eternity
To plainly manifest! ·

X

Whence, judge if he learn forthwith what the wind
    Means in its moaning — by the happy prompt
Instinctive way of youth, I mean; for kind
    Calm years, exacting their accompt   200
Of pain, mature the mind:

XI

And some midsummer morning, at the lull
    Just about daybreak, as he looks across
A sparkling foreign country, wonderful
    To the sea's edge for gloom and gloss,
Next minute must annul, —

XII

Then, when the wind begins among the vines,
    So low, so low, what shall it say but this?
"Here is the change beginning, here the lines
    Circumscribe beauty, set to bliss   210
The limit time assigns."

XIII

Nothing can be as it has been before;
    Better, so call it, only not the same.
To draw one beauty into our hearts' core,
    And keep it changeless! such our claim;
So answered, — Never more!

XIV

Simple? Why, this is the old woe o' the world;
    Tune, to whose rise and fall we live and die.
Rise with it, then! Rejoice that man is hurled
    From change to change unceasingly,   220
His soul's wings never furled!

XV

That's a new question; still replies the fact,
    Nothing endures: the wind moans, saying so;
We moan in acquiescence: there's life's pact,
    Perhaps probation — do *I* know?
God does: endure his act!

XVI

Only, for man, how bitter not to grave
    On his soul's hands' palms one fair good wise thing
Just as he grasped it! For himself, death's wave;
    While time first washes — ah, the sting! —   230
O'er all he'd sink to save.

7   Among the Rocks

I

Oh, good gigantic smile o' the brown old earth,
    This autumn morning! How he sets his bones
To bask i' the sun, and thrusts out knees and feet
For the ripple to run over in its mirth;
    Listening the while, where on the heap of stones
The white breast of the sea-lark twitters sweet.

II

That is the doctrine, simple, ancient, true;
    Such is life's trial, as old earth smiles and knows.
If you loved only what were worth your love,   240
Love were clear gain, and wholly well for you:
    Make the low nature better by your throes!
Give earth yourself, go up for gain above!

8 BESIDE THE DRAWING BOARD

I

"As like as a Hand to another Hand!"
 Whoever said that foolish thing,
Could not have studied to understand
 The counsels of God in fashioning,
Out of the infinite love of his heart,
This Hand, whose beauty I praise, apart
From the world of wonder left to praise,   250
If I tried to learn the other ways
Of love in its skill, or love in its power.
 "As like as a Hand to another Hand":
 Who said that, never took his stand,
Found and followed, like me, an hour,
The beauty in this, — how free, how fine
To fear, almost, — of the limit-line!
As I looked at this, and learned and drew,
 Drew and learned, and looked again,
While fast the happy minutes flew,   260
  Its beauty mounted into my brain,
  And a fancy seized me; I was fain
To efface my work, begin anew,
Kiss what before I only drew;
Ay, laying the red chalk 'twixt my lips,
  With soul to help if the mere lips failed,
  I kissed all right where the drawing ailed,
Kissed fast the grace that somehow slips
Still from one's soulless finger-tips.

II

'Tis a clay cast, the perfect thing,   270
 From Hand live once, dead long ago:
Princess-like it wears the ring
 To fancy's eye, by which we know
That here at length a master found
 His match, a proud lone soul its mate,
As soaring genius sank to ground,
 And pencil could not emulate

The beauty in this, — how free, how fine
To fear almost! — of the limit-line.
Long ago the god, like me   280
The worm, learned, each in our degree:
Looked and loved, learned and drew,
    Drew and learned and loved again,
While fast the happy minutes flew,
    Till beauty mounted into his brain
And on the finger which outvied
    His art he placed the ring that's there,
Still by fancy's eye descried,
    In token of a marriage rare:
    For him on earth, his art's despair,   290
For him in heaven, his soul's fit bride.

III

Little girl with the poor coarse hand
    I turned from to a cold clay cast —
I have my lesson, understand
    The worth of flesh and blood at last.
Nothing but beauty in a Hand?
    Because he could not change the hue,
    Mend the lines and make them true
To this which met his soul's demand, —
    Would Da Vinci turn from you?   300
I hear him laugh my woes to scorn —
"The fool forsooth is all forlorn
Because the beauty, she thinks best,
Lived long ago or was never born, —
Because no beauty bears the test
In this rough peasant Hand! Confessed!
'Art is null and study void!'
    So sayest thou? So said not I,
    Who threw the faulty pencil by,
And years instead of hours employed,   310
Learning the veritable use
    Of flesh and bone and nerve beneath
    Lines and hue of the outer sheath,
If haply I might reproduce
One motive of the powers profuse,
Flesh and bone and nerve that make
    The poorest coarsest human hand
    An object worthy to be scanned

A whole life long for their sole sake.
Shall earth and the cramped moment-space   320
Yield the heavenly crowning grace?
Now the parts and then the whole!
Who art thou, with stinted soul
    And stunted body, thus to cry
'I love, — shall that be life's strait dole?
    I must live beloved or die!'
This peasant hand that spins the wool
    And bakes the bread, why lives it on,
    Poor and coarse with beauty gone, —
What use survives the beauty?" Fool!   330

Go, little girl with the poor coarse hand!
I have my lesson, shall understand.

9 On Deck

I

THERE is nothing to remember in me,
    Nothing I ever said with a grace,
Nothing I did that you care to see,
    Nothing I was that deserves a place
In your mind, now I leave you, set you free.

II

Conceded! In turn, concede to me,
    Such things have been as a mutual flame.
Your soul's locked fast; but, love for a key,   340
    You might let it loose, till I grew the same
In your eyes, as in mine you stand: strange plea!

III

For then, then, what would it matter to me
    That I was the harsh ill-favored one?
We both should be like as pea and pea;
    It was ever so since the world begun:
So, let me proceed with my reverie.

IV

How strange it were if you had all me,
    As I have all you in my heart and brain,
You, whose least word brought gloom or glee,   350
    Who never lifted the hand in vain —
Will hold mine yet, from over the sea!

V

Strange, if a face, when you thought of me,
    Rose like your own face present now,
With eyes as dear in their due degree,
    Much such a mouth, and as bright a brow,
Till you saw yourself, while you cried " 'Tis She!"

VI

Well, you may, you must, set down to me
    Love that was life, life that was love;
A tenure of breath at your lips' decree,   360
    A passion to stand as your thoughts approve,
A rapture to fall where your foot might be.

VII

But did one touch of such love for me
    Come in a word or a look of yours,
Whose words and looks will, circling, flee
    Round me and round while life endures, —
Could I fancy "As I feel, thus feels he";

VIII

Why, fade you might to a thing like me,
    And your hair grow these coarse hanks of hair,
Your skin, this bark of a gnarled tree, —   370
    You might turn myself! — should I know or care
When I should be dead of joy, James Lee?

ABT VOGLER

*(After he has been extemporizing upon the musical
instrument of his invention.)*

I

WOULD that the structure brave, the manifold music I build,
    Bidding my organ obey, calling its keys to their work,
Claiming each slave of the sound, at a touch, as when Solomon willed
    Armies of angels that soar, legions of demons that lurk,
Man, brute, reptile, fly, — alien of end and of aim,
    Adverse, each from the other heaven-high, hell-deep removed, —
Should rush into sight at once as he named the ineffable Name,
    And pile him a palace straight, to pleasure the princess he loved!

II

Would it might tarry like his, the beautiful building of mine,
    This which my keys in a crowd pressed and importuned to raise!
Ah, one and all, how they helped, would dispart now and now combine,
    bine,   11
    Zealous to hasten the work, heighten their master his praise!
And one would bury his brow with a blind plunge down to hell,
    Burrow awhile and build, broad on the roots of things,
Then up again swim into sight, having based me my palace well,
    Founded it, fearless of flame, flat on the nether springs.

III

And another would mount and march, like the excellent minion he
    was,
    Ay, another and yet another, one crowd but with many a crest,
Raising my rampired walls of gold as transparent as glass,
    Eager to do and die, yield each his place to the rest: 20
For higher still and higher (as a runner tips with fire,
    When a great illumination surprises a festal night —
Outlining round and round Rome's dome from space to spire)
    Up, the pinnacled glory reached, and the pride of my soul was in
        sight.

IV

In sight? Not half! for it seemed, it was certain, to match man's birth,
    Nature in turn conceived, obeying an impulse as I;
And the emulous heaven yearned down, made effort to reach the earth,
    As the earth had done her best, in my passion, to scale the sky:
Novel splendors burst forth, grew familiar and dwelt with mine,
    Not a point nor peak but found and fixed its wandering star;   30
Meteor-moons, balls of blaze: and they did not pale nor pine,
    For earth had attained to heaven, there was no more near nor far.

V

Nay more; for there wanted not who walked in the glare and glow,
    Presences plain in the place; or, fresh from the Protoplast,
Furnished for ages to come, when a kindlier wind should blow,
    Lured now to begin and live, in a house to their liking at last;
Or else the wonderful Dead who have passed through the body **and**
    gone,
    But were back once more to breathe in an old world worth **their**
    new:
What never had been, was now; what was, as it shall be anon;
    And what is, — shall I say, matched both? for I was made perfect
    too.   40

VI

All through my keys that gave their sounds to a wish of my soul,
    All through my soul that praised as its wish flowed visibly forth,
All through music and me! For think, had I painted the whole,
    Why, there it had stood, to see, nor the process so wonder-worth:
Had I written the same, made verse — still, effect proceeds from
    cause,
    Ye know why the forms are fair, ye hear how the tale is told;
It is all triumphant art, but art in obedience to laws,
    Painter and poet are proud in the artist-list enrolled: —

VII

But here is the finger of God, a flash of the will that can,
    Existent behind all laws, that made them and, lo, they are!   50
And I know not if, save in this, such gift be allowed to man,
    That out of three sounds he frame, not a fourth sound, but a star.
Consider it well: each tone of our scale in itself is naught;
    It is everywhere in the world — loud, soft, and all is said:
Give it to me to use! I mix it with two in my thought:
    And, there! Ye have heard and seen: consider and bow the head!

VIII

Well, it is gone at last, the palace of music I reared;
  Gone! and the good tears start, the praises that come too slow;
For one is assured at first, one scarce can say that he feared,
  That he even gave it a thought, the gone thing was to go.   60
Never to be again! But many more of the kind
  As good, nay, better perchance: is this your comfort to me?
To me, who must be saved because I cling with my mind
  To the same, same self, same love, same God: ay, what was, shall
    be.

IX

Therefore to whom turn I but to thee, the ineffable Name?
  Builder and maker, thou, of houses not made with hands!
What, have fear of change from thee who art ever the same?
  Doubt that thy power can fill the heart that thy power expands?
There shall never be one lost good! What was, shall live as before;
  The evil is null, is naught, is silence implying sound;   70
What was good shall be good, with, for evil, so much good more;
  On the earth the broken arcs; in the heaven, a perfect round.

X

All we have willed or hoped or dreamed of good shall exist;
  Not its semblance, but itself; no beauty, nor good, nor power
Whose voice has gone forth, but each survives for the melodist
  When eternity affirms the conception of an hour.
The high that proved too high, the heroic for earth too hard,
  The passion that left the ground to lose itself in the sky,
Are music sent up to God by the lover and the bard;
  Enough that he heard it once: we shall hear it by-and-by.   80

XI

And what is our failure here but a triumph's evidence
  For the fulness of the days? Have we withered or agonized?
Why else was the pause prolonged but that singing might issue thence?
  Why rushed the discords in but that harmony should be prized?
Sorrow is hard to bear, and doubt is slow to clear,
  Each sufferer says his say, his scheme of the weal and woe:
But God has a few of us whom he whispers in the ear;
  The rest may reason and welcome: 'tis we musicians know.

XII

Well, it is earth with me; silence resumes her reign:
    I will be patient and proud, and soberly acquiesce.   **90**
Give me the keys. I feel for the common chord again,
    Sliding by semitones, till I sink to the minor, — yes,
And I blunt it into a ninth, and I stand on alien ground,
    Surveying awhile the heights I rolled from into the deep;
Which, hark, I have dared and done, for my resting-place is found,
    The C Major of this life: so, now I will try to sleep.

RABBI BEN EZRA

I

    Grow old along with me!
    The best is yet to be,
The last of life, for which the first was made:
    Our times are in His hand
    Who saith "A whole I planned,
Youth shows but half; trust God: see all nor be afraid!"

II

    Not that, amassing flowers,
    Youth sighed "Which rose make ours,
Which lily leave and then as best recall?"
    Not that, admiring stars,   **10**
    It yearned "Nor Jove, nor Mars;
Mine be some figured flame which blends, transcends them all!"

III

    Not for such hopes and fears
    Annulling youth's brief years,
Do I remonstrate: folly wide the mark!
    Rather I prize the doubt
    Low kinds exist without,
Finished and finite clods, untroubled by a spark.

IV

Poor vaunt of life indeed,
Were man but formed to feed   20
On joy, to solely seek and find and feast:
Such feasting ended, then
As sure an end to men;
Irks care the crop-full bird? Frets doubt the maw-crammed beast?

V

Rejoice we are allied
To That which doth provide
And not partake, effect and not receive!
A spark disturbs our clod;
Nearer we hold of God
Who gives, than of His tribes that take, I must believe.   30

VI

Then, welcome each rebuff
That turns earth's smoothness rough,
Each sting that bids nor sit nor stand but go!
Be our joys three-parts pain!
Strive, and hold cheap the strain;
Learn, nor account the pang; dare, never grudge the throe!

VII

For thence, — a paradox
Which comforts while it mocks, —
Shall life succeed in that it seems to fail:
What I aspired to be,   40
And was not, comforts me:
A brute I might have been, but would not sink i' the scale.

VIII

What is he but a brute
Whose flesh has soul to suit,
Whose spirit works lest arms and legs want play?
To man, propose this test —
Thy body at its best,
How far can that project thy soul on its lone way?

IX

Yet gifts should prove their use:
    I own the Past profuse   50
Of power each side, perfection every turn:
    Eyes, ears took in their dole,
    Brain treasured up the whole;
Should not the heart beat once "How good to live and learn"?

X

Not once beat "Praise be Thine!
    I see the whole design,
I, who saw power, see now love perfect too:
    Perfect I call Thy plan:
    Thanks that I was a man!
Maker, remake, complete, — I trust what Thou shalt do!"   60

XI

For pleasant is this flesh;
    Our soul, in its rose-mesh
Pulled ever to the earth, still yearns for rest;
    Would we some prize might hold
    To match those manifold
Possessions of the brute, — gain most, as we did best!

XII

Let us not always say
    "Spite of this flesh to-day
I strove, made head, gained ground upon the whole!"
    As the bird wings and sings,   70
    Let us cry "All good things
Are ours, nor soul helps flesh more, now, than flesh helps soul!"

XIII

Therefore I summon age
    To grant youth's heritage,
Life's struggle having so far reached its term:
    Thence shall I pass, approved
    A man, for aye removed
From the developed brute; a god though in the germ.

XIV

And I shall thereupon
Take rest, ere I be gone   80
Once more on my adventure brave and new:
Fearless and unperplexed,
When I wage battle next,
What weapons to select, what armor to indue.

XV

Youth ended, I shall try
My gain or loss thereby;
Leave the fire ashes, what survives is gold:
And I shall weigh the same,
Give life its praise or blame:
Young, all lay in dispute; I shall know, being old.   90

XVI

For note, when evening shuts,
A certain moment cuts
The deed off, calls the glory from the gray:
A whisper from the west
Shoots — "Add this to the rest,
Take it and try its worth: here dies another day."

XVII

So, still within this life,
Though lifted o'er its strife,
Let me discern, compare, pronounce at last,
"This rage was right i' the main,   100
That acquiescence vain:
The Future I may face now I have proved the Past."

XVIII

For more is not reserved
To man, with soul just nerved
To act to-morrow what he learns to-day:
Here, work enough to watch
The Master work, and catch
Hints of the proper craft, tricks of the tool's true play.

XIX

As it was better, youth
   Should strive, through acts uncouth,   110
Toward making, than repose on aught found made:
   So, better, age, exempt
   From strife, should know, than tempt
Further. Thou waitedest age: wait death nor be afraid!

XX

Enough now, if the Right
   And Good and Infinite
Be named here, as thou callest thy hand thine own,
   With knowledge absolute,
   Subject to no dispute
From fools that crowded youth, nor let thee feel alone.   120

XXI

Be there, for once and all,
   Severed great minds from small,
Announced to each his station in the Past!
   Was I, the world arraigned,
   Were they, my soul disdained,
Right? Let age speak the truth and give us peace at last!

XXII

Now, who shall arbitrate?
   Ten men love what I hate,
Shun what I follow, slight what I receive;
   Ten, who in ears and eyes   130
   Match me: we all surmise,
They this thing, and I that: whom shall my soul believe?

XXIII

Not on the vulgar mass
   Called "work," must sentence pass,
Things done, that took the eye and had the price;
   O'er which, from level stand,
   The low world laid its hand,
Found straightway to its mind, could value in a trice:

XXIV

But all, the world's coarse thumb
And finger failed to plumb,   140
So passed in making up the main account;
    All instincts immature,
    All purposes unsure,
That weighed not as his work, yet swelled the man's amount:

XXV

Thoughts hardly to be packed
Into a narrow act,
Fancies that broke through language and escaped;
    All I could never be,
    All, men ignored in me,
This, I was worth to God, whose wheel the pitcher shaped.   150

XXVI

Ay, note that Potter's wheel,
That metaphor! and feel
Why time spins fast, why passive lies our clay, —
    Thou, to whom fools propound,
    When the wine makes its round,
"Since life fleets, all is change; the Past gone, seize to-day!"

XXVII

Fool! All that is, at all,
Lasts ever, past recall;
Earth changes, but thy soul and God stand sure:
    What entered into thee,
    That was, is, and shall be: 160
Time's wheel runs back or stops: Potter and clay endure.

XXVIII

He fixed thee 'mid this dance
Of plastic circumstance,
This Present, thou, forsooth, wouldst fain arrest:
    Machinery just meant
    To give thy soul its bent,
Try thee and turn thee forth, sufficiently impressed.

XXIX

What though the earlier grooves
   Which ran the laughing loves   **170**
Around thy base, no longer pause and press?
    What though, about thy rim,
    Skull-things in order grim
Grow out, in graver mood, obey the sterner stress?

XXX

Look not thou down but up!
   To uses of a cup,
The festal board, lamp's flash and trumpet's peal,
    The new wine's foaming flow,
    The Master's lips a-glow!
Thou, heaven's consummate cup, what need'st thou with earth's wheel?

XXXI

But I need, now as then,   **181**
   Thee, God, who mouldest men;
And since, not even while the whirl was worst,
    Did I, — to the wheel of life
    With shapes and colors rife,
Bound dizzily, — mistake my end, to slake Thy thirst:

XXXII

So, take and use Thy work:
   Amend what flaws may lurk,
What strain o' the stuff, what warpings past the aim!
    My times be in Thy hand!   **190**
    Perfect the cup as planned!
Let age approve of youth, and death complete the same!

CALIBAN UPON SETEBOS; OR, NATURAL
THEOLOGY IN THE ISLAND

"Thou thoughtest that I was altogether such a one as thyself."

['WILL sprawl, now that the heat of day is best,
Flat on his belly in the pit's much mire,
With elbows wide, fists clenched to prop his chin.
And, while he kicks both feet in the cool slush,
And feels about his spine small eft-things course,
Run in and out each arm, and make him laugh:
And while above his head a pompion-plant,
Coating the cave-top as a brow its eye,
Creeps down to touch and tickle hair and beard,
And now a flower drops with a bee inside,   10
And now a fruit to snap at, catch and crunch, —
He looks out o'er yon sea which sunbeams cross
And recross till they weave a spider-web
(Meshes of fire, some great fish breaks at times)
And talks to his own self, howe'er he please,
Touching that other, whom his dam called God.
Because to talk about Him, vexes — ha,
Could He but know! and time to vex is now,
When talk is safer than in winter-time.
Moreover Prosper and Miranda sleep   20
In confidence he drudges at their task,
And it is good to cheat the pair, and gibe,
Letting the rank tongue blossom into speech.]

Setebos, Setebos, and Setebos!
'Thinketh, He dwelleth i' the cold o' the moon.

'Thinketh He made it, with the sun to match,
But not the stars; the stars came otherwise;
Only made clouds, winds, meteors, such as that:
Also this isle, what lives and grows thereon,
And snaky sea which rounds and ends the same.   30

'Thinketh, it came of being ill at ease:
He hated that He cannot change His cold,

Nor cure its ache. 'Hath spied an icy fish
That longed to 'scape the rock-stream where she lived,
And thaw herself within the lukewarm brine
O' the lazy sea her stream thrusts far amid,
A crystal spike 'twixt two warm walls of wave;
Only, she ever sickened, found repulse
At the other kind of water, not her life,
(Green-dense and dim-delicious, bred o' the sun)   40
Flounced back from bliss she was not born to breathe,
And in her old bounds buried her despair,
Hating and loving warmth alike: so He.
'Thinketh, He made thereat the sun, this isle,
Trees and the fowls here, beast and creeping thing.
Yon otter, sleek-wet, black, lithe as a leech;
Yon auk, one fire-eye in a ball of foam,
That floats and feeds; a certain badger brown
He hath watched hunt with that slant white-wedge eye
By moonlight; and the pie with the long tongue   50
That pricks deep into oakwarts for a worm,
And says a plain word when she finds her prize,
But will not eat the ants; the ants themselves
That build a wall of seeds and settled stalks
About their hole — He made all these and more,
Made all we see, and us, in spite: how else?
He could not, Himself, make a second self
To be His mate; as well have made Himself:
He would not make what he mislikes or slights,
An eyesore to Him, or not worth His pains: 60
But did, in envy, listlessness or sport,
Make what Himself would fain, in a manner, be —
Weaker in most points, stronger in a few,
Worthy, and yet mere playthings all the while,
Things He admires and mocks too, — that is it.
Because, so brave, so better though they be,
It nothing skills if He begin to plague.
Look now, I melt a gourd-fruit into mash,
Add honeycomb and pods, I have perceived,
Which bite like finches when they bill and kiss, —   70
Then, when froth rises bladdery, drink up all,
Quick, quick, till maggots scamper through my brain;
Last, throw me on my back i' the seeded thyme,
And wanton, wishing I were born a bird.
Put case, unable to be what I wish,
I yet could make a live bird out of clay:

Would not I take clay, pinch my Caliban
Able to fly? — for, there, see, he hath wings,
And great comb like the hoopoe's to admire,
And there, a sting to do his foes offence,   80
There, and I will that he begin to live,
Fly to yon rock-top, nip me off the horns
Of grigs high up that make the merry din,
Saucy through their veined wings, and mind me not.
In which feat, if his leg snapped, brittle clay,
And he lay stupid-like, — why, I should laugh;
And if he, spying me, should fall to weep,
Beseech me to be good, repair his wrong,
Bid his poor leg smart less or grow again, —
Well, as the chance were, this might take or else   90
Not take my fancy: I might hear his cry,
And give the mankin three sound legs for one,
Or pluck the other off, leave him like an egg,
And lessoned he was mine and merely clay.
Were this no pleasure, lying in the thyme,
Drinking the mash, with brain become alive,
Making and marring clay at will? So He.

'Thinketh, such shows nor right nor wrong in Him,
Nor kind, nor cruel: He is strong and Lord.
'Am strong myself compared to yonder crabs   100
That march now from the mountain to the sea;
'Let twenty pass, and stone the twenty-first,
Loving not, hating not, just choosing so.
'Say, the first straggler that boasts purple spots
Shall join the file, one pincer twisted off;
'Say, this bruised fellow shall receive a worm,
And two worms he whose nippers end in red;
As it likes me each time, I do: so He.

Well then, 'supposeth He is good i' the main,
Placable if His mind and ways were guessed,   110
But rougher than His handiwork, be sure!
Oh, He hath made things worthier than Himself,
And envieth that, so helped, such things do more
Than He who made them! What consoles but this?
That they, unless through Him, do naught at all,
And must submit: what other use in things?
'Hath cut a pipe of pithless elder-joint
That, blown through, gives exact the scream o' the jay

When from her wing you twitch the feathers blue:
Sound this, and little birds that hate the jay 120
Flock within stone's throw, glad their foe is hurt:
Put case such pipe could prattle and boast forsooth
"I catch the birds, I am the crafty thing,
I make the cry my maker cannot make
With his great round mouth; he must blow through mine!"
Would not I smash it with my foot? So He.

But wherefore rough, why cold and ill at ease?
Aha, that is a question! Ask, for that,
What knows, — the something over Setebos
That made Him, or He, may be, found and fought, 130
Worsted, drove off and did to nothing, perchance.
There may be something quiet o'er His head,
Out of His reach, that feels nor joy nor grief,
Since both derive from weakness in some way.
I joy because the quails come; would not joy
Could I bring quails here when I have a mind:
This Quiet, all it hath a mind to, doth.
'Esteemeth stars the outposts of its couch,
But never spends much thought nor care that way.
It may look up, work up, — the worse for those 140
It works on! 'Careth but for Setebos
The many-handed as a cuttle-fish,
Who, making Himself feared through what He does,
Looks up, first, and perceives he cannot soar
To what is quiet and hath happy life;
Next looks down here, and out of very spite
Makes this a bauble-world to ape yon real,
These good things to match those as hips do grapes.
'Tis solace making baubles, ay, and sport.
Himself peeped late, eyed Prosper at his books 150
Careless and lofty, lord now of the isle:
Vexed, 'stitched a book of broad leaves, arrow-shaped,
Wrote thereon, he knows what, prodigious words;
Has peeled a wand and called it by a name;
Weareth at whiles for an enchanter's robe
The eyed skin of a supple oncelot;
And hath an ounce sleeker than youngling mole,
A four-legged serpent he makes cower and couch,
Now snarl, now hold its breath and mind his eye,
And saith she is Miranda and my wife: 160
'Keeps for his Ariel a tall pouch-bill crane

He bids go wade for fish and straight disgorge;
Also a sea-beast, lumpish, which he snared,
Blinded the eyes of, and brought somewhat tame,
And split its toe-webs, and now pens the drudge
In a hole o' the rock and calls him Caliban;
A bitter heart that bides its time and bites.
'Plays thus at being Prosper in a way,
Taketh his mirth with make-believes: so He.
His dam held that the Quiet made all things   170
Which Setebos vexed only: 'holds not so.
Who made them weak, meant weakness He might **vex**.
Had He meant other, while His hand was in,
Why not make horny eyes no thorn could prick,
Or plate my scalp with bone against the snow,
Or overscale my flesh 'neath joint and joint,
Like an orc's armor? Ay, — so spoil His sport!
He is the One now: only He doth all.
'Saith, He may like, perchance, what profits Him.
Ay, himself loves what does him good; but why?   180
'Gets good no otherwise. This blinded beast
Loves whoso places flesh-meat on his nose,
But, had he eyes, would want no help, but hate
Or love, just as it liked him: He hath eyes.
Also it pleaseth Setebos to work,
Use all His hands, and exercise much craft,
By no means for the love of what is worked.
'Tasteth, himself, no finer good i' the world
When all goes right, in this safe summer-time,
And he wants little, hungers, aches not much,   190
Than trying what to do with wit and strength.
'Falls to make something: 'piled yon pile of turfs,
And squared and stuck there squares of soft white chalk,
And, with a fish-tooth, scratched a moon on each,
And set up endwise certain spikes of tree,
And crowned the whole with a sloth's skull a-top,
Found dead i' the woods, too hard for one to kill.
No use at all i' the work, for work's sole sake;
'Shall some day knock it down again: so He.

'Saith He is terrible: watch His feats in proof!   200
One hurricane will spoil six good months' hope.
He hath a spite against me, that I know,
Just as He favors Prosper, who knows why?
So it is, all the same, as well I find.

'Wove wattles half the winter, fenced them firm
With stone and stake to stop she-tortoises
Crawling to lay their eggs here: well, one wave,
Feeling the foot of Him upon its neck,
Gaped as a snake does, lolled out its large tongue,
And licked the whole labor flat; so much for spite.   210
'Saw a ball flame down late (yonder it lies)
Where, half an hour before, I slept i' the shade:
Often they scatter sparkles: there is force!
'Dug up a newt He may have envied once
And turned to stone, shut up inside a stone.
Please Him and hinder this? — What Prosper does?
Aha, if He would tell me how! Not He!
There is the sport: discover how or die!
All need not die, for of the things o' the isle
Some flee afar, some dive, some run up trees;   220
Those at His mercy, — why, they please Him most
When . . . when . . . well, never try the same way twice!
Repeat what act has pleased, He may grow wroth.
You must not know His ways, and play Him off,
Sure of the issue. 'Doth the like himself:
'Spareth a squirrel that it nothing fears
But steals the nut from underneath my thumb,
And when I threat, bites stoutly in defence:
'Spareth an urchin that contrariwise,
Curls up into a ball, pretending death   230
For fright at my approach: the two ways please.
But what would move my choler more than this,
That either creature counted on its life
To-morrow and next day and all days to come,
Saying, forsooth, in the inmost of its heart,
"Because he did so yesterday with me,
And otherwise with such another brute,
So must he do henceforth and always." — Ay?
Would teach the reasoning couple what "must" means!
'Doth as he likes, or wherefore Lord? So He.   240

'Conceiveth all things will continue thus,
And we shall have to live in fear of Him
So long as He lives, keeps His strength: no change,
If He have done His best, make no new world
To please Him more, so leave off watching this, —
If He surprise not even the Quiet's self
Some strange day, — or, suppose, grow into it

As grubs grow butterflies: else, here are we,
And there is He, and nowhere help at all.

'Believeth with the life, the pain shall stop.   250
His dam held different, that after death
He both plagued enemies and feasted friends:
Idly! He doth His worst in this our life,
Giving just respite lest we die through pain,
Saving last pain for worst, — with which, an end.
Meanwhile, the best way to escape His ire
Is, not to seem too happy. 'Sees, himself,
Yonder two flies, with purple films and pink,
Bask on the pompion-bell above: kills both.
'Sees two black painful beetles roll their ball   260
On head and tail as if to save their lives:
Moves them the stick away they strive to clear.

Even so, 'would have Him misconceive, suppose
This Caliban strives hard and ails no less,
And always, above all else, envies Him;
Wherefore he mainly dances on dark nights,
Moans in the sun, gets under holes to laugh,
And never speaks his mind save housed as now:
Outside, 'groans, curses. If He caught me here,
O'erheard this speech, and asked "What chucklest at?"   270
'Would, to appease Him, cut a finger off,
Or of my three kid yearlings burn the best,
Or let the toothsome apples rot on tree,
Or push my tame beast for the orc to taste:
While myself lit a fire, and made a song
And sung it, *"What I hate, be consecrate*
To celebrate Thee and Thy state, no mate
For Thee; what see for envy in poor me?"
Hoping the while, since evils sometimes mend,
Warts rub away and sores are cured with slime,   280
That some strange day, will either the Quiet catch
And conquer Setebos, or likelier He
Decrepit may doze, doze, as good as die.

[What, what? A curtain o'er the world at once!
Crickets stop hissing; not a bird — or, yes,
There scuds His raven that has told Him all!

It was fool's play this prattling! Ha! The wind
Shoulders the pillared dust, death's house o' the move,
And fast invading fires begin! White blaze —
A tree's head snaps — and there, there, there, there, there, 290
His thunder follows! Fool to gibe at Him!
Lo! 'Lieth flat and loveth Setebos!
'Maketh his teeth meet through his upper lip,
Will let those quails fly, will not eat this month
One little mess of whelks, so he may 'scape!]

CONFESSIONS

I

WHAT is he buzzing in my ears?
        "Now that I come to die,
Do I view the world as a vale of tears?"
        Ah, reverend sir, not I!

II

What I viewed there once, what I view again
        Where the physic bottles stand
On the table's edge, — is a suburb lane,
        With a wall to my bedside hand.

III

That lane sloped, much as the bottles do,
        From a house you could descry   10
O'er the garden-wall: is the curtain blue
        Or green to a healthy eye?

IV

To mine, it serves for the old June weather
        Blue above lane and wall;
And that farthest bottle labelled "Ether"
        Is the house o'ertopping all.

V

At a terrace, somewhere near the stopper,
        There watched for me, one June,
A girl: I know, sir, it's improper,
        My poor mind's out of tune.   20

VI

Only, there was a way . . . you crept
    Close by the side to dodge
Eyes in the house, two eyes except:
    They styled their house "The Lodge."

VII

What right had a lounger up their lane?
    But, by creeping very close,
With the good wall's help, — their eyes might strain
    And stretch themselves to Oes,

VIII

Yet never catch her and me together,
    As she left the attic, there,   30
By the rim of the bottle labelled "Ether,"
    And stole from stair to stair,

IX

And stood by the rose-wreathed gate. Alas,
    We loved, sir — used to meet:
How sad and bad and mad it was —
    But then, how it was sweet!

PROSPICE

FEAR death? — to feel the fog in my throat,
    The mist in my face,
When the snows begin, and the blasts denote
    I am nearing the place,
The power of the night, the press of the storm,
    The post of the foe;
Where he stands, the Arch Fear in a visible form,
    Yet the strong man must go:
For the journey is done and the summit attained,
    And the barriers fall,   10
Though a battle's to fight ere the guerdon be gained,
    The reward of it all.

I was ever a fighter, so — one fight more,
    The best and the last!
I would hate that death bandaged my eyes, and forbore,
    And bade me creep past.
No! let me taste the whole of it, fare like my peers
    The heroes of old,
Bear the brunt, in a minute pay glad life's arrears
    Of pain, darkness and cold.   20
For sudden the worst turns the best to the brave,
    The black minute's at end,
And the elements' rage, the fiend-voices that rave,
    Shall dwindle, shall blend,
Shall change, shall become first a peace out of pain,
    Then a light, then thy breast,
O thou soul of my soul! I shall clasp thee again,
    And with God be the rest!

YOUTH AND ART

I

It once might have been, once only:
    We lodged in a street together,
You, a sparrow on the housetop lonely,
    I, a lone she-bird of his feather.

II

Your trade was with sticks and clay,
    You thumbed, thrust, patted and polished,
Then laughed "They will see some day
    Smith made, and Gibson demolished."

III

My business was song, song, song;
    I chirped, cheeped, trilled and twittered,   10
"Kate Brown's on the boards ere long,
    And Grisi's existence embittered!"

IV

I earned no more by a warble
    Than you by a sketch in plaster;
You wanted a piece of marble,
    I needed a music-master.

V

We studied hard in our styles,
    Chipped each at a crust like Hindoos,
For air looked out on the tiles,
    For fun watched each other's windows.   20

VI

You lounged, like a boy of the South,
    Cap and blouse — nay, a bit of beard, too;
Or you got it, rubbing your mouth
    With fingers the clay adhered to.

VII

And I — soon managed to find
    Weak points in the flower-fence facing,
Was forced to put up a blind
    And be safe in my corset-lacing.

VIII

No harm! It was not my fault
    If you never turned your eye's tail up,   30
As I shook upon E *in alt,*
    Or ran the chromatic scale up:

IX

For spring bade the sparrows pair,
    And the boys and girls gave guesses,
And stalls in our street looked rare
    With bulrush and watercresses.

X

Why did not you pinch a flower
    In a pellet of clay and fling it?
Why did not I put a power
    Of thanks in a look, or sing it?   40

XI

I did look, sharp as a lynx,
    (And yet the memory rankles)
When models arrived, some minx
    Tripped up-stairs, she and her ankles.

XII

But I think I gave you as good!
    "That foreign fellow, — who can know
How she pays, in a playful mood,
    For his tuning her that piano?"

XIII

Could you say so, and never say
    "Suppose we join hands and fortunes,   **50**
And I fetch her from over the way,
    Her, piano, and long tunes and short tunes"?

XIV

No, no: you would not be rash,
    Nor I rasher and something over:
You've to settle yet Gibson's hash,
    And Grisi yet lives in clover.

XV

But you meet the Prince at the Board,
    I'm queen myself at *bals-paré,*
I've married a rich old lord,
    And you're dubbed knight and an R. A.   **60**

XVI

Each life unfulfilled, you see;
    It hangs still, patchy and scrappy:
We have not sighed deep, laughed free,
    Starved, feasted, despaired, — been happy.

XVII

And nobody calls you a dunce,
    And people suppose me clever:
This could but have happened once,
    And we missed it, lost it forever.

APPARENT FAILURE

"We shall soon lose a celebrated building."
PARIS NEWSPAPER

I

No, for I'll save it! Seven years since,
    I passed through Paris, stopped a day
To see the baptism of your Prince;
    Saw, made my bow, and went my way:
Walking the heat and headache off,
    I took the Seine-side, you surmise,
Thought of the Congress, Gortschakoff,
    Cavour's appeal and Buol's replies,
So sauntered till — what met my eyes?

II

Only the Doric little Morgue!   10
    The dead-house where you show your drowned:
Petrarch's Vaucluse makes proud the Sorgue,
    Your Morgue has made the Seine renowned.
One pays one's debt in such a case;
    I plucked up heart and entered, — stalked,
Keeping a tolerable face
    Compared with some whose cheeks were chalked:
Let them! No Briton's to be balked!

III

First came the silent gazers; next,
    A screen of glass, we're thankful for;   20
Last, the sight's self, the sermon's text,
    The three men who did most abhor
Their life in Paris yesterday,
    So killed themselves: and now, enthroned
Each on his copper couch, they lay
    Fronting me, waiting to be owned.
I thought, and think, their sin's atoned.

IV

Poor men, God made, and all for that!
    The reverence struck me; o'er each head
Religiously was hung its hat,   30
    Each coat dripped by the owner's bed,
Sacred from touch: each had his berth,
    His bounds, his proper place of rest,
Who last night tenanted on earth
    Some arch, where twelve such slept abreast, —
Unless the plain asphalt seemed best.

V

How did it happen, my poor boy?
    You wanted to be Buonaparte
And have the Tuileries for toy,
    And could not, so it broke your heart?   40
You, old one by his side, I judge,
    Were, red as blood, a socialist,
A leveller! Does the Empire grudge
    You've gained what no Republic missed?
Be quiet, and unclench your fist!

VI

And this — why, he was red in vain,
    Or black, — poor fellow that is blue!
What fancy was it turned your brain?
    Oh, women were the prize for you!
Money gets women, cards and dice   50
    Get money, and ill-luck gets just
The copper couch and one clear nice
    Cool squirt of water o'er your bust,
The right thing to extinguish lust!

VII

It's wiser being good than bad;
    It's safer being meek than fierce:
It's fitter being sane than mad.
    My own hope is, a sun will pierce
The thickest cloud earth ever stretched;
    That, after Last, returns the First,   60
Though a wide compass round be fetched;
    That what began best, can't end worst,
Nor what God blessed once, prove accurst.

EPILOGUE

First Speaker, *as David*

I

On the first of the Feast of Feasts,
  The Dedication Day,
When the Levites joined the Priests
  At the Altar in robed array,
Gave signal to sound and say, —

II

When the thousands, rear and van,
  Swarming with one accord
Became as a single man
  (Look, gesture, thought and word)
In praising and thanking the Lord, —   10

III

When the singers lift up their voice,
  And the trumpets made endeavor,
Sounding, "In God rejoice!"
  Saying, "In Him rejoice
Whose mercy endureth forever!" —

IV

Then the Temple filled with a cloud,
  Even the House of the Lord;
Porch bent and pillar bowed:
  For the presence of the Lord,
In the glory of His cloud,   20
  Had filled the House of the Lord.

Second Speaker, *as Renan*

Gone now! All gone across the dark so far,
  Sharpening fast, shuddering ever, shutting still,
Dwindling into the distance, dies that star
  Which came, stood, opened once: We gazed our fill

With upturned faces on as real a Face
    That, stooping from grave music and mild fire,
Took in our homage, made a visible place
    Through many a depth of glory, gyre on gyre,
For the dim human tribute. Was this true?   30
    Could man indeed avail, mere praise of his,
To help by rapture God's own rapture too,
    Thrill with a heart's red tinge that pure pale bliss?
Why did it end? Who failed to beat the breast,
    And shriek, and throw the arms protesting wide,
When a first shadow showed the star addressed
    Itself to motion, and on either side
The rims contracted as the rays retired;
    The music, like a fountain's sickening pulse,
Subsided on itself; awhile transpired   40
    Some vestige of a Face no pangs convulse,
No prayers retard; then even this was gone,
    Lost in the night at last. We, lone and left
Silent through centuries, ever and anon
    Venture to probe again the vault bereft
Of all now save the lesser lights, a mist
    Of multitudinous points, yet suns, men say —
And this leaps ruby, this lurks amethyst,
    But where may hide what came and loved our clay?
How shall the sage detect in yon expanse   50
    The star which chose to stoop and stay for us?
Unroll the records! Hailed ye such advance
    Indeed, and did your hope evanish thus?
Watchers of twilight, is the worst averred?
    We shall not look up, know ourselves are seen,
Speak, and be sure that we again are heard,
    Acting or suffering, have the disk's serene
Reflect our life, absorb an earthly flame,
    Nor doubt that, were mankind inert and numb,
Its core had never crimsoned all the same,   60
    Nor, missing ours, its music fallen dumb?
Oh, dread successson to a dizzy post,
    Sad sway of sceptre whose mere touch appalls,
Ghastly dethronement, cursed by those the most
    On whose repugnant brow the crown next falls!

THIRD SPEAKER

I

Witless alike of will and way divine,
How heaven's high with earth's low should intertwine!
Friends, I have seen through your eyes: now use mine!

II

Take the least man of all mankind, as I;
Look at his head and heart, find how and why   70
He differs from his fellows utterly:

III

Then, like me, watch when nature by degrees
Grows alive round him, as in Arctic seas
(They said of old) the instinctive water flees

IV

Toward some elected point of central rock,
As though, for its sake only, roamed the flock
Of waves about the waste: awhile they mock

V

With radiance caught for the occasion, — hues
Of blackest hell now, now such reds and blues
As only heaven could fitly interfuse, —   80

VI

The mimic monarch of the whirlpool, king
O' the current for a minute: then they wring
Up by the roots and oversweep the thing,

VII

And hasten off, to play again elsewhere
The same part, choose another peak as bare,
They find and flatter, feast and finish there.

VIII

When you see what I tell you, — nature dance
About each man of us, retire, advance,
As though the pageant's end were to enhance

IX

His worth, and — once the life, his product, gained —   90
Roll away elsewhere, keep the strife sustained,
And show thus real, a thing the North but feigned —

X

When you acknowledge that one world could do
All the diverse work, old yet ever new,
Divide us, each from other, me from you, —

XI

Why, where's the need of Temple, when the walls
O' the world are that? What use of swells and falls
From Levites' choir, Priests' cries, and trumpet-calls?

XII

That one Face, far from vanish, rather grows,
Or decomposes but to recompose,   100
Become my universe that feels and knows.

FROM *The Ring and the Book*
(1868-1869)

ᴧᴧᴧᴧᴧᴧᴧᴧᴧᴧᴧᴧᴧᴧᴧᴧᴧᴧᴧᴧᴧᴧᴧᴧᴧᴧ

GIUSEPPE CAPONSACCHI

ANSWER you, Sirs? Do I understand aright?
Have patience? In this sudden smoke from hell, —
So things disguise themselves, — I cannot see
My own hand held thus broad before my face
And know it again. Answer you? Then that means
Tell over twice what I, the first time, told
Six months ago: 'twas here, I do believe,
Fronting you same three in this very room,
I stood and told you: yet now no one laughs,
Who then . . . nay, dear my lords, but laugh you did,   10
As good as laugh, what in a judge we style
Laughter — no levity, nothing indecorous, lords!
Only, — I think I apprehend the mood:
There was the blameless shrug, permissible smirk,
The pen's pretence at play with the pursed mouth,
The titter stifled in the hollow palm
Which rubbed the eyebrow and caressed the nose,
When I first told my tale: they meant, you know,
"The sly one, all this we are bound believe!
Well, he can say no other than what he says.   20
We have been young, too, — come, there's greater guilt!
Let him but decently disembroil himself,
Scramble from out the scrape nor move the mud, —
We solid ones may risk a finger-stretch!"
And now you sit as grave, stare as aghast
As if I were a phantom: now 'tis — "Friend,
Collect yourself!" — no laughing matter more —
"Counsel the Court in this extremity,

306

Tell us again!" — tell that, for telling which,
I got the jocular piece of punishment,   30
Was sent to lounge a little in the place
Whence now of a sudden here you summon me
To take the intelligence from just — your lips!
You, Judge Tommati, who then tittered most, —
That she I helped eight months since to escape
Her husband, was retaken by the same,
Three days ago, if I have seized your sense, —
(I being disallowed to interfere,
Meddle or make in a matter none of mine,
For you and law were guardians quite enough   40
O' the innocent, without a pert priest's help) —
And that he has butchered her accordingly,
As she foretold and as myself believed, —
And, so foretelling and believing so,
We were punished, both of us, the merry way:
Therefore, tell once again the tale! For what?
Pompilia is only dying while I speak!
Why does the mirth hang fire and miss the smile?
My masters, there's an old book, you should con
For strange adventures, applicable yet,   50
'Tis stuffed with. Do you know that there was once
This thing: a multitude of worthy folk
Took recreation, watched a certain group
Of soldiery intent upon a game, —
How first they wrangled, but soon fell to play,
Threw dice, — the best diversion in the world.
A word in your ear, — they are now casting lots,
Ay, with that gesture quaint and cry uncouth,
For the coat of One murdered an hour ago!
I am a priest, — talk of what I have learned.   60
Pompilia is bleeding out her life belike,
Gasping away the latest breath of all,
This minute, while I talk — not while you laugh?

Yet, being sobered now, what is it you ask
By way of explanation? There's the fact!
It seems to fill the universe with sight
And sound, — from the four corners of this earth
Tells itself over, to my sense at least.
But you may want it lower set i' the scale, —
Too vast, too close it clangs in the ear, perhaps;   70
You'd stand back just to comprehend it more.

Well then, let me, the hollow rock, condense
The voice o' the sea and wind, interpret you
The mystery of this murder. God above!
It is too paltry, such a transference
O' the storm's roar to the cranny of the stone!

This deed, you saw begin — why does its end
Surprise you? Why should the event enforce
The lesson, we ourselves learned, she and I,
From the first o' the fact, and taught you, all in vain?   80
This Guido from whose throat you took my grasp,
Was this man to be favored, now, or feared,
Let do his will, or have his will restrained,
In the relation with Pompilia? Say!
Did any other man need interpose
— Oh, though first comer, though as strange at the work
As fribble must be, coxcomb, fool that's near
To knave as, say, a priest who fears the world —
Was he bound brave the peril, save the doomed,
Or go on, sing his snatch and pluck his flower,   90
Keep the straight path and let the victim die?
I held so; you decided otherwise,
Saw no such peril, therefore no such need
To stop song, loosen flower, and leave path. Law,
Law was aware and watching, would suffice,
Wanted no priest's intrusion, palpably
Pretence, too manifest a subterfuge!
Whereupon I, priest, coxcomb, fribble and fool,
Ensconced me in my corner, thus rebuked,
A kind of culprit, over-zealous hound   100
Kicked for his pains to kennel; I gave place
To you, and let the law reign paramount:
I left Pompilia to your watch and ward,
And now you point me — there and thus she lies!

Men, for the last time, what do you want with me?
Is it, — you acknowledge, as it were, a use,
A profit in employing me? — at length
I may conceivably help the august law?
I am free to break the blow, next hawk that swoops
On next dove, nor miss much of good repute?   110
Or what if this your summons, after all,
Be but the form of mere release, no more,
Which turns the key and lets the captive go?

I have paid enough in person at Civita,
Am free, — what more need I concern me with?
Thank you! I am rehabilitated then,
A very reputable priest. But she —
The glory of life, the beauty of the world,
The splendor of heaven, . . . well, Sirs, does no one move?
Do I speak ambiguously? The glory, I say,   120
And the beauty, I say, and splendor, still say I,
Who, priest and trained to live my whole life long
On beauty and splendor, solely at their source,
God, — have thus recognized my food in her,
You tell me, that's fast dying while we talk,
Pompilia! How does lenity to me,
Remit one death-bed pang to her? Come, smile!
The proper wink at the hot-headed youth
Who lets his soul show, through transparent words,
The mundane love that's sin and scandal too!   130
You are all struck acquiescent now, it seems:
It seems the oldest, gravest signor here,
Even the redoubtable Tommati, sits
Chop-fallen, — understands how law might take
Service like mine, of brain and heart and hand,
In good part. Better late than never, law
You understand of a sudden, gospel too
Has a claim here, may possibly pronounce
Consistent with my priesthood, worthy Christ,
That I endeavored to save Pompilia?

                          Then,   140
You were wrong, you see: that's well to see, though late:
That's all we may expect of man, this side
The grave: his good is — knowing he is bad:
Thus will it be with us when the books ope
And we stand at the bar on judgment-day.
Well then, I have a mind to speak, see cause
To relume the quenched flax by this dreadful light,
Burn my soul out in showing you the truth.
I heard, last time I stood here to be judged,
What is priest's-duty, — labor to pluck tares   150
And weed the corn of Molinism; let me
Make you hear, this time, how, in such a case,
Man, be he in the priesthood or at plough,
Mindful of Christ or marching step by step
With . . . what's his style, the other potentate

Who bids have courage and keep honor safe,
Nor let minuter admonition tease! —
How he is bound, better or worse, to act.
Earth will not end through this misjudgment, no!
For you and the others like you sure to come,   160
Fresh work is sure to follow, — wickedness
That wants withstanding. Many a man of blood,
Many a man of guile will clamor yet,
Bid you redress his grievance, — as he clutched
The prey, forsooth a stranger stepped between,
And there's the good gripe in pure waste! My part
Is done; i' the doing it, I pass away
Out of the world. I want no more with earth.
Let me, in heaven's name, use the very snuff
O' the taper in one last spark shall show truth   170
For a moment, show Pompilia who was true!
Not for her sake, but yours: if she is dead,
Oh, Sirs, she can be loved by none of you
Most or least priestly! Saints, to do us good,
Must be in heaven, I seem to understand:
We never find them saints before, at least.
Be her first prayer then presently for you —
She has done the good to me . . .
                              What is all this?
There, I was born, have lived, shall die, a fool!
This is a foolish outset: — might with cause   180
Give color to the very lie o' the man,
The murderer, — make as if I loved his wife,
In the way he called love. He is the fool there!
Why, had there been in me the touch of taint,
I had picked up so much of knaves'-policy
As hide it, keep one hand pressed on the place
Suspected of a spot would damn us both.
Or no, not her! — not even if any of you
Dares think that I, i' the face of death, her death
That's in my eyes and ears and brain and heart,   190
Lie, — if he does, let him! I mean to say,
So he stop there, stay thought from smirching her
The snow-white soul that angels fear to take
Untenderly. But, all the same, I know
I too am taintless, and I bare my breast.
You can't think, men as you are, all of you,
But that, to hear thus suddenly such an end
Of such a wonderful white soul, that comes

Of a man and murderer calling the white black,
Must shake me, trouble and disadvantage. Sirs,   200
Only seventeen!

       Why, good and wise you are!
You might at the beginning stop my mouth:
So, none would be to speak for her, that knew.
I talk impertinently, and you bear,
All the same. This is to have to do
With honest hearts: they easily may err,
But in the main they wish well to the truth.
You are Christians; somehow, no one ever plucked
A rag, even, from the body of the Lord,
To wear and mock with, but, despite himself,   210
He looked the greater and was the better. Yes,
I shall go on now. Does she need or not
I keep calm? Calm I'll keep as monk that croons
Transcribing battle, earthquake, famine, plague,
From parchment to his cloister's chronicle.
Not one word more from the point now!

                    I begin.
Yes, I am one of your body and a priest.
Also I am a younger son o' the House
Oldest now, greatest once, in my birth-town
Arezzo, I recognize no equal there —   220
(I want all arguments, all sorts of arms
That seem to serve, — use this for a reason, wait!)
Not therefore thrust into the Church, because
O' the piece of bread one gets there. We were first
Of Fiesole, that rings still with the fame
Of Capo-in-Sacco our progenitor:
When Florence ruined Fiesole, our folk
Migrated to the victor-city, and there
Flourished, — our palace and our tower attest,
In the Old Mercato, — this was years ago,   230
Four hundred, full, — no, it wants fourteen just.
Our arms are those of Fiesole itself,
The shield quartered with white and red: a branch
Are the Salviati of us, nothing more.
That were good help to the Church? But better still —
Not simply for the advantage of my birth
I' the way of the world, was I proposed for priest;
But because there's an illustration, late

I' the day, that's loved and looked to as a saint
Still in Arezzo, he was bishop of,   240
Sixty years since: he spent to the last doit
His bishop's-revenue among the poor,
And used to tend the needy and the sick,
Barefoot, because of his humility.
He it was, — when the Granduke Ferdinand
Swore he would raze our city, plough the place
And sow it with salt, because we Aretines
Had tied a rope about the neck, to hale
The statue of his father from its base
For hate's sake, — he availed by prayers and tears   250
To pacify the Duke and save the town.
This was my father's father's brother. You see,
For his sake, how it was I had a right
To the self-same office, bishop in the egg,
So, grew i' the garb and prattled in the school,
Was made expect, from infancy almost,
The proper mood o' the priest; till time ran by
And brought the day when I must read the vows,
Declare the world renounced and undertake
To become priest and leave probation, — leap   260
Over the ledge into the other life,
Having gone trippingly hitherto up to the height
O'er the wan water. Just a vow to read!

I stopped short awe-struck. "How shall holiest flesh
Engage to keep such vow inviolate,
How much less mine? I know myself too weak,
Unworthy! Choose a worthier stronger man!"
And the very Bishop smiled and stopped my mouth
In its mid-protestation. "Incapable?
Qualmish of conscience? Thou ingenuous boy!   270
Clear up the clouds and cast thy scruples far!
I satisfy thee there's an easier sense
Wherein to take such vow than suits the first
Rough rigid reading. Mark what makes all smooth,
Nay, has been even a solace to myself!
The Jews who needs must, in their synagogue,
Utter sometimes the holy name of God,
A thing their superstition boggles at,
Pronounce aloud the ineffable sacrosanct, —
How does their shrewdness help them? In this wise;   280
Another set of sounds they substitute,

Jumble so consonants and vowels — how
Should I know? — that there grows from out the old
Quite a new word that means the very same —
And o'er the hard place slide they with a smile.
Giuseppe Maria Caponsacchi mine,
Nobody wants you in these latter days
To prop the Church by breaking your back-bone, —
As the necessary way was once, we know,
When Diocletian flourished and his like.   290
That building of the buttress-work was done
By martyrs and confessors: let it bide,
Add not a brick, but, where you see a chink,
Stick in a sprig of ivy or root a rose
Shall make amends and beautify the pile!
We profit as you were the painfullest
O' the martyrs, and you prove yourself a match
For the cruelest confessor ever was,
If you march boldly up and take your stand
Where their blood soaks, their bones yet strew the soil,   300
And cry 'Take notice, I the young and free
And well-to-do i' the world, thus leave the world,
Cast in my lot thus with no gay young world
But the grand old Church: she tempts me of the two!'
Renounce the world? Nay, keep and give it us!
Let us have you, and boast of what you bring.
We want the pick o' the earth to practise with,
Not its offscouring, halt and deaf and blind
In soul and body. There's a rubble-stone
Unfit for the front o' the building, stuff to stow   310
In a gap behind and keep us weather-tight;
There's porphyry for the prominent place. Good lack!
Saint Paul has had enough and to spare, I trow,
Of ragged run-away Onesimus:
He wants the right-hand with the signet-ring
Of King Agrippa, now, to shake and use.
I have a heavy scholar cloistered up,
Close under lock and key, kept at his task
Of letting Fénelon know the fool he is,
In a book I promise Christendom next Spring.   326
Why, if he covets so much meat, the clown,
As a lark's wing next Friday, or, any day,
Diversion beyond catching his own fleas,
He shall be properly swinged, I promise him.
But you, who are so quite another paste

Of a man, — do you obey me? Cultivate
Assiduous that superior gift you have
Of making madrigals — (who told me? Ah!)
Get done a Marinesque Adoniad straight
With a pulse o' the blood a-pricking, here and there,   330
That I may tell the lady 'And he's ours!' "

    So I became a priest: those terms changed all,
I was good enough for that, nor cheated so;
I could live thus and still hold head erect.
Now you see why I may have been before
A fribble and coxcomb, yet, as priest, break word
Nowise, to make you disbelieve me now.
I need that you should know my truth. Well, then,
According to prescription did I live,
— Conformed myself, both read the breviary   340
And wrote the rhymes, was punctual to my place
I' the Pieve, and as diligent at my post
Where beauty and fashion rule. I throve apace,
Sub-deacon, Canon, the authority
For delicate play at tarocs, and arbiter
O' the magnitude of fan-mounts: all the while
Wanting no whit the advantage of a hint
Benignant to the promising pupil, — thus:
"Enough attention to the Countess now,
The young one; 'tis her mother rules the roast,   350
We know where, and puts in a word: go pay
Devoir to-morrow morning after mass!
Break that rash promise to preach, Passion-week!
Has it escaped you the Archbishop grunts
And snuffles when one grieves to tell his Grace
No soul dares treat the subject of the day
Since his own masterly handling it (ha, ha!)
Five years ago, — when somebody could help
And touch up an odd phrase in time of need,
(He, he!) — and somebody helps you, my son!   360
Therefore, don't prove so indispensable
At the Pieve, sit more loose i' the seat, nor grow
A fixture by attendance morn and eve!
Arezzo's just a haven midway Rome —
Rome's the eventual harbor, — make for port,
Crowd sail, crack cordage! And your cargo be
A polished presence, a genteel manner, wit
At will, and tact at every pore of you!

I sent our lump of learning, Brother Clout,
And Father Slouch, our piece of piety, 370
To see Rome and try suit the Cardinal.
Thither they clump-clumped, beads and book in hand,
And ever since 'tis meat for man and maid
How both flopped down, prayed blessing on bent pate
Bald many an inch beyond the tonsure's need,
Never once dreaming, the two moony dolts,
There's nothing moves his Eminence so much
As — far from all this awe at sanctitude —
Heads that wag, eyes that twinkle, modified mirth
At the closet-lectures on the Latin tongue 380
A lady learns so much by, we know where.
Why, body o' Bacchus, you should crave his rule
For pauses in the elegiac couplet, chasms
Permissible only to Catullus! There!
Now go to duty: brisk, break Priscian's head
By reading the day's office — there's no help.
You've Ovid in your poke to plaster that;
Amen's at the end of all: then sup with me!"

　　Well, after three or four years of this life,
In prosecution of my calling, I 390
Found myself at the theatre one night
With a brother Canon, in a mood and mind
Proper enough for the place, amused or no:
When I saw enter, stand, and seat herself
A lady, young, tall, beautiful, strange and sad.
It was as when, in our cathedral once,
As I got yawningly through matin-song,
I saw *facchini* bear a burden up,
Base it on the high-altar, break away
A board or two, and leave the thing inside 400
Lofty and lone: and lo, when next I looked,
There was Rafael! I was still one stare,
When — "Nay, I'll make her give you back your gaze" —
Said Canon Conti; and at the word he tossed
A paper-twist of comfits to her lap,
And dodged and in a trice was at my back
Nodding from over my shoulder. Then she turned,
Looked our way, smiled the beautiful sad strange smile.
"Is not she fair? 'Tis my new cousin," said he:
"The fellow lurking there i' the black o' the box 410
Is Guido, the old scapegrace: she's his wife,

Married three years since: how his Countship sulks!
He has brought little back from Rome beside,
After the bragging, bullying. A fair face,
And — they do say — a pocketful of gold
When he can worry both her parents dead.
I don't go much there, for the chamber's cold
And the coffee pale. I got a turn at first
Paying my duty: I observed they crouched
— The two old frightened family spectres — close   420
In a corner, each on each like mouse on mouse
I' the cat's cage: ever since, I stay at home.
Hallo, there's Guido, the black, mean and small,
Bends his brows on us — please to bend your own
On the shapely nether limbs of Light-skirts there
By way of a diversion! I was a fool
To fling the sweetmeats. Prudence, for God's love!
To-morrow I'll make my peace, e'en tell some fib,
Try if I can't find means to take you there."

That night and next day did the gaze endure,   430
Burnt to my brain, as sunbeam thro' shut eyes,
And not once changed the beautiful sad strange smile.
At vespers Conti leaned beside my seat
I' the choir, — part said, part sung — "*In ex-cel-sis* —
All's to no purpose; I have louted low,
But he saw you staring — *quia sub* — don't incline
To know you nearer: him we would not hold
For Hercules, — the man would lick your shoe
If you and certain efficacious friends
Managed him warily, — but there's the wife: 440
Spare her, because he beats her, as it is,
She's breaking her heart quite fast enough — *jam tu* —
So, be you rational and make amends
With little Light-skirts yonder — *in secula
Secu-lo-o-o-o-rum*. Ah, you rogue! Every one knows
What great dame she makes jealous: one against one,
Play, and win both!"
                         Sirs, ere the week was out,
I saw and said to myself "Light-skirts hides teeth
Would make a dog sick, — the great dame shows spite
Should drive a cat mad: 'tis but poor work this —   450
Counting one's fingers till the sonnet's crowned.
I doubt much if Marino really be
A better bard than Dante after all.

'Tis more amusing to go pace at eve
I' the Duomo, — watch the day's last gleam outside
Turn, as into a skirt of God's own robe,
Those lancet-windows' jewelled miracle, —
Than go eat the Archbishop's ortolans,
Digest his jokes. Luckily Lent is near:
Who cares to look will find me in my stall   460
At the Pieve, constant to this faith at least —
Never to write a canzonet any more."

So, next week, 'twas my patron spoke abrupt,
In altered guise. "Young man, can it be true
That after all your promise of sound fruit,
You have kept away from Countess young or old
And gone play truant in church all day long?
Are you turning Molinist?" I answered quick:
"Sir, what if I turned Christian? It might be.
The fact is, I am troubled in my mind,   470
Beset and pressed hard by some novel thoughts.
This your Arezzo is a limited world;
There's a strange Pope, — 'tis said, a priest who thinks.
Rome is the port, you say: to Rome I go.
I will live alone, one does so in a crowd,
And look into my heart a little." "Lent
Ended," — I told friends — "I shall go to Rome."

    One evening I was sitting in a muse
Over the opened "Summa," darkened round
By the mid-March twilight, thinking how my life   480
Had shaken under me, — broke short indeed
And showed the gap 'twixt what is, what should be, —
And into what abysm the soul may slip,
Leave aspiration here, achievement there,
Lacking omnipotence to connect extremes —
Thinking moreover . . . oh, thinking, if you like,
How utterly dissociated was I
A priest and celibate, from the sad strange wife
Of Guido, — just as an instance to the point,
Naught more, — how I had a whole store of strengths   490
Eating into my heart, which craved employ,
And she, perhaps, need of a finger's help, —
And yet there was no way in the wide world
To stretch out mine and so relieve myself, —
How when the page o' the Summa preached its best,

Her smile kept glowing out of it, as to mock
The silence we could break by no one word,
There came a tap without the chamber-door,
And a whisper; when I bade who tapped speak out.
And, in obedience to my summons, last   500
In glided a masked muffled mystery,
Laid lightly a letter on the opened book,
Then stood with folded arms and foot demure,
Pointing as if to mark the minutes' flight.

I took the letter, read to the effect
That she, I lately flung the comfits to,
Had a warm heart to give me in exchange,
And gave it, — loved me and confessed it thus,
And bade me render thanks by word of mouth,
Going that night to such a side o' the house   510
Where the small terrace overhangs a street
Blind and deserted, not the street in front:
Her husband being away, the surly patch,
At his villa of Vittiano.
                       "And you?" — I asked:
"What may you be?" "Count Guido's kind of maid —
Most of us have two functions in his house.
We all hate him, the lady suffers much,
'Tis just we show compassion, furnish help,
Specially since her choice is fixed so well.
What answer may I bring to cheer the sweet   520
Pompilia?"
                Then I took a pen and wrote
"No more of this! That you are fair, I know:
But other thoughts now occupy my mind.
I should not thus have played the insensible
Once on a time. What made you, — may one ask, —
Marry your hideous husband? 'Twas a fault,
And now you taste the fruit of it. Farewell."

"There!" smiled I as she snatched it and was gone —
"There, let the jealous miscreant, — Guido's self,
Whose mean soul grins through this transparent trick, —   530
Be balked so far, defrauded of his aim!
What fund of satisfaction to the knave,
Had I kicked this his messenger down stairs,
Trussed to the middle of her impudence,
And set his heart at ease so! No, indeed!

There's the reply which he shall turn and twist
At pleasure, snuff at till his brain grow drunk,
As the bear does when he finds a scented glove
That puzzles him, — a hand and yet no hand,
Of other perfume than his own foul paw!   540
Last month, I had doubtless chosen to play the dupe,
Accepted the mock-invitation, kept
The sham appointment, cudgel beneath cloak,
Prepared myself to pull the appointer's self
Out of the window from his hiding-place
Behind the gown of this part-messenger
Part-mistress who would personate the wife.
Such had seemed once a jest permissible:
Now I am not i' the mood."

                 Back next morn brought
The messenger, a second letter in hand.   550
"You are cruel, Thyrsis, and Myrtilla moans
Neglected but adores you, makes request
For mercy: why is it you dare not come?
Such virtue is scarce natural to your age.
You must love some one else; I hear you do,
The Baron's daughter or the Advocate's wife,
Or both, — all's one, would you make me the third —
I take the crumbs from table gratefully
Nor grudge who feasts there. 'Faith, I blush and blaze!
Yet if I break all bounds, there's reason sure.   560
Are you determinedly bent on Rome?
I am wretched here, a monster tortures me:
Carry me with you! Come and say you will!
Concert this very evening! Do not write!
I am ever at the window of my room
Over the terrace, at the *Ave*. Come!"

I questioned — lifting half the woman's mask
To let her smile loose. "So, you gave my line
To the merry lady?" "She kissed off the wax,
And put what paper was not kissed away,   570
In her bosom to go burn: but merry, no!
She wept all night when evening brought no friend,
Alone, the unkind missive at her breast;
Thus Philomel, the thorn at her breast too,
Sings" . . . "Writes this second letter?" "Even so!
Then she may peep at vespers forth?" — "What risk
Do we run o' the husband?" — "Ah, — no risk at all!

He is more stupid even than jealous. Ah —
That was the reason! Why, the man's away!
Beside, his bugbear is that friend of yours,   580
Fat little Canon Conti. He fears him,
How should he dream of you? I told you truth:
He goes to the villa at Vittiano — 'tis
The time when Spring-sap rises in the vine —
Spends the night there. And then his wife's a child:
Does he think a child outwits him? A mere child:
Yet so full grown, a dish for any duke.
Don't quarrel longer with such cates, but come!"

I wrote "In vain do you solicit me.
I am a priest: and you are wedded wife,   590
Whatever kind of brute your husband prove.
I have scruples, in short. Yet should you really show
Sign at the window . . . but nay, best be good!
My thoughts are elsewhere." "Take her that!"
                                                        "Again
Let the incarnate meanness, cheat and spy,
Mean to the marrow of him, make his heart
His food, anticipate hell's worm once more!
Let him watch shivering at the window — ay,
And let this hybrid, this his light-of-love
And lackey-of-lies, — a sage economy, —   600
Paid with embracings for the rank brass coin, —
Let her report and make him chuckle o'er
The break-down of my resolution now,
And lour at disappointment in good time!
— So tantalize and so enrage by turns,
Until the two fall each on the other like
Two famished spiders, as the coveted fly
That toys long, leaves their net and them at last!"
And so the missives followed thick and fast
For a month, say, — I still came at every turn   610
On the soft sly adder, endlong 'neath my tread.
I was met i' the street, made sign to in the church,
A slip was found i' the door-sill, scribbled word
'Twixt page and page o' the prayer-book in my place.
A crumpled thing dropped even before my feet,
Pushed through the blind, above the terrace-rail,
As I passed, by day, the very window once.
And ever from corners would be peering up
The messenger, with the self-same demand

"Obdurate still, no flesh but adamant?   620
Nothing to cure the wound, assuage the throe
O' the sweetest lamb that ever loved a bear?"
And ever my one answer in one tone —
"Go your ways, temptress! Let a priest read, pray,
Unplagued of vain talk, visions not for him!
In the end, you'll have your will and ruin me!"

One day, a variation: thus I read:
"You have gained little by timidity.
My husband has found out my love at length,
Sees cousin Conti was the stalking-horse,   630
And you the game he covered, poor fat soul!
My husband is a formidable foe,
Will stick at nothing to destroy you. Stand
Prepared, or better, run till you reach Rome!
I bade you visit me, when the last place
My tyrant would have turned suspicious at,
Or cared to seek you in, was . . . why say, where?
But now all's changed: beside, the season's past
At the villa, — wants the master's eye no more.
Anyhow, I beseech you, stay away   640
From the window! He might well be posted there."

I wrote — "You raise my courage, or call up
My curiosity, who am but man.
Tell him he owns the palace, not the street
Under — that's his and yours and mine alike.
If it should please me pad the path this eve,
Guido will have two troubles, first to get
Into a rage and then get out again.
Be cautious, though: at the *Ave!*"
                              You of the Court!
When I stood question here and reached this point   650
O' the narrative, — search notes and see and say
If some one did not interpose with smile
And sneer, "And prithee why so confident
That the husband must, of all needs, not the wife,
Fabricate thus, — what if the lady loved?
What if she wrote the letters?"
                              Learned Sir,
I told you there's a picture in our church.
Well, if a low-browed verger sidled up
Bringing me, like a blotch, on his prod's point,

A transfixed scorpion, let the reptile writhe,   660
And then said "See a thing that Rafael made —
This venom issued from Madonna's mouth!"
I should reply, "Rather, the soul of you
Has issued from your body, like from like,
By way of the ordure-corner!"
                              But no less,
I tired of the same long black teasing lie
Obtruded thus at every turn; the pest
Was far too near the picture, anyhow:
One does Madonna service, making clowns
Remove their dung-heap from the sacristy.   670
"I will to the window, as he tempts," said I:
"Yes, whom the easy love has failed allure,
This new bait of adventure tempts," — thinks he.
"Though the imprisoned lady keeps afar,
There will they lie in ambush, heads alert,
Kith, kin, and Count mustered to bite my heel.
No mother nor brother viper of the brood
Shall scuttle off without the instructive bruise!"

So I went: crossed street and street: "The next street's turn,
I stand beneath the terrace, see, above,   680
The black of the ambush-window. Then, in place
Of hand's throw of soft prelude over lute,
And cough that clears way for the ditty last," —
I began to laugh already — "he will have
'Out of the hole you hide in, on to the front,
Count Guido Franceschini, show yourself!
Hear what a man thinks of a thing like you,
And after, take this foulness in your face!' "

The words lay living on my lip, I made
The one-turn more — and there at the window stood,   690
Framed in its black square length, with lamp in hand,
Pompilia; the same great, grave, griefful air
As stands i' the dusk, on altar that I know,
Left alone with one moonbeam in her cell,
Our Lady of all the Sorrows. Ere I knelt —
Assured myself that she was flesh and blood —
She had looked one look and vanished.
                              I thought — "Just so:
It was herself, they have set her there to watch —
Stationed to see some wedding-band go by,

On fair pretence that she must bless the bride,   700
Or wait some funeral with friends wind past,
And crave peace for the corpse that claims its due.
She never dreams they used her for a snare,
And now withdraw the bait has served its turn.
Well done, the husband, who shall fare the worse!"
And on my lip again was — "Out with thee,
Guido!" When all at once she reappeared;
But, this time, on the terrace overhead,
So close above me, she could almost touch
My head if she bent down; and she did bend,   710
While I stood still as stone, all eye, all ear.

She began — "You have sent me letters, Sir:
I have read none, I can neither read nor write;
But she you gave them to, a woman here,
One of the people in whose power I am,
Partly explained their sense, I think, to me
Obliged to listen while she inculcates
That you, a priest, can dare love me, a wife,
Desire to live or die as I shall bid,
(She makes me listen if I will or no)   720
Because you saw my face a single time.
It cannot be she says the thing you mean;
Such wickedness were deadly to us both:
But good true love would help me now so much —
I tell myself, you may mean good and true.
You offer me, I seem to understand,
Because I am in poverty and starve,
Much money, where one piece would save my life.
The silver cup upon the altar-cloth
Is neither yours to give nor mine to take;   730
But I might take one bit of bread therefrom,
Since I am starving, and return the rest,
Yet do no harm: this is my very case.
I am in that strait, I may not dare abstain
From so much of assistance as would bring
The guilt of theft on neither you nor me;
But no superfluous particle of aid.
I think, if you will let me state my case,
Even had you been so fancy-fevered here,
Not your sound self, you must grow healthy now —   740
Care only to bestow what I can take.
That it is only you in the wide world,

Knowing me nor in thought nor word nor deed,
Who, all unprompted save by your own heart,
Come proffering assistance now, — were strange
But that my whole life is so strange: as strange
It is, my husband whom I have not wronged
Should hate and harm me. For his own soul's sake,
Hinder the harm! But there is something more,
And that the strangest: it has got to be   **750**
Somehow for my sake too, and yet not mine,
— This is a riddle — for some kind of sake
Not any clearer to myself than you,
And yet as certain as that I draw breath, —
I would fain live, not die — oh no, not die!
My case is, I was dwelling happily
At Rome with those dear Comparini, called
Father and mother to me; when at once
I found I had become Count Guido's wife:
Who then, not waiting for a moment, changed   **760**
Into a fury of fire, if once he was
Merely a man: his face threw fire at mine,
He laid a hand on me that burned all peace,
All joy, all hope, and last all fear away,
Dipping the bough of life, so pleasant once,
In fire which shrivelled leaf and bud alike,
Burning not only present life but past,
Which you might think was safe beyond his reach.
He reached it, though, since that beloved pair,
My father once, my mother all those years,   **770**
That loved me so, now say I dreamed a dream
And bid me wake, henceforth no child of theirs,
Never in all the time their child at all.
Do you understand? I cannot: yet so it is.
Just so I say of you that proffer help:
I cannot understand what prompts your soul,
I simply needs must see that it is so,
Only one strange and wonderful thing more.
They came here with me, those two dear ones, kept
All the old love up, till my husband, till   **780**
His people here so tortured them, they fled.
And now, is it because I grow in flesh
And spirit one with him their torturer,
That they, renouncing him, must cast off me?
If I were graced by God to have a child,
Could I one day deny God graced me so?

Then, since my husband hates me, I shall break
No law that reigns in this fell house of hate,
By using — letting have effect so much
Of hate as hides me from that whole of hate   790
Would take my life which I want and must have —
Just as I take from your excess of love
Enough to save my life with, all I need.
The Archbishop said to murder me were sin:
My leaving Guido were a kind of death
With no sin, — more death, he must answer for.
Hear now what death to him and life to you
I wish to pay and owe. Take me to Rome!
You go to Rome, the servant makes me hear.
Take me as you would take a dog, I think,   800
Masterless left for strangers to maltreat:
Take me home like that — leave me in the house
Where the father and the mother are; and soon
They'll come to know and call me by my name,
Their child once more, since child I am, for all
They now forget me, which is the worst o' the dream —
And the way to end dreams is to break them, stand,
Walk, go: then help me to stand, walk and go!
The Governor said the strong should help the weak:
You know how weak the strongest women are.   810
How could I find my way there by myself?
I cannot even call out, make them hear —
Just as in dreams: I have tried and proved the fact.
I have told this story and more to good great men,
The Archbishop and the Governor: they smiled.
'Stop your mouth, fair one!' — presently they frowned,
'Get you gone, disengage you from our feet!'
I went in my despair to an old priest,
Only a friar, no great man like these two,
But good, the Augustinian, people name   820
Romano, — he confessed me two months since:
He fears God, why then needs he fear the world?
And when he questioned how it came about
That I was found in danger of a sin —
Despair of any help from providence, —
'Since, though your husband outrage you,' said he,
'That is a case too common, the wives die
Or live, but do not sin so deep as this' —
Then I told — what I never will tell you —
How, worse than husband's hate, I had to bear   830

The love, — soliciting to shame called love, —
Of his brother, — the young idle priest i' the house
With only the devil to meet there. 'This is grave —
Yes, we must interfere: I counsel, — write
To those who used to be your parents once,
Of dangers here, bid them convey you hence!'
'But,' said I, 'when I neither read nor write?'
Then he took pity and promised 'I will write.'
If he did so, — why, they are dumb or dead:
Either they give no credit to the tale,   840
Or else, wrapped wholly up in their own joy
Of such escape, they care not who cries, still
I' the clutches. Anyhow, no word arrives.
All such extravagance and dreadfulness
Seems incident to dreaming, cured one way, —
Wake me! The letter I received this morn,
Said — if the woman spoke your very sense —
'You would die for me:' I can believe it now:
For now the dream goes to involve yourself.
First of all, you seemed wicked and not good,   850
In writing me those letters: you came in
Like a thief upon me. I this morning said
In my extremity, entreat the thief!
Try if he have in him no honest touch!
A thief might save me from a murderer.
'Twas a thief said the last kind word to Christ:
Christ took the kindness and forgave the theft:
And so did I prepare what I now say.
But now, that you stand and I see your face,
Though you have never uttered word yet, — well, I know,   860
Here too has been dream-work, delusion too.
And that at no time, you with the eyes here,
Ever intended to do wrong by me,
Nor wrote such letters therefore. It is false,
And you are true, have been true, will be true.
To Rome then, — when is it you take me there?
Each minute lost is mortal. When? — I ask."

I answered "It shall be when it can be.
I will go hence and do your pleasure, find
The sure and speedy means of travel, then   870
Come back and take you to your friends in Rome.
There wants a carriage, money and the rest, —

A day's work by to-morrow at this time.
How shall I see you and assure escape?"

She replied, "Pass, to-morrow at this hour.
If I am at the open window, well:
If I am absent, drop a handkerchief
And walk by! I shall see from where I watch,
And know that all is done. Return next eve,
And next, and so till we can meet and speak!"   880
"To-morrow at this hour I pass," said I.
She was withdrawn.
            Here is another point
I bid you pause at. When I told thus far,
Someone said, subtly, "Here at least was found
Your confidence in error, — you perceived
The spirit of the letters, in a sort,
Had been the lady's, if the body should be
Supplied by Guido: say, he forged them all!
Here was the unforged fact — she sent for you,
Spontaneously elected you to help,   890
— What men call, loved you: Guido read her mind,
Gave it expression to assure the world
The case was just as he foresaw: he wrote,
She spoke."
        Sirs, that first simile serves still, —
That falsehood of a scorpion hatched, I say,
Nowhere i' the world but in Madonna's mouth.
Go on! Suppose, that falsehood foiled, next eve
Pictured Madonna raised her painted hand,
Fixed the face Rafael bent above the Babe,
On my face as I flung me at her feet: 900
Such miracle vouchsafed and manifest,
Would that prove the first lying tale was true?
Pompilia spoke, and I at once received,
Accepted my own fact, my miracle
Self-authorized and self-explained, — she chose
To summon me and signify her choice.
Afterward, — oh! I gave a passing glance
To a certain ugly cloud-shape, goblin-shred
Of hell-smoke hurrying past the splendid moon
Out now to tolerate no darkness more,   910
And saw right through the thing that tried to pass
For truth and solid, not an empty lie:

"So, he not only forged the words for her
But words for me, made letters he called mine!
What I sent, he retained, gave these in place,
All by the mistress-messenger! As I
Recognized her, at potency of truth,
So she, by the crystalline soul, knew me,
Never mistook the signs. Enough of this —
Let the wraith go to nothingness again,   920
Here is the orb, have only thought for her!"

"Thought?" nay, Sirs, what shall follow was not thought:
I have thought sometimes, and thought long and hard.
I have stood before, gone round a serious thing,
Tasked my whole mind to touch and clasp it close,
As I stretch forth my arm to touch this bar.
God and man, and what duty I owe both, —
I dare to say I have confronted these
In thought: but no such faculty helped here.
I put forth no thought, — powerless, all that night   930
I paced the city: it was the first Spring.
By the invasion I lay passive to,
In rushed new things, the old were rapt away;
Alike abolished — the imprisonment
Of the outside air, the inside weight o' the world
That pulled me down. Death meant, to spurn the ground,
Soar to the sky, — die well and you do that.
The very immolation made the bliss;
Death was the heart of life, and all the harm
My folly had crouched to avoid, now proved a veil   940
Hiding all gain my wisdom strove to grasp:
As if the intense centre of the flame
Should turn a heaven to that devoted fly
Which hitherto, sophist alike and sage,
Saint Thomas with his sober gray goose-quill,
And sinner Plato by Cephisian reed,
Would fain, pretending just the insect's good,
Whisk off, drive back, consign to shade again.
Into another state, under new rule
I knew myself was passing swift and sure;   950
Whereof the initiatory pang approached,
Felicitous annoy, as bitter-sweet
As when the virgin-band, the victors chaste,
Feel at the end the earthly garments drop,
And rise with something of a rosy shame

Into immortal nakedness: so I
Lay, and let come the proper throe would thrill
Into the ecstasy and outthrob pain.

I' the gray of dawn it was I found myself
Facing the pillared front o' the Pieve — mine,   960
My church: it seemed to say for the first time
"But am not I the Bride, the mystic love
O' the Lamb, who took thy plighted troth, my priest,
To fold thy warm heart on my heart of stone
And freeze thee nor unfasten any more?
This is a fleshly woman, — let the free
Bestow their life-blood, thou art pulseless now!"
See! Day by day I had risen and left this church
At the signal waved me by some foolish fan,
With half a curse and half a pitying smile   970
For the monk I stumbled over in my haste,
Prostrate and corpse-like at the altar-foot
Intent on his *corona:* then the church
Was ready with her quip, if word conduced,
To quicken my pace nor stop for prating — "There!
Be thankful you are no such ninny, go
Rather to teach a black-eyed novice cards
Than gabble Latin and protrude that nose
Smoothed to a sheep's through no brains and much faith!"
That sort of incentive! Now the church changed tone —   980
Now, when I found out first that life and death
Are means to an end, that passion uses both,
Indisputably mistress of the man
Whose form of worship is self-sacrifice:
Now, from the stone lungs sighed the scrannel voice
"Leave that live passion, come be dead with me!"
As if, i' the fabled garden, I had gone
On great adventure, plucked in ignorance
Hedge-fruit, and feasted to satiety,
Laughing at such high fame for hips and haws,   990
And scorned the achievement: then come all at once
O' the prize o' the place, the thing of perfect gold,
The apple's self: and, scarce my eye on that,
Was 'ware as well o' the seven-fold dragon's watch.

Sirs, I obeyed. Obedience was too strange, —
This new thing that had been struck into me
By the look o' the lady, — to dare disobey

The first authoritative word. 'Twas God's.
I had been lifted to the level of her,
Could take such sounds into my sense. I said   1000
"We two are cognisant o' the Master now;
She it is bids me bow the head: how true,
I am a priest! I see the function here;
I thought the other way self-sacrifice:
This is the true, seals up the perfect sum.
I pay it, sit down, silently obey."

So, I went home. Dawn broke, noon broadened, I —
I sat stone-still, let time run over me.
The sun slanted into my room, had reached
The west. I opened book, — Aquinas blazed   1010
With one black name only on the white page.
I looked up, saw the sunset: vespers rang:
"She counts the minutes till I keep my word
And come say all is ready. I am a priest.
Duty to God is duty to her: I think
God, who created her, will save her too
Some new way, by one miracle the more,
Without me. Then, prayer may avail perhaps."
I went to my own place i' the Pieve, read
The office: I was back at home again   1020
Sitting i' the dark. "Could she but know — but know
That, were there good in this distinct from God's,
Really good as it reached her, though procured
By a sin of mine, — I should sin: God forgives.
She knows it is no fear witholds me: fear?
Of what? Suspense here is the terrible thing.
If she should, as she counts the minutes, come
On the fantastic notion that I fear
The world now, fear the Archbishop, fear perhaps
Count Guido, he who, having forged the lies,   1030
May wait the work, attend the effect, — I fear
The sword of Guido! Let God see to that —
Hating lies, let not her believe a lie!"

Again the morning found me. "I will work,
Tie down my foolish thoughts. Thank God so far!
I have saved her from a scandal, stopped the tongues
Had broken else into a cackle and hiss
Around the noble name. Duty is still
Wisdom: I have been wise." So the day wore.

At evening — "But, achieving victory,   1040
I must not blink the priest's peculiar part,
Nor shrink to counsel, comfort: priest and friend —
How do we discontinue to be friends?
I will go minister, advise her seek
Help at the source, — above all, not despair:
There may be other happier help at hand.
I hope it, — wherefore then neglect to say?"

There she stood — leaned there, for the second time,
Over the terrace, looked at me, then spoke:
"Why is it you have suffered me to stay   1050
Breaking my heart two days more than was need?
Why delay help, your own heart yearns to give?
You are again here, in the self-same mind,
I see here, steadfast in the face of you, —
You grudge to do no one thing that I ask.
Why then is nothing done? You know my need.
Still, through God's pity on me, there is time
And one day more: shall I be saved or no?"
I answered — "Lady, waste no thought, no word
Even to forgive me! Care for what I care —   1060
Only! Now follow me as I were fate!
Leave this house in the dark to-morrow night,
Just before daybreak: — there's new moon this eve —
It sets, and then begins the solid black.
Descend, proceed to the Torrione, step
Over the low dilapidated wall,
Take San Clemente, there's no other gate
Unguarded at the hour: some paces thence
An inn stands; cross to it; I shall be there."

She answered, "If I can but find the way.   1070
But I shall find it. Go now!"

                    I did go,
Took rapidly the route myself prescribed,
Stopped at Torrione, climbed the ruined place,
Proved that the gate was practicable, reached
The inn, no eye, despite the dark, could miss,
Knocked there and entered, made the host secure:
"With Caponsacchi it is ask and have;
I know my betters. Are you bound for Rome?
I get swift horse and trusty man," said he.

Then I retraced my steps, was found once more   1080
In my own house for the last time: there lay
The broad pale opened Summa. "Shut his book,
There's other showing! 'Twas a Thomas too
Obtained, — more favored than his namesake here, —
A gift, tied faith fast, foiled the tug of doubt, —
Our Lady's girdle; down he saw it drop
As she ascended into heaven, they say:
He kept that safe and bade all doubt adieu,
I too have seen a lady and hold a grace."

I know not how the night passed: morning broke;   1090
Presently came my servant. "Sir, this eve —
Do you forget?" I started. "How forget?
What is it you know?" "With due submission, Sir,
This being last Monday in the month but one
And a vigil, since to-morrow is Saint George,
And feast day, and moreover day for copes,
And Canon Conti now away a month,
And Canon Crispi sour because, forsooth,
You let him sulk in stall and bear the brunt
Of the octave . . . Well, Sir, 'tis important!"
                                    "True!   1100
Hearken, I have to start for Rome this night.
No word, lest Crispi overboil and burst!
Provide me with a laic dress! Throw dust
I' the Canon's eye, stop his tongue's scandal so!
See there's a sword in case of accident."
I knew the knave, the knave knew me.
                                    And thus
Through each familiar hindrance of the day
Did I make steadily for its hour and end, —
Felt time's old barrier-growth of right and fit
Give way through all its twines, and let me go.   1110
Use and wont recognized the excepted man,
Let speed the special service, — and I sped
Till, at the dead between midnight and morn,
There was I at the goal, before the gate,
With a tune in the ears, low leading up to loud,
A light in the eyes, faint that would soon be flare,
Ever some spiritual witness new and new
In faster frequence, crowding solitude
To watch the way o' the warfare, — till, at last,
When the ecstatic minute must bring birth,   1120

Began a whiteness in the distance, waxed
Whiter and whiter, near grew and more near,
Till it was she: there did Pompilia come:
The white I saw shine through her was her soul's,
Certainly, for the body was one black,
Black from head down to foot. She did not speak,
Glided into the carriage, — so a cloud
Gathers the moon up. "By San Spirito,
To Rome, as if the road burned underneath!
Reach Rome, then hold my head in pledge, I pay   1130
The run and the risk to heart's content!" Just that
I said, — then, in another tick of time,
Sprang, was beside her, she and I alone.

So it began, our flight thro' dusk to clear,
Through day and night and day again to night
Once more, and to last dreadful dawn of all.
Sirs, how should I lie quiet in my grave
Unless you suffer me wring, drop by drop,
My brain dry, make a riddance of the drench
Of minutes with a memory in each,   1140
Recorded motion, breath or look of hers,
Which poured forth would present you one pure glass,
Mirror you plain, — as God's sea, glassed in gold,
His saints, — the perfect soul Pompilia? Men,
You must know that a man gets drunk with truth
Stagnant inside him! Oh, they've killed her, Sirs!
Can I be calm?
                    Calmly! Each incident
Proves, I maintain, that action of the flight
For the true thing it was. The first faint scratch
O' the stone will test its nature, teach its worth   1150
To idiots who name Parian — coprolite.
After all, I shall give no glare — at best
Only display you certain scattered lights
Lamping the rush and roll of the abyss:
Nothing but here and there a fire-point pricks
Wavelet from wavelet: well!
                              For the first hour
We both were silent in the night, I know:
Sometimes I did not see nor understand.
Blackness engulfed me, — partial stupor, say —
Then I would break way, breathe through the surprise,   1160
And be aware again, and see who sat

In the dark vest with the white face and hands.
I said to myself — "I have caught it, I conceive
The mind o' the mystery: 'tis the way they wake
And wait, two martyrs somewhere in a tomb
Each by each as their blessing was to die,
Some signal they are promised and expect, —
When to arise before the trumpet scares:
So, through the whole course of the world they wait
The last day, but so fearless and so safe!   1170
No otherwise, in safety and not fear,
I lie, because she lies too by my side."
You know this is not love, Sirs, — it is faith,
The feeling that there's God, he reigns and rules
Out of this low world: that is all; no harm!
At times she drew a soft sigh — music seemed
Always to hover just above her lips,
Not settle, — break a silence music too.

In the determined morning, I first found
Her head erect, her face turned full to me,   1180
Her soul intent on mine through two wide eyes.
I answered them. "You are saved hitherto.
We have passed Perugia, — gone round by the wood,
Not through, I seem to think, — and opposite
I know Assisi; this is holy ground."
Then she resumed. "How long since we both left
Arezzo?" "Years — and certain hours beside."

It was at . . . ah, but I forget the names!
'Tis a mere post-house and a hovel or two;
I left the carriage and got bread and wine   1190
And brought it her. "Does it detain to eat?"
"They stay perforce, change horses, — therefore eat!
We lose no minute: we arrive, be sure!"
This was — I know not where — there's a great hill
Close over, and the stream has lost its bridge,
One fords it. She began — "I have heard say
Of some sick body that my mother knew,
'Twas no good sign when in a limb diseased
All the pain suddenly departs, — as if
The guardian angel discontinued pain   1200
Because the hope of cure was gone at last:
The limb will not again exert itself,
It needs be pained no longer: so with me,

— My soul whence all the pain is past at once:
All pain must be to work some good in the end.
True, this I feel now, this may be that good,
Pain was because of, — otherwise, I fear!"

She said, — a long while later in the day,
When I had let the silence be, — abrupt —
"Have you a mother?" "She died, I was born."   1210
"A sister then?" "No sister." "Who was it —
What woman were you used to serve this way,
Be kind to, till I called you and you came?"
I did not like that word. Soon afterward —
"Tell me, are men unhappy, in some kind
Of mere unhappiness at being men,
As women suffer, being womanish?
Have you, now, some unhappiness, I mean,
Born of what may be man's strength overmuch,
To match the undue susceptibility,   1220
The sense at every pore when hate is close?
It hurts us if a baby hides its face
Or child strikes at us punily, calls names
Or makes a mouth, — much more if stranger men
Laugh or frown, — just as that were much to bear!
Yet rocks split, — and the blow-ball does no more,
Quivers to feathery nothing at a touch;
And strength may have its drawback weakness 'scapes."

Once she asked "What is it that made you smile,
At the great gate with the eagles and the snakes,   1230
Where the company entered, 'tis a long time since?"
"— Forgive — I think you would not understand:
Ah, but you ask me, — therefore, it was this.
That was a certain bishop's villa-gate,
I knew it by the eagles, — and at once
Remembered this same bishop was just he
People of old were wont to bid me please
If I would catch preferment: so, I smiled
Because an impulse came to me, a whim —
What if I prayed the prelate leave to speak,   1240
Began upon him in his presence-hall
— 'What, still at work so gray and obsolete?
Still rocheted and mitred more or less?
Don't you feel all that out of fashion now?
I find out when the day of things is done!' "

At eve we heard the *angelus:* she turned —
I told you I can neither read nor write.
My life stopped with the play-time; I will learn,
If I begin to live again: but you —
Who are a priest — wherefore do you not read   1250
The service at this hour? Read Gabriel's song,
The lesson, and then read the little prayer
To Raphael, proper for us travellers!"
I did not like that, neither, but I read.

When we stopped at Foligno it was dark.
The people of the post came out with lights:
The driver said, "This time to-morrow, may
Saints only help, relays continue good,
Nor robbers hinder, we arrive at Rome."
I urged, "Why tax your strength a second night?   1260
Trust me, alight here and take brief repose!
We are out of harm's reach, past pursuit: go sleep
If but an hour! I keep watch, guard the while
Here in the doorway." But her whole face changed,
The misery grew again about her mouth,
The eyes burned up from faintness, like the fawn's
Tired to death in the thicket, when she feels
The probing spear o' the huntsman. "Oh, no stay!"
She cried, in the fawn's cry, "On to Rome, on, on,
Unless 'tis you who fear, — which cannot be!"   1270

We did go on all night; but at its close
She was troubled, restless, moaned low, talked at whiles
To herself, her brow on quiver with the dream:
Once, wide awake, she menaced, at arms' length
Waved away something — "Never again with you!
My soul is mine, my body is my soul's:
You and I are divided ever more
In soul and body: get you gone!" Then I —
"Why, in my whole life I have never prayed!
Oh, if the God, that only can, would help!   1280
Am I his priest with power to cast out fiends?
Let God arise and all his enemies
Be scattered!" By morn there was peace, no sigh
Out of the deep sleep.
                    When she woke at last,
I answered the first look — "Scarce twelve hours more,
Then, Rome! There probably was no pursuit,

There cannot now be peril: bear up brave!
Just some twelve hours to press through to the prize:
Then, no more of the terrible journey!" "Then,
No more o' the journey: if it might but last!   1290
Always, my life-long, thus to journey still!
It is the interruption that I dread, —
With no dread, ever to be here and thus!
Never to see a face nor hear a voice!
Yours is no voice; you speak when you are dumb;
Nor face, I see it in the dark. I want
No face nor voice that change and grow unkind."
That I liked, that was the best thing she said.

In the broad day, I dared entreat, "Descend!"
I told a woman, at the garden-gate   1300
By the post-house, white and pleasant in the sun,
"It is my sister, — talk with her apart!
She is married and unhappy, you perceive;
I take her home because her head is hurt;
Comfort her as you women understand!"
So, there I left them by the garden-wall,
Paced the road, then bade put the horses to,
Came back, and there she sat: close to her knee,
A black-eyed child still held the bowl of milk,
Wondered to see how little she could drink,   1310
And in her arms the woman's infant lay.
She smiled at me "How much good this has done!
This is a whole night's rest and how much more!
I can proceed now, though I wish to stay.
How do you call that tree with the thick top
That holds in all its leafy green and gold
The sun now like an immense egg of fire?"
(It was a million-leaved mimosa.) "Take
The babe away from me and let me go!"
And in the carriage "Still a day, my friend!   1320
And perhaps half a night, the woman fears.
I pray it finish since it cannot last:
There may be more misfortune at the close,
And where will you be? God suffice me then!"
And presently — for there was a roadside-shrine —
"When I was taken first to my own church
Lorenzo in Lucina, being a girl,
And bid confess my faults, I interposed
'But teach me what fault to confess and know!'

So, the priest said — 'You should bethink yourself: 1330
Each human being needs must have done wrong!'
Now, be you candid and no priest but friend —
Were I surprised and killed here on the spot,
A runaway from husband and his home,
Do you account it were in sin I died?
My husband used to seem to harm me, not . . .
Not on pretence he punished sin of mine,
Nor for sin's sake and lust of cruelty,
But as I heard him bid a farming-man
At the villa take a lamb once to the wood   1340
And there ill-treat it, meaning that the wolf
Should hear its cries, and so come, quick be caught,
Enticed to the trap: he practised thus with me
That so, whatever were his gain thereby,
Others than I might become prey and spoil.
Had it been only between our two selves, —
His pleasure and my pain, — why, pleasure him
By dying, nor such need to make a coil!
But this was worth an effort, that my pain
Should not become a snare, prove pain threefold   1350
To other people — strangers — or unborn —
How should I know? I sought release from that —
I think, or else from, — dare I say, some cause
Such as is put into a tree, which turns
Away from the north wind with what nest it holds, —
The woman said that trees so turn: now, friend,
Tell me, because I cannot trust myself!
You are a man: what have I done amiss?"
You must conceive my answer, — I forget —
Taken up wholly with the thought, perhaps,   1360
This time she might have said, — might, did not say —
"You are a priest." She said, "my friend."

                          Day wore,
We passed the places, somehow the calm went,
Again the restless eyes began to rove
In new fear of the foe mine could not see.
She wandered in her mind, — addressed me once
"Gaetano!" — that is not my name: whose name?
I grew alarmed, my head seemed turning too.
I quickened pace with promise now, now threat:
Bade drive and drive, nor any stopping more.   1370
"Too deep i' the thick of the struggle, struggle through!
Then drench her in repose though death's self pour

The plenitude of quiet, — help us, God,
Whom the winds carry!"
                    Suddenly I saw
The old tower, and the little white-walled clump
Of buildings and the cypress-tree or two, —
"Already Castelnuovo — Rome!" I cried,
"As good as Rome, — Rome is the next stage, think!
This is where travellers' hearts are wont to beat.
Say you are saved, sweet lady!" Up she woke.   1380
The sky was fierce with color from the sun
Setting. She screamed out "No, I must not die!
Take me no farther, I should die: stay here!
I have more life to save than mine!"
                         She swooned.
We seemed safe: what was it foreboded so?
Out of the coach into the inn I bore
The motionless and breathless pure and pale
Pompilia, — bore her through a pitying group
And laid her on a couch, still calm and cured
By deep sleep of all woes at once. The host   1390
Was urgent "Let her stay an hour or two!
Leave her to us, all will be right by morn!"
Oh, my foreboding! But I could not choose.

I paced the passage, kept watch all night long.
I listened, — not one movement, not one sigh.
"Fear not: she sleeps so sound!" they said: but I
Feared, all the same, kept fearing more and more,
Found myself throb with fear from head to foot,
Filled with a sense of such impending woe,
That, at first pause of night, pretence of gray,   1400
I made my mind up it was morn. — "Reach Rome,
Lest hell reach her! A dozen miles to make,
Another long breath, and we emerge!" I stood
I' the court-yard, roused the sleepy grooms. "Have out
Carriage and horse, give haste, take gold!" said I.
While they made ready in the doubtful morn, —
'Twas the last minute, — needs must I ascend
And break her sleep; I turned to go.
                        And there
Faced me Count Guido, there posed the mean man
As master, — took the field, encamped his rights,   1410
Challenged the world: there leered new triumph, there
Scowled the old malice in the visage bad

And black o' the scamp. Soon triumph suppled the tongue
A little, malice glued to his dry throat,
And he part howled, part hissed . . . oh, how he kept
Well out o' the way, at arm's length and to spare! —
"My salutation to your priestship! What?
Matutinal, busy with book so soon
Of an April day that's damp as tears that now
Deluge Arezzo at its darling's flight? —   1420
'Tis unfair, wrongs feminity at large,
To let a single dame monopolize
A heart the whole sex claims, should share alike:
Therefore I overtake you, Canon! Come!
The lady, — could you leave her side so soon?
You have not yet experienced at her hands
My treatment, you lay down undrugged, I see!
Hence this alertness — hence no death-in-life
Like what held arms fast when she stole from mine.
To be sure, you took the solace and repose   1430
That first night at Foligno! — news abound
O' the road by this time, — men regaled me much,
As past them I came halting after you,
Vulcan pursuing Mars, as poets sing, —
Still at the last here pant I, but arrive,
Vulcan — and not without my Cyclops too,
The Commissary and the unpoisoned arm
O' the Civil Force, should Mars turn mutineer.
Enough of fooling: capture the culprits, friend!
Here is the lover in the smart disguise   1440
With the sword, — he is a priest, so mine lies still.
There upstairs hides my wife the runaway,
His leman: the two plotted, poisoned first,
Plundered me after, and eloped thus far
Where now you find them. Do your duty quick!
Arrest and hold him! That's done: now catch her!"
During this speech of that man, — well, I stood
Away, as he managed, — still, I stood as near
The throat of him, with these two hands, my own, —
As now I stand near yours, Sir, — one quick spring,   1450
One great good satisfying gripe, and lo!
There had he lain abolished with his lie,
Creation purged o' the miscreate, man redeemed,
A spittle wiped off from the face of God!
I, in some measure, seek a poor excuse
For what I left undone, in just this fact

Thåt my first feeling at the speech I quote
Was — not of what a blasphemy was dared,
Not what a bag of venomed purulence
Was split and noisome, — but how splendidly　　　　1460
Mirthful, how ludicrous a lie was launched!
Would Molière's self wish more than hear such man
Call, claim such woman for his own, his wife,
Even though, in due amazement at the boast,
He had stammered, she moreover was divine?
She to be his, — were hardly less absurd
Than that he took her name into his mouth,
Licked, and then let it go again, the beast,
Signed with his slaver. Oh, she poisoned him,
Plundered him, and the rest! Well, what I wished　　　1470
Was, that he would go on, say once more
So to the world, and get his meed of men,
The fist's reply to the filth.　　And while I mused,
The minute, oh the misery, was gone!
On either idle hand of me there stood
Really an officer, nor laughed i' the least:
Nay, rendered justice to his reason, laid
Logic to heart, as 'twere submitted them
"Twice two makes four."
　　　　　　　　　　"And now, catch her!" he cried.
That sobered me. "Let myself lead the way —　　　　1480
Ere you arrest me, who am somebody,
Being, as you hear, a priest and privileged, —
To the lady's chamber! I presume you — men
Expert, instructed how to find out truth,
Familiar with the guise of guilt. Detect
Guilt on her face when it meets mine, then judge
Between us and the mad dog howling there!"
Up we all went together, in they broke
O' the chamber late my chapel. There she lay,
Composed as when I laid her, that last eve,　　　　1490
O' the couch, still breathless, motionless, sleep's self,
Wax-white, seraphic, saturate with the sun
O' the morning that now flooded from the front
And filled the window with a light like blood.
"Behold the poisoner, the adulteress,
— And feigning sleep too! Seize, bind!" Guido hissed.

She started up, stood erect, face to face
With the husband: back he fell, was buttressed there

By the window all a-flame with morning-red,
He the black figure, the opprobrious blur   1500
Against all peace and joy and light and life.
"Away from between me and hell!" she cried:
"Hell for me, no embracing any more!
I am God's, I love God, God —whose knees I clasp,
Whose utterly mòst just award I take,
But bear no more love-making devils: hence!"
I may have made an effort to reach her side
From where I stood i' the door-way, — anyhow
I found the arms, I wanted, pinioned fast,
Was powerless in the clutch to left and right   1510
O' the rabble pouring in, rascality
Enlisted, rampant on the side of hearth
Home and the husband, — pay in prospect too!
They heaped themselves upon me. "Ha! — and him
Also you outrage? Him, too, my sole friend,
Guardian and saviour? That I balk you of,
Since — see how God can help at last and worst!"
She sprang at the sword that hung beside him, seized,
Drew, brandished it, the sunrise burned for joy
O' the blade, "Die," cried she, "devil, in God's name!"   1520
Ah, but they all closed round her, twelve to one
— The unmanly men, no woman-mother made,
Spawned somehow! Dead-white and disarmed she lay.
No matter for the sword, her word sufficed
To spike the coward through and through: he shook,
Could only spit between the teeth — "You see?
You hear? Bear witness, then! Write down . . . but no —
Carry these criminals to the prison-house,
For first thing! I begin my search meanwhile
After the stolen effects, gold, jewels, plate,   1530
Money and clothes, they robbed me of and fled,
With no few amorous pieces, verse and prose,
I have much reason to expect to find."

When I saw that — no more than the first mad speech,
Made out the speaker mad and a laughing-stock,
So neither did this next device explode
One listener's indignation, — that a scribe
Did sit down, set himself to write indeed,
While sundry knaves began to peer and pry
In corner and hole, — that Guido, wiping brow   1540
And getting him a countenance, was fast

Losing his fear, beginning to strut free
O' the stage of his exploit, snuff here, sniff there, —
Then I took truth in, guessed sufficiently
The service for the moment. "What I say,
Slight at your peril! We are aliens here,
My adversary and I, called noble both;
I am the nobler, and a name men know.
I could refer our cause to our own Court
In our own country, but prefer appeal   1550
To the nearer jurisdiction. Being a priest,
Though in a secular garb, — for reasons good
I shall adduce in due time to my peers, —
I demand that the Church I serve, decide
Between us, right the slandered lady there.
A Tuscan noble, I might claim the Duke:
A priest, I rather choose the Church, — bid Rome
Cover the wronged with her inviolate shield."

There was no refusing this: they bore me off,
They bore her off, to separate cells o' the same   1560
Ignoble prison, and, separate, thence to Rome.
Pompilia's face, then and thus, looked on me
The last time in this life: not one sight since,
Never another sight to be! And yet
I thought I had saved her. I appealed to Rome:
It seems I simply sent her to her death.
You tell me she is dying now, or dead;
I cannot bring myself to quite believe
This is a place you torture people in:
What if this your intelligence were just   1570
A subtlety, an honest wile to work
On a man at unawares? 'Twere worthy you.
No, Sirs, I cannot have the lady dead!
That erect form, flashing brow, fulgurant eye,
That voice immortal (oh, that voice of hers!)
That vision in the blood-red daybreak — that
Leap to life of the pale electric sword
Angels go armed with, — that was not the last
O' the lady! Come, I see through it, you find —
Know the manœuvre! Also herself said   1580
I had saved her: do you dare say she spoke false?
Let me see for myself if it be so!
Though she were dying, a Priest might be of use,
The more when he's a friend too, — she called me

Far beyond "friend." Come, let me see her — indeed
It is my duty, being a priest: I hope
I stand confessed, established, proved a priest?
My punishment had motive that, a priest
I, in a laic garb, a mundane mode,
Did what were harmlessly done otherwise.   1590
I never touched her with my finger-tip
Except to carry her to the couch, that eve,
Against my heart, beneath my head, bowed low,
As we priests carry the paten: that is why
— To get leave and go see her of your grace —
I have told you this whole story over again.
Do I deserve grace? For I might lock lips,
Laugh at your jurisdiction: what have you
To do with me in the matter? I suppose
You hardly think I donned a bravo's dress   1600
To have a hand in the new crime; on the old,
Judgment's delivered, penalty imposed,
I was chained fast at Civita hand and foot —
She had only you to trust to, you and Rome,
Rome and the Church, and no pert meddling priest
Two days ago, when Guido, with the right,
Hacked her to pieces. One might well be wroth;
I have been patient, done my best to help:
I come from Civita and punishment
As friend of the Court — and for pure friendship's sake 1610
Have told my tale to the end, — nay, not the end —
For, wait — I'll end — not leave you that excuse!

When we were parted, — shall I go on there?
I was presently brought to Rome — yes, here I stood
Opposite yonder very crucifix —
And there sat you and you, Sirs, quite the same.
I heard charge, and bore question, and told tale
Noted down in the book there, — turn and see
If, by one jot or tittle, I vary now!
I' the color the tale takes, there's change perhaps;   1620
'Tis natural, since the sky is different,
Eclipse in the air now; still, the outline stays.
I showed you how it came to be my part
To save the lady. Then your clerk produced
Papers, a pack of stupid and impure
Banalities called letters about love —
Love, indeed, — I could teach who styled them so,

Better, I think, though priest and loveless both!
"— How was it that a wife, young, innocent,
And stranger to your person, wrote this page?" —   1630
"— She wrote it when the Holy Father wrote
The bestiality that posts thro' Rome,
Put in his mouth by Pasquin." "Nor perhaps
Did you return these answers, verse and prose,
Signed, sealed and sent the lady? There's your hand!"
"— This precious piece of verse, I really judge,
Is meant to copy my own character,
A clumsy mimic; and this other prose,
Not so much even; both rank forgery:
Verse, quotha? Bembo's verse! When Saint John wrote   1640
The tract *'De Tribus,'* I wrote this to match."
"— How came it, then, the documents were found
At the inn on your departure?" — "I opine,
Because there were no documents to find
In my presence, — you must hide before you find
Who forged them hardly practised in my view;
Who found them waited till I turned my back."
"— And what of the clandestine visits paid,
Nocturnal passage in and out the house
With its lord absent? 'Tis alleged you climbed . . ."   1650
"— Flew on a broomstick to the man i' the moon!
Who witnessed or will testify this trash?"
"— The trusty servant, Margherita's self,
Even she who brought you letters, you confess,
And, you confess, took letters in reply:
Forget not we have knowledge of the facts!"
"— Sirs, who have knowledge of the facts, defray
The expenditure of wit I waste in vain,
Trying to find out just one fact of all!
She who brought letters from who could not write,   1660
And took back letters to who could not read, —
Who was that messenger, of your charity?"
"— Well, so far favors you the circumstance
That this same messenger . . . how shall we say? . . .
Sub imputatione meretricis
Laborat, — which makes accusation null:
We waive this woman's: naught makes void the next.
Borsi, called Venerino, he who drove,
O' the first night when you fled away, at length
Deposes to your kissings in the coach,   1670
— Frequent, frenetic . . ." "When deposed he so?"

"After some weeks of sharp imprisonment . . ."
"— Granted by friend the Governor, I engage —"
"— For his participation in your flight!
At length his obduracy melting made
The avowal mentioned. . . ." "Was dismissed forthwith
To liberty, poor knave, for recompense.
Sirs, give what credit to the lie you can!
For me, no word in my defence I speak,
And God shall argue for the lady!"
       So   1680
Did I stand question, and make answer, still
With the same result of smiling disbelief,
Polite impossibility of faith
In such affected virtue in a priest;
But a showing fair play, an indulgence, even,
To one no worse than others after all —
Who had not brought disgrace to the order, played
Discreetly, ruffled gown nor ripped the cloth
In a bungling game at romps: I have told you, Sirs —
If I pretended simply to be pure,   1690
Honest and Christian in the case, — absurd!
As well go boast myself above the needs
O' the human nature, careless how meat smells,
Wine tastes, — a saint above the smack! But once
Abate my crest, own flaws i' the flesh, agree
To go with the herd, be hog no more nor less,
Why, hogs in common herd have common rights:
I must not be unduly borne upon,
Who just romanced a little, sowed wild oats,
But 'scaped without a scandal, flagrant fault. 1700
My name helped to a mirthful circumstance:
"Joseph" would do well to amend his plea:
Undoubtedly — some toying with the wife,
But as for ruffian violence and rape,
Potiphar pressed too much on the other side!
The intrigue, the elopement, the disguise, — well charged!
The letters and verse looked hardly like the truth.
Your apprehension was — of guilt enough
To be compatible with innocence,
So, punished best a little and not too much. 1710
Had I struck Guido Franceschini's face,
You had counselled me withdraw for my own sake,
Balk him of bravo-hiring. Friends came round,
Congratulated, "Nobody mistakes!

The pettiness o' the forfeiture defines
The peccadillo: Guido gets his share:
His wife is free of husband and hook-nose,
The mouldy viands and the mother-in-law.
To Civita with you and amuse the time,
Travesty us '*De Raptu Helenæ!*'   1720
A funny figure must the husband cut
When the wife makes him skip, — too ticklish, eh?
Do it in Latin, not the Vulgar, then!
Scazons — we'll copy and send his Eminence.
Mind — one iambus in the final foot!
He'll rectify it, be your friend for life!"
Oh, Sirs, depend on me for much new light
Thrown on the justice and religion here
By this proceeding, much fresh food for thought!

And I was just set down to study these   1730
In relegation, two short days ago,
Admiring how you read the rules, when, clap,
A thunder comes into my solitude —
I am caught up in a whirlwind and cast here,
Told of a sudden, in this room where so late
You dealt our law adroitly, that those scales,
I meekly bowed to, took my allotment from,
Guido has snatched at, broken in your hands,
Metes to himself the murder of his wife,
Full measure, pressed down, running over now!   1740
Can I assist to an explanation? — Yes,
I rise in your esteem, sagacious Sirs,
Stand up a renderer of reasons, not
The officious priest would personate Saint George
For a mock Princess in undragoned days.
What, the blood startles you? What, after all
The priest who needs must carry sword on thigh
May find imperative use for it? Then, there was
A Princess, was a dragon belching flame,
And should have been a Saint George also? Then,   1750
There might be worse schemes than to break the bonds
At Arezzo, lead her by the little hand,
Till she reached Rome, and let her try to live?
But you were law and gospel, — would one please
Stand back, allow your faculty elbow-room?
You blind guides who must needs lead eyes that see!
Fools, alike ignorant of man and God!

What was there here should have perplexed your wit
For a wink of the owl-eyes of you? How miss, then,
What's now forced on you by this flare of fact — 1760
As if Saint Peter failed to recognize
Nero as no apostle, John or James,
Till someone burned a martyr, made a torch
O' the blood and fat to show his features by!
Could you fail read this cartulary aright
On head and front of Franceschini there,
Large-lettered like hell's masterpiece of print, —
That he, from the beginning pricked at heart
By some lust, letch of hate against his wife,
Plotted to plague her into overt sin 1770
And shame, would slay Pompilia body and soul,
And save his mean self — miserably caught
I' the quagmire of his own tricks, cheats and lies?
— That himself wrote those papers, — from himself
To himself, — which, i' the name of me and her,
His mistress-messenger gave her and me,
Touching us with such pustules of the soul
That she and I might take the taint, be shown
To the world and shuddered over, speckled so?
— That the agent put her sense into my words, 1780
Made substitution of the thing she hoped,
For the thing she had and held, its opposite,
While the husband in the background bit his lips
At each fresh failure of his precious plot?
— That when at the last we did rush each on each,
By no chance but because God willed it so —
The spark of truth was struck from out our souls —
Made all of me, descried in the first glance,
Seem fair and honest and permissible love
O' the good and true — as the first glance told me 1790
There was no duty patent in the world
Like daring try be good and true myself,
Leaving the shows of things to the Lord of Show
And Prince o' the Power of the Air. Our very flight,
Even to its most ambiguous circumstance,
Irrefragably proved how futile, false . . .
Why, men — men and not boys — boys and not babes —
Babes and not beasts — beasts and not stocks and stones! —
Had the liar's lie been true one pin-point speck,
Were I the accepted suitor, free o' the place, 1800
Disposer of the time, to come at a call

And go at a wink as who should say me nay, —
What need of flight, what were the gain therefrom
But just damnation, failure or success?
Damnation pure and simple to her the wife
And me the priest — who bartered private bliss
For public reprobation, the safe shade
For the sunshine which men see to pelt me by:
What other advantage, — we who led the days
And nights alone i' the house, — was flight to find?   1810
In our whole journey did we stop an hour,
Diverge a foot from straight road till we reached
Or would have reached — but for that fate of ours —
The father and mother, in the eye of Rome,
The eye of yourselves we made aware of us
At the first fall of misfortune? And indeed
You did so far give sanction to our flight,
Confirm its purpose, as lend helping hand,
Deliver up Pompilia not to him
She fled, but those the flight was ventured for.   1820
Why then could you, who stopped short, not go on
One poor step more, and justify the means,
Having allowed the end? — not see and say
"Here's the exceptional conduct that should claim
To be exceptionally judged on rules
Which, understood, make no exception here" —
Why play instead into the devil's hands
By dealing so ambiguously as gave
Guido the power to intervene like me,
Prove one exception more? I saved his wife   1830
Against law: against law he slays her now:
Deal with him!

        I have done with being judged.
I stand here guiltless in thought, word and deed,
To the point that I apprise you, — in contempt
For all misapprehending ignorance
O' the human heart, much more the mind of Christ, —
That I assuredly did bow, was blessed
By the revelation of Pompilia. There!
Such is the final fact I fling you, Sirs,
To mouth and mumble and misinterpret: there!   1840
"The priest's in love," have it the vulgar way!
Unpriest me, rend the rags o' the vestment, do —
Degrade deep, disenfranchise all you dare —

Remove me from the midst, no longer priest
And fit companion for the like of you —
Your gay Abati with the well-turned leg
And rose i' the hat-rim, Canons, cross at neck
And silk mask in the pocket of the gown,
Brisk Bishops with the world's musk still unbrushed
From the rochet; I'll no more of these good things: 1850
There's a crack somewhere, something that's unsound
I' the rattle!
              For Pompilia — be advised,
Build churches, go pray! You will find me there,
I know, if you come, — and you will come, I know.
Why, there's a Judge weeping! Did not I say
You were good and true at bottom? You see the truth —
I am glad I helped you: she helped me just so.

But for Count Guido, — you must counsel there!
I bow my head, bend to the very dust,
Break myself up in shame of faultiness.   1860
I had him one whole moment, as I said —
As I remember, as will never out
O' the thoughts of me, — I had him in arm's reach
There, — as you stand, Sir, now you cease to sit, —
I could have killed him ere he killed his wife,
And did not: he went off alive and well
And then effected this last feat — through me!
Me — not through you — dismiss that fear! 'Twas you
Hindered me staying here to save her, — not
From leaving you and going back to him   1870
And doing service in Arezzo. Come,
Instruct me in procedure! I conceive —
In all due self-abasement might I speak —
How you will deal with Guido: oh, not death!
Death, if it let her life be: otherwise
Not death, — your lights will teach you clearer! I
Certainly have an instinct of my own
I' the matter: bear with me and weigh its worth!
Let us go away — leave Guido all alone
Back on the world again that knows him now!   1880
I think he will be found (indulge so far!)
Not to die so much as slide out of life,
Pushed by the general horror and common hate
Low, lower, — left o' the very ledge of things,
I seem to see him catch convulsively

One by one at all honest forms of life,
At reason, order, decency and use —
To cramp him and get foothold by at least;
And still they disengage them from his clutch.
"What, you are he, then, had Pompilia once   1890
And so forewent her? Take not up with us!"
And thus I see him slowly and surely edged
Off all the table-land whence life upsprings
Aspiring to be immortality,
As the snake, hatched on hill-top by mischance,
Despite his wriggling, slips, slides, slidders down
Hill-side, lies low and prostrate on the smooth
Level of the outer place, lapsed in the vale:
So I lose Guido in the lôneliness,
Silence and dusk, till at the doleful end,   1900
At the horizontal line, creation's verge,
From what just is to absolute nothingness —
Whom is it, straining onward still, he meets?
What other man deep further in the fate,
Who, turning at the prize of a footfall
To flatter him and promise fellowship,
Discovers in the act a frightful face —
Judas, made monstrous by much solitude!
The two are at one now! Let them love their love
That bites and claws like hate, or hate their hate   1910
That mops and mows and makes as it were love!
There, let them each tear each in devil's-fun,
Or fondle this the other while malice aches —
Both teach, both learn detestability!
Kiss him the kiss, Iscariot! Pay that back,
That smatch o' the slaver blistering on your lip,
By the better trick, the insult he spared Christ —
Lure him the lure o' the letters, Aretine!
Lick him o'er slimy-smooth with jelly-filth
O' the verse-and-prose pollution in love's guise!   1920
The cockatrice is with the basilisk!
There let them grapple, denizens o' the dark,
Foes or friends, but indissolubly bound,
In their one spot out of the ken of God
Or care of man, for ever and ever more!

Why, Sirs, what's this? Why, this is sorry and strange!
Futility, divagation: this from me
Bound to be rational, justify an act

Of sober man! — whereas, being moved so much,
I give you cause to doubt the lady's mind.   1930
A pretty sarcasm for the world! I fear
You do her wit injustice, — all through me!
Like my fate all through, — ineffective help!
A poor rash advocate I prove myself.
You might be angry with good cause: but sure
At the advocate, — only at the undue zeal
That spoils the force of his own plea, I think?
My part was just to tell you how things stand,
State facts and not be flustered at their fume.
But then 'tis a priest speaks: as for love, — no!   1940
If you let buzz a vulgar fly like that
About your brains, as if I loved, forsooth,
Indeed, Sirs, you do wrong! We had no thought
Of such infatuation, she and I:
There are many points that prove it: do be just!
I told you, — at one little roadside-place
I spent a good half-hour, paced to and fro
The garden; just to leave her free awhile,
I plucked a handful of Spring herb and bloom:
I might have sat beside her on the bench   1950
Where the children were: I wish the thing had been,
Indeed: the event could not be worse, you know:
One more half-hour of her saved! She's dead now, Sirs!
While I was running on at such a rate,
Friends should have plucked me by the sleeve: I went
Too much o' the trivial outside of her face
And the purity that shone there — plain to me,
Not to you, what more natural? Nor am I
Infatuated, — oh, I saw, be sure!
Her brow had not the right line, leaned too much,   1960
Painters would say; they like the straight-up Greek:
This seemed bent somewhat with an invisible crown
Of martyr and saint, not such as art approves.
And how the dark orbs dwelt deep underneath,
Looked out of such a sad sweet heaven on me!
The lips, compressed a little, came forward too,
Careful for a whole world of sin and pain.
That was the face, her husband makes his plea,
He sought just to disfigure, — no offence
Beyond that! Sirs, let us be rational!   1970
He needs must vindicate his honor, — ay,
Yet shirks, the coward, in a clown's disguise,

Away from the scene, endeavors to escape.
Now, had he done so, slain and left no trace
O' the slayer, — what were vindicated, pray?
You had found his wife disfigured or a corpse,
For what and by whom? It is too palpable!
Then, here's another point involving law:
I use this argument to show you meant
No calumny against us by that title   1980
O' the sentence, — liars try to twist it so:
What penalty it bore, I had to pay
Till further proof should follow of innocence —
Probationis ob defectum, — proof?
How could you get proof without trying us?
You went through the preliminary form,
Stopped there, contrived this sentence to amuse
The adversary. If the title ran
For more than fault imputed and not proved,
That was a simple penman's error, else   1990
A slip i' the phrase, — as when we say of you
"Charged with injustice" — which may either be
Or not be, — 'tis a name that sticks meanwhile.
Another relevant matter: fool that I am!
Not what I wish true, yet a point friends urge:
It is not true, — yet, since friends think it helps, —
She only tried me when some others failed —
Began with Conti, whom I told you of,
And Guillichini, Guido's kinsfolk both,
And when abandoned by them, not before,   2000
Turned to me. That's conclusive why she turned.
Much good they got by the happy cowardice!
Conti is dead, poisoned a month ago:
Does that much strike you as a sin? Not much,
After the present murder, — one mark more
On the Moor's skin, — what is black by blacker still?
Conti had come here and told truth. And so
With Guillichini; he's condemned of course
To the galleys, as a friend in this affair,
Tried and condemned for no one thing i' the world,   2010
A fortnight since by who but the Governor? —
The just judge, who refused Pompilia help
At first blush, being her husband's friend, you know.
There are two tales to suit the separate courts,
Arezzo and Rome: he tells you here, we fled
Alone, unhelped, — lays stress on the main fault,

The spiritual sin, Rome looks to: but elsewhere
He likes best we should break in, steal, bear off,
Be fit to brand and pillory and flog —
That's the charge goes to the heart of the Governor:　　　2020
If these unpriest me, you and I may yet
Converse, Vincenzo Marzi-Medici!
Oh, Sirs, there are worse men than you, I say!
More easily duped, I mean; this stupid lie,
Its liar never dared propound in Rome,
He gets Arezzo to receive, — nay more,
Gets Florence and the Duke to authorize!
This is their Rota's sentence, their Granduke
Signs and seals! Rome for me henceforward — Rome.
Where better men are, — most of all, that man　　　2030
The Augustinian of the Hospital,
Who writes the letter, — he confessed, he says,
Many a dying person, never one
So sweet and true and pure and beautiful.
A good man! Will you make him Pope one day?
Not that he is not good too, this we have —
But old, — else he would have his word to speak,
His truth to teach the world: I thirst for truth,
But shall not drink it till I reach the source.

Sirs, I am quiet again. You see, we are　　　2040
So very pitiable, she and I,
Who had conceivably been otherwise.
Forget distemperature and idle heat!
Apart from truth's sake, what's to move so much?
Pompilia will be presently with God;
I am, on earth, as good as out of it,
A relegated priest; when exile ends,
I mean to do my duty and live long.
She and I are mere strangers now: but priests
Should study passion; how else cure mankind,　　　2050
Who come for help in passionate extremes?
I do but play with an imagined life
Of who, unfettered by a vow, unblessed
By the higher call, — since you will have it so, —
Leads it companioned by the woman there.
To live, and see her learn, and learn by her,
Out of the low obscure and petty world —
Or only see one purpose and one will
Evolve themselves i' the world, change wrong to right:

To have to do with nothing but the true,   2060
The good, the eternal — and these, not alone
In the main current of the general life,
But small experiences of every day,
Concerns of the particular hearth and home:
To learn not only by a comet's rush
But a rose's birth, — not by the grandeur, God —
But the comfort, Christ. All this, how far away!
Mere delectation, meet for a minute's dream! —
Just as a drudging student trims his lamp,
Opens his Plutarch, puts him in the place   2070
Of Roman, Grecian; draws the patched gown close,
Dreams, "Thus should I fight, save or rule the world!" —
Then smilingly, contentedly, awakes
To the old solitary nothingness.
So I, from such communion, pass content . . .

O great, just, good God! Miserable me!

POMPILIA

I AM just seventeen years and five months old,
And, if I lived one day more, three full weeks;
'Tis writ so in the church's register,
Lorenzo in Lucina, all my names
At length, so many names for one poor child,
— Francesca Camilla Vittoria Angela
Pompilia Comparini, — laughable!
Also 'tis writ that I was married there
Four years ago: and they will add, I hope,
When they insert my death, a word or two, —   10
Omitting all about the mode of death, —
This, in its place, this which one cares to know,
That I had been a mother of a son
Exactly two weeks. It will be through grace
O' the Curate, not through any claim I have;
Because the boy was born at, so baptized
Close to, the Villa, in the proper church:
A pretty church, I say no word against,
Yet stranger-like, — while this Lorenzo seems
My own particular place, I always say.   20
I used to wonder, when I stood scarce high
As the bed here, what the marble lion meant,
With half his body rushing from the wall,
Eating the figure of a prostrate man —
(To the right, it is, of entry by the door)
An ominous sign to one baptized like me,
Married, and to be buried there, I hope.
And they should add, to have my life complete,
He is a boy and Gaetan by name —
Gaetano, for a reason, — if the friar   30
Don Celestine will ask this grace for me
Of Curate Ottoboni: he it was
Baptized me: he remembers my whole life
As I do his gray hair.

                    All these few things
I know are true, — will you remember them?
Because time flies. The surgeon cared for me,

To count my wounds, — twenty-two dagger-wounds,
Five deadly, but I do not suffer much —
Or too much pain, — and am to die to-night.

Oh how good God is that my babe was born,   40
— Better than born, baptized and hid away
Before this happened, safe from being hurt!
That had been sin God could not well forgive:
He was too young to smile and save himself.
When they took, two days after he was born,
My babe away from me to be baptized
And hidden awhile, for fear his foe should find, —
The country-woman, used to nursing babes,
Said "Why take on so? where is the great loss?
These next three weeks he will but sleep and feed,   50
Only begin to smile at the month's end;
He would not know you, if you kept him here,
Sooner than that; so, spend three merry weeks
Snug in the Villa, getting strong and stout,
And then I bring him back to be your own,
And both of you may steal to — we know where!"
The month — there wants of it two weeks this day!
Still, I half fancied when I heard the knock
At the Villa in the dusk, it might prove she —
Come to say "Since he smiles before the time,   60
Why should I cheat you out of one good hour?
Back I have brought him; speak to him and judge!"
Now I shall never see him; what is worse,
When he grows up and gets to be my age,
He will seem hardly more than a great boy;
And if he asks "What was my mother like?"
People may answer "Like girls of seventeen" —
And how can he but think of this and that,
Lucias, Marias, Sofias, who titter or blush
When he regards them as such boys may do?   70
Therefore I wish some one will please to say
I looked already old though I was young;
Do I not . . . say, if you are by to speak . . .
Look nearer twenty? No more like, at least,
Girls who look arch or redden when boys laugh,
Than the poor Virgin that I used to know
At our street-corner in a lonely niche, —
The babe, that sat upon her knees, broke off, —

Thin white glazed clay, you pitied her the more:
She, not the gay ones, always got my rose.   80

How happy those are who know how to write!
Such could write that their son should read in time,
Had they a whole day to live out like me.
Also my name is not a common name,
"Pompilia," and may help to keep apart
A little the thing I am from what girls are.
But then how far away, how hard to find
Will anything about me have become,
Even if the boy bethink himself and ask!
No father that he ever knew at all,   90
Nor ever had — no, never had, I say!
That is the truth, — nor any mother left,
Out of the little two weeks that she lived,
Fit for such memory as might assist:
As good too as no family, no name,
Not even poor old Pietro's name, nor hers,
Poor kind unwise Violante, since it seems
They must not be my parents any more.
That is why something put it in my head
To call the boy "Gaetano" — no old name   100
For sorrow's sake; I looked up to the sky
And took a new saint to begin anew.
One who has only been made saint — how long?
Twenty-five years: so, carefuller, perhaps,
To guard a namesake than those old saints grow,
Tired out by this time, — see my own five saints!

On second thoughts, I hope he will regard
The history of me as what someone dreamed,
And get to disbelieve it at the last:
Since to myself it dwindles fast to that,   110
Sheer dreaming and impossibility, —
Just in four days too! All the seventeen years,
Not once did a suspicion visit me
How very different a lot is mine
From any other woman's in the world.
The reason must be, 'twas by step and step
It got to grow so terrible and strange.
These strange woes stole on tiptoe, as it were,
Into my neighborhood and privacy,
Sat down where I sat, laid them where I lay;   120

And I was found familiarized with fear,
When friends broke in, held up a torch and cried
"Why, you Pompilia in the cavern thus,
How comes that arm of yours about a wolf?
And the soft length, — lies in and out your feet
And laps you round the knee, — a snake it is!"
And so on.

   Well, and they are right enough,
By the torch they hold up now: for first, observe,
I never had a father, — no, nor yet
A mother: my own boy can say at least   130
"I had a mother whom I kept two weeks!"
Not I, who little used to doubt . . . *I* doubt
Good Pietro, kind Violante, gave me birth?
They loved me always as I love my babe
(—Nearly so, that is — quite so could not be —)
Did for me all I meant to do for him,
Till one surprising day, three years ago,
They both declared, at Rome, before some judge
In some Court where the people flocked to hear,
That really I had never been their child,   140
Was a mere castaway, the careless crime
Of an unknown man, the crime and care too much
Of a woman known too well, — little to these,
Therefore, of whom I was the flesh and blood:
What then to Pietro and Violante, both
No more my relatives than you or you?
Nothing to them! You know what they declared.

So with my husband, — just such a surprise,
Such a mistake, in that relationship!
Everyone says that husbands love their wives,   150
Guard them and guide them, give them happiness;
'Tis duty, law, pleasure, religion: well,
You see how much of this comes true in mine!
People indeed would fain have somehow proved
He was no husband: but he did not hear,
Or would not wait, and so has killed us all.
Then there is . . . only let me name one more!
There is the friend, — men will not ask about,
But tell untruths of, and give nicknames to,
And think my lover, most surprise of all!   160
Do only hear, it is the priest they mean,

Giuseppe Caponsacchi: a priest — love,
And love me! Well, yet people think he did.
I am married, he has taken priestly vows,
They know that, and yet go on, say, the same,
"Yes, how he loves you!" "That was love" — they say,
When anything is answered that they ask:
Or else "No wonder you love him" — they say.
Then they shake heads, pity much, scarcely blame —
As if we neither of us lacked excuse,   170
And anyhow are punished to the full,
And downright love atones for everything!
Nay, I heard read out in the public Court
Before the judge, in presence of my friends,
Letters 'twas said the priest had sent to me,
And other letters sent him by myself,
We being lovers!
           Listen what this is like!
When I was a mere child, my mother . . . that's
Violante, you must let me call her so
Nor waste time, trying to unlearn the word . . .   180
She brought a neighbor's child of my own age
To play with me of rainy afternoons;
And, since there hung a tapestry on the wall,
We two agreed to find each other out
Among the figures. "Tisbe, that is you,
With half-moon on your hair-knot, spear in hand,
Flying, but no wings, only the great scarf
Blown to a bluish rainbow at your back:
Call off your hound and leave the stag alone!"
"— And there are you, Pompilia, such green leaves   190
Flourishing out of your five finger ends,
And all the rest of you so brown and rough:
Why is it you are turned a sort of tree?"
You know the figures never were ourselves
Though we nicknamed them so. Thus, all my life, —
As well what was, as what, like this, was not, —
Looks old, fantastic and impossible:
I touch a fairy thing that fades and fades.
— Even to my babe! I thought, when he was born,
Something began for once that would not end,   200
Nor change into a laugh at me, but stay
For evermore, eternally quite mine.
Well, so he is, — but yet they bore him off,
The third day, lest my husband should lay traps

And catch him, and by means of him catch me.
Since they have saved him so, it was well done:
Yet thence comes such confusion of what was
With what will be, — that late seems long ago,
And, what years should bring round, already come,
Till even he withdraws into a dream   210
As the rest do: I fancy him grown great,
Strong, stern, a tall young man who tutors me,
Frowns with the others "Poor imprudent child!
Why did you venture out of the safe street?
Why go so far from help to that lone house?
Why open at the whisper and the knock?"

Six days ago when it was New Year's-day,
We bent above the fire and talked of him,
What he should do when he was grown and great.
Violante, Pietro, each had given the arm   220
I leant on, to walk by, from couch to chair
And fireside, — laughed, as I lay safe at last,
"Pompilia's march from bed to board is made,
Pompilia back again and with a babe,
Shall one day lend his arm and help her walk!"
Then we all wished each other more New Years.
Pietro began to scheme — "Our cause is gained;
The law is stronger than a wicked man:
Let him henceforth go his way, leave us ours!
We will avoid the city, tempt no more   230
The greedy ones by feasting and parade, —
Live at the other villa, we know where,
Still farther off, and we can watch the babe
Grow fast in the good air; and wood is cheap
And wine sincere outside the city gate.
I still have two or three old friends will grope
Their way along the mere half-mile of road,
With staff and lantern on a moonless night
When one needs talk: they'll find me, never fear,
And I'll find them a flask of the old sort yet!"   240
Violante said "You chatter like a crow:
Pompilia tires o' the tattle, and shall to bed:
Do not too much the first day, — somewhat more
To-morrow, and, the next, begin the cape
And hood and coat! I have spun wool enough."
Oh what a happy friendly eve was that!

And, next day, about noon, out Pietro went —
He was so happy and would talk so much,
Until Violante pushed and laughed him forth
Sight-seeing in the cold, — "So much to see   250
I' the churches! Swathe your throat three times!" she cried,
"And, above all, beware the slippery ways,
And bring us all the news by supper-time!"
He came back late, laid by cloak, staff and hat,
Powdered so thick with snow it made us laugh,
Rolled a great log upon the ash o' the hearth,
And bade Violante treat us to a flask,
Because he had obeyed her faithfully,
Gone sight-see through the seven, and found no church
To his mind like San Giovanni — "There's the fold,   260
And all the sheep together, big as cats!
And such a shepherd, half the size of life,
Starts up and hears the angel" — when, at the door,
A tap: we started up: you know the rest.

Pietro at least had done no harm, I know;
Nor even Violante, so much harm as makes
Such revenge lawful. Certainly she erred —
Did wrong, how shall I dare say otherwise? —
In telling that first falsehood, buying me
From my poor faulty mother at a price,   270
To pass off upon Pietro as his child.
If one should take my babe, give him a name,
Say he was not Gaetano and my own,
But that some other woman made his mouth
And hands and feet, — how very false were that!
No good could come of that; and all harm did.
Yet if a stranger were to represent
"Needs must you either give your babe to me
And let me call him mine for evermore,
Or let your husband get him" — ah, my God,   280
That were a trial I refuse to face!
Well, just so here: it proved wrong but seemed right
To poor Violante — for there lay, she said,
My poor real dying mother in her rags,
Who put me from her with the life and all,
Poverty, pain, shame and disease at once,
To die the easier by what price I fetched —
Also (I hope) because I should be spared
Sorrow and sin, — why may not that have helped?

My father, — he was no one, any one, —   290
The worse, the likelier, — call him — he who came,
Was wicked for his pleasure, went his way,
And left no trace to track by; there remained
Nothing but me, the unnecessary life,
To catch up or let fall, — and yet a thing
She could make happy, be made happy with,
This poor Violante, — who would frown thereat?

Well, God, you see! God plants us where we grow.
It is not that because a bud is born
At a wild briar's end, full i' the wild beast's way,   300
We ought to pluck and put it out of reach
On the oak-tree top, — say "There the bud belongs!"
She thought, moreover, real lies were lies told
For harm's sake; whereas this had good at heart,
Good for my mother, good for me, and good
For Pietro who was meant to love a babe,
And needed one to make his life of use,
Receive his house and land when he should die.
Wrong, wrong and always wrong! how plainly wrong!
For see, this fault kept pricking, as faults do,   310
All the same at her heart: this falsehood hatched,
She could not let it go nor keep it fast.
She told me so, — the first time I was found
Locked in her arms once more after the pain,
When the nuns let me leave them and go home,
And both of us cried all the cares away, —
This it was set her on to make amends,
This brought about the marriage — simply this!
Do let me speak for her you blame so much! .
When Paul, my husband's brother, found me out,   320
Heard there was wealth for who should marry me,
So, came and made a speech to ask my hand
For Guido, — she, instead of piercing straight
Through the pretence to the ignoble truth,
Fancied she saw God's very finger point,
Designate just the time for planting me
(The wild-briar slip she plucked to love and wear)
In soil where I could strike real root, and grow,
And get to be the thing I called myself:
For, wife and husband are one flesh, God says,   330
And I, whose parents seemed such and were none,
Should in a husband have a husband now,

Find nothing, this time, but was what it seemed,
— All truth and no confusion any more.
I know she meant all good to me, all pain
To herself, — since how could it be aught but pain,
To give me up, so, from her very breast,
The wilding flower-tree-branch that, all those years,
She had got used to feel for and find fixed?
She meant well: has it been so ill i' the main?   340
That is but fair to ask: one cannot judge
Of what has been the ill or well of life,
The day that one is dying, — sorrows change
Into not altogether sorrow-like;
I do see strangeness but scarce misery,
Now it is over, and no danger more.
My child is safe; there seems not so much pain.
It comes, most like, that I am just absolved,
Purged of the past, the foul in me, washed fair, —
One cannot both have and not have, you know, —   350
Being right now, I am happy and color things.
Yes, everybody that leaves life sees all
Softened and bettered: so with other sights:
To me at least was never evening yet
But seemed far beautifuller than its day,
For past is past.

        There was a fancy came,
When somewhere, in the journey with my friend,
We stepped into a hovel to get food;
And there began a yelp here, a bark there, —
Misunderstanding creatures that were wroth   360
And vexed themselves and us till we retired.
The hovel is life: no matter what dogs bit
Or cats scratched in the hovel I break from,
All outside is lone field, moon and such peace —
Flowing in, filling up as with a sea
Whereon comes Someone, walks fast on the white,
Jesus Christ's self, Don Celestine declares,
To meet me and calm all things back again.
Beside, up to my marriage, thirteen years
Were, each day, happy as the day was long: 370
This may have made the change too terrible.
I know that when Violante told me first
The cavalier — she meant to bring next morn,
Whom I must also let take, kiss my hand —

Would be at San Lorenzo the same eve
And marry me, — which over, we should go
Home both of us without him as before,
And, till she bade speak, I must hold my tongue,
Such being the correct way with girl-brides,
From whom one word would make a father blush, —   380
I know, I say, that when she told me this,
— Well, I no more saw sense in what she said
Than a lamb does in people clipping wool;
Only lay down and let myself be clipped.
And when next day the cavalier who came —
(Tisbe had told me that the slim young man
With wings at head, and wings at feet, and sword
Threatening a monster, in our tapestry,
Would eat a girl else, — was a cavalier)
When he proved Guido Franceschini, — old   390
And nothing like so tall as I myself,
Hook-nosed and yellow in a bush of beard,
Much like a thing I saw on a boy's wrist,
He called an owl and used for catching birds, —
And when he took my hand and made a smile —
Why, the uncomfortableness of it all
Seemed hardly more important in the case
Than, — when one gives you, say, a coin to spend, —
Its newness or its oldness; if the piece
Weigh properly and buy you what you wish,   400
No matter whether you get grime or glare!
Men take the coin, return you grapes and figs.
Here, marriage was the coin, a dirty piece
Would purchase me the praise of those I loved:
About what else should I concern myself?

So, hardly knowing what a husband meant,
I supposed this or any man would serve,
No whit the worse for being so uncouth:
For I was ill once and a doctor came
With a great ugly hat, no plume thereto,   410
Black jerkin and black buckles and black sword,
And white sharp beard over the ruff in front,
And oh so lean, so sour-faced and austere! —
Who felt my pulse, made me put out my tongue,
Then oped a phial, dripped a drop or two
Of a black bitter something, — I was cured!
What mattered the fierce beard or the grim face?

It was the physic beautified the man,
Master Malpichi, — never met his match
In Rome, they said, — so ugly all the same!   420

However, I was hurried through a storm,
Next dark eve of December's deadest day —
How it rained! — through our street and the Lion's-mouth
And the bit of Corso, — cloaked round, covered close,
I was like something strange or contraband, —
Into blank San Lorenzo, up the aisle,
My mother keeping hold of me so tight,
I fancied we were come to see a corpse
Before the altar which she pulled me toward.
There we found waiting an unpleasant priest   430
Who proved the brother, not our parish friend,
But one with mischief-making mouth and eye,
Paul, whom I know since to my cost. And then
I heard the heavy church-door lock out help
Behind us: for the customary warmth,
Two tapers shivered on the altar. "Quick —
Lose no time!" cried the priest. And straightway down
From . . . what's behind the altar where he hid —
Hawk-nose and yellowness and bush and all,
Stepped Guido, caught my hand, and there was I   440
O' the chancel, and the priest had opened book,
Read here and there, made me say that and this,
And after, told me I was now a wife,
Honored indeed, since Christ thus weds the Church,
And therefore turned he water into wine,
To show I should obey my spouse like Christ.
Then the two slipped aside and talked apart,
And I, silent and scared, got down again
And joined my mother who was weeping now.
Nobody seemed to mind us any more,   450
And both of us on tiptoe found our way
To the door which was unlocked by this, and wide.
When we were in the street, the rain had stopped,
All things looked better. At our own house-door,
Violante whispered "No one syllable
To Pietro! Girl-brides never breathe a word!"
"— Well treated to a wetting, daggle-tails!"
Laughed Pietro as he opened — "Very near
You made me brave the gutter's roaring sea
To carry off from roost old dove and young,   460

Trussed up in church, the cote, by me, the kite!
What do these priests mean, praying folk to death
On stormy afternoons, with Christmas close
To wash our sins off nor require the rain?"
Violante gave my hand a timely squeeze,
Madonna saved me from immodest speech,
I kissed him and was quiet, being a bride.
When I saw nothing more, the next three weeks,
Of Guido — "Nor the Church sees Christ" thought I:
"Nothing is changed however, wine is wine   470
And water only water in our house.
Nor did I see that ugly doctor since
That cure of the illness: just as I was cured,
I am married, — neither scarecrow will return."

Three weeks, I chuckled — "How would Giulia stare,
And Tecla smile and Tisbe laugh outright,
Were it not impudent for brides to talk!" —
Until one morning, as I sat and sang
At the broidery-frame alone i' the chamber, — loud
Voices, two, three together, sobbings too,   480
And my name, "Guido," "Paolo," flung like stones
From each to the other! In I ran to see.
There stood the very Guido and the priest
With sly face, — formal but nowise afraid, —
While Pietro seemed all red and angry, scarce
Able to stutter out his wrath in words;
And this it was that made my mother sob,
As he reproached her — "You have murdered us,
Me and yourself and this our child beside!"
Then Guido interposed "Murdered or not,   490
Be it enough your child is now my wife!
I claim and come to take her." Paul put in,
"Consider — kinsman, dare I term you so? —
What is the good of your sagacity
Except to counsel in a strait like this?
I guarantee the parties man and wife
Whether you like or loathe it, bless or ban.
May spilt milk be put back within the bowl —
The done thing, undone? You, it is, we look
For counsel to, you fitliest will advise!   500
Since milk, though spilt and spoilt, does marble good,
Better we down on knees and scrub the floor,
Than sigh, 'the waste would make a syllabub!'

Help us so turn disaster to account,
So predispose the groom, he needs shall grace
The bride with favor from the very first,
Not begin marriage an embittered man!"
He smiled, — the game so wholly in his hands!
While fast and faster sobbed Violante — "Ay,
All of us murdered, past averting now!   510
O my sin, O my secret!" and such like.

Then I began to half surmise the truth;
Something had happened, low, mean, underhand,
False, and my mother was to blame, and I
To pity, whom all spoke of, none addressed:
I was the chattel that had caused a crime.
I stood mute, — those who tangled must untie
The embroilment. Pietro cried "Withdraw, my child!
She is not helpful to the sacrifice
At this stage, — do you want the victim by   520
While you discuss the value of her blood?
For her sake, I consent to hear you talk:
Go, child, and pray God help the innocent!"

I did go and was praying God, when came
Violante, with eyes swollen and red enough,
But movement on her mouth for make-believe
Matters were somehow getting right again.
She bade me sit down by her side and hear.
"You are too young and cannot understand,
Nor did your father understand at first.   530
I wished to benefit all three of us,
And when he failed to take my meaning, — why,
I tried to have my way at unaware —
Obtained him the advantage he refused.
As if I put before him wholesome food
Instead of broken victual, — he finds change
I' the viands, never cares to reason why,
But falls to blaming me, would fling the plate
From window, scandalize the neighborhood,
Even while he smacks his lips, — men's way, my child!   540
But either you have prayed him unperverse
Or I have talked him back into his wits:
And Paolo was a help in time of need, —
Guido, not much — my child, the way of men!
A priest is more a woman than a man,

And Paul did wonders to persuade. In short,
Yes, he was wrong, your father sees and says;
My scheme was worth attempting: and bears fruit,
Gives you a husband and a noble name,
A palace and no end of pleasant things.   550
What do you care about a handsome youth?
They are so volatile, and tease their wives!
This is the kind of man to keep the house.
We lose no daughter, — gain a son, that's all:
For 'tis arranged we never separate,
Nor miss, in our gray time of life, the tints
Of you that color eve to match with morn.
In good or ill, we share and share alike,
And cast our lots into a common lap,
And all three die together as we lived!   560
Only, at Arezzo, — that's a Tuscan town,
Not so large as this noisy Rome, no doubt,
But older far and finer much, say folk, —
In a great palace where you will be queen,
Know the Archbishop and the Governor,
And we see homage done you ere we die.
Therefore, be good and pardon!" — "Pardon what?
You know things, I am very ignorant:
All is right if you only will not cry!"

And so an end! Because a blank begins   570
From when, at the word, she kissed me hard and hot,
And took me back to where my father leaned
Opposite Guido — who stood eyeing him,
As eyes the butcher the cast panting ox
That feels his fate is come, nor struggles more, —
While Paul looked archly on, pricked brow at whiles
With the pen-point as to punish triumph there, —
And said "Count Guido, take your lawful wife
Until death part you!"

          All since is one blank,
Over and ended; a terrific dream.   580
It is the good of dreams — so soon they go!
Wake in a horror of heart-beats, you may —
Cry "The dread thing will never from my thoughts!"
Still, a few daylight doses of plain life,
Cock-crow and sparrow-chirp, or bleat and bell
Of goats that trot by, tinkling, to be milked;

And when you rub your eyes awake and wide,
Where is the harm o' the horror! Gone! Go here.
I know I wake, — but from what? Blank, I say!
This is the note of evil: for good lasts.   590
Even when Don Celestine bade "Search and find!
For your soul's sake, remember what is past,
The better to forgive it," — all in vain!
What was fast getting indistinct before,
Vanished outright. By special grace perhaps,
Between that first calm and this last, four years
Vanish, — one quarter of my life, you know.
I am held up, amid the nothingness,
By one or two truths only — thence I hang,
And there I live, — the rest is death or dream,   600
All but those points of my support. I think
Of what I saw at Rome once in the Square
O' the Spaniards, opposite the Spanish House:
There was a foreigner had trained a goat,
A shuddering white woman of a beast,
To climb up, stand straight on a pile of sticks
Put close, which gave the creature room enough:
When she was settled there he, one by one,
Took away all the sticks, left just the four
Whereon the little hoofs did really rest,   610
There she kept firm, all underneath was air.
So, what I hold by, are my prayer to God,
My hope, that came in answer to the prayer,
Some hand would interpose and save me — hand
Which proved to be my friend's hand: and, — blest bliss, —
That fancy which began so faint at first,
That thrill of dawn's suffusion through my dark,
Which I perceive was promise of my child,
The light his unborn face sent long before, —
God's way of breaking the good news to flesh.   620
That is all left now of those four bad years.
Don Celestine urged "But remember more!
Other men's faults may help me find your own.
I need the cruelty exposed, explained,
Or how can I advise you to forgive?"
He thought I could not properly forgive
Unless I ceased forgetting, — which is true:
For, bringing back reluctantly to mind
My husband's treatment of me, — by a light
That's later than my life-time, I review   630

And comprehend much and imagine more,
And have but little to forgive at last.
For now, — be fair and say, — is it not true
He was ill-used and cheated of his hope
To get enriched by marriage? Marriage gave
Me and no money, broke the compact so:
He had a right to ask me on those terms,
As Pietro and Violante to declare
They would not give me: so the bargain stood:
They broke it, and he felt himself aggrieved,   640
Became unkind with me to punish them.
They said 'twas he began deception first,
Nor, in one point whereto he pledged himself,
Kept promise: what of that, suppose it were?
Echoes die off, scarcely reverberate
For ever, — why should ill keep echoing ill,
And never let our ears have done with noise?
Then my poor parents took the violent way
To thwart him, — he must needs retaliate, — wrong,
Wrong, and all wrong, — better say, all blind!   650
As I myself was, that is sure, who else
Had understood the mystery: for his wife
Was bound in some sort to help somehow there.
It seems as if I might have interposed,
Blunted the edge of their resentment so,
Since he vexed me because they first vexed him;
"I will entreat them to desist, submit,
Give him the money and be poor in peace, —
Certainly not go tell the world: perhaps
He will grow quiet with his gains."

                  Yes, say   660
Something to this effect and you do well!
But then you have to see first: I was blind.
That is the fruit of all such wormy ways,
The indirect, the unapproved of God:
You cannot find their author's end and aim,
Not even to substitute your good for bad,
Your straight for the irregular; you stand
Stupefied, profitless, as cow or sheep
That miss a man's mind, anger him just twice
By trial at repairing the first fault.   670
Thus, when he blamed me, "You are a coquette,
A lure-owl posturing to attract birds,

You look love-lures at theatre and church,
In walk, at window!" — that, I knew, was false!
But why he charged me falsely, whither sought
To drive me by such charge, — how could I know?
So, unaware, I only made things worse.
I tried to soothe him by abjuring walk,
Window, church, theatre, for good and all,
As if he had been in earnest: that, you know,   680
Was nothing like the object of his charge.
Yes, when I got my maid to supplicate
The priest, whose name she read when she would read
Those feigned false letters I was forced to hear
Though I could read no word of, — he should cease
Writing, — nay, if he minded prayer of mine,
Cease from so much as even pass the street
Whereon our house looked, — in my ignorance
I was just thwarting Guido's true intent;
Which was, to bring about a wicked change   690
Of sport to earnest, tempt a thoughtless man
To write indeed, and pass the house, and more,
Till both of us were taken in a crime.
He ought not to have wished me thus act lies,
Simulate folly: but, — wrong or right, the wish. —
I failed to apprehend its drift. How plain
It follows, — if I fell into such fault,
He also may have overreached the mark,
Made mistake, by perversity of brain,
I' the whole sad strange plot, the grotesque intrigue   700
To make me and my friend unself ourselves,
Be other man and woman than we were!
Think it out, you who have the time! for me, —
I cannot say less; more I will not say.
Leave it to God to cover and undo!
Only, my dulness should not prove too much!
— Not prove that in a certain other point
Wherein my husband blamed me, — and you blame,
If I interpret smiles and shakes of head, —
I was dull too. Oh, if I dared but speak!   710
Must I speak? I am blamed that I forwent
A way to make my husband's favor come.
That is true: I was firm, withstood, refused . . .
— Women as you are, how can I find the words?

I felt there was just one thing Guido claimed
I had no right to give nor he to take;
We being in estrangement, soul from soul:
Till, when I sought help, the Archbishop smiled,
Inquiring into privacies of life,
— Said I was blamable — (he stands for God)   720
Nowise entitled to exemption there.
Then I obeyed, — as surely had obeyed
Were the injunction "Since your husband bids,
Swallow the burning coal he proffers you!"
But I did wrong, and he gave wrong advice
Though he were thrice Archbishop, — that, I know! —
Now I have got to die and see things clear.
Remember I was barely twelve years old —
A child at marriage: I was let alone
For weeks, I told you, lived my child-life still   730
Even at Arezzo, when I woke and found
First . . . but I need not think of that again —
Over and ended! Try and take the sense
Of what I signify, if it must be so.
After the first, my husband, for hate's sake,
Said one eve, when the simpler cruelty
Seemed somewhat dull at edge and fit to bear,
"We have been man and wife six months almost:
How long is this your comedy to last?
Go this night to my chamber, not your own!"   740
At which word, I did rush — most true the charge —
And gain the Archbishop's house — he stands for God —
And fall upon my knees and clasp his feet,
Praying him hinder what my estranged soul
Refused to bear, though patient of the rest:
"Place me within a convent," I implored —
"Let me henceforward lead the virgin life
You praise in Her you bid me imitate!"
What did he answer? "Folly of ignorance!
Know, daughter, circumstances make or mar   750
Virginity, — 'tis virtue or 'tis vice.
That which was glory in the Mother of God
Had been, for instance, damnable in Eve
Created to be mother of mankind.
Had Eve, in answer to her Maker's speech
'Be fruitful, multiply, replenish earth' —
Pouted 'But I choose rather to remain
Single,' — why, she had spared herself forthwith

Further probation by the apple and snake,
Been pushed straight out of Paradise! For see   700
If motherhood be qualified impure,
I catch you making God command Eve sin!
— A blasphemy so like these Molinists',
I must suspect you dip into their books."
Then he pursued " 'Twas in your covenant!"
No! There my husband never used deceit.
He never did by speech nor act imply
"Because of our souls' yearning that we meet
And mix in soul through flesh, which yours and mine
Wear and impress, and make their visible selves,   770
— All which means, for the love of you and me,
Let us become one flesh, being one soul!"
He only stipulated for the wealth;
Honest so far. But when he spoke as plain —
Dreadfully honest also — "Since our souls
Stand each from each, a whole world's width between,
Give me the fleshly vesture I can reach
And rend and leave just fit for hell to burn!" —
Why, in God's name, for Guido's soul's own sake
Imperilled by polluting mine, — I say,   780
I did resist; would I had overcome!

My heart died out at the Archbishop's smile;
— It seemed so stale and worn a way o' the world,
As though 'twere nature frowning — "Here is Spring,
The sun shines as he shone at Adam's fall,
The earth requires that warmth reach everywhere:
What, must your patch of snow be saved forsooth
Because you rather fancy snow than flowers?"
Something in this style he began with me.
Last he said, savagely for a good man,   790
"This explains why you call your husband harsh,
Harsh to you, harsh to whom you love. God's Bread!
The poor Count has to manage a mere child
Whose parents leave untaught the simplest things
Their duty was and privilege to teach, —
Goodwives' instruction, gossips' lore: they laugh
And leave the Count the task, — or leave it me!"
Then I resolved to tell a frightful thing.
"I am not ignorant, — know what I say,
Declaring this is sought for hate, not love.   800
Sir, you may hear things like almighty God.

I tell you that my housemate, yes — the priest
My husband's brother, Canon Girolamo —
Has taught me what depraved and misnamed love
Means, and what outward signs denote the sin,
For he solicits me and says he loves,
The idle young priest with naught else to do.
My husband sees this, knows this, and lets be.
Is it your counsel I bear this beside?"
"— More scandal, and against a priest this time! 810
What, 'tis the Canon now?" — less snappishly —
"Rise up, my child, for such a child you are,
The rod were too advanced a punishment!
Let's try the honeyed cake. A parable!
'Without a parable spake He not to them.'
There was a ripe round long black toothsome fruit,
Even a flower-fig, the prime boast of May:
And, to the tree, said . . . either the spirit o' the fig,
Or, if we bring in men, the gardener,
Archbishop of the orchard — had I time 820
To try o' the two which fits in best: indeed
It might be the Creator's self, but then
The tree should bear an apple, I suppose, —
Well, anyhow, one with authority said
'Ripe fig, burst skin, regale the fig-pecker —
The bird whereof thou art a perquisite!'
'Nay,' with a flounce, replied the restif fig,
'I much prefer to keep my pulp myself:
He may go breakfastless and dinnerless,
Supperless of one crimson seed, for me!' 830
So, back she flopped into her bunch of leaves.
He flew off, left her, — did the natural lord, —
And lo, three hundred thousand bees and wasps
Found her out, feasted on her to the shuck:
Such gain the fig's that gave its bird no bite!
The moral, — fools elude their proper lot,
Tempt other fools, get ruined all alike.
Therefore go home, embrace your husband quick!
Which if his Canon brother chance to see,
He will the sooner back to book again." 840

So, home I did go; so, the worst befell:
So, I had proof the Archbishop was just man,
And hardly that, and certainly no more.
For, miserable consequence to me,

My husband's hatred waxed nor waned at all,
His brother's boldness grew effrontery soon,
And my last stay and comfort in myself
Was forced from me: henceforth I looked to God
Only, nor cared my desecrated soul
Should have fair walls, gay windows for the world.   850
God's glimmer, that came through the ruin-top,
Was witness why all lights were quenched inside:
Henceforth I asked God counsel, not mankind.

So, when I made the effort, freed myself,
They said — "No care to save appearance here!
How cynic, — when, how wanton, were enough!"
— Adding, it all came of my mother's life —
My own real mother, whom I never knew,
Who did wrong (if she needs must have done wrong)
Through being all her life, not my four years,   860
At mercy of the hateful: every beast
O' the field was wont to break that fountain-fence,
Trample the silver into mud so murk
Heaven could not find itself reflected there.
Now they cry "Out on her, who, plashy pool,
Bequeathed turbidity and bitterness
To the daughter-stream where Guido dipt and drank!"

Well, since she had to bear this brand — let me!
The rather do I understand her now,
From my experience of what hate calls love, —   870
Much love might be in what their love called hate.
If she sold . . . what they call, sold . . . me her child —
I shall believe she hoped in her poor heart
That I at least might try be good and pure,
Begin to live untempted, not go doomed
And done with ere once found in fault, as she.
Oh and, my mother, it all came to this?
Why should I trust those that speak ill of you,
When I mistrust who speaks even well of them?
Why, since all bound to do me good, did harm,   880
May not you, seeming as you harmed me most,
Have meant to do most good — and feed your child
From bramble-bush, whom not one orchard-tree
But drew bough back from, nor let one fruit fall?
This it was for you sacrificed your babe?
Gained just this, giving your heart's hope away

As I might give mine, loving it as you,
If . . . but that never could be asked of me!

There, enough! I have my support again,
Again the knowledge that my babe was, is,   890
Will be mine only. Him, by death, I give
Outright to God, without a further care, —
But not to any parent in the world, —
So to be safe: why is it we repine?
What guardianship were safer could we choose?
All human plans and projects come to naught:
My life, and what I know of other lives,
Prove that: no plan nor project! God shall care!

And now you are not tired? How patient then
All of you, — Oh yes, patient this long while   900
Listening, and understanding, I am sure!
Four days ago, when I was sound and well
And like to live, no one would understand.
People were kind, but smiled "And what of him,
Your friend, whose tonsure the rich dark-brown hides?
There, there! — your lover, do we dream he was?
A priest too — never were such naughtiness!
Still, he thinks many a long think, never fear,
After the shy pale lady, — lay so light
For a moment in his arms, the lucky one!"   910
And so on: wherefore should I blame you much?
So we are made, such difference in minds,
Such difference too in eyes that see the minds!
That man, you misinterpret and misprise —
The glory of his nature, I had thought,
Shot itself out in white light, blazed the truth
Through every atom of his act with me:
Yet where I point you, through the crystal shrine,
Purity in quintessence, one dew-drop,
You all descry a spider in the midst.   920
One says "The head of it is plain to see,"
And one, "They are the feet by which I judge,"
All say, "Those films were spun by nothing else."

Then, I must lay my babe away with God,
Nor think of him again, for gratitude.
Yes, my last breath shall wholly spend itself
In one attempt more to disperse the stain.

The mist from other breath fond mouths have made,
About a lustrous and pellucid soul.
So that, when I am gone but sorrow stays,   930
And people need assurance in their doubt
If God yet have a servant, man a friend,
The weak a saviour and the vile a foe, —
Let him be present, by the name invoked,
Giuseppe-Maria Caponsacchi!
                              There,
Strength comes already with the utterance!
I will remember once more for his sake
The sorrow: for he lives and is belied.
Could he be here, how he would speak for me!

I had been miserable three drear years   940
In that dread palace and lay passive now,
When I first learned there could be such a man.
Thus it fell: I was at a public play,
In the last days of Carnival last March,
Brought there I knew not why, but now know well.
My husband put me where I sat, in front;
Then crouched down, breathed cold through me from behind,
Stationed i' the shadow, — none in front could see, —
I, it was, faced the stranger-throng beneath,
The crowd with upturned faces, eyes one stare,   950
Voices one buzz. I looked but to the stage,
Whereon two lovers sang and interchanged
"True life is only love, love only bliss:
I love thee — thee I love!" then they embraced.
I looked thence to the ceiling and the walls, —
Over the crowd, those voices and those eyes, —
My thoughts went through the roof and out, to Rome
On wings of music, waft of measured words, —
Set me down there, a happy child again
Sure that to-morrow would be festa-day,   960
Hearing my parents praise past festas more,
And seeing they were old if I was young,
Yet wondering why they still would end discourse
With "We must soon go, you abide your time,
And, — might we haply see the proper friend
Throw his arm over you and make you safe!"

Sudden I saw him; into my lap there fell
A foolish twist of comfits, broke my dream

And brought me from the air and laid me low,
As ruined as the soaring bee that's reached   970
(So Pietro told me at the Villa once)
By the dust-handful. There the comfits lay:
I looked to see who flung them, and I faced
This Caponsacchi, looking up in turn.
Ere I could reason out why, I felt sure,
Whoever flung them, his was not the hand, —
Up rose the round face and good-natured grin
Of one who, in effect, had played the prank,
From covert close beside the earnest face, —
Fat waggish Conti, friend of all the world.   980
He was my husband's cousin, privileged
To throw the thing: the other, silent, grave,
Solemn almost, saw me, as I saw him.

There is a psalm Don Celestine recites,
"Had I a dove's wings, how I fain would flee!"
The psalm runs not "I hope, I pray for wings," —
Not "If wings fall from heaven, I fix them fast," —
Simply "How good it were to fly and rest,
Have hope now, and one day expect content!
How well to do what I shall never do!"   990
So I said "Had there been a man like that,
To lift me with his strength out of all strife
Into the calm, how I could fly and rest!
I have a keeper in the garden here
Whose sole employment is to strike me low
If ever I, for solace, seek the sun.
Life means with me successful feigning death,
Lying stone-like, eluding notice so,
Foregoing here the turf and there the sky.
Suppose that man had been instead of this!"   1000

Presently Conti laughed into my ear,
— Had tripped up to the raised place where I sat —
"Cousin, I flung them brutishly and hard!
Because you must be hurt, to look austere
As Caponsacchi yonder, my tall friend
A-gazing now. Ah, Guido, you so close?
Keep on your knees, do! Beg her to forgive!
My cornet battered like a cannon-ball.
Good-bye, I'm gone!" — nor waited the reply.

That night at supper, out my husband broke,   1010
"Why was that throwing, that buffoonery?
Do you think I am your dupe? What man would dare
Throw comfits in a stranger lady's lap?
'Twas knowledge of you bred such insolence
In Caponsacchi; he dared shoot the bolt,
Using that Conti for his stalking-horse.
How could you see him this once and no more,
When he is always haunting hereabout
At the street-corner or the palace-side,
Publishing my shame and your impudence?   1020
You are a wanton, — I a dupe, you think?
O Christ, what hinders that I kill her quick?"
Whereat he drew his sword and feigned a thrust.
All this, now, — being not so strange to me,
Used to such misconception day by day
And broken-in to bear, — I bore, this time,
More quietly than woman should perhaps;
Repeated the mere truth and held my tongue.

Then he said, "Since you play the ignorant,
I shall instruct you. This amour, — commenced   1030
Or finished or midway in act, all's one, —
'Tis the town-talk; so my revenge shall be.
Does he presume because he is a priest?
I warn him that the sword I wear shall pink
His lily-scented cassock through and through,
Next time I catch him underneath your eaves!"
But he had threatened with the sword so oft
And, after all, not kept his promise. All
I said was "Let God save the innocent!
Moreover death is far from a bad fate.   1040
I shall go pray for you and me, not him;
And then I look to sleep, come death or, worse,
Life." So, I slept.

          There may have elapsed a week,
When Margherita, — called my waiting-maid,
Whom it is said my husband found too fair —
Who stood and heard the charge and the reply,
Who never once would let the matter rest
From that night forward, but rang changes still
On this the thrust and that the shame, and how
Good cause for jealousy cures jealous fools,   1050

And what a paragon was this same priest
She talked about until I stopped my ears, —
She said, "A week is gone; you comb your hair,
Then go mope in a corner, cheek on palm,
Till night comes round again, — so, waste a week
As if your husband menaced you in sport.
Have not I some acquaintance with his tricks?
Oh no, he did not stab the serving-man
Who made and sang the rhymes about me once!
For why? They sent him to the wars next day.   1060
Nor poisoned he the foreigner, my friend
Who wagered on the whiteness of my breast, —
The swarth skins of our city in dispute:
For, though he paid me proper compliment,
The Count well knew he was besotted with
Somebody else, a skin as black as ink
(As all the town knew save my foreigner)
He found and wedded presently, — 'Why need
Better revenge?' — the Count asked. But what's here?
A priest that does not fight, and cannot wed,   1070
Yet must be dealt with! If the Count took fire
For the poor pastime of a minute, — me —
What were the conflagration for yourself,
Countess and lady-wife and all the rest?
The priest will perish; you will grieve too late:
So shall the city-ladies' handsomest
Frankest and liberalest gentleman
Die for you, to appease a scurvy dog
Hanging's too good for. Is there no escape?
Were it not simple Christian charity   1080
To warn the priest be on his guard, — save him
Assured death, save yourself from causing it?
I meet him in the street. Give me a glove,
A ring to show for token! Mum's the word!"

I answered "If you were, as styled, my maid,
I would command you: as you are, you say,
My husband's intimate, — assist his wife
Who can do nothing but entreat 'Be still!'
Even if you speak truth and a crime is planned,
Leave help to God as I am forced to do!   1090
There is no other help, or we should craze,
Seeing such evil with no human cure.

Reflect that God, who makes the storm desist,
Can make an angry violent heart subside.
Why should we venture teach Him governance?
Never address me on this subject more!"

Next night she said "But I went, all the same,
— Ay, saw your Caponsacchi in his house,
And come back stuffed with news I must outpour.
I told him 'Sir, my mistress is a stone: 1100
Why should you harm her for no good you get?
For you do harm her — prowl about our place
With the Count never distant half the street,
Lurking at every corner, would you look!
'Tis certain she has witched you with a spell.
Are there not other beauties at your beck?
We all know, Donna This and Monna That
Die for a glance of yours, yet here you gaze!
Go make them grateful, leave the stone its cold!'
And he — oh, he turned first white and then red,   1110
And then — 'To her behest I bow myself,
Whom I love with my body and my soul:
Only a word i' the bowing! See, I write
One little word, no harm to see or hear!
Then, fear no further!' This is what he wrote.
I know you cannot read, — therefore, let me!
'My idol!' " . . .
            But I took it from her hand
And tore it into shreds. "Why join the rest
Who harm me? Have I ever done you wrong?
People have told me 'tis you wrong myself: 1120
Let it suffice I feel no wrong
Or else forgive it, — yet you turn my foe!
The others hunt me and you throw a noose!"

She muttered "Have your wilful way!" I slept.

Whereupon . . . no, I leave my husband out!
It is not to do him more hurt, I speak.
Let it suffice, when misery was most,
One day, I swooned and got a respite so.
She stooped as I was slowly coming to,
This Margherita, ever on my trace,   1130
And whispered — "Caponsacchi!"

If I drowned,
But woke afloat i' the wave with upturned eyes,
And found their first sight was a star! I turned —
For the first time, I let her have her will,
Heard passively, — "The imposthume at such head,
One touch, one lancet-puncture would relieve, —
And still no glance the good physician's way
Who rids you of the torment in a trice!
Still he writes letters you refuse to hear.
He may prevent your husband, kill himself,   1140
So desperate and all fordone is he!
Just hear the pretty verse he made to-day!
A sonnet from Mirtillo. '*Peerless fair . . .*'
All poetry is difficult to read,
— The sense of it is, anyhow, he seeks
Leave to contrive you an escape from hell,
And for that purpose asks an interview.
I can write, I can grant it in your name,
Or, what is better, lead you to his house.
Your husband dashes you against the stones;   1150
This man would place each fragment in a shrine:
You hate him, love your husband!"

                        I returned
"It is not true I love my husband, — no,
Nor hate this man. I listen while you speak,
— Assured that what you say is false, the same:
Much as when once, to me a little child,
A rough gaunt man in rags, with eyes on fire,
A crowd of boys and idlers at his heels,
Rushed as I crossed the Square, and held my head
In his two hands, 'Here's she will let me speak!   1160
You little girl, whose eyes do good to mine,
I am the Pope, am Sextus, now the Sixth;
And that Twelfth Innocent, proclaimed to-day,
Is Lucifer disguised in human flesh!
The angels met in conclave, crowned me!' — thus
He gibbered and I listened; but I knew
All was delusion, ere folk interposed
'Unfasten him, the maniac!' Thus I know
All your report of Caponsacchi false,
Folly or dreaming; I have seen so much   1170
By that adventure at the spectacle,

The face I fronted that one first, last time:
He would belie it by such words and thoughts.
Therefore while you profess to show him me,
I ever see his own face. Get you gone!"

"That will I, nor once open mouth again, —
No, by Saint Joseph and the Holy Ghost!
On your head be the damage, so adieu!"

And so more days, more deeds I must forget,
Till . . . what a strange thing now is to declare!   1180
Since I say anything, say all if true!
And how my life seems lengthened as to serve!
It may be idle or inopportune,
But, true? — why, what was all I said but truth,
Even when I found that such as are untrue
Could only take the truth in through a lie?
Now — I am speaking truth to the Truth's self:
God will lend credit to my words this time.

It had got half through April, I arose
One vivid daybreak, — who had gone to bed   1190
In the old way my wont those last three years,
Careless until, the cup drained, I should die.
The last sound in my ear, the over-night,
Had been a something let drop on the sly
In prattle by Margherita, "Soon enough
Gaieties end, now Easter's past: a week,
And the Archbishop gets him back to Rome, —
Every one leaves the town for Rome, this Spring, —
Even Caponsacchi, out of heart and hope,
Resigns himself and follows with the flock."   1200
I heard this drop and drop like rain outside
Fast-falling through the darkness while she spoke:
So had I heard with like indifference,
"And Michael's pair of wings will arrive first
At Rome, to introduce the company,
And bear him from our picture where he fights
Satan, — expect to have that dragon loose
And never a defender!" — my sole thought
Being still, as night came, "Done, another day!
How good to sleep and so get nearer death!" —   1210
When, what, first thing at daybreak, pierced the sleep
With a summons to me? Up I sprang alive,

Light in me, light without me, everywhere
Change! A broad yellow sunbeam was let fall
From heaven to earth, — a sudden drawbridge lay,
Along which marched a myriad merry motes,
Mocking the flies that crossed them and recrossed
In rival dance, companions new-born too.
On the house-eaves, a dripping shag of weed
Shook diamonds on each dull gray lattice-square,   1220
As first one, then another bird leapt by,
And light was off, and lo was back again,
Always with one voice, — where are two such joys? —
The blessed building-sparrow! I stepped forth,
Stood on the terrace, — o'er the roofs, such sky!
My heart sang, "I too am to go away,
I too have something I must care about,
Carry away with me to Rome, to Rome!
The bird brings hither sticks and hairs and wool,
And nowhere else i' the world; what fly breaks rank,   1230
Falls out of the procession that befits,
From window here to window there, with all
The world to choose, — so well he knows his course?
I have my purpose and my motive too,
My march to Rome, like any bird or fly!
Had I been dead! How right to be alive!
Last night I almost prayed for leave to die,
Wished Guido all his pleasure with the sword
Or the poison, — poison, sword, was but a trick,
Harmless, may God forgive him the poor jest!   1240
My life is charmed, will last till I reach Rome!
Yesterday, but for the sin, — ah, nameless be
The deed I could have dared against myself!
Now — see if I will touch an unripe fruit,
And risk the health I want to have and use!
Not to live, now, would be the wickedness, —
For life means to make haste and go to Rome
And leave Arezzo, leave all woes at once!"
Now, understand here, by no means mistake!
Long ago had I tried to leave that house   1250
When it seemed such procedure would stop sin;
And still failed more the more I tried — at first
The Archbishop, as I told you, — next, our lord
The Governor, — indeed I found my way,
I went to the great palace where he rules,
Though I knew well 'twas he who, — when I gave

A jewel or two, themselves had given me,
Back to my parents,— since they wanted bread,
They who had never let me want a nosegay, — he
Spoke of the jail for felons, if they kept   1260
What was first theirs, then mine, so doubly theirs,
Though all the while my husband's most of all!
I knew well who had spoke the word wrought this:
Yet, being in extremity, I fled
To the Governor, as I say, — scarce opened lip
When — the cold cruel snicker close behind —
Guido was on my trace, already there,
Exchanging nod and wink for shrug and smile,
And I — pushed back to him and, for my pains
Paid with . . . but why remember what is past?   1270
I sought out a poor friar the people call
The Roman, and confessed my sin which came
Of their sin, — that fact could not be repressed, —
The frightfulness of my despair in God:
And, feeling, through the grate, his horror shake,
Implored him, "Write for me who cannot write,
Apprise my parents, make them rescue me!
You bid me be courageous and trust God:
Do you in turn dare somewhat, trust and write
'Dear friends, who used to be my parents once,   1280
And now declare you have no part in me,
This is some riddle I want wit to solve,
Since you must love me with no difference.
Even suppose you altered, — there's your hate,
To ask for: hate of you two dearest ones
I shall find liker love than love found here,
If husbands love their wives. Take me away
And hate me as you do the gnats and fleas,
Even the scorpions! How I shall rejoice!'
Write that and save me!" And he promised — wrote   1290
Or did not write; things never changed at all:
He was not like the Augustinian here!
Last, in a desperation I appealed
To friends, whoever wished me better days,
To Guillichini, that's of kin, — "What, I —
Travel to Rome with you? A flying gout
Bids me deny my heart and mind my leg!"
Then I tried Conti, used to brave — laugh back
The louring thunder when his cousin scowled
At me protected by his presence: "You —   1300

Who well know what you cannot save me from, —
Carry me off! What frightens you, a priest?"
He shook his head, looked grave — "Above my strength!
Guido has claws that scratch, shows feline teeth;
A formidabler foe than I dare fret:
Give me a dog to deal with, twice the size!
Of course I am a priest and Canon too,
But . . . by the bye . . . though both, not quite so bold
As he, my fellow-Canon, brother-priest,
The personage in such ill odor here   1310
Because of the reports — pure birth o' the brain!
Our Caponsacchi, he's your true Saint George
To slay the monster, set the Princess free,
And have the whole High-Altar to himself:
I always think so when I see that piece
I' the Pieve, that's his church and mine, you know:
Though you drop eyes at mention of his name!"

That name had got to take a half-grotesque
Half-ominous, wholly enigmatic sense,
Like any by-word, broken bit of song   1320
Born with a meaning, changed by mouth and mouth
That mix it in a sneer or smile, as chance
Bids, till it now means naught but ugliness
And perhaps shame.
                    — All this intends to say,
That, over-night, the notion of escape
Had seemed distemper, dreaming; and the name, —
Not the man, but the name of him, thus made
Into a mockery and disgrace, — why, she
Who uttered it persistently, had laughed,
"I name his name, and there you start and wince   1330
As criminal from the red tongs' touch!" — yet now,
Now, as I stood letting morn bathe me bright,
Choosing which butterfly should bear my news, —
The white, the brown one, or that tinier blue, —
The Margherita, I detested so,
In she came — "The fine day, the good Spring time!
What, up and out at window? That is best.
No thought of Caponsacchi? — who stood there
All night on one leg, like the sentry crane,
Under the pelting of your water-spout —   1340
Looked last look at your lattice ere he leave
Our city, bury his dead hope at Rome.

Ay, go to looking-glass and make you fine,
While he may die ere touch one least loose hair
You drag at with the comb in such a rage!"

I turned — "Tell Caponsacchi he may come!"
"Tell him to come? Ah, but, for charity,
A truce to fooling! Come? What, — come this eve?
Peter and Paul! But I see through the trick!
Yes, come, and take a flower-pot on his head,   1350
Flung from your terrace! No joke, sincere truth?"

How plainly I perceived hell flash and fade
O' the face of her, — the doubt that first paled joy,
Then, final reassurance I indeed
Was caught now, never to be free again!
What did I care? — who felt myself of force
To play with silk, and spurn the horsehair-springe.

"But — do you know that I have bade him come,
And in your name? I presumed so much,
Knowing the thing you needed in your heart.   1360
But somehow — what had I to show in proof?
He would not come: half-promised, that was all,
And wrote the letters you refused to read.
What is the message that shall move him now?"

"After the Ave Maria, at first dark,
I will be standing on the terrace, say!"

"I would I had a good long lock of hair
Should prove I was not lying! Never mind!"

Off she went — "May he not refuse, that's all —
Fearing a trick!"

     I answered, "He will come."   1370
And, all day, I sent prayer like incense up
To God the strong, God the beneficent,
God ever mindful in all strife and strait,
Who, for our own good, makes the need extreme,
Till at the last He puts forth might and saves.
An old rhyme came into my head and rang
Of how a virgin, for the faith of God,
Hid herself, from the Paynims that pursued,

In a cave's heart; until a thunderstone,
Wrapped in a flame, revealed the couch and prey   1380
And they laughed — "Thanks to lightning, ours at last!"
And she cried "Wrath of God, assert His love!
Servant of God, thou fire, befriend His child!"
And lo, the fire she grasped at, fixed its flash,
Lay in her hand a calm cold dreadful sword
She brandished till pursuers strewed the ground,
So did the souls within them die away,
As o'er the prostrate bodies, sworded, safe,
She walked forth to the solitudes and Christ:
So should I grasp the lightning and be saved!   1390

And still, as the day wore, the trouble grew
Whereby I guessed there would be born a star,
Until at an intense throe of the dusk,
I started up, was pushed, I dare to say,
Out on the terrace, leaned and looked at last
Where the deliverer waited me: the same
Silent and solemn face, I first descried
At the spectacle, confronted mine once more.

So was that minute twice vouchsafed me, so
The manhood, wasted then, was still at watch   1400
To save me yet a second time: no change
Here, though all else changed in the changing world!

I spoke on the instant, as my duty bade,
In some such sense as this, whatever the phrase.
"Friend, foolish words were borne from you to me;
Your soul behind them is the pure strong wind,
Not dust and feathers which its breath may bear:
These to the witless seem the wind itself,
Since proving thus the first of it they feel.
If by mischance you blew offence my way,   1410
The straws are dropt, the wind desists no whit,
And how such strays were caught up in the street
And took a motion from you, why inquire?
I speak to the strong soul, no weak disguise.
If it be truth, — why should I doubt it truth? —
You serve God specially, as priests are bound,
And care about me, stranger as I am,
So far as wish my good, — that miracle
I take to intimate He wills you serve

By saving me, — what else can He direct? 1420
Here is the service. Since a long while now,
I am in course of being put to death:
While death concerned nothing but me, I bowed
The head and bade, in heart, my husband strike.
Now I imperil something more, it seems,
Something that's trulier me than this myself,
Something I trust in God and you to save.
You go to Rome, they tell me: take me there,
Put me back with my people!"

            He replied —
The first word I heard ever from his lips, 1430
All himself in it, — an eternity
Of speech, to match the immeasurable depth
O' the soul that then broke silence — "I am yours."

So did the star rise, soon to lead my step,
Lead on, nor pause before it should stand still
Above the House o' the Babe, — my babe to be,
That knew me first and thus made me know him,
That had his right of life and claim on mine,
And would not let me die till he was born,
But pricked me at the heart to save us both, 1440
Saying "Have you the will? Leave God the way!"
And the way was Caponsacchi — "mine," thank God!
He was mine, he is mine, he will be mine.

No pause i' the leading and the light! I know,
Next night there was a cloud came, and not he:
But I prayed through the darkness till it broke
And let him shine. The second night, he came.

"The plan is rash; the project desperate:
In such a flight needs must I risk your life,
Give food for falsehood, folly or mistake, 1450
Ground for your husband's rancor and revenge" —
So he began again, with the same face.
I felt that, the same loyalty — one star
Turning now red that was so white before —
One service apprehended newly: just
A word of mine and there the white was back!

"No, friend, for you will take me! 'Tis yourself
Risk all, not I, — who let you, for I trust
In the compensating great God: enough!
I know you: when is it that you will come?"　　　　　　1460

"To-morrow at the day's dawn." Then I heard
What I should do: how to prepare for flight
And where to fly.

　　　　　　That night my husband bade
"— You, whom I loathe, beware you break my sleep
This whole night! Couch beside me like the corpse
I would you were!" The rest you know, I think —
How I found Caponsacchi and escaped.

And this man, men call sinner? Jesus Christ!
Of whom men said, with mouths Thyself mad'st once,
"He hath a devil" — say he was Thy saint,　　　　　　1470
My Caponsacchi! Shield and show — unshroud
In Thine own time the glory of the soul
If aught obscure, — if ink-spot, from vile pens
Scribbling a charge against him — (I was glad
Then, for the first time, that I could not write) —
Flirted his way, have flecked the blaze!

　　　　　　For me,
'Tis otherwise: let men take, sift my thoughts
— Thoughts I throw like the flax for sun to bleach!
I did pray, do pray, in the prayer shall die,
"Oh, to have Caponsacchi for my guide!"　　　　　　1480
Ever the face upturned to mine, the hand
Holding my hand across the world, — a sense
That reads, as only such can read, the mark
God sets on woman, signifying so
She should — shall peradventure — be divine;
Yet 'ware, the while, how weakness mars the print
And makes confusion, leaves the thing men see,
— Not this man sees, — who from his soul, re-writes
The obliterated charter, — love and strength
Mending what's marred. "So kneels a votarist,　　　　　　1490
Weeds some poor waste traditionary plot
Where shrine once was, where temple yet may be,
Purging the place but worshipping the while,
By faith and not by sight, sight clearest so, —

Such way the saints work," — says Don Celestine.
But I, not privileged to see a saint
Of old when such walked earth with crown and palm,
If I call "saint" what saints call something else —
The saints must bear with me, impute the fault
To a soul i' the bud, so starved by ignorance,　　　　1500
Stinted of warmth, it will not blow this year
Nor recognize the orb which Spring-flowers know.
But if meanwhile some insect with a heart
Worth floods of lazy music, spendthrift joy —
Some fire-fly renounced Spring for my dwarfed cup,
Crept close to me, brought lustre for the dark,
Comfort against the cold, — what though excess
Of comfort should miscall the creature — sun?
What did the sun to hinder while harsh hands
Petal by petal, crude and colorless,　　　　1510
Tore me? This one heart gave me all the Spring!

Is all told? There's the journey: and where's time
To tell you how that heart burst out in shine?
Yet certain points do press on me too hard.
Each place must have a name, though I forget:
How strange it was — there where the plain begins
And the small river mitigates its flow —
When eve was fading fast, and my soul sank,
And he divined what surge of bitterness,
In overtaking me, would float me back　　　　1520
Whence I was carried by the striding day —
So, — "This gray place was famous once," said he —
And he began that legend of the place
As if in answer to the unspoken fear,
And told me all about a brave man dead,
Which lifted me and let my soul go on!
How did he know too, — at that town's approach
By the rock-side, — that in coming near the signs
Of life, the house-roofs and the church and tower,
I saw the old boundary and wall o' the world　　　　1530
Rise plain as ever round me, hard and cold,
As if the broken circlet joined again,
Tightened itself about me with no break, —
As if the town would turn Arezzo's self, —
The husband there, — the friends my enemies,
All ranged against me, not an avenue
To try, but would be blocked and drive me back

On him, — this other, . . . oh the heart in that!
Did not he find, bring, put into my arms
A new-born babe? — and I saw faces beam   1540
Of the young mother proud to teach me joy,
And gossips round expecting my surprise
At the sudden hole through earth that lets in heaven.
I could believe himself by his strong will
Had woven around me what I thought the world
We went along in, every circumstance,
Towns, flowers and faces, all things helped so well!
For, through the journey, was it natural
Such comfort should arise from first to last?
As I look back, all is one milky way;   1550
Still bettered more, the more remembered, so
Do new stars bud while I but search for old,
And fill all gaps i' the glory, and grow him —
Him I now see make the shine everywhere.
Even at the last when the bewildered flesh,
The cloud of weariness about my soul
Clogging too heavily, sucked down all sense, —
Still its last voice was, "He will watch and care;
Let the strength go, I am content: he stays!"
I doubt not he did stay and care for all —   1560
From that sick minute when the head swam round,
And the eyes looked their last and died on him,
As in his arms he caught me, and, you say,
Carried me in, that tragical red eve,
And laid me where I next returned to life
In the other red of morning, two red plates
That crushed together, crushed the time between,
And are since then a solid fire to me, —
When in, my dreadful husband and the world
Broke, — and I saw him, master, by hell's right,   1570
And saw my angel helplessly held back
By guards that helped the malice — the lamb prone,
The serpent towering and triumphant — then
Came all the strength back in a sudden swell,
I did for once see right, do right, give tongue
The adequate protest: for a worm must turn
If it would have its wrong observed by God.
I did spring up, attempt to thrust aside
That ice-block 'twixt the sun and me, lay low
The neutralizer of all good and truth.   1580
If I sinned so, — never obey voice more

O' the Just and Terrible, who bids us — "Bear!"
Not — "Stand by, bear to see my angels bear!"
I am clear it was on impulse to serve God
Not save myself, — no — nor my child unborn!
Had I else waited patiently till now? —
Who saw my old kind parents, silly-sooth
And too much trustful, for their worst of faults,
Cheated, brow-beaten, stripped and starved, cast out
Into the kennel: I remonstrated,   1590
Then sank to silence, for, — their woes at end,
Themselves gone, — only I was left to plague.
If only I was threatened and belied,
What matter? I could bear it and did bear;
It was a comfort, still one lot for all:
They were not persecuted for my sake
And I, estranged, the single happy one.
But when at last, all by myself I stood
Obeying the clear voice which bade me rise,
Not for my own sake but my babe unborn,   1600
And take the angel's hand was sent to help —
And found the old adversary athwart the path —
Not my hand simply struck from the angel's, but
The very angel's self made foul i' the face
By the fiend who struck there, — that I would not bear,
That only I resisted! So, my first
And last resistance was invincible.
Prayers move God; threats, and nothing else, move men!
I must have prayed a man as he were God
When I implored the Governor to right   1610
My parents' wrongs: the answer was a smile.
The Archbishop, — did I clasp his feet enough,
Hide my face hotly on them, while I told
More than I dared make my own mother know?
The profit was — compassion and a jest.
This time, the foolish prayers were done with, right
Used might, and solemnized the sport at once.
All was against the combat: vantage, mine?
The runaway avowed, the accomplice-wife,
In company with the plan-contriving priest?   1620
Yet, shame thus rank and patent, I struck, bare,
At foe from head to foot in magic mail,
And off it withered, cobweb-armory
Against the lightning! 'Twas truth singed the lies
And saved me, not the vain sword nor weak speech!

You see, I will not have the service fail!
I say, the angel saved me: I am safe!
Others may want and wish, I wish nor want
One point o' the circle plainer, where I stand
Traced round about with white to front the world. 1630
What of the calumny I came across,
What o' the way to the end? — the end crowns all.
The judges judged aright i' the main, gave me
The uttermost of my heart's desire, a truce
From torture and Arezzo, balm for hurt,
With the quiet nuns, — God recompense the good!
Who said and sang away the ugly past.
And, when my final fortune was revealed,
What safety while, amid my parents' arms,
My babe was given me! Yes, he saved my babe: 1640
It would not have peeped forth, the bird-like thing,
Through that Arezzo noise and trouble: back
Had it returned nor ever let me see!
But the sweet peace cured all, and let me live
And give my bird the life among the leaves
God meant him! Weeks and months of quietude,
I could lie in such peace and learn so much —
Begin the task, I see how needful now,
Of understanding somewhat of my past, —
Know life a little, I should leave so soon. 1650
Therefore, because this man restored my soul,
All has been right; I have gained my gain, enjoyed
As well as suffered, — nay, got foretaste too
Of better life beginning where this ends —
All through the breathing-while allowed me thus,
Which let good premonitions reach my soul
Unthwarted, and benignant influence flow
And interpenetrate and change my heart,
Uncrossed by what was wicked, — nay, unkind.
For, as the weakness of my time drew nigh, 1660
Nobody did me one disservice more,
Spoke coldly or looked strangely, broke the love
I lay in the arms of, till my boy was born,
Born all in love, with naught to spoil the bliss
A whole long fortnight: in a life like mine
A fortnight filled with bliss is long and much.
All women are not mothers of a boy,
Though they live twice the length of my whole life,
And, as they fancy, happily all the same.

There I lay, then, all my great fortnight long,   1670
As if it would continue, broaden out
Happily more and more, and lead to heaven:
Christmas before me, — was not that a chance?
I never realized God's birth before —
How He grew likest God in being born.
This time I felt like Mary, had my babe
Lying a little on my breast like hers.
So all went on till, just four days ago —
The night and the tap.

                    Oh it shall be success
To the whole of our poor family! My friends   1680
... Nay, father and mother, — give me back my word!
They have been rudely stripped of life, disgraced
Like children who must needs go clothed too fine,
Carry the garb of Carnival in Lent.
If they too much affected frippery,
They have been punished and submit themselves,
Say no word: all is over, they see God
Who will not be extreme to mark their fault
Or He had granted respite: they are safe.

For that most woeful man my husband once,   1690
Who, needing respite, still draws vital breath,
I — pardon him? So far as lies in me,
I give him for his good the life he takes,
Praying the world will therefore acquiesce.
Let him make God amends, — none, none to me
Who thank him rather that, whereas strange fate
Mockingly styled him husband and me wife,
Himself this way at least pronounced divorce,
Blotted the marriage-bond: this blood of mine
Flies forth exultingly at any door,   1700
Washes the parchment white, and thanks the blow.
We shall not meet in this world nor the next,
But where will God be absent? In His face
Is light, but in His shadow healing too:
Let Guido touch the shadow and be healed!
And as my presence was importunate, —
My earthly good, temptation and a snare, —
Nothing about me but drew somehow down
His hate upon me, — somewhat so excused
Therefore, since hate was thus the truth of him, —   1710
May my evanishment for evermore

Help further to relieve the heart that cast
Such object of its natural loathing forth!
So he was made; he nowise made himself:
I could not love him, but his mother did.
His soul has never lain beside my soul:
But for the unresisting body, — thanks!
He burned that garment spotted by the flesh.
Whatever he touched is rightly ruined: plague
It caught, and disinfection it had craved   1720
Still but for Guido; I am saved through him
So as by fire; to him — thanks and farewell!

Even for my babe, my boy, there's safety thence —
From the sudden death of me, I mean: we poor
Weak souls, how we endeavor to be strong!
I was already using up my life, —
This portion, now, should do him such a good,
This other go to keep off such an ill!
The great life; see, a breath and it is gone!
So is detached, so left all by itself   1730
The little life, the fact which means so much.
Shall not God stoop the kindlier to His work,
His marvel of creation, foot would crush,
Now that the hand He trusted to receive
And hold it, lets the treasure fall perforce?
The better; He shall have in orphanage
His own way all the clearlier: if my babe
Outlived the hour — and he has lived two weeks —
It is through God who knows I am not by.
Who is it makes the soft gold hair turn black,   1740
And sets the tongue, might lie so long at rest,
Trying to talk? Let us leave God alone!
Why should I doubt He will explain in time
What I feel now, but fail to find the words?
My babe nor was, nor is, nor yet shall be
Count Guido Franceschini's child at all —
Only his mother's, born of love not hate!
So shall I have my rights in after-time.
It seems absurd, impossible to-day;
So seems so much else, not explained but known!   1750

Ah! Friends, I thank and bless you every one!
No more now: I withdraw from earth and man
To my own soul, compose myself for God.

Well, and there is more! Yes, my end of breath
Shall bear away my soul in being true!
He is still here, not outside with the world,
Here, here, I have him in his rightful place!
'Tis now, when I am most upon the move,
I feel for what I verily find — again
The face, again the eyes, again, through all,   1760
The heart and its immeasurable love
Of my one friend, my only, all my own,
Who put his breast between the spears and me.
Ever with Caponsacchi! Otherwise
Here alone would be failure, loss to me —
How much more loss to him, with life debarred
From giving life, love locked from love's display,
The day-star stopped its task that makes night morn!
O lover of my life, O soldier-saint,
No work begun shall ever pause for death!   1770
Love will be helpful to me more and more
I' the coming course, the new path I must tread —
My weak hand in thy strong hand, strong for that!
Tell him that if I seem without him now,
That's the world's insight! Oh, he understands!
He is at Civita — do I once doubt
The world again is holding us apart?
He had been here, displayed in my behalf
The broad brow that reverberates the truth,
And flashed the word God gave him, back to man!   1780
I know where the free soul is flown! My fate
Will have been hard for even him to bear:
Let it confirm him in the trust of God,
Showing how holily he dared the deed!
And, for the rest, — say, from the deed, no touch
Of harm came, but all good, all happiness,
Not one faint fleck of failure! Why explain?
What I see, oh, he sees and how much more!
Tell him, — I know not wherefore the true word
Should fade and fall unuttered at the last —   1790
It was the name of him I sprang to meet
When came the knock, the summons and the end.
"My great heart, my strong hand are back again!"
I would have sprung to these, beckoning across
Murder and hell gigantic and distinct
O' the threshold, posted to exclude me heaven:
He is ordained to call and I to come!

Do not the dead wear flowers when dressed for God?
Say, — I am all in flowers from head to foot!
Say, — Not one flower of all he said and did,   1800
Might seem to flit unnoticed, fade unknown,
But dropped a seed, has grown a balsam-tree
Whereof the blossoming perfumes the place
At this supreme of moments! He is a priest;
He cannot marry therefore, which is right:
I think he would not marry if he could.
Marriage on earth seems such a counterfeit,
Mere imitation of the inimitable:
In heaven we have the real and true and sure.
'Tis there they neither marry nor are given   1810
In marriage but are as the angels: right,
Oh how right that is, how like Jesus Christ
To say that! Marriage-making for the earth,
With gold so much, — birth, power, repute so much,
Or beauty, youth so much, in lack of these!
Be as the angels rather, who, apart,
Know themselves into one, are found at length
Married, but marry never, no, nor give
In marriage; they are man and wife at once
When the true time is: here we have to wait   1820
Not so long neither! Could we by a wish
Have what we will and get the future now,
Would we wish aught done undone in the past?
So, let him wait God's instant men call years;
Meantime hold hard by truth and his great soul,
Do out the duty! Through such souls alone
God stooping shows sufficient of His light
For us i' the dark to rise by. And I rise.

THE POPE

LIKE to Ahasuerus, that shrewd prince,
I will begin, — as is, these seven years now,
My daily wont, — and read a History
(Written by one whose deft right hand was dust
To the last digit, ages ere my birth)
Of all my predecessors, Popes of Rome:
For though mine ancient early dropped the pen,
Yet others picked it up and wrote it dry,
Since of the making books there is no end.
And so I have the Papacy complete   10
From Peter first to Alexander last;
Can question each and take instruction so.
Have I to dare? — I ask, how dared this Pope?
To suffer? — Suchanone, how suffered he?
Being about to judge, as now, I seek
How judged once, well or ill, some other Pope;
Study some signal judgment that subsists
To blaze on, or else blot, the page which seals
The sum up of what gain or loss to God
Came of His one more Vicar in the world.   20
So, do I find example, rule of life;
So, square and set in order the next page,
Shall be stretched smooth o'er my own funeral cyst.

Eight hundred years exact before the year
I was made Pope, men made Formosus Pope,
Say Sigebert and other chroniclers.
Ere I confirm or quash the Trial here
Of Guido Franceschini and his friends,
Read, — How there was a ghastly Trial once
Of a dead man by a live man, and both, Popes: 30
Thus — in the antique penman's very phrase.

"Then Stephen, Pope and seventh of the name,
Cried out, in synod as he sat in state,
While choler quivered on his brow and beard,
'Come into court, Formosus, thou lost wretch,
That claimedst to be late Pope as even I!'

"And at the word the great door of the church
Flew wide, and in they brought Formosus' self,
The body of him, dead, even as embalmed
And buried duly in the Vatican   40
Eight months before, exhumed thus for the nonce.
They set it, that dead body of a Pope,
Clothed in pontific vesture now again,
Upright on Peter's chair as if alive.

"And Stephen, springing up, cried furiously
'Bishop of Porto, wherefore didst presume
To leave that see and take this Roman see,
Exchange the lesser for the greater see,
— A thing against the canons of the Church?'

"Then one — (a Deacon who, observing forms,   50
Was placed by Stephen to repel the charge,
Be advocate and mouthpiece of the corpse) —
Spoke as he dared, set stammeringly forth
With white lips and dry tongue, — as but a youth,
For frightful was the corpse-face to behold, —
How nowise lacked there precedent for this.

"But when, for his last precedent of all,
Emboldened by the Spirit, out he blurts
'And, Holy Father, didst not thou thyself
Vacate the lesser for the greater see,   60
Half a year since change Arago for Rome?'
'— Ye have the sin's defence now, Synod mine!'
Shrieks Stephen in a beastly froth of rage:
'Judge now betwixt him dead and me alive!
Hath he intruded, or do I pretend?
Judge, judge!' — breaks wavelike one whole foam of wrath.

"Whereupon they, being friends and followers,
Said 'Ay, thou art Christ's Vicar, and not he!
Away with what is frightful to behold!
This act was uncanonic and a fault.'   70

"Then, swallowed up in rage, Stephen exclaimed
'So, guilty! So, remains I punish guilt!
He is unpoped, and all he did I damn:
The Bishop, that ordained him, I degrade:
Depose to laics those he raised to priests:

What they have wrought is mischief nor shall stand,
It is confusion, let it vex no more!
Since I revoke, annul and abrogate
All his decrees in all kinds: they are void!
In token whereof and warning to the world,   80
Strip me yon miscreant of those robes usurped,
And clothe him with vile serge befitting such!
Then hale the carrion to the market-place:
Let the town-hangman chop from his right hand
Those same three fingers which he blessed withal;
Next cut the head off once was crowned forsooth:
And last go fling them, fingers, head and trunk,
To Tiber that my Christian fish may sup!'
— Either because of ΙΧΘΥΣ which means Fish
And very aptly symbolizes Christ,   90
Or else because the Pope is Fisherman,
And seals with Fisher's-signet.

                          "Anyway,
So said, so done: himself, to see it done,
Followed the corpse they trailed from street to street
Till into Tiber wave they threw the thing.
The people, crowded on the banks to see,
Were loud or mute, wept or laughed, cursed or jeered,
According as the deed addressed their sense;
A scandal verily: and out spake a Jew
'Wot ye your Christ had vexed our Herod thus?'   100
"Now when, Formosus being dead a year,
His Judge Pope Stephen tasted death in turn,
Made captive by the mob and strangled straight,
Romanus his successor for a month,
Did make protest Formosus was with God,
Holy, just, true in thought and word and deed.
Next Theodore, who reigned but twenty days,
Therein convoked a synod, whose decree
Did reinstate, repope the late unpoped,
And do away with Stephen as accursed.   110
So that when presently certain fisher-folk
(As if the queasy river could not hold
Its swallowed Jonas, but discharged the meal)
Produced the timely product of their nets,
The mutilated man, Formosus, — saved
From putrefaction by the embalmer's spice,
Or, as some said, by sanctity of flesh, —

'Why, lay the body again,' bade Theodore,
'Among his predecessors, in the church
And burial-place of Peter!' which was done.   120
'And,' addeth Luitprand, 'many of repute,
Pious and still alive, avouch to me
That, as they bore the body up the aisle,
The saints in imaged row bowed each his head
For welcome to a brother-saint come back.'
As for Romanus and this Theodore,
These two Popes, through the brief reign granted each,
Could but initiate what John came to close
And give the final stamp to: he it was
Ninth of the name, (I follow the best guides)   130
Who, — in full synod at Ravenna held
With Bishops seventy-four, and present too
Eude King of France with his Archbishopry, —
Did condemn Stephen, anathematize
The disinterment, and make all blots blank,
'For,' argueth here Auxilius in a place
De Ordinationibus, 'precedents
Had been, no lack, before Formosus long,
Of Bishops so transferred from see to see,
Marinus, for example:' read the tract.   140

"But, after John, came Sergius, reaffirmed
The right of Stephen, cursed Formosus, nay
Cast out, some say, his corpse a second time.
And here, — because the matter went to ground,
Fretted by new griefs, other cares of the age, —
Here is the last pronouncing of the Church,
Her sentence that subsists unto this day.
Yet constantly opinion hath prevailed
I' the Church, Formosus was a holy man."

Which of the judgments was infallible?   150
Which of my predecessors spoke for God?
And what availed Formosus that this cursed,
That blessed, and then this other cursed again?
"Fear ye not those whose power can kill the body
And not the soul," saith Christ, "but rather those
Can cast both soul and body into hell!"

John judged thus in Eight Hundred Ninety Eight,
Exact eight hundred years ago to-day.

When, sitting in his stead, Vice-gerent here,
I must give judgment on my own behoof.   160
So worked the predecessor: now, my turn!

In God's name! Once more on this earth of God's,
While twilight lasts and time wherein to work,
I take His staff with my uncertain hand,
And stay my six and fourscore years, my due
Labor and sorrow, on His judgment-seat,
And forthwith think, speak, act, in place of Him —
The Pope for Christ. Once more appeal is made
From man's assize to mine: I sit and see
Another poor weak trembling human wretch   170
Pushed by his fellows, who pretend the right,
Up to the gulf which, where I gaze, begins
From this world to the next, — gives way and way,
Just on the edge over the awful dark:
With nothing to arrest him but my feet.
He catches at me with convulsive face,
Cries "Leave to live the natural minute more!"
While hollowly the avengers echo "Leave?
None! So has he exceeded man's due share
In man's fit license, wrung by Adam's fall,   180
To sin and yet not surely die, — that we,
All of us sinful, all with need of grace,
All chary of our life, — the minute more
Or minute less of grace which saves a soul, —
Bound to make common cause with who craves time,
— We yet protest against the exorbitance
Of sin in this one sinner, and demand
That his poor sole remaining piece of time
Be plucked from out his clutch: put him to death!
Punish him now! As for the weal or woe   190
Hereafter, God grant mercy! Man be just,
Nor let the felon boast he went scot-free!"
And I am bound, the solitary judge,
To weigh the worth, decide upon the plea,
And either hold a hand out, or withdraw
A foot and let the wretch drift to the fall.
Ay, and while thus I dally, dare perchance
Put fancies for a comfort 'twixt this calm
And yonder passion that I have to bear, —
As if reprieve were possible for both   200
Prisoner and Pope, — how easy were reprieve!

A touch o' the hand-bell here, a hasty word
To those who wait, and wonder they wait long,
I' the passage there, and I should gain the life! —
Yea, though I flatter me with fancy thus,
I know it is but nature's craven-trick.
The case is over, judgment at an end,
And all things done now and irrevocable:
A mere dead man is Franceschini here,
Even as Formosus centuries ago.   210
I have worn through this sombre wintry day,
With winter in my soul beyond the world's,
Over these dismalest of documents
Which drew night down on me ere eve befell, —
Pleadings and counter-pleadings, figure of fact
Beside fact's self, these summaries to-wit, —
How certain three were slain by certain five:
I read here why it was, and how it went,
And how the chief o' the five preferred excuse,
And how law rather chose defence should lie, —   220
What argument he urged by wary word
When free to play off wile, start subterfuge,
And what the unguarded groan told, torture's feat
When law grew brutal, outbroke, overbore
And glutted hunger on the truth, at last, —
No matter for the flesh and blood between.
All's a clear rede and no more riddle now.
Truth, nowhere, lies yet everywhere in these —
Not absolutely in a portion, yet
Evolvible from the whole: evolved at last   230
Painfully, held tenaciously by me.
Therefore there is not any doubt to clear
When I shall write the brief word presently
And chink the hand-bell, which I pause to do.
Irresolute? Not I, more than the mound
With the pine-trees on it yonder! Some surmise,
Perchance, that since man's wit is fallible,
Mine may fail here? Suppose it so, — what then?
Say, — Guido, I count guilty, there's no babe
So guiltless, for I misconceive the man!   240
What's in the chance should move me from my mind?
If, as I walk in a rough country-side,
Peasants of mine cry "Thou art he can help,
Lord of the land and counted wise to boot:
Look at our brother, strangling in his foam,

He fell so where we find him, — prove thy worth!"
I may presume, pronounce, "A frenzy-fit,
A falling-sickness or a fever-stroke!
Breathe a vein, copiously let blood at once!"
So perishes the patient, and anon   250
I hear my peasants — "All was error, lord!
Our story, thy prescription: for there crawled
In due time from our hapless brother's breast
The serpent which had stung him: bleeding slew
Whom a prompt cordial had restored to health."
What other should I say than "God so willed:
Mankind is ignorant, a man am I:
Call ignorance my sorrow, not my sin!"
So and not otherwise, in after-time,
If some acuter wit, fresh probing, sound   260
This multifarious mass of words and deeds
Deeper, and reach through guilt to innocence,
I shall face Guido's ghost nor blench a jot.
"God who set me to judge thee, meted out
So much of judging faculty, no more:
Ask Him if I was slack in use thereof!"
I hold a heavier fault imputable
Inasmuch as I changed a chaplain once,
For no cause, — no, if I must bare my heart, —
Save that he snuffled somewhat saying mass.   270
For I am ware it is the seed of act,
God holds appraising in His hollow palm,
Not act grown great thence on the world below,
Leafage and branchage, vulgar eyes admire.
Therefore I stand on my integrity,
Nor fear at all: and if I hesitate,
It is because I need to breathe awhile,
Rest, as the human right allows, review
Intent the little seeds of act, my tree, —
The thought, which, clothed in deed, I give the world   280
At chink of bell and push of arrased door.

O pale departure, dim disgrace of day!
Winter's in wane, his vengeful worst art thou,
To dash the boldness of advancing March!
Thy chill persistent rain has purged our streets
Of gossipry; pert tongue and idle ear
By this, consort 'neath archway, portico.
But wheresoe'er Rome gathers in the gray,

Two names now snap and flash from mouth to mouth —
(Sparks, flint and steel strike) Guido and the Pope.   290
By this same hour to-morrow eve — aha,
How do they call him? — the sagacious Swede
Who finds by figures how the chances prove,
Why one comes rather than another thing,
As, say, such dots turn up by throw of dice,
Or, if we dip in Virgil here and there
And prick for such a verse, when such shall point.
Take this Swede, tell him, hiding name and rank,
Two men are in our city this dull eve;
One doomed to death, — but hundreds in such plight   300
Slip aside, clean escape by leave of law
Which leans to mercy in this latter time;
Moreover in the plenitude of life
Is he, with strength of limb and brain adroit,
Presumably of service here: beside,
The man is noble, backed by nobler friends:
Nay, they so wish him well, the city's self
Makes common cause with who — house-magistrate,
Patron of hearth and home, domestic lord —
But ruled his own, let aliens cavil. Die?   310
He'll bribe a jailer or break prison first!
Nay, a sedition may be helpful, give
Hint to the mob to batter wall, burn gate,
And bid the favorite malefactor march.
Calculate now these chances of escape!
"It is not probable, but well may be."
Again, there is another man, weighed now
By twice eight years beyond the seven-times-ten,
Appointed overweight to break our branch.
And this man's loaded branch lifts, more than snow,   320
All the world's cark and care, though a bird's nest
Were a superfluous burthen: notably
Hath he been pressed, as if his age were youth,
From to-day's dawn till now that day departs,
Trying one question with true sweat of soul
"Shall the said doomed man fitlier die or live?"
When a straw swallowed in his posset, stool
Stumbled on where his path lies, any puff
That's incident to such a smoking flax,
Hurries the natural end and quenches him!   330
Now calculate, thou sage, the chances here,
Say, which shall die the sooner, this or that?

"That, possibly, this in all likelihood."
I thought so: yet thou tripp'st, my foreign friend!
No, it will be quite otherwise, — to-day
Is Guido's last: my term is yet to run.

But say the Swede were right, and I forthwith
Acknowledge a prompt summons and lie dead:
Why, then I stand already in God's face
And hear "Since by its fruit a tree is judged,   340
Show me thy fruit, the latest act of thine!
For in the last is summed the first and all, —
What thy life last put heart and soul into,
There shall I taste thy product." I must plead
This condemnation of a man to-day.

Not so! Expect nor question nor reply
At what we figure as God's judgment-bar!
None of this vile way by the barren words
Which, more than any deed, characterize
Man as made subject to a curse: no speech —   350
That still bursts o'er some lie which lurks inside,
As the split skin across the coppery snake,
And most denotes man! since, in all beside,
In hate or lust or guile or unbelief,
Out of some core of truth the excrescence comes,
And, in the last resort, the man may urge
"So was I made, a weak thing that gave way
To truth, to impulse only strong since true,
And hated, lusted, used guile, forewent faith."
But when man walks the garden of this world   360
For his own solace, and, unchecked by law,
Speaks or keeps silence as himself sees fit,
Without the least incumbency to lie,
— Why, can he tell you what a rose is like,
Or how the birds fly, and not slip to false
Though truth serve better? Man must tell his mate
Of you, me and himself, knowing he lies,
Knowing his fellow knows the same, — will think
"He lies, it is the method of a man!"
And yet will speak for answer "It is truth"   370
To him who shall rejoin "Again a lie!"
Therefore these filthy rags of speech, this coil
Of statement, comment, query and response,*
Tatters all too contaminate for use,

Have no renewing: He, the Truth, is, too,
The Word. We men, in our degree, may know
There, simply, instantaneously, as here
After long time and amid many lies,
Whatever we dare think we know indeed
— That I am I, as He is He, — what else?   380
But be man's method for man's life at least!
Wherefore, Antonio Pignatelli, thou
My ancient self, who wast no Pope so long
But studiedst God and man, the many years
I' the school, i' the cloister, in the diocese
Domestic, legate-rule in foreign lands, —
Thou other force in those old busy days
Than this gray ultimate decrepitude, —
Yet sensible of fires that more and more
Visit a soul, in passage to the sky,   390
Left nakeder than when flesh-robe was new —
Thou, not Pope but the mere old man o' the world,
Supposed inquisitive and dispassionate,
Wilt thou, the one whose speech I somewhat trust,
Question the after-me, this self now Pope,
Hear his procedure, criticise his work?
Wise in its generation is the world.

This is why Guido is found reprobate.
I see him furnished forth for his career,
On starting for the life-chance in our world,   400
With nearly all we count sufficient help:
Body and mind in balance, a sound frame,
A solid intellect: the wit to seek,
Wisdom to choose, and courage wherewithal
To deal in whatsoever circumstance
Should minister to man, make life succeed.
Oh, and much drawback! what were earth without?
Is this our ultimate stage, or starting-place
To try man's foot, if it will creep or climb,
'Mid obstacles in seeming, points that prove   410
Advantage for who vaults from low to high
And makes the stumbling-block a stepping-stone?
So, Guido, born with appetite, lacks food:
Is poor, who yet could deftly play-off wealth:
Straitened, whose limbs are restless till at large.
He, as he eyes each outlet of the cirque
And narrow penfold for probation, pines

t, fill,: Rep

After the good things just outside its grate,
With less monition, fainter conscience-twitch,
Rarer instinctive qualm at the first feel 420
Of greed unseemly, prompting grasp undue,
Than nature furnishes her main mankind, —
Making it harder to do wrong than right
The first time, careful lest the common ear
Break measure, miss the outstep of life's march.
Wherein I see a trial fair and fit
For one else too unfairly fenced about,
Set above sin, beyond his fellows here:
Guarded from the arch-tempter all must fight,
By a great birth, traditionary name, 430
Diligent culture, choice companionship,
Above all, conversancy with the faith
Which puts forth for its base of doctrine just
"Man is born nowise to content himself,
But please God." He accepted such a rule,
Recognized man's obedience; and the Church,
Which simply is such rule's embodiment,
He clave to, he held on by, — nay, indeed,
Near pushed inside of, deep as layman durst,
Professed so much of priesthood as might sue 440
For priest's exemption where the layman sinned, —
Got his arm frocked which, bare, the law would bruise.
Hence, at this moment, what's his last resource,
His extreme stay and utmost stretch of hope
But that, — convicted of such crime as law
Wipes not away save with a worldling's blood, —
Guido, the three-parts consecrate, may 'scape?
Nay, the portentous brothers of the man
Are veritably priests, protected each
May do his murder in the Church's pale, 450
Abate Paul, Canon Girolamo!
This is the man proves irreligiousest
Of all mankind, religion's parasite!
This may forsooth plead dinned ear, jaded sense,
The vice o' the watcher who bides near the bell,
Sleeps sound because the clock is vigilant,
And cares not whether it be shade or shine,
Doling out day and night to all men else!
Why was the choice o' the man to niche himself
Perversely 'neath the tower where Time's own tongue 460
Thus undertakes to sermonize the world?

Why, but because the solemn is safe too,
The belfry proves a fortress of a sort,
Has other uses than to teach the hour:
Turns sunscreen, paravent and ombrifuge
To whoso seeks a shelter in its pale,
— Ay, and attractive to unwary folk
Who gaze at storied portal, statued spire,
And go home with full head but empty purse,
Nor dare suspect the sacristan the thief!   470
Shall Judas, — hard upon the donor's heel,
To filch the fragments of the basket, — plead
He was too near the preacher's mouth, nor sat
Attent with fifties in a company?
No, — closer to promulgated decree,
Clearer the censure of default. Proceed!

I find him bound, then, to begin life well;
Fortified by propitious circumstance,
Great birth, good breeding, with the Church for guide,
How lives he? Cased thus in a coat of proof,   480
Mailed like a man-at-arms, though all the while
A puny starveling, — does the breast pant big,
The limb swell to the limit, emptiness
Strive to become solidity indeed?
Rather, he shrinks up like the ambiguous fish,
Detaches flesh from shell and outside show,
And steals by moonlight (I have seen the thing)
In and out, now to prey and now to skulk.
Armor he boasts when a wave breaks on beach,
Or bird stoops for the prize: with peril nigh, —   490
The man of rank, the much-befriended-man,
The man almost affiliate to the Church,
Such is to deal with, let the world beware!
Does the world recognize, pass prudently?
Do tides abate and sea-fowl hunt i' the deep?
Already is the slug from out its mew,
Ignobly faring with all loose and free,
Sand-fly and slush-worm at their garbage-feast,
A naked blotch no better than they all:
Guido has dropped nobility, slipped the Church,   500
Plays trickster if not cut-purse, body and soul
Prostrate among the filthy feeders — faugh!
And when Law takes him by surprise at last,
Catches the foul thing on its carrion-prey,

Behold, he points to shell left high and dry,
Pleads "But the case out yonder is myself!"
Nay, it is thou, Law prongs amid thy peers,
Congenial vermin; that was none of thee,
Thine outside, — give it to the soldier-crab!

For I find this black mark impinge the man,   510
That he believes in just the vile of life.
Low instinct, base pretension, are these truth?
Then, that aforesaid armor, probity
He figures in, is falsehood scale on scale;
Honor and faith, — a lie and a disguise,
Probably for all livers in this world,
Certainly for himself! All say good words
To who will hear, all do thereby bad deeds
To who must undergo; so thrive mankind!
See this habitual creed exemplified   520
Most in the last deliberate act; as last,
So, very sum and substance of the soul
Of him that planned and leaves one perfect piece,
The sin brought under jurisdiction now,
Even the marriage of the man: this act
I sever from his life as sample, show
For Guido's self, intend to test him by,
As, from a cup filled fairly at the fount,
By the components we decide enough
Or to let flow as late, or staunch the source.   530

He purposes this marriage, I remark,
On no one motive that should prompt thereto —
Farthest, by consequence, from ends alleged
Appropriate to the action; so they were:
The best, he knew and feigned, the worst he took.
Not one permissible impulse moves the man,
From the mere liking of the eye and ear,
To the true longing of the heart that loves,
No trace of these: but all to instigate,
Is what sinks man past level of the brute   540
Whose appetite if brutish is a truth.
All is the lust for money: to get gold, —
Why, lie, rob, if it must be, murder! Make
Body and soul wring gold out, lured within
The clutch of hate by love, the trap's pretence!
What good else get from bodies and from souls?

This got, there were some life to lead thereby,
— What, where or how, appreciate those who tell
How the toad lives: it lives, — enough for me!
To get this good, — with but a groan or so,   550
Then, silence of the victims, — were the feat.
He foresaw, made a picture in his mind, —
Of father and mother stunned and echoless
To the blow, as they lie staring at fate's jaws
Their folly danced into, till the woe fell;
Edged in a month by strenuous cruelty
From even the poor nook whence they watched the wolf
Feast on their heart, the lamb-like child his prey;
Plundered to the last remnant of their wealth,
(What daily pittance pleased the plunderer dole)   560
Hunted forth to go hide head, starve and die,
And leave the pale awe-stricken wife, past hope
Of help i' the world now, mute and motionless,
His slave, his chattel, to first use, then destroy.
All this, he bent mind how to bring about,
Put plain in act and life, as painted plain,
So have success, reach crown of earthly good,
In this particular enterprise of man,
By marriage — undertaken in God's face
With all these lies so opposite God's truth,   570
For end so other than man's end.

                              Thus schemes
Guido, and thus would carry out his scheme:
But when an obstacle first blocks the path,
When he finds none may boast monopoly
Of lies and trick i' the tricking lying world, —
That sorry timid natures, even this sort
O' the Comparini, want not trick nor lie
Proper to the kind, — that as the gor-crow treats
The bramble-finch so treats the finch the moth,
And the great Guido is minutely matched   580
By this same couple, — whether true or false
The revelation of Pompilia's birth,
Which in a moment brings his scheme to naught, —
Then, he is piqued, advances yet a stage,
Leaves the low region to the finch and fly,
Soars to the zenith whence the fiercer fowl
May dare the inimitable swoop. I see.
He draws now on the curious crime, the fine

Felicity and flower of wickedness;
Determines, by the utmost exercise   590
Of violence, made safe and sure by craft,
To satiate malice, pluck one last arch-pang
From the parents, else would triumph out of reach,
By punishing their child, within reach yet,
Who, by thought, word or deed, could nowise wrong
I' the matter that now moves him. So plans he,
Always subordinating (note the point!)
Revenge, the manlier sin, to interest
The meaner, — would pluck pang forth, but unclench
No gripe in the act, let fall no money-piece.   600
Hence a plan for so plaguing, body and soul,
His wife, so putting, day by day, hour by hour,
The untried torture to the untouched place,
As must precipitate an end foreseen,
Goad her into some plain revolt, most like
Plunge upon patent suicidal shame,
Death to herself, damnation by rebound
To those whose hearts he, holding hers, holds still:
Such plan as, in its bad completeness, shall
Ruin the three together and alike,   610
Yet leave himself in luck and liberty,
No claim renounced, no right a forfeiture,
His person unendangered, his good fame
Without a flaw, his pristine worth intact, —
While they, with all their claims and rights that cling,
Shall forthwith crumble off him every side,
Scorched into dust, a plaything for the winds.
As when, in our Campagna, there is fired
The nest-like work that overruns a hut;
And, as the thatch burns here, there, everywhere,   620
Even to the ivy and wild vine, that bound
And blessed the home where men were happy once,
There rises gradual, black amid the blaze,
Some grim and unscathed nucleus of the nest, —
Some old malicious tower, some obscene tomb
They thought a temple in their ignorance,
And clung about and thought to lean upon —
There laughs it o'er their ravage, — where are they?
So did his cruelty burn life about,
And lay the ruin bare in dreadfulness,   630
Try the persistency of torment so
Upon the wife. that, at extremity,

Some crisis brought about by fire and flame,
The patient frenzy-stung must needs break loose,
Fly anyhow, find refuge anywhere,
Even in the arms of who should front her first,
No monster but a man — while nature shrieked
"Or thus escape, or die!" The spasm arrived,
Not the escape by way of sin, — O God,
Who shall pluck sheep Thou holdest, from Thy hand?   640
Therefore she lay resigned to die, — so far
The simple cruelty was foiled. Why then,
Craft to the rescue, let craft supplement
Cruelty and show hell a masterpiece!
Hence this consummate lie, this love-intrigue,
Unmanly simulation of a sin,
With place and time and circumstance to suit —
These letters false beyond all forgery —
Not just handwriting and mere authorship,
But false to body and soul they figure forth —   650
As though the man had cut out shape and shape
From fancies of that other Aretine,
To paste below — incorporate the filth
With cherub faces on a missal-page!

Whereby the man so far attains his end
That strange temptation is permitted, — see!
Pompilia wife, and Caponsacchi priest,
Are brought together as nor priest nor wife
Should stand, and there is passion in the place,
Power in the air for evil as for good,   660
Promptings from heaven and hell, as if the stars
Fought in their courses for a fate to be.
Thus stand the wife and priest, a spectacle,
I doubt not, to unseen assemblage there.
No lamp will mark that window for a shrine,
No tablet signalize the terrace, teach
New generations which succeed the old,
The pavement of the street is holy ground;
No bard describe in verse how Christ prevailed
And Satan fell like lightning! Why repine?   670
What does the world, told truth, but lie the more?

A second time the plot is foiled; nor, now,
By corresponding sin for countercheck,
No wile and trick that baffle trick and wile, —

The play o' the parents! here the blot is blanched
By God's gift of a purity of soul
That will not take pollution, ermine-like
Armed from dishonor by its own soft snow.
Such was this gift of God who showed for once
How He would have the world go white: it seems   680
As a new attribute were born of each
Champion of truth, the priest and wife I praise, —
As a new safeguard sprang up in defence
Of their new noble nature: so a thorn
Comes to the aid of and completes the rose —
Courage, to-wit, no woman's gift nor priest's,
I' the crisis; might leaps vindicating right.
See how the strong aggressor, bad and bold,
With every vantage, preconcerts surprise,
Leaps of a sudden at his victim's throat   690
In a byeway, — how fares he when face to face
With Caponsacchi? Who fights, who fears now?
There quails Count Guido, armed to the chattering teeth,
Cowers at the steadfast eye and quiet word
O' the Canon of the Pieve! There skulks crime
Behind law called in to back cowardice!
While out of the poor trampled worm the wife,
Springs up a serpent!
                     But anon of these.
Him I judge now, — of him proceed to note,
Failing the first, a second chance befriends   700
Guido, gives pause ere punishment arrive.
The law he called, comes, hears, adjudicates,
Nor does amiss i' the main, — secludes the wife
From the husband, respites the oppressed one, grants
Probation to the oppressor, could he know
The mercy of a minute's fiery purge!
The furnace-coals alike of public scorn,
Private remorse, heaped glowing on his head,
What if, — the force and guile, the ore's alloy,
Eliminate, his baser soul refined —   710
The lost be saved even yet, so as by fire?
Let him, rebuked, go softly all his days
And, when no graver musings claim their due,
Meditate on a man's immense mistake
Who, fashioned to use feet and walk, deigns crawl —
Takes the unmanly means — ay, though to ends
Man scarce should make for, would but reach thro' wrong, —

May sin, but nowise needs shame manhood so:
Since fowlers hawk, shoot, nay and snare the game,
And yet eschew vile practice, nor find sport   720
In torch-light treachery or the luring owl.

But how hunts Guido? Why, the fraudful trap —
Late spurned to ruin by the indignant feet
Of fellows in the chase who loved fair play —
Here he picks up the fragments to the least,
Lades him and hies to the old lurking-place
Where haply he may patch again, refit
The mischief, file its blunted teeth anew,
Make sure, next time, first snap shall break the bone.
Craft, greed and violence complot revenge: 730
Craft, for its quota, schemes to bring about
And seize occasion and be safe withal:
Greed craves its act may work both far and near,
Crush the tree, branch and trunk and root, beside.
Whichever twig or leaf arrests a streak
Of possible sunshine else would coin itself,
And drop down one more gold piece in the path:
Violence stipulates "Advantage proved,
And safety sure, be pain the overplus!
Murder with jagged knife! Cut but tear too!   740
Foiled oft, starved long, glut malice for amends!"
And what, craft's scheme? scheme sorrowful and strange
As though the elements, whom mercy checked,
Had mustered hate for one eruption more,
One final deluge to surprise the Ark
Cradled and sleeping on its mountain-top:
Their outbreak-signal — what but the dove's coo,
Back with the olive in her bill for news
Sorrow was over? 'Tis an infant's birth,
Guido's first born, his son and heir, that gives   750
The occasion: other men cut free their souls
From care in such a case, fly up in thanks
To God, reach, recognize His love for once:
Guido cries "Soul, at last the mire is thine!
Lie there in likeness of a money-bag
My babe's birth so pins down past moving now,
That I dare cut adrift the lives I late
Scrupled to touch lest thou escape with them!
These parents and their child my wife, — touch one,
Lose all! Their rights determined on a head   760

I could but hate, not harm, since from each hair
Dangled a hope for me: now — chance and change!
No right was in their child but passes plain
To that child's child and through such child to me.
I am a father now, — come what, come will,
I represent my child; he comes between —
Cuts sudden off the sunshine of this life
From those three: why, the gold is in his curls!
Not with old Pietro's, Violante's head,
Not his gray horror, her more hideous black —   770
Go these, devoted to the knife!"

                              'Tis done:
Wherefore should mind misgive, heart hesitate?
He calls to counsel, fashions certain four
Colorless natures counted clean till now,
— Rustic simplicity, uncorrupted youth,
Ignorant virtue! Here's the gold o' the prime
When Saturn ruled, shall shock our leaden day —
The clown abash the courtier! Mark it, bards!
The courtier tries his hand on clownship here,
Speaks a word, names a crime, appoints a price, —   780
Just breathes on what, suffused with all himself,
Is red-hot henceforth past distinction now
I' the common glow of hell. And thus they break
And blaze on us at Rome, Christ's birthnight-eve!
Oh angels that sang erst "On the earth, peace!
To man, good will!" — such peace finds earth to-day!
After the seventeen hundred years, so man
Wills good to man, so Guido makes complete
His murder! what is it I said? — cuts loose
Three lives that hitherto he suffered cling,   790
Simply because each served to nail secure,
By a corner of the money-bag, his soul, —
Therefore, lives sacred till the babe's first breath
O'erweights them in the balance, — off they fly!
So is the murder managed, sin conceived
To the full: and why not crowned with triumph too?
Why must the sin, conceived thus, bring forth death?
I note how, within hair's-breadth of escape,
Impunity and the thing supposed success,
Guido is found when the check comes, the change,   800
The monitory touch o' the tether — felt
By few, not marked by many, named by none
At the moment, only recognized aright

I' the fulness of the days, for God's, lest sin
Exceed the service, leap the line: such check —
A secret which this life finds hard to keep,
And, often guessed, is never quite revealed —
Needs must trip Guido on a stumbling-block
Too vulgar, too absurdly plain i' the path!
Study this single oversight of care,   810
This hebetude that marred sagacity,
Forgetfulness of all the man best knew, —
How any stranger having need to fly,
Needs but to ask and have the means of flight.
Why, the first urchin tells you, to leave Rome,
Get horses, you must show the warrant, just
The banal scrap, clerk's scribble, a fair word buys,
Or foul one, if a ducat sweeten word, —
And straight authority will back demand,
Give you the pick o' the post-house! — how should he,   820
Then, resident at Rome for thirty years,
Guido, instruct a stranger! And himself
Forgets just this poor paper scrap, wherewith
Armed, every door he knocks at opens wide
To save him: horsed and manned, with such advance
O' the hunt behind, why, 'twere the easy task
Of hours told on the fingers of one hand,
To reach the Tuscan frontier, laugh at home,
Light-hearted with his fellows of the place, —
Prepared by that strange shameful judgment, that   830
Satire upon a sentence just pronounced
By the Rota and confirmed by the Granduke, —
Ready in a circle to receive their peer,
Appreciate his good story how, when Rome,
The Pope-King and the populace of priests
Made common cause with their confederate
The other priestling who seduced his wife,
He, all unaided, wiped out the affront
With decent bloodshed and could face his friends,
Frolic it in the world's eye. Ay, such tale   840
Missed such applause, and by such oversight!
So, tired and footsore, those blood-flustered five
Went reeling on the road through dark and cold,
The few permissible miles, to sink at length,
Wallow and sleep in the first wayside straw,
As the other herd quenched, i' the wash o' the wave,
— Each swine, the devil inside him: so slept they,

And so were caught and caged — all through one trip,
One touch of fool in Guido the astute!
He curses the omission, I surmise,   850
More than the murder. Why, thou fool and blind,
It is the mercy-stroke that stops thy fate,
Hamstrings and holds thee to thy hurt, — but how?
On the edge o' the precipice! One minute more,
Thou hadst gone farther and fared worse, my son,
Fathoms down on the flint and fire beneath!
Thy comrades each and all were of one mind,
Thy murder done, to straightway murder thee
In turn, because of promised pay withheld.
So, to the last, greed found itself at odds   860
With craft in thee, and, proving conqueror,
Had sent thee, the same night that crowned thy hope,
Thither where, this same day, I see thee not,
Nor, through God's mercy, need, to-morrow, see.

Such I find Guido, midmost blotch of black
Discernible in this group of clustered crimes
Huddling together in the cave they call
Their palace outraged day thus penetrates.
Around him ranged, now close and now remote,
Prominent or obscure to meet the needs   870
O' the mage and master, I detect each shape
Subsidiary i' the scene nor loathed the less,
All alike colored, all descried akin
By one and the same pitchy furnace stirred
At the centre: see, they lick the master's hand, —
This fox-faced horrible priest, this brother-brute
The Abate, — why, mere wolfishness looks well,
Guido stands honest in the red o' the flame,
Beside this yellow that would pass for white,
Twice Guido, all craft but no violence,   880
This copier of the mien and gait and garb
Of Peter and Paul, that he may go disguised,
Rob halt and lame, sick folk i' the temple-porch!
Armed with religion, fortified by law,
A man of peace, who trims the midnight lamp
And turns the classic page — and all for craft,
All to work harm with, yet incur no scratch!
While Guido brings the struggle to a close,
Paul steps back the due distance, clear o' the trap
He builds and baits. Guido I catch and judge;   890

Paul is past reach in this world and my time:
This is a case reserved. Pass to the next,
The boy of the brood, the young Girolamo
Priest, Canon, and what more? nor wolf nor fox,
But hybrid, neither craft nor violence
Wholly, part violence part craft: such cross
Tempts speculation — will both blend one day,
And prove hell's better product? Or subside
And let the simple quality emerge,
Go on with Satan's service the old way?   900
Meanwhile, what promise, — what performance too!
For there's a new distinctive touch, I see,
Lust — lacking in the two — hell's own blue tint
That gives a character and marks the man
More than a match for yellow and red. Once more,
A case reserved: why should I doubt? Then comes
The gaunt gray nightmare in the furthest smoke,
The hag that gave these three abortions birth,
Unmotherly mother and unwomanly
Woman, that near turns motherhood to shame,   910
Womanliness to loathing: no one word,
No gesture to curb cruelty a whit
More than the she-pard thwarts her playsome whelps
Trying their milk-teeth on the soft o' the throat
O' the first fawn, flung, with those beseeching eyes,
Flat in the covert! How should she but couch,
Lick the dry lips, unsheathe the blunted claw,
Catch 'twixt her placid eyewinks at what chance
Old bloody half-forgotten dream may flit,
Born when herself was novice to the taste,   920
The while she lets youth take its pleasure. Last,
These God-abandoned wretched lumps of life,
These four companions, — country-folk this time,
Not tainted by the unwholesome civic breath,
Much less the curse o' the Court! Mere striplings too,
Fit to do human nature justice still!
Surely when impudence in Guido's shape
Shall propose crime and proffer money's-worth
To these stout tall rough bright-eyed, black-haired boys,
The blood shall bound in answer to each cheek   930
Before the indignant outcry break from lip!
Are these i' the mood to murder, hardly loosed
From healthy autumn-finish of ploughed glebe,
Grapes in the barrel, work at happy end,

And winter near with rest and Christmas play?
How greet they Guido with his final task · —
(As if he but proposed "One vineyard more
To dig, ere frost come, then relax indeed!")
"Anywhere, anyhow and anywhy,
Murder me some three people, old and young,   940
Ye never heard the names of, — and be paid
So much!" And the whole four accede at once.
Demur? Do cattle bidden march or halt?
Is it some lingering habit, old fond faith
I' the lord o' the land, instructs them, — birthright badge
Of feudal tenure claims its slaves again?
Not so at all, thou noble human heart!
All is done purely for the pay, — which, earned,
And not forthcoming at the instant, makes
Religion heresy, and the lord o' the land   950
Fit subject for a murder in his turn.
The patron with cut throat and rifled purse,
Deposited i' the roadside-ditch, his due,
Naught hinders each good fellow trudging home,
The heavier by a piece or two in poke,
And so with new zest to the common life,
Mattock and spade, plough-tail and wagon-shaft,
Till some such other piece of luck betide,
Who knows? Since this is a mere start in life,
And none of them exceeds the twentieth year.   960
Nay, more i' the background yet? Unnoticed forms
Claim to be classed, subordinately vile?
Complacent lookers-on that laugh, — perchance
Shake head as their friend's horse-play grows too rough
With the mere child he manages amiss —
But would not interfere and make bad worse
For twice the fractious tears and prayers: thou know'st
Civility better, Marzi-Medici,
Governor for thy kinsman the Granduke!
Fit representative of law, man's lamp   970
I' the magistrate's grasp full-flare, no rushlight-end
Sputtering 'twixt thumb and finger of the priest!
Whose answer to the couple's cry for help
Is a threat, — whose remedy of Pompilia's wrong,
A shrug o' the shoulder, and facetious word
Or wink, traditional with Tuscan wits,
To Guido in the doorway. Laud to law!
The wife is pushed back to the husband, he

Who knows how these home-squabblings persecute
People who have the public good to mind,   980
And work best with a silence in the court!

Ah, but I save my word at least for thee,
Archbishop, who art under, i' the Church,
As I am under God, — thou, chosen by both
To do the shepherd's office, feed the sheep —
How of this lamb that panted at thy foot
While the wolf pressed on her within crook's reach?
Wast thou the hireling that did turn and flee?
With thee at least anon the little word!

Such denizens o' the cave now cluster round   990
And heat the furnace sevenfold: time indeed
A bolt from heaven should cleave roof and clear place,
Transfix and show the world, suspiring flame,
The main offender, scar and brand the rest
Hurrying, each miscreant to his hole: then flood
And purify the scene with outside day —
Which yet, in the absolutest drench of dark,
Ne'er wants a witness, some stray beauty-beam
To the despair of hell.

                    First of the first,
Such I pronounce Pompilia, then as now   1000
Perfect in whiteness: stoop thou down, my child,
Give one good moment to the poor old Pope
Heart-sick at having all his world to blame —
Let me look at thee in the flesh as erst,
Let me enjoy the old clean linen garb,
Not the new splendid vesture! Armed and crowned,
Would Michael, yonder, be, nor crowned nor armed,
The less pre-eminent angel? Everywhere
I see in the world the intellect of man,
That sword, the energy his subtle spear,   1010
The knowledge which defends him like a shield —
Everywhere; but they make not up, I think,
The marvel of a soul like thine, earth's flower
She holds up to the softened gaze of God!
It was not given Pompilia to know much,
Speak much, to write a book, to move mankind,
Be memorized by who records my time.
Yet if in purity and patience, if

In faith held fast despite the plucking fiend,
Safe like the signet stone with the new name   1020
That saints are known by, — if in right returned
For wrong, most pardon for worst injury,
If there be any virtue, any praise, —
Then will this woman-child have proved — who knows? —
Just the one prize vouchsafed unworthy me,
Seven years a gardener of the untoward ground,
I till, — this earth, my sweat and blood manure
All the long day that barrenly grows dusk:
At least one blossom makes me proud at eve
Born 'mid the briers of my enclosure! Still   1030
(Oh, here as elsewhere, nothingness of man!)
Those be the plants, imbedded yonder South
To mellow in the morning, those made fat
By the master's eye, that yield such timid leaf,
Uncertain bud, as product of his pains!
While — see how this mere chance-sown, cleft-nursed seed,
That sprang up by the wayside 'neath the foot
Of the enemy, this breaks all into blaze,
Spreads itself, one wide glory of desire
To incorporate the whole great sun it loves   1040
From the inch-height whence it looks and longs! My flower,
My rose, I gather for the breast of God,
This I praise most in thee, where all I praise,
That having been obedient to the end
According to the light allotted, law
Prescribed thy life, still tried, still standing test, —
Dutiful to the foolish parents first,
Submissive next to the bad husband, — nay,
Tolerant of those meaner miserable
That did his hests, eked out the dole of pain, —   1050
Thou, patient thus, couldst rise from law to law,
The old to the new, promoted at one cry
O' the trump of God to the new service, not
To longer bear, but henceforth fight, be found
Sublime in new impatience with the foe!
Endure man and obey God: plant firm foot
On neck of man, tread man into the hell
Meet for him, and obey God all the more!
Oh child that didst despise thy life so much
When it seemed only thine to keep or lose,   1060
How the fine ear felt fall the first low word
"Value life, and preserve life for My sake!"

Thou didst . . . how shall I say? . . . receive so long
The standing ordinance of God on earth,
What wonder if the novel claim had clashed
With old requirement, seemed to supersede
Too much the customary law? But, brave,
Thou at first prompting of what I call God,
And fools call Nature, didst hear, comprehend,
Accept the obligation laid on thee,   1070
Mother elect, to save the unborn child,
As brute and bird do, reptile and the fly,
Ay and, I nothing doubt, even tree, shrub, plant
And flower o' the field, all in a common pact
To worthily defend the trust of trusts,
Life from the Ever Living: — didst resist —
Anticipate the office that is mine —
And with his own sword stay the upraised arm,
The endeavor of the wicked, and defend
Him who, — again in my default, — was there   1080
For visible providence: one less true than thou
To touch, i' the past, less practised in the right,
Approved less far in all docility
To all instruction, — how had such an one
Made scruple "Is this motion a decree?"
It was authentic to the experienced ear
O' the good and faithful servant. Go past me
And get thy praise, — and be not far to seek
Presently when I follow if I may!

And surely not so very much apart   1090
Need I place thee, my warrior-priest, — in whom
What if I gain the other rose, the gold,
We grave to imitate God's miracle,
Greet monarchs with, good rose in its degree?
Irregular noble 'scapegrace — son the same!
Faulty — and peradventure ours the fault
Who still misteach, mislead, throw hook and line,
Thinking to land leviathan forsooth,
Tame the scaled neck, play with him as a bird,
And bind him for our maidens! Better bear   1100
The King of Pride go wantoning awhile,
Unplagued by cord in nose and thorn in jaw,
Through deep to deep, followed by all that shine,
Churning the blackness hoary: He who made
The comely terror, He shall make the sword

To match that piece of netherstone his heart,
Ay, nor miss praise thereby; who else shut fire
I' the stone, to leap from mouth at sword's first stroke,
In lamps of love and faith, the chivalry
That dares the right and disregards alike   1110
The yea and nay o' the world? Self-sacrifice, —
What if an idol took it? Ask the Church
Why she was wont to turn each Venus here, —
Poor Rome perversely lingered round, despite
Instruction, for the sake of purblind love, —
Into Madonna's shape, and waste no whit
Of aught so rare on earth as gratitude!
All this sweet savor was not ours but thine,
Nard of the rock, a natural wealth we name
Incense, and treasure up as food for saints,   1120
When flung to us — whose function was to give
Not find the costly perfume. Do I smile?
Nay, Caponsacchi, much I find amiss,
Blameworthy, punishable in this freak
Of thine, this youth prolonged, though age was ripe,
This masquerade in sober day, with change
Of motley too, — now hypocrite's disguise,
Now fool's-costume: which lie was least like truth,
Which the ungainlier, more discordant garb
With that symmetric soul inside my son,   1130
The churchman's or the worldling's, — let him judge,
Our adversary who enjoys the task!
I rather chronicle the healthy rage, —
When the first moan broke from the martyr-maid
At that uncaging of the beasts, — made bare
My athlete on the instant, gave such good
Great undisguised leap over post and pale
Right into the mid-cirque, free fighting-place.
There may have been rash stripping — every rag
Went to the winds, — infringement manifold   1140
Of laws prescribed pudicity, I fear,
In this impulsive and prompt self-display!
Ever such tax comes of the foolish youth;
Men mulct the wiser manhood, and suspect
No veritable star swims out of cloud.
Bear thou such imputation, undergo
The penalty I nowise dare relax, —
Conventional chastisement and rebuke.
But for the outcome, the brave starry birth

Conciliating earth with all that cloud,   1150
Thank heaven as I do! Ay, such championship
Of God at first blush, such prompt cheery thud
Of glove on ground that answers ringingly
The challenge of the false knight, — watch we long
And wait we vainly for its gallant like
From those appointed to the service, sworn
His body-guard with pay and privilege —
White-cinct, because in white walks sanctity,
Red-socked, how else proclaim fine scorn of flesh,
Unchariness of blood when blood faith begs!   1160
Where are the men-at-arms with cross on coat?
Aloof, bewraying their attire: whilst thou
In mask and motley, pledged to dance not fight,
Sprang'st forth the hero! In thought, word and deed,
How throughout all thy warfare thou wast pure,
I find it easy to believe: and if
At any fateful moment of the strange
Adventure, the strong passion of that strait,
Fear and surprise, may have revealed too much, —
As when a thundrous midnight, with black air   1170
That burns, rain-drops that blister, breaks a spell,
Draws out the excessive virtue of some sheathed
Shut unsuspected flower that hoards and hides
Immensity of sweetness, — so, perchance,
Might the surprise and fear release too much
The perfect beauty of the body and soul
Thou savedst in thy passion for God's sake,
He who is Pity. Was the trial sore?
Temptation sharp? Thank God a second time!
Why comes temptation but for man to meet   1180
And master and make crouch beneath his foot.
And so be pedestaled in triumph? Pray
"Lead us into no such temptations, Lord!"
Yea, but, O Thou whose servants are the bold,
Lead such temptations by the head and hair,
Reluctant dragons, up to who dares fight,
That so he may do battle and have praise!
Do I not see the praise? — that while thy mates
Bound to deserve i' the matter, prove at need
Unprofitable through the very pains   1190
We gave to train them well and start them fair, —
Are found too stiff, with standing ranked and ranged,
For onset in good earnest, too obtuse

Of ear, through iteration of command,
For catching quick the sense ot the real cry, —
Thou, whose sword-hand was used to strike the lute,
Whose sentry-station graced some wanton's gate,
Thou didst push forward and show mettle, shame
The laggards, and retrieve the day. Well done!
Be glad thou hast let light into the world   1200
Through that irregular breach o' the boundary, — see
The same upon thy path and march assured,
Learning anew the use of soldiership,
Self-abnegation, freedom from all fear,
Loyalty to the life's end! Ruminate,
Deserve the initiatory spasm, — once more
Work, be unhappy but bear life, my son!

And troop you, somewhere 'twixt the best and worst,
Where crowd the indifferent product, all too poor
Makeshift, starved samples of humanity!   1210
Father and mother, huddle there and hide!
A gracious eye may find you! Foul and fair,
Sadly mixed natures: self-indulgent, — yet
Self-sacrificing too: how the love soars,
How the craft, avarice, vanity and spite
Sink again! So they keep the middle course,
Slide into silly crime at unaware,
Slip back upon the stupid virtue, stay
Nowhere enough for being classed, I hope
And fear. Accept the swift and rueful death,   1220
Taught, somewhat sternlier than is wont, what waits
The ambiguous creature, — how the one black tuft
Steadies the aim of the arrow just as well
As the wide faultless white on the bird's breast!
Nay, you were punished in the very part
That looked most pure of speck, — 'twas honest love
Betrayed you, — did love seem most worthy pains,
Challenge such purging, since ordained survive
When all the rest of you was done with? Go!
Never again elude the choice of tints!   1230
White shall not neutralize the black, nor good
Compensate bad in man, absolve him so:
Life's business being just the terrible choice.

So do I see, pronounce on all and some
Grouped for my judgment now, — profess no doubt

While I pronounce: dark, difficult enough
The human sphere, yet eyes grow sharp by use,
I find the truth, dispart the shine from shade,
As a mere man may, with no special touch
O' the lynx-gift in each ordinary orb: 1240
Nay, if the popular notion class me right,
One of well-nigh decayed intelligence, —
What of that? Through hard labor and good will,
And habitude that gives a blind man sight
At the practised finger-ends of him, I do
Discern, and dare decree in consequence,
Whatever prove the peril of mistake.
Whence, then, this quite new quick cold thrill, — cloudlike,
This keen dread creeping from a quarter scarce
Suspected in the skies I nightly scan?   1250
What slacks the tense nerve, saps the wound-up spring
Of the act that should and shall be, sends the mount
And mass o' the whole man's-strength, — conglobed so late —
Shudderingly into dust, a moment's work?
While I stand firm, go fearless, in this world,
For this life recognize and arbitrate,
Touch and let stay, or else remove a thing,
Judge "This is right, this object out of place,"
Candle in hand that helps me and to spare, —
What if a voice deride me, "Perk and pry!   1260
Brighten each nook with thine intelligence!
Play the good householder, ply man and maid
With tasks prolonged into the midnight, test
Their work and nowise stint of the due wage
Each worthy worker: but with gyves and whip
Pay thou misprision of a single point
Plain to thy happy self who lift'st the light,
Lament'st the darkling, — bold to all beneath!
What if thyself adventure, now the place
Is purged so well? Leave pavement and mount roof,   1270
Look round thee for the light of the upper sky,
The fire which lit thy fire which finds default
In Guido Franceschini to his cost!
What if, above in the domain of light,
Thou miss the accustomed signs, remark eclipse?
Shalt thou still gaze on ground nor lift a lid, —
Steady in thy superb prerogative,
Thy inch of inkling, — nor once face the doubt
I' the sphere above thee, darkness to be felt?"

Yet my poor spark had for its source, the sun;   1280
Thither I sent the great looks which compel
Light from its fount: all that I do and am
Comes from the truth, or seen or else surmised,
Remembered or divined, as mere man may:
I know just so, nor otherwise. As I know,
I speak, — what should I know, then, and how speak
Were there a wild mistake of eye or brain
As to recorded governance above?
If my own breath, only, blew coal alight
I styled celestial and the morning-star?   1290
I, who in this world act resolvedly,
Dispose of men, their bodies and their souls,
As they acknowledge or gainsay the light
I show them, — shall I too lack courage? — leave
I, too, the post of me, like those I blame?
Refuse, with kindred inconsistency,
To grapple danger whereby souls grow strong?
I am near the end; but still not at the end;
All to the very end is trial in life:
At this stage is the trial of my soul   1300
Danger to face, or danger to refuse?
Shall I dare try the doubt now, or not dare?

O Thou, — as represented here to me
In such conception as my soul allows, —
Under Thy measureless, my atom width! —
Man's mind, what is it but a convex glass
Wherein are gathered all the scattered points
Picked out of the immensity of sky,
To re-unite there, be our heaven for earth,
Our known unknown, our God revealed to man?   1310
Existent somewhere, somehow, as a whole;
Here, as a whole proportioned to our sense, —
There, (which is nowhere, speech must babble thus!)
In the absolute immensity, the whole
Appreciable solely by Thyself, —
Here, by the little mind of man, reduced
To littleness that suits his faculty,
In the degree appreciable too;
Between Thee and ourselves — nay even, again,
Below us, to the extreme of the minute,   1320
Appreciable by how many and what diverse
Modes of the life Thou madest be! (why live

Except for love, — how love unless they know?)
Each of them, only filling to the edge,
Insect or angel, his just length and breadth,
Due facet of reflection, — full, no less,
Angel or insect, as Thou framedst things.
I it is who have been appointed here
To represent Thee, in my turn, on earth,
Just as, if new philosophy know aught,   1330
This one earth, out of all the multitude
Of peopled worlds, as stars are now supposed, —
Was chosen, and no sun-star of the swarm,
For stage and scene of Thy transcendent act
Beside which even the creation fades
Into a puny exercise of power.
Choice of the world, choice of the thing I am,
Both emanate alike from Thy dread play
Of operation outside this our sphere
Where things are classed and counted small or great, —   1340
Incomprehensibly the choice is Thine!
I therefore bow my head and take Thy place.
There is, beside the works, a tale of Thee
In the world's mouth, which I find credible:
I love it with my heart: unsatisfied,
I try it with my reason, nor discept
From any point I probe and pronounce sound.
Mind is not matter nor from matter, but
Above, — leave matter then, proceed with mind!
Man's be the mind recognized at the height, —   1350
Leave the inferior minds and look at man!
Is he the strong, intelligent and good
Up to his own conceivable height? Nowise.
Enough o' the low, — soar the conceivable height,
Find cause to match the effect in evidence,
The work i' the world, not man's but God's; leave man!
Conjecture of the worker by the work:
Is there strength there? — enough: intelligence?
Ample: but goodness in a like degree?
Not to the human eye in the present state,   1360
An isoscele deficient in the base.
What lacks, then, of perfection fit for God
But just the instance which this tale supplies
Of love without a limit? So is strength,
So is intelligence; let love be so,
Unlimited in its self-sacrifice,

Then is the tale true and God shows complete.
Beyond the tale, I reach into the dark,
Feel what I cannot see, and still faith stands:
I can believe this dread machinery   1370
Of sin and sorrow, would confound me else,
Devised, — all pain, at most expenditure
Of pain by Who devised pain, — to evolve,
By new machinery in counterpart,
The moral qualities of man — how else? —
To make him love in turn and be beloved,
Creative and self-sacrificing too,
And thus eventually God-like, (ay,
"I have said ye are Gods," — shall it be said for naught?)
Enable man to wring, from out all pain,   1380
All pleasure for a common heritage
To all eternity: this may be surmised,
The other is revealed, — whether a fact,
Absolute, abstract, independent truth,
Historic, not reduced to suit man's mind, —
Or only truth reverberate, changed, made pass
A spectrum into mind, the narrow eye, —
The same and not the same, else unconceived —
Though quite conceivable to the next grade
Above it in intelligence, — as truth   1390
Easy to man were blindness to the beast
By parity of procedure, — the same truth
In a new form, but changed in either case:
What matter so intelligence be filled?
To a child, the sea is angry, for it roars:
Frost bites, else why the tooth-like fret on face?
Man makes acoustics deal with the sea's wrath,
Explains the choppy cheek by chymic law, —
To man and child remains the same effect
On drum of ear and root of nose, change cause   1400
Never so thoroughly: so my heart be struck,
What care I, — by God's gloved hand or the bare?
Nor do I much perplex me with aught hard,
Dubious in the transmitting of the tale, —
No, nor with certain riddles set to solve.
This life is training and a passage; pass, —
Still, we march over some flat obstacle
We made give way before us; solid truth
In front of it, what motion for the world?
The moral sense grows but by exercise.   1410

'Tis even as man grew probatively
Initiated in Godship, set to make
A fairer moral world than this he finds,
Guess now what shall be known hereafter. Deal
Thus with the present problem: as we see,
A faultless creature is destroyed, and sin
Has had its way i' the world where God should rule.
Ay, but for this irrelevant circumstance
Of inquisition after blood, we see
Pompilia lost and Guido saved: how long?   1420
For his whole life: how much is that whole life?
We are not babes, but know the minute's worth,
And feel that life is large and the world small,
So, wait till life have passed from out the world.
Neither does this astonish at the end,
That whereas I can so receive and trust,
Other men, made with hearts and souls the same,
Reject and disbelieve, — subordinate
The future to the present, — sin, nor fear.
This I refer still to the foremost fact,   1430
Life is probation and the earth no goal
But starting-point of man: compel him strive,
Which means, in man, as good as reach the goal, —
Why institute that race, his life, at all?
But this does overwhelm me with surprise,
Touch me to terror, — not that faith, the pearl,
Should be let lie by fishers wanting food, —
Nor, seen and handled by a certain few
Critical and contemptuous, straight consigned
To shore and shingle for the pebble it proves, —   1440
But that, when haply found and known and named
By the residue made rich for evermore,
These, — that these favored ones, should in a trice
Turn, and with double zest go dredge for whelks,
Mud-worms that make the savory soup! Enough
O' the disbelievers, see the faithful few!
How do the Christians here deport them, keep
Their robes of white unspotted by the world?
What is this Aretine Archbishop, this
Man under me as I am under God,   1450
This champion of the faith, I armed and decked,
Pushed forward, put upon a pinnacle,
To show the enemy his victor, — see!
What's the best fighting when the couple close?

Pompilia cries, "Protect me from the wolf!"
He — "No, thy Guido is rough, heady, strong,
Dangerous to disquiet: let him bide!
He needs some bone to mumble, help amuse
The darkness of his den with: so, the fawn
Which limps up bleeding to my foot and lies,   1460
— Come to me, daughter! — thus I throw him back!"
Have we misjudged here, over-armed our knight,
Given gold and silk where plain hard steel serves best,
Enfeebled whom we sought to fortify,
Made an archbishop and undone a saint?
Well, then, descend these heights, this pride of life,
Sit in the ashes with a barefoot monk
Who long ago stamped out the worldly sparks,
By fasting, watching, stone cell and wire scourge,
— No such indulgence as unknits the strength —   1470
These breed the tight nerve and tough cuticle,
And the world's praise or blame runs rillet-wise
Off the broad back and brawny breast, we know!
He meets the first cold sprinkle of the world,
And shudders to the marrow. "Save this child?
Oh, my superiors, oh, the Archbishop's self!
Who was it dared lay hand upon the ark
His betters saw fall nor put finger forth?
Great ones could help yet help not: why should small?
I break my promise: let her break her heart!"   1480
These are the Christians not the worldlings, not
The sceptics, who thus battle for the faith!
If foolish virgins disobey and sleep,
What wonder? But, this time, the wise that watch,
Sell lamps and buy lutes, exchange oil for wine,
The mystic Spouse betrays the Bridegroom here.
To our last resource, then! Since all flesh is weak,
Bind weaknesses together, we get strength:
The individual weighed, found wanting, try
Some institution, honest artifice   1490
Whereby the units grow compact and firm!
Each props the other, and so stand is made
By our embodied cowards that grow brave.
The Monastery called of Convertites,
Meant to help women because these helped Christ, —
A thing existent only while it acts,
Does as designed, else a nonentity, —
For what is an idea unrealized? —

Pompilia is consigned to these for help.
They do help: they are prompt to testify   1500
To her pure life and saintly dying days.
She dies, and lo, who seemed so poor, proves rich.
What does the body that lives through helpfulness
To women for Christ's sake? The kiss turns bite,
The dove's note changes to the crow's cry: judge!
"Seeing that this our Convent claims of right
What goods belong to those we succor, be
The same proved women of dishonest life, —
And seeing that this Trial made appear
Pompilia was in such predicament, —   1510
The Convent hereupon pretends to said
Succession of Pompilia, issues writ,
And takes possession by the Fisc's advice."
Such is their attestation to the cause
Of Christ, who had one saint at least, they hoped:
But, is a title-deed to filch, a corpse
To slander, and an infant-heir to cheat?
Christ must give up his gains then! They unsay
All the fine speeches, — who was saint is whore.
Why, scripture yields no parallel for this!   1520
The soldiers only threw dice for Christ's coat;
We want another legend of the Twelve
Disputing if it was Christ's coat at all,
Claiming as prize the woof of price — for why?
The Master was a thief, purloined the same,
Or paid for it out of the common bag!
Can it be this is end and outcome, all
I take with me to show as stewardship's fruit,
The best yield of the latest time, this year
The seventeen-hundredth since God died for man?   1530
Is such effect proportionate to cause?
And still the terror keeps on the increase
When I perceive . . . how can I blink the fact?
That the fault, the obduracy to good,
Lies not with the impracticable stuff
Whence man is made, his very nature's fault,
As if it were of ice the moon may gild
Not melt, or stone 'twas meant the sun should warm
Not make bear flowers, — nor ice nor stone to blame:
But it can melt, that ice, can bloom, that stone,   1540
Impassible to rule of day and night!
This terrifies me, thus compelled perceive,

Whatever love and faith we looked should spring
At advent of the authoritative star,
Which yet lie sluggish, curdled at the source, —
These have leapt forth profusely in old time,
These still respond with promptitude to-day,
At challenge of — what unacknowledged powers
O' the air, what uncommissioned meteors, warmth
By law, and light by rule should supersede?   1550
For see this priest, this Caponsacchi, stung
At the first summons, — "Help for honor's sake,
Play the man, pity the oppressed!" — no pause,
How does he lay about him in the midst,
Strike any foe, right wrong at any risk,
All blindness, bravery and obedience! — blind?
Ay, as a man would be inside the sun,
Delirious with the plenitude of light
Should interfuse him to the finger-ends —
Let him rush straight, and how shall he go wrong?   1560
Where are the Christians in their panoply?
The loins we girt about with truth, the breasts
Righteousness plated round, the shield of faith,
The helmet of salvation, and that sword
O' the Spirit, even the word of God, — where these?
Slunk into corners! Oh, I hear at once
Hubbub of protestation! "What, we monks,
We friars, of such an order, such a rule,
Have not we fought, bled, left our martyr-mark
At every point along the boundary-line   1570
'Twixt true and false, religion and the world,
Where this or the other dogma of our Church
Called for defence?" And I, despite myself,
How can I but speak loud what truth speaks low,
"Or better than the best, or nothing serves!
What boots deed, I can cap and cover straight
With such another doughtiness to match,
Done at an instinct of the natural man?"
Immolate body, sacrifice soul too, —
Do not these publicans the same? Outstrip!   1580
Or else stop race you boast runs neck and neck,
You with the wings, they with the feet, — for shame!
Oh, I remark your diligence and zeal!
Five years long, now, rounds faith into my ears,
"Help thou, or Christendom is done to death!"
Five years since, in the Province of To-kien,

Which is in China as some people know,
Maigrot, my Vicar Apostolic there,
Having a great qualm, issues a decree.
Alack, the converts use as God's name, not   1590
Tien-chu but plain *Tien* or else mere *Shang-ti*,
As Jesuits please to fancy politic,
While, say Dominicians, it calls down fire, —
For *Tien* means heaven, and *Shang-ti*, supreme prince,
While *Tien-chu* means the lord of heaven: all cry,
"There is no business urgent for despatch
As that thou send a legate, specially
Cardinal Tournon, straight to Pekin, there
To settle and compose the difference!"
So have I seen a potentate all fume   1600
For some infringement of his realm's just right,
Some menace to a mud-built straw-thatched farm
O' the frontier; while inside the mainland lie,
Quite undisputed-for in solitude,
Whole cities plague may waste or famine sap:
What if the sun crumble, the sands encroach,
While he looks on sublimely at his ease?
How does their ruin touch the empire's bound?

And is this little all that was to be?
Where is the gloriously-decisive change,   1610
Metamorphosis the immeasurable
Of human clay to divine gold, we looked
Should, in some poor sort, justify its price?
Had an adept of the mere Rosy Cross
Spent his life to consummate the Great Work,
Would not we start to see the stuff it touched
Yield not a grain more than the vulgar got
By the old smelting-process years ago?
If this were sad to see in just the sage
Who should profess so much, perform no more,   1620
What is it when suspected in that Power
Who undertook to make and made the world,
Devised and did effect man, body and soul,
Ordained salvation for them both, and yet . . .
Well, is the thing we see, salvation?
                          I
Put no such dreadful question to myself,
Within whose circle of experience burns
The central truth, Power, Wisdom, Goodness, — God:

I must outlive a thing ere know it dead:
When I outlive the faith there is a sun,   1030
When I lie, ashes to the very soul, —
Someone, not I, must wail above the heap,
"He died in dark whence never morn arose."
While I see day succeed the deepest night —
How can I speak but as I know? — my speech
Must be, throughout the darkness, "It will end:
The light that did burn, will burn!" Clouds obscure —
But for which obscuration all were bright?
Too hastily concluded! Sun-suffused,
A cloud may soothe the eye made blind by blaze, —   1640
Better the very clarity of heaven:
The soft streaks are the beautiful and dear.
What but the weakness in a faith supplies
The incentive to humanity, no strength
Absolute, irresistible, comports?
How can man love but what he yearns to help?
And that which men think weakness within strength,
But angels know for strength and stronger yet —
What were it else but the first things made new,
But repetition of the miracle,   1650
The divine instance of self-sacrifice
That never ends and aye begins for man?
So, never I miss footing in the maze,
No, — I have light nor fear the dark at all.

But are mankind not real, who pace outside
My petty circle, world that's measured me?
And when they stumble even as I stand,
Have I a right to stop ear when they cry,
As they were phantoms who took clouds for crags,
Tripped and fell, where man's march might safely move?   1660
Beside, the cry is other than a ghost's,
When out of the old time there pleads some bard,
Philosopher, or both, and — whispers not,
But words it boldly. "The inward work and worth
Of any mind, what other mind may judge
Save God who only knows the thing He made,
The veritable service He exacts?
It is the outward product men appraise.
Behold, an engine hoists a tower aloft:
'I looked that it should move the mountain too!'   1670
Or else 'Had just a turret toppled down,

Success enough!' — may say the Machinist
Who knows what less or more result might be:
But we, who see that done we cannot do,
'A feat beyond man's force,' we men must say.
Regard me and that shake I gave the world!
I was born, not so long before Christ's birth
As Christ's birth haply did precede thy day, —
But many a watch before the star of dawn:
Therefore I lived, — it is thy creed affirms,   1680
Pope Innocent, who art to answer me! —
Under conditions, nowise to escape,
Whereby salvation was impossible.
Each impulse to achieve the good and fair,
Each aspiration to the pure and true,
Being without a warrant or an aim,
Was just as sterile a felicity
As if the insect, born to spend his life
Soaring his circles, stopped them to describe
(Painfully motionless in the mid-air)   1690
Some word of weighty counsel for man's sake,
Some 'Know thyself' or 'Take the golden mean!'
— Forwent his happy dance and the glad ray,
Died half an hour the sooner and was dust.
I, born to perish like the brutes, or worse,
Why not live brutishly, obey brutes' law?
But I, of body as of soul complete,
A gymnast at the games, philosopher
I' the schools, who painted, and made music, — all
Glories that met upon the tragic stage   1700
When the Third Poet's tread surprised the Two, —
Whose lot fell in a land where life was great
And sense went free and beauty lay profuse,
I, untouched by one adverse circumstance,
Adopted virtue as my rule of life,
Waived all reward, loved but for loving's sake,
And, what my heart taught me, I taught the world,
And have been teaching now two thousand years.
Witness my work, — plays that should please, forsooth!
'They might please, they may displease, they shall teach,   1710
For truth's sake,' so I said, and did, and do.
Five hundred years ere Paul spoke, Felix heard, —
How much of temperance and righteousness,
Judgment to come, did I find reason for,
Corroborate with my strong style that spared

No sin, nor swerved the more from branding brow
Because the sinner was called Zeus and God?
How nearly did I guess at that Paul knew?
How closely come, in what I represent
As duty, to his doctrine yet a blank?   1720
And as that limner not untruly limns
Who draws an object round or square, which square
Or round seems to the unassisted eye,
Though Galileo's tube display the same
Oval or oblong, — so, who controverts
I rendered rightly what proves wrongly wrought
Beside Paul's picture? Mine was true for me.
I saw that there are, first and above all,
The hidden forces, blind necessities,
Named Nature, but the thing's self unconceived: 1730
Then follow, — how dependent upon these,
We know not, how imposed above ourselves,
We well know, — what I name the gods, a power
Various or one: for great and strong and good
Is there, and little, weak and bad there too,
Wisdom and folly: say, these make no God, —
What is it else that rules outside man's self?
A fact then, — always, to the naked eye, —
And so, the one revealment possible
Of what were unimagined else by man.   1740
Therefore, what gods do, man may criticise,
Applaud, condemn, — how should he fear the truth? —
But likewise have in awe because of power,
Venerate for the main munificence,
And give the doubtful deed its due excuse
From the acknowledged creature of a day
To the Eternal and Divine. Thus, bold
Yet self-mistrusting, should man bear himself,
Most assured on what now concerns him most —
The law of his own life, the path he prints, —   1750
Which law is virtue and not vice, I say, —
And least inquisitive where search least skills,
I' the nature we best give the clouds to keep.
What could I paint beyond a scheme like this
Out of the fragmentary truths where light
Lay fitful in a tenebrific time?
You have the sunrise now, joins truth to truth,
Shoots life and substance into death and void;
Themselves compose the whole we made before;

The forces and necessity grow God, — 1760
The beings so contrarious that seemed gods,
Prove just His operation manifold
And multiform, translated, as must be,
Into intelligible shape so far
As suits our sense and sets us free to feel.
What if I let a child think, childhood-long,
That lightning, I would have him spare his eye,
Is a real arrow shot at naked orb?
The man knows more, but shuts his lids the same:
Lightning's cause comprehends nor man nor child. 1770
Why then, my scheme, your better knowledge broke,
Presently re-adjusts itself, the small
Proportioned largelier, parts and whole named new:
So much, no more two thousand years have done!
Pope, dost thou dare pretend to punish me,
For not descrying sunshine at midnight,
Me who crept all-fours, found my way so far —
While thou rewardest teachers of the truth,
Who miss the plain way in the blaze of noon, —
Though just a word from that strong style of mine, 1780
Grasped honestly in hand as guiding-staff,
Had pricked them a sure path across the bog,
That mire of cowardice and slush of lies
Wherein I find them wallow in wide day!"

How should I answer this Euripides?
Paul, — 'tis a legend, — answered Seneca,
But that was in the day-spring; noon is now:
We have got too familiar with the light.
Shall I wish back once more that thrill of dawn?
When the whole truth-touched man burned up, one fire? 1790
— Assured the trial, fiery, fierce, but fleet,
Would, from his little heap of ashes, lend
Wings to that conflagration of the world
Which Christ awaits ere He makes all things new:
So should the frail become the perfect, rapt
From glory of pain to glory of joy; and so,
Even in the end, — the act renouncing earth,
Lands, houses, husbands, wives and children here, —
Begin that other act which finds all, lost,
Regained, in this time even, a hundredfold, 1800
And, in the next time, feels the finite love
Blent and embalmed with the eternal life.

So does the sun ghastlily seem to sink
In those north parts, lean all but out of life,
Desist a dread mere breathing stop, then slow
Re-assert day, begin the endless rise.
Was this too easy for our after-stage?
Was such a lighting-up of faith, in life,
Only allowed initiate, set man's step
In the true way by help of the great glow?   1810
A way wherein it is ordained he walk,
Bearing to see the light from heaven still more
And more encroached on by the light of earth,
Tentatives earth puts forth to rival heaven,
Earthly incitements that mankind serve God
For man's sole sake, not God's and therefore man's.
Till at last, who distinguishes the sun
From a mere Druid fire on a far mount?
More praise to him who with his subtle prism
Shall decompose both beams and name the true.   1820
In such sense, who is last proves first indeed;
For how could saints and martyrs fail see truth
Streak the night's blackness? Who is faithful now?
Who untwists heaven's white from the yellow flare
O' the world's gross torch, without night's foil that helped
Produce the Christian act so possible
When in the way stood Nero's cross and stake, —
So hard now when the world smiles "Right and wise!
Faith points the politic, the thrifty way,
Will make who plods it in the end returns   1830
Beyond mere fool's-sport and improvidence.
We fools dance thro' the cornfield of this life,
Pluck ears to left and right and swallow raw,
— Nay, tread, at pleasure, a sheaf underfoot,
To get the better at some poppy-flower, —
Well aware we shall have so much less wheat
In the eventual harvest: you meantime
Waste not a spike, — the richlier will you reap!
What then? There will be always garnered meal
Sufficient for our comfortable loaf,   1840
While you enjoy the undiminished sack!"
Is it not this ignoble confidence,
Cowardly hardihood, that dulls and damps,
Makes the old heroism impossible?

Unless . . . what whispers me of times to come?
What if it be the mission of that age
My death will usher into life, to shake
This torpor of assurance from our creed,
Re-introduce the doubt discarded, bring
That formidable danger back, we drove   1850
Long ago to the distance and the dark?
No wild beast now prowls round the infant camp:
We have built wall and sleep in city safe:
But if some earthquake try the towers that laugh
To think they once saw lions rule outside,
And man stand out again, pale, resolute,
Prepared to die, — which means, alive at last?
As we broke up that old faith of the world,
Have we, next age, to break up this the new —
Faith, in the thing, grown faith in the report —   1860
Whence need to bravely disbelieve report
Through increased faith i' the thing reports belie?
Must we deny, — do they, these Molinists,
At peril of their body and their soul, —
Recognized truths, obedient to some truth
Unrecognized yet, but perceptible? —
Correct the portrait by the living face,
Man's God, by God's God in the mind of man?
Then, for the few that rise to the new height,
The many that must sink to the old depth,   1870
The multitude found fall away! A few,
E'en ere new law speak clear, may keep the old,
Preserve the Christian level, call good good
And evil evil, (even though razed and blank
The old titles,) helped by custom, habitude,
And all else they mistake for finer sense
O' the fact that reason warrants, — as before,
They hope perhaps, fear not impossibly.
At least some one Pompilia left the world
Will say "I know the right place by foot's feel,   1880
I took it and tread firm there; wherefore change?"
But what a multitude will surely fall
Quite through the crumbling truth, late subjacent,
Sink to the next discoverable base,
Rest upon human nature, settle there
On what is firm, the lust and pride of life!
A mass of men, whose very souls even now
Seem to need re-creating, — so they slink

Worm-like into the mud, light now lays bare, —
Whose future we dispose of with shut eyes   1890
And whisper — "They are grafted, barren twigs,
Into the living stock of Christ: may bear
One day, till when they lie death-like, not dead," —
Those who with all the aid of Christ succumb,
How, without Christ, shall they, unaided, sink?
Whither but to this gulf before my eyes?
Do not we end, the century and I?
The impatient antimasque treads close on kibe
O' the very masque's self it will mock, — on me,
Last lingering personage, the impatient mime   1900
Pushes already, — will I block the way?
Will my slow trail of garments ne'er leave space
For pantaloon, sock, plume and castanet?
Here comes the first experimentalist
In the new order of things, — he plays a priest;
Does he take inspiration from the Church,
Directly make her rule his law of life?
Not he: his own mere impulse guides the man —
Happily sometimes, since ourselves allow
He has danced, in gayety of heart, i' the main   1910
The right step through the maze we bade him foot.
But if his heart had prompted him break loose
And mar the measure? Why, we must submit,
And thank the chance that brought him safe so far.
Will he repeat the prodigy? Perhaps.
Can he teach others how to quit themselves,
Show why this step was right while that were wrong?
How should he? "Ask your hearts as I ask mine,
And get discreetly through the morrice too;
If your hearts misdirect you, — quit the stage,   1920
And make amends, — be there amends to make!"
Such is, for the Augustin that was once,
This Canon Caponsacchi we see now.
"But my heart answers to another tune,"
Puts in the Abate, second in the suite,
"I have my taste too, and tread no such step!
You choose the glorious life, and may, for me!
I like the lowest of life's appetites, —
So you judge, — but the very truth of joy
To my own apprehension which decides.   1930
Call me knave and you get yourself called fool!
I live for greed, ambition, lust, revenge;

Attain these ends by force, guile: hypocrite,
To-day, perchance to-morrow recognized
The rational man, the type of common sense."
There's Loyola adapted to our time!
Under such guidance Guido plays his part,
He also influencing in the due turn
These last clods where I track intelligence
By any glimmer, these four at his beck   1940
Ready to murder any, and, at their own,
As ready to murder him, — such make the world!
And, first effect of the new cause of things,
There they lie also duly, — the old pair
Of the weak head and not so wicked heart,
With the one Christian mother, wife and girl,
— Which three gifts seem to make an angel up, —
The world's first foot o' the dance is on their heads!
Still, I stand here, not off the stage though close
On the exit: and my last act, as my first,   1950
I owe the scene, and Him who armed me thus
With Paul's sword as with Peter's key. I smite
With my whole strength once more, ere end my part,
Ending, so far as man may, this offence.
And when I raise my arm, who plucks my sleeve?
Who stops me in the righteous function, — foe
Or friend? Oh, still as ever, friends are they
Who, in the interest of outraged truth
Deprecate such rough handling of a lie!
The facts being proved and incontestable,   1960
What is the last word I must listen to?
Perchance — "Spare yet a term this barren stock
We pray thee dig about and dung and dress
Till he repent and bring forth fruit even yet!"
Perchance — "So poor and swift a punishment
Shall throw him out of life with all that sin:
Let mercy rather pile up pain on pain
Till the flesh expiate what the soul pays else!"
Nowise! Remonstrants on each side commence
Instructing, there's a new tribunal now   1970
Higher than God's — the educated man's!
Nice sense of honor in the human breast
Supersedes here the old coarse oracle —
Confirming none the less a point or so
Wherein blind predecessors worked aright
By rule of thumb: as when Christ said, — when, where?

Enough, I find it pleaded in a place, —
"All other wrongs done, patiently I take.
But touch my honor and the case is changed!
I feel the due resentment, — *nemini*   1980
Honorem trado is my quick retort."
Right of Him, just as if pronounced to-day!
Still, should the old authority be mute
Or doubtful or in speaking clash with new,
The younger takes permission to decide.
At last we have the instinct of the world
Ruling its household without tutelage:
And while the two laws, human and divine,
Have busied finger with this tangled case,
In pushes the brisk junior, cuts the knot,   1990
Pronounces for acquittal. How it trips
Silverly o'er the tongue! "Remit the death!
Forgive, . . . well, in the old way, if thou please,
Decency and the relics of routine
Respected, — let the Count go free as air!
Since he may plead a priest's immunity, —
The minor orders help enough for that,
With Farinacci's license, — who decides
That the mere implication of such man,
So privileged, in any cause, before   2000
Whatever Court except the Spiritual,
Straight quashes law-procedure, — quash it, then!
Remains a pretty loophole of escape
Moreover, that, beside the patent fact
O' the law's allowance, there's involved the weal
O' the Popedom: a son's privilege at stake,
Thou wilt pretend the Church's interest,
Ignore all finer reasons to forgive!
But herein lies the crowning cogency —
(Let thy friends teach thee while thou tellest beads)   2010
That in this case the spirit of culture speaks,
Civilization is imperative.
To her shall we remand all delicate points
Henceforth, nor take irregular advice
O' the sly, as heretofore: she used to hint
Remonstrances, when law was out of sorts
Because a saucy tongue was put to rest,
An eye that roved was cured of arrogance:
But why be forced to mumble under breath
What soon shall be acknowledged as plain fact,   2020

Outspoken, say, in thy successor's time?
Methinks we see the golden age return!
Civilization and the Emperor
Succeed to Christianity and Pope.
One Emperor then, as one Pope now: meanwhile,
Anticipate a little! We tell thee 'Take
Guido's life, sapped society shall crash,
Whereof the main prop was, is, and shall be
— Supremacy of husband over wife!'
Does the man rule i' the house, and may his mate   2030
Because of any plea dispute the same?
Oh, pleas of all sorts shall abound, be sure,
One but allowed validity, — for, harsh
And savage, for, inept and silly-sooth,
For, this and that, will the ingenious sex
Demonstrate the best master e'er graced slave:
And there's but one short way to end the coil, —
Acknowledge right and reason steadily
I' the man and master: then the wife submits
To plain truth broadly stated. Does the time   2040
Advise we shift — a pillar? nay, a stake
Out of its place i' the social tenement?
One touch may send a shudder through the heap
And bring it toppling on our children's heads!
Moreover, if ours breed a qualm in thee,
Give thine own better feeling play for once!
Thou, whose own life winks o'er the socket-edge,
Wouldst thou it went out in such ugly snuff
As dooming sons dead, e'en though justice prompt?
Why, on a certain feast, Barabbas' self   2050
Was set free, not to cloud the general cheer:
Neither shalt thou pollute thy Sabbath close!
Mercy is safe and graceful. How one hears
The howl begin, scarce the three little taps
O' the silver mallet silent on thy brow, —
'His last act was to sacrifice a Count
And thereby screen a scandal of the Church!
Guido condemned, the Canon justified
Of course, — delinquents of his cloth go free!'
And so the Luthers chuckle, Calvins scowl,   2060
So thy hand helps Molinos to the chair
Whence he may hold forth till doom's day on just
These *petit-maître* priestlings, — in the choir
Sanctus et Benedictus, with a brush

Of soft guitar strings that obey the thumb,
Touched by the beduide, for accompaniment!
Does this give umbrage to a husband? Death
To the fool, and to the priest impunity!
But no impunity to any friend
So simply over-loyal as these four   2070
Who made religion of their patron's cause,
Believed in him and did his bidding straight,
Asked not one question but laid down the lives
This Pope took, — all four lives together make
Just his own length of days, — so, dead they lie,
As these were times when loyalty's a drug,
And zeal in a subordinate too cheap
And common to be saved when we spend life!
Come, 'tis too much good breath we waste in words:
The pardon, Holy Father! Spare grimace,   2080
Shrugs and reluctance! Are not we the world,
Art not thou Priam? Let soft culture plead
Hecuba-like, *'non tali'* (Virgil serves)
'Auxilio' and the rest! Enough, it works!
The Pope relaxes, and the Prince is loth,
The father's bowels yearn, the man's will bends,
Reply is apt. Our tears on tremble, hearts
Big with a benediction, wait the word
Shall circulate thro' the city in a trice,
Set every window flaring, give each man   2090
O' the mob his torch to wave for gratitude.
Pronounce then, for our breath and patience fail!"

I will, Sirs: but a voice other than yours
Quickens my spirit. "*Quis pro Domino?*
Who is upon the Lord's side?" asked the Count.
I, who write —
                "On receipt of this command,
Acquaint Count Guido and his fellows four
They die to-morrow: could it be to-night,
The better, but the work to do, takes time.
Set with all diligence a scaffold up,   2100
Not in the customary place, by Bridge
Saint Angelo, where die the common sort;
But since the man is noble, and his peers
By predilection haunt the People's Square,
There let him be beheaded in the midst,
And his companions hanged on either side:

So shall the quality see, fear and learn.
All which work takes time: till to-morrow, then,
Let there be prayer incessant for the five!"

For the main criminal I have no hope   2110
Except in such a suddenness of fate.
I stood at Naples once, a night so dark
I could have scarce conjectured there was earth
Anywhere, sky or sea or world at all:
But the night's black was burst through by a blaze —
Thunder struck blow on blow, earth groaned and bore,
Through her whole length of mountain visible:
There lay the city thick and plain with spires,
And, like a ghost disshrouded, white the sea.
So may the truth be flashed out by one blow,   2120
And Guido see, one instant, and be saved.
Else I avert my face, nor follow him
Into that sad obscure sequestered state
Where God unmakes but to remake the soul
He else made first in vain; which must not be.
Enough, for I may die this very night:
And how should I dare die, this man let live?

Carry this forthwith to the Governor!

ЛЛЛЛЛЛЛЛЛЛЛЛЛЛЛЛЛЛЛЛЛЛЛЛ

HOUSE

I

SHALL I sonnet-sing you about myself?
   Do I live in a house you would like to see?
Is it scant of gear, has it store of pelf?
   "Unlock my heart with a sonnet-key?"

II

Invite the world, as my betters have done?
   "Take notice: this building remains on view,
Its suites of reception every one,
   Its private apartment and bedroom too;

III

"For a ticket, apply to the Publisher."
   No: thanking the public, I must decline.
A peep through my window, if folk prefer;
   But, please you, no foot over threshold of mine!

IV

I have mixed with a crowd and heard free talk
   In a foreign land where an earthquake chanced:
And a house stood gaping, naught to balk
   Man's eye wherever he gazed or glanced.

V

The whole of the frontage shaven sheer,
   The inside gaped: exposed to day,

10

Right and wrong and common and queer,
  Bare, as the palm of your hand, it lay.   20

VI

The owner? Oh, he had been crushed, no doubt!
  "Odd tables and chairs for a man of wealth!
What a parcel of musty old books about!
  He smoked, — no wonder he lost his health!

VII

"I doubt if he bathed before he dressed.
  A brazier? — the pagan, he burned perfumes!
You see it is proved, what the neighbors guessed:
  His wife and himself had separate rooms."

VIII

Friends, the goodman of the house at least
  Kept house to himself till an earthquake came: 30
'Tis the fall of its frontage permits you feast
  On the inside arrangement you praise or blame.

IX

Outside should suffice for evidence:
  And whoso desires to penetrate
Deeper, must dive by the spirit-sense —
  No optics like yours, at any rate!

X

"Hoity toity! A street to explore,
  Your house the exception! *'With this same key
Shakespeare unlocked his heart,'* once more!"
  Did Shakespeare? If so, the less Shakespeare he!   40

SHOP

I

So, friend, your shop was all your house!
  Its front, astonishing the street,
Invited view from man and mouse
    To what diversity of treat
    Behind its glass — the single sheet!

II

What gimcracks, genuine Japanese:
   Gape-jaw and goggle-eye, the frog;
Dragons, owls, monkeys, beetles, geese;
   Some crushed-nosed human-hearted dog:
   Queer names, too, such a catalogue!   10

III

I thought "And he who owns the wealth
   Which blocks the window's vastitude,
— Ah, could I peep at him by stealth
   Behind his ware, pass shop, intrude
On house itself, what scenes were viewed!

IV

"If wide and showy thus the shop,
   What must the habitation prove?
The true house with no name a-top —
   The mansion, distant one remove,
   Once get him off his traffic-groove!   20

V

"Pictures he likes, or books perhaps;
   And as for buying most and best,
Commend me to these City chaps!
   Or else he's social, takes his rest
   On Sundays, with a Lord for guest.

VI

"Some suburb-palace, parked about
   And gated grandly, built last year:
The four-mile walk to keep off gout;
   Or big seat sold by bankrupt peer:
   But then he takes the rail, that's clear.   30

VII

"Or, stop! I wager, taste selects
   Some out o' the way, some all-unknown
Retreat: the neighborhood suspects
   Little that he who rambles lone
   Makes Rothschild tremble on his throne!"

VIII

Nowise! Nor Mayfair residence
　Fit to receive and entertain, —
Nor Hampstead villa's kind defence
　From noise and crowd, from dust and drain, —
　Nor country-box was soul's domain!　　　　　　**40**

IX

Nowise! At back of all that spread
　Of merchandise, woe's me, I find
A hole i' the wall where, heels by head,
　The owner couched, his ware behind,
　— In cupboard suited to his mind.

X

For why? He saw no use of life
　But, while he drove a roaring trade,
To chuckle "Customers are rife!"
　To chafe "So much hard cash outlaid
　Yet zero in my profits made!　　　　　　　　**50**

XI

"This novelty costs pains, but — takes?
　Cumbers my counter! Stock no more!
This article, no such great shakes,
　Fizzes like wildfire? Underscore
　The cheap thing — thousands to the fore!"

XII

'Twas lodging best to live most nigh
　(Cramp, coffinlike as crib might be)
Receipt of Custom; ear and eye
　Wanted no outworld: "Hear and see
　The bustle in the shop!" quoth he.　　　　　**60**

XIII

My fancy of a merchant-prince
　Was different. Through his wares we groped
Our darkling way to — not to mince
　The matter — no black den where moped
　The master if we interloped!

XIV

Shop was shop only: household-stuff?
　　What did he want with comforts there?
"Walls, ceiling, floor, stay blank and rough,
　　So goods on sale show rich and rare!
　　'*Sell and scud home*' be shop's affair!"　　　　**70**

XV

What might he deal in? Gems, suppose!
　　Since somehow business must be done
At cost of trouble, — see, he throws
　　You choice of jewels, every one,
　　Good, better, best, star, moon and sun!

XVI

Which lies within your power of purse?
　　This ruby that would tip aright
Solomon's sceptre? Oh, your nurse
　　Wants simply coral, the delight
　　Of teething baby, — stuff to bite!　　　　**80**

XVII

Howe'er your choice fell, straight you took
　　Your purchase, prompt your money rang
On counter, — scarce the man forsook
　　His study of the "Times," just swang
　　Till-ward his hand that stopped the clang, —

XVIII

Then off made buyer with a prize,
　　Then seller to his "Times" returned;
And so did day wear, wear, till eyes
　　Brightened apace, for rest was earned:
　　He locked door long ere candle burned.　　　　**90**

XIX

And whither went he? Ask himself,
　　Not me! To change of scene, I think.
Once sold the ware and pursed the pelf,
　　Chaffer was scarce his meat and drink,
　　Nor all his music — money-chink.

XX

Because a man has shop to mind
     In time and place, since flesh must live,
Needs spirit lack all life behind,
     All stray thoughts, fancies fugitive,
     All loves except what trade can give?   100

XXI

I want to know a butcher paints,
     A baker rhymes for his pursuit,
Candlestick-maker much acquaints
     His soul with song, or, haply mute,
     Blows out his brains upon the flute!

XXII

But — shop each day and all day long!
     Friend, your good angel slept, your star
Suffered eclipse, fate did you wrong!
     From where these sorts of treasures are,
     There should our hearts be — Christ, how far!   110

HERVÉ RIEL

I

On the sea and at the Hogue, sixteen hundred ninety-two,
     Did the English fight the French, — woe to France!
And, the thirty-first of May, helter-skelter through the blue,
Like a crowd of frightened porpoises a shoal of sharks pursue,
     Came crowding ship on ship to Saint-Malo on the Rance,
With the English fleet in view.

II

'Twas the squadron that escaped, with the victor in full chase;
     First and foremost of the drove, in his great ship, Damfreville;
          Close on him fled, great and small,
          Twenty-two good ships in all;   10
And they signalled to the place
"Help the winners of a race!
     Get us guidance, give us harbor, take us quick — or, quicker still,
     Here's the English can and will!"

III

Then the pilots of the place put out brisk and leapt on board;
    "Why, what hope or chance have ships like these to pass!" laughed
        they:
"Rocks to starboard, rocks to port, all the passage scarred and
        scored, —
Shall the 'Formidable' here, with her twelve and eighty guns,
    Think to make the river-mouth by the single narrow way,
Trust to enter — where 'tis ticklish for a craft of twenty tons,   20
    And with flow at full beside?
    Now, 'tis slackest ebb of tide.
  Reach the mooring? Rather say,
While rock stands or water runs,
    Not a ship will leave the bay!"

IV

Then was called a council straight.
Brief and bitter the debate:
"Here's the English at our heels; would you have them take in tow
All that's left us of the fleet, linked together stern and bow,
For a prize to Plymouth Sound?   30
Better run the ships aground!"
    (Ended Damfreville his speech).
"Not a minute more to wait!
    Let the Captains all and each
    Shove ashore, then blow up, burn the vessels on the beach!
France must undergo her fate.

V

"Give the word!" But no such word
Was ever spoke or heard;
    For up stood, for out stepped, for in struck amid all these
— A Captain? A Lieutenant? A Mate — first, second, third?   40
    No such man of mark, and meet
    With his betters to compete!
    But a simple Breton sailor pressed by Tourville for the fleet,
A poor coasting-pilot he, Hervé Riel the Croisickese.

VI

And "What mockery or malice have we here?" cries Hervé Riel:
    "Are you mad, you Malouins? Are you cowards, fools, or rogues?
Talk to me of rocks and shoals, me who took the soundings, tell
On my fingers every bank, every shallow, every swell
    'Twixt the offing here and Grève where the river disembogues?

Are you bought by English gold? Is it love the lying's for?   50
    Morn and eve, night and day,
    Have I piloted your bay,
Entered free and anchored fast at the foot of Solidor.
    Burn the fleet and ruin France? That were worse than fifty
        Hogues!
    Sirs, they know I speak the truth! Sirs, believe me there's a
        way!
Only let me lead the line,
    Have the biggest ship to steer,
    Get this 'Formidable' clear,
Make the others follow mine,
And I lead them, most and least, by a passage I know well,   60
    Right to Solidor past Grève,
        And there lay them safe and sound;
    And if one ship misbehave, —
        — Keel so much as grate the ground,
Why, I've nothing but my life, — here's my head!" cries Hervé Riel.

VII

Not a minute more to wait.
"Steer us in, then, small and great!
    Take the helm, lead the line, save the squadron!" cried its chief.
Captains, give the sailor place!
    He is Admiral, in brief.   70
Still the north-wind, by God's grace!
See the noble fellow's face
As the big ship, with a bound,
Clears the entry like a hound,
Keeps the passage, as its inch of way were the wide sea's profound!
    See, safe thro' shoal and rock,
    How they follow in a flock,
Not a ship that misbehaves, not a keel that grates the ground,
    Not a spar that comes to grief!
The peril, see, is past.   80
All are harbored to the last,
And just as Hervé Riel hollas "Anchor!" — sure as fate,
Up the English come, — too late!

VIII

So, the storm subsides to calm:
    They see the green trees wave
    On the heights o'erlooking Grève.
Hearts that bled are stanched with balm.

"Just our rapture to enhance,
    Let the English rake the bay,
Gnash their teeth and glare askance   90
    As they cannonade away!
'Neath rampired Solidor pleasant riding on the Rance!"
How hope succeeds despair on each Captain's countenance!
Out burst all with one accord,
    "This is Paradise for Hell!
        Let France, let France's King
        Thank the man that did the thing!"
What a shout, and all one word,
    "Hervé Riel!"
As he stepped in front once more,   100
    Not a symptom of surprise
    In the frank blue Breton eyes,
Just the same man as before.

IX

Then said Damfreville, "My friend,
I must speak out at the end,
    Though I find the speaking hard.
Praise is deeper than the lips:
You have saved the King his ships,
    You must name your own reward.
'Faith, our sun was near eclipse!   110
Demand whate'er you will,
France remains your debtor still.
Ask to heart's content and have! or my name's not Damfreville."

X

Then a beam of fun outbroke
On the bearded mouth that spoke,
As the honest heart laughed through
Those frank eyes of Breton blue:
"Since I needs must say my say,
    Since on board the duty's done,
    And from Malo Roads to Croisic Point, what is it but a run? —
Since 'tis ask and have, I may —   121
    Since the others go ashore —
Come! A good whole holiday!
    Leave to go and see my wife, whom I call the Belle Aurore!"
    That he asked and that he got, — nothing more.

XI

Name and deed alike are lost:
Not a pillar nor a post
 In his Croisic keeps alive the feat as it befell;
Not a head in white and black
On a single fishing-smack,   130
In memory of the man but for whom had gone to wrack
  All that France saved from the fight whence England bore the
   bell.
Go to Paris: rank on rank
 Search the heroes flung pell-mell
On the Louvre, face and flank!
 You shall look long enough ere you come to Hervé Riel.
So, for better and for worse,
Hervé Riel, accept my verse!
In my verse, Hervé Riel, do thou once more
Save the squadron, honor France, love thy wife the Belle Aurore! 140

FROM *Dramatic Idyls*
(1879)

⊓⊔⊓⊔⊓⊔⊓⊔⊓⊔⊓⊔⊓⊔⊓⊔⊓⊔⊓⊔⊓⊔⊓⊔⊓⊔⊓⊔⊓⊔

IVÀN IVÀNOVITCH

"They tell me, your carpenters," quoth I to my friend the Russ,
"Make a simple hatchet serve as a tool-box serves with us.
Arm but each man with his axe, 'tis a hammer and saw and plane
And chisel, and — what know I else? We should imitate in vain
The mastery wherewithal, by a flourish of just the adze,
He cleaves, clamps, dovetails in, — no need of our nails and brads, —
The manageable pine: 'tis said he could shave himself
With the axe, — so all adroit, now a giant and now an elf,
Does he work and play at once!"
                                        Quoth my friend the Russ to me,
"Ay, that and more beside on occasion! It scarce may be   **10**
You never heard tell a tale told children, time out of mind,
By father and mother and nurse, for a moral that's behind,
Which children quickly seize. If the incident happened at all,
We place it in Peter's time when hearts were great not small,
Germanized, Frenchified. I wager 'tis old to you
As the story of Adam and Eve, and possibly quite as true."

In the deep of our land, 'tis said, a village from out the woods
Emerged on the great main-road 'twixt two great solitudes.
Through forestry right and left, black verst and verst of pine,
From village to village runs the road's long wide bare line.   **20**
Clearance and clearance break the else-unconquered growth
Of pine and all that breeds and broods there, leaving loth
Man's inch of masterdom, — spot of life, spirt of fire, —
To star the dark and dread, lest right and rule expire

460

Throughout the monstrous wild, a-hungered to resume
Its ancient sway, suck back the world into its womb:
Defrauded by man's craft which clove from North to South
This highway broad and straight e'en from the Neva's mouth
To Moscow's gates of gold. So, spot of life and spirt
Of fire aforesaid, burn, each village death-begirt   30
By wall and wall of pine — unprobed undreamed abyss.

Early one winter morn, in such a village as this,
Snow-whitened everywhere except the middle road
Ice-roughed by track of sledge, there worked by his abode
Iv`an Iv`anovitch, the carpenter, employed
On a huge shipmast trunk; his axe now trimmed and toyed
With branch and twig, and now some chop athwart the bole
Changed bole to billets, bared at once the sap and soul.
About him, watched the work his neighbors sheepskin-clad;
Each bearded mouth puffed steam, each gray eye twinkled glad   40
To see the sturdy arm which, never stopping play,
Proved strong man's blood still boils, freeze winter as he may.
Sudden, a burst of bells. Out of the road, on edge
Of the hamlet — horse's hoofs galloping. "How, a sledge?
What's here?" cried all as — in, up to the open space,
Workyard and market-ground, folk's common meeting-place, —
Stumbled on, till he fell, in one last bound for life,
A horse: and, at his heels, a sledge held — "Dm`itri's wife!
Back without Dm`itri too! and children — where are they?
Only a frozen corpse!"
                   They drew it forth: then — Nay,   50
Not dead, though like to die! Gone hence a month ago:
Home again, this rough jaunt — alone through night and snow —
What can the cause be? Hark — Droug, old horse, how he groans:
His day's done! Chafe away, keep chafing, for she moans:
She's coming to! Give here: see, mother-kin, your friends!
Cheer up, all safe at home! Warm inside makes amends
For outside cold, — sup quick! Don't look as we were bears!
What is it startles you? What strange adventure stares
Up at us in your face? You know friends — which is which?
I'm V`assili, he's Serge`i, Iv`an Iv`anovitch . . ."   60

At the word, the woman's eyes, slow-wandering till they neared
The blue eyes o'er the bush of honey-colored beard,
Took in full light and sense and — torn to rags, some dream
Which hid the naked truth — O loud and long the scream
She gave, as if all power of voice within her throat

Poured itself wild away to waste in one dread note!
Then followed gasps and sobs, and then the steady flow
Of kindly tears: the brain was saved, a man might know.
Down fell her face upon the good friend's propping knee;
His broad hands smoothed her head, as fain to brush it free   70
From fancies, swarms that stung like bees unhived. He soothed —
"Loukèria, Loùscha!" — still he, fondling, smoothed and smoothed.
At last her lips formed speech.

                                        "Ivàn, dear — you indeed!
You, just the same dear you! While I . . . O intercede,
Sweet Mother, with thy Son Almighty — let his might
Bring yesterday once more, undo all done last night!
But this time yesterday, Ivàn, I sat like you,
A child on either knee, and, dearer than the two,
A babe inside my arms, close to my heart — that's lost
In morsels o'er the snow! Father, Son, Holy Ghost,   80
Cannot you bring again my blessed yesterday?"

When no more tears would flow, she told her tale: this way.

"Maybe, a month ago, — was it not? — news came here,
They wanted, deeper down, good workmen fit to rear
A church and roof it in. 'We'll go,' my husband said:
'None understands like me to melt and mould their lead.'
So, friends here helped us off — Ivàn, dear, you the first!
How gay we jingled forth, all five — (my heart will burst) —
While Dmìtri shook the reins, urged Droug upon his track!

"Well, soon the month ran out, we just were coming back,   90
When yesterday — behold, the village was on fire!
Fire ran from house to house. What help, as, nigh and nigher,
The flames came furious? 'Haste,' cried Dmìtri, 'men must do
The little good man may: to sledge and in with you,
You and our three! We check the fire by laying flat
Each building in its path, — I needs must stay for that, —
But you . . . no time for talk! Wrap round you every rug,
Cover the couple close, — you'll have the babe to hug.
No care to guide old Droug, he knows his way, by guess,
Once start him on the road: but chirrup, none the less!   100
The snow lies glib as glass and hard as steel, and soon
You'll have rise, fine and full, a marvel of a moon.
Hold straight up, all the same, this lighted twist of pitch!
Once home and with our friend Ivàn Ivànovitch,

All's safe: I have my pay in pouch, all's right with me,
So I but find as safe you and our precious three!
Off, Droug!' — because the flames had reached us, and the men
Shouted 'But lend a hand, Dmìtri — as good as ten!'

"So, in we bundled — I, and those God gave me once;
Old Droug, that's stiff at first, seemed youthful for the nonce: 110
He understood the case, galloping straight ahead.
Out came the moon: my twist soon dwindled, feebly red
In that unnatural day — yes, daylight, bred between
Moon-light and snow-light, lamped those grotto-depths which screen
Such devils from God's eye. Ah, pines, how straight you grow
Nor bend one pitying branch, true breed of brutal snow!
Some undergrowth had served to keep the devils blind
While we escaped outside their border!

                        "Was that — wind?
Anyhow, Droug starts, stops, back go his ears, he snuffs,
Snorts, — never such a snort! then plunges, knows the sough's   120
Only the wind: yet, no — our breath goes up too straight!
Still the low sound, — less low, loud, louder, at a rate
There's no mistaking more! Shall I lean out — look — learn
The truth whatever it be? Pad, pad! At last, I turn —

" 'Tis the regular pad of the wolves in pursuit of the life in the sledge!
An army they are: close-packed they press like the thrust of a wedge:
They increase as they hunt: for I see, through the pine-trunks ranged
    each side
Slip forth new fiend and fiend, make wider and still more wide
The four-footed steady advance. The foremost — none may pass:
They are elders and lead the line, eye and eye — green-glowing brass!
But a long way distant still. Droug, save us! He does his best: 131
Yet they gain on us, gain, till they reach, — one reaches . . . How
    utter the rest?
O that Satan-faced first of the band! How he lolls out the length of
    his tongue,
How he laughs and lets gleam his white teeth! He is on me, his paws
    pry among
The wraps and the rugs! O my pair, my twin-pigeons, lie still and seem
    dead!
Stepàn, he shall never have you for a meal, — here's your mother
    instead!
No, he will not be counselled — must cry, poor Stiòpka, so foolish!
    though first

Of my boy-brood, he was not the best: nay, neighbors have called him
    the worst.
He was puny, an undersized slip, —a darling to me, all the same!
But little there was to be praised in the boy, and a plenty to blame.
I loved him with heart and soul, yes — but, deal him a blow for a
    fault,   141
He would sulk for whole days. 'Foolish boy! lie still or the villain will
    vault,
Will snatch you from over my head!' No use! he cries, screams, — who
    can hold
Fast a boy in a frenzy of fear! It follows — as I foretold!
The Satan-face snatched and snapped: I tugged, I tore — and then
His brother too needs must shriek! If one must go, 'tis men
The Tsar needs, so we hear, not ailing boys! Perhaps
My hands relaxed their grasp, got tangled in the wraps:
God, he was gone! I looked: there tumbled the cursed crew,
Each fighting for a share: too busy to pursue!   150
That's so far gain at least: Droug, gallop another verst
Or two, or three — God sends we beat them, arrive the first!
A mother who boasts two boys was ever accounted rich:
Some have not a boy: some have, but lose him, — God knows which
Is worse: how pitiful to see your weakling pine
And pale and pass away! Strong brats, this pair of mine!

"O misery! for while I settle to what near seems
Content, I am 'ware again of the tramp, and again there gleams —
Point and point — the line, eyes, levelled green brassy fire!
So soon is resumed your chase? Will nothing appease, naught tire 160
The furies? And yet I think — I am certain the race is slack,
And the numbers are nothing like. Not a quarter of the pack!
Feasters and those full-fed are staying behind . . . Ah why?
We'll sorrow for that too soon! Now, — gallop, reach home, and die,
Nor ever again leave house, to trust our life in the trap
For life — we call a sledge! Teriòscha, in my lap!
Yes, I'll lie down upon you, tight-tie you with the strings
Here — of my heart! No fear, this time, your mother flings . . .
Flings? I flung? Never! but think! — a woman, after all
Contending with a wolf! Save you I must and shall,   170
Terentìì!
        "How now? What, you still head the race,
Your eyes and tongue and teeth crave fresh food, Satan-face?
There and there! Plain I struck green fire out! Flash again?
All a poor fist can do to damage eyes proves vain!
My fist — why not crunch that? He is wanton for . . . O God,

Why give this wolf his taste? Common wolves scrape and prod
The earth till out they scratch some corpse — mere putrid flesh!
Why must this glutton leave the faded, choose the fresh?
Terentiì — God, feel! — his neck keeps fast thy bag
Of holy things, saints' bones, this Satan-face will drag   180
Forth, and devour along with him, our Pope declared
The relics were to save from danger!

                              "Spurned, not spared!
'Twas through my arms, crossed arms, he — nuzzling now with snout,
Now ripping, tooth and claw — plucked, pulled Terentiì out,
A prize indeed! I saw — how could I else but see? —
My precious one — I bit to hold back — pulled from me!
Up came the others, fell to dancing — did the imps! —
Skipped as they scampered round. There's one is gray, and limps:
Who knows but old bad Màrpha, — she always owed me spite
And envied me my births, — skulks out of doors at night   190
And turns into a wolf, and joins the sisterhood,
And laps the youthful life, then slinks from out the wood,
Squats down at door by dawn, spins there demure as erst
— No strength, old crone, — not she! — to crawl forth half a verst!

"Well, I escaped with one: 'twixt one and none there lies
The space 'twixt heaven and hell. And see, a rose-light dyes
The endmost snow: 'tis dawn, 'tis day, 'tis safe at home!
We have outwitted you! Ay, monsters, snarl and foam,
Fight each the other fiend, disputing for a share, —
Forgetful, in your greed, our finest off we bear,   200
Tough Droug and I, — my babe, my boy that shall be man,
My man that shall be more, do all a hunter can
To trace and follow and find and catch and crucify
Wolves, wolfkins, all your crew! A thousand deaths shall die
The whimperingest cub that ever squeezed the teat!
'Take that!' We'll stab you with, — 'the tenderness we met
When, wretches, you danced round — not this, thank God — not this!
Hellhounds, we balk you!'

                              "But — Ah, God above! — Bliss, bliss —
Not the band, no! And yet — yes, for Droug knows him! One —
This only of them all has said 'She saves a son!'   210
His fellows disbelieve such luck: but he believes,
He lets them pick the bones, laugh at him in their sleeves:
He's off and after us, — one speck, one spot, one ball
Grows bigger, bound on bound, — one wolf as good as all!

Oh but I know the trick! Have at the snaky tongue!
That's the right way with wolves! Go, tell your mates I wrung
The panting morsel out, left you to howl your worst!
Now for it — now! Ah me! I know him — thrice-accurst
Satan-face, — him to the end my foe!

                           "All fight's in vain:
This time the green brass points pierce to my very brain.   220
I fall — fall as I ought — quite on the babe I guard:
I overspread with flesh the whole of him. Too hard
To die this way, torn piecemeal? Move hence? Not I — one inch!
Gnaw through me, through and through: flat thus I lie nor flinch!
O God, the feel of the fang furrowing my shoulder! — see!
It grinds — it grates the bone. O Kìrill under me,
Could I do more? Beside he knew wolf's way to win:
I clung, closed round like wax: yet in he wedged and in,
Past my neck, past my breasts, my heart, until . . . how feels
The onion-bulb your knife parts, pushing through its peels,   230
Till out you scoop its clove wherein lie stalk and leaf
And bloom and seed unborn?

                         "That slew me, yes, in brief,
I died then, dead I lay doubtless till Droug stopped
Here, I suppose. I come to life, I find me propped
Thus — how or when or why, — I know not. Tell me, friends,
All was a dream: laugh quick and say the nightmare ends!
Soon I shall find my house: 'tis over there: in proof,
Save for that chimney heaped with snow, you'd see the roof .
Which holds my three — my two — my one — not one?

                                 "Life's mixed
With misery, yet we live — must live. The Satan fixed   240
His face on mine so fast, I took its print as pitch
Takes what it cools beneath. Ivàn Ivànovitch,
'Tis you unharden me, you thaw, disperse the thing!
Only keep looking kind, the horror will not cling.
Your face smooths fast away each print of Satan. Tears
— What good they do! Life's sweet, and all its after-years,
Ivàn Ivànovitch, I owe you! Yours am I!
May God reward you, dear!"

                        Down she sank. Solemnly
Ivàn rose, raised his axe, — for fitly, as she knelt,
Her head lay: well-apart, each side, her arms hung, — dealt   250

Lightning-swift thunder-strong one blow — no need of more!
Headless she knelt on still: that pine was sound at core
(Neighbors were used to say) — cast-iron-kernelled — which
Taxed for a second stroke Ivàn Ivànovitch.

The man was scant of words as strokes. "It had to be:
I could no other: God it was bade 'Act for me!' "
Then stooping, peering round — what is it now he lacks?
A proper strip of bark wherewith to wipe his axe.
Which done, he turns, goes in, closes the door behind.
The others mute remain, watching the blood-snake wind   260
Into a hiding-place among the splinter-heaps.

At length, still mute, all move: one lifts, — from where it steeps
Redder each ruddy rag of pine, — the head: two more
Take up the dripping body: then, mute still as before,
Move in a sort of march, march on till marching ends
Opposite to the church; where halting, — who suspends,
By its long hair, the thing, deposits in its place
The piteous head: once more the body shows no trace
Of harm done: there lies whole the Loùscha, maid and wife
And mother, loved until this latest of her life.   270
Then all sit on the bank of snow which bounds a space
Kept free before the porch for judgment: just the place!

Presently all the souls, man, woman, child, which make
The village up, are found assembling for the sake
Of what is to be done. The very Jews are there:
A Gipsy-troop, though bound with horses for the Fair,
Squats with the rest. Each heart with its conception seethes
And simmers, but no tongue speaks: one may say, — none breathes.

Anon from out the church totters the Pope — the priest —
Hardly alive, so old, a hundred years at least.   280
With him, the Commune's head, a hoary senior too,
Stàrosta, that's his style, — like Equity Judge with you, —
Natural Jurisconsult: then, fenced about with furs,
Pomeschìk, — Lord of the Land, who wields — and none demurs —
A power of life and death. They stoop, survey the corpse.

Then, straightened on his staff, the Stàrosta — the thorpe's
Sagaciousest old man — hears what you just have heard,
From Droug's first inrush, all, up to Ivàn's last word
"God bade me act for him: I dared not disobey!"

Silence   the Pomeschik broke with "A wild wrong way   290
Of righting wrong — if wrong there were, such wrath to rouse!
Why was not law observed? What article allows
Whoso may please to play the judge, and, judgment dealt,
Play executioner, as promptly as we pelt
To death, without appeal, the vermin whose sole fault
Has been — it dared to leave the darkness of its vault,
Intrude upon our day! Too sudden and too rash!
What was this woman's crime? Suppose the church should crash
Down where I stand, your lord: bound are my serfs to dare
Their utmost that I 'scape: yet, if the crashing scare   300
My children, — as you are, — if sons fly, one and all,
Leave father to his fate, — poor cowards though I call
The runaways, I pause before I claim their life
Because they prized it more than mine. I would each wife
Died for her husband's sake, each son to save his sire:
'Tis glory, I applaud — scarce duty, I require.
Iván Ivànovitch has done a deed that's named
Murder by law and me: who doubts, may speak unblamed!"

All turned to the old Pope. "Ay, children, I am old —
How old, myself have got to know no longer. Rolled   310
Quite round, my orb of life, from infancy to age,
Seems passing back again to youth. A certain stage
At least I reach, or dream I reach, where I discern
Truer truths, laws behold more lawlike than we learn
When first we set our foot to tread the course I trod
With man to guide my steps: who leads me now is God.
'Your young men shall see visions:' and in my youth I saw
And paid obedience to man's visionary law:
'Your old men shall dream dreams:' and, in my age, a hand
Conducts me through the cloud round law to where I stand   320
Firm on its base, — know cause, who, before, knew effect.

"The world lies under me: and nowhere I detect
So great a gift as this — God's own — of human life.
'Shall the dead praise thee?' No! 'The whole live world is rife,
God, with thy glory,' rather! Life then, God's best of gifts,
For what shall man exchange? For life — when so he shifts
The weight and turns the scale, lets life for life restore
God's balance, sacrifice the less to gain the more,
Substitute — for low life, another's or his own —
Life large and liker God's who gave it: thus alone   330
May life extinguish life that life may trulier be!

How low this law descends on earth, is not for me
To trace: complexed becomes the simple, intricate
The plain, when I pursue law's winding. 'Tis the straight
Outflow of law I know and name: to law, the fount
Fresh from God's footstool, friends, follow while I remount.

"A mother bears a child: perfection is complete
So far in such a birth. Enabled to repeat
The miracle of life, — herself was born so just
A type of womankind, that God sees fit to trust   340
Her with the holy task of giving life in turn.
Crowned by this crowning pride, — how say you, should she spurn
Regality — discrowned, unchilded, by her choice
Of barrenness exchanged for fruit which made rejoice
Creation, though life's self were lost in giving birth
To life more fresh and fit to glorify God's earth?
How say you, should the hand God trusted with life's torch
Kindled to light the world — aware of sparks that scorch,
Let fall the same? Forsooth, her flesh a fire-flake stings:
The mother drops the child! Among what monstrous things   350
Shall she be classed? Because of motherhood, each male
Yields to his partner place, sinks proudly in the scale:
His strength owned weakness, wit — folly, and courage — fear,
Beside the female proved male's mistress — only here.
The fox-dam, hunger-pined, will slay the felon sire
Who dares assault her whelp: the beaver, stretched on fire,
Will die without a groan: no pang avails to wrest
Her young from where they hide — her sanctuary breast.
What's here then? Answer me, thou dead one, as, I trow,
Standing at God's own bar, he bids thee answer now!   360
Thrice crowned wast thou — each crown of pride, a child — thy
    charge!
Where are they? Lost? Enough: no need that thou enlarge
On how or why the loss: life left to utter 'lost'
Condemns itself beyond appeal. The soldier's post
Guards from the foe's attack the camp he sentinels:
That he no traitor proved, this and this only tells —
Over the corpse of him trod foe to foe's success.
Yet — one by one thy crowns torn from thee — thou no less
To scare the world, shame God, — livedst! I hold He saw
The unexampled sin, ordained the novel law,   370
Whereof first instrument was first intelligence
Found loyal here. I hold that, failing human sense,
The very earth had oped, sky fallen, to efface

Humanity's new wrong, motherhood's first disgrace.
Earth oped not, neither fell the sky, for prompt was found
A man and man enough, head-sober and heart-sound,
Ready to hear God's voice, resolute to obey.
Ivàn Ivànovitch, I hold, has done, this day,
No otherwise than did, in ages long ago,
Moses when he made known the purport of that flow   380
Of fire athwart the law's twain-tables! I proclaim
Ivàn Ivànovitch God's servant!"

              At which name
Uprose that creepy whisper from out the crowd, is wont
To swell and surge and sink when fellow-men confront
A punishment that falls on fellow flesh and blood,
Appallingly beheld — shudderingly understood,
No less, to be the right, the just, the merciful.
"God's servant!" hissed the crowd.

                    When that Amen grew dull
And died away and left acquittal plain adjudged,
"Amen!" last sighed the lord. "There's none shall say I grudged   390
Escape from punishment in such a novel case.
Deferring to old age and holy life, — be grace
Granted! say I. No less, scruples might shake a sense
Firmer than I boast mine. Law's law, and evidence
Of breach therein lies plain, — blood-red-bright, — all may see!
Yet all absolve the deed: absolved the deed must be!

"And next — as mercy rules the hour — methinks 'twere well
You signify forthwith its sentence, and dispel
The doubts and fears, I judge, which busy now the head
Law puts a halter round — a halo — you, instead!   400
Ivàn Ivànovitch — what think you he expects
Will follow from his feat? Go, tell him — law protects
Murder, for once: no need he longer keep behind
The Sacred Pictures — where skulks Innocence enshrined,
Or I missay! Go, some! You others, haste and hide
The dismal object there: get done, whate'er betide!"

So, while the youngers raised the corpse, the elders trooped
Silently to the house: where halting, some one stooped,
Listened beside the door; all there was silent too.
Then they held counsel; then pushed door and, passing through,   410
Stood in the murderer's presence.

                        Ivàn Ivànovitch
Knelt, building on the floor that Kremlin rare and rich
He deftly cut and carved on lazy winter nights.
Some five young faces watched, breathlessly, as, to rights,
Piece upon piece, he reared the fabric nigh complete.
Stèscha, Ivàn's old mother, sat spinning by the heat
Of the oven where his wife Kàtia stood baking bread.
Ivàn's self, as he turned his honey-colored head,
Was just in act to drop, 'twixt fir-cones, — each a dome, —
The scooped-out yellow gourd presumably the home   420
Of Kolokol the Big: the bell, therein to hitch,
— An acorn-cup — was ready: Ivàn Ivànovitch
Turned with it in his mouth.

                        They told him he was free
As air to walk abroad. "How otherwise?" asked he.

FROM *Jocoseria*
(1883)

```
ППППППППППППППППППППППП
```

NEVER THE TIME AND THE PLACE

NEVER the time and the place
    And the loved one all together!
This path — how soft to pace!
    This May — what magic weather!
Where is the loved one's face?
In a dream that loved one's face meets mine,
    But the house is narrow, the place is bleak
Where, outside, rain and wind combine
    With a furtive ear, if I strive to speak,
    With a hostile eye at my flushing cheek,   10
With a malice that marks each word, each sign!
O enemy sly and serpentine,
    Uncoil thee from the waking man!
        Do I hold the Past
        Thus firm and fast
    Yet doubt if the Future hold I can?
This path so soft to pace shall lead
Thro' the magic of May to herself indeed!
Or narrow if needs the house must be,
Outside are the storms and strangers: we —   20
Oh, close, safe, warm sleep I and she,
    — I and she!

WHY I AM A LIBERAL

(1885)

"WHY?" Because all I haply can and do,
    All that I am now, all I hope to be, —
    Whence comes it save from fortune setting free
Body and soul the purpose to pursue,
God traced for both? If fetters, not a few,
    Of prejudice, convention, fall from me,
    These shall I bid men — each in his degree
Also God-guided — bear, and gayly too?

But little do or can the best of us:
    That little is achieved through Liberty.   10
Who, then, dares hold, emancipated thus,
    His fellow shall continue bound? Not I,
Who live, love, labor freely, nor discuss
    A brother's right to freedom. That is "Why."

FROM *Asolando*
(1889)

ЛЛЛЛЛЛЛЛЛЛЛЛЛЛЛЛЛЛЛЛЛЛЛЛЛ

SUMMUM BONUM

ALL the breath and the bloom of the year in the bag of one bee:
    All the wonder and wealth of the mine in the heart of one gem:
In the core of one pearl all the shade and the shine of the sea:
    Breath and bloom, shade and shine, — wonder, wealth, and —
        how far above them —
        Truth, that's brighter than gem,
        Trust, that's purer than pearl, —
Brightest truth, purest trust in the universe — all were for me
        In the kiss of one girl.

EPILOGUE *to* ASOLANDO

At the midnight in the silence of the sleep-time,
    When you set your fancies free,
Will they pass to where — by death, fools think, imprisoned —
Low he lies who once so loved you, whom you loved so,
      — Pity me?

Oh to love so, be so loved, yet so mistaken!
    What had I on earth to do
With the slothful, with the mawkish, the unmanly?
Like the aimless, helpless, hopeless, did I drivel
      — Being — who?   10

One who never turned his back but marched breast forward,
    Never doubted clouds would break,
Never dreamed, though right were worsted, wrong would triumph,
Held we fall to rise, are baffled to fight better,
      Sleep to wake.

No, at noonday in the bustle of man's work-time
    Greet the unseen with a cheer!
Bid him forward, breast and back as either should be,
"Strive and thrive!" cry "Speed, — fight on, fare ever
      There as here!"   20

NOTES

A selected bibliography of critical and scholarly studies of Browning's works appears on pages xxxi-ii, where full data are provided for each of them. These works are referred to in the notes that follow merely by author and page (for example, "Symons, p. 10").

Where the publishing history of a poem has any special complexity or importance, the facts are stated within the notes for the poem. Otherwise, the date of first publication is given after the title in the notes — for example, "Cleon (1855)" — and the collection in which it first saw print is that named in the left-hand running-heads of the proper pages of the text.

The reference in the text for each note is shown by two numbers: the first, in italics, is the page number; the second, the line number. Thus, "*125*, 39" refers to page 125, line 39.

PIPPA PASSES. *Page 3.*

This play was first published in April, 1841, as the initial number of *Bells and Pomegranates* (1841-46), a series of inexpensive pamphlets that Browning hoped would introduce his plays and poems to a wider audience than he could otherwise reach.

Browning had visited Asolo, the setting of his play, in the spring of 1838 on his first trip to Italy. The picturesque walled hilltown, thirty miles to the west of Venice, had fascinated him, and he had spent four days in and around it. In *Pippa Passes* Browning portrays the varied and colorful life of this Italian town, including its foreign art students, its political conspirators, and the Austrian police.

INTRODUCTION

5, 88. *martagon:* a kind of lily.

5, 90. *Turk bird:* turkey.

6, 100. *weevil and chafer:* small insects of the beetle family.

6, 131. *Possagno church:* Possagno is only four miles from Asolo. Its church, shaped in the circular form of a Roman temple, was designed by the sculptor Canova, who was born in Possagno. Jules, as a sculptor, might very well wish to be married in Canova's town and church.

8, 213. *cicala:* cicada, or locust.

477

I. Morning

9, 28. *Saint Mark's:* The cupolas and steeples of Venice thirty miles to the east can be seen from Asolo on clear days, and also the outline of Vicenza to the southwest and Padua, twenty-five miles to the south.

10, 53. *wittol:* a cuckold, a man whose wife is unfaithful.

10, 58. *Duomo:* cathedral.

11, 76. *proof-mark:* the sign on a print that shows it is one of the first impressions from the plate.

11, 83. *coil:* fuss or stir.

12, 119-20. The face of a murdered man, according to an old superstition, turns to look toward the sky for vengeance.

13, 170. *campanula:* Latin for "little bell," the name of the harebell, or bellflower.

15, 235. *heartsease:* a kind of violet.

18, 332. *Canova:* an Italian sculptor (1757-1822). See the note to line 131 of *Introduction* above.

18, 357. *Psiche-fanciulla:* This statue of Psyche as a young girl with a butterfly is considered one of Canova's finest works. It is in the gallery at Possagno (see the note to line 131 of *Introduction* above).

18, 361. *Pietà:* a statue of the Virgin Mary with the dead Christ in her arms. It is in the church at Possagno.

19, 375. *Malamocco:* a town near Venice, on an island of the same name.

19, 376. *Alciphron:* a Greek writer of about 200 A.D.

19, 379. *lire:* The *lira* (plural, *lire*) is an Italian coin formerly worth about twenty cents.

19, 381. *Tydeus:* one of the leaders in the expedition of the "Seven against Thebes" in Greek legend.

19, 381. *the Academy:* the Academy of Fine Arts at Venice.

19, 384. *the Fenice:* the Phoenix, a leading theater in Venice.

19, 401. *Hannibal Scratchy:* a garbled burlesque form of the name of the Italian artist, Annibale Caracci.

II. Noon

20, 26. *Psyche:* a mortal maiden so lovely that Venus was jealous of her beauty; she was beloved by Cupid.

21, 39-40. Coluthus was a sixth-century Greek poet; Cardinal Bessarion discovered one of his poems in the fifteenth century.

21, 46-47. Antinous: most arrogant of the suitors for Penelope, slain thus by Odysseus on his return from Troy.

21, 50. *Almaign:* German.

21, 54. *Hippolyta:* Queen of the Amazons.

21, 59. *bay-filleted:* crowned by bay, or laurel, leaves; *thunder-free* because a crown of laurel was supposed in ancient times to protect the wearer from lightning.

21, 60-61. *Hipparchus:* a tyrant of Athens. He was slain in 514 B.C. by assassins who had concealed their daggers in myrtle branches borne by them during the festival of the Panathenaea.

22, 92. Dryad: a tree nymph.

26, 258. Kate the Queen: Caterina Cornaro, a queen of the island of Cyprus in the fifteenth century, had been forced to abdicate by Venice in 1487 but had been given the castle at Asolo as a place of residence. Here she kept elaborate court for twenty years, surrounded by twelve maids of honor, eighty serving-men, and her favorite parrots, apes, peacocks, and hounds. She was loved by the people of Asolo for her many acts of charity.

26, 272. The Cornaro: See the preceding note.

28, 328. Bluphocks: Browning adds a footnote to his first use of the name in the play: "He maketh his sun to rise on the evil and on the good, and sendeth his rain on the just and on the unjust." The name is traditionally supposed to be a playful allusion to the *Edinburgh Review,* which was bound in a cover of blue fox.

28, 329. Intendant: superintendent (of the estates just inherited by the Bishop).

28, 334. grig: cricket.

28, 339. Chaldee: a Semitic dialect (parts of the books of Daniel and Ezra were written in it).

28, 345. Celarent, Darii, Ferio: The first three of a series of coined words employed by logicians as a device for memorizing the nineteen valid forms of the syllogism.

28, 347. posy: poesy, rhyme.

29, 355. Bishop Beveridge: He appears here merely as a pun on *beverage.* Bishop Beveridge (1626-1707) was a Calvinist divine.

29, 356-58. Charon in Greek mythology ferries the dead across the River Styx in the other world. A *wherry* is a small boat, and an *obolus* is a small Athenian coin.

29, 360. zwanzigers: Austrian coins (paid Bluphocks by the Austrian police).

29, 367. Prince Metternich: the chief Austrian statesman (1773-1859).

29, 391. Carbonari: a secret patriotic organization whose aim was to liberate Italy from Austria.

29, 392. Spielberg: an Austrian prison notorious for its severity.

III. EVENING

30, 6. Lucius Junius: Lucius Junius Brutus led the revolt which drove the Tarquins from Rome and established the Roman Republic (509 B.C.).

30, 14. old Franz: Francis I, emperor of Austria.

00, 10. *Pellicos. Silvio Pollico*, Italian patriot and member of the Carbonari, who was arrested by the Austrians and imprisoned for eleven years.

33, 122-23. *Andrea . . . Pier . . . Gualtier:* former conspirators against Austria.

33, 135. *How . . . the Austrians got these provinces:* The Austrian armies had taken the greater part of Northern Italy in the summer of 1813. The Congress of Vienna granted one concession after another until, by 1815, Austria held all of Italy.

33, 148-50. A quotation from the book of Revelation (2:28; 22:16).

34, 164-222. This song, in a somewhat different form, appeared in *The Monthly Repository* for November, 1835.

36, 236. *fig-peckers:* a kind of small bird that lives on figs.

36, 251. *Deuzans,* etc.: varieties of apples.

37, 293. *ortolans:* small singing birds, regarded as a great delicacy.

37, 295. *polenta:* a mush, or pudding, made of corn meal or chestnut meal.

IV. NIGHT

39, 3. *Benedicto benedicatur:* a form of blessing.

40, 74. *podere:* farm.

41, 87. *soldo:* a small Italian coin.

43, 180-81. *Miserere mei, Domine:* "Be merciful to me, O Lord!"

43, 83. *dray:* nest.

43, 186. *hedge-shrew:* field mouse; *lob-worm:* a worm resembling an earthworm, but larger.

44, 228. *trim:* costume.

45, 269. *Mavis* and *throstle* are thrushes; the *merle* is a blackbird.

45, 272. *howlet:* owlet.

45, 275. *complines:* the last religious service of the day, said after nightfall traditionally (sometimes earlier in the present).

CAVALIER TUNES (1842). *Page 47.*

The three songs express the gallantry and intrepidity of the Royalist followers of Charles I. As we know from his play, *Strafford* (1837), and from other evidence, Browning's stronger sympathies were with the supporters of Parliament, the adversaries of the Cavaliers. But Browning was already working his special vein as a poet, attempting insight into the minds of men and women, and speaking in his poetry from points of view other than his own.

A brief sketch of the historical background of the songs will identify several of the names that occur in them (which are italicized): The "Long Parliament," elected in 1640, was predominantly Puritan and opposed to the views of Charles I, especially in regard to religious issues and the extent of the powers of Parliament. John *Pym* and John *Hampden* were leaders of the opposition to Charles. They were supported by Sir Arthur *Hazelrig,* Nathaniel *Fiennes,* and *"young Harry,"* or Sir Henry Vane the younger. On August 22, 1642, the King raised the royal standard at *Nottingham,* an act tantamount to a declaration of war and a call to all loyal subjects to rally round his banner. His nephew, *Prince Rupert* of Bavaria, who joined him at Nottingham, became his great general of cavalry. The Parliamentary party were called *"crop-headed,"* or *"Roundheads,"* because they cropped their hair short, whereas the aristocratic Cavaliers wore long, flowing locks.

I. MARCHING ALONG

This song represents the Cavaliers gathering to the King's standard at Nottingham.

47, 3. pressing a troop: conscripting them for military service.

47, 7. carles: churls.

47, 8. parles: talk.

II. GIVE A ROUSE

This song represents a considerably later period in the struggle. It is sung by a dauntless old Cavalier who has seen his son George shot down at his side but who is still, "in hell's despite," determined to fight out the war for his king. A *rouse* is a toast, or cheer.

48, 16. Noll's damned troopers: Oliver Cromwell's famous Ironsides.

III. BOOT AND SADDLE

This song suggests the last period of the war, with the Cavaliers hard pressed. The speaker (or singer) is urging his troop to horse in order to break the Roundheads' siege of his own castle. Castle Brancepeth is situated near Durham in the northern part of England.

MY LAST DUCHESS. *Page 49.*

Originally published in *Dramatic Lyrics* (1842) under the title *Italy,* with *Count Gismond* following it as *France.*

The duke of the poem epitomizes the ruthless egoism, the pride in ancient family, the love of the arts representative of more than one ruler in Italy in the Renaissance. For the probable identification of the speaker in the poem with Alphonso II, a sixteenth-century duke of Ferrara, see Louis S. Friedland's highly interesting article in *Studies in Philology,* XXXIII (1936), 656-84.

49, 3. Frà Pandolf: an imaginary artist. *Frà* shows that he was a brother in a monastic order.

50, 45-56. When Browning was asked the meaning of these lines

many years later, he replied that the commands were to have her put
to death. "Or," he added after a pause, "he might have had her shut
up in a convent." *As if* of line 47 suggests that she is dead; and to
conclude a second marriage with his former wife alive would probably
under any circumstances have been awkward for the Duke.

51, 56. Claus of Innsbruck: an imaginary artist.

COUNT GISMOND. *Page 51.*

Count Gismond appeared originally in *Dramatic Lyrics* (1842) as
France following *My Last Duchess*, which bore the title *Italy*. The
count of this poem offers a strong contrast to the Renaissance Italian
duke of *My Last Duchess. Count Gismond* represents the chivalric
spirit of France in the middle ages, especially of Provence, the birthplace of the troubadours.

55, 124. tercel: a falcon. The line is, of course, addressed to Gismond, who has just entered, apparently hard upon the heels of the
announcer of his arrival in line 123.

INCIDENT OF THE FRENCH CAMP (1842). *Page 55.*

Browning stated that the story of the poem is true, the hero of
the incident being a man rather than a boy; but his source has never
been found. The anecdote is typical of the legends told of the devotion of Napoleon's soldiers to their emperor.

55, 1. Ratisbon: the Bavarian city of Regensburg, on the Danube,
stormed by Napoleon on April 23, 1809.

55, 11. Lannes: Napoleon's marshal, who led the assault in person.

SOLILOQUY OF THE SPANISH CLOISTER (1842). *Page 56.*

This poem is often presented with stress upon the intense and
vicious quality of the hatred of the speaker; but the mood seems less
grave than such an emphasis implies. The *Soliloquy* is a humorous
poem, though, as Arthur Symons says (p. 56), the humor is "grotesque, bitter and pungent." Browning has chosen details that portray
ineffectual malice rather than something more positively sinister. The
speaker has apparently contented himself, so far at least, with such
acts of vengeance as nipping Brother Lawrence's flowers "on the sly";
and his plans for damning the soul of his fellow monk suggest that he
has not thought them out at much length or weighed the implications
very seriously — he himself seems extremely well acquainted with his
obscene French novel that he supposes, nevertheless, to be able to
destroy Brother Lawrence's soul with a single glance at the "woeful

sixteenth print." His last, and absurdly anticlimactic, plot is for a tricky bargain with Satan to induce that Prince of Darkness to do nothing more ambitious in iniquity than to blast one of poor Brother Lawrence's favorite shrubs. The concluding three lines of the poem leave the reader with no sober sense of having looked into a revelation of evil but with an impression of comic irony.

57, 10. *Salve tibi:* "hail to thee."

57, 31. *Barbary corsair:* a pirate of the Barbary Coast of northern Africa.

58, 39. *Arian:* a heretic, a follower of Arius, fourth-century theologian who attacked the doctrine of the Trinity, holding that the Son, or Christ, was created by and inferior to the Father.

58, 49. Galatians 5:19-21 lists seventeen sinful practices. Or Browning may have in mind Galatians 3:10 — "Cursed is every one that continueth not in all things which are written in the book of the law to do them." Browning probably uses "twenty-nine" simply as a large and indefinite number, as the French use *trente-six* (Cooke, p. 364).

58, 56. *Manichee:* a heretic; specifically, a follower of Manes, a Persian, who attempted to combine Oriental philosophy with Christianity.

58, 70. *Hy, Zy, Hine:* The words are probably intended to indicate the ringing of the vesper bell at this point in the monologue.

58, 71-72. *Plena gratiâ, Ave, Virgo:* "Hail Virgin, full of grace." The words indicate the beginning of one of the prayers of the vesper service (usually *"Ave Maria, gratiâ plena"* — "Hail, Mary, full of grace").

IN A GONDOLA (1842). *Page 59.*

Browning composed the first seven lines of the poem to accompany a picture, *The Serenade,* by the artist Daniel Maclise, in the catalogue of an exhibition. Browning had not seen Maclise's canvas but had dashed off the verses at the urging of John Forster, a mutual friend, and according to Forster's description of the painting. When Browning did see the picture, he recalled much later, "I thought the Serenader too jolly somewhat for the notion I got from Forster — and I took up the subject in my own way."

In a Gondola has been admired for its opulence of fancy and color, its metrical magic, and its skill in conveying the mood of a love that knows it is only "an inch from Death's black fingers." The melodramatic ending probably owes something to Browning's attempts to write a successful play for the Victorian stage at the time of composing the poem.

59, 22. *the Three:* They are later called Paul, Gian, and Himself (i.e., the woman's husband).

60, 33. *cruce:* crucible.

60, 47. *wried:* wrung.

62, 106-107. See note to line 22.

62, 108. *stylet:* stiletto, or dagger.

62, 113. *Lido:* an island close to Venice which holds a Jewish cemetery. The graves are called *wet* because at highest tide the land holding them is flooded; *accursed* because they are the graves of heretics.

63, 127. *Giudecca:* a canal in Venice.

63, 141. *lory:* parrot.

64, 180. *dry limpet:* the limpet comes out of his shell when he hears the sound of the water (*lymph*).

64, 186. *Schidone:* Bartolomeo Schedone (1560-1616), an Italian painter.

64, 188. *Haste-thee-Luke:* Luca Giordana (1632-1705), a Neapolitan painter whose nickname is translated by Browning (*Luca-fa-presto*).

64, 190. *Castelfranco:* the painter Giorgio Barbarelli (1478-1511), usually called Giorgione, who was born at Castelfranco near Venice.

64, 192. *Ser:* Sir.

64, 193. *Tizian:* the most famous of Venetian painters, Titian, or Tiziano Vecellio (1477-1576).

65, 206-207. *Zorzi:* the lover's servant; *Zanze:* the woman's.

65, 222. *Siora:* Signora.

ARTEMIS PROLOGIZES (1842). *Page 66.*

Browning, according to Mrs. Orr, in 1842 wrote the following note regarding *Artemis Prologizes:* "I had better say perhaps that the above is nearly all retained of a tragedy I composed, much against my endeavour, while in bed with a fever two years ago — it went further into the story of Hippolytus and Aricia; but when I got well, putting only thus much down at once, I soon forgot the remainder."

The poem is based upon the *Hippolytus* of Browning's favorite Greek dramatist, Euripides (480?-406 B.C.); it was designed to serve as a prologue to Browning's projected continuation of the play. In *Artemis Prologizes,* Artemis (Diana) has removed the body of Hippolytus, unconscious and near death, to a secluded place in a forest and is nursing him back to life with the aid of Aesculapius, the physician. She tells the story of Hippolytus' misadventures as they occur in the tragedy of Euripides. Hippolytus, son of Theseus, a chaste youth, had always worshiped Artemis as goddess of chastity, and scorned Aphrodite (Venus) as goddess of love. As a devious punishment for this slight, Aphrodite had caused Phaedra, his stepmother, to fall desperately in love with him. Repulsed by Hippolytus,

Phaedra had hanged herself and left a note for Theseus falsely accusing her stepson of improper conduct toward her. Theseus in grief and wrath called upon the sea god Poseidon (Neptune) to avenge the supposed crime by sending a monster to terrify Hippolytus' horses as he drove along the shore. The youth was thrown from his chariot and dragged beneath it to the point of death. Theseus rejoiced in his revenge until Artemis appeared, to reveal to him that Hippolytus was innocent. The dying Hippolytus was brought before Theseus; the old love returned; and Hippolytus died in his father's arms.

Browning has carried the story beyond the point at which Euripides leaves it by following the legend as presented by Virgil (*Aeneid* vii, 765-77) and other authors, who say that Diana conveyed Hippolytus to the grove of the nymph Egeria near Aricia in Italy to restore him to life and that he there fell in love with the nymph. Browning apparently intended to employ this story in his continuation. Matthew Arnold pronounced *Artemis Prologizes* "one of the very best antique fragments" that he was familiar with, and felt that Browning would make a competent judge of *Merope*, his own attempt to write "a Greek tragedy in the English language."

In *Artemis Prologizes,* Browning first employed his eccentric theory for the spelling of Greek names in English, a theory he later elaborated in the preface to his translation of Aeschylus' *Agamemnon* in 1877.

66, 2. Here: Hera (Juno), queen of the gods.

66, 12. Athenai: Athens.

66, 13. Asclepios: Aesculapius.

66, 27. Amazonian stranger: Hippolyta, queen of the Amazons; former wife of Theseus and mother of Hippolytus.

68, 101. Phoibos: Phoebus (or Apollo), god of medicine and the arts.

RUDEL TO THE LADY OF TRIPOLI. *Page 69.*

First published in *Dramatic Lyrics* (1842), the poem there was paired with *Cristina* under the general title *Queen-Worship.*

Geoffrey Rudel, Prince of Blaye, or Blieux, was a troubadour of Provence in the twelfth century. Browning's poem is based upon the often-told story of Rudel's love for the Countess of Tripoli (a small duchy on the Mediterranean). Crusaders had brought back praises of her beauty and her wit. Rudel, in keeping with the best traditions of medieval Courtly Love, was seized by love for the Countess through the reports of her though he had never seen her; and he wrote some of his best songs in her honor. Later, according to the legend, Rudel set out in a pilgrim's garb for Tripoli. On the voyage he was overcome by a fatal malady. He died in the arms of the Countess, who had come to the vessel (or, in other accounts, the inn where he lay) on learning of his arrival. The legend is told in many versions with a variety of elaborations.

Browning has attempted in the language and especially the symbolism of the poem to catch the spirit of troubadour verse. His poem presents Rudel before he has set out on his fatal voyage. Rudel speaks to a pilgrim bound for the East, who will carry his words to the Countess.

69, 6. *Flower:* the sunflower (symbol of Rudel), which lives in adoration of the sun (symbol of his love for the Countess); but the Mount (his mistress, the Countess) remains cold and distant, unmindful of the sun that each day sheds his glory on her.

CRISTINA. *Page 70.*

When it first appeared, in *Dramatic Lyrics* (1842), *Cristina* was paired with *Rudel to the Lady of Tripoli* under the general title *Queen-Worship.*

Browning's Cristina was Christina Maria, Queen Regent of Spain from 1833 until 1840, when the scandal of her secret marriage to an army officer forced her abdication. Both as a royal princess and as queen, she was a notorious flirt, who is reported to have brought disaster to a number of men. Lord Malmesbury in his *Memoirs of an Ex-Minister,* recorded that she "was said at the time [1829] to be the cause of more than one inflammable victim languishing in prison for having too openly admired this royal coquette."

Browning's poem gives an unusual twist to the doctrine of "elective affinities" (the conception that a unique soul-mate awaits each person and that each will recognize and be drawn to the other upon sight) and to his belief in love as a revelation of truth or flash of insight for the lover. Compare *The Statue and the Bust* (lines 25-30) and *Caponsacchi* (lines 1162-75).

JOHANNES AGRICOLA IN MEDITATION. *Page 72.*

This poem and *Porphyria's Lover* were first published in the *Monthly Repository* for January, 1836. When they were republished in *Dramatic Lyrics* in 1842, Browning for the first time linked them together by means of a general caption, *Madhouse Cells.*

As a prefatory note in the *Monthly Repository,* Browning provided for *Johannes Agricola* the following quotation (somewhat altered) from Daniel Defoe's *Dictionary of All Religions* (1704): "Antinomians, so denominated for rejecting the Law as a thing of no use under the Gospel dispensation: they say, that good works do not further, nor evil works hinder salvation; that the child of God cannot sin, that God never chastiseth him, that murder, drunkenness, etc.

are sins in the wicked but not in him, that the child of grace being once assured of salvation, afterwards never doubteth . . . that God doth not love any man for his holiness, that sanctification is no evidence of justification, etc. Potanus, in his Catalogue of Heresies, says John Agricola was the author of this sect, A.D. 1535."

Both the *Dictionary* and the poem give an unfair picture of Johannes Agricola (1492-1566) and his doctrines, though some of the more fanatical of his followers could have sat for Browning's portrait of Johannes. In his state of cataleptic blessedness, Browning's character offers an interesting comparison with Lazarus in *An Epistle*. Both men, though in different ways, have been incapacitated for normal life by seeing heaven prematurely.

PORPHYRIA'S LOVER. *Page 73.*

First published, like *Johannes Agricola,* in the *Monthly Repository* for January, 1836, this poem was republished in *Dramatic Lyrics* (1842), where Browning for the first time paired it with *Johannes Agricola* under the general caption *Madhouse Cells.*

The characters are imaginary.

THE PIED PIPER OF HAMELIN (1842). *Page 75.*

Browning composed this poem, probably the most widely known of all his works, in the spring of 1842 for Willie, son of his friend, the noted tragedian William Charles Macready. The boy had fallen ill and the poet provided him with *The Pied Piper,* even as he had earlier provided him with another piece (*The Cardinal and the Dog*) to illustrate with drawings. Browning seems to have placed little value on *The Pied Piper;* he included it in *Dramatic Lyrics* only as filler when the printer asked for extra copy to complete a sheet.

Browning's first source for the story was probably the account given in Nathaniel Wanley's *Wonders of the Little World* (1678), a favorite book of his childhood; but his poem most resembles in its details another telling of the legend which he may have learned at second hand from his father. For an interesting study of the sources of the poem, see Arthur Dickson's article in *Studies in Philology,* XXIII (1926), 327-32. An excellent summary of the background of *The Pied Piper* is given in DeVane's *Handbook,* pp. 127-31.

77, 89. *Cham:* the ruler of Tartary.

77, 91. *Nizam:* the ruler of Hyderabad in India.

78, 123. According to legend, when Caesar's ship was captured at the siege of Alexandria in 48 B.C., he swam to safety with the manuscript of his *Commentaries on the Gallic Wars* in his hand.

78, 133. *train-oil-flasks:* flasks of whale oil.

78, 138. drusalteru: a place for selling pickled or salted foods.
78, 139. nuncheon: light luncheon.
78, 141. puncheon: cask.
79, 158. Names of famous wines.
79, 160. Rhenish: wine from the Rhine district of Germany.
79, 182. stiver: a small Dutch coin worth about two cents.
81, 258. text: Matthew 19:24.
82, 290. Transylvania: a district in Central Europe, formerly in Hungary.

"HOW THEY BROUGHT THE GOOD NEWS FROM GHENT TO AIX" (1845). *Page 83.*

Asked if this poem represented an historical event, Browning wrote in reply: "There is no sort of historical foundation about 'Good News from Ghent.' I wrote it under the bulwark of a vessel, off the African Coast, after I had been at sea long enough to appreciate even the fancy of a gallop on a certain good horse, 'York,' then in my stable at home. It was written in pencil on the fly-leaf of Bartoli's *Simboli*, I remember."

Later he stated in another letter that as he wrote the poem he had had in mind "a merely general impression of the characteristic warfare and besieging which abound in the Annals of Flanders. This accounts for some difficulties in the time and space occupied by the ride in one night." The distance between Ghent in Flanders and Aix-la-Chapelle in West Prussia is about one hundred miles in a direct route which includes all cities Browning mentions with the exception of Looz and Tongres. Including these would add about twenty miles.

Browning had been in Flanders in 1834 on his way to St. Petersburg in Russia and again in 1838. The poem was probably written during his second voyage to Italy, in 1844.

PICTOR IGNOTUS (1845). *Page 85.*

The title is Latin for "Unknown Painter." The speaker in this poem represents a striking contrast to Browning's later characterization of another artist — Fra Lippo Lippi with his fiery energy, his zest for experience, and his love for painting the world just as he sees it. Dean DeVane (*Handbook*, pp. 155-56) believes the speaker represents Browning's idea of the defense artists still in the medieval tradition of formal religious painting might make for themselves against the new vogue for realism in the early 1500's. *Pictor Ignotus* is a "belated traditionalist . . . left stranded by the change." Paul F. Jamieson (*Explicator* XI, Item 8) maintains that *Pictor Ignotus* is a timid individual, envious and self-deceiving, rather than a representative of an outworn movement.

86, 22. braved: attacked.

87, 67. travertine: limestone.

THE ITALIAN IN ENGLAND (1845). *Page 87.*

This poem probably reflects Browning's interest in an insurrection on the Neapolitan Coast of twenty-one young Italians only a few weeks before Browning visited Naples in the fall of 1844. However, the events of the poem could also have as their background the uprising in the north of Italy in 1823: they suggest the general spirit of Italy under Austrian domination rather than any specific uprising.

87, 19. Metternich: Prince Metternich (1773-1859), the famous statesman, was the prime force and chief symbol of Austrian oppression in Italy.

89, 75. duomo: the cathedral.

89, 76. Tenebrae: a service during Holy Week to commemorate the Passion and the Crucifixion.

THE ENGLISHMAN IN ITALY (1845). *Page 91.*

Piano di Sorrento is the plain of Sorrento, near the city of Naples. This poem, like the second section of *"De Gustibus,"* paints a vivid picture of southern Italy with its rich fertility and raw color.

91, 5. scirocco: the hot, dry wind that blows across the Mediterranean each autumn from North Africa.

92, 47. frails: baskets woven of rushes.

93, 87. love-apple: tomato.

93, 97. lasagne: macaroni.

94, 138. sorbs: trees of the apple family — service-trees.

95, 171. Calvano: a mountain near Naples.

95, 199. isles of the siren: According to legend, these are the three islands from which the Sirens sang to Ulysses (or Odysseus), as described in the *Odyssey.*

97, 250-51. the Feast of the Rosary's Virgin: A feast on October 7 to celebrate the date of the victory of the Christians over the Turks at Lepanto (1571).

97, 265. Bellini . . . Auber: Composers popular at the time of the poem.

97, 269. Corn-laws: These laws, which placed a high tariff on the importation of grain into the British Isles, made the price of bread high and caused much suffering among the poor. There was great agitation against the Corn Laws at the time the poem was written.

They were repealed in June, 1846, following a famine in Ireland. Allusions to contemporary events are rare in Browning's poetry.

THE LOST LEADER (1845). *Page 98.*

Thirty years after the poem first appeared, Browning confessed, "with shame and contrition," that he had thought of Wordsworth as his model for the Lost Leader when he wrote his poem. It seems clear, however, that Browning intended to write a poem that could be read without the reader's necessarily knowing anything of his particular model. In 1842, Wordsworth had accepted a Civil List pension of £300, and in 1843 he had become Poet Laureate. Browning later gladly conceded that such monetary rewards or honors did not influence Wordsworth's change in his political opinions. By 1845, however, Wordsworth had taken a position almost the exact reverse of the revolutionary sentiments of his youth.

The attitude of the speaker in the poem, it may be worth noting, is not so much anger or hostility as it is regret for the change in the Lost Leader and admiration for what the Lost Leader had once meant to the Liberal cause. It is very close to the attitude of Pym toward Strafford in Browning's drama *Strafford* (1837).

HOME-THOUGHTS, FROM THE SEA (1845). *Page 99.*

The scene of the poem is full of reminders of England's greatness. Cape Saint Vincent was the setting for Nelson's victory over the Spanish fleet on February 14, 1797; the Cape of Trafalgar was the place of Nelson's famous triumph over the French and Spanish joint fleet on October 21, 1805, and of his death in the battle; Gibraltar lies in the distance.

THE BISHOP ORDERS HIS TOMB AT SAINT PRAXED'S CHURCH (1845). *Page 100.*

John Ruskin in *Modern Painters* (vol. IV, chap. 20) praises Browning for capturing in this poem "the kind of admiration with which a southern artist regarded the *stone* he worked in; and the pride which populace or priest took in the possession of precious mountain substance, worked into the pavements of their cathedrals, and the shafts of their tombs." Later in the chapter he adds concerning the poem: "I know no other piece of modern English, prose or poetry, in which there is so much told, as in these lines, of the Renaissance spirit, — its worldliness, inconsistency, pride, hypocrisy, ignorance of itself, love of art, of luxury, and of good Latin. It is nearly all that I said of the Central Renaissance in thirty pages of the 'Stones of Venice' put into as many lines, Browning's being also the antecedent work."

100, 1. The Bishop is quoting loosely from Ecclesiastes 1:2.

100, 14. *Saint Praxed's:* The little church in Rome named for S. Prassede, the virgin daughter of a Roman senator who gave all her riches to the poor and to the Church. The edifice described in the poem seems much more spacious than the actual Saint Praxed's.

100, 21. *the epistle-side:* the right side, facing the altar, where the epistle is read during Mass.

100, 26. tabernacle: canopy.

100, 31. onion-stone: an inferior marble that peels off in layers.

101, 41. frail: basket.

101, 42. lapis lazuli: a semi-precious stone of a rich azure-blue color.

101, 46. Frascati: a beautiful town in the Alban Hills near Rome.

101, 51. a weaver's shuttle: See Job 7:6.

101, 53-54. The antique-black marble that the Bishop now demands is more beautiful and more costly than the basalt (also a black stone) that he had asked for his slab in line 25.

101, 58. thyrsus: a staff surmounted by a pine cone or ivy leaves, etc., associated with Bacchus and with satyrs.

101, 62. Moses with the tables: See Exodus 24-36.

101, 67. Gandolf from his tomb-top: Gandolf is carved in effigy on his tomb, even as the Bishop intends to be (see lines 87 ff.).

101, 77. Tully: Cicero (106-43 B.C.), whose full name was Marcus Tullius Cicero.

101, 79. Ulpian: Domitius Ulpian (170-228 A.D.), a Roman jurist, wrote at a time when Latin had lost the classical purity that had characterized it in Cicero's time.

102, 82. God made and eaten: in the sacrament of the Mass. The coarse materialism of the Bishop comes out vividly in his phrasing here and in such lines as 19, 43 ff., and 73 ff.

102, 89. mortcloth: funeral pall.

102, 95. The Bishop is growing delirious (though he seems to recover himself a few lines later).

102, 99. Elucescebat: "he was illustrious" as Ulpian wrote the word; but Cicero's classical Latin would have *elucebat.*

102, 108. vizor: a mask; *term:* a bust on a pedestal.

102, 116. Gritstone: a sandstone, cheap and perishable.

GARDEN FANCIES. *Page 103.*

The two poems under this general title first appeared in *Hood's Magazine* for July, 1844. They were republished in *Dramatic Ro-*

mances and Lyrics in 1845. The garden is probably that of Browning's mother at Hatcham, New Cross, Surrey. Arthur Symons (p. 72) praises discerningly the "varying ring and swing" of Browning's dactylic rhythms in these two pieces: "The easy flow, the careless charm of their versification, is by no means the artless matter it may seem to a careless reader." He singles out for special praise lines 21-24 of the first poem, where Browning contrives "to poise perfectly the loose lilt" of the verses.

II. SIBRANDUS SCHAFNABURGENSIS

Browning discovered the name for his special Dryasdust in one of his childhood's favorite books, Nathaniel Wanley's *Wonders of the Little World* (1678); but he makes Sibrandus of Aschafenburg a representative for all pedants.

104, 7. matin-prime: early morning hour.

105, 19. pont-levis: drawbridge.

105, 38-39. de profundis, etc.: Latin for "from the depths, with joyous accents, sing."

106, 52. right of trover: the discoverer's right to treasure trove.

106, 61. John Knox: the stern Scotch Calvinist leader (1505-72).

106, 67. sufficit: "it is sufficient."

THE LABORATORY. *Page 107.*

The poem first appeared in June, 1844, as a contribution to *Hood's Magazine.* It was republished in *Dramatic Romances and Lyrics* (1845). The subtitle *Ancien Régime* sets it in pre-revolutionary France in the court of one of the Louis. Dante Gabriel Rossetti's first water-color painting was an illustration of this poem.

THE BOY AND THE ANGEL. *Page 109.*

The poem first appeared in *Hood's Magazine* for August, 1844. It was republished in *Dramatic Romances and Lyrics* (1845). The story is without any historical basis. No pope has ever been named Theocrite.

MEETING AT NIGHT *and* PARTING AT MORNING (1845). *Pages 111, 112.*

In both of these companion poems the man is speaking. In line 3 of *Parting at Morning,* "him" refers to the sun.

TIME'S REVENGES (1845). *Page 112.*

The title comes from Shakespeare's *Twelfth Night* (V, i, 384): "And thus the whirligig of time brings in his revenges."
113, 46. the Florentine: Dante.

THE GLOVE (1845). *Page 114.*

The story of the poem had been told by various writers, notably by Schiller in his *Der Handschuh,* which Leigh Hunt translated under the title *The Glove and the Lions.* Hunt's poem (first published in *The New Monthly Magazine* for May, 1836) became highly popular, and Browning was surely thinking of it as he wrote his own. De Lorge had always been presented as the unquestioned hero of the story. Browning's conclusion is a fine early example of his practice in "special-pleading."

Pierre Ronsard, a French poet of the time of Francis I (1494-1547) supposedly speaks (*loquitur*) in the poem. There seems to be no particular reason for Browning's choosing Ronsard other than his being a poet at the French court.

114, 12. Naso: the Roman poet Ovid (43 B.C.-18 A.D.), author of *Metamorphoses.*

114, 14. Ixions: Ixion dared to love Hera, queen of the gods. Zeus formed a cloud into the shape of Hera (see *cloudlets* in line 13) and sent it to Ixion. The race of centaurs was the result of this union. For his presumption, Ixion in the underworld was fixed to a constantly turning wheel.

115, 45. Clement Marot: A French Protestant poet of the court of Francis I, famous for his sonnets and pastorals and his versifications of the Psalms.

115, 50. Illum Juda, etc.: "That lion of the Tribe of Judah."

116, 82. Marignan: an Italian town near Milan where Francis had won a great battle in 1515.

116, 96. Kaffir: The Kaffirs of South Africa were famous as lion hunters.

118, 162. Nemean: Slaying the ferocious lion of Nemea was one of the twelve labors Hercules had to perform.

118, 189. Venienti, etc.: "Go to meet the approaching evil."

118, 190. theorbo: an instrument like a lute. Peter Ronsard has been playing an accompaniment as he sings his poem.

LOVE AMONG THE RUINS (1855). *Page 119.*

The ruined city that Browning describes seems to be a composite with details from sources as varied as Herodotus' description of

Babylon, the Apocalypse of St. John, and the many accounts of excavations appearing in the eighteen-forties and early eighteen-fifties. Excavations were being made in such cities as Tarquinia, Thebes in Egypt, Nineveh, and those of the Roman Campagna, and there was an intense popular interest in archaeology throughout western Europe. Browning's principal source may well have been A. H. Layard's *Nineveh and Its Remains* (1849). See Johnstone Parr's "The Site and Ancient City of Browning's *Love Among the Ruins*," (*Publications of the Modern Language Association*, LXVIII [1953], 128-37) for a very interesting discussion of Browning's possible sources.

120, 39. caper: a low prickly shrub common in the Mediterranean region.

121, 65. causeys: raised paths, causeways.

EVELYN HOPE (1855). *Page 121.*

The idea of the individual's pursuing life after life in a series of incarnations is presented or implied in a number of Browning's poems. Compare especially *Cristina,* lines 35-40, where the idea is linked, as here, with the conception of "elective affinities" (see the general note to *Cristina*). In *Old Pictures in Florence* (stanza 21) the speaker succinctly describes the conception of an endless series of lives but rejects it for himself. The final stanza of *The Last Ride Together* presents a similar conception, but with an interesting difference. A sense of the attractiveness of "endless onward movement," as Henry Jones remarks (p. 330), colors much of Browning's best poetry.

UP AT A VILLA — DOWN IN THE CITY (1855). *Page 123.*

The scenery of the poem suggests the Tuscan countryside, and Browning is probably thinking, as Dean DeVane remarks (*Handbook,* p. 215) of his own jaunts into Siena from the villa the Brownings had taken during the fall of 1850 in the hills two miles above that city. Of course, Browning did not share the "Person of Quality's" dislike for the countryside, the beauty of which shows through the disparaging remarks of the speaker.

125, 39. diligence: stage-coach.

125, 42. Pulcinello-trumpet: the trumpet announcing the arrival of the puppet show, in which Pulcinello is the buffoon.

125, 44. liberal thieves: men of the revolutionary party against Austria. The "Person of Quality" (or the government notice) probably uses the word *thieves* loosely where revolutionists are concerned.

125, 51. our Lady: the Virgin; here, Our Lady of Sorrows, the seven swords symbolizing the seven great sorrows she endured.

A WOMAN'S LAST WORD (1855). *Page 126.*

The imagery of the poem derives from *Paradise Lost.* The Eve who speaks here, however, prefers marital concord, at the price of complete submission to her husband, over any trafficking with knowledge that would threaten her domestic Eden.

FRA LIPPO LIPPI (1855). *Page 127.*

Fra Lippo Lippi (1406-69) was a noted Florentine artist of the early Renaissance whose paintings suggest the zest for the pleasures of the world and the delight in realistic detail that Browning attributes to him. The artistic creed that the painter professes, however, was Browning's to a greater degree than it was Brother Lippo's; and the poem represents an eloquent though oblique exposition and defense of Browning's own artistic principles.

Browning found nearly all of the detail for his poem and the outlines of Fra Lippo's character in Giorgio Vasari's sixteenth-century *Lives of the Painters*, a gossipy and sometimes inaccurate work where the biography of Fra Lippo Lippi runs in part as follows:

> The Carmelite monk, Fra Filippo di Tommaso Lippi, was born at Florence in a bye street called Ardiglione, under the Canto alla Cuculia, and behind the convent of the Carmelites. By the death of his father he was left a friendless orphan at the age of two years, his mother having also died shortly after his birth. The child was for some time under the care of a certain Mona Lapaccia, his aunt, the sister of his father, who brought him up with very great difficulty till he had attained his eighth year, when, being no longer able to support the burden of his maintenance, she placed him in the above-named convent of the Carmelites. Here, in proportion as he showed himself dexterous and ingenious in all works performed by hand, did he manifest the utmost dullness and incapacity in letters, to which he would never apply himself, nor would he take any pleasure in learning of any kind. The boy continued to be called by his worldly name of Filippo; and, — being placed with others, who, like himself, were in the house of the novices, under the care of the master, to the end that the latter might see what could be done with him, — in place of studying, he never did anything but daub his own books, and those of the other boys, with caricatures, whereupon the prior determined to give him all means and every opportunity for learning to draw. . . .
>
> It is said that Fra Filippo was much addicted to the pleasures of sense, insomuch that he would give all that he possessed to

secure the gratification of whatever inclination might at the moment be predominant. . . . It was known that while occupied in the pursuit of his pleasures, the works undertaken by him received little or none of his attention; for which reason Cosimo de' Medici, wishing him to execute a work in his own palace, shut him up, that he might not waste his time in running about; but having endured this confinement for two days, he then made ropes with the sheets of his bed, which he cut to pieces for that purpose, and so having let himself down from a window, escaped, and for several days gave himself up to his amusements.

Fra Filippo was indeed so highly estimated for his great gifts, that many circumstances in his life which were very blamable received pardon, and were partly placed out of view, in consideration of his extraordinary abilities.

Fra Lippo Lippi is generally regarded as one of Browning's finest achievements in poetry. Many readers have agreed with Edward Dowden (p. 192) that in this poem "the dramatic monologue of Browning attains its perfection of life and energy."

127, 3. *Zooks:* "Gadzooks," a mild oath.

128, 17. *Cosimo of the Medici:* the great Florentine banker and patron of the arts, the real ruler of the city of Florence.

128, 23. *pilchards:* a common variety of Mediterranean fish.

128, 34. *John Baptist's head:* The painting described here, with a slave holding the head by the hair, seems to be Browning's own creation, though Vasari states that John the Baptist was a favorite subject of Lippo's, who did paint a picture in which the head of John the Baptist is carried on a charger by Salome. At her mother's urging, she had demanded his head as a reward from Herod for her dancing (see Matthew 14:1-12).

128, 53 ff. *Flower o' the broom,* etc.: Here and later in the poem Lippo's flower songs follow a type of Florentine folk song, the *stornello.*

129, 73. *Jerome:* Saint Jerome (340-420 A.D.), who made the Vulgate version of the Bible. Vasari notes that Lippo did such a picture for Cosimo di Medici. Browning seizes upon the fact to provide a fine ironic contrast of the ascetic saint with the worldly artist who is compelled to paint such a subject.

130, 121. *the Eight:* the eight magistrates who headed the government of Florence.

130, 130. *antiphonary:* the choir book containing the antiphons, or responses.

130, 140. *Preaching Friars:* the Dominicans.

131, 148. *cribs:* petty thefts.

131, 150. *safe:* since the victim's son (line 153) dares not kill him in the church.

131, 172. *funked:* went out in smoke.

132, 189 ff. Lippo is characterizing the medieval monastic ideal of painting against which his own zest for the pleasurable details of this world rebels.

132, 189. *Giotto:* the famous early medieval painter, sculptor, and architect (1266-1337).

132, 196. *Herodias:* mother of Salome (see note to line 34). The Prior confuses Herodias with her daughter, perhaps because Browning (or Fra Lippo) wishes to show the extent of the Prior's embarrassment.

132, 208 ff. Fra Lippo presents an artistic creed here and in lines 280 ff. and elsewhere that is clearly Browning's own as well as the painter's. Compare *How It Strikes a Contemporary* and *Rabbi Ben Ezra*, lines 49 ff.

133, 235. Fra Angelico (1387-1455) was the chief painter of the medieval monastic school, so devout in his art, it is said, that he knelt as he painted.

134, 277. *Hulking Tom:* Tommaso Guidi, or Masaccio (1401-29), whose nickname was Hulking Tom. Vasari correctly states that Masaccio was Lippo's predecessor, not his pupil. Browning, in an effort to correct Vasari, here follows another source, the ponderous (twenty-volume) *Delle Notizie de' Professori del Disegno da Cimabue*, by Filippo Baldinucci, published in the eighteenth century (1767-74).

134, 307. *cullion's hanging face:* Lippo refers to the guard who had seized his throat earlier (see lines 19-20). The face of this cullion, or rascal, Lippo says in effect, betrays a character that will cause him to die on the prison gallows. Compare *The Tempest* (I, i, 31-34): "I have great comfort from this fellow: methinks he hath no drowning mark upon him; his complexion is perfect gallows."

135, 323. *a Saint Laurence:* This martyr was broiled to death on a gridiron. According to the legend, he bore his suffering so well that he cried to his torturers to turn him over, since he "was done on one side."

135, 346. *Sant' Ambrogio's:* Lippo painted *The Coronation of the Virgin*, the picture described in the lines that follow, for this convent in Florence.

136, 375. *His camel-hair:* Saint John was "clothed with camel's hair" (Mark 1:6).

136, 377. *Iste perfecit opus:* "This man created the work," or "This man caused the work to be created." The words are painted on a scroll in the lower right hand of the picture near the head of the man Browning and contemporary critics supposed to be Fra Lippo Lippi. Modern scholarship indicates that the man represented was not the painter but the canon who caused the painting to be created for the altar of the church at Sant' Ambrogio's.

A TOCCATA OF GALUPPI'S (1855). *Page 136.*

Baldassare Galuppi (1706-85), a Venetian musician of great fame in his day, was a composer of toccatas, comic operas, church music, and sonatas. A toccata, or "touch piece," has a light, capricious movement resembling the freedom of an improvisation; it is designed to show off the technical virtuosity of the player rather than to develop a theme to its fullest possibilities of expression, as in a sonata. In *A Toccata of Galuppi's,* the speaker, a meditative Englishman of the mid-nineteenth century, sees the gaiety of Venice in her decadence reflected in Galuppi's coldly brilliant music; but as he plays he senses, too, a strong note of irony in what the music says to him, especially in stanza XIII.

137, 6. *St. Mark's:* the cathedral at Venice. *Doges:* the doge was the chief magistrate of Venice. In an annual ceremony first performed in 1000 A.D., the doge threw a ring into the Adriatic thus symbolizing the wedding of this sea to Venice.

137, 18. *clavichord:* a precursor of the piano, in which the strings were struck by metal blades or pins.

138, 32. *a secret wrung from nature's close reserve:* The speaker is a scientist either by profession or, more probably, by avocation. See lines 37-38.

138, 35-43. The quotation marks enclose the comments that Galuppi's music addresses to the speaker of the poem.

BY THE FIRE-SIDE (1855). *Page 138.*

The poem owes much to Browning's memory of his own love and courtship; it is autobiographical in spirit though not in its details. The "perfect wife, my Leonor" of the poem, is generally accepted to be Mrs. Browning; lines 258-59 paint her as she appears in portraits and photographs.

140, 43. *Pella:* a village.

141, 83. *grange:* granary,

141, 84. *wattled cote:* a light thatched shelter.

141, 89. *John in the Desert:* John the Baptist in the wilderness.

142, 101. *my Leonor:* Leonor is the faithful wife in Beethoven's opera *Fidelio.*

143, 132. *The great Word:* Revelation 21:5 — "And he that sitteth on the throne said, 'Behold, I make all things new.' "

144, 185. *chrysolite:* an olive-green stone. Transparent varieties are used as gems.

ANY WIFE TO ANY HUSBAND (1855). *Page 147.*

150, 77. Titian's Venus: probably the *Venus* in the Uffizi at Florence, painted by Titian (1477-1576) about 1538.

AN EPISTLE (1855). *Page 152.*

For the story of Jesus' raising of Lazarus from the dead, on which the poem is founded, see John 11:1-44. In *An Epistle* Browning's characteristic belief that ignorance, doubt, and struggle toward knowledge are basic conditions of human life is exemplified in a novel and ingenious way. Since Lazarus has actually been on the other side of the grave and has experienced eternal life, he is no longer a human being: he is outside the conditions of life in the world — "Professedly the faultier that he knows/ God's secret, while he holds the thread of life."

Karshish, the Arabian physician, and Abib, his master, are imaginary characters. The time of the poem is 66 A.D., the year the Roman emperor Vespasian invaded Jerusalem. Karshish is well-versed in the medical knowledge of his day, and his approach to the case of Lazarus is essentially that of a scientist. On the other hand, he is a child of the believing East; his mood as he tells the story of Lazarus vacillates between scientific skepticism and great wonder.

152, 17. snakestone: a stone believed to cure snake bites.

152, 21. Jericho: Karshish had written his last letter from this city northeast of Jerusalem.

152, 28. Vespasian: See the general note above.

153, 43. tertians: fevers that recur every third day.

153, 44. falling-sickness: epilepsy.

153, 55. gum-tragacanth: a medicinal gum produced by a shrub.

153, 60. Zoar: a city near the Dead Sea.

154, 109. fifty: Lazarus would be about sixty-five at the time of the poem. Karshish probably judges him to be fifty by his physical appearance, which, because of the man's freedom from ordinary cares, shows less wear than his years would otherwise have caused.

157, 252. the earthquake: the earthquake chronicled in Matthew 27:51 as occurring at the time of the Crucifixion.

158, 281. borage: a flowering plant assumed to have stimulating powers. *Aleppo:* a town in Syria.

A SERENADE AT THE VILLA (1855). *Page 159.*

This serenade of an unlucky lover who picks the worst of nights to sing to an aging and dispirited mistress offers a refreshing variation on an old theme.

"CHILDE ROLAND TO THE DARK TOWER CAME" (1855).
Page 162.

On New Year's Day, 1852, Browning made a resolution to "write something every day." On the second day of carrying out this vow, *Childe Roland* occurred to him as "a kind of dream." He felt, he said later, a compulsion to write it, and finished it on the same day. "I did not know then what I meant beyond that, and I'm sure I don't know now. But I am very fond of it." Browning did not, however, object to others' attempting to find a consistent allegory in the work, feeling that every man had a right to make of a poem what he could. The poem seems to develop a mood rather than any consistent allegory; and the keynote of the poem probably lies in lines 41-43. *Childe Roland* seems closer in manner to stream-of-consciousness writing of the twentieth century than it does to any norm of technique in the Victorian period. The unusual imagery of the poem has been shown to come from a great variety of sources, but chiefly, as Dean DeVane has demonstrated, from Gerard de Lairesse's *The Art of Painting in All its Branches,* Browning's favorite childhood book. De Lairesse's seventeenth chapter, "Of Things Deformed and Broken, Falsely Called Painter-like," contains or parallels many of the details of *Childe Roland.* For an excellent summary of the various studies of the sources of the poem, see DeVane's *Handbook* (pp. 228-32).

Edgar's song in "Lear": In *Lear,* III, iv, Edgar, as he sings, is pretending madness:

> "Childe Rowland to the dark tower came,
> His word was still, — Fie, foh, and fum
> I smell the blood of a British man."

163, 48. *estray:* an animal found strayed from its owner.
164, 66. *calcine:* turn to powder by means of heat.
164, 68. *bents:* coarse grasses.
164, 80. *colloped:* in folds.
165, 114. *bespate:* spattered.
166, 143. *Tophet:* a Hebrew name for Hell.
167, 160. *Apollyon:* the devil. See Revelation 9:11 — "And they had a king over them, which is the angel of the bottomless pit, [who] . . . in the Greek tongue hath his name Apollyon."
167, 161. *dragon-penned:* dragon-pinioned.
168, 203. *slug-horn:* a trumpet.

RESPECTABILITY (1855). *Page 169.*

The pair of lovers may be George Sand, the French writer, noted for her novels and plays and her unconventional life, and Jules

Sandeau, with whom she lived for some time in Paris after leaving her husband. The Brownings had seen George Sand on various occasions in Paris in 1852. The same place and year provided Browning with the incident he uses for contrast in the poem: "respectability" required that François Guizot, an eminent French statesman and historian, welcome Charles Montalembert upon the latter's election to the Academie Française, though the two were bitter political enemies.

169, 23. lampions: lamps. The lovers approach the lighted court of the Institute. The next line is, of course, spoken ironically, as if they, too, must concern themselves about "respectability."

A LIGHT WOMAN (1855). *Page 170.*

171, 26. basilisk: a creature of classical fable supposed to be able to kill his victim with a glance of his eyes.

THE STATUE AND THE BUST (1855). *Page 172.*

The Duke of the poem is Ferdinand di Medici (1549-1608), whose equestrian statue still looks up at the eastern window of the Palace of the Riccardi (now called the Palazzo Antinori). The bust which the woman of the poem causes to be placed beneath her window is Browning's addition to the legend, though an empty niche in the wall may well have suggested the idea of the bust to him. Also Browning's is the unorthodox moral of his conclusion, which has puzzled some readers, and disturbed others. But Browning, in this poem as in *The Grammarian's Funeral, Iv*à*n Iv*à*novitch, The Glove,* and often elsewhere, is indulging his love for making a case — for arguing his point from an extreme instance.

The poem has the rhyme scheme of *terza rima,* as in Dante's *Divine Comedy.*

172, 22. encolure: mane.

173, 33. the pile: the Grand Duke's palace.

173, 36. a crime: the crime of Cosimo di Medici in destroying the Republic of Florence by seizing the government in 1434. The Medici remained rulers of Florence for three centuries.

173, 57. catafalk: a pall-covered, coffin-shaped structure used at requiem masses performed after burial.

175, 94. Arno . . . Petraja: The Duke invites the couple to abandon Florence and the Arno River to visit his villa in the suburb of Petraja.

177, 169. Robbia's craft: The della Robbias, especially Luca della Robbia (1400-1482), were famous for their bas-relief sculptures in marble, bronze, and terra cotta. The last of the great artists of the name had died in 1566, but della Robbia ware continued to be made.

178, 202. John of Douay: the sculptor Giovanni da Bologna (1524-

1608), whose equestrian statue of the Duke still stands in the Annunziata Piazza in Florence.

179, 234. *the stamp of the very Guelph:* genuine coin with the stamp of the government upon it.

179, 250. *De te, fabula:* "concerning you, the fable!" (The story is told so that you may apply it to yourself.)

LOVE IN A LIFE *and* LIFE IN A LOVE. *Page 180.*

These companion poems were first published in *Men and Women* (1855). The idea of "elective affinities" (see the general note to *Cristina*) seems to underlie the speaker's search.

HOW IT STRIKES A CONTEMPORARY (1855). *Page 181.*

So far as is known, Browning had no first-hand acquaintance with the Spanish city of Valladolid, the scene of the poem. The speaker is a jolly Philistine who "could never write a verse." The man gives us a humorous and curiously left-handed description of the town's bard; but into it Browning has contrived to put some of his favorite ideas about the general nature and function of the poet. With Shelley (*Defence of Poetry*), Browning held that poets were the "unacknowledged legislators" of mankind. He believed, also, that a poet must have a higher aim in his verse than writing for the public at large. "A poet's affair is with God," he wrote Ruskin in 1855, "— to whom he is accountable, and of whom is his reward." The poet's duty, Browning states in his *Essay on Shelley* (1852), is "beholding with an understanding keenness the universe, nature and man, in their actual state of perfection in imperfection." The obscure poet of Valladolid, "The town's true master if the town but knew," who comprehends with an understanding keenness all that goes on around him and who writes his reports to "our Lord the King," shows himself a true representative of the poetic tradition. His death scene, with the spirits standing by his bed in "the heavenly manner of relieving guard," is reminiscent of Shelley's *Adonais,* where many poets, "inheritors of unfulfilled renown," have risen from obscure lives on earth to assume their thrones in heaven.

181, 19. *Moorish work:* Old buildings in this Spanish city would still bear witness to the days before the end of the fifteenth century when the Moors occupied much of Spain.

182, 28. *fly-leaf ballads:* ballads printed and sold separately on single sheets of paper.

182, 44. *our Lord the King:* In the first edition, all pronouns referring to the "King" were capitalized to underscore his identity in the general meaning of the poem.

183, 90. *corregidor:* the chief magistrate.

184, 115. *Prado:* the promenade, or chief walk of the city, where the fashionable congregate to see and be seen.

THE LAST RIDE TOGETHER (1855). *Page 184.*

The poem is a special favorite with many readers. Arthur Symons (pp. 109-110) is among them: "Thought, emotion and melody are mingled in perfect measure: it has the lyrical 'cry,' and the objectiveness of the drama. The situation, sufficiently indicated in the title, is selected with choice and happy instinct: the very motion of riding is given in the rhythm . . . in the last verse . . . the dramatic intensity strikes as with an electric shock."

186, 65. *scratch his name on the Abbey-stones:* honor him with burial in Westminster Abbey.

187, 101ff. A notable expression of Browning's idea that aspiration and action in themselves, movement toward a goal, not the experience of attaining a goal, constitute the best state in life. Compare *Rabbi Ben Ezra,* especially stanzas xxiii-xxv, and *Old Pictures in Florence,* stanza xxi.

THE PATRIOT (1855). *Page 187.*

The poem probably stems from Browning's witnessing of the rise and fall of heroes in Italy's premature struggle to free herself from Austria (1848-49). But the situation is "An Old Story" and all too universal in its application.

188, 19. *Shambles' Gate:* the place where animals are slaughtered.

BISHOP BLOUGRAM'S APOLOGY (1855). *Page 188.*

Browning made no secret of the fact that the model for his brilliant but comfort-loving and temporizing Bishop Blougram was Nicholas Wiseman, who, in 1850, had been made Archbishop of Westminster and Primate of the Roman Catholic Church in England. By a strange chance, Cardinal Wiseman himself reviewed the poem in *The Rambler,* a Roman Catholic journal, in January, 1856, apparently finding no reason to identify himself with Browning's portrait. He concluded his review with this statement: ". . . beneath the surface there is an undercurrent of thought that is by no means inconsistent with our religion; and if Mr. Browning is a man of will and action, and not a mere dreamer and talker, *we should never feel surprise at his conversion.*" Wilfrid Ward, biographer of Wiseman, finds the portrait quite unlike the Cardinal: "Subtle and true as the sketch is in itself, it really depicts some one else."

Critics are generally agreed that *Bishop Blougram* is one of Browning's cleverest and most successful dramatic monologues.

188, 3. our Abbey: Westminster Abbey, which had been lost to the Roman Catholic Church at the Reformation.

188, 6. brother Pugin's: A. W. N. Pugin (1812-52), a convert to Roman Catholicism, was a noted architect who did much to popularize Gothic architecture in Victorian England.

188, 13. Gigadibs: This clever, superficial journalist, thirty years old, who writes literary criticism and sprightly imitations of Dickens for *Blackwood's Magazine* and other journals (see lines 944ff.), does despise Blougram. He believes that for Blougram to be a bishop at so late a date as the middle of the nineteenth century means that he must be either a fool or a knave (line 405), since for reasoning men the age of faith is past. Gigadibs' scorn has rankled in the great Bishop's mind, and he now proceeds to annihilate the man along with his arguments, employing Gigadibs' own line of reasoning to do the work. Since Blougram possesses an intellect far subtler and more powerful than Gigadibs' own, he succeeds even better than he realizes. But, Browning suggests at the end of the poem, Blougram's mind has not been set at ease with itself for any length of time, though he has effectively silenced one of his critics.

189, 54. Count D'Orsay: a famous Victorian dandy and dictator of fashion.

190, 70. tire-room: dressing room.

190, 85. I would be merely much: Certainly a chief flaw in the Bishop's life, from Browning's point of view, is his failure to live earnestly, his emphasis on comfort rather than self-development or self-realization as an end in his life. Contrast *Rabbi Ben Ezra,* etc. Blougram so often employs the phrases and arguments characteristic of Browning in other poems that separating the Bishop's views from those of Browning can become a stimulating exercise.

191, 113. the Jerome: Correggio's picture of Saint Jerome in the Ducal Academy at Parma.

191, 117. the marvellous Modenese: Correggio studied at Modena, though he was not born in that city.

196, 316. Peter's creed . . . Hildebrand's: Blougram mentions St. Peter as the first pope; Hildebrand (Pope Gregory VII, who lived from 1073 to 1085) is mentioned as a representative of the Church in its full claim to temporal power.

198, 411. Schelling's way: Friedrich Wilhelm Joseph von Schelling (1775-1854), a German idealistic philosopher who held, with Kant, that what might seem true to the senses, or "Understanding," could be judged insubstantial and false by the "Reason."

201, 516. Giulio Romano . . . Dowland: The pictures of Romano, an Italian painter (1492-1546) who is mentioned in Shakespeare's

Winter's Tale (V, ii, 105); John Dowland (1563?-1626?), English lutenist and composer, is mentioned in *The Passionate Pilgrim* (a pirated anthology containing poems by Shakespeare and bearing his name on the title page).

201, 519. *King John* (III, i, 138).

201, 536. *St. Gothard:* The principal pass between Italy and Switzerland in the Alps.

202, 572. *Re-opens a shut book:* i.e., causes the Bible to be translated into the vernacular.

202, 577. *Strauss:* David Friedrich Strauss (1808-74). His *Life of Jesus* appeared in 1835. Blougram here uses Strauss to represent the whole movement of Higher Criticism in Biblical studies — the "next advance" in religious heterodoxy beyond Luther.

203, 640. *born in Rome:* Cardinal Wiseman was born of Anglo-Irish parents in Seville, Spain.

205, 703. *brother Newman:* John Henry Newman, leader of the Oxford Movement in the Anglican Church, had entered the Roman Catholic Church in 1845. He wrote in defense of a belief in miracles on many occasions. See, for example, his *Lectures on the Present Position of Catholics* (1851), where he defends belief in the "Naples liquefaction" (see line 728 below) and the motion of eyes in pictures of the Madonna.

205, 704. *the Immaculate Conception:* This doctrine of the Church holds that Mary, mother of Jesus, was conceived without sin. Pope Pius IX had appointed a commission to investigate the subject in 1851; he proclaimed the doctrine a dogma in 1854.

205, 715. *King Bomba:* a nickname for Ferdinand II, King of Sicily at the time of the poem; *lazzaroni:* beggars.

205, 716. *Antonelli:* Cardinal Antonelli was secretary to Pius IX.

206, 728. *Naples' liquefaction:* a small amount of the blood of Januarius, patron saint of Naples, preserved as a solid, is believed to liquefy each year on the day of the Feast of St. Januarius.

206, 744. *Fichte's clever cut at God himself:* Johann Gottlieb Fichte (1765-1814), a German philosopher, held that God was merely an idea in the mind of man.

211, 972 ff. *in partibus,* etc.: In 1850, the Pope re-established the Roman Catholic hierarchy in England. Wiseman's title was changed from titular Bishop of Melipotamus, *in partibus infidelium,* to Archbishop of Westminster.

212, 1014. *studied his last chapter of St. John:* Perhaps the most ingenious interpretation of this ambiguous line is that once offered by Mr. Charles Klingler, a graduate student, in a class of the present editor's: Gigadibs has given up the study of Higher Criticism and such matters. The gospel of John figured very prominently in the writings of Strauss and other Higher Critics.

MEMORABILIA (1855). *Page 213.*

Browning as a young man had worshiped Shelley; in *Pauline* (1833), his first published work, he had addressed Shelley in adulatory lines as "Sun-treader," and the poem is full of echoes of Shelley's poetry. *An Essay on Shelley* (1852) shows his continued admiration for the earlier poet. *Memorabilia* ("things worth remembering") had its origin in an incident which Browning later recounted to his friend W. G. Kingsland:

> "I was one day in the shop of Hodgson, the well-known Lon-
> don bookseller, when a stranger came in, who, in the course of
> conversation with the bookseller, spoke of something that Shelley
> had once said to him. Suddenly the stranger paused, and burst
> into laughter as he observed me staring at him with blanched
> face; and," the poet continued, "I still vividly remember how
> strangely the presence of a man who had seen and spoken with
> Shelley affected me."

213, 9. *moor:* a large area of marshy waste ground.

ANDREA DEL SARTO (1855). *Page 213.*

According to a well-established tradition, Browning wrote this poem in reply to the request of John Kenyon, his friend and bene-factor, for a photographic copy of Andrea del Sarto's portrait of himself and his wife. (The portrait still hangs in the Pitti Palace at Florence.) When Browning could not find a reproduction of the picture, he is said to have written and sent the poem as a substitute.

The poem is based largely upon the life of Andrea del Sarto con-tained in the first edition of Giorgio Vasari's *Lives of the Painters*. Vasari had known both Andrea and Lucrezia well when he was Andrea's apprentice. Andrea d'Angelo Francesca (1486-1531) was the son of a tailor (hence the nickname *del Sarto*) who through his technical skill became known early in his career as the "Faultless Painter." He was already an artist of some importance when, in 1513, he married Lucrezia. Vasari provides the following account of Andrea's marriage:

> At that time there was a most beautiful girl in the Via di San
> Gallo, who was married to a capmaker, and who, though born of
> a poor and vicious father, carried about her as much pride and
> haughtiness as beauty and fascination. She delighted in trapping
> the hearts of men, and among others ensnared the unlucky
> Andrea, whose immoderate love for her soon caused him to

neglect the studies demanded by his art, and in great measure to discontinue the assistance which he had given to his parents.

Now it chanced that a sudden and grievous illness seized the husband of this woman, who rose no more from his bed, but died thereof. Without taking counsel of his friends, therefore; without regard to the dignity of his art or the consideration due to his genius, and to the eminence he had attained with so much labor; without a word, in short, to any of his kindred, Andrea took this Lucrezia di Baccio del Fede, such was the name of the woman, to be his wife; her beauty appearing to him to merit thus much at his hands, and his love for her having more influence over him than the glory and honor towards which he had begun to make such hopeful advances. But when this news became known in Florence, the respect and affection which his friends had previously borne to Andrea changed to contempt and disgust, since it appeared to them that the darkness of this disgrace had obscured for a time all the glory and renown obtained by his talents.

But he destroyed his own peace as well as estranged his friends by this act, seeing that he soon became jealous, and found that he had besides fallen into the hands of an artful woman, who made him do as she pleased in all things. He abandoned his own father and mother, for example, and adopted the father and sisters of his wife in their stead; insomuch that all who knew the facts mourned over him, and he soon began to be as much avoided as he had been previously sought after. His disciples still remained with him, it is true, in the hope of learning something useful, yet there was not one of them, great or small, who was not maltreated by his wife, both by evil words and despiteful actions; none could escape her blows, but although Andrea lived in the midst of all that torment, he yet accounted it a high pleasure.

Though Browning's interpretation of Andrea expresses his characteristic ideas in regard to the "philosophy of the imperfect" (see the note to line 81 of *Old Pictures in Florence*), Vasari gave him an excellent foundation for his reading of the painter's character:

In Andrea del Sarto nature and art combined to show all that may be done in painting, when design, coloring and invention unite in one and the same person. Had this master possessed a somewhat bolder and more elevated mind; had he been as much distinguished for higher qualifications as he was for genius and depth of judgment in the art he practiced, he would, beyond all doubt, have been without an equal. But there was a certain timidity of mind, a sort of diffidence and want of force in his

nature, which rendered it impossible that those evidences of
ardor and animation which are proper to the more exalted character, should ever appear in him; nor did he at any time display
one particle of that elevation which, could it have been added
to the advantages wherewith he was endowed, would have
rendered him a truly divine painter: wherefore the works of
Andrea are wanting in those ornaments of grandeur, richness, and
force, which appear so conspicuously in those of many other
masters. His figures are, nevertheless, well drawn, they are
entirely free from errors, and perfect in their proportions, and are
for the most part simple and chaste; the expression of his heads
is natural and graceful in women and children, while in youths
and old men it is full of life and animation. The draperies of
this master are beautiful to a marvel, and the nude figures are
admirably executed, the drawing is simple, the coloring is most
exquisite, nay, it is truly divine.

Andrea del Sarto has always been one of the most-admired of
Browning's dramatic monologues; some critics consider the poem his
finest single work.

214, 15. *Fiesole:* a suburb on a hill three miles to the west of
Florence.

215, 93. *Morello:* a peak of the Apennine Mountains north of
Florence.

216, 105. *The Urbinate:* Raphael Sanzio (1483-1520), the great
Italian painter, who was born in Urbino.

216, 130. *Agnolo:* Michelangelo (1475-1564).

217, 149. *Francis:* Francis I of France, who, in 1518, persuaded
Andrea to accept his invitation to visit his court at Fontainebleau.
Andrea did excellent work there and was much honored. According
to Vasari, however, Lucrezia wrote him letters from Florence filled
with bitter complaints, so that, taking with him a sum of money
entrusted to him by Francis for the purchase of pictures and statues in
Italy, "he set off . . . having sworn on the Gospels to return in a few
months. Arrived in Florence, he lived joyously with his wife for some
time, making presents to her father and sisters, but doing nothing for
his own parents, who died in poverty and misery. When the period
specified by the king had come . . . he found himself at the end not
only of his own money but . . . of that of the king." Modern scholars
clear Andrea of this charge, believing that the story arose from his
serving Francis as a messenger to carry a sum of money to certain
citizens of Florence.

217, 178. *the Roman:* Raphael, who spent his last years painting
for the Pope.

218, 210. *cue-owls:* a species of small owls whose cry (*ki-yu*) suggests their name.

219, 261. *the New Jerusalem:* heaven. See Revelation 21:10-21.

219, 263. *Leonard:* Leonardo da Vinci (1452-1519).

OLD PICTURES IN FLORENCE (1885). *Page 221.*

"Robert has been picking up pictures at a few pauls each," Mrs. Browning wrote her friend Mrs. Jameson from Florence on May 4, 1850, " 'hole and corner' pictures which the 'dealers' had not found out. . . ." His great triumph had been the discovery of five old pictures in a grain shop where they had lain "among heaps of trash." Mr. Kirkup, a friend who enjoyed some reputation as a judge of early art, spoke seriously of the possibility of their being the work of such noted early masters as Cimabue or Ghirlandajo. A scene of the crucifixion painted on a banner he had pronounced "Giottesque, if not Giotto."

Old Pictures in Florence has four more or less distinct themes that separate and blend as the poem progresses: (a) Browning's quarrel with Giotto, the great medieval Italian master, who has recently allowed another enthusiast for old paintings, and not Browning, to rediscover a little picture of his, "a certain precious little tablet," that had dropped from sight since the sixteenth century; (b) the neglect that the somewhat unpolished but eloquent early masters have suffered, their paintings now allowed to moulder in out-of-the-way places; (c) the question whether perfection (as in Greek art) is an adequate ideal in art, as opposed to an aim for fuller expression at the cost of imperfect execution (as in the early Italian masters); (d) — really an extension of (b) — the question whether Italy's neglect of her early masters is not caused by her subjection to Austria. Browning ends by prophesying that once the Austrians are driven out, Italy will be united and Giotto's unfinished bell tower (which has been the chief symbol throughout the poem for great incomplete works that are the nobler for their aspiring beyond limits that could be brought to completion) will soar up a further fifty cubits in gold, perfected by the citizens of a free Florence.

This poem, with its headlong, grotesque rhymes, shows Browning in one of his favorite manners, and at his virtuoso best.

221, 15. *bell-tower:* the campanile of the cathedral in Florence, designed by Giotto (1276-1337), greatest of early Florentine artists in painting and in architecture.

222, 44. *One:* the ghost of the painter.

222, 51. *Michaels:* Michelangelo (1475-1564).

223, 64. *Dellos:* Dello di Niccolo Delli, an obscure painter of the fifteenth century.

223, 69. *Stefano:* a pupil of Giotto's.

223, 72. *Vasari:* Giorgio Vasari praised Stefano in his *The Lives of the Painters.*

223, 76. *sic transit: sic transit gloria mundi,* "thus passes away the glory of the world."

223, 81. In stanzas xi-xx, Browning expounds the "philosophy of the imperfect," a doctrine widely held in the nineteenth century and usually identified, as here, with the much-debated question whether ancient Greek art is superior to Western art. Ruskin had given the doctrine a famous exposition in his *Stones of Venice* (vol. II, chap. 6). Those works that "are more perfect in their kind," Ruskin holds (to quote a part of his summary statements),

> are always inferior to those which are, in their nature, liable to more faults and shortcomings . . . we are . . . not to set the meaner thing, in its narrow accomplishment, above shattered majesty; not to prefer mean victory to honourable defeat; not to lower the level of our aim, that we may the more surely enjoy the complacency of success.
> . . . accurately speaking, no good work whatever can be perfect, and *the demand for perfection is always a sign of a misunderstanding* of the ends of art. . . . no great man ever stops working till he has reached his point of failure; that is to say, his mind is always far in advance of his powers of execution, and the latter will now and then give way in trying to follow it. . . .
> Accept this then for a universal law, that neither architecture nor any other noble work of man can be good unless it be imperfect. . . .

Other poems in which Browning's "philosophy of the imperfect" plays an important part include *A Grammarian's Funeral, Andrea del Sarto, Rabbi Ben Ezra,* and *Abt Vogler.*

223, 84. *in fructu:* "as fruit."

224, 98. *Theseus:* Browning is thinking of the great statue of Theseus, once a part of the frieze of the Parthenon, now in the British Museum.

224, 99. *Son of Priam:* One of the famous sculptures on the island of Aegina depicted Paris, son of Priam, kneeling and drawing a bow.

224, 103. *Racers' frieze:* on the Parthenon.

225, 135. *O!:* Asked by the envoy of Pope Benedict XI for an example of his skill, Giotto with one stroke, free-hand, drew a perfect circle. His great bell tower, on the other hand, Giotto began late in life and was forced to leave unfinished.

226, 179. *Nicolo the Pisan:* an early Italian architect and sculptor (1207-78), especially famous for his carved pulpit in the Baptistery at Pisa.

226, 180. *Cimabue:* Giovanni Cimabue (1240-1302), earliest of the great Italian painters. According to legend, Cimabue was the discoverer of Giotto, whose genius he recognized when he saw the young shepherd draw the outline of a sheep on a rock with a sharp stone.

226, 182. *Ghiberti and Ghirlandajo:* Lorenzo Ghiberti (1381-1455) designed the eastern doors of the Baptistery at Florence; Domenico Bigordi, or Ghirlandajo (1449-94), was a facile and sophisticated painter, famous for his frescoes. He was the teacher of Michelangelo.

227, 198. *dree:* endure, suffer.

227, 201. *Bigordi:* Ghirlandajo (see note to line 182).

227, 201-232. The many names occurring in these lines seem adequately explained by the context. Browning honors the great artists among them but does not expect to be lucky enough to find any of their paintings. On the other hand, he feels that the ghost of one of the lesser painters he mentions might grant him a discovery.

227, 206. *intonaco:* the plaster background for fresco painting.

228, 218. *barret:* a flat cap.

228, 233-40. The "precious little tablet" was a painting of the Last Supper supposed to be by Giotto that had been rediscovered recently in Florence. Buonarotti (Michelangelo) had admired it.

228, 241. *San Spirito:* a church in Florence which had earlier possessed the "precious little tablet."

228, 244. *Detur amanti:* "Let it be given to the one who loves it."

228, 245. *Koh-i-noor:* the "Mountain of Light," one of the largest and most famous diamonds of the world, given to Queen Victoria in 1850.

229, 249. *a certain dotard:* Ferdinand, Grand-Duke of Tuscany. Browning hopes to see him pitched over the Alps to the Austrians, whose tool he is.

229, 255. *Radetzky:* the Austrian field marshal who held Italy in subjection.

229, 256. *Morello:* a mountain in the Apennines, north of Florence.

229, 258. *the stone of Dante:* a stone on which Dante was supposed often to have sat; it was made a political rallying point in nineteenth-century Florence.

229, 259. *Witanagemot:* the council of the Anglo-Saxon kings.

229, 260. *"Casa Guidi": Casa Guidi Windows* was a poem published by Mrs. Browning in 1851 dedicated to the cause of Italian liberty; *quod videas ante:* "which you may have seen before."

229, 264. *Orgagna:* Andrea di Cione (1315-76), a noted painter of the school of Giotto, who flourished in the days when Florence was free.

229, 274. *"issimo":* the superlative ending for adjectives in Italian.

229, 275. *tale of Cambuscan:* Chaucer's *Squire's Tale,* which he left uncompleted.

229, 276. *alt to altissimo:* "high to highest."

229, 277. *beccaccia:* woodcock.

229, 279. *braccia:* cubits. Giotto's plans called for a spire fifty cubits high.

SAUL. *Page 230.*

At Elizabeth Barrett's urging, Browning had published the first nine sections of *Saul,* roughly one-third of the total poem, in *Dramatic Romances and Lyrics* (1845), though the piece was a fragment ending with David's celebration of earthly joys and marked, at the conclusion, "End of Part the First." The completed poem, with considerable alteration of section IX, was first published in *Men and Women* (1855). In the intervening years, Browning had written *Christmas-Eve and Easter-Day* (1850) and had worked out more fully his ideas concerning a religion of love and the meaning of the Incarnation, ideas that are developed at length in the last two-thirds of the poem. They also figure prominently in *An Epistle* and *Cleon,* both published, like *Saul,* in the collection of 1855. The basic source of *Saul* is the Biblical narrative in I Samuel (16:14-23), where Saul is troubled with an evil spirit and David is sent for to drive it away by playing on his harp. For an interesting discussion of Browning's indebtedness to Christopher Smart's *Song to David* and the preface to Smart's *Ode to Musick on Saint Cecilia's Day,* see Dean DeVane's *Handbook,* pp. 254-57.

230, 1. *Abner:* Saul's uncle and the commander of Saul's army.

231, 31. *king-serpent:* the boa constrictor, waiting to slough off his skin.

231, 45. *jerboa:* a small rodent, remarkable for its long, swift leaps, so that in the next line Browning calls it "half bird."

236, 188. *paper-reeds:* a plant of the sedge family, from the pith of which papyrus was made.

236, 203. *Hebron:* a mountain in Judaea, where stood a city of the same name.

236, 204. *Kidron:* a brook near Jerusalem.

236, 213. *error:* Saul had lost favor with Jehovah when he had refused to destroy utterly the Amalekites and all their property, as the Lord had commanded. Saul had kept their king, Agag, and the best of their cattle.

238, 291. *Sabaoth:* armies.

239, 300 ff. Through insight into God's love that he has gained from his own desire to help Saul, Browning's David has evolved the idea of the Incarnation and the Crucifixion as Browning characteristically views them in his poetry. Compare especially the conclusion of *An Epistle,* lines 304-312.

"DE GUSTIBUS —" (1855). *Page 240.*

The Latin proverb that provides Browning with his title runs: *De gustibus non est disputandum,* "there is no use disputing tastes." It is possible that Browning's own ghost would have had a hard time choosing which of the scenes he would most like to revisit. Compare, on the one hand, *Home Thoughts from Abroad* and, on the other, *The Englishman in Italy.*

240, 4. *cornfield:* a field of grain — not, as in American usage, a field of Indian maize.

240, 22. *cicala:* cicada, or locust.

241, 36. *liver-wing:* right arm.

241, 40. *Queen Mary's saying:* When, in 1558, the English lost Calais to the French, the Queen in her grief said that after her death "Calais would be found written on her heart."

CLEON (1855). *Page 241.*

Browning has set this poem in the decline of Greek civilization, not long after 50 A.D.; Cleon and Protus (both fictitious characters) have heard of the Apostle Paul, who began his preaching among the Greeks about that time. Browning's motto following the title comes from Acts 17, which tells of Paul's speaking from the Areopagus at Athens at the invitation of various Stoic and Epicurean philosophers. Verse 28 of this chapter runs in full: "For in him we live and move and have our being; as certain also of your own poets have said. For we are also his offspring." Browning has made his Cleon such a poet and has endowed him with the characteristic Greek view of life — an intense consciousness, heightened by cultivation of the arts, of the joys in living; and, at the same time, a tragic sense of life's brevity. Cleon also possesses the intellectual pride of his people, which makes him reject impatiently the idea that "a mere barbarian Jew, As Paulus proves to be," can have anything of value to say toward a solution of Protus' problem and Cleon's own — how to "fear death less."

241, 1. *sprinkled isles:* probably the Sporades, a scattered group of islands off the Greek coast, near Crete.

241, 4. *his Tyranny:* Protus is an absolute ruler of a tyranny — a province or district. The word as used here does not imply that Protus is a despotic or oppressive ruler.

242, 51. *phare:* lighthouse.

242, 53. *the Poecile:* the portico or covered colonnade at Athens, painted with battle scenes.

242, 60. combined the moods: in Greek music the scales were called *moods* or *modes.*

243, 83-84. rhomb . . . lozenge . . . trapezoid: These are all four-sided figures, but each is different from the others in the relation of its sides and angles. Laid "on a level" — side by side rather than superimposed — these figures combine to form a picture.

244, 132. drupe: the wild plum, as contrasted with the cultivated variety.

244, 138. soul: Cleon uses the word *soul* here and elsewhere to denote man's consciousness as opposed to his physical being, but without the spiritual overtones usually associated with the word. Cleon thinks of the soul as independent of man's physical powers, but he does not expect it to survive them.

244, 140-41. Terpander: a musician of Lesbos (7th century B.C.); *Phidias:* the great Athenian sculptor (5th century B.C.).

246, 232. Watch-tower: The soul of man climbs the tower to rise above the flatland of animal life. It attains a height where it can look around itself, achieving self-consciousness and becoming aware of both the possibilities for joy in life and the tragic brevity of the time the body allows for such enjoyment. Cleon plays on this figure throughout lines 227-242.

247, 252. Naiad: water-nymph. As the one thin tube of the fountain allows only so much water for the water-bow it throws upward, so man's body allows him only so many years to live regardless of the soul's capacities for enjoying a longer span.

247, 273ff. The last point now: Cleon finds little satisfaction in the idea that while his body dies, he lives on in a sense in his artistic creations. Browning as he wrote these lines was almost certainly thinking of his own time and the various skeptics (especially the Utilitarians and the Comtists) who rejected the idea of personal immortality but offered as a substitute the sort of "vicarious immortality" in one's contributions to mankind that Cleon describes in lines 273-77.

POPULARITY (1855). *Page 249.*

Through his image of the murex, Browning offers his tribute to John Keats, who was so original and so intense a poet that the readers of his day let him go unrecognized, while the poetasters of the next generation flourished by giving the public suitably watered-down imitations of his poetry.

250, 18-20: a paraphrase of John 2:1-10.

250, 24. Tyre: a city of Phoenicia. Tyrian purple, or blue, came to be employed as the color of royalty. This dye was produced from a colorless secretion of the murex, a shellfish with an especially rough shell.

250, 29. *Astarte:* a goddess of fertility and of sexual love worshiped by the Phoenicians.

251, 41ff. See I Kings 6-7 for a description of Solomon's cedar house. The Spouse was Pharaoh's daughter.

TWO IN THE CAMPAGNA (1855). *Page 252.*

The Campagna is the area surrounding Rome. The seat of many ancient cities, it contains at the time of the poem only ruins overrun with weeds and grasses that afford rich pasture for sheep and cattle.

Two in the Campagna expresses the sense of loneliness and helplessness of a woman who wishes she could lose her doubts and hesitancies in order to fall completely in love with the man of the poem. In the morning, on the Campagna, she had almost managed to do so; but, as always, the "good minute" went. She was thrown back once more upon her fears, her self-conscious intellectualizings. Around her the fennel scattering its seed, the endless feathery grasses, the flowers in pollen-time (one with five blind green beetles feeding on the gold dust in its cup) offered by way of a powerful ironic contrast the easy, unreflecting profusion of life and love in nature.

A GRAMMARIAN'S FUNERAL (1855). *Page 254.*

As the subtitle suggests, this poem is set in the early Renaissance; it conveys the adventurous spirit, the hunger for knowledge, among the pioneer scholars who did much to restore the learning of ancient Greece and Rome to the modern world. The poem is also a notable expression of Browning's "philosophy of the imperfect" (see the note to line 81 of *Old Pictures in Florence*) and a good example of Browning's love for case-making, for arguing his point from an extreme instance. The old grammarian, despite the narrow limits of his actual achievements, leads the life of a hero.

> "The union of humour with intense seriousness, of the grotesque with the stately, is one that only Mr. Browning could have compassed, and the effect is singularly appropriate. As the disciples of the old humanist bear their dead master up to his grave on the mountain-top, chanting their dirge and eulogy, the lines of the poem seem actually to move to the steady climbing rhythm of their feet." — Arthur Symons (p. 102).

254, 3. *crofts:* enclosed fields; *thorpes:* villages.

255, 50. *gowned him:* donned the gown, symbol of academic life; turned to scholarship.

256, 86-88. *Calculus:* the stone (gallstones); *Tussis:* a bad cough.

256, 95. *hydroptic:* overthirsty.

257, 127. *the rattle:* the death rattle.

257, 129-30. *Hoti, Oun, De:* Greek particles meaning "that," "therefore," and "toward." *De,* when it is enclitic, is pronounced as part of the word that precedes it.

"TRANSCENDENTALISM: A POEM IN TWELVE BOOKS"
(1855). *Page 257.*

The title suggests the sort of long, prosy, pretentious work that is described and protested against in the body of the poem. Browning may have been thinking of Martin Farquhar Tupper's *Proverbial Philosophy* (1838-42), a bleak Victorian bestseller consisting of page after page of rhymed commonplaces; or of Philip James Bailey's long and prosy philosophical poem *Festus,* first published in 1839, which aimed at offering the reader "a sketch of world-life and a summary of its combined moral and physical conditions, estimated on a theory of spiritual things. . . ." Both works — and other Victorian poems in a similar vein — emphasized stark thought rather than pleasurable sights and sounds.

Though sometimes attacked for freighting his own pieces with too much gray argument, Browning believed that the essential function of the poet must be to make his scene and characters come alive before the reader. In *"Transcendentalism"* Browning favors the method of the magician John of Halberstadt, who, instead of writing arid volumes about roses like Jacob Boehme, "vents a brace of rhymes" and causes his audience to behold the roses themselves.

257, 1. This line is spoken by the poet who chooses to write "stark-naked thought." All the remainder of the poem is the reply of the poet who is addressed in the first line.

258, 12. *six-foot Swiss tube:* a wooden megaphone.

258, 22. *German Boehme:* Jacob Boehme (1575-1624), a German shoemaker, writer of several mystical treatises. One day, observing the sunshine falling with great brilliance upon a pewter dish, Boehme fell into a mood in which he seemed to penetrate the deepest secrets of life. When he went outside, he found that he could gaze "into the very heart of things, the very herbs and grass." He recorded his experiences in *De Signatura Rerum,* the "tough book" Browning refers to in line 30.

258, 37-38. *John of Halberstadt:* Johannes Teutonicus, a canon of Halberstadt and student of medieval science. He was supposed to possess a "vegetable stone" which could make plants grow at will.

ONE WORD MORE. *Page 259.*

First published as the concluding poem in *Men and Women* (1855), *One Word More* dedicates the volume to Elizabeth Barrett Browning. As he seems to promise in line 28, Browning never again used the meter employed here.

259, 1-2. There were fifty poems in *Men and Women,* not counting *One Word More.*

259, 5. According to a tradition at least in part apocryphal, Raphael (1483-1520) fell in love with a young girl named Margherita, or La Fornacina, to whom he remained faithful throughout his life, making her the model for his madonnas and writing a hundred sonnets to her. Only three sonnets and part of a fourth are known to exist; these are written on the backs of studies for paintings.

260, 27. The book Guido Reni (1575-1642) guarded and loved was a collection of Raphael's drawings, not his sonnets.

260, 32. *Dante:* In his *Vita Nuova* (XXXV), Dante tells how, in the year 1291 on the first anniversary of the death of Beatrice, he commenced to paint her portrait from memory, portraying her as an angel: "And while I was drawing, I turned my eyes and saw at my side certain people of importance. They were looking on what I did, and as I heard afterwards, they had been there some time before I was aware of it. When I saw them, I arose, and greeting them, said, 'Another was with me just now, and because of that I was abstracted.'" It is improbable that Dante, as Browning imagines, was writing the *Inferno* as early as 1291, and there is no indication in the *Vita Nuova* that the people who interrupted him seized him or intended to do him any harm.

260, 57. *Bice:* short for *Beatrice.*

261, 74. *He who smites the rock:* Browning compares the artist, bringing truth to mankind, with Moses smiting the rock to bring forth water for an ungrateful people thirsting in the wilderness. See Exodus 16-19 and Numbers 12 and 20.

261, 95. *Egypt's flesh-pots:* "Would that we had died by the hand of the Lord in the land of Egypt, when we sat by the flesh pots, when we did eat bread to the full; for ye have brought us forth into this wilderness, to kill this whole assembly with hunger." — Exodus 16: 3-4.

262, 97. *Sinai . . . brilliance:* God appeared to Moses on Mount Sinai amid lightning and thunder. See Exodus 19 and 35.

262, 101. *Jethro's daughter:* Zipporah, the wife of Moses (see Exodus 2 and 18). Moses had also married an Ethiopian slave (see Numbers 12:1).

263, 146. *thrice-transfigured:* a reference to the three phases of the moon — new, full, and old. Here and later in his poetry the moon becomes Browning's symbol for his wife.

263, 148. *Fiesole:* a hillside town overlooking Florence from the east.

263, 150. *Samminiato:* San Miniato, a church in the hills near Florence.

263, 160. *mythos:* the legend of the love of Diana, the moon goddess, for Endymion.

263, 163. *Zoroaster:* (589-513 B.C.), founder of the Persian religion, which involves worship (and observation) of the heavenly bodies.

263, 165. Homer's *Hymn to Artemis* (which Shelley translated) appears in the *Iliad*, book XXI. Keats wrote *Endymion* (see note to line 160).

264, 174-76. "Then went up Moses, and Aaron, Nadab, and Abibu, and seventy of the elders of Israel; and they saw the God of Israel; and there was under his feet as it were a paved work of a sapphire stone, and as it were the body of heaven in his clearness." — Exodus 24: 9-10.

JAMES LEE'S WIFE (1864). *Page 265.*

Browning wrote the series of lyrics that make up *James Lee's Wife* in 1862 when he was living at Ste. Marie, near Pornic, on the coast of Brittany. The scenery and the mood of the Breton coast pervade the poems; so does Browning's sense of his wife's death scarcely a year earlier. As C. H. Herford observed (*Robert Browning* [1905], p. 154), the problem of James Lee's wife was essentially Browning's own — "how to live when answering love was gone." The successive lyrics deal with the unhappy life of a couple newly married and living in seclusion on the seacoast in a foreign land. The wife records her moods and impressions as the estrangement continues to grow.

III. IN THE DOORWAY

The second stanza contains a fairly accurate description of Browning's own view from his house at Ste. Marie, in Brittany.

V. ON THE CLIFF

270, 137. *barded and chanfroned:* armed and plumed.
270, 183. *quixote-mage:* a quixotic magician.

VI. READING A BOOK, UNDER THE CLIFF

The "young man" whose poem is quoted in the first six stanzas is Browning himself. He had published the stanzas as a separate poem twenty-eight years earlier in *The Monthly Repository* for May, 1836.

VIII. BESIDE THE DRAWING BOARD

Lines 270-330 were added in the edition of 1868.

ABT VOGLER (1864). *Page 278.*

Abt (or Abbé) George Joseph Vogler (1749-1814) was a noted German musician under whom Browning's own music teacher, John Relfe, had once studied. Browning probably chose Vogler as the subject of this poem because of his devoutness and his fame as an extemporizer (i.e., a musician who improvises music even as he is playing it, creating unique melodies that will never be heard again); the meaning of the poem hinges on the fact that the Abbé, even as he speaks, is extemporizing. The "musical instrument of [Vogler's] own invention" was called the Orchestrion, an organ of considerable range which could be packed into nine cubic feet of space.

278, 3. Solomon willed: According to Jewish and Moslem legends, Solomon held dominion over demons of earth and air through possession of a seal bearing the "ineffable name" of God.

278, 21-23. as a runner tips with fire: The dome of St. Peter's at Rome is illuminated thus on the nights of important festivals.

279, 34. fresh from the Protoplast: fresh from the first-created ancestor of the species.

279, 52. not a fourth sound, but a star: i.e., a chord or harmony unlike any of the notes sounded separately and as miraculous-seeming as a star.

280, 66. houses not made with hands: "For we know that if our earthly house of this tabernacle were dissolved, we have a building of God, an house not made with hands, eternal in the heavens." — II Corinthians 5:1.

281, 91 ff. The general meaning is not difficult: Vogler has risen to spiritual heights in his improvisation; now he slides by semitones to a minor key, rests a while on the "alien ground" or level of a ninth chord, surveying from this level below them the heights he had recently scaled, and then descends farther to take his stand on "The C Major of this life" — the level ground of ordinary living. For a detailed discussion of the musical terms in this passage, see Helen J. Ormerod's "Abt Vogler, the Man," *Browning Society's Papers*, II, 221-36, or the note to *Abt Vogler* in the Florentine Edition of Browning's works, edited by Charlotte Porter and Helen A. Clarke (1898).

RABBI BEN EZRA (1864). *Page 281.*

Abraham Ibn Ezra, or Abenezra (1092-1167), was a philosopher, scientist, and theologian. Born in Toledo, Spain, he traveled extensively throughout Europe and the Near East. The second half of his life was more productive and probably happier than the first.

It is not likely that Browning had read widely in the works of Ibn Ezra, but he was familiar with the general doctrine presented in them.

The Rabbi's philosophy, based on Platonism and modified by his reading in Arabian thinkers and in the early Neo-Platonists, has strong resemblances to Browning's own ideas. Ibn Ezra believed that man is a microcosm-created with a soul that is of like nature to God. The soul descends from heaven as a *tabula rasa,* or blank tablet; it desires to return to heaven, but it can do so only if it secures for itself a fullness of wisdom while on earth. Learning, acquiring wisdom, is the purpose of the soul in its sojourn in the body.

There are parallels in the writings of Ibn Ezra, therefore, for several of the ideas that Browning's Rabbi expounds in the poem: that all life is a process of learning; that the last of life, when a man has attained wisdom, is better than the first; that aspiring in itself, rather than success in the world's terms, is the important fact in living; that doubts and difficulties are to be welcomed as part of the soul's process of attaining wisdom. The historical Ibn Ezra, on the other hand, believed that the soul is a stranger and prisoner in the body and that the desires of the flesh must be vanquished as enemies; whereas Browning and the Rabbi of his poem (stanzas XI-XII) regard life as no prison house but rather as a pleasant inn, or school.

Probably, as Dean DeVane suggests (*Handbook,* pp. 293-94), Browning had read Edward Fitzgerald's *The Rubaiyat of Omar Khayyam* before he wrote *Rabbi Ben Ezra* and intended his poem to serve as a reply to Omar's *carpe diem* hedonism. It may be that Matthew Arnold, in turn, intended his poem *Growing Old* (1867) to be a reply to Browning's poem.

Rabbi Ben Ezra has always been a favorite with readers of Browning. It is often associated with *Abt Vogler* and the book of the Pope in *The Ring and the Book* as one of the loftiest achievements of Browning in metaphysical verse.

283, 57. see now love perfect too: The idea that God's love is as illimitable and perfect as his power and his intelligence is central to Browning's religious thinking. Compare especially *Saul, An Epistle,* and the book of the Pope in *The Ring and the Book,* lines 1354-79.

284, 81. adventure brave and new: i.e., in an afterlife.

285, 133-50. A notable expression of Browning's "philosophy of the imperfect." (See the note to line 81 of *Old Pictures in Florence.*)

286, 151. The metaphor of the potter's wheel appears frequently in the Bible (see Isaiah 64:8 and Jeremiah 18:2-6, for examples); but Browning may very well have intended his lines as an answer to Fitzgerald's employment of the figure in *The Rubaiyat of Omar Khayyam,* stanzas 82-90. See the general note above.

CALIBAN UPON SETEBOS (1864). *Page 288.*

Browning found Caliban in *The Tempest,* though Shakespeare's character, half man, half beast (the name is possibly an anagram for *cannibal*), does not speculate at any length on theology. Browning's satire in *Caliban Upon Setebos* seems to cut more than one way. In one direction it may well represent an oblique attack on the sterner aspects of Calvinism with its doctrines of predestination and eternal punishment and its presentation of a god who "extendeth or witholdeth mercy as He pleaseth, for the glory of His sovereign power over His creatures, to pass by, and to ordain them to dishonour and wrath for their sin, to the praise of His glorious grace" (Westminster Confession of Faith). In another direction, *Caliban Upon Setebos* seems to be a satire upon contemporary critics of the Bible (Strauss and Renan among them) whose works state or imply that the Christian idea of God is the product of collective human thinking rather than divine inspiration. Caliban's Setebos, Browning seems to invite the reader to infer, is the sort of god mankind would arrive at through "natural theology" and the kind of thinking implied in the motto that follows the title: the Christian idea of the Incarnation and of God's love could come only through divine revelation. (For still other possibilities in the meaning of *Caliban*, see C. R. Tracy's "Caliban Upon Setebos," *Studies in Philology*, XXXV [1938], 487-99.)

In the background of the poem, certainly, is Browning's awareness of Darwin's *Origin of Species*, published only five years before the poem. The famous debate on evolution between Bishop Samuel Wilberforce of Oxford and Thomas Huxley had taken place in 1860, and discussions of primitive man, the "missing link," and man's relation to the animals were very much in the air.

The motto following the title is quoted from Psalms 50:21.

288, 5. eft-things: newts, or little lizard-like creatures.

288, 7. pompion-plant: a wild vine of the pumpkin species.

288, 16. his dam: Sycorax, Caliban's mother in *The Tempest*, worshiped a god named Setebos.

288, 20. Prosper and Miranda: Prospero in *The Tempest* is the magician who has made Caliban his unwilling servant; Miranda is Prospero's daughter.

288, 27. But not the stars: See lines 137-39.

289, 50. pie: magpie.

289, 71. bladdery: in bubbles.

289, 75. Put case: assume that.

290, 83. grigs: grasshoppers.

291, 137. This Quiet: Caliban is forced to allow for two gods, one of which is so remote, feeling neither joy nor grief, as to be without any real meaning for him. (In Browning's own belief, the idea of the Incarnation as a means of God's revealing his love for man resolved the dilemma. Compare *An Epistle* and *Saul*.)

291, 148. hips: haws, hawthorn berries.

291, 156-57. oncelot, or *ounce:* a mountain leopard.

291, 101. *Ariel.* an any spirit who serves Prospero in *The Tempest*.

292, 177. *orc:* a carnivorous sea-beast, the killer whale.

293, 229. *urchin:* hedgehog.

294, 266 ff. Browning seems to be satirizing the idea of propitiating the Deity through self-inflicted punishment.

PROSPICE. *Page 296.*

This poem first appeared in the *Atlantic Monthly* for June, 1864, but was published only a short time later in *Dramatis Personae* (1864). Probably written not long after the death of Mrs. Browning, the poem is frankly autobiographical. The title (pronounced pros'pisē) means "look forward."

297, 27. *thou soul of my soul:* addressed to Browning's wife, who had died on June 29, 1861.

YOUTH AND ART (1864). *Page 297.*

The setting is probably the artists' colony in Rome, but the speakers are English. For the doctrine of "elective affinities" which underlies the idea of the poem, see the general note to *Cristina*.

297, 8. *Gibson:* a noted English sculptor (1790-1866) who had his studio in Rome.

297, 12. *Grisi:* Giulia Grisi (1811-69), an Italian operatic soprano.

298, 31. *E in alt:* high E.

299, 58. *bals-paré:* fancy-dress balls.

299, 60. *R.A.:* a member of the Royal Academy.

APPARENT FAILURE (1864). *Page 300.*

The items mentioned in the first stanza as having been current events seven years earlier indicate that Browning wrote *Apparent Failure* in 1863 and that his visit to the Morgue in Paris took place in 1856. (The Brownings had been living in Paris since October, 1855, and left the city in June, 1856.) With Browning's belief here that "what began best, can't end worst," compare the concluding lines (2122-25) of the book of the Pope in *The Ring and the Book*.

300, 3. *baptism of your Prince:* Prince Louis Napoleon, the only son of Napoleon III, was baptised in June, 1856.

300, 7 ff. *the Congress,* etc.: The Imperial Congress met in Paris early in 1856 to conclude the Crimean War. Prince Alexander Gortschakoff (1798-1883) was the Russian minister of foreign affairs, an important figure at the Congress. Count Buol-Schauenstein (1797-

1865) was the chief Austrian diplomat. Count Cavour (1810-61), as prime minister of Piedmont, succeeded in persuading the great powers at the conference to recognize this small principality.

300, 12. Petrarch's Vaucluse: Petrarch, the famous Italian poet (1304-74), lived for a time in the village of Vaucluse in Southern France at the source of the Sorgue.

301, 39. Tuileries: the royal palace in Paris, burned in 1871.

301, 46-47. red . . . black: an allusion to the gambling game *rouge-et-noir*, named from the colors on the table.

EPILOGUE. *Page 302.*

This poem concluded *Dramatis Personae* (1864).

The first two speakers present contrasting attitudes both widely held in later Victorian religious thought. The "First Speaker, *as David*," expresses the ritualistic position of the Roman Catholic Church and of High Church Anglicanism. Browning probably had in mind as well the Oxford Movement and its powerful influence in making ritualism and sacerdotalism live issues in the religious thinking of the time. The Church, the House of the Lord, is from David's (or John Henry Newman's) point of view the dwelling-place of God; and worship is associated with elaborate ritual — "Priest's cries, and trumpet-calls."

The "Second Speaker, *as Renan*," expresses the position of the modern rationalist, and especially the higher critics of the Scriptures. Ernest Renan, whose *Vie de Jésus* Browning had read with disapproval in 1863, has been driven reluctantly by his researches to believe that the sense of the Lord's presence in or out of the temple must inevitably dwindle and die for mankind as historical knowledge increases and as warrant for belief in the supernatural disappears. He views the loss with grief and even hopelessness.

The "Third Speaker" is clearly Browning himself. His own belief is based upon the spiritual drama that he sees enacted in the heart of every man — even the lowest, or "least man of all mankind."

302, 2. Dedication Day: the day of the dedication of the Temple (actually built and dedicated by Solomon rather than David). See I Kings 8,9, and II Chronicles, 5,6,7.

302, 3. Levites: sons of the tribe of Levi, members of which were traditionally chosen to aid the priests in the care of sacred objects and in performing rituals.

303, 26. a Face: the face of Christ.

303, 55 ff. Renan dreads a universe devoid of personality. His fear is very like that of Carlyle's Teufelsdrökh in "The Everlasting No" (*Sartor Resartus*).

THE RING AND THE BOOK. *Page 306.*

[The three books included here are given in the order of their appearance in *The Ring and the Book* with *Caponsacchi* therefore preceding *Pompilia*. However, since *Pompilia* represents a much simpler and a much fuller setting-forth of the chief incidents of Browning's poem, the reader who is unfamiliar with the total work may very well choose to read *Pompilia* first.]

This poem, generally regarded as Browning's masterpiece (as he intended it should be), was published in four volumes — the first and second in 1868 and the third and fourth in 1869.

Browning found the original for *The Ring and the Book* in 1860 in the square of San Lorenzo at Florence. Here, amid fire irons, mirror sconces, chalk drawings, old tapestry, picture frames, and the multitudinous odds and ends sold by second-hand vendors in their booths cramming the square, he picked up for a *lira* a vellum-covered book "part print part manuscript" which, according to its Latin title, contained "A Setting-forth of the entire Criminal Cause against *Guido Franceschini*, Nobleman of Arezzo, and his Bravoes, who were put to death in Rome, February 22, 1698. The first by beheading, the other four by the gallows. . . ." This book of 250 pages contained twenty-one items — part pamphlets, part letters addressed to one Cencini, a Florentine lawyer who probably was responsible for having the whole bound into a volume now known as The Old Yellow Book.*

Some years (probably four years) later, Browning hit upon his plan for telling the story in a series of dramatic monologues, allowing not only the three chief participants in the action but also six other persons to give their interpretations of the events that led to the final scene of this Roman murder tale. The story of the poem is briefly as follows:

Count Guido Franceschini, a nobleman of Arezzo, down at the heel and ugly but of an ancient family, had wasted the best years of his life vainly seeking preferment at the Papal Court. Under the guidance of a younger and more politic brother, Guido, already aging, finally decided to recover his fortunes by marriage. He addressed himself to the family of Pompilia, thirteen-year-old daughter of Pietro and Violante Comparini, a middle-class couple who were falsely reputed to be wealthy. The father, Pietro, made inquiries into the state of Guido's fortune and declined the offer. Violante, however, was dazzled by the thought of an aristocratic marriage and secretly led

* It is easily available, edited and translated by C. W. Hodell, in an Everyman's Library edition.

Pompilia to church for a hasty wedding. Faced with an accomplished fact, Pietro accepted Guido as his son-in-law and made over to him the family's possessions with the understanding that Pietro and Violante would come to live as part of Guido's household at Arezzo.

The arrangement soon became an impossible one. The castle at Arezzo turned out to be a dilapidated pile with mouldy and threadbare furnishings. Pietro and Violante voiced their complaints about their food and housing not only to Guido and his family but also to the townspeople. Guido, wishing to rid himself of the old couple, made their lives unendurable by petty persecutions. At the end of four months, Pietro and Violante returned to Rome; shortly thereafter they began court proceedings for the return of Pompilia's dowry.

This suit hinged upon a fact which Violante had kept hidden from Pietro up to the time of their return from Arezzo: Pompilia was not really their daughter. Violante had pretended that the baby was her own in order to secure an inheritance that she and Pietro could claim only if they had a child. She had secretly procured the newborn infant from a woman of the streets.

The chief sufferer through the suit and its revelation was Pompilia. Guido, already tyrannical in his treatment of her, was now infuriated by his awareness of her base birth and by the threat of losing her dowry. As the lawsuit dragged on from court to court, he shaped a plan to rid himself of his wife, but in such a manner as not to relinquish any property rights he could claim by the marriage. He began to treat Pompilia with increasing cruelty, at the same time laying snares for her elopement. Pompilia made many futile attempts to obtain help, including appeals to the Archbishop and to the Governor. Finally, in desperation and despite the fact that she was with child, Pompilia fled toward Rome with the assistance of Canon Giuseppe Caponsacchi, a chivalric young priest. On the road to Rome, at Castelnuovo, they were overtaken by Guido, who had them arrested on the charge of adultery. They were brought before a Papal court (Castelnuovo being within the Papal dominion), which decreed that Caponsacchi be banished to Civita Vecchia for three years and that Pompilia, for a time, be sent to the Scalette, a convent that took charge of penitent women. From this place the court soon permitted her to retire to the home of Pietro and Violante; and here she gave birth to her son.

The birth of Pompilia's child brought matters to a crisis. Guido saw that by securing his son, the heir, and doing away with Pompilia and her foster parents, he might at one stroke obtain his revenge and keep the property now challenged by lawsuit. Accordingly he enlisted the aid of four ruffians, laborers on his estate. Having first spied out the movements of the Comparini family, he and his fellows proceeded, on the day following New Year's Day, an hour after sunset, to their home, just outside the walls of Rome. Violante, answering Guido's knock, asked who wished admission. "Caponsacchi," Guido answered, and Violante opened the door. In the terrible scene that followed, Pietro and Violante were both stabbed to death. Pompilia, though she received twenty-two wounds from Guido's dagger and was left for dead, survived almost miraculously for four days to give evidence against her husband. Guido and his fellows had begun their flight back to Arezzo but were swiftly taken.

Guido's lawyers argued that though Guido and his men had indeed committed the triple slaying, Guido was justified by the offenses the Comparini had committed against him and particularly by the alleged adultery of Pompilia (". . . whether and when a Husband may kill his adulterous Wife without incurring the ordinary penalty . . ." runs part of the lengthy title of the Old Yellow Book). The court rejected Guido's plea; it decreed that his accomplices be hanged and Guido, as a nobleman, be executed by beheading. Guido's lawyers made appeal to the Pope, but the Pope affirmed the sentence of the court. On February 22, 1698, in the Piazza del Popolo at Rome, a large platform having been raised for the occasion, Guido was beheaded by guillotine. "Many stands were constructed," states a contemporary account, "for the convenience of those who were curious to witness such a terrible act of justice; and the concourse was so great that some windows fetched as much as six dollars each." Later, in a suit against Pompilia's property, the court judged her innocent of adultery and established her son, Gaetano, as heir to her estate.

The relation of Browning's characters in *The Ring and the Book* to their originals in the pamphlets and letters of the Old Yellow Book and in a secondary source, a seventeenth-century pamphlet Browning procured in 1862, is a fascinating question on which there are a variety of opinions. (An excellent account of them is given in DeVane, *Handbook,* pp. 338-43.) It is clear, however, that Browning read his sources as a poet rather than as an historian and that his characters are in good part his own brilliant creations, despite the fact that Browning was convinced they appeared in the documents very much as he had drawn them. It is clear, too, that his own rescue of Elizabeth Barrett from the impossible situation in her father's house colors his interpretation of Caponsacchi's rescue of Pompilia from her plight in Guido's household. The Pompilia of *The Ring and the Book* owes much to Browning's memories of Elizabeth Barrett Browning.

The title of the poem comes from an elaborate metaphor with which Browning introduces his work. The "book" (the Old Yellow Book), Browning asserts, was the gold from which he shaped the "ring" of his poem. His own contribution was merely to give the tale its form.

The Ring and the Book is divided into twelve books. In the first, Browning introduces the poem. The next three present the story from three different points of view as it is seen by three representatives of the Roman Republic. The next three books are devoted to the monologues of the chief participants, Guido, Caponsacchi, and Pompilia. There follow the three monologues of the Law, in which the chief counsel for Guido, the chief lawyer for the prosecution, and the Pope present their judgments. Guido again speaks in book eleven as he awaits execution. In book twelve Browning in his own person concludes the poem. There is far less repetition in the many tellings of the story than one might imagine: each character speaks from a perspective, and dwells upon aspects of the tale, determined by his special temperament and situation.

GIUSEPPE CAPONSACCHI.* *Page 306.*

Caponsacchi addresses the court during Guido's trial, about four days after Guido's murder of the Comparini. Browning has invented the scene; there is no evidence in the original accounts for Caponsacchi's appearing at Guido's trial. Caponsacchi speaks while he is still seized by his first wild grief at being told that Pompilia is dying. His mood as he speaks ranges widely from sorrow, pity, and love for Pompilia to loathing and hatred for Guido; from excited, spontaneous utterance to self-repressed calm. Six months earlier he had appeared before the same judges when Guido had charged Pompilia and Caponsacchi with adultery.

307, 49 ff. *an old book:* Accounts of the soldiers' casting lots for the coat, or cloak, of Christ at the Crucifixion are given in John 19:23,24 and Matthew 27:35.

309, 151. *Molinism:* a heresy condemned by the Roman Catholic Church in 1687. For a fuller account see the note to line 1863 of *The Pope.*

311, 226 ff. Dante (*Paradiso* 15:139-48 and 16:122-22) makes an ancestor of Caponsacchi's who was killed in the second crusade say that by his time the family "already had descended from Fiesole to the Market" (i.e., to the Mercato Vecchio in Florence, as in line 234).

312, 245. *Ferdinand:* Ferdinand II, Grand Duke of Tuscany (1621-70).

312, 279. *ineffable sacrosanct:* A Jewish and Mohammedan tradition forbade uttering in public the name of God. *Jehovah* is a word contrived from the true name by making a "jumble" of "consonants and vowels" (line 281).

---

* Line numbers for *Caponsacchi* and the two other books that follow are given in accordance with the text of the Florentine Edition (see textual note on page xxv). Some texts, including that of the Centenary Edition, follow Browning's unusual practice of assigning a new number to the second half of a broken line.

313, 200. Diocletian: Roman emperor (204-005 A.D.). The last persecutions of the Christians occurred in his reign.

313, 314. Onesimus: Referred to in the Bible, Philemon 11-18.

313, 316. Agrippa: Acts 25-26 tells how Paul defended himself before the sympathetic King Agrippa.

313, 319. Fénelon: a French ecclesiastic, archbishop of Cambrai (1651-1751). He adopted the heretical doctrines of Molinos (see note to line 151).

314, 329. Marinesque Adoniad: Giovanni Battista Marino (1569-1625), a popular Neapolitan poet, had published his enormous epic *Adone* in 1623.

314, 342. Pieve: the church of Santa Maria della Pieve, in Arezzo, of which Caponsacchi was a canon.

314, 345. at tarocs: a fashionable card game of the seventeenth century.

315, 384. Catullus: The noted Latin poet (87-47 B.C.) made unorthodox pauses in his lines by leaving syllables unelided.

315, 385-87. break Priscian's head . . . Ovid: break the rules of classical Latin grammar. Priscian was a renowned grammarian of the sixth century A.D. Caponsacchi would have to read the day's service of his church in the less pure medieval Latin, but he could heal the damage to his sensibilities by reading the polished and secular verse of Ovid (43 B.C.-18 A.D.).

315, 398. facchini: porters.

316, 434. In the lines that follow, Conti while he is talking to Caponsacchi attempts at the same time to keep up with the Latin of the vesper service.

316, 452. Marino: See note to line 329.

317, 479. Summa: the *Summa Theologiae* of Saint Thomas Aquinas.

319, 551. Thyrsis and Myrtilla: The love letters which were brought as evidence in the trial of Caponsacchi and Pompilia were filled with such conventional names derived from pastoral love poetry.

319, 574. Philomel: According to the legend of Philomela, Tereus, and Procne, the maiden Philomela was transformed into a nightingale which sang of the griefs she had suffered.

328, 946. Cephisian reed: The Cephisus was one of the rivers of Athens.

329, 973. corona: rosary.

329, 987. fabled garden: the fabled garden of the Hesperides, where a golden apple was guarded by a dragon.

332, 1086. Our Lady's girdle: The Virgin, according to the Legend, loosened her girdle on her ascent to heaven and threw it down as proof into the hands of Saint Thomas, who had doubted the Assumption of the Virgin, an event at which he had not been present.

333, 1143. God's sea, glassed in gold: "And there were seven lamps of fire burning before the throne, which are the seven Spirits of God;

and before the throne, as it were a glassy sea like unto crystal; and in the midst of the throne, and round about the throne, four living creatures full of eyes before and behind." — Revelation 4:6-7.

333, 1151. who name Parian — coprolite: who confuse the pure marble of Paros with *coprolite,* a petrified dung of carnivorous reptiles.

334, 1185. Assisi . . . holy ground: as the birthplace of Saint Francis.

338, 1367. Gaetano: This is the name Pompilia is to give her son. (See *Pompilia,* lines 99-104.)

340, 1434. Vulcan pursuing Mars: the story (as in Homer) of Vulcan's hunting out the trysting place of Venus, his unfaithful spouse, and her lover Mars.

340, 1436. my Cyclops: Though in the *Odyssey* the Cyclopes appear as Sicilian shepherds, a later fable makes them forgers of thunderbolts for Vulcan.

341, 1462. Molière's self: Caponsacchi alludes to Molière's *Don Juan,* where a libertine husband claims Donna Elvire, a nun, as his wife.

344, 1594. the paten: the sacred bread of the communion service is carried on a plate, or *patine.*

345, 1633. Pasquin: the name given to a statue in Rome on which anonymous satires were often posted (hence the word *pasquinade*).

345, 1640. Bembo: The word is spoken in scorn and disbelief (i.e., "You might as well tell me these clumsy lines were written by Bembo."). Pietro Bembo (1470-1547) was an eminent Italian writer, Cardinal, and secretary to Pope Leo X.

345, 1665. Sub imputatione, etc.: "Labors under the reputation of being a prostitute."

346, 1702-5. Joseph . . . Potiphar: The story of Joseph and Potiphar's wife occurs in Genesis 39.

347, 1720. De Raptu Helenae: "The Rape of Helen," a rather weak poem in Greek hexameters by Coluthus of Lycopolis in Egypt (*ca.* 500 A.D.).

347, 1724. Scazons: iambic verses of six feet with a spondee in the sixth foot.

351, 1921. cockatrice . . . basilisk: Both are mythical creatures supposed to be able to kill the beholder with a glance.

353, 1984. Probationis ob defectum: "for lack of adequate proof."

354, 2031-2. Augustinian . . . who writes: Father Celestine, the confessor of Pompilia. For his testimony regarding Pompilia's character, see the general note to *Pompilia.*

POMPILIA. *Page 356.*

Pompilia speaks from her deathbed in the hospital, "the good house that helps the poor to die." It has been only two weeks (in Brown-

ing's sources, three) since the birth of her child, and a simple pride
in her motherhood is strong in her consciousness, though she is dying
and though the terrible scene at the villa of the Comparini had taken
place just four days earlier. Her great remaining desire, aside from
the welfare of her son Gaetano, is to defend the name of her
rescuer, Caponsacchi.

The gentle, sad, compassionate, and, in its way, profound personality of *The Ring and the Book* owes more to Browning's creative
powers than to the materials of his sources. Browning's memory of
his wife enters largely into his portrait of Pompilia. However, Browning was certainly encouraged in his conception of Pompilia by his
belief in the deposition of Father Celestine, the confessor of Pompilia,
a document contained in the pamphlet that served as a secondary
source for *The Ring and the Book:*

> I, the undersigned, barefooted Augustinian priest, pledge my
> faith that inasmuch as I was present, helping Signora Francesca
> Comparini from the first instant of her pitiable case, even to the
> very end of her life, I say and attest on my priestly oath, in the
> presence of the God who must judge me, that to my own
> confusion I have discovered and marvelled at an innocent and
> saintly conscience in that ever-blessed child. During the four
> days she survived, when exhorted by me to pardon her husband,
> she replied with tears in her eyes and with a placid and compas-
> sionate voice: 'May Jesus pardon him, as I have already done
> with all my heart.' But what is more to be wondered at is that,
> although she suffered great pain, I never heard her speak an
> offensive or impatient word, nor show the slightest outward
> vexation either toward God or those near by. . . .
>
> You should therefore say that this girl was all goodness and
> modesty, since with all ease and gladness she performed virtuous
> and modest deeds even at the very end of her life. Moreover she
> has died with strong love for God, with great composure, with
> all the sacred sacraments of the Church, and with the admiration
> of all bystanders, who blessed her as a saint. I do not say more
> lest I be taxed with partiality. I know very well that God alone
> is the searcher of hearts, but I also know that from the abundance
> of the heart the mouth speaks; and that my great St. Augustine
> says: 'As the life, so its end.'
>
> Therefore, having noted in that ever blessed child saintly
> words, virtuous deeds, most modest acts, and the death of a
> soul in great fear of God, for the relief of my conscience I am
> compelled to say, and cannot do otherwise, that necessarily she
> has ever been a good, modest, and honourable girl, etc.

This tenth of January, 1698,

> I, Fra Celestino Angelo of St. Anna, barefooted Augustinian, affirm as I have said above, with my own hand.

356, 4. Lorenzo in Lucina: the church in the heart of Rome where Pompilia had been baptized and where she had been married to Guido. It was also the church in which the bodies of Pietro and Violante lay in state after the murder. It is described at length by "Half-Rome" at the opening of his monologue.

356, 31. Don Celestine: Pompilia's confessor. See the general note to *Pompilia* for his testimony as to Pompilia's character.

358, 102. a new saint: Saint Gaetan, or Cajetan (1480-1547) was founder of the order of Theatins. He had been canonized in 1671.

359, 143. a woman known too well: a prostitute.

360, 183. ı tapestry on the wall: The tapestry offers different subjects. It pictures Diana, the goddess of the chase, and Daphne, a nymph who, pursued by Apollo, was changed at her own entreaty into a laurel tree. A third subject in the tapestry is described in lines 386-89.

361, 227. Our cause is gained: presumably the suit against Guido for return of Pompilia's dowry. However, the Comparini had not actually won either of their two "causes" in the courts by the time of their death.

363, 320. Paul: Guido's suave older brother, Father Paolo Franceschini, who had first suggested to Guido that he marry for money and who had conducted negotiations with Violante. He was holder of an important position in the Church as secretary of the Order of St. John of Malta.

364, 357. journey with my friend: the flight from Arezzo with Caponsacchi.

365, 386. slim young man: Perseus rescuing Andromeda from the dragon.

366, 423. Lion's-mouth: a street in Rome, the *Via di Bocca di Leone.*

372, 685. could read no word of: Pompilia in her deposition in the Old Yellow Book stated that she could neither read nor write at the time the letters were written. Modern scholars are inclined to believe that she had actually written the letters.

373, 728. twelve years old: Pompilia was actually thirteen.

374, 763. Molinists': an heretical sect condemned in 1687. See the note to *The Pope,* line 1863.

374, 765. in your covenant: in the terms of the marriage ceremony.

374, 792. God's Bread!: an oath.

376, 879. them: the Comparini.

378, 944. Carnival: the period of merrymaking preceding Lent.

379, 980-81. *Conti . . . cousin:* Conti was a "cousin" only in the more general sense of the word; his brother had married Guido's sister.

379, 1008. *cornet:* a conical twist of paper.

383, 1135. *imposthume:* abscess.

383, 1143. *Mirtillo:* a conventional name for a lover in pastoral poetry. Compare *Thyrsis* and *Myrtilla* in *Caponsacchi,* line 551.

385, 1254. *the Governor:* Marzi-Medici, governor of Arezzo.

387, 1315-16. *Pieve:* There is a statue of St. George by Vasari in the church of Santa Maria della Pieve, where Caponsacchi and Conti were canons.

388, 1357. *horsehair springe:* a noose trap made of coarse horsehair. Pompilia feels she is a match for the crude traps laid for her by Margherita, and is even ready for coping with subtler traps (made of silk).

390, 1434-46. *star . . . the House o' the Babe:* the Star in the East that led the Three Kings to Bethlehem.

391, 1470. *"He hath a devil":* The charge the Pharisees brought against Jesus when he cast out devils (Matthew 9:34).

392, 1501. *blow:* bloom.

394, 1619 ff. Pompilia took Guido's sword (merely *a* sword, not necessarily Guido's, in the Old Yellow Book) and brandished it at him. See *Caponsacchi,* lines 1514 ff. Compare *Half-Rome*'s account (lines 1021-31):

> Her defence? This. She woke, saw, sprang upright
> I' the midst and stood as terrible as truth,
> Sprang to her husband's side, caught at the sword
> That hung there useless, — since they held each hand
> O' the lover, had disarmed him properly, —
> And in a moment out flew the bright thing
> Full in the face of Guido: but for help
> O' the guards who held her back and pinioned her
> With pains enough, she had finished you my tale
> With a flourish of red all round it, pinked her man
> Prettily; but she fought them one to six.

398, 1776. *Civita:* Civita Vecchia, the city north of Rome where Caponsacchi had been relegated as punishment following the flight from Arezzo.

398, 1791. *name of him:* When, on the night of the murder, there was a knock at the door, Violante asked who was without. Guido replied, "Caponsacchi."

THE POPE. *Page 400.*

Most critics agree with Hugh Walker that among the books of *The Ring and the Book* "the palm of greatness belongs to *The Pope*,"* though there are some who feel with Stopford Brooke** that so much intellectualizing and theological disquisition as the last part of this book contains represents a distinct falling-off from the earlier parts in which the Pope pronounces judgment on the characters of the poem. The Old Yellow Book has little to say of Pope Innocent XII, to whom Guido made appeal after the court had sentenced him; it gives scarcely a hint of the Pope's reasons for rejecting Guido's plea or his opinions on other aspects of the case. The searching analysis of the motives of the characters which takes up a major part of *The Pope* is largely Browning's own creation and represents his personal evaluations of the characters in the story. The form of *The Ring and the Book* demanded some such summing up of the evidence, a feature lacking in the Old Yellow Book. From pronouncing judgment on the case and the characters, the Pope proceeds to a general exposition of his reading of life. The views which he expresses are both unorthodox for a pope and such as reflect the intellectual problems of the nineteenth century rather than the seventeenth. They are the views of Robert Browning, and the section of the poem which presents them affords what is often regarded as Browning's finest expression of his philosophical and religious ideas. In an important sense, *The Pope* is more intimately Browning's own monologue than either the first or the last book of the poem, where he speaks in his own person.

The Pope is not, however, simply a mouthpiece for the poet's opinions, but a memorable personality, dramatically conceived, with more than a touch of grandeur in him. He is a very old man, "with winter in his soul beyond the world's," past caring greatly for the issues of the moment. His powers of judgment are keen, and his vision of the world is the clearer for his living in habitual awareness of the outer limits of life and the mystery of what lies beyond them. Browning had a basis in the biographical sources he consulted for making Innocent XII, whose secular name was Antonio Pignatelli, a good man and one capable of making penetrating judgments. Elevated to the papacy in 1691, after a long and varied career in the Church, he established important reforms during his nine-year reign, lived abstemiously, and was always easily accessible to the humble and the needy. "He has nothing in his thoughts," the Venetian envoy reported, "but God, the poor, and the reform of abuses."

400, 1. *Ahasuerus:* a wealthy and powerful king of the Old Testa-

---

* *The Literature of the Victorian Era* (1931), p. 432.
** *The Poetry of Robert Browning* (1902), p. 411. See also A. K. Cook's discussion (pp. 198 ff.) of critical estimates of *The Ring and the Book.*

ment who, when he could not sleep, had the chronicles read to him. See Esther 1:1 and 6:1.

400, 11. St. Peter was the first pope; Alexander VIII, who died in 1691, was succeeded by Innocent XII, who is speaking.

400, 23. *funeral cyst:* coffin.

400, 24-156. The 132 lines that follow illustrate the sort of degradation that the papacy suffered between 867 and the accession of Hildebrand in 1073. In the two centuries there were over fifty popes; many of them died by violence. Browning seems to give all the data concerning the popes mentioned that is essential for an intelligent reading of the poem. The especially curious reader may consult Platina's *Lives of the Popes.*

402, 89. IXΘΥΣ: The letters of this Greek word (signifying *fish*) represent the initials of the Greek words for Jesus Christ, of God, Son, Saviour. The fish was a secret symbol employed by early Christians for recognizing each other.

402, 91. *Pope is Fisherman:* as the successor to Peter, the fisherman whom Christ said he would make a fisher of men (Mark 1:17).

403, 121. *Luitprand:* a chronicler of the papacy and Bishop of Cremona in the tenth century.

403, 133. *Eude:* (or Odo) King of France (888-98).

403, 136. *Auxilius:* a French theologian of the tenth century who wrote concerning Stephen's decision.

404, 168-69. *from man's assize to mine:* Guido had taken minor orders and could claim some connection with the Church. When he received a death sentence from the regular court, he therefore made an appeal to be tried before an ecclesiastical tribunal as a member of the clergy.

405, 211. *wintry day:* The day on which the Pope rejected Guido's appeal was the twenty-first of February.

405, 220. *chose defence should lie:* i.e., what line of defense Guido's advocates thought it the best course to take.

405, 227. *a clear rede:* a clear pattern

407, 292. *the sagacious Swede:* What person Browning had in mind is still a puzzle to scholars. Swedenborg was suggested by Dr. Berdoe; but Swedenborg was only ten years old at the time the Pope spoke and he is not known to have had any special knowledge of the Theory of Probability.

407, 296-97. The Pope refers to the *sortes Virgilianae,* or Virgilian lots. Opening a copy of Virgil at random, the person seeking guidance would, without looking, let the tip of his finger come to rest somewhere on the page. He then read the line and tried to interpret it as some sort of advice relevant to his problem.

407, 327. *posset:* a drink made of hot milk curdled by ale or wine, and spiced.

409, 375. *He:* Christ.

409, 385-86. *diocese . . . legate-rule:* a bishopric at home (in Italy), and a nunciature, or position as representative of the pope, abroad.

409, 416. *cirque:* arena.

411, 465. *paravent:* screen from wind; *ombrifuge:* shelter from rain (a word apparently coined by Browning).

411, 474. *attent with fifties:* "And he commanded them that all should sit down by companies upon the green grass. And they sat down in ranks, by hundreds, and by fifties." — Mark 6:39-40, where Jesus feeds the multitude with five loaves and two fishes.

412, 509. *soldier-crab:* or hermit crab, a creature that occupies the empty shells of snails and other mollusks.

413, 578. *gor-crow:* carrion crow.

415, 652. *Aretine:* inhabitant of Arezzo. The Pope refers to Pietro Aretino (1492-1556), a Renaissance author of scandalous plays and sonnets, famed for his mastery of ribald language.

415, 662. *for a fate to be:* The Pope refers to astrology, the belief that the stars govern human destinies. Browning has added the idea of stars in conflict to determine the outcome of a particular human issue.

416, 695. *the Pieve:* the church in Arezzo where Caponsacchi was a canon.

416, 697-98. Pompilia brandished a sword at Guido in the inn at Castelnuovo. See the more detailed note to *Pompilia,* lines 1619 ff.

417, 745-49. See Genesis 8. The dove on its second flight from Noah's Ark, which was resting on Mt. Ararat, brought back an olive branch, evidence that the flood had subsided.

418, 777. *when Saturn ruled:* In Greek mythology, the golden age was the early idyllic age preceding the rule of Zeus. The Pope is satirizing the poets' attribution of virtue to rustics because they supposedly lead a simple life.

419, 811. *hebetude:* obtuseness, stupidity.

419, 814-28. Guido had neglected to obtain a warrant, or pass, to enter or leave the city gates. Such a pass, easily obtained, would have allowed him the "pick o' the posthouse," or the choice of horses for his trip back across the Tuscan frontier (Arezzo was in the duchy of Tuscany).

419, 832. *Rota:* the supreme court.

420, 877. *Abate:* Guido's brother Paul, an abbot in the church.

421, 891. Paolo Franceschini left Rome in 1697 before the murder. He had probably departed because the Order of Malta had forced him to resign his secretaryship, his conduct in arranging the marriage of Guido having become known.

421, 903-5. Girolamo Franceschini had also fled. Pompilia charged that he had made improper advances to her. See *Pompilia,* lines 802-809.

423, 987. *crook's:* the bishop's crosier, resembling a shepherd's staff, symbolizing his office as shepherd of the people.

423, 1006. *splendid vesture:* i.e., that will be hers in Heaven.

423, 1017. *memorized:* memorialized, recorded for posterity.

424, 1020. *signet . . . name:* See Revelation 7:2-4.

424, 1060. *only thine:* before she realized she was to give birth to a child. See the memorable passage in *Pompilia,* lines 1210 ff.

425, 1080. *Him:* Caponsacchi.

425, 1092. *the other rose, the gold:* On the fourth Sunday in Lent, the Pope traditionally blesses a golden rose and has it sent to a king (line 1094) or another notable person or group.

425, 1096. *ours the fault:* i.e., the Church's fault.

425, 1098. *leviathan:* the enormous whale of Job 41.

426, 1112-22. The Pope regrets that Caponsacchi cannot give his love and service directly to the Church rather than to the human being, Pompilia, even as a half-pagan Roman in early Christian times could not worship the Madonna except through images that had formerly been representations of Venus. Nevertheless, he admires the self-sacrifice in Caponsacchi's action.

426, 1119. *nard:* spikenard, a fragrant ointment.

426, 1126. *masquerade:* The Pope deplores the fact that Caponsacchi instead of serving Pompilia in his proper garb as a priest disguised himself in lay costume.

426, 1132. *Our adversary:* Satan.

429, 1240. *lynx-gift:* the gift of sharp eyes, like those of a lynx; *orb:* eye.

429, 1266. *misprision:* mistake.

430, 1303 ff. The religious and philosophical ideas presented in the lines that follow are essentially Browning's own. See the general note to *The Pope.* For an excellent discussion of Browning's religious ideas, see W. O. Raymond, "Browning and Higher Criticism," in *The Infinite Moment* (1950).

431, 1330. *new philosophy:* new science, or "natural philosophy," as science used to be called, even in Browning's time and later.

431, 1334. *Thy transcendent act:* the Incarnation. Browning regards the coming of Christ, through which God revealed His love for man, as the pivotal doctrine in his religious beliefs. Compare *Saul, Cleon,* and especially *An Epistle.*

431, 1343. *a tale of Thee:* the New Testament.

431, 1346. *discept:* reject.

431, 1361. *isocele:* an isoceles triangle in which the three sides are of equal length. In Browning's triangle, the sides represent Power, Intelligence, and Love.

432, 1383 ff. Browning here suggests that the figure of Christ, as representative of a god of love, is the key to life whether it is accepted as an historical fact or as a spiritual symbol.

432, 1398. *choppy:* chapped.

434, 1467-80. An Augustinian monk had promised Pompilia to write to the Comparini in her behalf; but the Comparini received no message.

434, 1494. *Convertites:* This nunnery had been founded to help and reform immoral women. It had legal right to the possessions of all such women if they died in Rome. The Convertites laid claim to Pompilia's property, but the court rejected the claim, judging her innocent of adultery. The historical Pompilia had actually been put into the custody of the convent Scalette rather than in the charge of the Convertites.

435, 1513. *the Fisc:* Dr. Johannes-Baptista Bottinius. He had been the official prosecutor against Guido and, to that extent, a defender of Pompilia. He is the speaker in Book IX of *The Ring and the Book.*

436, 1561 ff. See Ephesians 6:13-17.

436, 1586. *To-kien:* Fukien.

437, 1588. *Maigrot:* Vicar-Apostolic in China. In 1693 he condemned the Jesuit policy of tolerating Chinese elements in interpreting Christian truth.

437, 1598. *Tournon:* a papal legate to India, later sent to China. He was not actually made a cardinal until 1707.

437, 1614. *adept of the . . . Rosy Cross:* a Rosicrucian. The Rosicrucians claimed to possess the secret of transmuting baser metals into gold.

437, 1615. *Great Work:* transmutation (see note to line 1614).

438, 1664 ff. Euripides, the famous tragic poet (born 480 B.C.), Browning's favorite Greek dramatist, is imagined as speaking the next 120 lines.

439, 1701. *the Two:* Aeschylus and Sophocles.

439, 1712. *Paul spoke, Felix heard:* Paul explained Christian teachings to Felix, governor in Jerusalem. See Acts 34.

440, 1716-17. Euripides attacked the morality of some of the Greek legends.

440, 1724. *Galileo's tube:* the telescope.

441, 1786. Paul, according to legend, corresponded with Seneca, the Roman philosopher (4 B.C.?-65 A.D.).

442, 1827. *Nero's cross:* for punishment by crucifixion.

443, 1863. *Molinists:* Miguel de Molinos (1627-1696) was a Spanish priest who gained a great reputation as a mystic and spiritual adviser in Rome. In 1675 he published his most famous work, *The Spiritual Guide,* which stresses a passive mystical state in which the soul neither desires nor fears anything. Once the person attains this state, Molinos held, the sacraments, good works, and the fear of eternal punishment are all meaningless. His heresies were condemned in 1687. Molinism caused a great popular stir for some time, especially in and shortly before 1687; but the excitement seems to have subsided even before Molinos' death in prison in 1696.

444, 1898. *antimasque:* a comic interlude between the acts of a masque; *kibe:* heel.

444, 1904. *first experimentalist:* Caponsacchi.

444, 1919. *morrice:* an intricate dance, the "maze" of line 1911.

445, 1936. *Loyola:* St. Ignatius Loyola (1491-1556), founder of the Society of Jesus (the Jesuits).

446, 1980,81. *nemini honorem trado:* "I entrust my good name to no man's keeping."

446, 1998. *Farinacci:* a Renaissance authority on canon law.

447, 2050. *Barabbas:* When, in honor of the feast, Pontius Pilate offered to give freedom to either Jesus or Barabbas, the Jews cried out for Barabbas. See Matthew 27:15-26.

447, 2054. *three little taps:* Upon the death of a pope, the cardinal camerlengo (or chamberlain) traditionally taps three times upon the forehead of the corpse with a silver mallet, each time asking the pope to answer. The cardinal then formally announces that the pope is dead.

447, 2063. *petit-maître priestlings:* petty, wordly priests.

447, 2064. *Sanctus et Benedictus:* "Holy and blessed."

448, 2082-83. *Priam* was the aged last king of Troy; *Hecuba* was his wife.

448, 2083-84. *"non tali auxilio":* "not with such help . . ." (*Aeneid,* II, 521). In context, the gist is that the desperate times call for no such feeble aid or defense as the aged king is prepared to give.

448, 2104. *the People's Square:* the Piazza del Popolo, where Guido was beheaded next day, February 22, 1698.

HOUSE. *Page 450.*

First published in *Pacchiarotto,* Browning's volume of 1876.

Browning in this poem argues that the artist, like other human beings, has a right to privacy — that his own poems are dramatic in principle and should not be inspected as revelations of his own life. Browning takes exception to Wordsworth's statement in his "Scorn not the sonnet" (itself a sonnet) that Shakespeare "unlocked his heart" with his famous sonnet cycle. Browning himself, of course, did not keep the shades of his house drawn as consistently as the poem implies.

Dean DeVane presents a most interesting case (*Handbook,* pp. 400-01) for Browning's being moved to write this poem by his disapproval of Dante Gabriel Rossetti's intimate revelations in his sonnet sequence *The House of Life,* which had been published in 1870.

450, 4. See the general note above.

SHOP. *Page 451.*

This poem immediately followed *House* in *Pacchiarotto* (1876) and has the same theme. See the general note to *House*.

452, 23. City chaps: business men.

452, 35. Rothschild: the famous Jewish banking family.

453, 36. Mayfair: the fashionable residential section of London.

453, 38. Hampstead: a middle-class residential section, in the suburbs of London at the time Browning wrote.

453, 40. country-box: a small country house.

455, 109-110. Compare Matthew 6:21 — "For where your treasure is, there will your heart be also."

HERVE RIEL. *Page 455.*

Republished in *Pacchiarotto* (1876), the poem had first been published in the *Cornhill Magazine* for March, 1871. Browning contributed the poem with the understanding that the hundred guineas he received for it were to go to the Paris Relief Fund to provide food for the people starving as an aftermath of the siege of Paris in the Franco-Prussian War. The poem in its first appearance was dated from Le Croisic, France, September 30, 1867. Le Croisic is a small fishing village and seaside resort on the Breton coast, where Browning had spent the late summer of 1866 and the summer of 1867. Browning had found his subject matter for the poem in a guide book, *Notes sur le Croisic,* par Caillo jeune. He gives the facts as he found them except for his having apparently misread the account in one particular. Hervé Riel asked for and received as his reward not a day's leave but a complete discharge from the French navy.

455, 1-2. Louis XIV had fitted out a large expedition under Admiral Tourville with the purpose of putting James II once more on the throne of England. In the battle the English destroyed a great part of the French fleet.

455, 5. Saint-Malo: a seaport at the mouth of the Rance River, in Brittany.

455, 8. Damfreville: the commander of the largest ship, the *Formidable.*

456, 30. Plymouth Sound: a large naval station on the south coast of England.

456, 43. pressed: conscripted for war. Tourville was admiral of the French fleet.

456, 46. Malouins: natives of St. Malo.

456, 49. Grève: the treacherous sands off the French coast from St. Malo to Mont St. Michel; *disembogues:* empties.

457, 53. *Solidor:* the fortified town at the mouth of the Rance River.

459, 129. *head:* figurehead.

459, 132. *bore the bell:* came off the victor.

459, 135. *Louvre:* the famous art museum in Paris.

IVAN IVANOVITCH. *Page 460.*

First published in *Dramatic Idyls* (1879).

The scenery and atmosphere of the poem probably owe a good deal to Browning's own visit to Russia as a young man in the spring of 1834, though the source of the poem seems to be the story as told in *An Englishwoman in Russia,* an anonymous book published in 1855. The concluding words of this tale as told by "An Englishwoman" suggest how much Browning has added to the vividness and meaning of the narrative in his retelling:

> "And did you *throw them all* to the wolves, even the little baby you held in your arms?" exclaimed the horrorstricken peasant. "Yes, all!" was the reply. The words had scarcely escaped from the white lips of the miserable mother, when the man laid her dead at his feet with a single blow of the axe with which he was cleaving wood when she arrived. He was arrested for murder, and the case was decided by the Emperor, *who pardoned* him, wisely making allowance for his agitation and the sudden impulse with which horror and indignation at the unnatural act had inspired him.

460, 14. *Peter's time:* Peter the Great (1672-1725).

460, 19. *verst:* The *verst* is about two-thirds of a mile.

461, 28. *Neva's mouth:* The River Neva flows into the Gulf of Finland at Leningrad (formerly St. Petersburg).

461, 53. *Droug:* Russian for "friend."

465, 181. *our Pope:* the village priest.

467, 281. *Commune's head:* the mayor or bailiff.

467, 286. *thorpe:* village.

468, 317 and 319. The quotations are from Acts 2:17.

470, 404. *Sacred Pictures:* the sacred ikons, usually images of the saints, or of Christ, or of the Virgin Mary.

471, 412. *Kremlin:* the famous fortress and palace at Moscow.

471, 421. *Kolokol the Big:* the great bell of the Kremlin.

NEVER THE TIME AND THE PLACE. *Page 472.*

This lyric was first published in Browning's volume *Jocoseria* (1883). It is traditionally assumed to be "an expression of love and longing with some memory in it of Mrs. Browning," who had died in 1861 (Cooke, p. 214). The "enemy sly and serpentine" is probably best interpreted as time, or change, or the hold of the present upon the speaker.

WHY I AM A LIBERAL. *Page 473.*

This poem, which expresses Browning's characteristic belief in extreme individualism, first appeared as a contribution to *Why I Am a Liberal* (1885), a book compiled by Andrew Reid. In his use of the word *liberal* in the sonnet, Browning clearly has in mind a general view rather than the Liberal Party in Parliament, though he usually sided with the Liberals in English political issues.

SUMMUM BONUM. *Page 474.*

Summum Bonum appeared for the first time in *Asolando* (1889). Browning's Latin title means "the highest good," a phrase frequently used in philosophical discussions.

EPILOGUE *to* ASOLANDO. *Page 475.*

This epilogue concludes *Asolando,* Browning's final volume, published on the day of his death, December 12, 1889. The *Pall Mall Gazette* of February 1, 1890, carried the following account concerning the third stanza of the poem: "One evening, just before his death-illness, the poet was reading this from a proof to his daughter-in-law and sister. He said: 'It almost looks like bragging to say this, and as if I ought to cancel it; but it's the simple truth; and as it's true, it shall stand.'"

INDEX OF TITLES

Abt Vogler, 278
Andrea del Sarto, 213
Any Wife to Any Husband, 147
Apparent Failure, 300
Artemis Prologizes, 66

Bishop Blougram's Apology, 188
Bishop Orders His Tomb at Saint
 Praxed's Church, The, 100
Boot and Saddle, 49
Boy and the Angel, The, 109
By the Fire-side, 138

Caliban Upon Setebos, 288
Caponsacchi, Giuseppi, 306
Cavalier Tunes, 47
"Childe Roland to the Dark Tower
 Came," 162
Cleon, 241
Confessions, 295
Count Gismond, 51
Cristina, 70

"De Gustibus —," 240

Englishman in Italy, The, 91
Epilogue: "On the first of the Feast
 of Feasts," 302
Epilogue to Asolando, 475
Epistle Containing the Strange Medi-
 cal Experience of Karshish, the
 Arab Physician, An, 152
Evelyn Hope, 121

Flower's Name, The, 103
Fra Lippo Lippi, 127

Garden Fancies, 103
Giuseppe Caponsacchi, 306
Give a Rouse, 48
Glove, The, 114
Grammarian's Funeral, A, 254

Hervé Riel, 455
Home-Thoughts, from Abroad, 99
Home-Thoughts, from the Sea, 99
House, 450
How It Strikes a Contemporary, 181
"How They Brought the Good News
 from Ghent to Aix," 83

In a Gondola, 59
Incident of the French Camp, 55
In Three Days, 220
Italian in England, The, 87
Ivàn Ivànovitch, 460

James Lee's Wife, 265
Johannes Agricola in Meditation, 75

Laboratory, The, 107
Last Ride Together, The, 184
Life in a Love, 180
Light Woman, A, 170
Lost Leader, The, 98
Love Among the Ruins, 110
Love in a Life, 180

Marching Along, 47
Meeting at Night, 111
Memorabilia, 213
My Last Duchess, 49
My Star, 161

Never the Time and the Place, 472

Old Pictures in Florence, 221
One Word More, 259

Parting at Morning, 112
Patriot, The, 187
Pictor Ignotus, 85
Pied Piper of Hamelin, The, 75
Pippa Passes, 3
Pompilia, 356
Pope, The, 400
Popularity, 249
Porphyria's Lover, 73
Prospice, 296

Rabbi Ben Ezra, 281
Respectability, 169
Ring and the Book, The, 306
Rudel to the Lady of Tripoli, 69

Saul, 230
Serenade at the Villa, A, 159
Shop, 451
Sibrandus Schafnaburgensis, 104
Soliloquy of the Spanish Cloister, 56
Statue and the Bust, The, 172
Summum Bonum, 474

Time's Revenges, 112
Toccata of Galuppi's, A, 136
"Transcendentalism," 257
Two in the Campagna, 252

Up at a Villa — Down in the City, 123

Why I Am a Liberal, 473
Woman's Last Word, A, 126

Youth and Art, 297

JAY

Sexuality - a principal dramatic metaphor for philosophical & psychological crisis

Dramatic monologue vs Romantic lyric - split between author & speaker

analyze the speaking subjects

Culture & society replace nature as the setting for investigations of the soul,

Historical allusions & timeless truth beyond events of time

Bloom — Map of Misreading 114

degeneration of the west
Tithonus - Cumaean sybil

Clio - intersection of poetic tradition
Prufrock's non-identity
soliloquy on procrastination deferral of the Word by words